A Dynamic Approach to Language Arts

Lillian M. Logan

and

Virgil G. Logan

Brandon University, Manitoba

McGRAW-HILL COMPANY OF CANADA LIMITED

TORONTO New York London Sydney Johannesburg Mexico

A DYNAMIC APPROACH TO LANGUAGE ARTS

Library of Congress Catalog Card Number: 67-27416

94846

1 2 3 4 5 6 7 8 9 0   D-67 9 8 7

The text of this book—9 on 11, and 10 on 12 Times
Roman—was set on an Intertype Monarch Linecasting
machine driven by computer justified six-level tape.
Times Roman italic and Optima were used for the
chapter heads.

Printed and bound in Canada.

Foreword

In teaching the language arts methods courses over a period of years the authors have searched but failed to find a textbook which blends dynamically the findings of research with the teaching-learning situation in the elementary classroom. *A Dynamic Approach to Language Arts* is based on research involving the nature of the development of the child who is learning the language skills, the role of creativity in language expression, the sequence in which the child develops linguistic skills, the concept of readiness as an integral part of the environment, and a spiral curriculum organization which involves the mastery of skills through an ever broadening and deepening confrontation with them at the different educational levels. An understanding of language arts as the dynamic central core of the child's experiences enables the teacher to make the child's natural need for creative communication a powerful ally in teaching the language arts.

Research stresses that the child's oral facility sets the pattern for his written expression and language development. All too frequently language arts texts lead to drill on rules and mechanics of grammar to the exclusion of oral language activities. The child is propelled into writing long before his eyes are filled with print and his ears with words. As he talks, so shall he read. Yet we rush into a reading program without providing the needed background of experiences in expressing orally what he feels, sees, or experiences.

In teaching the tools of writing, spelling, handwriting, and grammar many textbooks have failed to take into account the significant findings in linguistics which can make the language the child uses to express his ideas an exciting adventure instead of a sheer drudgery. The area of linguistics offers much in the teaching of reading as well as composition and spelling.

Too many textbooks on the market present a pedantic, plodding, pusillanimous method of teaching the language arts. This results all too often in a program which is dull, debilitating, and disenchanting. Consequently the child who expectantly came to the elementary school leaves some years later sans eagerness, sans imagination, and sans talent.

Key concepts in each of the specific disciplines of listening, speaking, reading, and writing; their inter-relatedness; organization of learning experiences; and innovations in methodology based on findings of research will be investigated.

The spiral curriculum design advocated by the authors involves the mastery of skills at each educational level which in turn becomes more complex and challenging as the child advances up the educational ladder. As he gains control of the disciplines involved and confidently expresses his ideas, the deepening and enrichment of earlier understanding is his intrinsic reward. Throughout the text the teacher's task of selecting, planning, organizing, developing, and evaluating the learning experiences is clarified. Differentiated projects and activities are provided for the college student at the end of each chapter. The text will have fulfilled its purpose to the extent that the reader brings children and language together in a way that leads to the goal of language arts—enriched creative communication.

Preface

The teacher who guides children as they develop the arts of language and the skills of communication must keep in mind the significance of discovering within each child the spark of creativity and nurture it so the spark bursts into flame—to become for that child a medium of communication and an avenue of creative expression.

The program in the language arts should provide more than a means of sharing experiences and influencing those with whom children come in contact. It should fulfill the need of the child to experiment, to create, to invent, and to communicate. The use of language, both as a tool for communication and as a medium for creative expression, should be a paramount concern to the teacher as he guides children in their learning experiences in listening, speaking, reading, and writing.

The teacher of tomorrow's adults must recognize the need for today's child to listen both creatively and critically, to speak both fluently and logically, to read both appreciatively and analytically, and to write expressively and concisely.

Central to this book is the concept that creative communication, the goal of the language arts, is attained best through the nurture of each child's creative potential melded with the linguistic skills essential to his purpose. The aim of the book is to guide the prospective teacher and the experienced teacher alike in teaching the skills of communication and the arts of language. Although the elementary school cannot anticipate all the information and skills needed for coping with an uncertain future, it must provide the basic skills of communication and avenues for creative thinking and expression.

Out of the combined experience of some fifty years working in the language arts areas in the public schools and in colleges the authors deal with principles and methods essential to success in teaching the language arts of listening, speaking, reading, and writing. While guiding children through learning experiences in the discrete areas emphasis is placed on the interrelatedness of the language arts. In harmony with the child's mode of learning language, his need of freedom to experiment, the necessity of guidance as he develops the disciplines of the language arts, and encouragement as he uses the tools to develop his unique mode of creativity this book is written. Literature assumes the role of the catylist that moves the child to further creativity and aesthetic experiences. The problem of evaluation as a continuing thread consistent with the concept of teaching the language arts in an environment in which the child is motivated to think, to experience, to create, to communicate, to express is examined from the developmental viewpoint of children's growth in language expression.

Table of Contents

Dedicated to

John E. Robbins

a scholar who demonstrates the power of language

PART ONE: Language Arts and the Children We Teach

1
Through the Language Arts
to Creativity

It is doubtful whether a human being can create, without wishing to share his creation.

Carl R. Rogers

Creative communication is a multiple process in which the individual thinks creatively, plans purposively, organizes logically, and speaks or writes expressively. He is conscious both of his audience and of his purpose. In a world in which creative ideas are essential not alone for self-realization but for survival of the race, the need for developing skill in creative communication has never been greater. The essential linguistic skills for creative expression must be taught to every elementary school child.

There is today a growing body of evidence that creativity is not confined to a favoured few, nor does it manifest itself in the arts alone. *All children are creative.* Within each is a well-spring of potential creativity waiting to be released. All children have a need to communicate. Creative communication begins with cognition, an awareness of the need, however vague, to express an idea or to solve a problem. It is carried through to the moment of communication. It begins in the mind of the individual and is urged along by an irresistable force demanding expression in the communication of the original idea.

THE NEED FOR COMMUNICATION

The elusive quality of creativity has perturbed and long puzzled those who seek to understand it. The mysteries of both the quality and the process become less formidable, however, as the significance of the continuum from cognition to communication is realized in creativity. The child does not communicate in a vacuum. He must have experiences to draw on for his ideas. "The compulsion of the creative mind is primarily to feed on that experience and knowledge out of which it may create."[1] However, knowledge and experiences are not enough. His powers of awareness must be developed if he is to gain satisfaction from his efforts to communicate. This sense of awareness is important in any area of human endeavor.

Every child has a right to an environment rich with language experiences which will not only help him discover his particular inclination toward creative expression, but will encourage him to *want* to pursue it—to create again and again. He enjoys the feeling of exhilaration that comes when the creative process is completed and his product—a poem, a story, an essay, the solution to a problem—is shared and understood by at least one other person. The teacher must realize that although the child has completed the "product", the total goal is not achieved nor is his feeling of completeness fulfilled until the idea is communicated. A seven-year-old expressed this concept when he said, "I hear a voice. I have to say it to see if that is what I want to write." Observe the ten-year-old as his expression changes from puzzlement to elation when he finds the precise word in the dictionary that expresses his exact meaning. He is delighted by the creative effect he has achieved, but he is not satisfied until he communicates the expression of his idea.

Rogers recognizes this need for communication as an integral part of creativity. "It is doubtful," he states, "whether a being can create, without wishing to share his creation. It is the only way he can assuage the anxiety of separateness and assure himself that he belongs to the group. He may confine his theories only to his private diary. He may put his discoveries in some cryptic code. He may conceal his poems in a locked drawer. He may put away his paintings in a closet. Yet he desires to communicate with a group which will understand him. . . . He does not create in order to communicate, but once having created he desires to share his new aspect of himself-in-relation-to-his-environment with others."[2]

The experience of the five-year-old Jimmie illustrates this need to communicate. After listening to the story of *Karl's Wooden Horse* Jimmie went to the easel and painted a picture. When he finished he hurried over to his teacher. "Come and see Karl's Wooden Horse—his beautiful magic horse." As soon as he had a response from his teacher—a smile, a nod, and an appreciative comment, "You *are* an artist"—he was content. He had communicated his idea to one who was ready to receive it. Later his painting was shown to one who was not ready to comprehend it. At the close of school his mother was waiting for him at the curb. He hurried over to her and held up his picture proudly. Mother looked at the picture in bewilderment and asked, "What in the world is *that?*" "It's Karl's Wooden Horse. Don't you know the story?" He excitedly related the story in his own words. The blue horse became his Pegasus to creative communication.

When a child is able to communicate his ideas he is motivated to continue in creative endeavors. This is an extremely important factor in developing communication. Not only must the child *want* to communicate, he must have someone to receive his communication. He will be more willing to come out of his emotional shell and express his ideas spontaneously if he knows that they will be understood and appreciated. Success leads to success and satisfaction to satisfaction as he moves confidently from tentative excursions in language to creative expression and effective communication.

NON-VERBAL COMMUNICATION

If the hypothetical "average person" is asked what is meant by communication he will usually respond by telling you that it means talking to someone or reading what someone has written. If he probes a bit further he will recall that he knew that Kris was despondent, even though he hadn't talked to him, because of the way he walked into the office and sat at his desk. An investigation of how we learn about people and things reveals that a considerable share of our knowledge comes to us through non-verbal communication. We "read" a person's posture, we interpret the tone of his voice. We understand the slight shrug of the shoulders or the lift of an eyebrow. In other words, his actions often speak louder than his words and give us a clue to situations which mere words cannot do.

Non-verbal communication is not limited to the familiar use of the body as cues to meaning and mood. The musician is "sent" by his favourite performer, the lover of art finds his soul refreshed after a day in the museum, the mathematician and scientist read symbols that are incomprehensible to the layman, and understand what they mean.

We are becoming more fully aware of the variety and significance of non-verbal communication, gestures, facial expression, tactile contacts, and the immense range of signs, symbols, and signals by which messages are conveyed, ideas are transmitted, and communication understood. Non-verbal communication may reinforce, weaken, or contradict the verbal message just as the tone of the voice may distort or negate what is being said. "What you are speaks so loudly that I can't hear what you say."

The extent to which gestures are useful in communicating is vividly brought to mind when one attempts to communicate in a foreign tongue via the telephone, only to discover to his dismay that without the use of the non-verbal cues communication is well-nigh impossible—unless one is expert in the foreign language.

Concepts About Non-Verbal Communication

Visible or sign language is the first level of communication. The only avenue through which the very young child can express his creativity is in non-verbal communication. He is not bound by conformity to previous patterns of speech. He makes use of the tools he has to express himself. He communicates spontaneously with gestures long before he knows what words mean. From time immemorial various types of non-verbal communication have served man well. "When Columbus discovered America he found copper-skinned natives who had been separated from peoples of the Old World. . . . They spoke approximately 100 distinctly different word-languages, none of them related to the languages of Europe or Asia, *but these newly discovered natives shook their heads for 'no' and nodded their heads for 'yes', exactly as did Columbus' crew of Mediterranean sailors and as had the Greeks, Romans, Egyptians, Mesopotamians and all the others.* These newly discovered natives raised their right arm to greet an approaching stranger, as had the knights of Medieval Europe. They turned palms down to express disapproval, palms up to express approval, and lifted their hands in supplication—as did people everywhere in the world. They had a universal sign language by which they could talk to members of other tribes—and this sign language was almost identical with that used in other parts of the world. . . .

Visible, or sign language is older than the spoken word. It is more uniform. It is written more deeply into our organisms, and carries more basic meanings. We use spoken words for refined thought, but for broad, deep basic meanings we use action. We are civilized, yes; but the eye is still quicker than the ear."[3]

EMPATHY: *A form of non-verbal communication.* Empathy is the physical and emotional response to situations and ideas. It implies a "feeling in with". This feeling of empathy is the basis for the phenomenal success of spectator sports. It is the explanation for the exhilaration experienced by the spectator as he empathizes with muscles tensed, body forward, and hands clenched while he plays the game with the team—on the football field, the basket ball court, or the hockey rink. Empathy is involved not only in the sports, but also in the arts. One is exhilarated by a hilarious comedy or exhausted by a tense tragedy.

DANCE: *A refined form of non-verbal communication.* Dance is an imaginative non-verbal language in which ideas and feelings are communicated through the organization of rhythm, movement, colour, space, shape, form, and level. The ability of the dancer to transform subjective experiences into non-verbal, imaginative, visual language is often more effective in communicating human thoughts and feelings than the more familiar verbal types of communication.

The core of the creative process lies in the ability to mold experience into creative forms that communicate the experience to another—translating the idea, the impression of the artist into imaginative and at times non-verbal language. "The artist in search of his subject looks about him with the eyes of the painter, the sculptor, the dancer, or the poet, responding to what fits his form."[4]

The forces operating within a given individual who is creating at a particular period in time and those operating within that society will influence the specific art forms. Communication of creative ideas in whatever form they take or whatever medium is used for the creation, has a spiritual significance in that it releases within us forces that are universal. To the extent that one becomes aware of this power and utilizes it, the esthetic response can be more fully developed. Creativity is a developmental process. The ability to communicate creatively develops with the ability to utilize both the non-verbal and verbal forms of communication.

No barrier of language impedes the comprehension of the viewer of the dance. No archaic vocabulary hinders his appreciation. The dancer interprets life as he views it. "For life is not an occasional, partial affair, but a constant balancing on the point of intersection where past and future meet."[5]

VERBAL COMMUNICATION

Human beings are difficult to understand merely through non-verbal forms of communication. What is needed for clearer understanding of the refinements of social behaviour is verbal communication. It is the highest form of the meeting of minds. "We see, feel, and sense those aspects of the cosmos which our language habits predispose us to interpret. . . . The verbal symbol itself does not tell us what this behaviour should be, but it has alerted us to observe both the verbal and nonverbal behaviour of the individual . . ."[6]

Verbal communication is the most refined means for stimulating thoughts, ideas, and concepts. The highest purpose of language is meaningful communication. When we listen we respond in terms of our experience. When we speak or write we share our ideas and experiences with others. We are communicating through verbal media. "Communication is the key that unlocks the mind and puts it in the service of society."[7]

"The ability to . . . express ideas clearly and succinctly, to listen courteously but critically, and to evaluate introspectively yet objectively is important in a democratic society. In fact it is to people who develop such skills, and who are able to get along with others, that we look for leadership."[8] The world in which we live is a verbal one. "Without words our imagination cannot retain distinct objects and their relations, but out of sight is out of mind. . . . The transformation of experience into concepts, . . . not the elaboration of symbols and signs, is the motive for language."[9]

By the time the child enters school, language is his most important activity. "He reaches out for language with a hunger that often exceeds his physical desire for food. Food he eats occasionally; speech is his ceaseless activity in waking moments."[10] We are not blessed with a birthright of vocabularies and syntaxes. Children must be provided with an environment in which they are stimulated and helped to communicate.

Without skill in verbal communication today's children will be unprepared to meet the demands of living in tomorrow's world. The role of the various media of communication, international conferences, and world planning in modern society points up the need for developing communication skills and the arts of language in the classroom. Without ability to express himself creatively through language the individual fails in finding this avenue for attaining self-realization, an essential need of every human being.

CONCLUDING STATEMENT

Long before the child comes to school, long before he meets a teacher who assumes the responsibility of teaching him linguistic skills, the child has discovered that language is a powerful weapon. He has already learned much about people and places. He has learned to use language as a means of persuasion. He has learned to read adults by their actions and tone of voice as well as by their words. He has learned to use and understand both verbal and non-verbal language—movement, gestures, and voice quality.

He comes to the door of the school with a language of his own, a set of tools for expression. He has, in fact, accomplished a remarkable intellectual feat in acquiring the basic language system which, in his particular circumstances, will develop increasingly into an avenue for creative communication.

In an environment where the inter-relatedness of language arts and creativity are appreciated, the child will find opportunities for building upon those language skills he already possesses. The teacher should recognize that the basis of the language arts program for the elementary school is a sound oral language program. The child will first be encouraged to express his ideas and experiences orally and informally. Opportunities should be provided, however, for him to have many experiences in such non-verbal activities as rhythms, dance, pantomime, and dramatic play before he encounters the advanced activities of the language arts.

Such an environment will reflect the significant role of the language arts in providing the child with the tools for communication skills and the avenue for creative expression. It will reflect the importance of building the language arts program in harmony with the developmental nature of the child's ability to listen, speak, read, and write. Finally, such an approach will emphasize the inter-relatedness of the language arts while at the same time it delineates the unique elements of each of the disciplines which go to make up the language arts curriculum.

REFERENCES

1. Stephen Spender, "Poets and Critics: The Forgotten Difference," *Saturday Review,* 46:17, p. x.
2. By permission from Carl R. Rogers, "Toward a Theory of Creativity," in Sydney J. Parnes and Harold H. Harding (eds.), *A Source Book for Creative Thinking,* Charles Scribner's Sons, New York, 1962, p. 32.
3. William N. Brigance, *Speech: Its Techniques and Disciplines in a Free World.* Copyright, 1952, by Appleton-Century-Crofts, Inc. Reprinted by permission of Appleton-Century-Crofts, Division of Meredith Publishing Company, pp. 323, 324.
4. R. Arnheim, *Art and Visual Perception: A Psychology of the Creative Eye,* University of California Press, Berkeley, 1954, p. 408.
5. C. W. Ceram, *Gods, Graves, and Scholars,* tr. E. B. Garside, Alfred A. Knopf, New York, 1952, p. 20.
6. Emma Marie Birkmaier, "Modern Languages: Vehicle for the Humanities," *Educational Leadership,* 20:239, January, 1963.
7. Louis A. Fliegler, *Curriculum Planning for the Gifted,* Prentice-Hall, Inc., Englewood Cliffs, 1961, p. 43.
8. By permission from Lillian M. Logan and Virgil G. Logan, *Teaching the Elementary School Child,* Houghton Mifflin Company, Boston, 1961, p. 226.
9. Susanne K. Langer, *Philosophy in a New Key,* rev., The New American Library, New York, 1958, p. 113.
10. Harry R. Warfel, "Structural Linguistics and Composition," *College English,* 20:209, February, 1959.

2

The Creative Potential of the Children We Teach

Creativity is the most basic manifestation of man's fulfilling his own being in his world.

Rollo May

Children come to school with various stages of language development. Linda, a five-year-old, was being interviewed by the school psychologist. The first part of the interview proceeded without incident. Cooperative, interested, and capable, she talked freely. When asked the question, "Why is it better to use brick than wood as a building material?" she answered, "We haven't yet established that it is better in terms of purpose, locality, and availability of materials."

A father reported reading *Mother Goose* to his four-year-old son. "I started with 'Tom, Tom, The Piper's Son.' Right away he started interrupting. 'Was Tom about my age? What is a piper? Was Tom's father poor? Is that why Tom stole the pig? If he was my age, how did he carry a pig? If the pig was so small, how did it kill a goose? What's a calaboose?' "

Another father told of answering as best he could his seven-year-old son's questions about what things are made of. The next day he had a call from the second grade teacher, complaining of Tommy's disruptive behaviour. "I'm afraid he is being over-stimulated at home," she said. "When he came into class today, he said, 'You're nothing but a bunch of molecules.' "[1]

Creativity is expressed in so many different ways that identification of the creative individual is no simple task. What distinguishes the individual who upon walking through the quiet countryside, or crowded city streets, contemplates the grandeur of the sunset and later expresses in a poem or an essay what he thinks or feels? What force impels one individual to extract from the world around him the elements which he transforms into creative content and another to be content to view and comment merely, "How beautiful"? What impels one individual to look at a complicated problem from an original viewpoint while another merely seeks for a solution in a traditional way?

Tentative answers to such questions can be found in the results of research and from empirical evidence. These will provide a framework for understanding and interpreting the linguistic behaviour of boys and girls. It is in this expression of the creative impulse that the individual attains self-fulfillment. To the teacher is given much of the responsibility for identifying the specific talents of the child and provid-

9

ing avenues through which he may express his creativity. Knowledge gained from research gives the teacher more than empirical evidence as his basis for observation, identification, and nurture of the creative talent of the individual.

CHARACTERISTICS OF THE CREATIVE INDIVIDUAL: FINDINGS FROM RESEARCH

An examination of the literature reveals that cognitive factors and personality-motivational elements loom large as clues for identifying the creative individual. A multidimensional approach will reveal some characteristics which will serve as clues for the teacher as he seeks to recognize creativity.

As early as 1916 Chassell[2] compared a hundred students at Northwestern University with an inventor of international reputation to ascertain the relationships between creativity and cognitive factors by means of tests devised to discover and rank the individuals studied on the degree of originality they exhibited. The inventor was found not to be particularly original, but proved to be industrious and persevering.

Hargreaves[3] (1927) hypothesized that the "unknown" common denominator found in his tests of imagination were cognitive in nature.

More recently Guilford summarized his own thinking and research findings as well as that of his colleagues in the area of creativity. His approach to the problem was through trait concepts, defined by means of his own factor-analysis. These traits he discusses and defines. He provides examples of tests used to measure them. The following aptitude traits have been found to be related to creativity: "(a) ability to see problems (while this factor plays no constructive part in productive thinking, productive thinking cannot begin without it); (b) fluency of thinking, which involves four factors—word fluency, associational fluency, expressional fluency, and ideational fluency; (c) flexibility of thinking, which includes two factors—spontaneous flexibility and adaptive flexibility; (d) originality; (e) redefinition; (f) elaboration."[4] Identifying creativity involves a study of personality and motivational factors in addition to the cognitive factors emphasized in the I.Q. tests.

PERSONALITY STUDIES OF HIGHLY CREATIVE INDIVIDUALS

Most of the early research on creativity centered around adults. Only recently is there a concentrated effort to study the creative child. Various researchers from their studies of highly creative individuals have drawn portraits of the creative individual, each from his particular point of view. Since creativity, like growth, is an ongoing process, a view of the creative adult will hold value for those guiding creative development in children—the teacher, the counselor, the parent, and the prospective educator. In the search for identifying the creative individual not one possible clue should be overlooked.

Protrait by Barron

A study, under the direction of Frank Barron, Research Psychologist at the Institute of Personality Assessment and Research of the University of California, in which the characteristics of a large number of individuals in a group composed of artists, writers, physicians, physicists, biologists, economists, and anthropologists brought to light some interesting findings. The degree of creativeness of the individuals studied was estimated on the basis of opinions of colleagues or by experts in their particular medium of expression. Based on this and similar studies, Barron paints the following portrait of creative artists, and perhaps also of creative scientists:

> Creative people are especially observant, and they value accurate observation (telling themselves the truth) more than other people do.
> They often express part-truths, but this they do vividly; the part they express is the generally unrecognized; by displacement of accent and apparent disproportion in statement they seek to point to the usually unobserved.
> They see things as others do, but also as others do not.
> They are thus independent in their cognition, and they also value clearer cognition. They will suffer great personal pain to testify correctly.
> They are motivated to this value and to the exercise of this talent (independent, sharp observation) both for reasons of self-preservation and in the interest of human culture and its future.
> They are born with greater brain capacity; they have more ability to hold many ideas at once, and to compare more ideas with another—hence to make a richer synthesis.
> In addition to unusual endowment in terms of cognitive ability, they are by constitution more vigorous and have available to them an exceptional fund of psychic and physical energy.
> Their universe is thus more complex, and in addition they usually lead more complex lives, seeking tension in the interest of the pleasure they obtain upon its discharge.
> They have more contact than most people do with the life of the unconscious—with fantasy, reverie, the world of the imagination.
> They have exceptionally broad and flexible awareness of themselves. . . . The creative person is both more primitive and more cultured, more destructive and more constructive, crazier and saner, than the average person.
> When the distinction between subject (self) and object is most secure, the distinction can with most security be allowed to disappear for a time (as in mysticism and in deep love. . .).
> The objective freedom of the individual is at maximum when this capacity exists, and creative potential is directly a function of freedom.[5]

"Perhaps most of all," states Barron, "creative persons are moved by an intense commitment of an almost metaphysical sort that impels them to search for new forms of artistic vision."[6]

Portrait by Guilford

Guilford in his research at the University of Southern California as Director of the Project on Aptitudes of High-level Personnel, sponsored by the Office of Naval Research, has received world-wide acclaim for his more than ten year study of creativity. In these studies of architects, scientists, and engineers Guilford, through factor analysis, identified specific abilities related to creative thinking. He considered the specific qualities, abilities, and other traits which characterize the creative individual and reports some of these in the portrait of the creative individual:

> The creative individual is a fluent, flexible, and elaborate thinker. Much of his success, however, is dependent upon his fund of special information in the field of his endeavor.
>
> A creative person is inclined toward impulsive behavior. He lets his feelings and emotion dictate action, but is capable of reflective thinking. He likes to ponder over philosophical themes and over the nature of human behavior. He is an independent thinker.
>
> The creative individual is self-assertive, self sufficient, tolerant of ambiguity, and cozy with disorder and complexity.
>
> Possession of the attributes or aptitudes cited will not guarantee that the individual will be creative. Other traits, needs, interests and attitudes, and of temperament are also important in developing creativity. It takes motivation and hard work to excel in performance and to exhibit a high level of output. Nothing takes the place of faithful application to the creative task.[7]

Portrait by Taylor

Calvin Taylor, principal investigator for the National Science Foundation, sponsored a series of research conferences on the Identification of Creative Scientific Talent at the University of Utah. From an analysis of the data these characteristics have been identified:

> COMMUNICATION ABILITIES.   Communication abilities tests reveal the importance of ability to sense problems, adeptness in recognizing ambiguity, and skill in effective questioning sometimes described as questing, or curiosity in action.
>
> MOTIVATIONAL CHARACTERISTICS.   Among the motivational characteristics which have implications for the classroom teacher are curiosity, inquiry, liking to think, liking to toy with ideas, liking to manipulate elements, intellectual persistence, need for variety, need for recognition for achievement, willingness to take long-range risks, effective work habits, and high energy level.
>
> Other personality characteristics cited by Taylor include: commitment to autonomy, self-sufficiency, independence, complex personality, self-accepting, resourcefulness, originality, adventurous, self-controlled, sensitive, introverted but confident.[8]

Portrait by Lowenfeld

At Penn State University Viktor Lowenfeld and his associates developed over a period of years some "criteria for creativity" based on a study of artists and art students. Note the similarity of these findings concerning the creative characteristics of artists and those identified by Guilford in a study of architects, scientists, and engineers.

The most effective individuals were found to possess the following qualities:

The creative person readily adapts or adjusts to new situations, a quality defined as "flexibility".

A creative person exhibits fluency of ideas, not alone in verbal expression but in a variety of art media. (Non verbal communication.)

A creative person is original in thought and expression as opposed to "conforming". (The non-creative child fastens his clothing with a button. For a creative child buttons become elephant eyes or other spring-boards to imagination.)

A creative person gives uncommon responses to questions and offers unusual solutions to problems. The solutions appear to come from the depths of their minds rather than from the top layer.

A creative person tends to substitute functions of the materials he uses. He is adept at combining materials in some organized fashion, using materials in unique ways and searching for original ideas.

A creative person is capable of synthesizing—that is combining—several elements in a meaningful fashion to create something new.

A creative person is skillful in coherent organization. He has the ability to weave the necessary elements into a meaningful coherent whole. Whether it be the case of the artist who skillfully arranges colour, line, and shape; the musician who works with melody, rhythm, harmony, and relates movements of a symphony or other monumental composition; or the mathematician who uses the steps of logic to solve the problem confronting him—the principle of coherent organization is operating.

The creative person is unusually sensitive to what he sees, hears, and touches.

The creative person empathizes with people of other cultures and races.

The creative person has social awareness to a great degree.[9]

PERSONALITY PORTRAITS OF HIGHLY CREATIVE ADOLESCENTS

Counsellors, teachers, and parents are becoming more concerned with finding out all they can about the characteristics which distinguish the creative adolescent. They are recognizing that development is a continuous process and that patterns of development in creativity proceed in harmony with each child's unique growth pattern. Because children progress through similar stages of development at different rates and at their own pace some of the traits which characterize the creative adolescent may appear in the elementary school child.

Attempts to identify creativity in adolescents have been made largely in terms of such factors as achievement, teacher judgment, and academic grades. Intellectual factors, motivation, and personality factors have also received the attention of researchers. One of the most interesting recent studies is that of Elizabeth Drew.

Portrait by Drew

Elizabeth Drew of Michigan State University in an eight year study of the records, interests, creative products of some thousand gifted high school students conducted in the public schools of Lansing, Michigan and Boston, Massachusetts attempted to describe superior adolescents. Her objective was to "depict the disparate styles, tempos, and patterns of the gifted and to bring test data and reality closer together."[10] Drew compiled the results which evolved from the study into the following four categories: the high-achieving studious, the social leaders, the creative intellectuals, and the rebels. The students—dramatically different from each other—were able to describe themselves according to these types:

THE HIGH-ACHIEVING STUDIOUS. These students are known by such terms as "egg-heads", "grinds".

Twice as many girls are high-achievers as boys in terms of grades, although on standardized achievement tests they tend to rank equally.

High-achievers conform to the suggestions and/or demands of teachers and parents readily, putting their school work ahead of pleasure.

They are dependable in completing assignments, and are highly productive in volume of output of work, but not necessarily outstanding in creativity and originality.

They want assignments which are explicit, lectures which are well organized, and prefer the textbook-workbook method.

They have a high sense of organization, a feeling for logic, and are oriented to means rather than ends.

High-achieving studious read to improve their grades and their knowledge rather than for pleasure.

High-achievers are not often school leaders, and rate recreation lowest in relation to other interests checked and compared to choices made by other groups.

Teachers are often favourably predisposed to the high-achieving studious since they enjoy school, are interested in school subjects, and are eager to please.

Many of the girls in this group expect to become teachers. The boys prefer mathematics and science and tend to be drawn toward engineering.

Punctual, punctilious, persevering, neat, attractive, hard working, and conscientious they make fine citizens. They will be excellent employees. They may not scintillate at parties but they will shine on their monthly reports.

THE SOCIAL LEADERS. Social leadership requires the communication skills which often characterize a type of the highly creative individual. This type of gifted child, the social leader type, is said to epitomize popularity. He is the one who shines in social relationships.

As a group the social leaders tend to conform more to peer mores than to teacher expectations.

The social interests of this group come first although they achieve well enough and sometimes very well academically. (While the studious study for exams and the intellectuals are reading about existentialism, the social leaders are getting people elected to office, or more important, getting elected themselves.)

Fluent, personable, charming, and social they are the "campus wheels".

As a group they begin to date early and are quite at home in the country club. The offspring of young, handsome, well educated, well connected parents, their basic values tend to be materialistic, rounded out with hedonism.

Community minded, they are crusaders of popular causes, but not too interested in India's starving population.

Well liked, popular, agreeable, they will probably become corporation executives, lawyers, doctors. As one of the intellectual students said, "There isn't a teacher or a minister or a scientist or a real genuine attic-prone artist in the lot of them. They want jobs that pay."

THE CREATIVE INTELLECTUAL. The creative intellectual is a nonconformist. (He does not conform either to the teacher's standards or those set by other students.)

The creative intellectual is found in the entire socio-economic range of society. The creative intellectually inclined is interested in a wide variety of areas: literature, philosophy, psychology, music, science, art, extra-sensory perception.

The creative intellectuals form the large core of future scientists, artists, writers, musicians, and scholars-at-large.

The creative intellectual revolves in his orbit. He is usually not a leader and has no interest in becoming one.

The creative intellectual is fluent and highly original in creativity tests, has a sense of humour, and a subtle "zing" which allows creativity to come into full play.

The feminine creative intellectual finds it difficult to be accepted by fellow students or teachers. Social prejudices and traditions operate to prolong this attitude.

The creative intellectual tends to ask beneath the surface questions. He is concerned with basic issues, and problems plaguing mankind rather than with immediate questions such as who will win the student election.

The creative intellectual is eager to take responsibility for learning: he wants freedom in assignments, freedom to explore, freedom to formulate standards and rules.

The creative intellectual reads widely. He purchases books and has broad interests beyond the usual perusal of encyclopedia, current news magazines. He reads science fiction, religion and biography, Russian translations, French in the original, free verse, classics, and plays. He sees education as a continuing process, not just a course of study and a series of grades on report cards.

The creative intellectual combines a skepticism with a deep seated idealism.

He has a deep sense of commitment. Drew cites one student who remarked, "I would be willing to kill myself for the discovery of one small segment of truth, even if only one person in the world understood it."

The creative intellectual has more social conscience than social inclination. He rarely dates.

The creative intellectual is more concerned with the process than the product— with inner life more than the external evidences—with intrinsic rather than extrinsic rewards.

THE REBEL. The rebel, or the individualistic creative non-intellectual, is the fourth type of able students indentified by Drew. He exhibits the following characteristics:

The creative non-intellectual is identified chiefly by a general nonconformity which serves as a means of showing his dislike for regimentation at all levels.

He attaches little value to things intellectual or social.

He is in most cases of the masculine sex who is low in social responsibility and high on the delinquency scales and comprises a very small group of the population surveyed.

The rebel is predominantly of the lower socio-economic class origin whose parents are often "outsiders".

The rebel ranks high in technical skills. He has potential for success in the entertainment and sports world.

The rebel is a "do-it-yourself" fan. He may be clever with his hands.

The rebel, although lacking fluency in a verbal situation, is highly creative in his special areas of interest.

The rebel, while at odds with society as a result of rejection, may sometimes respond to novel ideas and challenging problems which are significant to him.

If given the appropriate direction the rebel may become more socialized, more human, and more positively directed.[11]

Portrait by Getzels and Jackson

A study of able students was carried on by Getzels and Jackson of the University of Chicago. In an effort to broaden the base for the identification of the gifted and differentiate the characteristics unique to the high-creatives as compared with the high-intellectuals, they examined various types of giftedness. The students studied ranged from the sixth grade through the senior high school. The academic achievement of the two groups—highly creative and highly intelligent—was equally superior to the total school population. Among the characteristics identified in the high-creatives were the following:

The high-creatives have a highly developed sense of humour. On fantasy production the creative individual makes greater use of stimulus-free themes, surprise endings, humour, and playfulness. He tends to structure a task in his own terms and is less bound to the specific details of the instructions.

The high-creatives exhibit a certain mocking attitude toward conformity and "conventional success". Sixty-two per cent of the high-creatives chose unconventional occupations such as adventurer, writer, inventor, and artist.

The high-creatives express more violence along with humour in their verbal and non-verbal imaginative productions. They are more in contact with impulses from within that are denied expression in overt action but may be expressed in creative activity.

The high-creatives appear to enjoy the risk and uncertainity of the unknown. They are drawn toward the untried, the unexplored, the uncertain. They tend to use imagination.

The high-creatives tend to produce new forms, conjoin elements that are ordinarily regarded as dissimilar and to "go off" in new directions.

The high-creatives are independent of teachers and adults in their measure of adult success.

In short, Getzels and Jackson found that the outstanding quality of the creative individual as compared with the non-creative is the ability to toy with ideas, elements, and concepts.[12]

Portrait by Hammer

In an exploratory investigation of the personalities of gifted adolescent artists in the eleventh and twelfth grades, E. F. Hammer attempted to contrast the genuinely creative with the merely facile personality. Eighteen subjects were selected, five of whom were identified as "truly creative" and five as "merely facile". On the basis of psychological studies the following characteristics were ascribed to the "truly creative":

> They exhibited deeper feelings than the merely facile.
> They displayed greater original responsiveness.
> They showed a distinct preference for the role of the observer over that of the participant.
> They had stronger determination, ambition, and perseverance.
> They displayed greater integration of feminine and masculine traits.
> They possessed greater independence of thought and action.
> They were more rebellious.
> They had a deep sense of self-awareness.
> They appeared to have greater needs for creative self-expression.
> They possessed a more complete range of emotional expression.
> They were able to withstand personal discomfort when engaged in a project.[13]

It is important that the teacher, the counsellor, the parent recognize that the highly creative has even greater problems and more of them than the so-called "average" child. He is generally more sensitive, more temperamental, and often misunderstood. He compensates in various ways for the rough spots in his work-a-day world. He may indulge in flights of fancy and be criticized for being lazy, bored, withdrawn. He may rebel because his assignments in school hold little challenge or interest for him. He may cause trouble in the classroom by negative, disruptive behaviour. On the other hand, when he discovers a special interest in science, art, music, literature, drama through which to express his creative drive he has unbounded energy and can work hours on end without feeling fatigue or being bored.

IDENTIFYING THE CREATIVE CHILD

Although all children are creative, creativity varies in kind as well as in degree. It is essential for the teacher to know the characteristics of the creative child in order to recognize such characteristics in whatever degree they may be found in the children he teaches. Among these are curiosity, flexibility, sensitivity to problems, originality, insight, ability to see relationships, and self-directedness.

Unless the teacher is equipped with such knowledge he may never uncover the range of creativity which exists in the children in his classroom. Creativity which is not discovered and motivated tends to atrophy. Creative abilities determine the potential for creative behaviour; motivation and tempermental traits determine whether one will realize his potential.

To be deplored is the lack of attention to the creative individual in the classroom. "Many of our present academic programs are stressing non-creative activities so that work habits which are being developed are strongly ingrained and are valuable in accomplishing non-creative things. Some of these successful persons may show real resistance and perhaps emotional disturbances if late in their education, or anytime afterwards on the job, they are asked to be creative. They may resist this late change 'in the nature of the ball game' even though they may have high, though uncultivated, potential to be creative. Such conflicts might be avoided if creativity training and encouragement had occured much earlier or even throughout their entire academic training."[14]

A study by the authors of one hundred twenty kindergarten boys and girls designed to identify creativity through art experiences reveals findings which have significance to teachers of young children. The control group were matched for sex, intelligence, class (teacher), and age with the creative subjects. Evaluations were based on the California Test of Mental Maturity, Draw-a-House-Tree-Person Test, Easel Age Scale, peer nominations of creative products, teacher nominations based on observation, and individual self-evaluation.

Five personality characteristics appeared to dominate the creatives:

> The creatives were more self-reliant. They immediately went ahead with a project, used their own ideas without waiting to see what someone else was doing.
> The creatives evidenced a greater concern for detail.
> The creatives displayed a variety in the modes of expression.
> The creatives gained great satisfaction from the process as well as the product.
> The creatives displayed originality, "tongue in cheek" expression, humour, playfulness, lack of stereotype when they shared their product with the group.

Personality traits observed in the creatives gave evidence that these children were: attracted to the mysterious, desirous of excelling, adventurous, emotionally sensitive, energetic, curious, receptive to external stimuli, tempermental, preoccupied with a problem until they found a solution which satisfied them, highly communicative, impatient, willful, and self-assertive.

Unfortunately, a highly creative child is often unpopular, not only with his classmates, but with his teachers. Many teachers tend to prefer children who are conforming, who do not upset the equilibrium of the classroom, who are more academically inclined, and who are satisfied with the usual routine of the class. Many a creative child is bored by the classroom activities and reacts by becoming disruptive, silly, uncooperative, or naughty. He may even be classed as a slow learner or under-achiever because he fails to respond to the accepted patterns of behaviour. He may prefer concentrating on his individual projects to working on some dull, meaningless assignment which fails to challenge him. At times he conforms in self-defence and deliberately sublimates his creativity in an effort to be one of the group.

A great need is the teacher who values creativity, helps the child appreciate his unique gift, aids him to accept his limitations as well as his strengths, understands how to guide the development of his creative talents, creates a climate in which creativity can develop, provides the necessary materials and conditions, and plans activities which encourage self-expression and keeps alive the creative spark. Specific suggestions for aiding teachers in meeting these responsibilities will be given in later chapters.

IDENTIFYING SPECIAL TALENTS IN CHILDREN

Mere knowledge of the general characteristics which distinguish creativity does not equip the teacher to identify the specific avenue whereby the child might express this creativity. It is important to identify as early as possible the child who has a special interest in art, music, writing, drama, science, leadership skill, and other areas.

Identifying Artistic Talent

The child talented in art, exhibits to a marked degree the following behaviour: He

Is eager to express himself in a variety of art media

Paints or draws a wide variety of things—not limited to people, animals, houses, trees, jets, or rockets

Finds satisfaction in creating with art media—concentrates as he works

Organizes pictures and gives attention to balance, colour, line, and design

Is original in content and process in art expression—does not imitate work of the other children

Selects art whenever he has an opportunity to choose an activity

Is eager to experiment with new media, materials, and art activities

Uses art as a medium for expressing creatively his feelings, ideas, and experiences

Likes to model with clay, carve with soap, make collages, work with many forms of dimensional art

Experiments with less conventional materials such as old newspapers, wire, cement, sand, metal, cardboard

Shows an unusual interest in art of other people, but maintains his originality in content and process as he creates

Is sensitive to his environment, more imaginative in his responses, and eager to express himself in an art medium

Derives keen pleasure from visiting art museums and other places where art objects are exhibited.

Because children express themselves creatively in painting, modeling, and sculpture does not guarantee that they will become artists, or even indicate that they have exceptional artistic talent. It means merely that paint and clay at the moment are the avenues through which they can express their creativity. In later life they may be creative in such other fields as science, medicine, business, or teaching. "Artistic development is a slow process that is wrapped up in the development of the individual student, his whole pattern of perceiving, creating, and living."[15]

The teacher first gets a clear picture of the general characteristics which mark the creative child and looks for evidences of the specific talent whereby he best expresses his creativity. Such an approach in no way ignores other factors in guiding creativity such as understanding the process of creating or the environment in which creativity flourishes, nor even the product created. It takes all of these into consideration at some point and to some degree, but the initial focus must be on the person—the child who is creating. Only THEN can we provide every child with his rightful heritage.

Identifying Musical Talent

Musical talent may be first discovered by the classroom teacher who provides opportunities for children to explore, to experiment, to express themselves through a variety of musical activities. The alert teacher opens doors to musical enjoyment.

The child with musical talent gives evidence of some of these behaviours:

> Responds with bodily movement when he hears music
> Reacts eagerly, spontaneously, and with originality to rhythm and melody
> Shows a strong curiosity and sustained interest in music, accompanied by a desire to create musical sounds via some particular medium
> Possesses tonal memory and draws on this skill in creating original tunes, accompaniements, and patterns in music
> Evidences the ability to reproduce melodies as well as ability to compose original ones at an early age
> Enjoys improvising, composing, and transposing music into various keys
> Is ready for musical instruction at the preschool age
> Shows evidence of creative imagination and emotional sensitivity
> Is interested in music; listens to recordings; attends concerts; puts himself out to hear music
> Enjoys singing in groups and harmonizing with others
> Performs well on at least one instrument.

Identifying Talent for Writing

"Painting is silent poetry, and poetry is painting with the gift of speech." (Simonides) One of the distinguishing marks of the gifted child is his unusual fluency in language. He is an artist with words. He talks earlier than the average child; acquires a colourful, vivid, and extensive vocabulary early; uses more complex forms of expression; blends rhymes, rhythm, and ideas in a highly poetic and original manner. Clues indicating a flair for imaginative writing reveals that the talented child:

Is sensitive to the world of nature and the world of people and to the phenomena he observes as he interacts with his environment

Has a keen perception of details, coupled with a memory which enables him to recall minutia

Has a flair for perceiving, recording and expressing the uncommon in an original, unique, and often "tongue in cheek" quality

Gives a refreshing twist even to old ideas

Is flexible in modifying an accepted idea, an established pattern, through a unique approach

Gives wholehearted attention and concentrated effort to the writing task

Shows complete absorption in the activity even under the most unfavourable conditions

Accepts discipline necessary to perfect any art, realizing that mastery of an art requires tools and techniques

Is conscious of the need to do his best work at all times

Finds satisfaction in the creative process—not alone in the product

Writes from a sense of urgency to create—not to fulfill the requirements of an assignment.

Identifying Dramatic Talent

Universal with children in every clime and in every land is the desire to "make believe". Dramatic talent appears early in the child's development and he expresses this talent as he "tries on life". "The world and I" might well be the theme of his creative activity. This talent can be observed to some degree in every child; it can be observed to a remarkable degree is some children. Evidences of dramatic ability can be seen in every classroom and playground.

These children:

Display more than the customary amount of alertness, attentiveness, and responsiveness to the world of people, situations, events

See relationships of social situations immediately and respond readily

Give evidence of intuitive and insightful behaviour which coupled with ease in verbalization and comprehension makes dramatic expression a natural avenue for creativity

Possess empathy—a physical and emotional response to situations—the ability to "feel in with" an individual

Have skill in creating and maintaining a mood

Are poised and at ease in handling various situations

Have high ability to visualize and dramatize situations and to identify completely with the character they portray

Show originality in creating the role—using both non-verbal and verbal means of communicating emotions and ideas in response to the situation

Have a flair for the dramatic in staging from the standpoint of design, colour, and balance.

Discovering Leadership Talent

Although all leaders exhibit some traits which can be identified, it is clear that leadership is not a single trait or ability. Children possessing high potential for social leadership exhibit many of the following characteristics:

Show understanding of others and have tact in working with them
Have ability to release tensions
Demonstrate high level skill in communication, both oral and written
Have confidence in themselves
Facilitate a feeling of group solidarity
Help the group organize and carry out projects
Have ability to assess and state the needs and purposes of the group
Demonstrate skill in eliciting positive action from the group
Have the ability to think quickly
Possess the ability to be impartial
Have an understanding of how groups work
Are well informed on a wide variety of matters
Show willingness to accept responsibility and follow through to the completion
Possess sensitivity to the needs and feelings of the group
Utilize effective problem-solving skills
Avoid dominating the group
Keep the main issues before the group

INTELLIGENCE AND CREATIVITY

The relationship between intelligence and creativity is the basis of much conjecture, investigation, and disputation. The need for reliable information on this issue as well as a broader base for identifying the creative individual has led to investigations.

One of the most widely quoted studies concerned with the relationships between intelligence and creativity is that conducted by Getzels and Jackson. They set out to explore the meaning of intelligence specifically as it related to creativity; investigate various types of giftedness, not merely cognitive excellence; broaden the base for examining intellectual and social excellence in children; and free the concept of giftedness from its one-sided attachment to the IQ metric.

The IQ test which has been the most widely used instrument for evaluating cognition or intellectual functions required that the individual taking the test respond to a stimulus for which there is only one accepted answer. He must know the accepted solution to a problem, the usual association to a stimulus. There is no room for invention, innovation, speculation, or originality. Since the conventional

IQ test tends to measure those cognitive processes identified with convergent thinking rather than those identified with divergent thinking, Getzels and Jackson sought to discover whether or not the two processes were so closely interrelated that it would be impossible to differentiate between the individuals who are high in one and not equally high in the other. "For analytic purposes, however, in order to make the various factors more manageable, it is possible to begin by identifying two basic cognitive or intellective modes. The one mode tends toward retaining the known, learning the predetermined and conserving what is. The second mode tends toward revising the known, exploring the undetermined, and constructing what might be."[16]

The high IQ's tend to converge on sterotyped meanings, to perceive personal success by conventional standards, to move toward the model provided by teachers, to seek out careers that conform to what is expected of them. The high creatives tend to diverge from stereotyped meanings, to move away from the model provided by teachers, to seek out careers that do not conform to what is expected of them.[17]

CONCLUDING STATEMENT

The challenge to identify creativity in every individual is facilitated by an examination of the portraits of creativity. That creativity exists in many forms and in varying degrees is supported by an examination of the literature. As the teacher guides each child in his development of curiosity, flexibility, adaptability, originality, and sensitivity he aids him to develop his own design for expressing creativity.

The task of the school is to help each child to develop his creative potential. The task of the teacher is to know the general characteristics of creativity and the specific characteristics which distinguish special abilities, and apply this knowledge as he creates an environment in which creativity is valued, nurtured, and rewarded. The significance of discovering and nurturing creativity cannot be overestimated. Until each child is encouraged to become his best creative self, the teacher's mission remains unfilled and the child's potential unrealized.

REFERENCES

1. By permission from John Kord Lagemann, "How We Discourage Creative Children," *Red Book*, 120:123, March, 1963. (Adapted.)
2. L. N. Chassell, "Tests for Originality," *Journal of Educational Psychology*, 7:317-29, 1916, in Morris I. Stein and Shirley J. Heinze, *Creativity and the Individual*, Glencoe Free Press, Glencoe, 1960, pp. 153, 154.
3. H. M. Hargreaves, "The Faculty of Imagination," *British Journal of Psychology*, Monograph Supplement, 3:10, 1927.
4. J. P. Guilford, "Traits of Creativity," in H. H. Anderson (ed.), *Creativity and Its Cultivation*, Harper & Sons, New York, 1959, pp. 142-161.
5. Frank Barron, "The Psychology of Imagination," in Sydney J. Parnes and Harold H. Harding (eds.), *A Source Book for Creative Thinking*, Charles Scribner's Sons, New York, 1962, pp. 236, 237.

6. Frank Barron, "Creative Vision and Expression," in Alexander Frazier (ed.) *New Insights and the Curriculum*, Yearbook for the ASCD, Washington: NEA, 1963, p. 305.
7. J. P. Guilford, "Psychology of Creativity," *Creative Crafts*, 1:4-8, April-May, 1960. (Adapted.)
8. Calvin W. Taylor, "A Tentative Description of the Creative Individual," in Walter Waetjen (ed.), *Human Variability and Learning*, ASCD, Washington, 1961, pp. 62-79. (Adapted.)
9. Viktor Lowenfeld, "Creativity: Education's Stepchild," in Sydney J. Parnes and Harold H. Harding (eds.), *op. cit.*, pp. 12-14. (Adapted.)
10. By permission from Elizabeth Drew, "The Four Faces of Able Adolescents," *Saturday Review*, 46:69, January 19, 1963.
11. *Ibid.*, pp. 68-70. (Adapted.)
12. By permission from Jacob W. Getzels and Philip W. Jackson, *Creativity and Intelligence: Explorations with Gifted Students*, John Wiley and Sons, New York, 1962, pp. 54-60. (Adapted.)
13. E. Paul Torrance, *Guiding Creative Talent*, Prentice-Hall, Inc., Englewood Cliffs, 1962, p. 82. (Adapted.)
14. W. Lambert Brittain, "Creative Art," in Louis Fliegler (ed.), *Curriculum Planning for the Gifted*, Prentice-Hall, Inc., Englewood Cliffs, 1961, p. 296.
15. *Ibid.*, p. 299.
16. Jacob Getzels and Philip Jackson, *op. cit.*, pp. 13, 14.
17. *Ibid.*, pp. 60, 61.

3

Creating an Environment
for Learning

The overall task is to get research off the library shelves, beyond the theory, and into the classroom.

Nagol

If every child is to be encouraged to reach his potential it is essential that all possible avenues for creativity be explored, understood, and utilized. For too many, creativity has been limited to creativity in the arts. The time is ripe to relate the findings of research pertinent to creativity to the entire elementary school curriculum. Thus every child can find his particular avenues for self-expression. However, for any individual, the creative process does not stop with mere self-expression. He finds within himself the desire to communicate in some way to others.

The curriculum must be vitalized if every child is to express his creative urge. Some will express primarily through the creative arts—the dance, play and panto-mime, the brush, a bit of clay, a song which may be a remembered fragment, the echo of some half-forgotten melody, or a poem that writes itself out of the figment of the imagination or a memorable experience. Creativity, however, is broader than this. It manifests itself also through a problem solved, an idea exploited, a product invented, or (for him) a principle discovered. Creativity is also the applying of principles of creative thinking in the sciences, the quest for discovery in mathematics, and the spirit of inquiry and adventure in the social sciences. Creativity exists, too, in one of the least considered but most important facets of creative behaviour—creative leadership.

An attitude of open-mindedness toward using the knowledge from research will enable the teacher to create a climate in which every learner will express and develop his creative potential through the processes as well as the content of the learning experiences. The task of the modern educator is that of nurturing creativity in a culture that tends to reward conformity and to convert the individual into a cog in a machine. Through placing high value on creative self-expression, independent thinking, the spirit of inquiry, learning through discovery, reflective thinking, and problem-solving the school can through its curriculum and creative teaching fulfill its task.

With today's child, content as well as process must be updated and revitalized to meet the demands of living creatively in a period of interstellar exploration.

"Consider the child who knows the difference between a rocket trajectory and a satellite orbit, who can distinguish among hundreds of brands of cereals, soaps, and deodorants, who knows the families of automobiles with mytho-poetic names; consider this and appreciate his disappointment. We offer him a cup of magic, filled with tap-water."[1]

Learning will come alive when children create, experiment, and discover and communicate their own generalizations. Today's child cannot afford to delay in developing skill in asking crucial questions, selecting and organizing relevant data, and drawing conclusions which lead to the formulation of new questions. He uses intuitive thinking and the creative process in the way that best serves his purposes in a given situation. Through an acquaintance with various procedures for learning and for solving problems the child learns early to select the appropriate procedure on the basis of the problems he faces.

This will demand a fresh approach to curriculum and new teaching procedures and materials in the classroom. Both the content and process will be selected on the basis of significant priorities. Under these conditions the child will be free to move to creativity from cognition through communication in his encounters with learning in the various curriculum areas.

The challenge has been flung and the creative teacher stands ready to accept the challenge of bridging the gap from research to application in the classroom. Thus he assumes "the heightened responsibility of the school of our time to guide youth's dynamic creativity into constructive and growth-giving channels through which the young may come into their unique and vigorous heritage as worthily creative men."[2]

Creativity is the integrating thread the teacher employs to weave the strands of the curriculum areas into a harmonious design for self-realization of the children he teaches. To accomplish this he:

> Meets the children's developmental needs
> Creates a climate in which creativity, originality, and initiative are valued
> Creates a setting for creative learning
> Motivates children to learn creatively
> Selects and organizes the learning experiences around problems of significance
> Utilizes a concept of evaluation which shares the responsibility for appraisal with the learner.

To the extent that these objectives are realized successfully, creativity permeates every area of the curriculum from the child's initial excursions in the arts to the broadened ventures into the realms of leadership, problem-solving, scientific inventiveness, and global relationships.

As teachers broaden their concept of creativity, as they catch the enthusiasm of developing creativity, as they increase their knowledge of the creative process and the creative approaches to guiding children's learning, they will acquire new insights, gain greater courage, and catch a vision of what can happen when a child and teacher enter into a conspiracy which sparks the child's innate creativity and exploits the teacher's potential creative capacity.

MEETING CHILDREN'S NEEDS

In fostering creativity the teacher must assume responsibility much like that of the farmer whose work only begins when the seed is sown. It remains for him to supply the nurturing conditions which will permit the development of the potentialities of the seed. Both internal factors and external conditions will influence the direction and extent of growth possible. The nurture for the child is provided through the most propitious physical environment for growth plus the most propitious climate for social-emotional development.

Personal-Social Needs

The child's need for acceptance, affection, recognition, and identification are well known. They are important considerations in promoting a climate for growth. Personal-social needs can be fulfilled only through social experiences. The extent to which these needs are successfully met will determine the child's confidence in himself, and in turn his confidence in others.

Acceptance

Unless the teacher can accept every child as a unique, valued individual he has undoubtedly chosen the wrong profession. Even in the face of unacceptable actions the teacher has a responsibility to help the child to move toward socially approved and individually satisfying behaviour. It is the teacher's attitude toward the child which shows that he is accepted as an important individual. Although the teacher may disapprove of the child's actions, he does not disapprove of the child himself. To the degree that a child is accepted by those whom he values is he able to accept himself.

Affection

When children's emotional needs are met they learn more effectively. The importance of a teacher-child relationship based on mutual respect and understanding cannot be overemphasized. "Giving love means giving security, affection, respect for the child's personality, and understanding of his point of view and feelings."[3]

Recognition

The child needs recognition if he is to develop an adequate image of himself and function at his optimum level. This places the responsibility on the teacher to discover an area, academic or non-academic, in which the child can achieve. A case in point is the eighth grade pupil whose only achievement was the ability to distribute and collect papers more efficiently and organize them more neatly than any other child in the class. For this he received recognition from both the students and the teacher. Other students received their recognition through their academic excellence, creative endeavors, and social or athletic abilities.

Identification

The child needs a teacher who understands him and peers with whom he can identify himself. Understanding used in this sense means entering into the inner world of the child and still being able to take that individual as he is. In such a situation the child is free to express his ideas, feelings, and thoughts without being ridiculed or laughed at. He feels no need for a facade, sham, or pretense. To be with others and contribute to the general welfare is an important part of the child's development. The language arts curriculum provides numerous opportunities for a wide range of group activities. The good life is a cooperative one.

Integrative Needs

Children express their creative drive when the atmosphere is conducive to self-direction, self-realization, and creative expression. In an atmosphere of support, encouragement, and stimulation the child is impelled toward an increasingly higher level of learning. Free to use his energy, he develops his powers of awareness. He learns new techniques to meet his developing standards of excellence. The teacher is there to help him when he needs help—in encouragement and in more complex technical assistance. In such an environment he is able to operate as an integrated individual. All of him is able to experience, to express, and to create.

PROVIDING A CLIMATE WHERE CREATIVITY CAN FLOURISH

To create a climate in which children are free to express themselves creatively it is essential to give opportunity for developing both the esthetic and creative powers as well as intellectual, verbal, and technical. The learning experiences which contribute to the development of the child's awareness, sense of perception, imagination, emotional sensitivity, and bodily poise and control have centered chiefly around the so-called creative arts. It is in this area that the child expresses his creativity in the dance, music, drama, and visual arts.

Growth in the esthetic phase of the child's life is fostered in an environment in which the child is given the time, materials, experiences, stimulation, and skills to translate his imaginings, feelings, and ideas into some artistic medium through which he expresses and communicates to another. Children need what Carl Rogers has termed "psychological safety"[4] if they are to venture forth freely with new ideas.

It is in the moments of creating that the child moves beyond the boundaries of the every-day world and soars to outer limits. This he is unable to do unless he is free from the threat of embarrassment should his expression fail to be valued. Experiences in the creative arts give the child opportunity to express thoughts, imaginings, feelings, and rhythms that he has never before experienced and impel him to broaden his horizons.

PROVIDING A SETTING FOR CREATIVE LEARNING

The teacher who provides a curriculum with many opportunities for creative expression is providing the most obvious conditions for creative learning. Learning creatively is the child's most natural way of learning. It also brings the greatest satisfaction. The child who is led to discover something he has not known before, rather than to accept something by fiat, is motivated to continue his questing behaviour.

Torrance compares creative learning with the cat's compulsive curiosity, and routine learning with the dog's submissive acceptance of authority. He conceives creative learning as taking place "in the process of sensing problems or gaps in information, making guesses or hypotheses about these deficiencies, testing these guesses, revising and retesting them, and communicating the results."[5]

The teacher who would provide conditions for creative learning must plan learning experiences which involve the application of the creative ways of problem-solving, the techniques of discovery, and the spirit of inquiry. This implies a knowledge of these teaching processes as well as the ability to organize the learning experiences from the standpoint of content as well as process in the various areas of the curriculum.

Creativity is expressed when learning experiences are challenging. Creative self-expression is developed in an environment in which creativity is prized, originality rewarded, and stimulating experiences abound. In such a climate inducements for learning are equated with the child's natural inclination for discovery and challenge.

MOTIVATING CREATIVE LEARNING

Too often extrinsic rewards only such as grades, gold stars, monetary rewards, bribes, and so forth have been used to create motivation for learning. The creative teacher makes use of both the child's innate motives of curiosity and what White calls "competency motive".[6] One approach to motivation that capitalizes on the competency motive as a drive for learning behaviour is that of "learning by discovery". Although this approach has been largely tied to mathematics and science it should be used in all areas of the curriculum. The creative child should be guided to make use of a number of ways of learning. Then he will solve his problems through the particular way which appears to be appropriate to the occasion.

Motivation plays an important part in learning. Since creative learning occurs in response to an awareness of a need to solve a problem, interest and motivation are high. Curiosity, drive, interest, awareness—all of these "built-in" factors are capitalized on by the teacher. Since the creative process provides the child with the tools for viewing situations, solving problems creatively, grasping the essential concepts, principles, and generalizing, this experience makes transfer of response to similar or new situations well nigh automatic. The child who is successful in confronting problems over a period of time has a predisposition toward learning.

SELECTING AND ORGANIZING CHALLENGING EXPERIENCES

It is not enough to create a climate wherein creativity can flourish nor yet to provide a situation which facilitates creative learning. Unless the learning experiences selected offer a richer, deeper experience for the child little development will occur. The theory that an environment replete with the creative arts and the services of good teachers is sufficient for the discovery and development of creativity is unconvincing. What is essential are learning experiences in every curriculum area based on the needs, interests, and abilities of children, a concern for the development of the creative potential of each child, and the use of effective methods of guiding the special abilities of each child. Learning experiences that are broad in scope, balanced in content, flexible in programming, and integrated in structure must be provided. The learning experiences must encompass a broad program commensurate with the needs of the children. Experiences should be selected which will provide depth and balance, continuity and integration of experience.

One of the most significant tasks of the teacher is that of organizing the learning experiences in such a way that children are motivated to develop their creative abilities. Activities should be organized in such a way that children, ideas, materials, and experiences are woven into a design in which creativity is the warp and content the woof. "The effectiveness of curriculum organization in facilitating integration depends upon the extent to which it aids the student in perceiving relationships among phenomena and ideas, in sensing the meaning and significance of his feelings, and in developing abilities, skills, and courses of action which are guided by comprehensive knowledge and through and by disciplined feelings."[7]

The teacher should create an environment and structure the situation so as to evoke a response and utilize creativity as an integrating thread. Units may be organized around such centers as persistent problems, significant ideas, concepts, and genre.

DEVELOPING AND UTILIZING EVALUATION

Research indicates that creative thinking is not a unitary ability. Multiple abilities are involved. A single index is ineffectual in measuring creativity. Such general abilities as originality, sensitivity to problems, fluency of ideas, flexibility, elaboration, and redefinition are involved.

Creativity in the preschool child has been measured by eliciting responses through such activities as dramatic play, imaginative play, art activities, samples of children's art, picture tests, inkblots, easel products, verbalization while painting, and standardized problem situations.

For the elementary school child the variety of tasks in assessing creative thinking abilities is greater. Among these are: picture construction from dots, circles, squares, parallel lines, incomplete figures, and shapes of coloured paper; verbalization while painting; perceptions of ink blots; symbolizations of words by lines, designs from standarized materials, ideas for product improvement (e.g., toys and common objects); consequence problems, asking and guessing; creative writing; and guessing sounds or constructing images from sounds. Performances are generally scored for such qualities as originality, flexibility, fluency, and elaboration.[8]

As the concept of the dimensions of the human mind expand and the understanding of creativity grows experiences will be provided for the elementary school child which call for the development of skills required in creative thinking and learning—skills and strategies of inquiry, discovery, and creative problem solving. Opportunities should be provided for creative learning through content which demands independent research skills, creative activity, self-initiated and directed projects, and experimentation.[9] Such a curriculum should provide a balance of both internal and external evaluation. When the individual finds himself in an environment where he is not being continually evaluated by some external standard he is free to be creative.

Children need opportunity to create, to learn, to discover without threat of immediate external evaluation. As they develop confidence through perfecting skills needed to express their creativity they will come to the place where the evaluation by another is merely an opportunity to share ideas. At what point an individual reaches this stage of maturity can be judged only on the basis of understanding the child who is creating. This is one of the characteristics that mark the perceptive teacher and often forms the basis of a creative relationship with the child.[10]

CONCLUDING STATEMENT

To fulfill the teacher's role in creating an environment in which children are encouraged to communicate creatively and to develop the skills needed to make of language a power for expression of ideas he must: meet the children's developmental needs; value spontaneity, originality, and initiative; provide a setting for creative learning; organize significant learning experiences; utilize the concept of evaluation in which the responsibility for evaluation is shared by the teacher and learner.

The extent to which the teacher achieves the goal is dependent upon his understanding of the physical and psychological needs of the child, the teacher's own creativeness and the degree of sensitiveness he possesses, and the flexibility of his relationships to the environment and his ability to empathize with the children he teaches. Teachers who set out to stimulate learning in those they teach must be responsive both to the physical and social environment in which they operate.

REFERENCES

1. Frank G. Jennings, "Textbooks and Trapped Idealists," *Saturday Review*, 47:57, January 18, 1964.
2. Lorrene L. Ort, *A Matter of Fences: An Essay*, ASCD, Washington, 1963, p. 1.
3. Dorothy Barclay, "Rearing a Child of Goodwill," *The New York Times Magazine*, February 21, 1960, Section 6, p. 62.
4. See Carl Rogers, *Client Centered Therapy*, Houghton Mifflin Company, Boston, 1951.
5. E. Paul Torrance, "Creativity," *What Research Says to the Teacher*, Department of Classroom Teachers, AERA of the NEA, Washington, Bulletin 28, April, 1963, p. 19.
6. R. W. White, "Motivation Reconsidered: the Concept of Competence," *Psychological Review*, 66:297 ff., September, 1959.
7. Ralph Tyler, "Curriculum Organization," in Nelson B. Henry (ed.), *The Integration of Educational Experiences*, Fifty-seventh Yearbook, National Society for the Study of Education, University of Chicago Press, Chicago, 1958, p. 10.
8. See R. E. Meyers and E. P. Torrance, *Can You Imagine?* (and Teacher's Guide), *Invitation to Speaking and Writing Creatively* (and Teacher's Guide) and *Invitations to Thinking and Doing* (and Teacher's Guide), Ginn and Co., Boston, 1965. See also Calvin W. Taylor and Frank E. Williams, *Instructional Media and Creativity*, John Wiley & Sons, Inc., New York, 1966.
9. See E. P. Torrance, *Gifted Children in the Classroom*, Macmillan Co., New York, 1965.
10. See Patricia Schwartz Golarski, "Creativity: Student Teachers' Perception of Approaches to Classroom Teaching," *The Journal of Creative Behaviour*, The Creative Education Foundation Inc., 1:65, January, 1967.

PART TWO: The Curriculum

Prologue to the Language Arts Curriculum

A dynamic language arts curriculum is based on a two pronged approach, (1) the fostering of creative ideas, and (2) the development of the skills essential for the expression of those ideas.

In Part One the relationship between creativity and language was examined, portraits of creative children were presented, clues to creative behaviour were delineated, and formulae for structuring the climate for creative learning were suggested.

In Part Two the various areas of the language arts curriculum will be examined and suggestions for their implementation will be given. In planning, organizing, and developing activities which stimulate the child to creative expression and effective communication, basic principles are needed. Creative teachers are constantly on the alert to try new ways of teaching when information and knowledge point toward an improved curriculum. Curriculum decisions should be made on the basis of the findings of research as well as promising practices developed out of experience and empirical evidence. The teacher who fails to use these sources effectively may be enticed to climb aboard an inappropriate bandwagon. There are those who always follow along like the folk song which says:

> Come along, children, come along,
> While de moon's shinin' bright, shinin' bright,
> Git on board, down de river float.

Fortunately, most teachers are looking for guidance in deciding which bandwagon to climb aboard. The following principles will serve as a basis for wise decision making in the language arts program.

PRINCIPLES UNDERLYING THE LANGUAGE ARTS PROGRAM

The development of the creative potential of every child should be the paramount concern in the language arts program. The development of the skills in various areas of the language are a necessary prologue to the maximum creative expression.

Language development is dependent upon experiences. An environment rich in both first hand and vicarious experiences contributes to language growth. Children will express their ideas freely and welcome suggestions for improving their skills when they have something interesting to express.

Language arts are an integral part of the daily curriculum, and must be given priority. Provision should be made for (1) integrating the language arts with other curriculum areas, (2) teaching each as a separate discipline, and (3) correlating them with other curriculum areas. The concepts of integration and correlation will be examined in the succeeding chapters. Language learning increases a child's competency in all areas of the curriculum. In turn, these areas provide motivation and content for language activites.

The language arts program should stimulate an increasing understanding of the forms, function, and structure of the English language. As children grow in their understanding of the structure of language, they will discover the relationships of linguistics to spelling, reading, and composition. The "wonder of words" which so intrigues the young child will not be lost as he progresses in the educational program. The fluid nature of the language, the varied ways of experimenting with words will open new doors.

Freedom in bodily movement leads to freedom in speech. A controlled body is essential to effective speech. Bodily movement, gestures, pantomime, and dramatic play afford a natural introduction to oral language. Not only does creative movement and dramatic play promote freedom in bodily action, it enhances the spoken word and reduces the inhibitions children feel in speech activities.

Oral language development is fundamental to the other language arts. Children who express themselves effectively in speech, whose oral language is above average, tend to exceed other children in reading ability as they progress through the elementary school. Written communication, too, is enhanced when it comes as the outgrowth of rich and frequent opportunities for speech activities. As a child speaks, so shall he read—is no longer merely a truism.

Linguistic skills develop more effectively through a spiral curriculum design. The spiral curriculum affords opportunity to develop increasingly complex skills in language growth through recurring confrontation with language arts activities in harmony with the child's needs, abilities, interests, and educational level. It provides, too, for individual differences which must be met in every classroom.

The mechanics of expression—grammar, punctuation, spelling, and form—are most readily mastered in connection with the need at a specific time in the educational growth of the child. The close relationships of interest, need, and learning should guide the teacher in understanding motivation for learning certain skills. Skills should be taught in the context of meaningful and purposeful activity applied to significant experiences. They should be taught when they can be put to immediate use in the learning activities of the school day. The spiral organization of the curriculum provides for the recurring needs for language skills among the children at different educational levels. The challenge to the teacher is to see that the skills are both refined and broadened as the child progresses along the educational ladder.

Standards for proficiency at each educational level should be determined. Levels of proficiency of skills should be determined by the staff of a particular school on the basis of the linguistic and cultural needs of the community. To demand the same level of proficiency in all sectors is out of harmony with what is known about child development, language learning, and social morés. To demand the same level of proficiency for each child within a classroom is also questionable in the light of child development and linguistic research.

Continuous evaluation is essential for growth in the skills of communication. Self-evaluation and teacher-evaluation are essential to growth in creative expression. The child must become skillful in evaluating his growth in terms of objectives and purposes cooperatively planned. Through guided experiences and participation in individual and group enterprises the child will grow in his ability to evaluate his progress in terms of the objectives.

Language learning is imitative. The teacher must be a model for the child by speaking effectively and communicating clearly. The child tends to follow the model provided for him. However, the teacher must be aware that ". . . in the daily linguistic experience of, say, the child of twelve, the interplay of language which goes on within the school during the five hours of formal instruction is by no means as extensive or as natural as the communication which takes place in the eight or nine hours which he spends on the playground and in the home. In some situations the classroom teacher, representing the principal cultured or quasi-cultured contact which the child encounters, may exercise a linguistic influence of considerable proportions."[1]

REFERENCES

1. Albert Marckwardt, "Research Methods of the Linguist Which May Be Useful in Educational Research," *Research Design and the Teaching of English*, Proceedings of the San Francisco Conference, National Council of Teachers of English, Champaign, 1964, p. 50.

4

Developing the Skills

of Listening

Only as individuals learn to understand, analyze, and improve the world in which they live can they be said to be truly educated.

Nagol

"To the school is assigned the task of releasing the individual's language potential, of cultivating his talents, of correcting his imperfections, and of developing in him an attitude favourable for future growth. Such an obligation carries with it the responsibility for developing effective communication." "Effective communication at home and abroad is the chief means by which men will find a way of living together around the world in harmony with our belief in the inherent dignity of man and the worth of the individual."[1]

There is no deeper craving of the human heart than the hunger for understanding. Prime Ministers, statesmen, teen agers, and children all suffer from a common complaint—they say "No one understands me". To a great extent this is true. The cliché, "Each man is an island" is not completely true: each man is at least a peninsula connected to the mainland of humanity by the common bonds of education and communication.

Sojourner Truth was born in slavery. Because she was an alert child she was sent to the plantation school to learn the rudiments of reading and writing so she could be a house slave. Many statesmen, the rich and the famous visited her owners. As she unobtrusively went about her duties she *listened*, observed, and learned. She was proud of her heritage as the descendent of a great African chief. She determined to gain her freedom and work for her people.

In the confusion of the Civil War she escaped to Washington. Here her untiring work among the escaping and freed slaves brought her into contact with President Lincoln. He recognized her great compassion and encouraged her to devote her life to bringing about a greater understanding between her race and those who had been their captors.

It was in the 1880's that she visited the campus. By now Sojourner Truth had become a national figure. The students were eager to hear this former slave who had become the friend of statesmen. She was introduced, then stepped forward. She was a commanding figure as she stood before the students in her simple gray gown.

The notebooks snapped open and pencils were poised, ready to record every

38

word that this great—but simple—woman uttered. She smiled, looked at them for a moment, then said, "Young men and ladies, will you put away your notebooks and pencils? If you listen with your pencils you will not remember what I have to say. If you will listen with your ears and hearts you will always remember Sojourner and what she told you about her people."

"That day," said one of the students who heard her, "was one of the most significant of my life. I learned the true importance of listening to understand and remember. After fifty years I can still recall much of her speech."

As pupils learn to listen to speeches, stories, poems, plays, or music the teacher should be aware that their understanding is in direct proportion to the background that they bring to the experience and the concentration with which they listen. As they learn to listen they will come to look upon listening as the other side of the coin of speaking. By early becoming aware of listening-speaking as related aspects of one process, children will simultaneously develop skills of listening and speaking. In developing listening skills in an environment where listening takes its place as a significant language art the child learns not only to listen for enjoyment and for ideas, but he also learns to observe the speaker's use of his voice, his articulation, and his poise. As he participates in meaningful listening-speaking activities he becomes a creator of ideas, an appreciative listener, a more effective learner, and a discriminating critic. In a classroom in which the listening climate is structured for language learning as a creative process which requires mastery of skills, the teacher gives evidence that listening is the dominant means of sensory comprehension. Today's children listen much more than they read as a means of acquiring information, ideas, and attitudes. "For every fact which a student can trace to a book, there are many more that can be traced to the spoken word."[2]

In an era in which the spoken word is so vital, in which its significance is no longer questioned, the teacher of the language arts must give specific and systematic instruction in listening. Teaching of effective listening is based on:

An understanding of the nature of listening
A knowledge of formulating of objectives based on the concept of listening as a tool for learning
Ability to apply the findings of research which have implications for teaching children to listen
Awareness of the misconceptions about listening
Recognition of the factors which influence listening effectiveness
Acquaintance with guides to effective listening
Establishing purposes for listening
Organization of activities which develop skills in listening for a specific purpose
Ensuring balance in the listening program
Self-evaluation technique for the teacher

THE NATURE OF LISTENING

Before we can formulate objectives for the teaching of effective listening it is essential to get a clear understanding of listening as a tool, as one of the communication skills, as an art, and as a process.

There have been many definitions of listening, each of which has implications for the language arts teacher.

Jacobs defines listening in behavioural terms as he states: "In listening, the individual hears familiar sound combinations to which, in terms of his experience, he brings meaning and from which he simultaneously takes meaning, and acquires, thereby, sources for reaction, interpretation, and knowing."[3]

Logan and Logan define listening as "a combination of what we hear, what we comprehend, and what we remember; it is the assimilation of aural plus visual clues."[4]

Alice Duer Miller describes listening as responding. "Listening is not merely talking, though even that is beyond most of our powers; it means a vigorous human interest in what is being told us. We can listen like a blank wall or like a splendid auditorium where every sound comes back fuller and richer."

"The best listener I ever knew was the late Clarence Day, author of *Life With Father*. He did not listen in silence. He laughed, he groaned, he roared: his eyes shone with surprise and delight. However mild the anecdote you might be relating, it became significant through his exciting interest."[5]

Irwin and Rosenberger delineate four steps in the listening process: (1) hearing, (2) understanding, (3) evaluating, and (4) responding. According to these authorities ". . . first you *hear* a series of sounds which you call words. Second, you *understand* the meaning of those words in the context in which you hear them. Third, you *evaluate* . . . the meaning to decide whether you accept or reject the idea expressed. Fourth, you *respond*—that is, you convey your reaction to the meaning by bodily movement, facial expression, or audible response to a great or small degree, as the occasion warrants."[6]

Thus effective listening requires that the individual "receive a message intact, understand its full meaning, bounce it back and forth in his mind before deciding whether to hold on to it or throw it away, and convey to the speaker some suggestion of his response."[7]

Fest and Cobin stress the reciprocity of listening and speaking, and the role of the listener in the speaking situation. "Most frequently the speaker's purpose is to secure a response from the listener, . . . For the listener to respond effectively he must have sensory adequacy, interest that goes beyond the most elementary attention, some capacity for interpretation of the message, and both a willingness and a capacity to change relationships."[8] Dominic Barbara emphasizes selectivity in listening. "To listen effectively, it is imperative that we be free and spontaneous enough to be selective in the communicative situation and not feel coerced into interpreting what we feel was meant to be said. . . . If we are to learn how to listen well, we must proceed as we would in learning any other art such as music, painting, architecture or acting. The art of listening requires discipline, concentration, active participation, comprehension and evaluation."[9]

Neville also holds to the belief that "Listening is an art, and must be practised as an art; therefore, the techniques and skills of the art must be understood and practiced before the speaker-listener experience can be fully realized."[10]

Nichols defines listening in terms of aural-oral communication. "Obviously hearing and listening are not identical. They are most clearly conceived as two distinguishable phases, the hearing of sound and the interpreting of sound, of a total process usually called aural assimilation. If the first phase, hearing is identified as the perception of sound only, then it is the second phase of the process—the attachment of meaning to the aural symbols perceived—which has come to be largely accepted as the definition of listening."[11]

From this cursory examination of the nature of listening it is evident that listening is a complex process in itself which must be taught as a discrete skill. Underlying the objectives of listening is the concept that the all important, central contribution to be made by effective listening to the individual growth and development is that of making learning easier, more pleasant, and more economic.

As the child listens to learn, listens to enjoy, listens to evaluate, listens to discriminate sounds he will be perfecting skills which will enable him to use listening, not alone as a tool for effective communication, but as an avenue for creative expression and self-fulfillment.

OBJECTIVES FOR TEACHING LISTENING

"Language is the only means of communication between specialities as far apart as every individual's unique experience of his own life. . . . Life attains significance through the consciousness of the individual who lives it and who is able to understand that significance through comparing his own experiences with those of other people."[12] Creative communication requires the cooperation of at least two individuals, a speaker and a listener or a writer and a reader. Expressing so that another understands what one feels, believes, or observes is the core of communication.

The mastery of skills of listening tends to improve the skills of speaking and vice versa. In listening to learn, as well as learning to listen, the process is cyclic. "The basic purposes of speaking and listening are demonstrated in the active process of communication when two or more individuals are expressing themselves concerning an idea, feeling, or desire. The speaker wishes through his speaking to impart knowledge, to reveal emotion, and to entertain. . . . The listener, on the other hand, hopes that by listening he will increase his knowledge, understand the revealed emotion, and be entertained. Through the information gained and the reason for the emotion understood, he may accept a belief or decide upon a course of action."[13]

A well organized language arts program will provide children with many opportunities to listen to learn (for information or directions), listen to enjoy (for pleasure or entertainment), listen to evaluate (for critical judgment), listen to appreciate (for esthetic judgment), listen to discriminate and recognize speech sounds (for speech improvement).

Among the specific objectives which the teacher keeps in mind in providing experiences in listening are:

To develop a respect for listening as a medium of learning
To gain an appreciation of the role of the listener in the speaking-listening situation
To develop the basic skills, concepts, and attitudes essential to effective listening habits
To progress toward the elimination of poor listening habits previously acquired
To select the type of listening essential to the purpose
To distinguish between hearing and listening.

Such objectives negate the belief held by some that listening need not be taught. If these objectives are to be achieved the teacher must plan specific listening activities which motivate children to listen attentively, intelligently, creatively, and critically.

WHAT RESEARCH TELLS US ABOUT LISTENING

What we know and what we practice in education do not always go hand in hand. What we know about listening can be of great value to the classroom teacher. However, until the research is taken off the library shelves and made available to the elementary teachers it will be as valueless as it has been in the past. One earmark of the effective teacher is the interest he takes in research findings.

As early as 1928, Rankin found that the amount of time devoted to the language arts is inversely related to their social utility in human affairs. He found that our daily communication time is divided in this manner: 70% of our waking day is spent in verbal communication. Of this communication time, 45% is spent listening, 30% in speaking, 16% in reading, and 9% in writing.[14]

In spite of this finding, schools went on teaching children to read, teaching children to write, and occasionally teaching children to speak. Instruction in listening was limited to the admonition, "Put your feet on the floor, fold your hands, sit up straight, and listen."

The last twenty years have brought an increased interest in listening as one of the language arts. Goldstein[15] in 1940 completed a significant study from which two important observations emerged. First, that a person can listen to speech at a rate of more than three times that at which he normally hears it, without significant loss of comprehension, and second, that schools have overlooked a very important phase of the child's educational development—that of teaching youngsters how to listen. Shortly thereafter Hubbel published a book in which he stated "without equivocation 98% of all man learns in a lifetime he learns through his eyes or through his ears."[16]

As recently as 1948 Nichols discovered that only three experimental scientific researches had been published in the area of listening comprehension as compared with over 3,000 scientific studies in the parallel learning medium of reading comprehension.

However, the decade between 1950 and 1960 saw a dramatic increase in interest in listening. Today leading universities not only teach listening, they are at last carrying on graduate research in this field. Training in listening in the schools receives steady support from the National Council of Teachers of English and the Speech Association of America. Their help in preparing language arts guides is considerable. "Typically, these guides give equal emphasis to the four communication skills of reading, writing, speaking and listening."[17]

In 1950 Wilt made a significant study of the listening time of elementary school children and found that they were expected to listen 57.5% of the time they were in the classroom, but were given no systematic listening instruction. The following chart shows that out of a five-hour-day children were listening more than two and one half hours. The distribution of listening time has implications for the classroom teacher.

TABLE III[18]
Distribution of Listening Time
(Children listening to)

	%
a. Teacher-talk	33.0
b. Teacher-read	3.5
c. Teacher-child conversation	6.0
d. Questions-answers	14.5
e. Child-talk	6.0
f. Child-read	9.5
g. Child-child conversation	6.5
h. Group discussion	6.0
i. Dramatization	—
j. Radio talk	7.0
k. Sound film	—
l. Choric activities	1.0
m. Public address system	—
n. Singing	7.0

Most significant in the implications for the classroom teacher is the recommendation that "a wide variety of listening experiences should be introduced into classrooms if children are to learn to adapt the kind of listening they do to that type which will best serve the purpose of the activity."[19]

Hogan[20] reported superior gains made by the experimental group over a six week period of listening to readings, radio programs, sound motion pictures, individual and group reports, discussions of standards of listening, and differentiating between fact and opinion in radio advertising.

Edgar[21] used two matched groups of fourth, fifth, and sixth grade children in which the experimental group used ten half-hour recorded lessons and the control group read the same material and answered the same questions. Analogy, exposition, vocabulary practice, and the "story" approach were used. On a post-test eight weeks after the pre-test Edgar found that significant gains were evident in listening in all methods used, but that the analogies seemed to be the most effective of the devices used.

Devine[22] used two matched groups of ninth graders in an effort to improve critical listening abilities. He found a significant gain by the experimental group in recognizing the bias of a speaker, determining the competence of a speaker, distinguishing between opinion and fact, and discriminating between report and emotive language.

Lundsteen[23], in a study involving 263 fifth and sixth grade students found that they gave evidence of the existence of critical listening abilities as distinct from general listening ability and verbal fluency. Through factor analysis the following four components of critical listening ability were revealed: (1) general analysis and inference, (2) reasons for fallacies in arguments, (3) value judgments regarding propaganda, and (4) factual judgments of arguments.

On the assumption that there may be a constellation of interrelated listening abilities and that critical listening may be included in the constellation, Lundsteen recently carried on an experiment in critical listening designed to identify, define, teach, and test certain abilities in critical listening. Working again with fifth and sixth grade students from families of middle to high socioeconomic levels the pupils in the experimental group were taught two lessons a week of forty minutes each. On the first lesson of the week they developed concepts in critical listening; the second lesson enriched the learnings and provided further practice. The content included three major areas or abilities: identification of the speaker's purpose, analysis and judgment of propaganda, and analysis and judgment of arguments. Applications of the study suggest that "the content, the concepts, the processes, and the abilities in critical listening appear to be amenable to empirical analysis and can be improved by practice."[24]

In a study involving fifth grade students Trivette[25] reports that when specific training was given in listening for main ideas, details, and inferences not only were gains in these skills significant, but other skills, such as getting word meaning and following directions, also showed improvement.

In another study involving fifth graders Canfield[26] compared three groups: one experimental group received direct instruction and practice in listening for main ideas, important details, opinions, relevant and irrelevant details, and transitional phrases; a second experimental group received indirect instruction by listening to selections and discussing their content; the third group, a control group, received only the usual language arts program. The direct-instruction group made the most significant gains, and the control group showed no significant gains.

In a study involving eighth grade students, a series of taped lessons designed to improve both listening and reading skills was used. The experimental group showed a significant gain in listening, reading, and English skills as measured by standardized tests. Especially outstanding gains were made in following directions in both listening and reading.[27]

The significance of critical listening in the lives of children and adults points to the need for developing these abilities through a planned program instead of the usual program in English which provides no regular instruction in critical listening. Closely related to the child's need for developing abilities in listening is the need of the teacher to see listening in its proper perspective in the language arts program.

A study of the behaviour of elementary school teachers during the language arts period reveals that teachers accounted for more than 50% of the talk in the classroom and that most student talk was in response to teacher questions. "Although a large number of teachers were included each teacher was observed for only forty-five minutes. Using supervisory ratings as a criterion of teaching excellence, Amidon and Giammatteo (1965) compared the interaction patterns of 30 'superior' teachers with 150 randomly selected teachers in eleven elementary school districts. Using Flander's categories they found that superior teachers talked less, accepted more student ideas, encouraged more pupil-initiated participation, and gave fewer directions than did the average teachers."[28]

The Flanders' rule of two-thirds should be kept in mind by the teacher as he plans his classroom activities and the learning experiences of his students. "In the average classroom someone is talking two-thirds of the time; two-thirds of this is teacher talk; and two-thirds of teacher talk consists of direct influence (lecture, direction-giving, or criticism)."[29] The goal of good teaching should be to avoid the "average" classroom. Research on listening highlights the lag between the findings of research and the classroom implication. The implications and recommendations suggest some solutions to the problem.

IMPLICATIONS AND RECOMMENDATIONS FOR THE TEACHER

Based upon the studies surveyed and similar studies, the following implications and recommendations are presented:

Teachers should become aware of the fact that listening is an important area of the language arts and a skill that can and should be taught.

Students who receive instructions in listening give evidence of significant improvement in listening ability, whereas those who do not receive such instruction do not.

Listening is a skill which can be improved through specific directed instruction.

Reading comprehension is significantly related to listening ability.

Listening ability is significantly related to the entire curriculum.

The language arts curriculum should provide challenging activities which motivate all types of listening experience. At every educational level the teacher should provide listening activities, materials, and instruction which will be meaningful and rewarding to each child.

The content of textbooks in the language arts should be based on the findings of research so as to contribute toward the listening needs of children.

Greater emphasis should be placed on improvement of listening skills in teacher education programs so that future and current teachers are well informed about the significance of teaching listening skills and the importance of keeping up-to-date on the findings of research.

Materials (other than text books) should aid the teacher in implementing the integration of listening instruction with the other areas of language arts and the social studies.

An increased awareness of the interrelatedness of listening comprehension and reading comprehension skills should be fostered in the classroom. The development of these skills should be the responsibility of each teacher.

MISCONCEPTIONS ABOUT LISTENING

In view of the findings of research as to the significance of listening comprehension, why is there so little emphasis placed on teaching the listening skills in the elementary school? The answer seems to lie in certain unfounded assumptions.

Listening Is Closely Related to Intelligence

One misconception about listening which has done much to deter a systematic listening program in the schools is that listening is largely a matter of intelligence. Although there is a positive correlation between listening ability and intelligence, as there is between intelligence and behaviour in response to situations, the relationship between listening and intelligence is not nearly so significant as many have assumed. It is more correct to say "We listen with our experience" than "We listen with our intelligence". Observe how one "pricks up his ears" when the conversation turns to a subject in which he can speak from experience. How well we listen is determined by the extent to which we develop and utilize skills required for effective listening. The well-educated teacher does not accept the concept that the bright student will learn without training in listening and that the dull one won't learn anyway.

Listening Ability Determined by Hearing Acuity

Another widely held misconception is that children's listening ability is determined by hearing acuity. This has been responsible for retarding the program of teaching listening. As a matter of fact, only three to six percent of the school population suffers from hearing defects severe enough to impair learning in the classroom. What is regarded as a hearing loss is often merely a matter of inattention, boredom, or indifference. Individual listening comprehension differs as widely among children as does any other trait, ability, or competency.

Listening Is Automatic

Perhaps even more serious than the other two misconceptions about listening is the belief that children listen automatically, that daily exposure to teacher-talk eliminates the need for training in listening. Many teachers are convinced that since more than fifty percent of the time in school is spent in their talking that there is no need to give *formal* training in listening. They put their faith in such well-worn phrases as, "Now class, I want you to listen", "Stop wool gathering and pay attention", or "Sit up and pay attention".

Teaching Reading Is More Important Than Teaching Listening

Most educators believe that learning to read is more important than learning to listen. They believe that an individual is more influenced by what he reads than by what he hears. This may well be the most detrimental of the misconceptions in the light of the significance of modern communications media. It is now generally agreed that this is a false assumption, as unfounded as the other three. Not only do we listen three times as much as we read, but listening has more influence upon human behaviour than reading. In the years ahead we shall be influenced even more by what we hear than by what we read.

"It is important to know that assimilation through the ear is multi-directional while that through the eye must be focused; that the ear is more sensitive than the eye, requiring a smaller amount of energy for activation; that reaction time for sound is faster than for light; and that the ear appears to be much more durable than the eye, with a much greater capacity for continuous use."[30]

As educators become aware of the misconceptions which have retarded the development of formal instruction in listening they will make use of the findings of research. Thus they will discover for themselves that factors other than intelligence influence listening performance, that most of these factors outweigh listening acuity, that listening can be taught through carefully graded and guided experiences, and that to be taught effectively it cannot be left to incidental teaching.

FACTORS WHICH INFLUENCE LISTENING

Listening requires a mind set in order to get the most out of a given situation. If we want to become good listeners we must assume the role of the good listener. We must be conscious of the extent to which environmental, physical, psychological, and experiential factors affect the quality of listening.

Environmental Factors

The teacher should be aware of both the physical environment of the classroom and the social climate of the class. Each is important. Each is essential to a satisfying situation for learning.

PHYSICAL ENVIRONMENT. In considering the physical environment of the classroom as a factor in motivating listening it is essential that the acoustics are such that the child is able to hear without strain. The teacher should arrange the tables or desks in such a manner that every child has the same opportunity to hear and be heard. Placing work areas close together so children can communicate when necessary encourages good listening. Too great a distance between speaker and listener impedes communication. The teacher should use a pleasant voice, give clear, concise directions, and be a good listener himself.

The teacher should provide activities which motivate children to shift easily between the roles of listener and speaker. Through such activities as working on committees of various sizes; engaging in panel discussions, symposiums, and role playing; being members of audiences and speakers for groups the children may alternate between the roles of leader and follower—of listener and speaker.

SOCIAL ENVIRONMENT. Children readily sense an atmosphere in which they are encouraged to express their ideas with the knowledge that their contributions will be respected. Children who have an opportunity to be heard will more readily listen when some one else has the floor. An atmosphere which encourages children to experience, to express, and to evaluate ideas is imperative if the communication skills and the arts of language are to develop. This must be the basis for planned experiences and informal activities which require communication.

Obviously the climate in which the teacher plans experiences through which children will be able to utilize the classroom situation to improve their communication skills is of significance in the total curriculum planning. The teacher should set an example for listening as well as provide opportunities for teaching listening and plan specific activities to promote it.

Physical Factors

Physical conditions within the listener may impede his listening. If he is fatigued, hungry, worried, or ill he will find listening extremely difficult. It is not only the hard-of-hearing who presents problems in listening. It is also the undernourished, the disadvantaged, the chronically ill child. The child who is in excellent physical condition is potentially a better listener than one in poor physical condition. Frequently the class before lunch or the class that is held late in the afternoon suffers because children are physically not up to par and find it well-nigh impossible to listen. A mid-morning snack, especially for young children, helps bring the class up to a higher level of listening skill. It takes energy to listen, and it takes food to provide the energy.

Psychological Factors

Psychological factors involving personality traits, attitudes, and biases may also contribute to poor listening. Among psychological "deaf-spots" are areas of sensitivity when the listener is caught up in the emotion-laden words used by the speaker. These cause him to react emotionally and listening comprehension deteriorates. Poor listeners, on the whole, are more biased than good listeners. The poor listener has less emotional control, broods about what the speaker is doing to destroy his pet theory, stops listening to the speaker, and concentrates on organizing a rebuttal of his own. On the other hand, the good listener tends to listen with an open mind, weighs all the evidence before making a judgment, and gives the speaker courteous attention until he has heard him out before making up his mind. In other words, the good listener tends to use the problem solving technique and scientific attitude in his listening.

Experiental Factors

We listen with our experience. Observe a group of people in the midst of a conversation. Notice how the eyes light up, the body becomes alive, and the expression of the listener changes when the topic shifts to personal interests. Knowing the interests of all the children is helpful in planning the listening program. The child who has had varied and rich experiences is interested in many facets of living when he comes to school. Others whose experiences are limited will need to find in the curriculum itself broadening experiences and new horizons. It is only as the child broadens his experiences that he is interested enough in a specific subject or area of the curriculum to gain the most in listening to learn. As he enjoys new experiences, he will become not only a better listener, a better conversationalist, but a more effective student.

GUIDES TO EFFECTIVE LISTENING

In recent years research has emphasized the positive approach to negative listening factors and has concentrated on replacing poor listening habits with effective skills as the central concern of the listening programs. Of significance to the elementary school teacher as an individual and as a teacher of children are the following guides to effective listening based on research carried on at the University of Minnesota and reported by Nichols.[31]

FIND AREAS OF INTEREST. Whereas poor listeners after the first few sentences declare the subject dry, and stop listening, good listeners who find the subject dry, instead of getting up and walking out, look for something in the speech they can put to use. Chesterton summarized this philosophy when he stated. "There is no such thing as an uninteresting subject; there are only uninterested people." Use is the key to the matter of interest in a topic.

JUDGE CONTENT, NOT DELIVERY. Essentially we listen with our experience. If this is true, the fact that the speaker may be inept in his delivery should not rob us of the message he has to give us. True, the speaker may have his faults, but we can get something out of the talk if we are interested in finding out what he knows that we need to know. We might not like the way he says it, but we *can* learn from what he says.

HOLD YOUR VIEW. We must learn not to get too emotional about a speaker's point until we are certain we thoroughly understand it. This calls for withholding evaluation until our comprehension is complete. Over-stimulation either in support of the speaker's point or in opposition reflects a desire to enter into the argument immediately instead of following the development of the speaker's ideas.

LISTEN FOR IDEAS. We are all familiar with the situation of being asked about a speech or sermon we have heard and replying, "It was very good". "I was really impressed" or some such comment. Upon further questioning we have been embarrassed by our failure to answer, "What was it about?"

Good listeners focus on central ideas; they are able to remember the main idea of the speech, to distinguish between fact and opinion, idea and example, evidence and argument. It is a significant fact that only about twenty-five percent of the people listening to a formal speech are able to grasp the speaker's central idea. "To develop these skills," says Nichols, "requires an ability to recognize conventional organizational patterns, transitional language, and the speaker's use of recapitulation. Fortunately, all of these items can be readily mastered with a bit of effort."[32]

BE FLEXIBLE. Some of the best listeners never take notes. Instead, they concentrate on listening and later attempt to recall or reconstruct the speech they heard. With programmed material, taped lectures, and other audio-aids it is possible to check on the progress one makes in this type of skill development.

There is, interestingly enough, some evidence to indicate that the volume of notes taken and their value to the taker are inversely related. In any event, it is the ability to take meaningful notes that is important. The old chestnut about the notes going from the notebook of the professor to the notebook of the student without going through the minds of either is an exaggerated statement indicative of the need for flexibility in note-taking in terms of the organizational pattern of the speech to which they listen.

WORK AT LISTENING. Poor listeners refuse to spend any energy in listening. "College students, by their own testimony, frequently enter classes all worn out physically; assume postures which only seem to give attention to the speaker, and then proceed to catch up on needed rest or to reflect upon purely personal matters."[33]

As a courtesy to the speaker as well as a favour to ourselves it is important to give the speaker our conscious attention. Not only does such behaviour help the speaker in expressing his ideas more clearly, we gain by better understanding the improved communication we have helped the speaker to achieve. The mere act of behaving as though we were listening is not enough. It is necessary to establish eye contact and maintain it, to indicate by posture and facial expression that the speaker's efforts are a matter of concern to us, and that we are listening at a high level of comprehension.

RESIST DISTRACTIONS. The good listener tends to adjust quickly to adverse situations. He instinctively fights distractions. It is the courteous listener who closes the door, turns off the radio, shuts the window, puts his hand to his ear indicating the need for more projection on the part of the speaker, changes his seat, and if all else fails, concentrates more deeply on the topic at hand.

EXERCISE YOUR MIND. The poor listener is inexperienced in listening to anything that requires more effort on his part than the "soap opera," or light, recreational material. Listening to anything that requires response to technical, expository, difficult material is too much for such an individual. He may recognize that listening is hard work—but hard work is not for him. Such an individual is using only a limited amount of his mental capacity as well as his listening skill. He is a poor risk in the classroom, the office, *or* the factory. Good listeners are challenged by material that requires mental effort.

KEEP YOUR MIND OPEN. Closely related to the blind spots which impair our sight are the psychological deaf spots which impair our ability to perceive or understand. Effective listeners make an effort to identify the "red flag" words or phrases which tend to upset them emotionally, and try to rationalize those which are most upsetting to them. Words which cause communication to drop to zero are well known and vary with the region, the socioeconomic level, and cultural background of the individual.

CAPITALIZE ON THOUGHT SPEED. The rate at which a person speaks and the rate at which he thinks differ considerably. There is evidence to show that if thought were measured in words per minute, most of us think easily at about four times as fast as we speak. This lag is responsible for much of the "day-dreaming" that goes on in the classroom as well as the embarrassing moment when the conversation is turned in our direction and we have been "woolgathering" and can't pick up the conversational thread.

Nichols suggests capitalizing on thought speed by developing the following pattern:

A. Try to anticipate what a person is going to talk about. On the basis of what he had already said, ask yourself: "What's he trying to get at? What point is he going to make?"

B. Mentally summarize what the person has been saying. What point has he made already, if any?

C. Weigh the speaker's evidence by mentally questioning it. As he presents facts, illustrative stories and statistics, continually ask yourself: "Are they accurate? Do they come from an unprejudiced source? Am I getting the full picture, or is he telling me only what will prove his point?"

D. Listen between the lines. The speaker doesn't always put everything that's important into words. The changing tones and volume of his voice may have a meaning. So may his facial expressions, the gestures he makes with his hands, the movement of his body.[34]

PLANNING THE LISTENING PROGRAM

Any attempt to help children develop skills in listening must take into account the various levels, types, and purposes for listening. Although objectives for developing skills will be in the mind of the teacher, he must recognize that children move from the tentative and early skills of listening in the preschool stage to the higher levels only if there is continual guidance throughout the elementary school years. The development of listening skills and behaviour is outlined below:

Levels of Listening

1. Little conscious listening on the part of the child and then only when he is the center of interest; easily distracted by people and things.
2. Half-listening; the child more interested in his own ideas, waiting to "break in".
3. Passive listening; the child just sitting there, with little or no reaction.
4. Sporadic listening; the child showing interest if the conversation is closely related to his own experience, but shutting off the current when the conversation turns away from him.
5. Listening; some reaction shown through comments or questions.
6. Listening; indication of sincere emotional and intellectual response.
7. Highest level of listening; complete understanding of what is being said.[35]

Children listen at one or more of these levels throughout the day. They need guidance if they are to acquire the highest levels of listening skills.

Purposes for Listening

Just as there are different levels of listening, so there are different purposes for listening. There are numerous classifications of the purposes of listening. Through research and empirical evidence in working with children and teachers in elementary classrooms the following purposes for listening have been established.

Listening to follow directions
Listening for information
Listening for enjoyment
Listening to evaluate
Listening to appreciate
Listening to communicate
Listening to discriminate sounds

There is an art to teaching listening just as there is to teaching any other area of the language arts curriculum. There is skill in selecting, organizing, directing, and evaluating learning experiences which will help children achieve skills needed for each purpose for listening. It is as necessary to develop skills in listening for specific purposes as it is to develop skills in reading for specific purposes. For the teacher it is essential to realize that these skills will be used at every level of education according to the situation and the demands of the moment. Throughout the elementary school the purposes for listening should provide continuity, balance, and integration of learning experiences.

Purposeful listening, like purposeful reading, is more successful than that which is without purpose. To help children develop the various skills needed for listening it is essential to provide a systematic and regularly scheduled training program.

Although there is a sequence in which the listening skills tend to develop, experience with children shows that many are needed simultaneously. The teacher must be able to meet the listening needs of the children in terms of the purposes required at a specific time.

Listening to Follow Directions

In teaching listening skills related to the various purposes the teacher will find the following steps useful in the procedure:

Make the student aware of his need to develop greater listening effectiveness
Motivate him to improve his listening power
Provide specific listening experiences which will give him practice in developing a specific type of skill both in the classroom and outside
Devise techniques whereby his development may be evaluated
Give him suggestions for further training

The teacher can do very little teaching without getting and maintaining the attention of the group while directions, explanations, and announcements are given. The need to learn to follow instructions or directions is a listening purpose which is essential throughout a lifetime. If all the time and money lost in the course of a single day because of failure to follow oral instructions were calculated it would be an impressive amount. In the classroom the student who does not learn to listen to follow instructions is well on the road to becoming a failure, not only in the academic years, but later in life when even more dire consequences may result.

Successful procedures which are useful in teaching listening for the specific purpose of following instructions, directions, and explanations are cited by Tressler:[36]

1. Listen to each detail carefully
2. In your mind, picture each
3. If convenient, jot down notes on important points
4. If given chance, ask questions about doubtful points
5. If possible, say out loud the directions, explanations, or instructions
6. In the case of instructions, repeat the directions as you carry them out. The quickest and surest way to learn a new job is to repeat your instructions as you practice, audibly or silently.

In initial experiences in listening to follow directions it is well worth while to work toward the "once only" rule, so that value is placed on listening the first time. One elementary school student expressed his reaction this way, "Why listen to Miss Tarnowski the first time? She always says it three times anyway."

Listening for Information

Another purpose for listening is for information—facts, ideas, principles—with recall as the goal. Listening for information is one of the most significant purposes for listening. It has been discovered that students will recall more facts if they are told beforehand the purpose for listening, the follow-up activities, and/or the relation of the material to their interests and needs. Hedde and Brigance[37] list seven basic principles which will guide the teacher in teaching children to listen for information:

1. Get ready to listen.
2. Start listening with the first sentence.
3. Get the central idea.
4. Get the chief supporting facts.
5. Separate the important from the unimportant.
6. Make mental summaries.
7. Analyze what you hear.

Sooner or later in the elementary grades the problem of taking notes will arise and instructions will have to be given to facilitate their use. Weaver and Borchers[38] give the following suggestions:

1. Have pencil or pen and notebook ready when the speaker begins.
2. Do not try to make a full word-by-word record of any considerable part of the speech. Listen and note words, phrases, and figures which will help in recalling the most important statements.
3. Be especially on the alert for points which the speaker himself emphasizes in his presentation. If he is a good speaker, he will indicate the relative importance of the various parts of his speech by the way in which he delivers them.
4. When the speaker has finished the discussion of one point, watch carefully for what he says concerning his next point; often he will state this in a topic sentence.
5. It is usually more helpful to put down a striking phrase than it is to write out a complete sentence.

Listening for Enjoyment

Language is like music. It must be heard not only as discrete words, but as melody of real life. "It is not so much the question whether heard melodies are sweet and those unheard are sweeter; we must aim to equip our students with the ability to hear melodies where before they heard mere sounds; experience enjoyment where before they were bored; enjoy every living moment where before they merely existed. Such is the essence of listening for enjoyment."[39]

The ability to enjoy listening to stories, plays, poetry, essays, and/or music must be developed. The somewhat common belief that no training is needed in listening for enjoyment is ill-founded. The student may believe that he knows what he likes to listen to and he needs no one else to tell him what he likes or what he should like. However, this is coloured by his experiential background. The teacher may broaden his enjoyment by discussions about what constitutes humour and wit with examples that one finds in communication media. The enjoyment of laughter can stimulate greater learning as well as increased enjoyment in listening.

Nor must humour be the only measure of enjoyment. Sounds, words, apt phrases can give pleasure to those who have taken the time to become acquainted with the world's great writers. The student misses much who is not given the opportunity to extend his horizons in listening to the rhythm and melody of words as well as the rhythm and harmony of music. Pupils must be shown that enjoyment stems from the arrangement and harmony of the artist's manipulation of the tools of expression whether the artist be the poet, musician, or the graphic artist.

Lewis and Nichols point out that "Pleasurable listening derives from complex sources. A bird call, for instance, may give us intense pleasure because it reminds us of summer, vacation, freedom, the out-of-doors, hunting, pleasant associations. On the other hand, we may take intellectual pleasure in being able to identify the bird, know its habits, and its life history. It is possible, of course, simply to enjoy the virtuosity of the bird—the music of its call. Similar factors may play a part in the enjoyment of music, listening to the reading of drama, verse, even the diction of a foreign language we cannot understand intellectually."[40]

Listening to Evaluate

Important as listening for comprehension and enjoyment is, of even greater significance is listening for evaluation. Unless children are taught to develop skills in critical listening, the cause of democracy may well be lost. Unless critical listening is developed, our civilization may be destroyed. Critical listening involves weighing the evidence in the face of techniques of persuasion which men may use to influence decision making *before* the listener has had the time or the background of information to make up his mind. Wendall Johnson presents graphically the dilemma of the individual confronted with decisions in the midst of a world in which the true and the false, the genuine, and the charlatan, the orator and the spellbinder vie for our attention. "The act of listening holds for us the desparate hope of withstanding the spreading ravages of commercial, nationalistic, and ideological persuasion. Unless the gentle watchword, "Listen!" becomes an arresting command, we may not halt in time the stampede of humanity in its pursuit of the enchanting tooting of the Pied Piper of Doom."[41]

The discriminating listener must be taught to compare points made by the speaker, to get at the basis of contradiction, to check the authenticity of the information, to ascertain the bias of the speaker. He must immediately and continually weigh and test the evidence or lack of it used to support each argument. Questions which should become habitual in listening critically are: What does the speaker mean? How does he know? What is he leaving out?

From the early beginnings in the elementary school children should be taught to listen attentively, accurately, and critically. Not only should they listen for the ideas the speaker is trying to convey, but they should be judging the worth of what he is saying. From the beginning they should examine the reasoning to make sure that the speaker's inferences as well as his statements are sound and that he has support which is acceptable for his ideas. Thus children will learn early that whenever they hear an assertion they must check its veracity with evidence which can be identified and verified.

Listening to Appreciate

Appreciative listening requires more complex skills than does listening for enjoyment. After each return to a truly great poem, drama, or musical composition the pleasure which we first experienced and enjoyed should be intensified. Appreciative listening requires effort—it depends chiefly upon our willingness to learn. It depends upon our conscious effort to deepen our understanding by finding out all we can about the object of our appreciation. To listen for more than enjoyment of words, to listen for more than enjoyment of the melody, we move toward deeper involvement and thus gain deeper satisfaction from the experiences. In poetry and drama we can improve our appreciation by listening to good actors or good readers, either live or on recordings. The teacher who is gifted has an advantage in holding students spellbound by his beautiful interpretation. However, thanks to the magic of recordings, television, and radio children can listen as well to a wide variety of interpretations. And yet, in spite of the availability of the technical devices to assist in teaching listening, no machine will ever be a substitute for the artist-teacher. This points to the need for pre-service training in oral interpretation.

Listening to oral reading by both teachers and pupils, participating in choral speaking, listening to radio, television, and motion pictures, listening to a play or poetry opens the way for a growing appreciation of the beauties of the spoken language, whether this beauty exists in a story interpreted by an artist-teacher, in a poem by a classical or contemporary author, or in the dialogue of a master novelist or playwright. Appreciative listening must be developed—it does not "just happen". This is the teacher's responsibility from the preschool through the academic years. The fact that appreciation is acquired through guided experience places the responsibility on the teacher for knowing the children he teaches well enough to help each child experience frequently those types of listening which bring him both enjoyment and esthetic satisfaction. In doing this he broadens and extends his appreciative listening as he grows toward maturity.

Listening to Communicate

Listening to communicate is perhaps the most important purpose for learning to listen. When we consider that an individual spends some 45% of his communication time in listening and another 30% in speaking, then the skills required of the

good listener and good conversationalist are significant enough to warrant attention. In order to improve our social relationships it is necessary to learn to listen,
and to learn when and how to come into the conversation. Communicative listening
is an important attribute of effective conversation. Communicative listening can
well have its roots in the dialogue of the child and teacher, the child and child, and
the child and a small group. It is one of the responsibilities of the school to provide
informal situations in which social discourse between two or three individuals can
take place.

Listening to Discriminate Sounds

Listening to discriminate speech sounds involves not only the recognition of the
phonetic elements of the language (vowels and consonants), but also the various
elements of voice such as quality, force, time, and pitch. Learning to discriminate
speech sounds is a continuous process of a lifetime—starting when the child first
identifies single sounds and reproduces them and stopping only when the last breath
is taken.

The child imitates the sound he perceives—first in a rather gross form with the
result that the speech is full of errors (baby talk). As he develops his listening and
imitative skills his speech pattern improves. The classroom teacher must take the
child where he is and help him to discriminate not only the phonetic elements of
speech but also the desirable expressive elements of quality, force, time, and pitch.
As the child develops he should consistently be made aware of the ever finer
shadings of meanings that can be given by an expressive voice.

With the use of a tape recorder it is possible for the child to listen to his own
voice and compare it to good models so that he becomes aware of his need, makes an
effort to improve, and learns to evaluate achievement in terms of progress in harmony with his own limitations and goals.

LISTENING ACTIVITIES WHICH DEVELOP SKILLS FOR A SPECIFIC PURPOSE

The focus of the teacher's concern is at this point the organization of activities
which will motivate the development of skills essential to each purpose of listening
the child encounters in the elementary years. It is necessary that the activities
selected are in harmony with the objectives. Thus the purpose determines the skills
to be developed, the activities to be organized, and the evaluation whereby progress
is measured. The listening skills and activities are organized into seven categories:

Listening to follow directions
Listening for information
Listening for enjoyment
Listening to evaluate
Listening for appreciation

Listening to communicate
Listening to discriminate speech sounds

Listening to Follow Directions

Successful teachers will use a wide variety of techniques, activities, and materials to help children listen with increased attention and discrimination in following directions. The teacher can help children develop a "set" for listening with comprehension by:

A. Objectives
   1. Putting distracting materials out of sight
   2. Listening from the beginning
   3. Listening actively for the who-what-when-where
B. Techniques of the Teacher
   1. Waiting until every one is attentive
   2. Speaking simply, with clear, simple phrases
   3. Giving directions once only
   4. Checking to see that the children understand
   5. Organizing material so it is systematic, explicit, and brief
   6. Making use of visual aids to support the auditory experience
C. Activities (designed to achieve the objectives)
   1. Listening to directions and announcements
   2. Playing such games as "Simon Says"
   3. Following instructions for cutting and folding paper, drawing pictures, or writing according to oral directions
   4. Listening to and repeating directions that might be given to a traveller on a journey to an imaginary place
   5. Listening to and repeating directions that might be given to a traveller on a journey to a specific, real place
   6. Having students, on a prepared worksheet, follow directions such as "Put an X . . ," "Circle . . ," "Cross out . . ," "Underline . . ".
   7. Playing "Do As I Say". Give three or more directions in sequence and choose a child to carry them out. For example: "Go to the back of the room, turn around three times, pick up a book from the library table, give it to John, walk over to the pencil sharpener, count to ten, and take your seat." In the early experiences the game must be simple. Increase the complexity as the year progresses—or as the individual is able to accomplish it. When a child makes an error another child is chosen
   8. Listening to a list of action words. At a signal perform the designated actions
   9. Responding automatically to signals for fire drills, change of classes, dismissal, gymnasium signals, and so forth
D. Evaluation (Cooperative endeavor by teacher and pupils)
   1. Did the speaker wait until the children were ready to listen before making announcements or giving directions?
   2. Did everyone in the room listen courteously as well as attentively?

3. Did the children stop what they were doing and "Pay attention"?
4. Did they remember what was said and give evidence of it by their subsequent behaviour?
5. Did they listen for the clue words of who-when-where-what?
6. Did they distinguish the signals and respond quickly and in an orderly manner?
7. Did they share in the listening experience with real interest and enthusiasm?
8. Do they give evidence of listening to directions with increasing efficiency as the school year progresses?

Children should evaluate their own progress in any learning experience. When they can cooperatively set up goals for the various purposes of listening they will be more apt to attempt to achieve those goals. As early as kindergarten children enjoy taking responsibility for improving their ability to listen. The following criteria set up by a group of kindergartners did much to help them achieve the necessary listening skills.

1. We listen when the teacher gives directions
2. We wait for the children who aren't ready to listen
3. We stop what we are doing. We look at the speaker. We keep quiet
4. We think before we speak so our directions are clear
5. We listen until the directions are completed
6. We give a signal for silence if someone is talking
7. We listen when someone reads to us
8. We listen and respond to specific signals (teacher's whistle on the playground, class bells, fire drills, piano chord to stop talking).

Listening for Information

Before children learn to read they are entirely dependent on listening for information, both in and out of the classroom. Even after reading skills are developed they still must depend upon listening for much of their information. In the average classroom two-thirds of the time someone is talking, two-thirds of the time this someone is the teacher. This makes listening for information vital.

A. Objectives
   To help children listen to recall facts, ideas, and principles with accuracy by:
   1. Developing an interest in the subject or project
   2. Listening actively to what is said
   3. Noting sequence of ideas
   4. Holding the thread of the discourse in mind
   5. Watching for transitional phrases and change of subject
   6. Reserving evaluation until the speech is concluded
   7. Listening for the central idea
   8. Relating supporting ideas
   9. Making mental summaries periodically
   10. Analyzing what is heard.

B. Techniques of the Teacher
   1. Establishing a specific purpose for listening
   2. Telling students beforehand what to listen for
   3. Teaching children how to take notes efficiently
   4. Training in listening for points which the speaker emphasizes as important
   5. Emphasizing the organization of the talk heard
   6. Showing how to extract the main ideas
   7. Demonstrating how to distinguish the significant idea from the unimportant
   8. Guiding children to reserve judgment when various points of view are presented
   9. Having children listen to share what was heard
   10. Making intelligent and pertinent observations at the conclusion of the talk after hearing the observations of the children.

C. Activities
   These can be accomplished through:
   1. Sharing period, show and tell, conversations
   2. Carrying on dialogues between teacher-child and child-child
   3. Discussing, planning, and evaluating projects
   4. Answering the telephone and delivering the message accurately
   5. Listening to a short selection and suggesting a title
   6. Reading a short story to the group and asking the students to tell what happened in a one-sentence summary statement
   7. Reading three statements, one containing the main idea and the other two containing subordinate ideas. Have the students select the one that contains the main idea. Example:

   All life on earth is dependent on the sun.
   The sun provides us with heat during the day.
   Ocean plants get their energy from the sun.

   8. Reading a series of paragraphs and having students select the main idea from a number of choices. Have them discuss their choice in terms of specificity, relevancy, and accuracy.
   9. Having students listen to a description of an object, a place, or a person, knowing that they will complete an outline based on this description. The description should be read again, one sentence at a time. After each sentence, the students should enter information in appropriate places on the partially structured outline form.
   10. Having students listen to a selection that contains information that could be categorized. After listening to the selection, the students should be given a prepared worksheet containing the basic structure. Re-read the selection again, sentence by sentence, allowing time for the students to fill in the chart.
   11. Having students listen to a story and asking them to write an original story based on a similar personal experience.
   12. Giving the students prepared worksheets containing an outline form with at least one topic and subtopic filled in as a guide. After listening to a simple selection the students are to fill in the information that they remember.
   13. Having pupils listen as announcements are being read over the school's

public address system. Have them compare what they remember. Finally, have them check their information with the copy which the announcer read.

14. Reading a description of a landscape, then asking the children to draw the landscape from their memories of what was read.
15. Having the children listen to a television program without looking at it. How much can they picture imaginatively from what they have heard?
16. Following the school assembly, have the children tell how much they remember of the announcements made.
17. Exchanging tape recording with another grade in your school on which interesting and informative topics have been recorded. Send a copy of the script with the tape. After listening to the tape, have the children note significant and interesting facts. Check back against the tape script.

D. Evaluation
   1. Did the children understand the purpose for which they were listening? Did they remember the information?
   2. Did the children act on the information they received? (If action was necessary.)
   3. Did they use the information in constructive ways?
   4. Did they work independently as they were listening for the information? As they recorded their information?
   5. Did they discuss and evaluate on an increasingly mature level?

Listening for Enjoyment

Among the high moments for children in the elementary school are those in which they listen for sheer pleasure and enjoyment, be it listening to poetry with its flowing rhythm and rhyme, television with its variety of programs, prose with its sequence of happenings, or drama with its exciting climax. Here the teacher has opportunity to share his enthusiasm with the children and help them catch the joy such listening brings.

A. Objectives
   1. Providing a wealth of experiences in listening upon which to build for appreciative listening
   2. Helping children listen to enjoy music, plays, poetry, and prose
   3. Helping children develop enjoyment in listening to the sounds of nature
   4. Developing in children a sense of the esthetic.
B. Techniques of the Teacher
   1. Creating an environment in which listening for enjoyment is valued
   2. Securing equipment needed for listening to recordings, transcriptions, radio, television, sound films, and so forth
   3. Providing time for listening to music, drama, speech programs, both live and recorded.
C. Activities
   1. Listening to good vocal and instrumental music, drama, poetry, and prose

2. Responding rhythmically to music
3. Planning original ending to a story read by the teacher
4. Arranging instrumentation for the class orchestra
5. Listening to selected radio and television programs
6. Listening to music for relaxation and during self-chosen activities
7. Sketching an original cartoon of a character or situation portrayed in a story the teacher reads to the group
8. Using puppets, or pantomiming, or dramatizing as an outgrowth of a story just listened to
9. Creating sound effects with such instruments as finger cymbals, bells, triangles, etc. as an accompaniment to a story or poem read by the teacher
10. Creating sound effects to accompany a "radio" play read into the tape recorder
11. Composing the "developing story" in which each participant carries on from the point at which the preceding speaker stopped
12. Making up the second act of a play which the children have seen presented by a committee. In creative dramatics the acts will differ with each group as will the interpretation of the story
13. Reading to children from the great literature of the ages as well as from contemporary literature that meets high standards.

D. Evaluation
1. Did the children enjoy their listening experience?
2. Did they extend their base for listening for enjoyment?
3. Did they make an effort to listen to music, drama, stories, poems, with increasing frequency as the year progressed?
4. Did they grow in their interest in listening for enjoyment as evidenced by such activities as: polling the class members for television listening preferences, personal "hit parades" of stories or poems listened to during the preceding month, greater selection of music, poetry, drama recordings during the self-chosen period, request for stories the teacher read to the group, and number of books checked out from the library, read, and enjoyed?
5. Did they spend more time in listening to programs other members of the class enjoyed and recommended?
6. Did they spend some of their allowances on recordings, books and share them with the class?
7. Did they give evidence of enjoyment of literature read to them by the teacher?

Through listening to stories, drama, poetry, and music, both live and recorded, children will grow in listening enjoyment. It is the responsibility of the teacher to provide both a literary and a cultural environment for his classroom.

Listening to Evaluate (Critical Listening)

"It is time to begin a more scientific, systematic, and developmental approach to the teaching of critical listening. . . . It should be an integrated one commingling all the language arts. Long range planning is needed, spiraling through the elementary school with varied teaching strategies and devices. . . . Devices such as the following . . . role playing to illustrate attitudes and fallacies, partner practice in judging samples, abstraction ladders, and a rumour clinic."[42]

A. Objectives
1. Helping children to arrive at conclusions by critical listening
2. Helping children to understand what is meant by critical listening
3. Helping children to develop a questioning attitude
4. Helping children to analyze what they hear and judge the material on the basis of criteria regarding the evidence presented.

B. Techniques of the Teacher
1. Evaluating literature by teaching children to distinguish between truth and fancy, fact and fiction in literature. Older children should be taught to recognize and evaluate propaganda.
2. Making use of technological resources such as radio, television, recordings, and tape recordings to present children with opportunities for critical listening at varying levels of difficulty
3. Reading material (of varying levels of difficulty) which calls for critical evaluation
4. Demonstrating through his classroom behaviour that the teacher himself listens critically
5. Setting up standards for listening to lectures, speeches, or discussions in which speakers have strong opinions or views. These standards could be based on questions such as:
   a. What is the speaker's motive or purpose?
   b. What emotionally laden words or phrases does he use?
   c. Does he base his views on fact or opinion?
   d. Does he present his points through using propaganda techniques? Logic?
   e. Do his statements agree or conflict with presented evidence?
   f. Is the evidence he presents too old to be valid?
   g. Is the evidence reliable in terms of its source?
   h. Does the speaker have anything personal to gain by having his evidence accepted?

C. Activities
1. Discriminating between fact and fancy in listening to "tall tales". Children enjoy the flights of fancy in such stories as "Mulberry Street" by Dr. Suess. The child's vivid imagination causes him to hear a lion roaring or leopard stalking
2. Role playing "off the cuff" press conferences, then getting facts to prove the oral statements
3. Listening to panel discussions in which there are conflicting opinions. If possible, get scripts and tape recordings of radio or television programs. Have a before and after opinion poll. Use the script to refer to disputed points

4. Clipping or formulating statements in which fact and opinion are inter-twined. Ask pupils to listen first for opinions and then for facts which are indisputable

5. Reading statements of personal opinion aloud with the assignment that the students are to reinforce them by gathering factual evidence. Example: "I think the cost of living has gone up rapidly this past year." The students gather comparative costs of selected items

6. Listening to radio and television commercials and note techniques of propa-ganda. Classify the appeals used

7. Listening to speeches for evidence of any of the following devices or basic techniques of propaganda:

   a. Name calling. Essentially this consists of denouncing a person or thing by giving it the label of something widely condemned.

   b. Glittering generalities. This device seeks acceptance of ideas or propo-sitions through association with words widely accepted or approved.

   c. Transfer. Transfer is the device of citing respected sources of authority, prestige, or reverence in a way to make it appear they sanction the new proposal at hand.

   d. Plain folks. Identification with the so-called "plain folks". This device is evident in such behaviour of candidates for political office being photographed milking cows to prove they support the farmers and have a "dirt-farmer" background; kissing babies to show they love children.

   e. Card stacking. This technique is one built of half-truths. By careful selection of favourable evidence and an equally careful omission of contrary evidence, the listener is lulled into making a false conclusion.

   f. Testimonial. The use of testimonials from famous people to build confidence in a product or proposition. Many professional athletes "recommend" cereals, cigarettes, sports clothes.

   g. Band wagon. The appeal here is based on the premise that if every-body else is going along with a certain idea that we ought to join the movement or "climb aboard" ourselves. It is well to remember Anatole France's "If fifty million people say a foolish thing, it is still a foolish thing."[43]

8. Listening to a speech with a single purpose in mind. (Perhaps to judge the intent of the speaker.)

9. Analyzing the sales psychology that underlies advertisements on television, radio, in newspapers and/or magazines. Watch for sensory appeal, status appeal, physical prowess or well-being

10. Comparing the news reports and commentaries on radio and television in terms of their party affiliations. Do the same with newspaper stories.

Listening to Appreciate (*To make esthetic judgments*)

When does listening for enjoyment become listening for appreciation? Listen-ing, like poetry, begins in wonder and ends in appreciation *if* it is built upon a foundation of listening for enjoyment. The better we understand what we are listening to, the greater the possibility for potential satisfaction and pleasure. The more we know about what we are listening to, the more capable we are of listening to appreciate in the sense of making an esthetic judgment.

A. Objectives
1. Helping children grow from listening for enjoyment to listening to make an esthetic judgment. This can be achieved by helping children move from a purely emotional response to both emotional and intellectual response.

B. Techniques of the Teacher
1. Creating an environment in which the creative arts are valued
2. Providing equipment and time for listening experiences at the levels of listening appreciation of the children in the class
3. Providing listening experiences which challenge children to grow in appreciation of the beauties of poetry, drama, speech, and music. These activities will be explored in later chapters
4. Evidencing interest through attending performances of drama, opera, music, ballet
5. Informing pupils of forthcoming radio and television programs of special value for esthetic growth
6. Informing and urging attendance at live performances of esthetic value locally and in nearby communities
7. Being on the alert and searching for new esthetic experiences and expression.

C. Activities
1. Having children listen to skilfully interpreted poems, plays, readings, and speeches by gifted professionals
2. Reading for the children from some of the literary classics for them to observe at first hand the inter-relationships of movement, gestures, voice, inflection, cadence, and emphasis
3. Having children listen to a specific recording with a view to making esthetic judgments about the material and performance
4. Reading to the students stories, poems, plays, or essays that are high in sensory impact. Ask the children to prepare a selection of their own choice to read to the group
5. Organizing a readers theatre and having children develop a program centering around their favourite poems, excerpts from plays, or prose they have enjoyed
6. Inviting another class in and trying to determine the level of listening which the other class evidenced
7. Having students listen to a recording of a drama they are studying, noting the personal style of delivery of a selected actor
8. Listening to the same recording, this time noting characteristics of theme, plot, setting
9. Obtaining different recording of the same play and comparing the two
10. Having students listen to a poem read by the teacher or a record by an artist and listening for such details as:
   a. the voice qualities

b. inflectional patterns

c. imagery

d. emotional level

11. Having children listen to various types of sounds from different sizes of bells, then listen to a musical composition in which bells are used to appreciate the composer's method of blending them into the work

12. Keeping a record of the children's most frequently called for poems. At the end of a term have them analyze the qualities that made them select these particular ones

13. Appointing a committee to give advance notice of programs of quality to be presented in a local concert hall, theatre, auditorium or on radio or television

14. Discussing the program in class, forming esthetic judgments.

D. Evaluation

1. Did the children grow in their ability to make esthetic judgments?

2. Did the children listen with increasing frequency to programs which offered an opportunity to make esthetic judgments?

3. Did the children grow in their desire to attend programs which would demand this type of listening?

Listening to Communicate

The primary function of language is to communicate. "The most important single psychological principle underlying all speech instruction is that of the "circuit response". The essence of this concept is that communication is always a two-way affair. The listener is always of equal importance to the speaker and makes an equally significant contribution to the successful sharing of material."[44]

The good conversationalist is the good listener. The good listener inspires good conversation. He exerts a great influence upon the speaker and increases or decreases his effectiveness by his attitude. It is the good listener who lends a sympathetic ear to the speaker. He responds in an animated and cooperative manner. In turn, the speaker, warmed by such response, proceeds to communicate with improved ability.

As the child moves from the ego-centered individual toward the maturing individual he discovers that one of the surest routes to social acceptance is the ability to understand another human being. To understand it is essential to listen to what is being said. Conversation between individuals is an alternating process in which at least one speaker and one listener exchange roles as readily as they exchange ideas. The speaker becomes the listener who in turn becomes the speaker. The give and take of the situation has an exhilarating effect upon the individuals. Within the broad aim of listening to communicate the listener keeps the thread of conversation in mind so that he will be guided in knowing how to respond when he is the speaker. He is alive, interested, alert. It is an exhilarating experience to be a contributing member of a stimulating conversational group. The art of conversation is still one of the greatest of the Arts. The Age of Enlightenment was the age of great conversationalists. Gracious living implies gracious listening.

A. Objectives
   1. Developing listening skills for effective communication
   2. Holding the thread of conversation in mind
   3. Watching for transitional phrases and change of subject
   4. Being courteous, especially when one disagrees
   5. Listening actively to what is being said
   6. Refraining from monopolizing the conversation
   7. Entering the conversation at appropriate times. Avoiding rude interruptions.
B. Techniques of the Teacher
   1. Creating an atmosphere where conversation is valued
   2. Listening courteously to a child when he speaks
   3. Providing time for conversation as well as for formal speaking activities
   4. Reading interesting conversations from literature
   5. Using scenes from plays to analyze good conversation (or bad).
C. Activities
   1. Having a designated time each day for "share and tell", conversation, and/or discussion
   2. Providing time in the daily schedule for dialogue or conversations for teacher and child
   3. Discussing, planning, and evaluating classroom activities
   4. Working in groups and committee assignments
   5. Telephoning
   6. Role playing situations in which conversation is significant
   7. Engaging in conversations on specific topics
   8. Writing conversation in stories
   9. Creating conversation in creative dramatics.
D. Evaluation
   1. Did the children give evidence of courteous listening in everyday activities?
   2. Did the children set standards for courteous listening?
   3. Did the children take responsibility for participating in both phases of conversation—speaking and listening?
   4. Did the children act on the information gained through conversations?
   5. Did they converse on an increasingly mature basis?
   6. Did they broaden their interests and extend their horizons by engaging in conversations with older students and adults?
   7. Did they grow in their discussion and evaluation abilities as a result of their improved skills in conversation and courteous listening?

Listening to Discriminate Sounds

Listening to discriminate sounds is involved in listening for oral improvement. Even though the child's hearing may be normal he may not perceive all the speech sounds accurately. Thus he reproduces the sound as he perceives it—not necessarily as he hears it. To help this child improve his speech he must first be helped to perceive and reproduce accurately, in isolation, sounds with which he has difficulty. Before he is expected to reproduce the sound in words he already uses (where the sound is distorted or another is substituted) he should be helped to attain proficiency in perceiving and then making the sound first in isolation, then in numerous combinations in nonsense syllables and words. No effort should be made at this stage to correct the sound in the words already in his daily vocabulary. Not until he has attained consistent confidence in making the sound in nonsense combinations should he be guided to make the sound in words. The sound should first be introduced into words through words not normally in the child's vocabulary. Only when he has gained confidence and skill with new words should the teacher guide him to make the substitution of the approved speech sound in familiar words. New habits must now be substituted for old ones.

Most children will learn correct pronunciation of new words and use them readily through the normal oral activity of the classroom rather than in isloated drills. If, however, the child's language environment has been impoverished the teacher should provide opportunities for language experiences, for listening, and for group speech work that will make him feel a part of the group and enjoy improving his speech in spite of himself. The classroom teacher has the responsibility to provide an environment where language experiences are rich, and where the child feels psychologically safe. If then the decision is made to call in the speech therapist, it is the result of the considered opinion of a teacher who understands the distinction between speech improvement in the class room and speech therapy. Speech improvement is the province of the classroom teacher; speech therapy is the province of the specialist.

A. Objectives
   1. Helping children learn acceptable pronunciation through listening carefully to the way words are sounded
   2. Helping children to listen to individual speech sounds with discrimination and understanding
   3. Teaching children to listen to the way educated people in the community talk
   4. Helping children with errors of pronunciation previously acquired through poor listening habits
   5. Training the child to produce a sound properly after learning to perceive it correctly.
B. Techniques of the Teacher
   1. Setting an example of accurate pronunciation, clear enunciation, and precise articulation
   2. Providing a classroom environment in which listening to discriminate sounds is habitual
   3. Making use of the tape recorder so children are aware of the sounds they make
   4. Being aware of mispronunciations in one's own speech (Teachers who pronounce pen "pin" cannot expect children to pronounce it correctly.)
   5. Analyzing problems children have in listening accurately to speech sounds and providing exercises and listening games to alleviate the faults

  6. Referring the child who has severe or persistent problems to a speech therapist or to the speech clinic.
C. Activities
  1. Giving direct practice to develop an awareness of sounds as an aid to discriminating listening:
     a. Having students concentrate on everyday sounds around them until they can describe them in detail
     b. Having students listen to contrasting sounds, e.g., noise and music, loud and soft, and note their effect on the listener
     c. Having students analyze sounds according to pitch, rhythm, timbre, loudness in order to learn to distinguish among these various characteristics
     d. Having them listen to voices of others and study elements that make them pleasant or unpleasant to the listener
  2. Developing an awareness of pleasing voices by listening critically to those of announcers, actors, professional speakers
  3. Recording the pupils' voices and listening analytically to them played back to help them become conscious of their own needs for improvement
  4. Developing specific procedures for improving the voices through group speech games, poems, and varied speech activities
  5. Playing speech games to develop listening skills
  6. Listing all the aural impressions that they can identify during a specified period (traffic sounds, birds, machinery, movements)
  7. Listening to a series of sounds recorded on tape and identify them (rain, clatter of dishes, starting a car, paper rattling etc.)
  8. Identifying designated sounds from material read by the teacher
  9. Giving the children a specific speech sound and having them respond with words in which the sound comes first in an initial position, then medial, and then final. Have the words put on the board (g as in girl, figure, fog. Remember—the emphasis is on sound, NOT spelling).
D. Evaluation
  1. Did the children develop auditory discrimination through the exercises and games?
  2. Did the children learn to discriminate in listening to sounds placed in different positions in a word?
  3. Did the children make a sincere effort to make their sounds correctly after the teacher called attention to mistakes and gave concrete suggestions for improvement?
  4. Did the children look forward with anticipation to the speech improvement activities? Were they fun?
  5. Did the classroom atmosphere contribute toward listening with discrimination?

ENSURING BALANCE IN THE LISTENING PROGRAM

In the Primary Grades

The teacher who recognizes listening as a vital factor in the language arts program will provide opportunities for listening as an integral part of the day's experiences. The following activities which children normally engage in during the first years of school provide a well-rounded program wherein not alone the specific skills of listening are taught, but where the normal activities utilize those skills in a continuous, integrated language program.

1. Conversation and telephoning (a real phone if possible, otherwise a toy one)
2. Sharing experiences
3. Discussing, planning, evaluating
4. Directions and announcements
5. Story telling and dramatizations
6. Poetry and choral speaking
7. Listening to music
8. Reporting on excursions, science experiments, book reports
9. Oral reading in order to share what one has enjoyed
10. Introducing guests when they visit the school
11. Listening to programs and assemblies in the auditorium
12. Listening to sound films, recordings, transcriptions, radio and television
13. Listening to and identifying the various sounds in the environment
14. Listening creatively for imaginary sensory experiences.

Providing individual and group experiences in listening will involve:

1. Personal Experiences
   Sharing with the class weekend experiences, parties, trips, visits
   Showing and telling about a possession, toy, clothing, pet, science project
   Listening to and carrying out directions
   Listening to and relaying messages
   Listening and conversing over the telephone
   Listening to original stories, poems, and rhymes
   Listening to a story read by the teacher or another child
2. Group Experiences
   Planning a group activity
   Discussing a new game, a holiday, a celebration
   Developing an experience chart based on an excursion, movie, science experiment
   Contributing as a member of a committee delegated to perform a specific mission
   Planning and reporting an interview with a distinguished visitor
   Evaluating an excursion, movie, television or radio program
   Participating as a listener or player in creative dramatics
   Cooperating as a participant in teacher-pupil planning of work and group studies
3. Observing the Social Amenities
   Listening courteously when anyone is speaking
   Contributing to the conversation of the group of which one is a member
   Sensing occasions when listening is a requirement: when someone is speaking, in the theatre, at a program, in church

In the Intermediate and Upper Grades

Time must be provided throughout the intermediate and upper grades for both informal and formal listening activities. These should include experiences in listening discriminately, critically, and appreciatively. The teaching of listening must continue throughout the elementary school as an integral part of the curriculum. Listening must become habitual and automatic with the child if he is to meet the increased pressures of the curriculum. The demands of the intermediate and upper grades require ever more complex and refined skills in listening. One sixth grade teacher who was having difficulty getting the children to listen attentively motivated them to devise the following code for listening:

We identify the specific purpose for which we are listening
We listen actively
We listen with respect
We evaluate the speeches we hear—radio, television, student rallies
We listen analytically to oral reports by members of the class
We listen respectfully to all points of view—even those which are in direct opposition to our own cherished views
We listen appreciatively to literature read orally.

Typical activities which develop listening skills:

Listening to speeches
Participating in discussions
Interviewing people
Role playing situations
Symposiums followed by open forums
Creative dramatics and improvisations
Story telling
Choral speaking
Oral interpretation of poetry and prose
Readers' Theatre.

SELF EVALUATION FOR THE TEACHER

Under the pressures of the crowded curriculum and class room routines, teachers all too often fail to evaluate their listening program as an integral part of the curriculum. Periodic self evaluation is the key to success in teaching. Self evaluation is the key to a successful listening program.

1. Do I provide a classroom climate which fosters good listening habits?
2. Do I provide opportunity for the development of a wide variety of listening skills?
3. Do I provide a listening center where children may go to carry on listening activities that is comparable to the art center, music center, the arithmetic center, the library?
4. Do I arrange for the use of the language laboratory for practice in improving listening skills?
5. Do I record stories and programs for use in the listening center?
6. Do I use tapes of educational radio programs available?

7. Do I keep alert to the special needs of those children who need to replay the tape, record, or film?
8. Do I encourage children to carry on some of their listening activities in small groups at the listening center?
9. Do I plan as carefully to help children learn to listen for various purposes as I do to help them learn to read for various purposes?
10. Do I make use of listening activities for self-teaching and self-testing?
11. Do I listen to children as courteously as I should?
12. Do I initiate activities for various purposes for listening in terms of the interests, abilities, and needs of the children?
13. Do I get the attention of everyone before I start speaking?
14. Do I teach the children to be courteous listeners at all times?
15. Do I involve the children in setting standards for listening?
16. Do I guide the children in developing an appreciation and awareness of the sounds in our language?
17. Do I keep in mind that children spend more time in listening than in other communication skills?
18. Do I develop a balanced program in which listening skills are taught consistently and practiced through such specific activities as: listening to evaluate an idea or point of view, listening for directions, listening for main and subordinate ideas, listening for enjoyment, listening to appreciate poetry, prose, and music, listening courteously to communicate and engage in conversation, listening to learn to discriminate sounds?
19. Do I understand the factors that influence listening?
20. Do I keep a record of each child's listening progress based on a form such as the following?

PROGRESS CHART FOR LISTENING

Name of Child _____
Grade _____
School _____
Name of teacher _____

Item	Comments	Date
1. He evidences a readiness for listening with a purpose		
2. He disregards distractions in the environment		
3. He comprehends what he hears		
4. He listens courteously		
5. He listens critically for evidence, logic, main ideas		

6. He listens for enjoyment

7. He listens appreciatively

8. He follows the thread of the conversation

9. He makes good use of the differential in time between thought and speech

10. He reinforces the speaker by showing an interest in the topic

CONCLUDING STATEMENT

Listening to learn rather than merely learning to listen should be a goal of the language arts program. The child does not automatically listen. He must be taught to listen for a variety of purposes. He should participate in a well planned, well articulated, well balanced, and well directed developmental listening program. This should begin in the kindergarten and continue throughout the elementary school. He must achieve ever increasing mastery of this tool for learning if he is to live successfully in a society that demands a citizen who can listen critically as well as appreciatively, who can listen with comprehension as well as enjoyment, who can make judgments as well as follow directions, and who can listen to communicate as well as to discriminate sounds and words.

The imperative need for listening purposefully, effectively, and efficiently in a wide range of listening situations will be met only if the school assumes its responsibility in this area. This necessitates preparing teachers to carry out a well planned program of training in listening. In a classroom oriented to listening the child develops the auditory sensitivity and the functional facility that ensures that he will be equal to purposeful listening and effective learning with a minimum expenditure of time and energy and a maximum measure of enjoyment, satisfaction, and reward.

"Through listening the student experiences satisfactions in hearing beautiful phrases and artistic expression; he enhances his appreciation of poetry, drama, and various forms of literature; he grows more discriminative in evaluating the language he hears and thereby extends and improves his own usage; he becomes better able to recall information and ideas; he learns to react critically and become selective as he learns."[45]

REFERENCES

1. By permission of National Council of Teachers of English, *The English Language Arts*, Appleton-Century-Crofts, Inc., New York, 1952, pp. 273, 271.

2. Joseph Mersand, "Developing Competence in Listening in Secondary Schools," *The Speech Teacher*, 7:301, November, 1958.
3. Leland B. Jacobs, "Speaking and Listening," in Helen McCracken Carpenter (ed.), *Skill Development in Social Studies*, National Council for the Social Studies, NEA, Washington, 1963, p. 141.
4. Lillian M. Logan and Virgil G. Logan, *Teaching the Elementary School Child*, Houghton Mifflin Company, Boston, 1961, p. 212.
5. Quoted in John Irwin and Marjorie Rosenberger, *Modern Speech*, Holt, Rinehart, and Winston, Inc., New York, 1961, p. 41.
6. *Ibid.*, p. 42
7. *Ibid.*, p. 42
8. Thorrel B. Fest and Martin T. Cobin, *Speech and Theatre*, The Center for Applied Research in Education, Washington, 1964, p. 14.
9. Dominic Barbara, "Listening With a Modest Ear," *Today's Speech*, 9:3, February, 1961.
10. Mark A. Neville, "Listening Is an Art: Practice It," *Elementary English*, 36:226, April, 1959.
11. By permission from Thomas R. Lewis and Ralph G. Nichols, *Speaking and Listening*, William C. Brown Company, Publishers, Dubuque, 1965, p. 6.
12. Stephen Spender, "The Age of Overwrite and Underthink," *Saturday Review*, 49:21, March 12, 1966.
13. Thomas R. Lewis and Ralph G. Nichols, *op. cit.*, p. 28.
14. Paul T. Rankin, "The Importance of Listening Ability," *English Journal* (College Edition), 17:623-630, 1928.
15. Harry Goldstein, "Reading and Listening Comprehension at Various Controlled Rates," *Contributions to Education*, Teachers College, Columbia University, New York, No. 28, 1940, p. 56.
16. By permission from Ralph G. Nichols, "Do We Know How to Listen?" *The Speech Teacher*, 10:119, March, 1961.
17. *Ibid.*
18. By permission from Miriam Wilt, "A Study of Teacher Awareness of Listening as a Factor in Elementary Education," *Journal of Educational Research*, 43: 626-636, April, 1950.
19. *Ibid.*, p. 635.
20. Ursala Hogan, "An Experiment in Improving Listening Skills of Fifth and Sixth Grade Pupils," masters thesis, University of California, Berkeley, 1953.
21. E. K. F. Edgar, "The Validation of Four Methods of Improving Listening Abilities," doctoral dissertation, University of Pittsburgh, Pittsburgh, 1961.
22. T. C. Devine, "The Development and Evaluation of a Series of Recordings for Teaching Certain Critical Listening Abilities," unpublished doctoral dissertation, Boston University, Boston, 1961.
23. Sara Lundsteen, "Teaching Abilities in Critical Listening in the Fifth and Sixth Grades," doctoral dissertation, University of California, Berkeley, 1963.
24. Sara Lundsteen, "Critical Listening: An Experiment," *The Elementary School Journal*, 66:315, March, 1966.
25. Sue E. Trivette, "The Effect of Training in Listening for Specific Purposes," *Journal of Educational Research*, 54:276-277, March, 1961.

26. Robert G. Canfield, "How Useful Are Lessons on Listening?" *Elementary School Journal*, 62:146-151, December, 1961.
27. Robert E. Kraner, "A Comparison of Two Methods of Listening Instruction in an Eighth Grade Language Arts Program," doctoral dissertation, University of Texas, Austin, 1963.
28. By permission from Edmund Amidon and Anita Simon, "Teacher-Pupil Interaction," *Review of Educational Research*, 35:132, April, 1965.
29. *Ibid.*, p. 132.
30. Thomas R. Lewis and Ralph G. Nichols, *op. cit.*, p. 9.
31. Ralph G. Nichols, "Do We Know How to Listen? Practical Helps in a Modern Age," *The Speech Teacher*, 10:120-124, March, 1961.
32. *Ibid.*, p. 122.
33. *Ibid.*
34. *Ibid.*, p. 124.
35. By permission from Lillian M. Logan, *Teaching the Young Child*, Houghton Mifflin Company, Boston, 1960, p. 176.
36. J. C. Tressler, *English in Action*, Course III, Fifth Edition, D. C. Heath and Company, 1950, p. 83.
37. Wilhelmina G. Hedde and William Brigance, *American Speech*, J. P. Lippincott Company, Chicago, 1950, quoted in Martha Gray and Clarence W. Hach, *English for Today*, J. P. Lippincott Company, Chicago, 1950, pp. 189-190.
38. By permission from Andrew T. Weaver and Gladys L. Borchers, *Speech*, Harcourt, Brace Company, New York, 1946, p. 171.
39. Joseph Mersand, "Developing Competence in Listening in Secondary Schools," *The Speech Teacher*, 7:301, November, 1958.
40. Thomas R. Lewis and Ralph G. Nichols, *op. cit.*, p. 187.
41. Wendall Johnson, "Do You Know How to Listen?" *ETC—A Review of General Semantics*, 7:3-9, Autumn, 1949.
42. Sara Lundsteen, "Teaching and Testing Critical Listening in the Fifth and Sixth Grades," *Elementary English*, 47:747, November, 1964.
43. Propaganda techniques adapted from Thomas R. Lewis and Ralph G. Nichols, *op. cit.*, pp. 56-58.
44. *Ibid.*, p. 23.
45. Lillian M. Logan and Virgil G. Logan, *op. cit.*, p. 223.

5

Freeing the Child for Effective Speaking

A controlled body gives
a controlled voice.
Carrie Rasmussen

Bodily activity is the very basis of speech. Since words themselves are produced with muscles, the muscles of the body must be controlled to have effective speech. It takes a controlled body to produce a controlled voice.

Teaching children to speak effectively begins with attention to bodily movement and rhythmic activity, developing through pantomime into creative dramatics. The relationship between bodily movement and speech has long been recognized by those of the world of the theatre. It was early recognized by Señorita Zapata, Chief of Preschool Education in Mexico for more than fifty years. It was her conviction that there was a close relationship between bodily action and speech. She stated, "When children say 'Buenos Dias' they should say it with their eyes, their voice, and their bodies. There must be a correlation among voice, language, ideas, and bodily action. This has been my belief and practice. [The three year preschool curriculum] offered numerous opportunities for speaking, listening, discussion, creative dramatics, rythms, storytelling, puppetry, and other types of oral expression."[1] An excellent approach to speech in the elementary school is through a developmental program in which rhythmic activity, creative movement, pantomime, and dramatic play introduce the child gradually to the wonderful world of creative speech.

The child is enthralled with the discovery that the body is an instrument through which he can express without words his moods, emotions, and ideas. He finds, however, that soon he must add words to his actions to communicate better what he is thinking, feeling, and experiencing. Pantomime combines readily with activities in the dramatic play of the young child. Dramatic play leads naturally into creative dramatics, a perfect vehicle for creative expression.

Experience in rhythms and pantomime gives the child the expressive body so essential for expressive speech. Thus non-verbal communication forms the bridge for the later speech activities of dramatization, oral interpretation of literature, the planning and organization of speeches, panel discussions, and other related speech skills. When the teacher realizes the importance of freeing the child to use his body spontaneously, creatively, and joyously he is paving the way for every child in his class to develop self-confidence, poise, and ease. Movement, rhythms, pantomime, and dramatic play afford the opportunities for language and conceptual growth as well as creative expression.

CREATIVE MOVEMENT

Creative movement is as natural to the child as breathing. He expresses his joy of living as he sways, bends, and dances; as he skips, runs, and prances. He moves, not because it is physically impossible to remain still, but to express his feelings, ideas, and aspirations. For him physical response is an integral part of the rhythm of life. "With the first breath and the first heartbeat, rhythm becomes an urge demanding response. . . . If no words are said and no songs sung, there are other ways of responding to the inner urge of rhythm."[2]

The ancient Greeks recognized this principle as they harmonized rhythm with the art of living. Man has always expressed his deepest feelings, his strongest emotions, his most significant moments in movement. In the rituals of the dance, in the processional, in the recessional, in the most solemn occasions response to the measured beat is essential. Movement free or movement patterned in regular rhythmic sequence of recurring beat remains throughout life one of the greatest avenues for self-expression.

How to capitalize on this inner urge to rhythm is the challenge to the teacher who guides children's rhythmic response from tentative movements to bold communication of ideas. Observe the young child as he responds to the rhythm of the marching band, the ballet, or the ocean waves. His body is an instrument for expression. He does not need to be told to march, to fly like a bird, lumber like an elephant, or float like a cloud. He *is* the bird flying across the sky or hopping across the green to get a worm, or the elephant lumbering along in the circus parade or stampeding across the veldt. He *is* the cloud floating lazily across the sky. He identifies as readily with the elements of nature as he does with the creatures of the world of nature. Through movement alone he can express his moods, feelings, and concepts about life.

CREATING AN ENVIRONMENT CONDUCIVE TO PRE-SPEECH ACTIVITIES

The teacher must create a receptive environment in which originality, spontaneity, and creative expression can flourish. Children must be free to explore, to experiment, to create, to express ideas, and to create patterns of movement, knowing that their contribution will be valued and that they will not be laughed at. They must recognize, too, that within the framework of freedom of expression many activities require specific techniques. A favourable attitude on the part of the teacher does much to encourage children to express themselves freely in movement.

The teacher must provide *space* in which to move freely. If space in the classroom is limited he should find a time when the playground is free, the auditorium or activity room is unoccupied, or the gymnasium is empty. However, the gymnasium may be too large to establish a feeling of rapport so evident when the space is right. Enough space for rhythmic activity may be found in the classroom if the furniture is rearranged. The resourceful teacher is alert to possibilities for providing space; he knows the importance of movement not only for creative expression and recreation, but also as an antidote to tension, fatigue, and negative behaviour.

Through integrating activities the teacher can provide *time* for a balanced program in which children respond to rhythm, plan group activity in movement, create new forms and designs in rhythms and dance. Time is needed for planning, participating, and evaluating.

The teacher must have *skills* for guiding activities. Children need guidance. They cannot develop without it. They need a teacher who has the skills that will enable him to direct the various phases of the program in such a way that growth, not chaos, results. They need a teacher who has a creative imagination, a sense of rhythm, and ingenuity in providing an accompaniment. They need a teacher who enjoys movement.

ESSENTIAL SKILLS FOR THE TEACHER

CREATIVE IMAGINATION. More essential than the other requisites for guidance is that of a creative imagination. A teacher must be able to inspire children to create; this is possible only if he himself is creative. He must know how to develop the child's imagination and encourage him to use his own ideas. He must remember what it is to be a child; to keep alive the wonder and the awe of experiencing something new. The teacher should participate in creative experiences himself in order to understand their value. The creative teacher does not teach the same song, the same dances in the same way, at the same time. One teacher kept a record over a period of 23 years and prided herself on the fact that she never failed to teach the identical songs, games, and rhythms on the same day of the same week each year. Leap year was always a problem for her.

A SENSE OF RHYTHM. Most people have a sense of rhythm. They respond spontaneously if they are asked to move on the beat or off-beat. They can keep time with the music and swing and sway, hop and skip, march and dance. Those who feel a lack in this area should avail themselves of the opportunity to develop their rhythmic skills through pre-service or in-service experiences in a class in rhythms or dancing.

INGENUITY IN PROVIDING AN ACCOMPANIMENT. Running, skipping, marching, walking, and other basic rhythmic activities may be accompanied not only by the piano but the auto-harp, the drum, or other percussion instruments. Instrumental music is essential to accompaniment in folk dances and can be an invaluable aid in guiding rhythmic response. However, there are activities in which the beat of the drum or the tom-tom, the music of the tambourine or triangle, or the regular recurring beat of the rhythm sticks can serve to accompany the children in rhythmic activity.

ENJOYMENT OF MOVEMENT. Children are delighted when the teacher actually does a skip, a slide, a polka, or a folk dance step. Children like to watch him. Not only must he be willing to guide rhythmic expression, he must be enthusiastic about it. In addition to skills he must also have a sense of enjoyment. Music and movement should offer the child an exciting adventure throughout the elementary school years. It should stir the creative impulse of the teacher as well as the children. It should add zest to living.

Among the rhythmic activities that children enjoy are: creative rhythms; fundamental movements (locomotor and non-locomotor); ideas; dramatizing nursery rhymes, poems, and songs; singing games; dancing (folk, creative, and social).

Creative movement offers an excellent avenue for creative expression. Many children are led to an appreciation of rhythm through the physical response to music, the beat of the tom-tom, or the rhythm of the sticks. With little motivation other than the sound of the music many children will move out to the center of the floor and begin to dance. Those who are more timid respond to "acting out" songs. All, however, are eager to participate in such basic locomotor activities as walking, running, skipping—the primary rhythms. Secondary locomotor rhythms are hopping, jumping, leaping, galloping, sliding. Non-locomotor rhythms that they enjoy are swinging, bending, rocking, swaying, stretching, pulling-pushing, twisting-turning, reaching-stretching, rising-falling, bending-lifting.

As primary children grow into intermediate children they create designs which become more precise and more complex. Throughout the elementary school, children need a balance of rhythmic activities that afford opportunity for individual and group creativity. In guiding rhythmic response the teacher must keep in mind freedom of motion, originality of expression, spontaneity of movement, sensitivity of emotional response, and communication of ideas.

HELPING CHILDREN GET STARTED IN CREATIVE MOVEMENT. An important skill that encourages the teacher to use his own creativity as well as that of the children is that of helping children get started in creative movement. There is no magic formula, no one sequence for introducing children to creativity through movement. Here the teacher can employ the strategy of inquiry to bring the children to the delight of discovery. Questions, cues, and experiences used to motivate a particular group must be based on the teacher's knowledge of that group. He might start with a simple question about a skip and build on this basic movement. Further questioning could lead to more complex designs employing other basic locomotor activities such as a jump, walk, hop, and so forth. Another way could be to question axial movements such as swinging or a combination of movements such as rocking horses (push and pull). "We discover many possibilities concerning the movement, how we do it, what we are doing, how we can do it better, what it reminds us of, how it feels and how it looks."[3]

It is important that the teacher know his group, that he be aware of various approaches he might use, and that he is willing to adapt the approach to the specific needs of a specific group at a specific time. Never should the approach become crystallized at the level of a technique. The ingenuity of the teacher and the creativity of the children should merge to make of every rhythmic experience a creative one.

Unlike the physical education teacher who teaches movement with emphasis on physical development, the teacher of speech emphasizes movement as it prepares the child for speech skills. An evaluation of the effectiveness of the program will focus on such questions as are listed below.

Does the child use free bodily movements in his activity? The child's body tells us much about his experiences. Does his body seem tense, his movements jerky? Is he relaxed and able to use his body freely? Is there a sureness in his movements and muscular coordination? Does he move his arms and hands freely as a part of an integral whole body which moves rhythmically in any creative activity?

Does he verbalize during any phase of the creative expression? Does he talk, hum, sing, or use nonsense words? Does he giggle, laugh, shout? Is his voice shrill, tense, aggressive; soft, excited, enthusiastic, matter-of-fact? Does he try to communicate what the creative activity means to him? What specifically does he say in his own words? Does any relationship exist between what he says and what he is expressing with his body? What appears to be the purpose of his verbalization? Does the activity seem to require verbalization?

Questions such as these may serve to give the clue to the teachable moment when the child and/or the group is ready to move toward activities related to using more specifically planned movements to express ideas.

RHYTHMIC ACTIVITY

One of the most successful ways of getting children to express themselves creatively is through listening to music and interpreting it in free bodily activity. In creative rhythms the emphasis is on responding to the mood of the music. The music itself motivates each child to move in his individual way. The music should be highly rhythmic, strongly accented, and contrasting in mood. If children are expressing themselves to music that has variety they will show greater originality.

In responding creatively to music children should listen first, then move out on the floor spontaneously, and in a completely individual interpretation express themselves to the music they hear. As they become aware of unity, balance, and climax in the music they integrate these elements into a design that is a creative experience for them. Rhythmic activities of this type prepare the child for responding to the rhythms of poetry and the more subtle rhythms of prose. "Unless certain basic skills are mastered, later, more elaborated ones become increasingly out of reach."[4] Rhythm is basic to all the language arts.

In creative rhythms the emphasis is on originality of expression, not conformity to another's concept of interpretation. Teachers will find this a rewarding approach when they create a favourable environment, are enthusiastic about creative movement, understand the children they teach, and have the necessary skills to blend these elements in such a way that response is natural, spontaneous, and vital. Most young children have few inhibitions about expressing themselves through creative movement. When they are given ample opportunity to express creatively through this avenue they grow in enjoyment. It is vital that this should continue to be an integral part of the education of all children as an aid in achieving their potential speech skills. Findley states, ". . . bodies should be as plastic, as responsive as their voices. . . . The actor who has a finely tuned rhythmic body will have a perfect instrument for the expression of his art."[5] This is as true for the speaker and reader as for the actor.

Fundamental Rhythms

The approach to rhythms may also be made through the basic locomotor skills. Children walk, march, run, skip, slide, gallop, jump, and hop. When the spirit is willing and the body is ripe comes the moment when the child wants to express himself through these basic movements. Physical maturation as well as the willingness to try influence the child's success in such activities. Allowance should be made for individual differences in the fundamental rhythms. There are children who feel initially more at ease with fundamental movements such as walking, running, hopping, leaping, skipping, and galloping.

Some activities in fundamental rhythms are:

WALKING
    (1) clapping or tapping out the beats
    (2) walking to music
    (3) dramatizing different types of walk
    (4) marching to music

RUNNING
    (1) begin by walking
    (2) gradually increase the rate of the music or drum beat until the children are running
    (3) combine running, marching, and walking movements
    (4) have different children set the tempo and others follow their lead

HOPPING
    (1) suggest that the children be a favourite animal that hops around
    (2) use such activities as skipping rope
    (3) dramatize one of the nursery rhymes that requires a hop
    (4) play hop-scotch or similar games that require a hop
    (5) create a group pattern in which walking, running, and hopping are combined

LEAPING
    (1) develop from a long run
    (2) jump as though jumping over a puddle

    (3) create a ballet movement

    (4) combine a leap with other movements

SKIPPING

    (1) clap out the rhythm of a skip

    (2) respond to the rhythm of a skip—long, short; long, short

    (3) move with a long and short step, getting upon toes, and then off the floor

    (4) dramatize nursery rhymes in which skipping is suggested

GALLOPING

    (1) clap out the rhythm of long and short beat (heavy-light)

    (2) use coconut shells to create the sound of horses galloping

    (3) dramatize horses galloping

    (4) combine movements in a creative design

Ideas

Ideas afford an excellent approach to rhythmic response. They form an important motivation for movement. Instead of initiating the activity by playing music that evokes the basic rhythms of walking, running, jumping, or hopping, the teacher might begin by asking the children how they would walk if—"there were pebbles under your feet and you are barefooted"?—"the sidewalk is hot and there is a hole in the sole of one shoe"? Other leading questions could be:

> Can you think of a musical instrument you would like to be and show with your body how you make music? (The children might be a music box, a spinning top, an accordion, a trombone.)
>
> Can you think of Christmas toys you could be? See if we can guess what the toys are? (Bouncing ball, train, robot, doll.)
>
> Can you think of new ways to stretch and bend your body?
>
> Can you demonstrate in movement some type of activity observed at the zoo?
>
> Can you show me how the animals at the zoo move?

Lengthy discussion is not effective with young children. For the younger child the urge is to respond immediately. Suggestions for improvement come better after the movement is under way.

However, as children grow in this type of response they will be eager to suggest ways of improving. For example, Tommy might think of a variety of ways birds would fly in getting to their nests. Jimmy might suggest a new way for flying a jet. Marilyn might try a new movement for the dancer on the top of the music box, and Lucille might suggest getting some one to dance a ballet while the others watched the music box as it was being wrapped up for a gift. Some of the children get their inspiration for creativity from a poem; others get it from the music; still others seem to have it within them and respond to any approach to rhythm.

Older children may be motivated by such suggestions as:

> Find an area where you can move without interfering with any one else and work out an idea using your arms, your legs, head, or torso

What activities can you work out if you stay in one spot?

What activities can be integrated in a complex situation such as a circus, a carnival, ball game, railway station, or airport?

Ideas for creative expression in movement may come at times when children are not even participating in rhythmic activities. They may originate in other curriculum areas. For example: "A group of fifth grade children were working with chalk, experimenting with ways of getting different degrees of intensity in color. David, while thinking about what to do next, yawned and stretched. Then with a sudden outburst he said, 'Say, I've got an idea—watch me.' As the children watched, he explained and demonstrated a stretch that could be intense, while the recoil could be just the opposite. 'Couldn't we put this on paper?' he asked. This idea led to an interesting combination of experimenting with movement, color, and line in which all the boys and girls became interested. In an informal way, some worked alone, first 'feeling', then 'drawing'. Others worked in twos, one child 'doing' and the other getting it down on paper. Some started with the 'drawing' and then translated it into movement. Soon, this particular group listened to some favourite music and then transferred what they felt 'inside' to movement and paper."[6]

Poetry

Bodily response to poetry offers the child essential activity correlated with the rhythm and rhyme. He responds to the moods in the poetry as he moves to the rhythm. Among the poems the authors have found effective are:

GALLOPING. "I Had a Little Pony", "Ride a Cock Horse", "The Huntsman", "To Market", "Little Boy Blue", "Lucy Locket", "I Saw a Ship a-Sailing".

JUMPING AND HOPPING. "Jack Be Nimble", "Diddle, Diddle, Dumpling". "Hoppity", "Once I Saw a Little Bird".

MARCHING. "The Brave Old Duke of York", "Yankee Doodle".

RUNNING. "Wee Willie Winkie", "Hickory, Dickory, Dock", "Tom, Tom, the Piper's Son".

CLAPPING AND TAPPING. "Pease Porridge Hot", "Mrs. Peck Pigeon", "Pat-a-Cake".

ROCKING. "Rock-a-Bye- Baby", "Hush-a-Bye Baby".

FLYING. "Bless You, Bless You, Burnie-bee".

SKIPPING. "Little Miss Muffet", "Little Jack Horner", "Jack Sprat", "Peter, Peter, Pumpkin Eater", "Pop Goes the Weasel".

SWINGING AND SWAYING. "The Swing".

WALKING. "One Misty, Moisty Morning", "Hot Cross Buns", "There Was an Old Woman Who Lived in a Shoe".[7]

There is a wealth of children's literature that can be used to motivate rhythmic response. Action and pantomime may be suggested by the words. The teacher should be sure that the children are familiar with the rhyme and have an opportunity to discuss it before dramatizing it. The highly creative child is not limited by the text, but spontaneously adds much in pantomime to the bare outline suggested by the words.

PANTOMIME

Long before a child communicates in words he communicates through movement. He uses his entire body to express himself. Thus pantomime is a natural avenue for creative expression. Children come by pantomime naturally. Pantomime as an art form, however, requires concentrated effort and is not usually perfected at the elementary school level.

Strickland recognizes the close relationship between the actor's control of his body and the poet's choice of words in the following statement: "The poet's selection of specific words to express his thoughts and feelings is similar to the actor's selection of specific actions through which he, too, may reveal his thoughts and feelings. . . ."[8]

Pantomine involves action and/or gestures without words as a means of creative expression. It is one of the most effective modes of non-verbal communication. Children pantomime spontaneously in dramatic play. Pantomime is an outlet for the imagination. The child, like the poet, expresses himself in whatever media he chooses at a particular moment. In creative movement the child uses his entire body as an instrument of expression. This is particularly true in pantomime. As children develop skills in this medium they become increasingly adept in relating an experience or telling a simple or complex story wholly through action.

Pantomime affords excellent oportunity for the creative expression of children through doing, feeling, and reacting. The child, for instance, may use pantomime to depict what he is *doing*. Instead of concern about words to express his ideas, he demonstrates with his body.

DOING

Camping or picnicking

Exploring a cave

Searching for a lost article. After searching earnestly, finding it, showing through pantomine what it is

Receiving a birthday gift, unwrapping it, showing pleasure (or disappointment), showing through pantomine what it is

Showing favourite activities of the different seasons of the year

Selecting a favourite toy and playing with it

Participating in any sport

Going to a circus, observing and/or being the various acts in the big tent, the side shows, the midway

Passing a tray of food. Each child takes something, and portrays what it is by the way he holds and eats it.

FEELING

After initiatory experiences the teacher may introduce the next step in pantomimic action—feeling. The actions suggested above should show how a person feels while he is doing it. For example, the pantomime of the eating should be extended to find out if the person likes or dislikes what he is eating. This opens up a variety of participation activities to stimulate the emotional state of mind and the physical response.

REACTING

Here the important factor is the ability to empathize and identify with the action from the *inside out*, to feel the part, to be aware of every possible detail which clothes the pantomime with reality. For example, if a child picks up a basket one should be able to tell if it is filled or empty by the muscle tension employed. As children develop, the feeling and reaction steps usually precede the doing. They are ready to discuss and plan the characterizations in more detail. For the young child, "the play's the thing".

Refinement in this art does not come all at once. It is the result of much experience in developing powers of awareness, sense reactions, characterizations, and playing out simple situations creatively.

Educators are no longer satisfied to leave the child alone and let him create in the mistaken belief that all that is needed is a climate of psychological safety which frees the child so his emotional and psychic energy will fill the void and he will create. Without some specific techniques and skills, be it in dramatics, art, or writing, the growing child will be at a loss. Although it is true that the very young child in no way senses a need for technique nor skill in expressing what he feels and experiences, as he matures he is no longer so confident about expressing his creativity. It is at this point that the child will feel the need for help in the skills. According to Eisner, "Creative ability is, to a significant degree, specific to the subject matter. . . . a person must be able to control the syntax and techniques of the discipline within which he is working if he is to use it creatively".[9]

Through pantomime and impersonation the child develops specifically in (1) imagination, (2) awareness, (3) sensitivity, and (4) communication of a nonverbal nature.

DEVELOPING IMAGINATION. Children naturally imagine and create. They are endowed by nature with the creative spirit. They need, however, opportunities for developing the aptitudes for creativity which they possess. As the imagination takes over the child uses his imagination spontaneously as he transforms a sandpile and a few old pans and well-worn blocks into a railroad terminal. The imagination, too, is developed as the child decides on a characterization he wishes to portray with bodily actions alone. Through insight, perception, and developing technique in the dramatic skills he becomes increasingly adept at portraying imaginatively.

Swartz defines imagination as "The recall to consciousness of mental pictures produced through the senses, without the present stimulation of these senses in the original way".[10]

DEVELOPING POWERS OF AWARENESS. Pantomime offers the child a built-in avenue for developing his powers of awareness. He must in pantomime not only give the impression of walking up the stairs, he must show through the movements of his body, his muscles, the weight exerted by the body in going up the stairs. Developing awareness is a responsibility of every teacher. A good teacher makes children aware of their environment through sense training. For example, the teacher calls attention to such impressions as smelling rain and bonfires, feeling the touch of velvet and other fabrics, listening to voices, pleasant and unpleasant, tasting sweet and sour, enjoying beautiful cloud formations, snowflakes falling, and other such common experiences. In every possible way the child should be encouraged to cultivate awareness of detail, sensitivity, and the quality of perceptive reaction to stimuli. Awareness implies vigilance in observing or in drawing inferences from what one hears, sees, smells, touches, and so on.

An experience such as a visit to the farm can provide many opportunities for developing awareness as well as stimulating the imagination as the experience is recreated. The children may recapture the impressions of holding the warm, soft, baby chicks, throwing corn to the chickens, cobs to the pigs, (showing that this requires greater strength and control as the cobs are heavier than the grain) squealing like baby pigs, neighing like horses, frolicking like baby lambs, and prancing like ponies.

Specific activities for developing sense awareness include:

Sewing and sticking self with needle
Smelling several kinds of perfume and deciding on which to give mother for her birthday
Tasting a dish of jello and discovering that it is only egg white beaten without sugar added
Coming upon the witch's house in *Hansel and Gretel*
Crackling of twigs when you are walking in the woods while you are trying to observe a deer; when you are lost and it is getting late

DEVELOPING SENSITIVITY. Pantomime, to be effective, requires the individual to have a clear understanding of the situation to be portrayed. The individual, in order to portray a character, must search for clues to inner motivations expressed in a person's overt actions. "He must gain insight into a character's inner life *if* he is to understand the turbulence beneath the facade of appearance."[11] To portray the character intuitively and with sensitivity the child must *become* the character. There must be an interaction of doing and feeling as he works out the situation. Sensitivity implies the capacity to respond quickly and acutely to actions of others, to impressions, and/or external stimuli.

COMMUNICATION OF A NON-VERBAL NATURE. Pantomime offers excellent opportunities for communication of a non-verbal type. Action is not mere random activity. Pantomime must be purposeful, expressive, and significant. "The quality of the action reveals the dramatic intent. . . . Much of the significance of language results from the actor's delivery, which includes gesture, posture, facial expression, and movement".[12]

Non-verbal communication is intensified by pantomiming characterizations (always from the inside out), *feeling* the emotion, *reacting* to the emotion, and getting the audience to *respond empathically.*

Some suggestions are:

A miser counting his money
A witch stirring her brew
A peddler selling his wares
A beggar finding a purse
A mother receiving word of a son lost in battle
A villain plotting an evil deed
A person receiving a telegram—good news!

Guidelines for the Teacher

Teachers frequently ask what they can do to help the child develop skills in pantomime. They are conversant with their responsibility for providing an environment in which children are free to express themselves creatively through many avenues. However, they are aware that for each creative medium there is a body of knowledge, a discipline, some specific skills and techniques which if understood can facilitate the quality of the creative expression.

The following brief suggestions will be helpful in guiding activities in pantomime. The child should be encouraged to:

Use spontaneous action, not planned action. Pay no attention to rules, elegance, or correctness, but act on impulse. (This is especially true in the early attempts. As skill is gained the pantomime will become more polished.)
Use abundant action. Avoid timid, stereotyped, restrained, or halfhearted movements
Use the entire body as an instrument of expression
Express genuine thought and feeling. Characterization requires a "from the inside out" approach
Understand the difference between *covert and overt action.* Overt action involves the whole body in large movements like walking, nodding the head, curtseying, gesturing. Covert action is more subtle and oftentimes may go unnoticed as action. It consists of the muscle sets and tensions that reveal the inner feelings, the mood, the emotional state of the character.

Brigance gives an excellent example of covert action. "A child stands in front of a window filled with candy. He is standing stock still; and at first you might say 'He's not doing anything', or 'He's looking at the candy'. But a second look will tell you that his posture and face are saying, 'I want that candy', and you know his salivary glands are overworking, his stomach is contracting and expanding, his blood pressure is up, and his endocrine glands are pumping fluids into his blood. You don't see this terrific internal activity; you do see the hungry look in the boy's face and posture. What you see is *covert* action. Rather it is the outward sign of covert action; and when you see these outward signs you infer the inner action and react to it."[13]

And so it is in pantomime. It is not enough to catch the overt action. One must also capture and relate the covert action—the body set, tilt of the head, total muscular tension—to convey the intense feeling within. When the body catches and reveals the muscle sets and tensions the audience reacts with empathy.

As the child develops in the art of pantomime he tries to recreate the feelings of the character in his imagination. Good pantomime requires a fine sensitiveness to situation. Stanislavsky held the belief that to make the public aware of the fine shades of your feelings, you have to experience them intensely yourself.

For the teacher who would guide children's creativity through pantomime an understanding of the importance of sensitivity to a situation is vital. To the child the important thing is that he can show exactly how he feels without saying a word.

DRAMATIC PLAY

Variously termed the "mirror of the child", "trying on life", "imitation of life", and "orientation to life", dramatic play *is* life for the child. The child through instantaneous, spontaneous, unstructured free activity of "make-believe" utilizes his sense of the dramatic. The play life of the child is a mirror which reflects not only his relationships with the external world; it is a mirror reflecting his inner self. Through such activity he is unrestricted in the use of his imagination as he takes on the role of the person, phenomena, animal he wishes at a particular moment to identify with. There is no need for plot, no audience, nor external direction. The younger the child, the more able he is to identify, to shift from one role to another. In the space of a morning he may be a pilot, a captain, a passenger, a fireman, a tree, a mother, father, brother or baby sister, bird, a jet, or an astronaut.

One has merely to observe a group of children at play to realize the intensity and spontaneity with which they absorb the happenings of the day and react to the environment; the swiftness with which they respond to crises; the eagerness with which they absorb radio and television; the wholeheartedness with which they identify with the world of people, places, and things; the boundless energy which they bring to their activities. Listen to a group of five-year-olds as they drone out "ten, nine, eight, seven, six, five, four, three, two, one. BLAST OFF."

"Wait," shouts Johnny. "I'm Glenn, the first orbiting astronaut, blasting off into outer space in Friendship VII."

"No! You're not!" insists Glenn. "I'm Shephard and I'm going first."

"You can be the countdown man. He's important."

At that moment of indecision Nancy runs up and throws her arms around Johnny. That settles the argument. "I'm Mrs. Glenn. I'll be praying for you. Do be careful."

And off John goes into space. Allen, content to remain with Nancy and be the countdown man *this* time, drones out, "Ten, nine, eight, seven, six, five, four, three, two, one. BLAST OFF!"

Never mind that you're the countdown man this time. Next time you can be Glenn. In dramatic play you can be anything you want to be. If you're fat you can be thin; if you're short you can be tall; if you're homely you can be handsome; if you're as poor as a church mouse you can be rich as Croesus. You can be what you want to be.[14]

By dramatizing, by acting out his ideas, feelings, emotions the child communicates his concept of the "world and I". Regardless of the role he is playing he is working out some of his feelings and frustrations about this world. He is assimilating on his own level of understanding events which are happening all around him. In this way they take on meaning for him and extend his understanding about the complex world.

Essential to dramatic play is a creative teacher who encourages the children to use their imagination, who provides exciting activities which stimulate the imagination, rewards original responses and ideas, gives children time to think, to imagine, to play with ideas, and to equip them with needed tools of expression *when* and *if* the child is ready for them. Critical thinking and evaluation of play activities are an essential part of dramatic play if it is not to deteriorate into chaos and confusion.

The usual patterns of dramatic play of young children include: (1) play centering around activities of the home, such as building, furnishing, playing house, cooking, eating, entertaining at parties, taking care of younger brothers and sisters, being fathers, mothers, and grandparents; (2) buying and selling at the super market or neighbourhood store; (3) transportation: building and playing in boats, trains, airplanes, cars, busses, being captains, engineers, pilots, bus drivers, running gas stations, and assuming duties of employees at air terminals or railroad stations; (4) community helpers: policemen, firemen, postmen; (5) playing legendary persons: Santa Claus, Easter Bunny, St. Valentine; and (6) being animals, particularly pets such as cats, dogs, and birds.

"Playing house" is the universal favourite of the preschool years. The sophistication with which the child reproduces the conversation as well as the tone of voice and mannerisms of the person whose role he is taking on is revealed in the following scene.

"This is a nail file to do your hands. I'll put it on the dresser. I bought it down town. You really call it an emery board, but filing nails is what it does. Why don't you sit down and do your nails before we go to the party with the Nelsons? O, just a minute. There's the telephone now. That's probably them calling. What time will you be ready? O.K."

Jim smiles gaily at Ann as he answers the phone. "Yes, Mrs. Nelson. Ann is home, but she's busy doing her nails. I got her a new emery board. *Emery* board— you know, what you use to file your nails with. NOT ironing board. She likes it fine.

Oh, just a moment, she'll be right here to talk to you. Then you two can get together on the time."

Today Jim is the father, but yesterday he was the little boy.[15]

This is dramatic play, a forerunner of creative dramatics. In dramatic play verbal expression is incidental. The child becomes the individual he is characterizing—whether child, adult, animal, or tree. "Older children, on the other hand, participate in creative dramatics in which . . . they dramatize stories they have heard or read, movies or television shows they have seen. Instead of playing that they are people of everyday life, they play that they are fairies, Indians, "G" men, or bandits. . . . Each year as the child grows older, he pays more and more attention to details."[16]

THE ROLE OF BODILY ACTION IN THE INTERMEDIATE AND UPPER GRADES

Bodily movement is as vital in effective communication of pupils in the intermediate and upper grades as it is to children in the preschool and primary grades. Freedom of movement is essential if the speaker is to communicate his ideas and feelings effectively. In communicating with others it is the total response, the total interaction which determines the quality of understanding and communication. Not alone the words people speak, but the subtle, covert actions convey ideas and feelings. The non-verbal communication—the actions of the speaker—help or hinder his attempt to communicate effectively because the listener interprets the action as well as the words. "As psychiatrists and psychologists remind us, one gets to know something of mental and organic states by noting the type, directions, and force of bodily activity. How do we recognize the brain-injured, the drunk, the tired individuals? In the absence of direct signs, and often in addition to them, we rely on evidence furnished by bodily action. The underlying neurological control of spoken communication may often be obscure, but bodily action is nevertheless an important part of the entire process."

"As employed in this discussion, the term 'bodily action' is differentiated from random activity regardless of the complexity involved. For us *action is that observable physical activity which occurs as a result of reflection and motive.*"[17]

A prerequisite to effective communication is control of bodily action in order to release the individual to speak more freely and fluently, think more efficiently, and move with greater ease and freedom. Achievement of motivated bodily action helps the individual gain poise—so essential in effective communication of ideas through verbal and non-verbal means. An absence of motivated bodily action in relation to speech often leads to sluggishness, lack of self-confidence, and random movements.

The teacher must keep in mind the need for the student at all educational levels to develop coordination and bodily poise as a prerequisite to effective speaking.

Controlled and properly employed, bodily action clarifies meaning, provides emphasis, and permits the audience to empathize with the speaker. The lines of the popular song, "Every Little Movement Has a Meaning of Its Own" is a case in point.

In helping students reveal meaning through bodily action the teacher might well emphasize in the intermediate and upper grades pantomime and improvisation. "Overt activity supplies an important link in speaker-listener relations. In *Hamlet* (Act III, Scene 2) Shakespeare offers some sage advice to the aspiring actor and to the discerning citizen as well: 'suit the action to the word and word to the action'. As did the philosophers and rhetoricians who espoused this view some 1500 years before he was born, Shakespeare underscores the thought that every human being gives two speeches at the same time: that which is heard and that which is seen. Effective speakers mold these to form *one* which is stronger than either singly."[18]

In both pantomime and improvisation posture gives the first clue to characterization. For instance, in "The Emperor's New Clothes" posture should immediately distinguish the Emperor from the weavers. In "Rumplestilskin" when the miller's daughter becomes the queen she immediately assumes the queenly bearing.

Exercises centering around posture, gestures, and movement should not be practiced in isolation but as an outgrowth of meaningful situations. When this is done they will result in animation, spontaneity, co-ordination, and creativity. As the student gains in his control of bodily action he will readily and easily integrate his movements and speech as he interprets feelings, emotions, and ideas creatively.

Suggested activities appropriate for the pupils in the intermediate and upper grades designed to free the body for effective speaking are:

A. Pantomime
   1. Individual pantomimes
      a. A traffic policeman
      b. A waiter taking an order
      c. A person watching a hockey game
   2. Group pantomimes
      a. Scenes from movies
      b. Photographer taking a family picture
      c. A club meeting
B. Exercises for spontaneity and co-ordination
   1. You have a baseball in one hand. You see a window. You are tempted. Throw the ball
   2. You are a graceful dancer. You are trying to teach another person to dance
   3. You overhear a story that is false. You cry out, "That's a lie! Go!"
C. Exercises for the development of posture
   1. Walk to the front of the room, assume good standing position, ask a question, and return to your seat
   2. Walk to a chair at the front, pick up a book, be seated, open the book and read from it; close the book, rise, put it in the chair, and return to your seat

    3. Step forward to indicate, "therefore", "also", and "furthermore"
    4. Walk to different parts of the room. Indicate a different mood as you change directions
    5. Say five short sentences, shifting weight on each sentence
  D. Exercises for the development of gestures (group exercises)
    1. You, there in the front row, and you by the door, listen to this!
    2. Hand me the book, please
    3. I shall have nothing to do with you
    4. All of you, stand up, sit down
    5. Look out of the window. What do you see?
    6. The box was this long, and this high
    7. Don't speak to me!
    8. I can give you three reasons
  E. Speech involving action
    1. Tell a story and act out the characters
    2. Explain how to do something; use visual aids if you wish
    3. Give a talk in which you handle an object or use materials in a demonstration
    4. Defend some person or cause
    5. Dramatize action in social situations (introductions, telephoning, etc.).[19]

The importance of bodily action for effective speaking cannot be over-emphasized. In the physical education classes the training designed to help the individual develop the control, co-ordination and bodily poise so essential for success in games is equally vital for effective communication. It is necessary, however, for the classroom teacher to help children to make use of the bodily control gained in physical education classes for more effective communication. The activities suggested here provide the teacher with some idea of what should be accomplished in the intermediate and upper elementary grades in helping pupils gain the needed physical skills necessary to speech. In the chapter "Helping Children Appreciate Literature" the topics of improvisations, dramatics, and drama will explore further the relationships between bodily activity and effective communication.

CONCLUDING STATEMENT

Through rhythmic response children express the creative urge as spontaneously as they breathe. For them movement provides a release for the imagination, sensitivity, feelings, and ideas. They move, not because they are pressured, but because movement gives them a tremendous lift, a sense of freedom, exhilaration akin to flying high above the waters, above the clouds, above the earth, and into the sky.

The teacher creates the environmental conditions for such response; the child provides the expression. The teacher provides the propitious climate; the child brings with him the urge to move—and so it goes. For the child the movement, the expression, the creative process is the important element of the rhythmic activity. For the teacher the climate for the expression of ideas, giving guidance in the essential skills, and encouraging growth in creative expression are means to the all important end—creative communication.

Creative communication is fostered through varied activities: free bodily movement approached through creative rhythmic response which impels a child to express his feelings, ideas, emotions; participating in locomotor movement of various types and modifications which the child originates; moving to the chanting of poems and ballads; creating new rhythmic designs; expressing emotions and moods through pantomime; and enjoying dramatic play. Just as the child crawls before he walks—so should he experience the creative expression of the rhythmic impulse as an aid to understanding the rhythmic nature of speech.

The teacher should capitalize on the inspiration of the moment whenever that is possible: the first snow fall which sends children scurrying to the window and leaves them breathless a moment before they dance out on the floor; the quiet rain as it patters on the roof; the music of the masters that evokes from the children the beautiful dance of the Sugar Plum Fairy; or the beat of the tom-tom which is the catalyst for the Indian dance. The creative teacher provides the climate, the inspiration, the guidance; the creative children do the rest. Nowhere more than in creative rhythmic activity can children translate their dreams and use their imaginations which they have in such abundance—*if* they are encouraged to do so. Communication is a revelation of the inner self.

In guiding children toward effective communication they must be freed to use their bodies as avenues for expression of their ideas. Whether the child expresses himself through pantomime or dramatic play he communicates by the use of the entire body. When the child becomes adept at expressing in pantomime and dramatic play he is ready to move confidently toward speech as an art. Before he can command his voice to speak as he wishes, his body must be free.

REFERENCES

1. Virgil G. Logan, "Speech Education in Mexico," *The Speech Teacher,* 11 : 228, September, 1962.
2. Edna Johnson, Evelyn R. Sickles, and Frances Clarke Sayers, *Anthology of Children's Literature,* 3rd ed., Houghton Mifflin Company, Boston, 1959, p. 1001.
3. Gladys Andrews, *Creative Rhythmic Movement for Children,* Prentice-Hall, Inc., Englewood Cliffs, 1954, p. 55.
4. Jerome Bruner, "Education As Social Invention," *Saturday Review,* 49:72, February 19, 1966.
5. Elsie Findley, "Rhythmic Practice," *Theatre Arts,* September, 1927, p. 41, quoted in Loren E. Taylor, *Informal Dramatics for Young Children,* Burgess Publishing Company, Minneapolis, 1965, p. 61
6. Gladys Andrews et al., *Physical Education for Today's Boys and Girls,* Allyn and Bacon, Inc., Boston, 1960, p. 51. Reprinted by permission of the publishers.
7. These poems are all available in Edna Johnson et al., *Anthology of Children's Literature,* 3rd ed., Houghton Mifflin Company, Boston, 1959, pp. 6-21.

8. F. Cowles Strickland, *The Technique of Acting,* McGraw-Hill Book Company, Inc., New York, 1956, pp. 22, 23.
9. Elliot W. Eisner, "Fostering Creativity in the Classroom," *The Instructor,* 72:92, May, 1963.
10. D. Swartz, "Developing Creative Imagination," *High Points,* 14:43-46, 1932, in Morris I. Stein and Shirley J. Heinze, *Creativity and the Individual,* The Free Press of Glencoe, Glencoe, 1960, pp. 407, 408.
11. Theodore W. Halten, *Orientation to the Theatre,* Appleton-Century-Crofts, New York, 1962, p. 24.
12. *Ibid.,* p. 23.
13. William N. Brigance, *Speech: Its Techniques and Disciplines in a Free World,* Copyright, 1952, by Appleton-Century-Crofts, Inc. Reprinted by permission of Appleton-Century-Crofts, Division of Meredith Publishing Company, p. 334.
14. Lillian M. Logan, "What Are Today's Children Like?" in William Crowder (ed.), *Social Education of Young Children,* rev. ed., National Council for the Social Studies, Washington, in publication.
15. By permission from Lillian M. Logan and Virgil G. Logan, *Teaching the Elementary School Child,* Houghton Mifflin Company, Boston, 1961, p. 519.
16. Elizabeth Hurlock, *Child Development,* 3rd ed., McGraw-Hill Book Company, Inc., New York, 1956, p. 330.
17. By permission from Horace G. Rahskopf, *Basic Speech Improvement,* Harper and Row, New York, 1965, p. 214.
18. *Ibid.,* p. 224.
19. Adapted from "Fundamentals of Speech: A Basic Course for High Schools", *The Speech Teacher,* 8:96, March, 1959.

6

Teaching the Speech Skills: The Primary Grades

> Talking and eloquence are not the same; to speak, and to speak well, are two things.
>
> Ben Jonson

Twenty-five hundred years ago Confucius was asked how he would begin to govern his nation if he were placed in power. He answered: "I would begin by establishing correct use of speech". He went on to explain how destructive incorrect speech is to the social and political structure. He concluded by saying: "A gentleman never uses his speech indiscriminately."

Quintilian defined an orator as "a good man skilled in speaking". From the lips of a good man speech is a force for right. From the lips of a demagogue it is a force for evil. . . . In a society in which group action is an integral part of the pattern of life, it is essential that all the members recognize the power of communication skill—and recognize too that with power goes responsibility for using it to improve society."[1]

George Orwell, in looking to the future in his *1984* paints a picture of the final ruin of a free society by a totalitarian tyranny whose secret weapon is degrading society to the level of robots through a distorted, controlled, and ever shrinking vocabulary.

As the world shrinks, communication becomes ever more important. Ability to express ideas clearly and succinctly, to listen courteously but critically, and to evaluate introspectively yet objectively, is imperative in a democratic society. It is to individuals who possess skills of communication, who work well with others, that we look for leadership.

The best defense against the ever-present danger of misunderstanding is, in fact, to speak in words which have the power to communicate clearly. Abstract language which fails to reach the listener is as empty as an unkept promise and as futile as a broken reed.

Speaking is the other side of the coin of listening. Both are essential for communication. How the teacher develops the experiences determines whether the emphasis is to be on listening or speaking in a given situation. In speaking, the child *gives* information; in listening, the child *gets* information. The good listening habits children are developing in the listening program will be reflected in better speaking habits, because children imitate the speech they hear. Thus the arts of language and the skills of communication complement one another. They overlap and cannot be, nor should they be completely isolated one from another.

Activities which give children opportunity to share experiences, to converse, to interview, to give talks, to participate in formal and informal discussions, and/or practice parliamentary procedure require both a listener and a speaker. Each child through such experiences communicates his needs, ideas, and feelings. Through speech he clarifies his thinking, shares his information and beliefs, and learns to control his environment.

Guiding children in the development of one of the most powerful instruments for both self-fulfillment and social utility requires that the teacher:

> Understand the basic concepts in speaking to communicate
> Develop effective guide lines for teaching speech
> Organize a balanced speech program
> Direct speech activities which implement the defined objectives
> Be aware of the relationship between creative thought and speech
> Develop and utilize instruments of evaluation of speech competency
> Understand the sequence of learning experiences

BASIC CONCEPTS IN SPEAKING TO COMMUNICATE

Speaking and listening are reciprocal activities. The speaker and the listener engage in a reciprocal activity interchanging roles spontaneously and easily. The speaker is concerned with securing a response from the listener, and the listener, in order to respond effectively, must have sensory adequacy, interest, and experiential background in order to catch the conversational ball and bounce it back and forth in his mind before deciding whether to hold on to it or toss it back to the sender (speaker).

Speech is a process by which individuals communicate. "Central to the academic discipline that concerns itself with this subject (speech) as its primary focus is the process by which men adapt their bodies as linguistic vehicles to serve their communicative needs in exploring, controlling, and adjusting to the environment in which they exist."[2] A child uses speech to adapt to his social environment. He uses speech to influence and control others in his environment, and in turn is influenced by them. Speech is for every individual the most important tool for communication.

Speech is creative expression. Through creative speech man is doing more than expressing ideas. He is manifesting his unfolding personality. Not only does he use the magic of the spoken word to say what he wants to say; he says it with originality, fluency, sparkle, and spontaneity. His growing perception and sensitivity coupled with increasing skill in communication stimulates him to achieve at the highest level of creative and intellectual expression. Choral speaking, interpretative reading, creative dramatics and drama challenge the child's most creative abilities.

Equally stimulating are activities which demand creative thinking—role playing, brainstorming, group discussion, and problem solving. "Depending upon the capacity of the speaker, oral communication [speech] can be creative in the best sense of that term, or it can degenerate into banality."[3] Thus speech is more than a means of communicating ideas already conceptualized; it is our principal medium for creating and formulating new ideas.

Speech behaviour. "The behaviour known as speech is an extraordinarily complex form of human activity, which often embraces in a single, unified human action a variety of behaviours of quite different sorts. Part of what occurs is expressive—a symbolization of the speaker's internal state; part is dynamic in the sense that it involves the speaker's purposes toward events around him—toward a listener, or an object."[4]

Speech is a learned behaviour. Most children have acquired speech before they come to school. Although children express themselves orally before they are formally taught by a teacher, they need guidance in the development of skills in speaking. They learn to speak through frequent opportunities to speak in a variety of speech situations in a speech-oriented environment. Such skills include articulation, voice control, bodily control, pronunciation, word choice, appropriate usage, and organization of ideas.

Speech is stimulated by rich experiences. Children who have had rich and varied experiences are eager to talk about them. The child who has experienced little, who feels that what he has to say is unimportant is reticent. In one culturally deprived area the kindergarten children had their sharing period at the close of the morning session. When asked why they waited until the end of the morning, the director replied, "The children have nothing to say when they come to school. After we have had some interesting experiences here they want to talk—all at one time, perhaps, but they want to talk!" Children need experiences before they talk, and time to think, discuss, and share ideas.

Speech is a means of extending horizons. Speech not only helps the child to express his ideas, feelings, and imagination; it helps him to extend his horizons and to increase his knowledge. How eagerly he asks questions before the adults around him have taught him to refrain from questioning. "What?", "Why?", "When?", "Where?", "How?". Questions that call for answers; questions that lead to discovery; questions that help him think aloud. Through observing, through a growing awareness of the environment, through involvement in the world about him the young child learns by asking, by searching, by discovery. Speech helps him to understand himself and the world in which he lives.

Linguistic skills and environment are inter-related. The child is a product of his environment. If he finds people who talk to him, who are concerned with the questions he asks, who provide an environment in which speaking, listening, reading, and writing are integral parts of the daily activity the child will come to school with an eagerness to continue his excursions into the world of words and ideas. On the other hand, if he is in an environment in which linguistic activities are at a minimum, in which there is little if any dialogue between members of the family, and in which communication is forgotten or ignored he will bear the mark of that sterile speech environment. Too, if he is surrounded by slovenly, illiterate speech, he will come to school bringing with him the habits formed in the pre-school years.

Speech reflects personality. Speech is an index to personality. Voice quality, tone, pitch, and rate are indicators of the emotional state of an individual. The high-pitched, shrill, unpleasant voice of the anxiety ridden neurotic adult has its counterpart in the child's voice in a fit of temper or a moment of tension. The child who is worried, tense, strained shows it in his voice. As the violin string is tightened to produce a higher tone, so the tightening of the throat muscles produces a high-pitched unpleasant voice. A pleasing voice is one in which the qualities of pitch, rate, rhythm, and articulation reflect an integrated, self-reliant, alert personality.

Effective Guides to Teaching Speech

That teacher is most effective in teaching children to communicate who is adept at arranging an environment in which there is encouragement, time, stimulation, and guidance. The teacher who makes a difference in the lives of children is one who understands the importance of the process of speech as well as the content. For him the primary function of all language is communication. Because he realizes the significance of speech in the life of the individual he utilizes this knowledge in establishing objectives for teaching speech effectively. Such a teacher demonstrates a knowledge of speech as an academic discipline as well as a process.

The Speech Association of America in 1963 prepared an official document entitled "The Field of Speech: It's Purposes and Scope in Education". In part the document states:

> The use of the term "speech" to identify an academic discipline emerged in the first two decades of this century. . . . Although its name is a coinage of this century, Speech as a field of study grew from an academic tradition as old as the history of Western education. The study of the theory and practice of public discussion, under the name *rhetoric*, was a central concern of Greek, Roman, medieval, renaissance, and early modern education. Subjects allied to rhetoric also flourished in the Western educational tradition: argumentative dialogue and logical inquiry, usually called *dialectic;* literature which was inseparably linked to rhetoric; and speculative inquiry into the nature and function of language.
>
> Growing thus from a major educational tradition, the field of speech has shared in the unparalleled expansion of knowledge characteristic of this century, and in the specialization of research and instruction. . . .
>
> Despite their manifest specializations, teachers and scholars in the field of speech share these assumptions . . . :
>
> (a) Speech is man's most distinctive and significant behavior. Speech is learned, and it is learned from teachers. The "teachers" include all members of

the social groups in which the child moves as well as the persons who give direct attention to speech instruction in formal educational settings. The learning of speech and the form and efficiency of the habits developed are matters of utmost consequence to the individual and his society. Speaking is prerequisite to the child's development of a sense of identity. It is a behavior inseparably linked to the processes of thought and communication. Speech habits mirror the form and quality of one's thought, the nature of his social identifications, and the form and quality of his interaction with his physical environment and with other persons. Speech habits are important to vocational success and effective citizenship. Speech is thus *central* to the nature of man, to the development of the person, and to the functioning of political, economic, and social institutions. . . . No one can be said to be knowledgeable about himself and his environment unless he understands speech, its nature, structure, and functioning.

(b) An educated person needs more than an understanding of speech behavior. He should be capable of transmitting his meanings with accuracy, correctness, and clarity. . . . In the education of such a man, knowledge and skill meld inextricably. . . .

(c) Man cannot avoid being essentially and significantly a communicator. . . .

(d) The acts and arts of communication in speech and language are humanistic. . . .

The learning of speech begins before formal education, and the development of knowledge about speech behavior and the development of skill in speaking are necessarily continuous processes. At every level of education the speech and language skills of the student both limit and are limited by the kind and extent, the breadth and depth, of the student's knowledge. The growth, refinement, and permanence of communication habits parallel the development of the knowledge built into the process. Hence continuity of instruction in speech is of primary concern in formal education. . . .

. . . Despite massive evidence to the contrary, the assumption that speaking skill can be expected to develop as a by-product of instruction in reading and writing seems still to be prevalent. In too many schools, instruction in speech is represented only in extracurricular endeavor.

. . . Innumerable graduates of the common schools have practically no knowledge of speech behavior and of the arts of communication, only the most superficial acquaintance with any of the "literature" of public address and discussion, and no experience at all in rhetorical analysis and appraisal. Large numbers of graduates face a variety of situations requiring ready speech with powers far under their abilities. Such an attenuated and unbalanced treatment of the study of language and the development of language skills is a most serious problem in . . . education. Teachers of speech and English must recognize their related problems in the curriculum in the English language arts and confront them co-operatively.[5]

Improved Communication is the Chief Purpose of Speech Training

The central concern of speech instruction should be to help each child develop his speech skills to his maximum potential. Whatever the activity in which the child is participating—conversing, giving a talk, discussing, oral interpretation, creative dramatics, role-playing, and so forth, the objective should be to improve the personal skills of the student.

Failure to communicate effectively, both through verbal language and non-verbal expression, may result in lack of understanding that may lead to irreparable consequences. "The relationship that exists between you and others . . . permanently or at the moment of communicating . . . colors the reception of everything you say or hear. In a climate of good will much is permissable; much will be understandable; much will be acceptable that otherwise would be productive of irritation, confusion, and rejection. And the way you communicate will, in the long run, greatly affect the climate between you and others."[6]

Developing skills in speech requires persistent, conscious guided effort. Children must not only learn the theory of how to speak more effectively, they must learn these things "in a way that will take root in their way of living. . . . The knowledge they need is not the sort that is merely learned; it must be *appropriated*. And it is only learning that has been appropriated which can take root in behaviour."[7] If the child is to improve his skills in speaking he must be motivated. He must be so consciously involved in the speech activity that speaking effectively becomes habitual behaviour.

Speech training must be an integral part of the daily program. Speech training in specific skills must be carried on in a functional setting. It is not enough to plan separate activities which offer opportunities for children to practice certain speech skills; neither is it enough to offer an incidental speech program. An effective speech program requires planned settings, situations, and experiences. Content for speech activities will be drawn from all the curriculum areas. Throughout the daily program the teacher will be conscious of the children's need to develop skills in communication.

Each individual develops his unique style of speaking. Each person should develop his own personal style of expressing his ideas orally. Good speaking is not merely a question of accuracy in reporting an event. It is a matter of organizing ideas in a way that gives evidence of appropriate style and usage, vividness of expression, clarity of tone, and originality of content and presentation. As the child gains confidence in speaking, he will use words, phrases, and sentences to communicate in terms of his own unique personality. Knowledge of the subject, sincerity, and individuality, together with a mastery of the techniques of speaking, mark the effective speaker.

Students gain confidence in speaking by speaking. Practice makes permanent. It does not necessarily make perfect. Mere practice, without effective guidance will not of itself improve the child's speaking ability. Although it is essential to give the student opportunity to practice speaking in various situations that are meaningful, it is necessary to provide direct teaching in a planned program. As the child learns speech skills he will use them in the other curriculum areas. Confidence grows as he feels the satisfaction which comes from giving a good speech, participating effectively in interpreting poetry through choral speaking, dramatizing a story, leading discussion, or conducting a meeting with dispatch.

There must be a concerted attack on common language difficulties. Growth in speaking effectively is facilitated when special teachers, too, recognize the child's speech needs. If speaking is to be an integral part of the daily experiences of the child, every teacher *must* be interested in helping him express his ideas in a form that is appropriate to the occasion. Children should learn to "be at home" with the correct forms of usage and to improve their vocabularies through experiences in which they have a common interest and in which common difficulties in the language arts are solved.

It is important for every teacher to be aware of the child's need to express ideas clearly, concisely, and expressively. Since much of the language growth in primary children comes through activities involving oral expression, *every teacher* must be concerned with helping children communicate thoughts and feelings effectively. It is, however, the province of the child's language arts teacher, if there is one, or the classroom teacher in a self-contained classroom, to organize and direct a balanced, developmental program of speech activities which are geared to the level of the children, the abilities of the group, and their specific needs for effective speaking. The teacher responsible for their growth in communicating ideas must plan a well organized program.

Organizing Learning Experiences in Harmony with Varied Abilities of Children

The proficiency expected of each child should be commensurate with his level of development, his need for improvement of a particular skill at each level, and his potential for improvement. Helping the child to develop skills in oral language is of such importance that the teacher must be aware of each child's specific needs and abilities so he can take advantage of every occasion for meaningful oral experiences. It is only when the child has ample opportunity for self-expression through speech under the guidance of a capable, understanding teacher will he realize his potential. The teacher must keep in mind simultaneously the objectives of the speech program, guides to teaching speech effectively, and the needs of the children. Only then can he plan an adequate program that gives children the freedom to grow but at the same time provides experiences which stimulate them to achieve higher levels of thought and usage.

The primary teacher finds a wide range of individual differences among children in their competence with respect to speaking as with listening. Some six-year-olds have meager vocabularies and are immature in their understanding and use of language patterns. Others, because of better opportunities or abilities, can speak and listen at higher levels of achievement. Moreover, personality differences are also apparent, and the teacher is likely to find among her pupils the good listener who is too shy to speak, the chatterbox who seldom listens, and the withdrawn child who seldom speaks or listens.

At the other extreme, the teacher finds pupils who listen and understand at a high level of competence and who express their ideas in mature language patterns with good habits of speech. No six-year-old child, however, has reached his highest potential. Each is growing in his own way and all are at various stages of accomplishment on the way toward learning to listen and speak. There is a continuous, sequential development in the arts of listening and speaking just as there is in reading and writing.[8]

The teacher must create a climate for speech activities. Before the teacher can successfully teach children to improve their linguistic skills he must create a climate which values this skill. This he does by encouraging the children to carry on oral communication throughout the day. In a friendly, supporting atmosphere he draws out the shy child, helps the loquacious one give way to another child, and provides an environment in which talk is natural, spontaneous, and fluent.

Young children must become free in their oral expression before the teacher begins direct teaching of speech skills. To encourage the child to talk about his home, his pets, his family, his trips, his possessions is often an entering wedge into the broader area of speech. As the child gets older he must extend his horizons and improve his skills in speaking in order to express abstract concepts, as well as concrete experiences. "As children mature they display a growing interest in ideas. They begin to talk less about people and more about ideas."[9]

ORGANIZING THE SPEECH PROGRAM IN THE ELEMENTARY SCHOOL

"The time has come, the walrus said,
   to talk of many things:
Of shoes—and ships—and sealing wax—
   of cabbages—and kings. . . ."
    Lewis Carroll

An understanding of the term speech is essential to the teacher in organizing a speech program. "For our purposes speech may be defined as the communication of thought and emotion by means of voice, language, and/or bodily action. By speech we can mean conversation, discussion, public speaking, reading aloud, or even booing, hissing, heckling, or sign language. Effective speech is not a thing but an interaction that occurs among people when both the speaker and the listeners are participating knowledgeably, responsibly, and communicatively."[10]

Organization of a speech program must consider at the outset the basic abilities and attitudes to be developed in the speaking situations and activities in the classroom. Important speech attitudes and skills to be developed through the speech program in the elementary school curriculum are:

1. A desire to express worth-while ideas effectively
2. The skill to select and organize ideas efficiently
3. The ability to use words which express ideas clearly and accurately

4. The skill to use voice and articulation so that speech will be heard and understood
5. The skill to use appropriate bodily actions to reinforce the speaker's message
6. The ability to adapt speech behaviour and speech organization to group situations such as conversations, discussions, etc.
7. The skill to communicate thought and mood of the author through oral reading, choral speaking, and dramatic activities.

Scope of the Program

Before organizing the speech activities the teacher must have a clear understanding of the *scope* of the program. Simply defined, scope is the *what* of the curriculum. From preschool onward the child must be given opportunity to participate in a wide range of speech activities. This will involve a balanced program of speech activities; both in informal and formal situations.

"Nowhere in the elementary school is the guiding of language experiences more rewarding than in the kindergarten and primary grades. At this stage children develop rapidly in speech skills and vocabulary. The teacher should keep in mind objectives of oral communication [speech] as he organizes stimulating activities in meaningful situations.

One of the most significant changes in speech education during the 20th century has been the new emphasis upon informal speaking. Since it is this form of communication which we employ largely throughout most of our waking hours, and by which we are most often judged, speech teachers should feel a challenge to help students to increase their skills in using the speech of everyday life."[11]

Informal Activities

Through informal speaking situations the child makes his first excursions into the social environment of the school. As he shares his personal experiences, follows directions, participates in the give and take of conversations and discussions, he learns to express his ideas. He soon discovers that if he wants to influence his peers he must speak clearly and accurately. The teacher sets the stage for informal speaking situations. The very young child develops his speech skills most readily through sharing experiences, conversing, planning, and participating in social situations.

The teacher must provide guidance to help children in developing the needed speech skills. He provides this guidance through such techniques as asking questions that elicit critical and creative thinking, giving a word of encouragement when needed, and providing motivation for exploration of concepts and ideas.

The school has a two-fold responsibility in organizing the informal speech activities—to create a need for interesting and effective communication through enriching, expanding, and utilizing those activities which involve oral communication, and to teach directly those speech skills essential to fulfill this need.

Among the informal speech activities which should be an integral part of the primary curriculum are:

sharing experiences   making introductions
conversing   telephoning
telling the news   giving directions, explanations,
making announcements   instructions

The teacher who is conscious of the significance of speech education will create an atmosphere in the classroom which stimulates informal speaking. For example, arranging a bulletin board to keep posted on the latest news events is an open door to informal discussion. Placing copies of children's books and magazines where they will be "discovered" motivates informal speaking. Arranging maps, dictionaries, supplementary materials where they can be explored and discussed is an open sesame to conversation. Motivating interest in a new unit through pictures, realia, art objects; planning excursions such as trips to the farm, the market, the railway station, the airport—all these stimulate discussion. Placing captions such as "Come and See," "Come and Discuss," "Come and Share Ideas" at strategic places is a catalyst for expression of ideas. A classroom that is speech oriented is filled with many interesting activities which literally cry for expression.

GUIDING INFORMAL SPEECH ACTIVITIES IN PRIMARY GRADES

Although the child's basic speech is established by the time he enters the primary school, he must be provided with numerous opportunities and a variety of activities to improve his speech skills. Teachers have the responsibility for providing both informal and formal speech activities throughout the elementary school years to meet the child's need for developing skill in communication.

Specific suggestions for informal speech activities are presented as guides for the teacher.

Sharing Experiences

"Share and Tell" is an activity which should give the child an opportunity to use language creatively. This can become a significant part of the daily living and learning at school *if* the teacher uses some simple guide lines to motivate the experience. When the children understand that listening is as much a part of "sharing" as speaking it helps to ease the frustrations and tensions that too often exist where there are large groups. Sharing interesting happenings which occur in the home, at school, and out of school offer opportunities for developing creative communication.

Sharing experiences, as any other type of speech situation, requires standards to be set if the performances are not to deteriorate into a waste of time. "Share and

Tell" also stimulates observation, critical thinking, and reporting needed in imaginative and expository writing and in creative and critical thinking.

An effective sharing period is the result of careful planning, group evaluation, and standards in harmony with the developmental level of the children. However, the teacher should be careful lest the experience degenerate into a monologue in which the teacher does the sharing and the child the listening. The following is a verbatim account of one such experience.

> Teacher: Oh, Dorothy, you brought your new doll to show the class. Isn't that wonderful! Did your mother get her for you?
>
> Dorothy: Unh unh.
>
> Teacher: Did Santa bring her?
>
> Dorothy: Unh huh.
>
> Teacher: How do you like her? Does she close her eyes? Oh, my! She walks, too. Did everyone see Dorothy's doll? Thank you for sharing her with us and helping us get acquainted.
>
> Dorothy: Her name is Sarah.
>
> Teacher: Oh, she has a name and I forget to ask what it is. I'm sorry. Next time we will not be so rushed and you can tell us more about her. (And Dorothy is pushed aside to make way for Tommy who is rushing up with his robot.)

In contrast, another group of children and their teacher facilitated the development of creative language and skill in communication as an outgrowth of their mutual discovery of the following standards for their "share and tell".

The Speaker	The Listeners
Wait to speak until everyone is ready	Listen courteously
Have something interesting to tell	Keep your mind on the speaker
Think before you speak	Respond to the enthusiasm of the speaker
Show interest in the experience	
Use colourful words	Do not interrupt
Organize the ideas in sequence	Ask good questions when the speaker invites them
Give interesting details	
Have an interesting conclusion	Listen to the whole thing
Look at the audience	Avoid anything that might distract the speaker
Speak clearly and forcefully so everyone can hear you	
Be alive! Use expressive gestures	Watch for evidence of non-verbal communication through gestures and bodily movements
Finish speaking before starting back to your seat.	
	Show genuine appreciation through such non-verbal means of communication as smiling, nodding, shaking the head, and having an attitude of listening carefully.

To the extent that the speaker succeeds in getting and holding the attention of the audience his communication is effective. To the degree that the speaker finds increasing satisfaction in oral communication will it become a significant medium for creative self-expression.

Conversing

Unfortunately, the type of speech that individuals will engage in more than any other type is rarely provided for in the curriculum. Genuine sparkling conversation, which has been termed the poetry of the literate, needs both time and opportunity if it is to flourish into full bloom as the child becomes an adult. Conversation is dialogue in discovery, for through such an experience one individual discovers another individual and engages in one of the most fascinating creative experiences possible. However, an entire class is too large for genuine discovery to take place. Artificiality results when groups are assigned to engage in conversation about a specific subject. Conversation is an art which develops best when a few individuals have genuine need to share experiences, ideas, and aspirations, serious or humorous. Opportunity should be provided for this phase of the language arts program throughout the elementary school years. It is not enough to provide time for children to talk with children. Most children on their own will find time for this. Time must also be planned for child-adult dialogue.

Conversations between children and adults is an avenue along which children travel toward self-understanding and maturity. Even a child is stimulated by the give and take of spirited conversation. Conversing should become an intellectual adventure to which children look forward eagerly.

Schreiber emphasizes the impact of such experiences: "Thinking back to my own childhood, I could relive dialogue of discovery, those snatches of conversation that excited my growing imagination. To my amazement, I realized that these conversations with their special words had yielded the very words that today I use most and with greatest affection. To my everlasting wonder I could find that the thoughts, the emotions, the values those first words I heard had instilled were with me still."[12]

Where children grow up without interchange of ideas they often develop a negative self-image that leaves the mark of cultural deprivation upon them.

The role of dialogue has achieved an even greater significance as travel is facilitated, boundaries are erased, and the population of nations is in a state of mobility. Political tensions will be increased or lessened in proportion to the ability of man to communicate effectively with man. "Effective communication at home and abroad is the chief means by which men will find a way of living together around the world in harmony with our belief in the inherent dignity of man and the worth of the individual."[13]

Helping Children Participate in Conversation

"Said a second grader to an entering first grader whom he was orienting. 'There's just one thing to remember and that is not to talk.' In many schools a tremendous value is placed on quietness. We teach children *not* to talk. We threaten them if they do talk and then we initiate elaborate lessons to stimulate them to speak."[14] Such inconsistencies do not go unrecognized by the school child; they should not go unrecognized by the teacher.

Why not capitalize on the child's natural inclination to talk? Some ways in which a teacher can help children participate effectively in conversation are: use every opportunity to motivate children to converse, involve individual children in conversational groups, help children develop skills in conversing with ease, and encourage them to evaluate their strengths and weaknesses.

Developing Skills in Conversation

A. Objectives
   1. To instruct pupils in conversational techniques
   2. To help pupils use conversational skills in their social contacts
   3. To help pupils identify and correct their weaknesses
B. Techniques of the Teacher
   1. Have children dramatize some situations requiring conversation
   2. Discuss the attributes of good conversation; spontaneity, fluency, respect for others' ideas, alert listening, pleasant voice
   3. Discuss conversation as an informal speech activity
      a. Importance of conversation
      b. Consideration of others in conversation
      c. What to talk about
      d. Keeping well informed about happenings
      e. How to avoid awkward pauses
      f. Learning from conversationalists in real life and in literature
C. Activities
   1. Dramatize specific situations
   2. Divide into pairs and select an interesting problem for the dialogue
   3. Have the students suggest appropriate topics for conversation
   4. Compose an imaginary conversation with an imaginary character of one's choice
   5. Have pupils listen to and evaluate television programs involving conversations and/or dialogues on subjects of general interest
   6. Have each student bring to class, to be read aloud, the best conversation that he has found in his reading recently
   7. Have the class draw up a list of ways to become better class conversationalists
   8. Tape several of the best conversations. Have the class listen to them and evaluate them on the basis of the criteria set up
   9. Have the students report to the class on a conversation in which they took part
D. Evaluation
   Ask questions such as:
   1. Did all of the children participate in the conversation?

2. How many times did each person participate?
3. Did anyone tend to monopolize the conversation?
4. Did the conversation capture and maintain interest?
5. Were the contributions worthwhile?
6. What effect did the conversation have on others in the group?
7. Did the contributions promote successful group living?
8. Were the participants thoughtful, courteous, and kind in their remarks?

Telling the News and Making Announcements

What is more exciting for a child than telling his favourite news and/or making an announcement of great import? It need not necessarily take on the mien of a great public event. As a matter of fact, in the preschool years the announcements may be made to the group in which the child is a member. It may be the announcement of a new baby in the family; a birthday party for the group; an invitation to the child's home to see the baby martins who have just arrived. At this level it may be little more than the mention—very briefly—of a new possession, a happening, or a memorable occurrence. It may not be earth shaking to the group; it *is* to the child.

As the child progresses in school the typical announcement becomes connected with use of the public address system, closed-circuit television, the tape recorder, the school assembly. These experiences offer opportunity for emphasis on such speech objectives as clear articulation, moderate rate, logical organization of ideas, and projection of the voice.

A formula for organizing the information in making a public announcement is What? Who? When? Where?

Social Situations

Social situations offer excellent motivation for meaningful informal speech activities. When social forms are taught functionally, as they are needed in response to a real situation the children learn them readily and eagerly. The kindergarten child is as anxious to learn correct forms of introducing his parents as is the intermediate child. The first grader is eager to learn how to be an effective host or hostess, how to extend invitations, and how to acknowledge introductions as well as to make introductions properly. Children should be taught in a functional setting how to accept thanks graciously or how to accept congratulations modestly after winning an award at the speech festival, athletic event, or music contest.

A. Objectives
   1. To help children improve their skills in human relations
   2. To instruct students in social situations in a functional setting
   3. To give students practical experience through dramatizing situations
B. Techniques of the Teacher
   1. Point out to the students the social amenities

2. View a film which demonstrates correct social behaviour
3. Discuss the need for knowing what to do in specific situations
4. Use creative dramatics as a preparation for the "real" experience
5. Have children introduce parents, relatives, visitors, friends

ORDER OF INTRODUCTION

Manner of Introduction	Introduce first the person who because of age or sex is entitled to greater respect. A girl is introduced first when being introduced to a person of the opposite sex. "Mary, this is Dan Mabrey. Dan, this is my cousin, Mary Davis".
Correct Phrases	"May I present?" "This is my Mother".
Response	"How do you do?" *not* "I'm pleased to meetcha" or "Charmed".
When to Shake Hands	If a boy is introduced to a girl, he waits for her to initiate the action of shaking hands. Men always shake hands.
When to Rise	In the presence of an older or distinguished guest one always rises. A boy always rises in the presence of a girl or woman.
How to introduce a person to a group	Present the honoured person to the entire group at once.
How to proceed easily from the introduction into conversation	Add a comment telling something about the individual you are introducing that will give a clue to or spring-board for conversation.
ex.	"Miss Jenson, this is my friend Alice. She has just moved to Manitoba. She lived in Ohio before she came here." "How do you do, Ann? Do you find the climate here quite a contrast to that of Ohio?"

C. Activities
1. Draw up a list of suggestions for making introductions.
2. Practice the procedure for making introductions by introducing a classmate
   to your mother
   a relative to your teacher
   your mother to your teacher
   a boy to a girl
   two girls to each other
   one group to another group
3. Dramatize the following introductions:
   (a) The Prime Minister of the province or mayor of the town to the class
   (b) Judge Brown, senior resident, to your teacher
   (c) A friend to a member of your family
4. View a film demonstrating correct procedure for making introductions and note how well the introductions were "cued in" to start a conversation, how well the cues were picked up, and so forth.
5. Dramatize: You are sitting at your desk and your mother comes to the door. You present your teacher to her.

    6. Have students pair off and select types of introductions they wish to demonstrate for the class

D. Evaluation
Have the class evaluate the correctness of the introductions

Telephoning

Telephoning is a special type of conversation which requires specific behaviour. Instruction in the use of the telephone should emphasize the fact that other people may need to use the phone. Under any circumstances, prolonged conversation is thoughtless. When the telephone clicks showing someone needs the line, it is a mark of considerateness to hang up and release the line.

A. Objectives
To teach children:
1. To speak with clarity and expressiveness
2. To use correct form in answering the phone
3. To use correct form in: calling home, calling a friend, calling the school
4. To distinguish between correct forms used in business and social calls
5. That courtesy in the use of the telephone is essential to developing good manners

B. Techniques of the Teacher
Develop the following concepts through direct instruction to help children establish standards for telephone use:
1. Speak directly into the transmitter
2. The use of the telephone for prolonged social conversation is seldom legitimate
3. Certain formal procedures in answering the telephone will greatly increase the efficiency of conversations
4. Telephone conversation requires more careful articulation than does face-to-face conversation
5. The person initiating a telephone conversation should plan his remarks carefully before calling
6. The use of "thank you" and "you're welcome" in telephone conversation is one way to smile
7. It is always a mistake to shout

C. Activities
1. View one or more films such as:

                    Speech: *Conversation*, 11 min.
                    Young America Films.
                    Telephone Courtesy, 25 min. each
                    Thanks for Listening
                    Bell Telephone Co.

2. Have the class draw up a "Code for Using the Telephone" which combines courtesy and efficiency

3. Dramatize emergency situations:

        Set a timer, so that conversation is limited, in each case, to three minutes

  (a) Calling in a fire-alarm

  (b) Calling an ambulance

  (c) Report to the proper city official the presence of the stray dog on the playground

  (d) Call the family doctor

  (e) Report a fire

4. Dramatize social situations:

  (a) Invite a friend to a party

  (b) Ask a friend for a homework assignment

  (c) Call mother to get permission to purchase a ticket to the play

  (d) Call a friend to talk about a party, a movie, a new dress, a hockey game

D. Evaluation

  1. Have the class evaluate the performance using the code for telephoning drawn up by the class

Giving Directions

In helping children become oriented to the world in which they live, it is essential that they understand relationships of space as well as time. For example, they must develop the ability to give precise directions for finding a specific address. The young child should be taught to recognize the familiar landmarks which tell him he is near home, near the school, etc. He should have the clues which enable him to direct a person to reach the desired destination.

In giving directions, instructions, and explanations effectively children must learn to express themselves with precision, accuracy, terseness, and logic. Careful thinking, concise speaking, and a well-ordered, clear picture in one's mind as he speaks is essential if this informal speech activity is to be fruitful. Perhaps of all the informal types of speech situations and language activities, giving clear directions gives a true reflection of the child's ability to organize his thinking, clearly, logically and concisely and offers opportunity for developing the thought processes of children.

A. Objectives

  1. To develop habits of logical thinking

  2. To develop ability to organize ideas in narrative sequence

  3. To give directions and explanations concisely and clearly

B. Techniques of the Teacher

  1. To make use of child's interest in his environment to teach him the skills of order, logic, sequence in relation to his world

  2. To provide a natural outlet for the child to explain, give directions and instruction

  3. To provide activities that will enable the child to use knowledge about his physical environment, the people in his environment, and the desire to explore

C. Activities
   1. Have children give directions for getting to their house
   2. Take a walk to a home of a child within walking distance of the school following the directions given earlier
   3. Make a map showing the location of a park, store, post-office or a public building within walking distance of the school
   4. Take a walk to the specified location using a commercially printed map as a guide
   5. Compare the map and the diagram made by the children
   6. Select a specified place for the class to visit and make a diagram of the bus route
   7. Have a child explain how to make a certain object
   8. Have a child explain a process and have the children carry out each step as he explains it—e.g. proper folding, cutting, etc., arithmetic problem, making a kite, assembling a model airplane, etc.
   9. Give some clues about a hobby and have the children guess what it is
   10. Explain how you arrived at the answer to an arithmetic problem using the new math

D. Evaluation
   Among the questions to be asked are:
   1. Did we tell things in the right order?
   2. Did we organize ideas in narrative sequence?
   3. Did we learn to use spatial sequence organization?
   4. Did we arrive at the correct destination by using the directions given?
   5. Did we make use of diagrams and maps to make our directions clear?
   6. Did we learn the difference between chronological, logical and spatial sequence?
   7. Did our knowledge of logic, order, and sequence contribute to our enjoyment in going to and from school, in going to town, and/or taking trips?
   8. Did we learn to listen more carefully in order to carry out the directions, explanations, or instructions given us?
   9. Did we become more accurate, concise, and terse in our speaking as a result of experiences in this phase of speaking?

FORMAL SPEECH ACTIVITIES IN THE PRIMARY GRADES

It is not enough to provide time for children to express ideas in informal situations only. Planned formal situations must also be provided. "The total oral communication skills must be taught well at all levels of instruction so that pupils may develop proficiency not only for adequate participation in society but also for self-fulfillment."[15]

This gives a mandate to the primary teacher to equip himself with the knowledge of the speech curriculum in order to teach effectively. The language behaviours of children are formed early, are formed solidly, and are formed regardless of whether there is an able teacher or not. Even if oral language or speech is included in the curriculum guide, in the final analysis what is taught is what the teacher knows and can teach well; what the teacher knows about what should be taught, when it should be taught, and how it should be taught.

Among the formal speech activities that should be developed in the primary grades are:

giving talks	discussion
planning and evaluating	parliamentary procedure
interviewing	storytelling

Giving Talks

As children develop interest in sharing experiences with the group, it soon becomes evident that their eagerness to talk sometimes exceeds their skills of expression. They enjoy telling what they did during the work period. They want the group to hear what happened over the weekend, they like to explain the process they used in building a boat, making a kite, constructing an airplane. They can tell how to get to the post office, the library, the playground, the recreation building. They develop standards for a particular activity. They can talk about trips, hobbies, and activities. They need help, however, in moving from tentative expression of ideas to carefully planned and organized talks. This involves guidance in selecting an interesting topic, collecting material for the talk, organizing the material, and presenting the material.

The extent to which the teacher gives such help in the primary grades will be dependent upon his knowledge of speech, his understanding of the needs of children, his ability to create situations in which children become aware of their needs of increased speech skills, and his ability to give direct instruction in the skills of oral communication through planned speech activities.

The young child is content to talk about topics such as pets, games, excursions, people, places, and things. He subconsciously chooses subjects with which he is familiar, is interested in, and has some enthusiasm for. As he grows in linguistic skills and experience he learns to express ideas in a more colourful, imaginative, and vivid manner. He finds that his audience of children listen with greater interest. He learns, too, that if he is going to hold the interest of the group, he will need a plan of organization.

The teacher can give guidance by suggesting they have a plan for the talk. Even kindergartners and first graders can readily work out simple plans for a talk. For example, they can relate in sequence what they saw on a trip; or they can indicate the steps to take in making jello in the school cafeteria. Third and fourth graders can make an outline and list the main points they intend to cover in the talk. Fifth and sixth graders are ready to make a more detailed outline showing the main points and the subpoints. By the time the children complete the elementary school they should be able to use sentence outlines and plan carefully so they can decide the particular type of organization they wish to use. At all educational levels the teacher should be alert to the child's need to include the necessary facts, omit unrelated details that detract from the talk, and organize the ideas in a logical manner and tell it in an interesting, exciting fashion.

Planning and Evaluating

Participation in planning the activities throughout the day should begin early in the child's school experience. When the children are familiar with the timetable; when they know what comes the first thing in the morning; what happens after recess; what the afternoon session holds they feel a sense of security. They can move readily from one activity to another without consulting the teacher at each turn. A daily schedule on the chalkboard goes a long way toward enabling each child to look ahead and help plan his day's activities.

Before the day begins there should be time for conscious planning with the children in order for them to understand the specific goals for the day, and to share in long range planning such as deciding on some of the activities that involve special programs for parents, giving a program for another group, taking a field trip, setting standards for behaviour, drawing up plans to simplify routines, deciding on committee responsibility.

Evaluation, too, is an important daily oral activity for which there must be planned time and guidance. The teacher and children should plan time to check their progress toward stated goals. They should be helped to formulate such questions as: "What do we hope to accomplish today in Social Studies?" "What do we need to do to get ready for the music festival?" "How can we improve our creative dramatics program before our mothers come to hear us?" "What needs to be done to help our class improve its record of behaviour on the playground?" Evaluation of activities should be a continuous process. Teachers should keep in mind such dimensions of evaluation as the progress each child is making toward his individual goals, the progress the child is making toward his group goals, and the progress the entire group is making toward defined goals.

Involving children in evaluation affords an excellent avenue for oral expression. One primary group set up a standard for evaluating their own progress in giving talks:

We speak in a conversational tone
We speak so we can be heard
We look at the audience when we talk
We have worthwhile content
We organize our talk clearly
We make it interesting so people will want to listen

When children have a part in setting standards, when they know what they are to be judged on, the desired behaviour becomes the basis for evaluation. If children have a part in setting up goals, in working together to achieve them, and in evaluating progress, skills in speaking will improve *and* so will behaviour.

Interviewing

Children learn in many ways. They observe, read, experiment, explore. Very early in life they discover that one way to find answers is to ask someone who knows. This is the simplest form of interviewing. Interviewing as a speech activity is the natural outgrowth of the child's quest for knowledge. He becomes more effective in his questions when he learns what to do, what to say, how to say it, and how to terminate the interview. He discovers that a successful interview requires both a friendly manner and careful preparation. This means that he must have a specific purpose, a planned procedure, and criteria for the selection of the person to be interviewed.

If the children are studying the community they might well choose to interview a public official. They may wish to interview a school inspector, a mayor, a chief of police, or a city manager. They should be aware that the person they choose to interview has no time to waste. Thus they will plan carefully to the last detail. Since the reputation of the group is involved, they should select one of the most able and capable pupils to carry on the interview. Why? Because each interview entails a series of experiences in oral expression: opening the topic with the interviewee; formulating questions that elicit information desired; introducing new aspects of the subject as the interview proceeds; adapting the inquiries to new or unexpected turns in the developing interview; attentive listening; and tactful, courteous behaviour throughout the interview.

Role-playing before the interview is an excellent practice in getting children to understand the challenge of the give-and-take situation inherent in the interview.

The following suggests four steps in the interviewing procedure:

1. Greet the interviewee politely and express your pleasure at his willingness to be interviewed. Look directly at him during the interview.
2. State the purpose of the interview clearly to refresh the interviewee's memory as soon as his cue allows you to do so.
   "Mr. Blank, we are studying conservation and there is a difference of opinion as to the policy we should follow to conserve wild life in the province. What do you think should be our attitude?"
3. "I have a list of questions which our class prepared and I would appreciate your commenting on them." (The interviewee will be pleased that you have taken time to draw up questions, but you may not have to follow them rigidly.) It is possible that in discussing the first question he will have answered several others. Perhaps by the time he pauses for breath you will know his stand on the questions you have written down. If not, select those items that his answers have not clarified. Be flexible, but try to get a clear picture of the situation.
4. When you have the desired information, the interview should terminate. Follow the clue. If he gives no clue to end the interview, take the initiative. This you may do by saying, "That should give me all the information we need. Thank you for your time and help. I know the members of the class will appreciate it."

Remember that each interview with a member of the community is an important means of public relations. It is well to remember that the courteous, intelligent behaviour of the interviewer reflects positively in the school's interest.

Things to do in Interviewing Practice

1. Dramatize the following situations which entail an interview for information.
   (a) A person who has just returned from Europe; your class is studying Switzerland
   (b) A person who has won a trip to the Capital
   (c) A student who won the poetry writing contest
   (d) A foreign student who has just enrolled in the school
   (e) Tape an interview to use for evaluation
   (f) A new principal has been appointed; you are asked to interview him about his hobbies, family, interests
2. Evaluating the experience
   Did the interviewer report the facts accurately?
   Did he seem to get the point of view?
   Did the attitudes of the interviewee come through in a clear and unbiased picture?
   Did the interviewee appear to be comfortable during the questioning?
   Did the interviewer remember to be courteous, friendly, and natural during the interview?
   Did the behaviour of the interviewee prove helpful to the interviewer?

Discussion

Beginning in the kindergarten discussion is a significant part of the language arts curriculum. Throughout the day children talk about questions of common interest. They make plans for their work. They make preparations for trips and then they discuss it afterwards. They decide on presenting a puppet show and make arrangements for the entire school to see it. In this way, they find answers to their own inquiries. A well organized program of discussion is an important facet of the elementary curriculum. "The spirit of inquiry brought about by a willingness to talk things over freely, accounts in many cases for the successful management of a classroom".[16]

In the primary grades discussion takes on the procedure of talking over problems such as how to get along, how to prepare for a specific event, how to plan a program for mothers, how to spend the money allocated for the class by the home and school association, etc. Here the teacher starts with group discussion as an informal opinion sharing experience on common topics or problems of interest to the class.

Primary grade children should be taught basic facts about discussion. Discussion involves two or more people, listening and speaking interchangeably, thinking interactively, and working cooperatively to solve a common problem or concern. It is not a debate in which children take sides—pro-and-con. Neither should it be a pooling of ignorance. Under the guidance of the teacher the children can engage in problem-solving situations which will accomplish the aim they seek—that of solving the problem at hand using the best thinking of the group in terms of predetermined criteria and careful, critical thinking. Specific techniques for problem solving at a more mature level will be presented in the chapter on the speech activities for the intermediate grades.

A Discussion in a Second Grade

An illustration of a second grade group who solved a problem cooperatively follows:

The children in Miss Lang's group had planned a party for Valentine's Day. The problem was how to finance the party. They decided to make and sell valentines. This created many new problems. Among these were: how to announce the sale, how to make the valentines, where to get the needed materials, when to begin the sale, how to handle the money, how to plan the schedule for the children who would sell the valentines each day, and what to do if they ran out of time, materials and valentines before the announced sale ended.

On the first day they seriously set about solving the problems they had previously listed. They started with the one that dealt with the announcement of their project—the sale of valentines. They came up with several ideas and then Nan said: "Why don't we have two of us dress up to look like the Queen of Hearts" and go to each of the rooms and announce the valentine sale?" John chimed in, "I couldn't be the Queen of Hearts, but I could be the Knave of Hearts and go with you. I could hold up a poster for everyone to read." "Who would make the poster?" questioned the teacher. "I would," said Ralph, "and if I need help I'm sure Mother would help me". "I could be the Knave's servant." At this point Andy said, "Why don't we send a small group in to say 'The Queen of Hearts'—you know, choral speaking—like we did for the speech festival, last year. Remember our class did well."

At that point Miss Lang summarized, "We have really had some excellent ideas. Let's write them down." This is what she wrote:

A valentine sale in the second grade.
Announcement by the Queen of Hearts.
Poster carried by the Knave of Hearts.
Poster made by John—the servant of the Knave of Hearts.
Choral speaking—group to be selected to say "The Queen of Hearts".

The following day the children attacked the problem of making the valentines. Jill suggested that they get help from Miss Jackson, the art teacher. Jack volunteered to bring some "boughten" ones from his father's store to use for ideas.

Miss Lang suggested they turn to the next problem—when to begin the sale. Janice wisely questioned "Won't that depend on how quickly we can have some ready?" It was decided that perhaps Miss Jackson could give some suggestions to

Miss Lang so they could get started on the project. Because the agreement came readily it was possible to discuss another problem—what to do about the schedule for selling the valentines once they were finished. Ann suggested that the children who had the highest grades in arithmetic should sell the valentines so they would be able to make correct change. Jim suggested that they get permission to open the "store" each morning about fifteen minutes before school started and at noon, ten minutes before the tardy bell rang. This discussion took time because of the decision to get permission from the principal. It was suggested by Tony that the class write a letter to ask permission. However, Lester suggested a personal interview with the principal might expedite matters.

On the following day they were ready to grapple with another problem—what to do if they ran out of valentines *before* the sale was scheduled to close. Again Jack came to the rescue by offering to take out on consignment four dozen valentines from the store. "Because", as he said, "our sale at school will be over before Valentine's Day, so my dad can still sell the valentines—unless they are soiled". That brought up the problem of care of merchandise. "We'll choose people with clean hands to handle the merchandise". This from Nina, who was always careful about washing her hands.

Discussion of the final problem—what kind of a party to have—was postponed until the sale was over so they would know how much money they had to spend. The two weeks passed quickly as they were all busy working on the project in one capacity or another. What surprised them was the enthusiasm of the whole school in their project. Big brothers and sisters from the upper grades came to buy their wares and the children were delighted. Their project was highly successful, for they made $25.00. "Of course", said Jack, "my father donated the valentines he loaned us. He wanted us to have a good party". "Yes", said Miss Lang, "but the valentines that were sold first were the ones you people made yourselves".

The final discussion was concerned with the party to be held on Valentine's Day. They talked it over and finalized plans. (1) We will make the cookies ourselves, (2) we will invite our mothers, (3) we will have punch with the cookies, (4) we will serve the punch and cookies when the mothers come in. Each one will escort his mother to the punch table. (5) We will sing some valentine songs. (6) We will dramatize the "Queen of Hearts". (7) We will open the valentine box and choose a postman.

Obviously, the valentine project provided numerous opportunities for learning and using the techniques for successful discussion at their level of development. Teacher and children pooled their information to solve the problems involved.

Group discussion serves the elementary teacher and children in four ways: (1) it provides an opportunity for purposeful oral expression, (2) it encourages children to pool information, (3) it stimulates children to seek and find solutions to a problem, and (4) it motivates critical thinking.

Through group discussion children and the teacher cooperatively study the various aspects of a problem. In doing this they state the problem, analyze its various aspects, discover the possible solutions, decide which is the best, and recommend ways of carrying it out. Both in pooling information and in seeking a solution to a problem, children are stimulated to think critically as well as reflectively, creatively as well as analytically, cooperatively as well as individually.

Parliamentary Procedure

Parliamentary procedure is the term applied to those rules in accordance with which any organization attempts to carry on its business in an orderly and democratic manner. In a democratic society such as Canada and the U.S. the citizens are great "joiners". Logically, children follow the example set by the adults. In the primary grades this takes the form of class meetings, clubs, and organizations of various types. In order to be a contributory member one must have an understanding of the simple basic procedure for conducting meetings and expediting business.

In a sense, parliamentary procedure simply provides one set of rules within which debate, discussion, or public speaking may take place. Including parliamentary procedure in the elementary curriculum rests on the premise that it is useful to the individual to have some knowledge of and skill in using the procedures which facilitate decision making. "Most students will be participating in class and club organizations in which business will be expedited if members have a knowledge of parliamentary law. . . . Most adults will be similarly involved in meetings, clubs, or societies requiring some measure of adherence to parliamentary procedure for the efficient conduct of their business."[17]

Without knowledge of basic parliamentary procedure groups are almost inevitably inefficient. With a knowledge of procedures for conducting meetings, however, even primary grade group organizations can be efficient and effective.

If children are taught the purpose of rules in conducting meetings, if they are guided to understand that in a democratic society there must be opportunity for free discussion of opinions, they will grow in appreciation as well as skill in using the parliamentary techniques for worthy ends.

Such rules contribute to orderliness, efficiency, fairness, and courteous behaviour and organized thinking. Thus parliamentary procedure protects the rights of each individual to participate in a meeting; no one can monopolize in a meeting in which rules and regulations are understood and obeyed.

Primary children frequently organize into a class organization or club. They write and adopt a constitution (rules to live by), elect officers, and propose action. This action may range from such simple behaviour as wording a motion, amending a motion, and voting on the motion at the primary level to becoming skilled in the intricacies of main, subsidiary and priveleged motions by the end of the elementary school.

Even first graders can be taught how to make a motion, amend a motion, and that only one person can have the floor at a time, and that only one item of business can be taken up at one time. No new business may be initiated until the motion on hand is disposed of.

The teacher helps children follow proper procedure and use correct terminology. For example he may say:

Keep your remarks pertinent to the topic. Not—stick to the point.

Kindly keep personalities out. Not—don't be rude.

Amend the motion. Not—change the motion.

Delete the words. Not—take out the words.

A Third-Grade Meeting

During the spring of the year Mr. Tarnrushè's class decided to organize as a club. The teacher suggested that he be the parliamentarian in order to guide the group. Officers were elected, weekly meetings were scheduled, plans for organizing the meetings were accepted, and the time came to have the second meeting of the club.

Meeting on March 3.

Chairman: Will the meeting come to order please? Will the secretary please read the minutes of the last meeting?

Secretary: (Reads minutes)

Chairman: Are there any additions or corrections? If not, all in favour of approving the minutes raise your hand.

Children respond.

Chairman: Those opposed? (None) The minutes are approved as read.

May we hear treasurer's report?

Treasurer: (Reads report)

Chairman: Are there any errors or omissions? If not, all in favour of accepting the report please raise your hand?

Children respond.

Chairman: Those opposed? (Pause.) The report is accepted.

Are there any reports of standing committees? (Listens to reports on social events, supplies, monitors, etc.)

Is there any old business? (Pause.) Since there is no old business we can consider new business.

(Each speaker addresses the chair and waits to be recognized before he speaks).

Child: Mr. Chairman, I think we should plan a Mother's Day Tea.

Child: I think we should too; the third grade always plans one.

Child: How much would it cost?

Child: When should we have it? On the Friday before Mother's Day?

Child: Should we have it in the morning or afternoon?

Teacher: Mr. Chairman, since there seem to be so many questions, I suggest that we appoint a committee to look into the idea for us. Perhaps they could contact Miss Jones who taught the third grade last year. Will someone move that we appoint a committee of five to get as much information about last year's Mother's Day Tea as possible and report at our next meeting?

Child: Mr. Chairman, I move that the executive appoint a committee of five to investigate last year's Mother's Day Tea and report back to the group.

Chairman: It has been moved and seconded that the executive appoint a committee of five to get as much information as possible from Miss Jones about last year's Mother's Day Tea.

Is there any discussion? (Pause.) Since there is no discussion, all in favour of the motion raise your hands. (Counts hands.)

Those opposed? (None.) The motion is passed.

Teacher: Mr. Chairman, I am afraid our time is up.

Chairman: Is there a motion to adjourn?

Child: I move that we adjourn.

Chairman: Is there a second?

Child: I second the motion.

Chairman: All in favour of the motion to adjourn, raise your hands.

All opposed. The same. (Pause.) (No dissenting votes)

Chairman: The meeting stands adjourned.

These children had many prior experiences in informal and problem solving discussions before they were able to manage the formal business meeting. As can be noted this class followed the traditional pattern of a meeting. The chairman called the meeting to order, followed by secretary's report, treasurer's report, committee reports, old business, and discussion of new business. Technically, discussion of new business should not be permitted until *after* a motion has been made. The teacher will have to use judgement in deciding when a group is ready for the more complicated procedures such as amending motions, referring to committees, etc. Participation in class or club meetings should be a right of the primary child as a way of becoming an effective member of a democratic society. This is possible if the teacher keeps in mind that previous participation in discussions is a prerequisite to participation in parliamentary procedure.

The more complex aspects will be presented at the intermediate and upper grade levels.

Storytelling

Storytelling is an activity that is for many children an avenue to effective communication as well as to creative expression with literature. Many a child enjoys telling a story he knows, sharing it with his classmates, and because he enjoys it so much, he is able to communicate more effectively than in other activities of oral expression. Watch him as he forgets himself in the telling of the tale, the building up of the events leading to the exciting climax or the satisfying conclusion. Here he uses his body readily as a medium of communication. He talks with his hands, his eyes, his entire body. As he watches the interest of his audience he is stimulated to so identify with the story that he and the characters become one as it were; and it is only when he is playing the role of the narrator that he assumes an objective attitude toward the story he is relating.

Although story telling is a formal speech activity it depends upon literature for its content and will be considered in detail in the chapter on literary appreciation.

Giving Oral Reports

The teacher who is really concerned about helping children express their ideas effectively and interestingly will begin in the kindergarten and primary grades to motivate children to give oral reports effectively. True, reports become a major responsibility of the intermediate grade teacher, but the intermediate grade teacher merely builds upon the foundation the primary teacher lays. A kindergarten child who had visited a filtering plant over the weekend reported on the experience with as clearly organized report as any adult who had had a similar initial experience. He began by getting the interest of his audience by an anecdote that demanded and received attention. During the presentation the listeners were entranced to follow his plan of organization, his selection and sequence of ideas, his discrimination in the selection of incidents and information that carried their interest as he literally took them with him from the moment he got into his father's red convertible, drove down the highway to the new filtering plant, followed the guide as he took them through the plant, used effective gestures that told more clearly than mere words what he had seen and heard on the excursion.

If a kindergarten child can be taught the elements of presenting a vivid, exciting, stimulating, and informative report, it is certainly the responsibility of the primary teacher to equip children with skills which will change the report from a dull, lifeless, tedious, boring session to one that is vital, alive, and worthwhile.

This requires that the child is:

1. Interested in the topic
2. Is selective in the material he chooses
3. Decides on the main ideas he wants to present
4. Selects supporting material to implement and support his main idea
5. Organizes the information in an interesting manner
6. Presents the report making use of colourful language and visual aids.

A good report is no accident; it is the result of careful, organized planning coupled with skill in communicating ideas to an interested group. An effective plan for presenting the report follows:

Get the attention. For example, begin with a startling statement or visual aids that arouse curiosity. Be sure that these are pertinent.

Create or point out a need in the audience for the report. Relate the speech to *their* interests or problems.

Present the report. Have the report organized in your own mind so you can develop it naturally, spontaneously, and vividly.

Keep the sequence in mind. Memorize the sequence. Use a key-word outline.

Conclude with a summary or recapitulation.

Sequence in the Program

In addition to knowing the activities to be included in the speech program the teacher frequently asks, "How can I decide the sequence of the activities?" Sequence refers to the *when* of the curriculum and determines the placement of a particular learning experience. One of the most effective methods of determining sequence or placement of activities is based on the language development of the children we teach. Such a criteria takes into consideration: objectives in teaching communication, language growth of children in the preschool-primary years, and specific speech activities designed to implement the objectives in terms of the children's developmental growth patterns.

A chart of suggested sequence of speech activities from the kindergarten through the primary grades follows. The speaking activities listed are not all inclusive; they are merely suggestive. If they are reinforced with directions for teaching presented throughout this chapter the teacher can develop a basic speech curriculum. The activities should be selected in terms of the experiental background of the children in the class, their linguistic development, and their growing interests and needs.

The chart is based on research concerning what to expect of children at various age levels. These are approximations and should be regarded as such. Standards of what to include at each level have been organized, not as infallible guides, but as aids in understanding sequences of linguistic development and appropriate activities.

CONCLUDING STATEMENT

Today's society depends more and more on the spoken word as a means of communication. "Don't write, telephone" is a common axiom. From the time the child is born into a world of words he begins a gradual, complex process of learning to understand and use words to communicate. The increasing importance of speech or oral communication in our world suggests that emphasis be placed on direct teaching of oral communication skills from the time the child enters the kindergarten throughout his educational experience.

Children use speech daily for sharing information, influencing and analyzing ideas and actions, solving problems, and pooling ideas as well as for enjoyment and appreciation. Through oral communication the child shares information so it will be understood readily and remembered by listeners. He combines logic and evidence when he gives a talk. He learns to evaluate what he hears when others are speaking and he develops the skills of communicating with others through appropriate speech behaviour.

Throughout the primary school years he should be provided with experiences which require him to perfect his skills of communication. The manner as well as the content of the speech of his teachers and his peers, the quality of the learning activities in speech, and the opportunities the daily program provides for the development and use of oral communication determine the pattern of speech behaviour which will be the basis for improving his skills in the ensuing years. Whatever his future plans, during much of his life he is involved in improving, extending, and

Speech Development[18]

Aims in Teaching Communications	Language Growth of Children Five to Nine Years Old	Speaking Activities
	IN THE KINDERGARTEN	
To talk fluently about experiences. To listen appreciatively to others.	Fives like to talk. Conversation is ego-centred—pets, hobbies, and arguments. They like to tell what happened at home, on trips.	Conversation about items of interest to the child, such as home activities, family, birthdays, holidays, play activities, weather, pets, trips, visits, new clothes, new experiences.
To use speech as a tool to adjust to social situations. To take advantage of opportunities for developing language through a variety of experiences.	Fives greet friends, say "Please," "Thank you," "I beg your pardon," "Excuse me." They introduce mother or friend, acknowledge introductions, invite visitors to come in.	Greeting each other and strangers. Introducing parents or friends. Serving as hosts or hostesses to mothers or children from other grades. Saying "Thank You," "Please," and other forms of the social amenities. Dictating a letter to the parent who went with the children to the zoo, or to the firemen who showed them around the fire-station, or to a child who is in the hospital.
To listen to stories appreciatively. To tell a short, simple story. To participate in choral speaking of favorite poems. To tell the story ending when the teacher asks them to do this.	Fives like to listen to stories. Some like to read. Children of five can narrate a complete occurrence and repeat a familiar story in sequence.	Listening to the teacher tell and read stories. Listening to the children tell stories. Creating stories and dictating to the teacher. "Reading" the stories from the chart. Repeating with the teacher favorite refrains of nursery rhymes or stories. Retelling a simple story to the group.

Aims in Teaching Communications	Language Growth of Children Five to Nine Years Old	Speaking Activities
		Participating in choral speaking.
To contribute information to the class.	Fives seek information. They ask innumerable questions. Fives are interested in using new, large and colorful words.	Explaining the work accomplished during the work period. Explaining how to do a certain task or how to get to a particular place. Explaining standards of behaviour on trips. Explaining and interpreting the picture painted during the work period. Telling why they did work as they did.
To begin to take part in group planning.	Fives like to make decisions. They exhibit increasing willingness to share and are beginning to be interested in the welfare of others.	Planning the work of the class. Planning the work of small groups. Planning the standards of the group. Planning activities for entertaining parents. Discussing the behaviour of the group during the fire drill or trip.
To express oneself in dramatic play.	Children of five are highly dramatic. They like to imitate adults. Both girls and boys play in the doll house and take the roles of adults. Boys and girls choose the same activities in the kindergarten. Fives are highly imaginative, but some are beginning to distinguish fact from fancy.	Dramatic play in the doll house. Role playing of events such as going to the dentist. Dramatizing stories. Dramatizing nursery rhymes. Using hand or stick puppets to tell nursery rhymes and stories.

Aims in Teaching Communications	Language Growth of Children Five to Nine Years Old	Speaking Activities
	IN THE PRIMARY GRADES	
To talk freely and easily about new experiences. To listen with increasing ability to get other's point of view. To increase fund of ideas through listening to literature, listening to music, looking at and "reading" pictures, taking trips, listening to people who come in to talk to the group.	Children of six, seven, and eight are interested in almost everything. Sixes use language aggressively. Sevens are more introspective. They like to talk about themselves. They are likely to use language to complain. Eights talk a great deal. They tell tales, boast, exaggerate. Some prefer to talk to adults and engage in real social conversation with adults. Nines talk things over with adults.	Conversation about topics of mutual interest or class activities. Relating personal experiences. Talking over the trip on returning from an excursion.
To use the telephone correctly.	Sixes use the telephone with ease. Sevens do considerable phoning. They call home to see about lunch money or after-school plans. They use the phone for helping mother with grocery list. They receive and send messages.	Using the telephone to give and receive invitations. Using the telephone to deliver simple messages. Ordering supplies. Taking simple messages.
To respond easily to simple social situations.	Sixes enjoy offering and receiving hospitality from their peers. Some sevens like to introduce their mothers to their friends. Eights use language fluently. Nines are more cooperative and make plans far in advance, without adult direction.	Giving and receiving invitations. Making introductions. Serving as host and hostess to visitors. Responding to introductions. Greeting guests. Showing visitors around the room. Carrying on an interesting conversation with visitors.

Aims in Teaching Communications	Language Growth of Children Five to Nine Years Old	Speaking Activities
To tell stories for others. To listen appreciatively to stories.	Primary children respond to humor. Primary children can listen to stories for twenty minutes with courtesy and obvious enjoyment. Sixes like legends and fables as well as stories about themselves and the activities of other children. Sevens have wider interests; they are interested in stories about nature, animals, space ships and rockets, children of other countries. They like myths, legends, some fanciful tales, and stories about grown-up occupations. Eights shows interest in primitive cultures. They also are turning to stories of adventure and humor. They still enjoy stories of children, animals, and wee folk. Nines love adventure stories.	Listening to stories read or told by the teacher. Telling stories to the group. Telling stories the children have created. Listening to a story the teacher reads and making up the ending.
To tell an experience. To report an event or activity in an orderly manner. To stick to the main point and develop the point by means of a simple sequence of ideas.	Sixes show a marked interest in construction, transportation, and science. Sevens want to acquire knowledge of natural and social sciences, through excursions, projects, and celebration of holidays. Eights show a greater interest in people of foreign lands and like to read about	Participating in a sharing period. Reporting materials read. Explaining pictures they have painted or colored. Explaining a game or process. Reporting on events, seen or heard. Reporting on individual or group activities.

Aims in Teaching Communications	Language Growth of Children Five to Nine Years Old	Speaking Activities
	strange and distant places. They are extremely interested in nature and science and they have numerous hobbies.	
To read aloud a simple poem or story and share it with the group.	Sixes, sevens, and eights like to read aloud to the group.	Reading a story or poem aloud.
		Reading reports aloud.
	Nines are getting to be avid readers. Some nines also like choral speaking.	Choral speaking with children selecting the poem and deciding on the interpretation.
To select a topic for discussion.	Children cannot plan far in advance.	Planning activities (both of the class as a whole and sub-groups).
To share information by means of group discussion.	Sixes need help in making choices. They should not be confronted with too many alternatives.	
To settle issues through group discussion.	Sevens find it easier to make up their minds but harder to change. They engage in genuine argument in which they put forth reasons in support of the assertions they make.	Planning and preparing for trips and excursions.
		Talking about the trips.
	Sevens are methodical and like to plan their day.	Talking about the benefits gained from the trips.
	Sevens are very critical.	Discussing the work of the members of the class.
	Eights make up their minds easily but they listen to reason and are willing to change their minds.	Evaluating work.
		Settling an issue through group discussion.
	Eights verbalize ideas and concerns. They begin to understand relationships of cause and effect.	

Aims in Teaching Communications	Language Growth of Children Five to Nine Years Old	Speaking Activities
	Eights take criticism if it is sincerely given. They want to improve in what they do. Nines listen to others.	Dramatizing every-day occurrences. Pantomiming. Playing a story or poem with stick or hand puppets.
To engage in dramatic play. To dramatize a story so that the listeners can follow it readily and enjoy it.	Children from six to nine enjoy dressing up and playing appropriate roles, which they not only play but live. Several children will make up a play, work on it by themselves, and present it to the group. Sixes increase in ability to tell fact from fantasy. They like spontaneous dramatic play and creative dramatics, not a formal play. They pretend to be a pony, an airplane or a space ship. For them, a block or piece of furniture can be anything they want it to be. They play school, house, library, grocery store, travelling by boat, train, bus, or plane. Outdoors they choose more active games. Sevens want realism in their play. They play transportation activities, community helpers such as postman, fireman, policeman, grocery man. Outdoor games are active. Girls tend to be dancers and prima donnas; boys tend toward television stars and gun play. Sevens, eights, and nines all enjoy putting	Dramatic play in the room using doll house and later building post offices, florist shops, markets, stations, airports, in the room. Dramatizing puppet plays. Choral speaking.

Aims in Teaching Communications	Language Growth of Children Five to Nine Years Old	Speaking Activities
	on a show or playing a dramatic role. Each age group participates in dramatizing events and activities. They impersonate things and people as well as animals. Nines enjoy dramatization and creative play.	

refining the oral communication skills. Communication is a basic process, profoundly affecting success, not alone in his years in the elementary school, but throughout his life.

Speech as a social and vocational tool contributes to a well rounded development of the individual. The child who learns early not only what to say but how to say it effectively is at a distinct advantage over his associates.

Finally, acceptance or rejection not alone of his ideas but acceptance or rejection of himself by others often depends to a great extent on the impression one makes as he uses the spoken word.

In the written word, in the world of letters, an individual has time to re-write, to re-organize his thinking, to re-structure his thoughts before they are presented to public view. In the spoken word, however, the child must learn through direct teaching the techniques of organizing his thoughts, presenting his ideas, and communicating them to others without having time to re-write, re-structure, or re-organize. In a world of words and letters, learning to communicate effectively is a life-long process which must begin in the preschool and continue throughout life.

REFERENCES

1. By permission from Lillian M. Logan and Virgil G. Logan, *Teaching the Elementary School Child,* Houghton Mifflin Company, Boston, 1961, p. 226.
2. Thorrel B. Fest and Martin T. Cobin, *Speech and the Theatre,* The Center for Applied Research in Education, Inc., Washington, 1964, p. 4.
3. Robert G. Gunderson, "Teaching Critical Thinking," *The Speech Teacher,* 10:100, March, 1961.
4. Donald K. Smith, "What Are the Contemporary Trends in Teaching Speech?" *The Speech Teacher,* 10:89, March, 1961.
5. By permission from *The Field of Speech: It's Purpose and Scope in Education,* The Speech Association of America, Statler Hilton Hotel, New York (Pamphlet).
6. John Von Arnold, "Communication Is More Than Words," *Today's Speech,* 11:15, November, 1963.
7. Donald K. Smith, "What Are the Contemporary Trends in Teaching Speech?" *The Speech Teacher,* 10:90, 91, March, 1961.
8. Marian Monroe Cox, "The Relationship of Speech and Reading in an Elementary School Program," *The Speech Teacher,* 8:213, September, 1959.
9. Mardel Ogilvie, *Speech in the Elementary School,* McGraw-Hill Book Company, Inc., New York, 1954, p. 130.
10. Milton Dickens, *Speech: Dynamic Communication,* 2nd ed., Harcourt, Brace & World, New York, 1963, p. 5.
11. "Fundamentals of Speech: A Basic Course for High Schools," *The Speech Teacher,* 8:96, March, 1959.
12. Flora Rheta Schreiber, "How to Talk to Children," *Today's Speech,* 11:9, April, 1963.
13. *The English Language Arts,* Commission of the English Curriculum of the National Council of Teachers of English, Appleton-Century-Crofts, Inc., New York, 1952, p. 271.

14. Lucile Lindberg, "Oral Language or Else," *Elementary English*, 42:760, December, 1965.
15. William E. Buys, "Speech Curricula for All American Youth," *The Speech Teacher*, 15:25, January, 1966.
16. Mardel Ogilvie, *op. cit.*, p. 173.
17. Andrew Weaver, Gladys Borchers, and Donald Smith, *The Teaching of Speech*, Prentice-Hall, Inc., New York, 1952, p. 284.
18. By permission from Lillian M. Logan, *Teaching the Young Child*, Houghton Mifflin Company, Boston, 1960, pp. 225-232.

7

Teaching the Speech Skills: The Intermediate and Upper Grades

As the child speaks, so will the man.

Anon.

The student who develops to his highest potential in oral communication during his intermediate and upper school years has a distinct advantage over his peers throughout his lifetime. Our future leaders will be found among those who not only have something significant to say, but also have the ability to say it well. Such an attainment does not come automatically. It is the result of a clearly articulated, well organized, and well taught speech curriculum in the intermediate and upper grades. It consists of more than a conglomeration of oral activities which are auxiliary tools in imparting and reinforcing learning experiences in "real" disciplines. It must go beyond the conversation hour, the book report, the occasional panel discussion in the social studies class, the six-weeks oral English unit, or the sporadic choral reading, creative dramatics, orations, and dramatic presentations to get ready for the Speech Festival. "When we sacrifice the development of critical and intellectual skills for practice in telephone talking and conversation, . . . and when, for all our tools of communication we share so few ideas and materials capable of uplifting the quality of . . . speech education, *we* have failed."[1]

If the future needs of society are to be met effectively it is time to prepare teachers who understand the nature of speech and its relationship to children of all ages and abilities and who apply this knowledge, not only in organizing speech activities, but in looking at speech as a discipline worthy of intellectual involvement of the students they teach. It is during the intermediate years that the skills initiated in the primary school demand a curriculum commensurate with the added maturity, increased skills, broadened interests, and greater needs for expression.

SCOPE OF THE SPEECH PROGRAM IN THE INTERMEDIATE AND UPPER GRADES

"Speech, when distinguished from oral English, is concerned with the development of significant skills and techniques. It has its own liberal content and its own responsibility to the language development of students. Development and control of the voice, enunciation, pronunciation, bodily movement, gestures, the planning

133

and organization of speeches, the interpretation of oral literature, pantomime, dramatization, play production, with its many special skills, . . . panel discussion, and the conduct of public meetings are among its peculiar offerings. These are enriched by the great literature of speech."[2]

The importance of total bodily movement was emphasized in a preceding chapter. Development and control of the voice, enunciation, and pronunciation will be dealt with in the next chapter. The oral interpretation of literature both through reading and dramatics will form the central core of the chapter "Appreciating Literature Through Experiencing".

PLANNING AND ORGANIZING SPEECHES

Speech-making is as old as Western Civilization. The Greeks used the term *Rhetoric* basically referring to speaking and oral communication. This usage predominated down to modern times. The organizational pattern of rhetoric was applicable to writing as well as to speaking. And with the development of the modern printing press, the term gradually became applied to written communication almost exclusively. However, recently the term rhetoric is returning to its original connotation of oral communication without losing its implication for written communication as well. For many, thus, rhetoric has a dual meaning and a dual application. For example, organization of material according to purpose, is similar both in speaking and writing. The authors accept I. A. Richards still broader concept of rhetoric: "rhetoric not only as speech but as part of the communication process, whether the person is speaking, listening, writing, or reading to achieve efficient comprehension."[3]

To achieve the aims of speech instruction it is essential that the teacher have a clear understanding of both the theory and practice of public speaking. This includes:

The purpose of speaking before a group
The relationship between the general purposes of speech and the value standards of the individual
Speeches for special occasions
Types of organization of speeches
Organizing a speech effectively
Giving the talk
Evaluating the talk

The Purpose of Speaking Before a Group

There are two kinds of speakers, those who "have something to say" and "those who have to say something". The first has a purpose in speaking, the second merely fulfills an obligation. Too many teachers fail to help the student distinguish between them. Selecting the specific purpose for the speech is an important factor in the effectiveness of the speech. The speaker must also be aware of the general purposes for which people make speeches: to entertain, to inform, to stimulate, to convince, and to actuate.

The speech to entertain has as its sole purpose to get and hold the attention of the audience. Any information that is given is purely incidental. The speech is characterized by humour, spontaneity, excitement, or adventure.

The speech to inform is one of the most widely used purposes. Children spend much time in explaining or giving information which is not already known by the class. This speech is fundamentally one of explanation: how to do something, how to make something and how it works, clarifying plans, relating details of an experience. The speech to inform is basically the simplest for children. However, it requires that the information be given in such a way that it is clearly understood by the audience, that it is interesting as well as informative, that it contains illustrative material as well as facts. Flavouring the facts with humour, with vivid language, and with visual aids lends a refreshing touch to this type of speech.

The speech to stimulate, sometimes known as the speech to inspire, has as its goal arousing interest in doing what the listeners know they should do. The belief already exists, but the urge to do something about it is lacking. This type of speech is more complex than either the speech to entertain or inform. Without both interest and information it fails to stimulate. The speech must be developed on the basis of the needs, wants, hopes, and aspirations of the audience in order to vitalize their behaviour.

The speech to convince has as its purpose changing the attitudes of the listeners who may be indifferent or opposed to the proposal. Not only must the speaker stimulate the listener, he must motivate him to change his attitude or to alter his opinions. He must present evidence to show the logic of his cause. He must give reasons that will help his listeners to change their minds.

The speech to actuate may be the outgrowth of either the speech to stimulate or to convince. Here the group is stimulated to take action. They go out to support the campaign, to vote for the candidate, to sign the petition, to go to the game following the rally, or to participate in the Speech Festival.

Relationships Between the Purpose of Speech and Individual Value Standards

In teaching children to give speeches there are opportunities for helping them change their behaviour through understanding the relationship existing between the basic general objectives of speech and the values of the axiology. "Thus, for example, . . . the values of *well-being, affection,* and *rectitude* are typically nurtured by the speech to *inspire*; those of *respect* and *power* by the speech to *convince*; those of *wealth* and *skill* by the speech to *activate*; and the value of *enlightenment* by the speech to *inform*."[4]

The teacher who is concerned with helping children integrate learning experiences will help them select topics and issues which involve them in questions of value both in preparing for talks they will give and in the group discussions in which they will participate. Thus topics and issues taken from the disciplines of literature, political science, history, art, ethics, will not only help children integrate their learnings but *also* help them make wise choices in the realm of human values. They will better comprehend the definition of Quintilian. "An orator is a good man skilled in speaking". Students can profitably prepare and deliver speeches on great persons in various areas of human endeavor of both the past and the present. "We are equal", says Gerald W. Johnson, "to all that we can understand; and to the extent that we can understand true greatness as it appears in men, and how and why it appears, we have the radiant hope of employing that force to carry us forward, not into a new world, but a new universe of power, beauty, and truth."[5]

Speeches for Special Occasions

"If you become an eloquent and sought-after speaker, there will be times when a whole world of choices lies before you, when you are free to decide whether you want to entertain, inform, persuade or inspire, send your audience away relaxed or on fire for a cause, dazzled by your wit, glowing with complacency, or beating their breasts for their sins. Speaking realistically, however, most of you will speak most of the time under conditions that call for prescribed types of talks. Many of these situations are so rigidly structured that if you master the pattern of an acceptable talk, you can produce a good one nearly every time."[6]

In our society, numerous occasions arise in which one must be prepared to give brief speeches for special occasions both in and out of school. If he has developed the skills he will enjoy these challenges.

The speech of presentation. Frequently awards or trophies are presented to or from a group, and someone is required to make a speech. Such an occasion should be prepared for ahead of time—just in case. It calls for dignity, clarity, and precision. Since there is an audience of some size it is necessary that the audience be able to hear, understand and enjoy the remarks.

A three-part formula for a speech of presentation is:
1. State the occasion for the award and the reason for making it.
2. Tell the major reason or reasons for awarding it to this specific person or group.
3. Express the pleasure of the donors in making this award. This formula is short, simple, and concise. It is possible to treat the three elements simultaneously—not necessarily in a consecutive order. For example the following speech includes all the essentials:

"Each year the Imperial Order of the Daughters of the Empire presents a trophy to the group demonstrating the best performance of a dramatic portrayal of a literary classic. In keeping with the tradition, excellence is understood to involve two factors: creativity and effective communication. This year the award goes to the students in the fourth grade of the Earl Oxford School for their excellent portrayal of 'The Emperor's New Clothes.' Their performance showed creativity, effective communication, and total class involvement. It is with real pleasure that I present this trophy from the local chapter of the IODE to the fourth grade group in Miss——————'s room."

Should one wish to amplify the speech, it would be possible to stress the background or history of the award, the names of previous winners, and the honour which goes with it.

Displaying the award or gift is an added attraction. Describing the gift if it is uniquely appropriate, or if it is a radio presentation is also suggested. Be sure to congratulate the recipient as he steps up to accept the reward. A handshake is appropriate at this point.

The acceptance speech. A speech of acceptance should be short, particularly if the award is unexpected. In such a case a simple "Thank you" expressed clearly and sincerely is more appropriate than a polished, lengthy acceptance speech. If one is really surprised it would seem awkward to give a major address in saying thank you. A simple "Thank you, Madam President—thank you very much", or "Thank you—I appreciate this very much" is sufficient. If however, he was informed about the award beforehand he might extend the speech:

"Thank you, Madam President. To me, the award from the Imperial Order of the Daughters of the Empire is the highest honour a student at—————— could aspire to achieve. It is my sincere hope that I will be worthy of the honour and will do my best to carry out the traditions of those who have won this award in previous years."

The speech of farewell. When a pupil who has been active in a class leaves the vicinity he may be called upon to make a speech of farewell. Another occasion for a speech of this type may be giving up responsibility for some office—club or class president, for example. In either case, the speech should include the expression of:

1. Appreciation for the gift or award, if one has been received
2. Regret over leaving the vicinity or the office
3. Pleasure in the associations of the past year or years
4. Thanks for the cooperation given by classmates or club members
5. Reminiscences of memorable occasions or episodes

The essence of a farewell speech is to express sincere appreciation for having been an integral part of the class, community, or club and to thank them for making it a memorable experience.

The after-dinner speech. Although less frequently needed by elementary school children, there are occasions in the upper elementary grades when an after-dinner speech is demanded. Speakers on such occasions are expected to give a speech that is at once humorous, amusing, provocative, filled with surprise, and delivered with élan.

"The best after-dinner speeches carry a message, communicate an idea, but build up to it gracefully and lightly. The light touch is evident in the very title of the after-dinner speech. It should never be prosy, heavy-handed, and over earnest; such topics as 'The Conquest of Space' or 'Adult Education' need rephrasing to 'Shooting the Moon' or 'Have Books, Will Travel'.[7]

The speech of introduction. The most common speech for special occasions is the speech to introduce. The purpose of a speech of introduction involves (1) setting the stage, (2) preparing the audience for what will be said by the speaker, and (3) establishing a spirit of rapport between the speaker and his audience. The formality, the length of the introduction, and the manner of the presentation are determined by the occasion, the type of program, and the known reputation of the speaker.

A formula for an effective introduction is:

Be brief. The introduction should not detract from the main speaker. Therefore brevity is important. Give the name and office of the speaker clearly and distinctly.

Be relevant. Be sure that the introduction leads into the speech by mentioning the topic to be discussed, and that background of the speaker which is relevant to the speech.

Be provocative. Arouse the interest of the audience in the speaker and/or the speech by giving pertinent and provocative information which:

1. *Gives prominence to the speaker by*:
   (a) telling briefly about the speaker's career
   (b) expressing the honour and pleasure of having him speak to the group
   (c) introducing him with the title of the talk

OR

2. *Gives prominence to the subject by*:
   (a) emphasizing timeliness of the subject
   (b) the achievements of the speaker in this field
   (c) introducing him with the title of the talk

Be sincere in your praise. Your role as a good host is to make the speaker comfortable. Complement, but don't flatter. Over-praise is obnoxious to an effective speaker.

Be conscious of the audience. Don't address your remarks to the speaker. Remember you are talking to the audience about the speaker. When you complete your introduction, turn to the speaker and mention his name.

Be alert to the situation. Remain standing where you are until the speaker acknowledges the introduction, comes forward to the microphone and nods, smiles or gives you a word of thanks. If there is applause, it is proper to join in with it. Then take your seat as quietly as possible.

The mood of the introduction should be appropriate to the occasion. Like all good speeches of introduction, it gets the attention of the audience, brings speaker and audience together, and leads directly into the subject. Funny stories are incongruous as a prelude to a serious speech. The reverse is also true.

The nomination. With the early interest in politics at all levels, especially in class organization, it is essential that children be taught early the correct form for making a nomination speech. The nominating speech is a specialized form of praise or eulogy, a eulogy with a specific, practical design, and immediate purpose. It may vary in length from the short impromptu speech which is made on the spur of the moment to a distinctive oration, polished to the last pause. A formula for an effective nomination speech includes: specific qualifications of the candidate for the office: (1) the character, personality, education, background, and experience which fits him for the office under consideration, (2) the need of the class, the community and/or the country for an individual of such accomplishments, personality, and spirit, (3) the willingness of the individual to be considered for such an auspicious position, (4) a positive statement attesting to the support of the candidate for the office.

Types of Organization of Speeches

Speeches in the elementary school may be organized on any of the following patterns: chronological (time sequence), spatial (space or location sequence), causal relations (effect and cause), need and plan, personal experience, order-of-importance sequence, string-of-beads, and topical.

Chronological. The chronological pattern is one of the simplest for the elementary school child. He arranges ideas or events in the time order in which they happened. It is useful in describing a vacation trip by telling what happened every day. It is especially successful in topics focusing on history, biography, travel, and adventure. In a report on the founding and development of a province, the student would begin with the early explorers and follow through in sequential order with selected significant events. In planning a speech on the biography of an individual one could organize it according to the early years, the middle years, and the sunset years.

Spatial. In the spatial organization the child has several choices. Spatial refers to the division that can be made within any given area of space; from north to south, from left to right, from back to front, from bottom to top. Space-sequence helps in describing a place, talking about geographical subjects, or location of objects. The child tells what he sees step by step. If he is describing his school he will start with the view when he turns the corner and sees it, then the close-up description of the grounds, the entrance to the building, the hall leading to his room, and the sequence as he goes to his desk. He may wish to describe the school in terms of (bottom to top) first floor, second floor, third floor. Or he could use spatial order to describe only his classroom. He could begin at the left side of the room and proceed with all the items from left to right. The spatial pattern is an excellent way to organize a speech to inform.

Cause and effect (or logical order). This is commonly used for organizing a speech to persuade. The central idea is stated first and then the speaker proceeds to prove it. "The central idea is supported by two or more main points, each of which in turn may be supported by two or more sub-ideas. Each main heading, therefore, ends with the word 'because', and all subheads are reasons for the main heads above them."[8] In this organization the student examines the causes to see what logical effect may be expected.

In the Cause and Effect pattern, commonly used in persuasive speech, the student states the problem, (the effect) and then goes on to tell the various causes that he has found leading up to it. In arguments from effect to cause the conclusion shows an observed phenomenon was caused by certain other observed facts or events. An example of effect to cause: The present difficulties of the party in power are due to unsuccessful attempts in the last campaign to purge the party of certain individuals who were opposed to policies to strengthen the federal government.

The need and plan. This speech is excellent for the elementary school child at every level. Children frequently give this type of speech without being conscious of making a speech. A classic example is the annual picnic. Here is a need—a felt need. The need is explained, a picnic. The class makes plans designed to make the picnic a success. Johnny has investigated the situation early. He remembers the last picnic when it rained. This time he wants it in the park close to the school. He uses the need (the picnic) and the plan (where to have it) as his type of organization. This development is used for the speech to inform, stimulate, or convince.

The personal experience. This speech forms an excellent basis for informal speeches. It is appropriate for the young child as he relates experiences he has had in the home, on trips, shopping, or sight-seeing in the community. To entertain or inform is the purpose of the speech which is used as a stepping stone to speeches of more complex organizational patterns appropriate for older children. However, for children in the intermediate grades transferring from schools where they have had little or no formal speech activities the *personal experience speech* is a good one to help them get their bearings in a public-speaking situation.

Order-of-importance. The order-of-importance speech pattern is helpful to the student who chooses to speak about things in terms of priority. In progressing from the least important to the most important, or starting with the most important and going to the least is an interesting way to organize a speech. For example, in discussing favourite hobbies, if collecting rocks was the least important a speaker should start here, go on to creative dramatics, playing the accordion, and finishing with his favourite—building model trains. In discussing the cities in a province one could take Manitoba and go from the largest—Greater Winnipeg, down through Brandon, Portage la Prairie, Flin Flon, Dauphin.

The "string-of-beads". This is a favourite with the new-comer to the speech program as well as to the younger child. It consists of a series of incidents or stories tied together or related to a single theme—the "string" on which the beads are strung. If the string (or theme) on which the beads are strung is thin the speech will fail to be effective. If it is a strong one it makes an excellent speech to entertain or interest an audience.

The visual aid or demonstration speech. This speech gives the child a perfect setting for demonstrating how the toy he received at Christmas works, whether a simple or complicated mechanism or principle operates it. He can show step by step how to make a puppet, a theatre. He can point out on the map the route the family took to the Orient and relate details of the trip. He can demonstrate how to use a back-hand drive in tennis, demonstrate the stance for putting in golf, and how to block a goal in hockey. This, too, makes a good speech to inform or to entertain. Although the speech to demonstrate is a pattern within itself, it does not preclude the use of visual aids in the other speech patterns.

Topical. The topical organization is useful for the speech that does not seem to fit any of the other classifications. For instance, in explaining how a combustion engine works the speaker would explain the functions of the various parts, carburetor, spark plugs, and so on. A Home Economics student might explain the principles involved in redecorating her room.

Organizing the Speech

The traditional method of organizing a speech is: the introduction, body and conclusion. Monroe, however, has taken a different approach to this task in the development of a speech organization based on the "motivated sequence". He focuses on the reaction of the audience to the speech whereas the traditional organization focuses on the speech itself. It is his belief that the impact of a speech will be greater if the student plans in advance how to direct the audience's attention to the subject at the beginning and how to maintain that attention throughout the entire speech. States Monroe, " . . . The speech must be built with the specific audience always in mind, and the structure of the speech must conform to the thinking process of the listener. To do otherwise is as foolish as trying to make a man fit a suit."[9]

A speech structure to motivate audience response. "In daily conversation most of us speak to get a certain response from our hearer. We may shout 'Hey!' simply to get a friend's attention, we may tell him that he needs a haircut, or we may ask him to help us with our work. In each case we had an objective in mind, one that we tried to reach by speaking.

The public speaker also seeks a definite response when he faces an audience. Because public speaking situations are generally more complex and formal than private conversations, however, he must organize and construct his speech beforehand so that it will have the best chance of achieving his purpose. The motivated sequence is a method to help him do this successfully."[10]

The popularity of this motivated sequence is attested to by thousands and thousands of students who have been introduced successfully to the experience of speaking to motivate audience response through this method.

The five steps which make up the complete motivated sequence form a basic plan which is applicable to almost all types of public speech and can be modified to fit the general purpose of a particular talk.

Step I   Attention
Step II   Need
Step III Satisfaction
Step IV   Visualization
Step V   Action

In the elementary school a modified motivated sequence is sufficient to meet the requirements for most speeches; in the chart which follows the role of each step in getting an audience response is clearly evident.

The Motivated Sequence Applied to Entertaining Speeches[11]

STEP	FUNCTION	AUDIENCE RESPONSE
1. Attention Step	Getting attention and re-taining interest through entertainment	"I want to listen, and I'll continue listening because I'm enjoying myself."

The speech to entertain consists entirely of an expanded attention step. The other four steps are omitted.

The Motivated Sequence Applied to Informative Speeches[12]

STEP	FUNCTION	AUDIENCE RESPONSE
1. Attention Step	Getting attention	"I want to listen"
2. Need Step	Demonstrating the need to know	"I need information on this subject".
3. Satisfaction Step	Presenting the information itself.	"The information being presented helps me under-stand the subject more sat-isfactorily."

The speech to inform requires only the first three steps in order to achieve its purpose. In fact only when the purpose of the speech is to *stimulate,* to *convince* or to *actuate* are all five steps used.

The Motivated Sequence Applied to Persuasive Speeches[13]
(. . . to stimulate, to convince, to actuate.)

STEP	FUNCTION	AUDIENCE RESPONSE
1. Attention Step	Getting attention	"I want to listen"
2. Need Step	Showing the need: describing the problem	"Something needs to be done (decided or felt)."
3. Satisfaction Step	Satisfying the need: presenting the solution	"This is what to do (believe, or feel) to satisfy the need."
4. Visualization Step	Visualizing the result	"I can see myself enjoying the satisfaction of doing (believing, or feeling) this."
5. Action Step	Requesting action or approval	"I will do (believe, or feel) this".

From the above charts it is evident that each step of the motivated sequence has a particular function to perform in stimulating audience response. The ideas and supporting material included in each step therefore must contribute to the achievement of the purpose of that step.

Developing the Speech

Once the student has decided upon the pattern of organization he wishes to use for his speech he is ready go about organizing the speech itself. Although the introduction of the speech is presented first, it should be planned last. The *body* of the speech should be planned first. He decides upon the main point or points of the speech and then finds supporting materials to reinforce these points. The purpose of supporting materials is to develop the main points by using explanations, illustrations, examples, statistics, authority, and quotations.

The difference between dull, dry, disorganized speeches and sparkling, stimulating, and sagacious speeches often lies in the development of the main ideas. It is not enough to simply state the main and subordinate points in a speech (a fault common to the novice). The speaker needs supporting materials—illustrations, examples, statistics, quotations. Supporting materials develop the main and subordinate points in the speech.

Supporting Materials

A speech with only main points is very much like a skeleton with no flesh. Although the skeleton is necessary, it lacks grace and beauty. The supporting materials give the clarity, the beauty, the logic that the main points need to make the speech acceptable. Among the most used types of supporting material are:

explanation, illustration, examples, statistics, documentation, testimony, and comparison.

Explanation. Explanation as a type of supporting material consists chiefly in reiterating, discussing, and extending the main points, saying them in different words, going into greater detail, and amplifying the original concepts. By observing the audience closely it is possible to tell when it gets the point and clearly understands what you are saying.

Illustrations. An illustration is an elaborated incident with enough detail to make it clearer and interesting. Illustrations may be factual or hypothetical, which ever is needed to get the point across to the audience.

Examples. Examples are sometimes called specific instances. They differ from illustrations in the fact that they are merely mentioned, but not elaborated. The examples should be familiar to the listeners so that they may fill in the details. At times the speaker may prefer to give many examples rather than a few illustrations.

Statistics. It is true that statistics can be boring to an audience. They need not be. Used with discrimination, they aid greatly in supporting a point. The speaker should be accurate in his use of figures. If possible, they should be placed on a chalk board or projected with an overhead projector. If charts are used, they should be large enough to be easily read.

Documentation. Documentation is a vital form of supporting material in many speeches. Library facilities, journals, magazines, as well as encyclopedias and books are essential if students are to give evidence which is authoritative and authentic. Quoting from authorities in the field lends support and credence to the ideas presented. In quoting documentary evidence, it is necessary to give credit for the quotation. The source, book, journal, magazine, or other, should be cited with the correct date and page number if possible.

Testimony. Testimony is evidence based on an individual's reputation. Unfortunately, the reputation is often gained in a field far removed from the area of concern. Hockey players, for instance, are seldom nutritional experts. When the person whose testimony is quoted is noted in the field in which he gives testimony the effect is usually convincing to the listening audience.

Comparison. Comparison points out the similarities between what is already known or believed and that which is not. Sometimes the comparison is literal, but equally effective may be a figurative comparison. Comparisons are weak as proof because of the many factors which may be different in the items compared. They may show a high degree of probability, however.

Developing the Speech

In developing a speech and getting ideas organized the following sequence will facilitate the task. Because speeches should in the early stages reflect the interests of the speaker:

Start with the knowledge the speaker already has
Get information from people conversant with the topic
Make use of personal observation
Read widely to broaden knowledge

In helping a child prepare a speech it is very important that the child should begin with what he knows. This is the reason the speeches that deal with personal experiences are effective in helping beginners express their ideas vividly, interestingly, and effectively. The child should be encouraged to go back into the halls of memory and try to recall experiences, bringing to mind examples, observations, and specific instances which will put life into the speech; which will clothe the skeletal frame with flesh and blood and make it come alive. This is only the first step.

The speaker must be helped to go beyond his limited knowledge. He should extend his knowledge by talking with others about the topic and getting other viewpoints. He may get this information through conversation, discussion, interviewing, and critical listening.

In addition, the speaker makes use of personal observation to gain greater insight and understanding of the problem. Finally, he must read widely to verify the tentative conclusions he has reached based on the previous knowledge, interviews, and observations. As he finds interesting, relevant material for developing his main ideas he should take notes in such a manner that the material is readily accessible. This involves careful documentation in the notes so he can quote with authority, secure in the knowledge that he can give the source. He should plan to have more information than needed to give the speech. Then he will be able to organize the information in such a way that he can discard irrelevant material.

Streeter suggests a practical seven-step sequence for preparing a speech.[14]

a. *Subject.* Select the subject

b. *Central thought.* First decide on the general purpose for your speech. Then work out your specific purpose and phrase it into a carefully worded central thought.

c. *Material.* Divide your central thought into two or three main points. Select interesting material to develop these points. Try to have at least two of the different kinds of supporting material in your speech: statistics, illustrations, examples, quotations, explanations, authority, testimony, and so on.

d. *Speaker's notes.* Prepare your notes for the body of the speech. . . do not plan to take your full outline to the speaker's stand for this speech. Use "Speaker's Notes". (5" × 8" cards)

e. *Conclusion.* Plan your introduction now that you know what you have to introduce.

f. *Practice.* Rehearse the speech many times.

Giving the Talk

"Isn't it peculiar that the human brain begins to function from the moment you are born, improves as you grow older, then stops completely when you stand up to talk?" This oft-quoted saying, loved by after dinner speakers, all too well expresses the feeling all of us have had in the first few moments of facing an audience.

Organization alone is not sufficient. Effective speaking is not automatic. Aristotle expressed this concept when he wrote, "It is not enough to know what to say, but it is necessary to know how to say it." Knowing how to say it, or giving the talk in a manner that the speaker communicates effectively, and the audience responds favourably, can be facilitated through a three dimensional approach.

The oral dimension. The oral dimension is concerned with the voice. The inexperienced speaker tends to speak without expression. He needs to cultivate variety, not for the sake of variety, but to give meaning to his ideas. Variety is obtained by varying the force of the voice, the pitch of the voice, the quality of the voice, the rate of speaking, and the total design in which these elements are combined to give emphasis to words, variety to the voice, and conviction to the concepts.

The visual dimension. Every speaker gives two speeches simultaneously—one with his voice and one with his body. Nowhere is the truism, "Actions speak louder than words," more self-evident than in the delivery of a speech. The listener may ignore the words and concentrate on the actions. Therefore the speaker must be sure that the speech in action corresponds with the speech in word.

In terms of the visual dimension of the speech, the speaker must be aware of the importance of eye contact, facial expression, gestures, movement, and posture.

The psychological dimension. This is one of the most fascinating dimensions of giving a speech. It deals with the psychological elements within the speaker which determine the attitude of the audience toward what he has to say. While one is speaking the audience is evaluating the person as much as the words he utters and the gestures he uses. As Irwin expresses it, "You must deliver *yourself* in an effective manner if you expect your ideas to arrive in perfect condition. How well you succeed depends upon your attitude."[15]

Some guidelines Irwin suggests for evoking response are: (a) be sincere, (b) be poised, (c) be friendly, (d) be positive, and (e) be forceful. Although these are self-explanatory, yet how often do we see speakers who fail to get their ideas accepted, not because the ideas are worthless, but because they lack the personal qualities that combine to make the speaker effective. Some speakers inspire confidence through their ethical appeal, some through their poise and self-assurance. Others are accepted immediately because of their friendliness. "A smile will go a long, long way" is the title of an old favourite song, not because of an outstanding melodic line or words of high literary quality, but because of the veracity of the statement. A genial personality is an asset not only in salesmanship, but in any speaking situation. In an ideal situation positiveness should go hand in hand with sincerity. The definition of the orator as a good man speaking implies that truth, sincerity, and positive belief are companions.

If for no other reason than keeping the audience awake the admonition to be forceful is worthwhile. At a Speech Festival listen to the same oration delivered by different speakers. Who gets the attentive listening, the response, the thunderous applause? The person who is listless, disinterested, and dull? Delivering a speech in a dynamic manner requires energy, strength, and power.

Methods of Delivery

The question "What method of delivery should be used—the impromptu, the extemporaneous, the memorized, or reading from manuscript—frequently arises. The answer depends upon the occasion and the purpose of the speech. The four differ primarily in the manner of delivery.

The extemporaneous method. Most successful speakers use the extemporaneous method. The method calls for thorough research, completely outlined, and rehearsed from the outline. At no two rehearsals is the attempt made to use exactly the same wording. The advantage of the extemporaneous method is that only the outline is memorized and allows for spontaneity in delivery, flexibility in adapting to audience, and to time limit. The outline is used to fix the sequence of ideas firmly in mind. Thus delivery has the advantage of being polished without being stilted or disorganized.

Speeches which lend themselves readily to this method include anecdotes, explanations using visual aids, informative talks, and in fact, all except the most formal of speeches. The elementary school child is unlikely to have an occasion when the extemporaneous method is unsuitable.

Reading from manuscript. A second method is that of reading from a manuscript. The speech has been written out verbatim. The disadvantage of this method of delivery is that few students can communicate with the audience effectively. Concentrating on the reading usually blocks audience contact. The danger of a monotonous, dull, uninspiring delivery is ever present in this method. Only a skilful reader is likely to use sufficient emphasis and vocal variety to give life to his ideas. Most readers sound as though they are reading a speech (which they are) instead of communicating with the audience.

Only on occasions where a slip of the tongue could bring dire consequences, or serious misunderstanding, or where time limits must be observed, such as in television or radio, is it wise to use this technique. Even then, the attempt should be made to adopt a conversational rather than a reading delivery.

The memorized speech. Here the speech is not only written out but it is committed to memory. The method of memorization is a risky one. In case memory fails, the speaker is embarrased and builds up a block against speaking in public. Even where the memory is a servant rather than a master, the fear of forgetting places a strain on the speaker which detracts from the effectiveness of the delivery, and a strain on the audience as they empathize with the reciter. Too often the result is a stilted, inflexible, and artificial presentation. This is not an advisable method for the elementary or secondary school pupil.

The impromptu method. The impromptu method is characterized by lack of formal preparation. The student has to rely on his general knowledge and skill; the ability to speak impromptu has little value except in an emergency. Speaking on the spur of the moment, speaking "off the cuff", speaking from "the top of the head", is disastrous for all except the most experienced speakers, and even these did not acquire their skill from this method. The impromptu method has no place in an educational program.

Evaluation

Evaluation should include both teacher and self evaluation. Unless pupils understand the specific areas in which they are evaluated it is difficult if not impossible for them to develop skill in self-evaluation. The ability to improve in any of the linguistic skills is influenced by a knowledge of the specific points which are to be evaluated.

A rating scale which is clear about the weaknesses pupils need to overcome in developing communication skills is helpful both to the teacher and the pupil. Such a scale enables the teacher to check frequently recurring weaknesses in student speaking. Detecting the specific weakness of the pupil is more difficult for the average individual than to give a generalized statement of approval or disapproval of the speech. With a minimum amount of effort the teacher can indicate to the student his weakness or weaknesses.

In the rating scale opposite the scale from 1 - 5 makes rating simple. Space is given for brief comments which should emphasize the strong points of the speaker. Of special significance is the fact that the negative qualities listed in the rating scale have been found to distinguish good from poor speakers; scales of this type are especially helpful to teachers who are trying to help every pupil develop at least minimal powers in oral communication. Simplicity, comprehensiveness, and utility are the characteristics which make such a device of inestimable value to the classroom or the special language arts teacher.

TEACHING GROUP DISCUSSION IN THE ELEMENTARY CLASSROOM

"I was going to say something, but somebody else made another comment, then I was afraid my idea was too late."

"Ed Page and Mary Farmer and some of the other kids talk so easily that I don't feel I can keep up with them . . . so I don't try."

Comments such as these are less frequent when the teacher is aware of the values, the types, and the methods of teaching group discussion. With such a teacher it becomes a vital part of the school curriculum—not alone in language arts, but in other curriculum areas as well.

Rating Scale for Giving a Talk

Name		Date
Subject of Talk		Grade

CRITERIA FOR EVALUATION	RATE 1—5	COMMENTS

Attitude of Speaker   Rating

Indifferent	Apologetic
Tense	Antagonistic
Flustered	Artificial

Bodily Action   Rating

Random Movements	Weak
Slovenly posture	Monotonous
Exaggerated gestures	Unmotivated

Voice and Articulation   Rating

Weak	Loud
Monotonous	Indistinct
Poor quality	Poor articulation
Non-Rhythmic	
Poor pitch	Dialect

Language Usage   Rating

Slang	Stilted
Incorrect Usage	Inexpressive
Ambiguous	Limited vocabulary

Content   Rating

Lacks clarity	Inaccurate
Insignificant	Lacks imagination
Dull	Lacks unity
Limited material	Lacks coherence

Organization   Rating

Lacks purpose	Insufficient supporting
Poor introduction	material
Central thought	Weak transitions
not clear	Sequence not clear
	Weak conclusion

Projection to audience   Rating

Eye contact	Gestures
Facial Expression	Communicates

Audience Response   Rating

Fails to get attention	Fails to get confidence
Fails to maintain interest	Ignores audience
Fails to consider audience	Avoids audience analysis

General Effectiveness   *Total Rating*

Values of Group Discussion

Two closely related values of discussion are the development of critical and creative thinking. Learning to write or speak is essentially the process of learning to think. Thus contrary to the popular stereotype, rhetoric is not the art of saying nothing well; it involves finding, organizing, phrasing, and presenting information and ideas. Depending upon the capacity of the speaker, oral communication can be creative in the best sense of that term, or it can degenerate into banality. President Nathan M. Pusey of Harvard says that the job of the schools is "to educate free, independent, and vigorous minds, capable of analyzing events, of exercising judgment, of distinguishing facts from propaganda, and truth from half-truth and lies".[16]

Although critical and creative thinking may be applied in any of the areas of the curriculum, it is in the language arts that it is taught as a specific process. This can be achieved in the classrooms through providing more activities in oral communication analagous to those students will meet in modern society. Greater emphasis should be placed on problem solving, research techniques, and methods of enquiry; not as ends in themselves but as means for enabling students to search for new facts, to discover how to use those he already possesses, and to relate his own experience to problems he attempts to solve. We need to provide him with the problems which demand critical and creative thinking. This in turn requires the knowledge and skills necessary for their solution. "Experimental studies have demonstrated that critical thinking can be encouraged by constant reference to errors in reasoning".[17]

Brown and Pruis attest to the values of discussion. "Discussion ought to be one of the teacher's most effective devices. It adds variety to classroom activity, and it gives students a sense of belonging, a stake in the class. At a more important level, discussion forces students to use their knowledge and ideas and thus to test and exercise their thinking powers. Class discussion brings out, as no other means can, the wide range of attitudes and interpretations that exist on most subjects. Under proper direction, discussion teaches open-mindedness, and appreciation of other people's views. In short, discussion is a legitimate teaching device when the objective is to develop or test the student's ability to apply information, to learn from other students, or to appreciate a multiplicity of judgments."[18]

TYPES OF DISCUSSION

The classroom teacher should keep in mind that there are two purposes for discussion—one an informal searching for information and the pooling of ideas, and the other, the more formal, structured problem-solving techniques. Both have their place and should be widely used in all classrooms.

Informal Discussion

The classroom that is organized on the basis of a miniature democratic society has a built-in motivation for discussion and problem solving techniques. "The democratic society is made up of individuals; it is also made up of groups. Such a society functions best when its parts mesh together, when agreement can be reached on common goals, and cooperation can be sustained in striving toward the achievement of these goals. [Speech] education plays its part in improving the functioning of both individuals and groups . . . the school, as a formalized institution of education, must provide ample opportunities for the development of individuals within a group setting. Not only individual opportunity, but cooperative experience in group projects allows the individual to emerge, well-rounded and attuned to the fulfillment of his own needs and those of society."[19]

Many of the problems that arise in day-by-day living in the classroom can find their solution through the group discussion process under the guidance of a teacher who is concerned with helping children develop skill in critical thinking, reasoning, and problem-solving. The following account of an informal procedure shows how a group and teacher function in talking over common problems:

> Getting out "The Mission Star", the sixth grade classroom newspaper in a school in San Bernardino County, California, was the task at hand. In the left-hand column is an account of what was said and done when the group gathered to evaluate and plan after a 40 minute work session. In the column to the right are comments about the groups. Considerable restraint was exercised by the author when he refrained from comment in this column about the teacher's development of direct and concomitant learnings in skills and content. Since the intent of this piece is to study the teacher's utilization of group forces, comments are focused upon the group with special emphasis upon the teacher's leadership function.

DISCUSSION	COMMENTS ON PROCEDURE
Teacher: During our planning periods many important and special problems and plans were discussed. Perhaps others have arisen?	The class is a group and a combination of groups. Each individual is also a member of one or more subgroups.
Murray: I had some real help today. Brownie and Ricky met with the city editor and reporter of the primary page. Did everything work out okay, Brownie?	
Brownie: Fay can tell you about the meeting she had about the drawing on the primary page.	
Fay: Well, we had the meeting, but only three reporters came. Still, we decided on something.	Duties and responsibilities of members must be decided upon.
Teacher: Do you remember that Penny	

suggested that everyone should have an opportunity to come?

Fay: No editors came!

Teacher: Let's consider the matter briefly. Why, in your opinion, was it possible for the reporters to come and not for the editors?

Rose: The reporters were interested.

Judy: Well, we could come too, because we didn't have to go out on assignments.

Penny: All the editors were very busy, and probably couldn't leave their work.

Teacher: One of the reasons for the success of our paper has been the sharing of responsibility. Our policies may be determined by the large group but often a few can help make other decisions. Fay, what was the decision of your group?

Fay: We decided we had enough stories to fill up all but one-fourth of our primary page. We can put Larry's drawing in that space.

George: That's still too much for a drawing.

Teacher: Why will we not be able to accept any more suggestions for this page?

John: The meeting for the suggestions is over.

Teacher: We shall say, then, that the editor of our primary page is reporting the final suggestions.

Ricky: Fay may be little, but she is sure stubborn.

Teacher: Is it necessary to be stubborn at times? When is it necessary?

Murray: In the city editor's case!

Penny: I'll say! He can't always let people do what they want or our paper wouldn't meet the deadline. Also, I think, Fay knows what little children would like about drawing for the primary page. She talked to the primary teachers.

Teacher: Sometimes people think of stubborn behavior as bad behavior, but synonyms for the word are: determined, persistent, and tenacious, as well as holding firmly. If one believes in certain principles

The teacher helps the group to understand its members.

To be successful, groups set policies by which they are guided.

To achieve goals, channels of communication are left open.

Group activities foster cohesion.
Difficulties can be dealt with as a problem for the group.

The teacher leads the group towards an understanding of the deviate.

or ideas, it is often necessary to be determined or tenacious. Other times it is necessary to compromise, or adjust our ideas in order to work out plans together. Our evaluation and planning periods often require us to be persistent, or to compromise. Incidentally, how would you explain the meaning of evaluation?

Carolyn: Our evaluation period usually involves a problem and how we worked it out, or sometimes we sum up our progress, and what we did.

George: We look over what else is needed.

Babs: We always talk over our work and how good it is, or how we could do better.

> The teacher guides the members of the group in an evaluation of their work.

Teacher: Your understanding is excellent. Were there evidences that other things were needed in today's work period?

> The teacher asks for, and gets, an additional problem.

Ricky: Mrs. Allyn's husband is being transferred to Pasadena. She's leaving; so is Mr. Aring (secretary and gardener).

Teacher: How we shall miss them! What is significant also about this in relation to "The Mission Star"?

Sue: Mrs. Allyn has always helped us so much. She showed us how to type correctly.

Carolyn: And she's our librarian.

Carl: When I cut my forehead she fixed me up.

> Some irrelevancies arise before attention is applied to the problem facing the group.

Margie: We couldn't list all the things she has done for us; it would take all day.

Murray: Couldn't we put something in the paper to show our appreciation?

Lynette: I think we could make a manuscript in appreciation. She'd like that. (This sixth grade had made illuminated manuscripts as an industrial arts activity related to their social studies experience—Modern Press and the History of Records. They were very proud of them and enjoyed decorating them in the style of the monks of the middle ages.)

Rose: Let's ask Larry to paint the one for Mrs. Allyn.

Babs: And Margie could do the manuscript printing.

> Informal planning.
> Group agreements without need for voting.

Teacher: How about writing a cooperative note of appreciation during the Language Arts period today—in addition to the manuscript? (The class approved this plan.) Carolyn, what was the outcome of the work period regarding the editorial page?

Carolyn: Babs, Judy and I got our ideas worked out for the second page. We can start typing the master copy pretty soon. On the overflow page we have our appreciation to the custodians and Miss Kims' third grade poetry. George also wants some of his sports news on this page.

Subgroups permit interaction not otherwise possible.

Teacher: Do you think the problem would have been solved in this way on a large city newspaper? Would a sports item be carried over to an editorial page?

Teacher helps group to clarify its problems.

Leroy: Well, big newspapers have several pages for sports.

Teacher: Can anyone define the biggest difference between a school newspaper and a city newspaper?

Danny: Most big papers have lots of pages.

Penny: That's because they use A.P., I.P., and U.P. news coverage.

Teacher writes on board:

> School Newspaper
> small
> school news
> > City Newspaper
> large, many pages
> local news, and A.P., I.P.,
> and U.P. coverage

An occasional summary helps the group to solve its problem.

Susan: The city paper is out for profit; we're a nonprofit paper.

Teacher: Would you amplify, or extend your statement, Susan? What is the meaning of non-profit?

Clarification of terms helps communication among group members.

Susan: Well, we're not making money with "The Mission Star" because we don't charge for it. (Teacher adds profit and non-profit to the list on the chalkboard.)

Teacher: There are many other differences between our school paper and a city paper. If you think of more later, we'll add to our list. Were any other problems solved?

LeRoy: When I was running the galley-proof press, I noticed a word I thought was spelled wrong. I couldn't figure out what it was, but I just thought it was wrong. Connie helped me find out what was wrong.

Teacher: You're a fine printer, LeRoy, to recognize the need for a copyreader's help. Is it a good idea to think there may be need for improvement in one's work?

John: Yes, we should look into the matter.

Teacher: Margie, did you work out a solution to your story about the manuscripts?

Margie: I read over Ramona's story about the manuscripts, too. I think it is clearer than mine, so if we need any story to fill in, we might use hers.

The group learns to be task-centered in decision making.

Murray: Why not read both stories so we can decide, Margie? (Margie reads both stories.)

Penny: Both of the stories are very good, and they have excellent information. Perhaps we can use them both.

Carolyn: Margie tells about the decorating and writing, and Ramona tells about the making of inks and colors.

Teacher: Does anyone have an opinion on how both stories may be used in our paper? Connie, you read both stories carefully as a copyreader. What do you think?

Teacher helps group draw out and develop potentials of members.

Connie: Maybe they could be put together to make one article.

Joey: Then Margie and Ramona could both be the writers of the story.

The group often helps its members attain goals which they could not achieve otherwise.

Murray: Couldn't Alan put the stories together? He's our rewrite man.

Teacher: Alan, what is your opinion?

Alan: They'd make a very good article; I'll do the rewriting.

Teacher: Another reason for the success of the Star is your ability to accept suggestions and figure out, or analyze the situation. Sometimes 11- and 12-year-olds do this better than many adults. Are there any other questions and suggestions?

Encouragement strengthens the group.

Desire for group approval leads to high standards of workmanship. Cooperation among members strengthens the group. Teacher's praise encourages group members and helps set group standards.

This session with the staff of "The Mission Star" obviously does not illustrate all the factors of group structure and function. Just as obviously, another teacher might have taught the lesson differently, but the fact remains that "The Mission

Star" group did illustrate a few important ideas about how groups can function effectively. The manner in which the teacher encouraged, helped and challenged the group may be worth special attention. Without knowing the group better, it is difficult to know whether the teacher offered too many opinions or made too many judgements. Perhaps the leadership might have come more from group members in a group that had worked together successfully over a longer period. By the same token, a group with less experience in group work might have needed even more teacher direction than was given here. How would you have done it?[20]

Formal Discussion

Although all discussion occurs in face-to-face situations, the formal discussion is more highly structured, both in format and techniques. The formal discussion usually has a leader who has the responsibility of guiding the discussion toward predetermined goals.

Discussion seeks to accomplish any or all of the following purposes: locating and defining the problem, analyzing the problem, exploring possible solutions, and in some instances reaching a single or preferred solution.

Formal discussion normally has one of three purposes, to investigate facts, to analyze problems, and to formulate solutions.

Among the most commonly used types of formal discussion are:

The committee. The committee is a selected group of individuals appointed to carry out specific functions. The leader presents the problem and guides the group in seeking a solution. The secretary or recorder takes notes on what is said and later presents a summary to the group for their consideration. The committee has become an integral part of democratic living. Students who have learned to accept responsibility for the various committee functions will have a decided advantage throughout their educational and professional careers.

The panel. The panel is a situation in which four to eight *informed* individuals are chosen to represent various viewpoints of the group. They should be "specialists" in specific phases of the problem, and carry on a conversational discussion before an audience. After careful research (reading, interviewing, and studying), they discuss the problem under the leadership of a moderator. No one presents a set speech. A panel is a give-and-take situation in which no one monopolizes. If possible, the group meets ahead of time for a planning session in which they decide on the scope of the discussion, definition of terms, the points of view, and a time budget. Panels are frequently used in classrooms, for the culmination of units, in Home and School, and in school assemblies.

Dialogue. The dialogue as a term applied to discussion is fairly recent. It is a conversation between two people in the presence of an audience. One person, usually designated as the chairman, questions a second person, usually designated as the respondent, in order to seek information which an audience may need or want. It is essential to the success of this form of discussion that the respondent be an expert in the specific area under discussion. The responsibility of the chairman is to understand what the audience wants to know, and to be able to phrase his questions effectively and appropriately to elicit this information.

The dialogue differs from the interview in that the dialogue takes place before an audience, making the information immediately accessible. Following the dialogue, the audience may direct questions to one or both of the participants.

The round table. The most commonly used type of discussion in the classroom is the round table. Children and teacher work together to solve a particular problem. Together they define, analyze, and attempt to reach conclusions. The round table discussion involves the entire classroom under the direction of a leader. In the early grades or in the initial experiences in the higher grades the teacher should be the leader.

The symposium. In the symposium, three to six students give *prepared* talks on various aspects of a problem. Each speaker is an *expert* in his phase of the problem, is specifically prepared, and gives a set speech. The speaking time for each participant as well as the total time alloted for the symposium must be predetermined and strictly adhered to. The length of each speech should be planned in terms of the number participating. Ten to fifteen minutes is the customary length. Each person presents a different point of view, or aspects of the problem. It should be determined in the preplanning that each speaker contributes to the clarification of the problem as a whole. The chairman makes the necessary transitions and correlations, and conducts the question and answer period.

The forum. The unique feature of the forum, whether presented alone or in combination with other discussion methods, is the role the audience plays. The forum may be combined with the panel, dialogue, symposium, lecture, or film as a means of involving the audience in participation.

The chairman or moderator presides, directs the questions from the audience to the various members of the panel, the symposium, or to the person being questioned in a dialogue. He makes transitional remarks. The functions of the chairman are to: explain the specific procedure to the participants and audience, stimulate the audience to ask questions, rephrase the questions when necessary, repeat the questions so they can be heard by all the audience, close the meeting at the determined time. The duties of the audience are to: ask pertinent questions, ask answerable questions, phrase questions well, allow various members to ask questions. The duties of the members being questioned are to: answer the questions to the best of their abilities, be brief, avoid making a speech in answering the questions.

Problem Solving: The Process of Discussion

Every classroom teacher should be aware of the process of problem solving, both from the analytical and creative viewpoints. The analytical approach involves: recognizing and defining the problem; clarifying the problem through defining the terms, distinguishing between facts and assumptions; collecting and organizing data; formulating possible solutions or hypotheses (explanations); selecting one or more promising hypotheses for testing and verification; and stating tentative solutions.

The classroom teacher should provide a variety of situations which require problem solving techniques for their solutions.

The following outline for analytical problem-solving sequence has been successfully used by elementary teachers in many parts of the country:

1. Phrase the problem as a question
   a. Question may concern a matter of fact. What method of teaching reading are we using?
   b. Question may concern a matter of value. What are the advantages of our present approach to the teaching of reading?
   c. Question may concern a matter of policy. How can we improve our present reading program?
2. Define the problem
   a. Determine the objectives
   b. Define the terms
   c. Reach an agreement upon acceptable definitions
3. Determine the extent of the problem
   a. Explore the scope of the problem
   b. Limit the scope to the ability of the group
   c. Limit the scope to the time available
4. Set up tentative solutions to the problem
   a. Begin with known information
   b. Locate the possible sources of information
   c. Collect additional data needed
   d. Organize the data into tentative solutions
   e. Suggest the possible solutions
5. Choose the best solutions
   a. Analyze and interpret all solutions, checking each against the objectives
   b. Choose the solutions which best meet the objectives
6. Carry out or recommend the chosen solutions.

Participating in Discussion

As Miss Jonison, the language arts specialist, came into the teacher's lounge she overhead Miss Simon say, "I don't know how I can teach discussion when the day is already crowded. I have to teach reading, writing, spelling, social studies, science, and mathematics". Mrs. Peters interrupted, "Don't forget art, music, literature, and physical education". "If I take time to teach discussion too, *when* will I teach the content subjects?" Miss Jonison entered the room and took up the conversation where it had abruptly ended. "The question, simply put, is 'Why teach discussion techniques—is that it?' " The next few minutes were spent in developing with the two teachers the values of discussion and the techniques in which the skills of group discussion using critical and creative thinking could be integrated into the curriculum.

Among the values Miss Jonison pointed out were: developing the ability to express one's ideas increasingly effectively, promoting critical and creative thinking on the part of the group, fostering interest in attacking problems, developing improved relationships among members of the group, learning to distinguish fact from fiction, learning to evaluate, making sure of data before coming to conclusions, and applying problem solving techniques in their classes in science, social studies, mathematics and reading as well as in language arts.

"There are still a few wrinkles to iron out," admitted Miss Lamson, who had been very quiet up to this point. "I need a few ideas about selecting a good problem for discussion, being sure of the role of the leader in the discussion, and the role of the members. Once I get this straightened out I'll go into it with zest."

Selecting the Problem for Discussion

The place to start in selecting a problem or subject for discussion is the group itself. Not only must the group be interested in the question, they must have knowledge, opinions, and feelings about it. In addition, it must be within the capabilities of the group and have within its scope the need for critical thinking.

Finally, the problem should be significant enough to warrant research, study, and discussion. It should be either timely or timeless. It should have more than one point of view. Obviously a problem with a clearcut "yes" and "no" answer should be avoided. In a capsule form the problem for discussion should:

1. Be within the range of the experiences of the members of the group
2. Be concerned with a problem of significance to the group
3. Be controversial in nature, except where the purpose is merely to impart information
4. Serve as a basis for planning and solving problems in the classroom
5. Be a vehicle for critical and/or creative thinking

The Role of the Leader

Several qualifications are required for a successful discussion leader. The most important qualifications are personal. Among these are: intelligence, pleasant personality, optimism, enthusiasm, tact, sense of timing, awareness of others, energy, effective speech, and experience in oral communication—particularly in discussion.

Specific responsibilities of the leader in a discussion group include the following:

1. Understanding the discussion process and the responsibilities of group leadership
2. Knowledge of the subject matter of the discussion topic or problem

3. Planning the discussion with the participants, following the general steps for the problem-solving sequence. The planning session may vary from a few ideas jotted down, to a full-scale planning session depending on the particular situation
4. Introducing the speakers to each other and to the audience
5. Opening the discussion by: (a) announcing the topic, (b) explaining its nature and importance, (c) informing the audience of anything necessary for an understanding of the problem
6. Keeping the discussion moving
7. Establishing and maintaining an atmosphere of informality and of pleasant relationship
8. Exerting leadership through not dominating the meeting, but through encouraging and guiding the participants to contribute their ideas. It is the function of the leader not only to guide but also to be aware of the types of people in his group and deal with them wisely—the shy, the aggressive, the hostile, the monopolizer, etc.
9. Closing the discussion effectively. Summarizing the main points briefly, and stating the decision if one has been reached
10. Making sure that the physical conditions such as size of room, seating arrangements, ventilation, microphone, will be taken care of. If no one has been designated to do this, it may be necessary for the leader to assume the responsibility.

Evaluation

In teaching discussion it is necessary to add two final steps—evaluation of the leader and evaluation of the participants.

The role of the leader. Did the leader:
state the problem clearly?
encourage the group to think critically?
involve everyone in the discussion?
elicit the needed information?
handle conflict skillfully?
summarize frequently?
help the group to reach solutions to the problem?

The role of the participants. Did each participant show:
familiarity with the problem solving sequence?
a desire to help other members of the group form ideas?
a willingness to admit his own errors and to credit the contribution of the others?
a willingness to answer the question of others directly?
ability to present ideas conversationally, concisely, and in a friendly spirit?
a willingness to stick to the subject?
a willingness to avoid monopolizing by giving others their fair share of discussion time?
skill in using facts and pertinent information objectively?
ability to weigh critically the contributions made by himself and others?
a willingness to follow the leadership of the moderator or chairman?

a willingness to help the group to explore its chosen solution, even if opposed to it?

ability to differ without losing one's temper?

As the students participate, they will become skilled in using the process of critical thinking, as a way of solving problems. They will find, too, that not only in the confines of the school, but in life outside the school, many of the problems can best be solved through critical thinking.

CREATIVE THINKING

In a committee-oriented society such as ours it is imperative that all citizens develop skill in originating, presenting, and discussing worth-while ideas as they seek to solve problems creatively, either individually or collectively in groups of varying size and complexity. "The art of creative thinking," says Whiting, "is the term generally applied to the body of principles and techniques which have evolved to accomplish this end."[21]

The question of how people can be taught to solve problems creatively is being asked with increasing frequency. It is important that each individual develop this capability in order to function as a contributing member of society. To the schools is delegated the responsibility for teaching children to develop the ability to think creatively as well as critically as they seek to solve problems in daily living and learning in and out of the classroom.

It is vital that the classroom teacher recognize opportunities for developing creative thinking abilities through problem-solving situations. This involves an understanding of varied approaches to creative thinking ranging from the formally structured method of reflective (critical) thinking to the informal, unstructured intuitive process.

Creative Thinking as Reflective Thought

Dewey held the belief that creative thinking involves a series of steps in which the sequences are delineated as reflection indicates they have occurred.

In the complete act of reflective thought Dewey perceived five logically distinct steps: "(i) a felt difficulty; (ii) its location and definition; (iii) suggestion of possible solution; (iv) development by reasoning of the bearings of the suggestion; (v) further observation and experiment leading to its acceptance or rejection, that is, the conclusion of belief or disbelief."[22]

Reflective thinking is an analytical approach to thought and proceeds characteristically a step at a time. "Such thinking," says Bruner, "proceeds with relatively full awareness of the information and operations involved. It may involve careful and deductive reasoning, often using mathematics or logic and an explicit play of attack. Or it may involve a step-by-step process of induction and experiment, utilizing principles of research design and statistical analysis."[23]

Creative Thinking as Intuitive Thought

At the other end of the continuum is intuitive (creative) thinking. Intuitive thinking is characterized by "disarray, complexity, ferment, and turmoil. Processes overlap, ebb and flow, and intermix to an extent scarcely compatible with notions of fixed stages and sequences."[24]

Bruner describes intuitive thinking as "the intellectual technique of arriving at plausible but tentative formulations without going through the analytic steps by which such formulations would be found to be valid or invalid conclusions. Intuitive thinking, the training of hunches, is a much neglected and essential feature of productive thinking not only in formal academic disciplines but also in everyday life. The shrewd guess, the fertile hypothesis, the courageous leap to a tentative conclusion—these are the most valuable coin of the thinker at work, whatever his line of work."[25]

Platt quotes the late Dr. Alexis Carrel of the Rockefeller Institute of Medical Research: "We are led to our goal when we do not know how to attain it or even where it is located. This is close to clairvoyance, to a sixth sense. It is the creator of much scientific discovery."[26]

In this type of intuitive thinking the individual engages in the act of discovery on the basis of a hunch. He makes a "courageous leap into the unknown" as he attempts to link the present situation to some similar situation in the past and projects it into the future. Through rapid deduction, the adding up of observable evidence, coupled with highly developed powers of awareness, sensitivity, and observation intuitive thinking is consummated.

It must be recognized that it is only when the person has some background, some knowledge of the area of concern that he is able to leap about, skip steps, and take short cuts in coming to a solution. Later rechecking by a more analytic method may be necessary for the skeptic.

The crux of intuitive thinking lies in the ability of the thinker to focus on the problem as a whole without advancing on it step by step or phase by phase. Rarely can one tell the specific way in which he has arrived at the solution or even the specific aspects of the problem situation to which he responded.

Certain problems can often be dealt with through the analytical step-by-step process of critical thinking. They fall neatly into the framework of this analytical procedure. Other problems, however, may be more easily solved without going through the step-by-step process of defining, questioning, observing, predicting, and testing.

Creative Process as Creative Thinking

Even as the concept of the creative process from cognition to communication has been successfully applied to the curriculum areas, so can it be employed to bridge the gap between the theorists of the laboratories and the pragmatists of the classroom in stimulating creative thinking in the elementary school. Thus the task of the teacher is facilitated as he attempts to develop an eagerness in the child to discover, confront, and solve problems creatively. Even more important, the child's penchant for imagining, discovering, creating, and communicating is the catalyst which stimulates creative thinking.

In solving a problem creatively the individual begins with the recognition of a need which is not satisfied until he communicates the solution. The idea must be conceived, developed, tested, and communicated before the process of creative thinking is completed. During the process he calls up his past experience, wrestles with it, inverts it perhaps, combines and recombines it into new patterns, arrangements, configurations to the end that there is something brought to bear which did not exist previously. At times the phases may be merged or telescoped, at others each phase is a distinct entity. "The new pattern that results exhibits what we call synergy, the new value is greater than the sum of the parts. A multiplying rather than an adding process has taken place. The stamp of the innovator . . . has transformed the often prosaic components into a new unity which, while it bears resemblance to its antecedents, has discrete new properties of its own and greatly increased value."[27]

By capitalizing on the problems which already exist in the elementary curriculum which demand solving, the teacher will help each child achieve his creative potentiality. He will provide opportunity for the pupil to develop an awareness of a problem and skill in the ability to verbalize this awareness into a problem statement (cognition). He will provide time for children to search materials and for ideas to ripen, and opportunity to compare insights with others (conception). At some point, sometimes quickly and sometimes only after a great struggle, a spark ignites. The moment of discovery bursts upon the child. He is drawn as toward a magnet to the best of the solutions (combustion.) "You listen silently and the sacred power that is within you dictates and you obey; and that is called creation."[28]

For some the most difficult task is to express clearly in words the "moment of discovery". The truth is within them—bound to their experiences, beliefs, and prejudices. The tragedy is that all too often it remains there—unexpressed. For many this (consumation) is the most difficult phase. "I have forgotten the word I intended to say, and my thought, unembodied, returns to the realm of shadows."[29]

Although some may be satisfied when the consumation is reached and the idea is perfectly expressed, the creative act is not completed until the idea is shared (communication). It is at this point that the individual achieves self-realization and the particular creative experience is brought to its full term.

The Relationship Between Creative Thought and Speech

An understanding of creative thinking is clarified by an understanding of the relationship between thought and speech. Psychologists have long wrestled with the definition of thinking and the role speech plays in the formulation of thought.

"At one time, the early behavorists felt that thinking was merely sub-audible speech, that and nothing else. Various researchers have shown that this proposition is not true. Some thinking seems to have no verbal coding. Einstein claims to have thought in visual symbols of his mathematics. Artists report aesthetic experiences which require contours and color and lines for their formulation. Musicians compose with tones and postures. Perhaps the closest we can come to grips with the nature of thinking is to view it as covert symbolic behavior. It is covert because it is hidden, invisible, private. It is symbolic since experience is somehow coded and transformed and translated into representative symbols. Finally these symbols are bits of behavior. . . . Much thinking consists of covert speech behavior . . . not all thinking is inner speech, but much of it is."[30] One might safely say that with elementary school children most thinking is done with words.

Vygotsky theorizes on the relationship between thought and speech and makes the following pertinent observations: "The relation between thought to word is not a thing but a process, a continual movement back and forth from thought to word and from word to thought. In that process the relation of thought to word undergoes changes which themselves may be regarded as development in the functional sense. Thought is not merely expressed in words; it comes into existence through them. Every thought tends to connect something to something else, to establish a relationship between things. Every thought moves, grows and develops, fulfills a function, solves a problem."[31]

Without an understanding of the significant relationship between the spoken word, thought, and creative problem solving teachers may inadvertently limit the development of the power of creative thinking in the children they teach. Too often teachers equate creativity through the spoken word only with dramatics, puppetry, oral reading, and so forth and fail to realize the wealth of opportunity there is to stimulate creative thinking through the various techniques of discussion.

Speech Activities for Stimulating Creative Thinking

The teachers who would guide children's learning in solving problems should be conversant with a wide variety of techniques for stimulating creative thinking. This requires specific training. Creative problem solving, perhaps more than in any other single activity involving oral communication, presents the individual with an opportunity to break from the stereotyped, routinized ways of thinking and branch out in new and different directions in solving problems. In the creative process the individual proceeds from cognition—the awareness of the need to solve a problem—through the phase of conception in which he is searching out many possible solutions and the stage at which, if successful, he has enough insight to move on to the phase of combustion when the plausible solution to which he is being drawn becomes conscious. Brainstorming, checklists, Phillips 66 (buzz session), and synectics are some of the techniques that have been developed to free the individual for creative thinking.

In order to help children develop creative thinking abilities it is important to give them opportunity and training in creative problem solving as well as creative self-expression in the art forms of speech. "While some general traits, such as flexibility and tolerance for ambiguity, seem to be conducive to creative thinking, a person must be able to control the syntax and techniques of the discipline within which he is working if he is to use it creatively."[32]

Brainstorming. Brainstorming is the term used to describe the novel and exciting problem-solving conference method originated and popularized by Osborn. The rapid-fire, spontaneous suggestions which come from a group participating in this activity is exciting to children as well as adults. Unlike reflective thinking where producing ideas and evaluating ideas take place concurrently, thereby slowing down the tempo at which ideas are generated and expressed, in brainstorming the two activities of producing and evaluating ideas are completely separated.

The momentum of rapid-fire conception of ideas carries those children along with the current who normally have little, if anything, to contribute to group discussion. The opportunity to participate in the spontaneous solution of specific problems, limited in scope, without receiving adverse criticism and having to defend one's ideas the moment they are given makes it a fun activity for children as well as adults. It is important that the leader make sure that the rules are not disregarded and that the group not break down into sub-groups. Later the list of suggestions is carefully scrutinized for fruitful ideas. If some five percent of the ideas are accepted the session is considered a success and the children or adults are happy over the outcome.

Some basic rules for brainstorming are:

1. All ideas are accepted, impractical as they may seem
2. Quantity rather than quality is emphasized
3. All criticism of ideas is prohibited in the early stages
4. Combination of ideas is encouraged
5. Evaluation is deferred until after the ideas-producing stage

Among the obvious advantages of brainstorming are the elimination of criticism and all evaluation during the idea-producing stage, the encouragement of every idea—good or bad—to be heard, and the conservation of time because of the rapidity with which ideas are produced.

What brainstorming purports to do is to provide a psychological climate in which encouragement, respect for the ideas of others, and excitement of group success is fostered.

Checklists. Another technique which proves valuable in searching for new ideas in problem solving is that of using checklists. A typical example of this device is that developed by Osborn and described in his book *Applied Imagination.*[33] Here he suggests nine basic categories for modifying an existing idea. It is evident that the checklist can be a useful tool in brainstorming or other creative problem-solving techniques, and for developing a multiplicity of ideas which can be applied to the problem at hand. The checklist as developed by Osborn is listed below.

Put to Other Uses? New ways to use it as is? Other uses if modified?

Adapt?   What else is like this? What other ideas does this suggest? Does past offer parallel? What could I copy? Whom could I emulate?

Modify?   New Twist? Change meaning, color, motion, odor, form, shape? Other changes?

Magnify?   What to add? More time? Greater frequency? Stronger? Larger? Thicker? Extra value? Plus ingredient? Duplicate? Multiply? Exaggerate?

Minify?   What to substitute? Smaller? Condensed? Miniature? Lower? Shorter? Lighter? Omit? Streamline? Split up? Understate?

Substitute? Who else instead? What else instead? Other ingredient? Other materials? Other process? Other power? Other place? Other approach? Other tone of voice?

Rearrange?   Interchange components? Other pattern? Other layout? Other sequence? Transpose cause and effect? Change pace? Change schedule?

Reverse?   Transpose positive and negative? How about opposites? Turn it backward? Turn it upside down? Reverse roles? Change shoes? Turn tables? Turn other cheek?

Combine?   How about a blend, an alloy, an assortment, an ensemble? Combine units? Combine purposes? Combine appeals? Combine ideas?[34]

Another useful type of checklist is that developed by G. Polya of Stanford University for guidance in solving single answer mathematical problems. With a creative teacher it can be modified to apply to multi-answer creative problems.

FIRST

You have to understand the problem.

UNDERSTANDING THE PROBLEM

What is the unknown? What are data? What is the condition? Is it possible to satisfy the condition? Is the condition sufficient to determine the unknown? Or is it insufficient? Or redundant? Or contradictory? Draw a figure. Introduce suitable notation. Separate the various parts of the condition. Can you write them down?

SECOND

Find the connection between the data and the unknown.

You may be obliged to consider auxiliary problems if an immediate connection cannot be found. You should obtain eventually a plan of the solution.

DEVISING A PLAN

Have you seen it before? Or have you seen the same problem in a slightly different form? Do you know a theorem that could be useful? Look at the unknown? Try to think of a familiar problem having the same or a similar unknown.

Here is a problem related to yours and solved before. Could you use it? Could you use its results? Could you use its method? Should you introduce some auxiliary element in order to make its use possible? Could you restate the problem? Could you restate it still differently? Go back to definitions.

If you cannot solve the proposed problem try to solve first some related problem. Could you imagine a more accessible related problem? A more general problem? A more special problem? An analogous problem? Could you solve a part of the problem? Keep only a part of the condition, drop the other part; how far is the unknown then determined, how can it vary? Could you derive something useful from the data? Could you think of other data appropriate to determine the unknown? Could you change the unknown or the data, or both, if necessary, so that the new unknown and the new data are nearer to each other? Did you use all the data? Did you use the whole condition? Have you taken into account all essential notions involved in the problem?

THIRD
CARRYING OUT THE PLAN
Carrying out your plan of the solution, check each step. Can you see clearly that the step is correct? Can you prove that it is correct?

FOURTH
EXAMINE THE SOLUTION OBTAINED
Can you check the result? Can you check the argument? Can you derive the result differently? Can you see it at a glance? Can you use the result or the method for some other problem?[35]

Phillips 66 (Buzz Session). Developed by J. Donald Phillips of Hillsdale College, this technique has been termed a "mass brainstorming session". It is so called because it is merely the application of the brainstorming technique as a way of facilitating problem solving within a large group. Following a lecture, panel, movie, or excursion the audience is divided into as many groups of six persons as are required to give every individual a place within a group. A chairman is appointed from within each group. It is imperative that the chairman understands the technique of the buzz session.

Once the groups have been formed and the brainstorming technique explained fully, each group is on its own for the brainstorming session. The length of time is predetermined and six to ten minutes is usually adequate. At a signal from the leader each group stops producing ideas and moves into the phase of evaluating and selecting the ideas which seem to have merit. If possible, within the time limit the one most meritorious idea is selected. When the evaluation phase is completed the chairman of each group is called upon to present the ideas selected to the entire audience.

The success of this technique depends upon the ability of the leader to organize the whole group in buzz groups rapidly, and the briefing of the audience on the brainstorming technique effectively within the time alloted, and the willingness of the members to contribute.

Synectics. Closely related to brainstorming is the technique developed by William J. Gordon, first called the Gordon technique and later *synectics.* Unevaluated free-flowing discussion is encouraged, but the technique is more complex than that of brainstorming. Synectics defines creative process as "the mental activity in problem stating, problem-solving situations where artistic or technical inventions are the result. . . . The Synectic mechanisms are intended to induce appropriate psychological states and thus promote creative activity. . . . Synectics is an attempt to describe those conscious, preconscious and subconscious psychological states which are present in any creative act."[36]

The proponents of the synectics theory hold that creative efficiency in people can be markedly increased if they understand the psychological processes by which they operate, and that in the creative process the emotional component is more important than the intellectual, the irrational more important than the rational.

Synectics puts its faith in the mechanisms which are purported to increase the probability of success when creative solutions to problems are called for. A member of a synectics group cited the psychological states (aspects of the creative process) that entered into the solution of a problem in a synectics group.

"(1) Deferment: Look first for viewpoints rather than solutions. (2) Autonomy of object: Let the problem take on a life of its own. (3) Use of the commonplace: Take advantage of the familiar as a springboard to the strange. (4) Involvement/detachment: Alternate between entering into the particulars of the problem and standing back from them, in order to see them as instances of a universal. (5) Use of metaphor: Let apparently irrelevant, accidental things suggest analogies which are sources of new viewpoints."[37]

In capsule form, the synectic process involves (1) making the strange familiar and (2) making the familiar strange. That is to say, in confronting a problem with a view to solving it one must first view it in a new way, a fresh viewpoint which in turn embodies the possibility for a new solution. Instead of looking at the problem from the usual angle, try looking at it from an "upside down" point of view. In making the familiar strange the trick is to invert, distort, transpose, modify the ordinary way of looking, responding, and solving problems and thus take an "upside-down, inside-out, out-of-focus" look at what has been the familiar world.

Developing Creative Thinking in the Classroom

The importance of developing creative thinking in children during the elementary school years cannot be overestimated. A knowledge of techniques for stimulating creative thinking is vital. In addition, the conviction of the importance of developing this ability must be brought home to the teacher and the potential teacher. Torrance, in a speech delivered to the Minneapolis Teachers League, emphasized the responsibility for developing children's ability in creative thinking as they plan, organize, and evaluate learning experiences for the children they teach.

"First," says Torrance, "it is important from the standpoint of personality development and mental health. . . . There is little question that prolonged enforced repression of the creative desire may lead to actual breakdown of the personality. . . . Secondly, there seems to be little doubt that creative thinking contributes importantly to the acquisition of information and may ultimately be demonstrated to be as important in this respect as memory and similar intellectual functions. Third, creative thinking is certainly essential in the application of knowledge to personal and professional problems. . . . Fourth, I believe it is tremendously important to society that our creative talent be identified, developed, and utilized. The future of our civilization depends upon the quality of the creative imagination of our next generation."[38]

In conclusion, Torrance advanced suggestions to the teacher which he believed could be put into practice in the daily classroom activities and would provide training for creative thinking.

1. Value creative thinking
2. Make children more sensitive to environmental stimuli.
3. Encourage manipulation of objects and ideas.
4. Teach how to test systematically each idea.
5. Develop tolerance of new ideas.
6. Beware of forcing a set pattern.
7. Develop a creative classroom atmosphere.
8. Teach the child to value his creative thinking.
9. Teach skills for avoiding peer sanctions.
10. Give information about the creative process.
11. Dispel the sense of awe of masterpieces.
12. Encourage and evaluate self-initiated learning.
13. Create "thorns in the flesh".
14. Create necessities for creative thinking.
15. Provide for active and quiet periods.
16. Make available resources for working out ideas.
17. Encourage the habit of working out the full implication of ideas.
18. Develop acquisition of knowledge in a variety of fields.
19. Develop adventurous-spirited teachers.[39]

In guiding children into creative thinking it is essential to: (1) create a classroom climate favourable for creative expression and creative problem-solving; (2) provide broad experiences for children to give them something out of which to create; (3) plan learning experiences which compel them to confront and solve problems; (4) plan a daily schedule which allows for creative thinking and creative expression of ideas; (5) teach children the techniques for solving problems through reflective thinking, intuitive thinking, and creative problem solving; (6) evaluate progress in terms of the activity; and (7) teach creatively.

In utilizing guidelines such as those presented the teacher will find success in working effectively *if* he realizes that curiosity about the world in which he lives is as an important magic ingredient in creativity for him as it is for the child. The teacher who is alive to new ideas, new ways of looking at problems, and who finds in creative teaching, creative expression, and creative thinking an avenue for self-realization is on the way to success in stimulating creative behaviour in the children he teaches.

CONDUCTING A MEETING

> Which motions have the most success?
> For which do persons yearn?
> One is the motion to recess,
> The other, to adjourn.
>
> Richard Armour

"Mr. Chairman, I move that . . ." "I rise to a point of order!" "I move to amend by . . ." "I move to refer to a committee . . ." "I favour this motion because . . ." "I move to adjourn". A knowledge of parliamentary procedure is essential in a democratic society. The individual who understands and uses parliamentary procedure can present his views, protect his rights, and help secure wise decisions in any organization of which he is a part. It prepares him, too, to execute his duties of office effectively should he be elected.

Basic Principles of Parliamentary Procedure

The basic aim of parliamentary procedure is to provide for a group to come to a decision in the simplest and most direct manner while providing free debate, protecting the rights of the minority, and ensuring the rule of the majority. This aim is accomplished in several ways.

"Only one proposal may be debated at a time; every subject is entitled to full debate; each member has an equal right to propose subjects for consideration, to speak on a subject, to vote as he pleases, and to have information supplied about the proper procedure; order is necessary so that these procedures are possible; members must cooperate, only one may speak at any one time, and each must speak to the specific matter before the group; each member has an equal vote in reaching any decision; through the written rules of the group and the customs of parliamentary procedure a method is established to provide for these rights in a natural and uniform way."[40]

Order of Business

Through the years a uniform procedure for conducting a meeting has evolved. Groups have found that business is facilitated when there is a procedure common to most organizations. Unless the by-laws call for a different pattern, the following is the order of business that will be followed: call to order by the chairman, roll call by the secretary (if attendance records are kept), reading and approving of the minutes of the previous meeting (corrections when necessary), announcements, reports by officers, standing and special committees, unfinished business, new business, adjournment.

The chairman calls the meeting to order by standing, rapping his gavel, and stating, "The meeting will please come to order". If the group decides to include a brief prayer, is should be given at this time. The chairman asks the secretary to call the roll, he declares that a quorum is (or isn't) present. Then the secretary reads the minutes. After the minutes have been read, the chairman asks, "Are there any corrections or additions to the minutes as read?" If there is no response, he states, "The minutes will stand approved as read."

In the event of a correction or addition, the member addresses the chairman, waits for recognition, and states his point. After conferring with the secretary the chairman announces his decision and asks if there is any objection. If there is an objection, the matter must be brought to a vote for a group decision. After suggested changes have been determined the chairman states, "If there are no further objections, the minutes will stand approved as corrected." The secretary then writes at the conclusion of the minutes, "approved" followed by the date and his signature.

The chairman then calls for announcements (some organizations have the announcements just before adjournment to catch the late comers). The order of reports usually has a set order, again varying from group to group, but usually the treasurer reports first to determine available funds. The standing committees report in the order in which they are listed in the by-laws. The special committees report in the order in which they were named, unless there is a special reason to shift the order. Each chairman presents his report and moves the acceptance. If there is no special recommendation for action the chairman usually states, "If there is no objection, the report will be filed as read." If there is a recommendation for action, the chairman of the committee moves its adoption. This is treated like any main motion when new business is considered, and in the order in which the committees report. The group may adopt, modify, reject, or request the committee to give the report further study.

Following the committee reports, any business left from the last meeting is considered. This does not mean business disposed of by vote at the last meeting and postponed. It is business that was uncompleted by adjournment with no action being taken.

Under the heading of new business will be motions that were postponed definitely to this meeting. If more than one was postponed, the motions will be read by the secretary in the order in which they were disposed. If a motion was tabled, it must be brought before the group by a special main motion when no other business is before the house. If no business has been postponed, the chairman will entertain motions for new business. Main motions will be introduced by the member standing, receiving recognition by the chair, and then stating, "I move that . . ." If the motion is long or complicated it should be written out and handed to the secretary. The chairman restates the motion and asks for a second. This is necessary to insure that at least two people want to consider the motion. If there is no second the chairman states, "The motion dies for lack of a second". If there is a second the motion is before the group for consideration.

When there is no further business, or there is a definite lag in presenting motions, the chairman says, "Is there any further business to come before the group? If not, the chair will entertain a motion to adjourn." However, if there is a fixed time for adjournment (such as the end of a class period), the chairman states, "The fixed hour for adjournment is here. I declare the meeting adjourned."

The chairman may call for a vote in one of four ways: by a show of hands, by asking members to stand, by voice vote, and by secret ballot. Normally the chairman has no vote except to break a tie or to create a tie. If the vote is by secret ballot, however, he must vote at the time the group votes.

Types of Motions

Motions are proposals submitted for decision by the group and may serve many different functions. A brief look at their functions will serve to clarify them. There are four types: main, subsidiary, incidental, and privileged.

Main motions. Main motions are initial proposals for action. They introduce a subject for the group to act upon. Any motion is treated as a main motion when there is no other business before the group.

Subsidiary motions. Subsidiary motions are those which act directly upon the main motion in some fashion. Their purpose is to change its content or to dispose of it temporarily or permanently. The purposes of the subsidiary motions are: to change the debate on the main motion, as by amending it; to dispose of the question for that particular meeting, as by postponing the motion by laying it on the table, or by referring it to a committee; to postpone action until a definite time; to stop debate; to limit or extend debate. Subsidiary motions must be considered and disposed of in the order of their precedence before the main motion may be considered.

Incidental motions. Incidental motions are tools that provide a means for a correction or changing of the procedure under which motions are handled. For example, a member may feel that the chairman has made a decision contrary to parliamentary law and may wish an appeal from his decision. Another member may wish additional information from the maker of a motion. Or he may wish to rise to point of order (to enforce rules) etc.,

Privileged motions. The purpose of privileged motions is to protect the rights and comfort of members of the group. They involve such problems as taking a recess, adjourning, heating and lighting in the room, calling for the orders of the day. They require the direct and immediate attention of the group because of their importance. They have precedence over subsidiary motions and the main motion.

For all business meetings the procedures should be as simple as possible. The machinery of parliamentary procedure should not get in the way of expediting business. The degree of formality with which a meeting is conducted depends largely on the group involved. The presiding officers should master the procedures in order to conduct business with dispatch in an orderly, organized, yet democratic manner. The chairman and parliamentarian should always have at hand (and understand) a chart indicating the classification of motions and how they should be handled.

Frequently Used Parliamentary Motions[41]
(Listed in the order of precedence)

TYPE	MOTION	PURPOSE	MAY INTERRUPT A SPEAKER?	SECOND REQUIRED?	DEBATABLE?	AMENDABLE?	VOTE REQUIRED?
Privileged	20. Fix Time for Reassembling	To arrange time of next meeting	No	Yes	No	Yes	Majority
	19. Adjourn	To dismiss the meeting	No	Yes	No	No	Majority
	18. To Recess	To dismiss the meeting for a specific length of time	No	Yes	No	Yes	Majority
	17. Rise to a Question of Privilege	To make a personal request during debate	Yes	No	No	No	Decision of Chair
	16. Call for the Orders of the Day	To force consideration of a postponed motion	Yes	No	No	No	Decision of Chair
Incidental	15. Appeal a Decision of the Chair	To reverse the decision of the chairman	Yes	Yes	No	No	Majority
	14. Rise to a Point of Order or Parliamentary Inquiry	To correct a parliamentary error or ask a question	Yes	No	No	No	Decision of Chair
	13. To Call for Division of the Assembly	To verify a voice vote	Yes	No	No	No	Majority*
	12. Object to the Consideration of a Question	To suppress action	Yes	No	No	No	Two-Thirds
	11. Leave to Withraw a Motion	To allow the maker of a motion to withdraw it	No	No	No	No	Majority
	10. To Suspend the Rules	To take action contrary to standing rules	No	Yes	No	No	Two-Thirds

* Requires no vote unless a formal motion is offered to force the chairman to make a division.

Subsidiary	9. To Lay on the Table	To defer action	No	Yes	No	No	Majority
	8. To Call the Previous Question	To force an immediate vote	No	Yes	No	No	Two-Thirds
	7. To Limit or Extend Debate	To modify freedom of debate	No	Yes	No	Yes	Two-Thirds
	6. To Postpone to a Definite Time	To defer action	No	Yes	Yes	Yes	Majority†
	5. To Refer to a Committee	For further study	No	Yes	Yes	Yes	Majority
	4. To Amend an Amendment	To modify an amendment	No	Yes	Yes	No	Majority
	3. To Amend	To modify a motion	No	Yes	Yes	Yes	Majority
	2. To postpone Indefinitely	To suppress action	No	Yes	Yes	No	Majority
Main	1. Main Motion	To introduce business	No	Yes	Yes	Yes	Majority
Specific Main Motions	A. To take from the Table	To consider tabled motions	No	Yes	No	No	Majority
	B. To rescind	To reverse previous action	No	Yes	Yes	Yes	Majority
	C. To Reconsider	To consider a defeated motion again	Yes	Yes	Yes	No	Majority

† Majority vote required for general order; two-thirds vote required for special order.

Duties of Officers

When the officers have a clear understanding of their duties and responsibilities and are willing to fulfill them the organization is fortunate. The by-laws will usually state the qualifications for and duties of the various offices. There are certain general duties commonly assigned to the chairman and secretary. The other officers duties will vary with the organization.

The Chairman. If the president of an organization or the chairman of a committee has already been chosen he automatically becomes the presiding officer. When no such officer has been selected, the first duty of the group is to nominate and elect by a majority vote a chairman from among the members.

The chief function of the chairman is to expedite business. To avoid confusion speakers are required to address the chairman and be recognized by him before speaking. Only one person may speak at a time. It is the responsibility of the chairman to be familiar with the order of the business of the meeting and to understand the order of precedence of motions. In informal groups the chairman may enter the discussion and vote on proposals which are presented. He may also remain seated during much of the meeting. It is proper for him to stand as he calls the meeting to order, as he puts questions to the vote, and as he gives decisions. In formal meetings the chairman may stand much of the time. In informal meetings he sits much of the time.

A good chairman should be able to speak well. He should help the group expedite business with the minimum amount of formality. For example, contrary to strict parliamentary procedure, he may permit the discussion and modification of business before a formal motion is placed before the group for voting. If however, extraneous matters are introduced the chairman must call for a main motion. Technically, nothing can be declared out of order if there is no motion before the group.

The Secretary. The secretary is responsible for keeping the minutes of each meeting. These should include:

1. Name of the organization
2. Kind of meeting (regular, special, etc.)
3. Date, time, and place of meeting
4. Name and title of presiding and recording officers
5. Fact that a quorum was present
6. Notation as to the reading and approval of the minutes
7. Record of the reports by officers and committees
8. Record of all main motions, except those withdrawn, name of mover
9. Record of all other motions including their order of disposition, name of mover
10. Record of all votes taken
11. Time and type of adjournment
12. Signature of the secretary.

The minutes should be written in ink or typed. A loose-leaf notebook, size 8½" by 11", is quite convenient. It is wise to allow wide margins so that any changes may be legibly entered in the margins. The secretary's book becomes part of the permanent records of an organization.

In addition to keeping the minutes, the secretary may handle the correspondence, prepare the agenda for meetings, coordinate committee work, and perform such other duties as prescribed by the constitution or bylaws.

The Parliamentarian. Ordinarily the parliamentarian is appointed to advise the Chair on procedural matters. He cannot rule on any questions, but merely advises the Chair who is free to disregard the advice. Since the teacher is likely to be the best informed parliamentarian in the group it is recommended that he take over this responsibility.

As parliamentarian the teacher can use discretion in deciding how much depth to attempt in experiences in conducting meetings according to procedures cited. It is well to keep in mind that it is necessary to plan in terms of a specific group of children, and to draw up a special set of rules which fit the needs of a particular group. "While unstructured democracy may end in anarchy, yet guides of parliamentary rule protect the individual, the minority, and the majority from failure to be heard or from unfair treatment by chairman and other members. It may be tiresome to 'Plod' through the usual forms, but it is still the method of getting the business of the group accomplished with legality and with the approval of tomorrow. Differences of opinion made clear through discussion and debate are thus channelled into decision which is then to become the policy of this group (until and) unless revised by this group."[42]

SEQUENCE OF SPEECH ACTIVITIES IN THE INTERMEDIATE AND UPPER GRADES

In the placement of activities throughout the intermediate and upper grades the authors have kept in mind the aims of oral communication, the language development of pupils, and the need for the refinement of linguistic skills for the expression of ideas and the freeing of creative potential. They have also been cognizant of the individual differences of children at each developmental level and have suggested a variety of activities from which the teacher can choose in order to meet the needs, interests, and abilities of the group. Some of the children will be ready for the activities at an earlier time than others. Children grow differently; they react to their environment differently; they have different skills. It is the responsibiity of the teacher to provide a speaking environment which will challenge all children and which will have for each child the particular activity that best meets his abilities and growing needs. Although children develop some speech skills through group activities, opportunities must also be provided for personalized speech activities for both individual growth and evaluation.

CONCLUDING STATEMENT

The child learns to speak before he comes to school, before his formal education begins. However, his skills in speaking are far from perfected. The development of skill in speaking is a continuous process. Throughout the child's educational experience his speech and language skills both limit and are limited by his experiential background, native abilities, and instruction. "The growth, refinement, and permanence of communication habits parallel the development of knowledge built into the process. Hence continuity of instruction in speech is of primary concern in formal education."[43]

It is through speech that a child first expresses his ideas. It is through speech that he makes his wants known and develops a sense of identity. It is through speech that the quality of his thoughts, that the form and worthwhileness of his relationships with others is mirrored. It is in the elementary school that he has his first direct training in transmitting his ideas with accuracy, correctness, and clarity; that he learns to speak in ways that help resolve misunderstanding and aids in

Sequence in Speech Activities in the Intermediate and Upper Grades

AIMS IN TEACHING ORAL COMMUNICATION IN THE INTERMEDIATE GRADES	LANGUAGE GROWTH OF CHILDREN IN FOURTH THROUGH EIGHTH GRADES	SPEAKING ACTIVITIES
To converse intelligently To have something to say To say it well To respond actively to another's conversation To listen courteously and critically	Children: Show definite interest in communicating with their peers Are improving in speech skills Are critical of their own and others speech Are increasing vocabularies	**CONVERSATION** Participate in conversation Choose subjects for conversation Learn how to carry on conversation Plan how to change the subject Discuss how to be interesting listeners Demonstrate this knowledge
To speak courteously and effectively on the telephone To know how to begin and end a telephone conversation		**TELEPHONING** Take messages accurately Ask for information Carry on business over the telephone Ask permission to visit a market or institution by means of the telephone
To interview to gain specific information	Recognize need for increased language facility	**INTERVIEWING** Plan an interview Dramatize interviews Conduct an interview in front of the class Conduct an interview outside of the class and make a report to the class
To participate in social situations with ease To learn to be considerate of guests	Children are ready to begin to learn and practice social amenities Classmates set standards of manners Children from nine to eleven are ready for widening social contacts	**SOCIAL SITUATIONS** Serve as host or hostess in school functions Welcome the guests Express sympathy and congratulations

(Sequence in Speech Activities, continued)

AIMS IN TEACHING ORAL COMMUNICATION IN THE INTERMEDIATE GRADES	LANGUAGE GROWTH OF CHILDREN IN FOURTH THROUGH EIGHTH GRADES	SPEAKING ACTIVITIES
To give speeches to entertain, to inform, to stimulate, convince, actuate. To collect and arrange material for a talk. To provide supporting material To organize ideas To develop research techniques To know where to look to find information	Reasoning based on direct observation. Begin to make assumptions, generalizations, deductions Use research methods in collecting data	GIVING TALKS Give short talks to inform, entertain, stimulate, convince, actuate Make and use simple outline for speech Find specific facts for talks from magazines, books and journals Evaluate own and peers talks
To cooperate in informal group discussion To think critically about what others are saying To be willing to change one's mind. To stick to a point To participate constructively in formal group discussion To experiment with creative ways of solving problems To know which type of group discussion techniques will best serve a specific purpose To serve as an effective discussion leader	Children are eager for activities which require them to make decisions and cooperate in planning They are eager to think independently and critically The predolescent is quite willing to express his ideas He has not yet become fixed in his ideas In planning, children at this age can be guided to set up standards for discussion and follow through Children enjoy contributing ideas without evaluating first as in brainstorming The predolescent likes to make guesses and state hunches He is beginning to discriminate in types of discussions to meet a particular problem or question	DISCUSSION Participate in informal planning sessions of class routines Plan activities of the class Pool information Participate in various forms of discussion: committee, round table, panel, symposium, forum Participate in planning and carrying through different types of discussion in terms of the needs of the situation Be a discussion leader Follow the problem solving sequence in a discussion
To conduct a meeting by means of simple parliamentary procedure	The intermediate grade child is gregarious and enjoys organizing a club and being a vital part of it	ORGANIZING A CLUB. Conduct club meetings following the correct order of business Use the correct form for making the various motions

Speech in the Upper Grades (7-8)

AIMS IN TEACHING ORAL COMMUNICATION IN THE UPPER GRADES	LANGUAGE DEVELOPMENT OF SEVENTH AND EIGHTH GRADES	SPEAKING ACTIVITIES
To gain greater skill in conversing with peers and adults about a variety of topics	Increased complexity in sentence structure and greater vocabulary development	CONVERSING Converse with adults Study the characteristics of a successful conversation Select broad range of topics for conversation
To use the telephone in a mature manner	More concern with approved usage	TELEPHONING Arrange interviews by telephone Ask a favor Invite a resource person to the school Plan a class activity Express sympathy over the telephone Order materials Make a business complaint Plan to visit a telephone office
To plan an interview, carry it through courteously and effectively		INTERVIEWING Study interview techniques Participate in an interview Dramatize an interview: as an interviewer—as an interviewee
To be a cooperative, social member of the group, considering others and making them feel at ease	Early adolescents are eager to learn correct vocabulary and usage required by the various social amenities	SPEAKING IN SOCIAL SITUATIONS Study what is required in different social situations in the way of speech Role-play social situations demonstrating effectively used correct form

(Speech in the Upper Grades, continued)

AIMS IN TEACHING ORAL COMMUNICATION IN THE UPPER GRADES	LANGUAGE DEVELOPMENT OF SEVENTH AND EIGHTH GRADES	SPEAKING ACTIVITIES
To participate with increasing effectiveness in discussion To listen critically, and courteously To participate in critical thinking To participate in creative problem solving To be a discussion leader To participate in parliamentary procedure To be a parliamentarian	Early adolescents are anxious to have their ideas accepted in group planning They see clearer cause and effect relationships They can solve problems involving concrete situations They enjoy role-playing situations, brainstorming, and buzz sessions as an aid to finding solutions They analyze, "talk-out" problems, and clarify through group thinking. They tend to draw conclusions from limited data unless they are guided	DISCUSSION Participate in pupil-teacher planning Plan the work of the class in units Plan activities of the group Use discussion technique in social studies, science and mathematics as well as in oral communication Discuss problems of concern to the group, the community, the province, and the world Follow the steps of problem solving Participate in critical thinking and creative problem solving Be a discussion leader Conduct a meeting using approved procedures

bringing groups to worthwhile decisions. Here he is introduced to the study of speech processes and forms, and develops speaking skills in functional, meaningful and creative situations. The elementary teacher must have the preparation which will enable him to guide children effectively in the skills and art of communication.

Opportunities for developing creativity through the medium of the spoken word abound in the classroom. However, the teacher must be aware of the need of the child to think, express, experiment, create, and communicate. He must also be able to guide him through the many types of communication such as sharing experiences, conversing, giving talks, discussing problems, and conducting meetings. The child, by the time he completes the elementary school years, has found in this area of the curriculum one of the most significant as well as effective means for developing and realizing his creative potential.

Through the spoken word the child finds an effective answer to his need for releasing creativity, communicating with his peers, and developing his personality. He learns to confront problems with eagerness, born of confidence in using the techniques for critical thinking, group discussion and creative problem solving. As he learns to communicate his ideas effectively he finds the bridge between him and other individuals is spanned and understanding ensues.

REFERENCES

1. Ronald R. Allen, "The New Speech Educator: Philosophy and Standards," *The Speech Teacher*, 15: 18, 19, January, 1966.
2. By permission from Robert Pooley, "Oral Communication in the English Curriculum," *The Speech Teacher*, 15:28, January, 1966.
3. Daniel Fogarty, "I. A. Richard's Theory," in Joseph Schwartz and John A. Rycenga, (eds.), *The Province of Rhetoric*, The Ronald Press, New York, 1965, p. 346.
4. Ralph T. Eubanks and Virgil L. Baker, "Toward an Axiology of Rhetoric," in Joseph Schwartz and John Rycenga (eds.), *op. cit.*, p. 342.
5. Gerald W. Johnson, "Emerson's Scholar: A New Chapter in His Biography," *The Key Reporter*, 23:3, July, 1958.
6. Reprinted by permission from *Speech for Today*, by Hibbs, Fessenden, Larson and Wagner. Copyright © 1965 by McGraw-Hill Inc., Manchester, 1965, p. 273.
7. *Ibid.*, p. 283.
8. Used by special permission of publishers, Holt, Rinehart, and Winston, Inc., from *Modern Speech* by John Irwin and Marjorie Rosenberger, copyright 1961. All rights reserved, p. 175.
9. Reprinted from *Principles and Types of Speech* by Allan Monroe. Copyright 1962 by Scott, Foresman and Company, Chicago, 1962, 5th ed., p. 281.
10. *Ibid.*, p. 285.
11. *Ibid.*, p. 290.
12. *Ibid.*, p. 289.
13. *Ibid.*, p. 287.
14. Donald C. Streeter, *A Speech Handbook for Teachers*, © 1964. Reprinted by permission of Prentice-Hall Inc., Englewood Cliffs, New Jersey, 1964, p. 9.

15. John V. Irwin and Majorie Rosenberger, *op. cit.*, p. 246.

16. Robert G. Gunderson, "Teaching Critical Thinking," *The Speech Teacher*, 10:100, March, 1961.

17. Winston L. Brembeck, "The Effects of a Course in Argumentation on Critical Thinking Ability," *Speech Monographs*, 16:177-189, September, 1949.

18. By permission from Charles T. Brown and John J. Pruis, "Encouraging Participation in Classroom Discussion," *The Speech Teacher*, 7:344, November, 1958.

19. By permission from Murray M. Horowitz, "The Teacher Utilizes Group Forces," *Learning and the Teacher* 1959 Yearbook, Association for Supervision and Curriculum Development, NEA, Washington, 1959, pp. 117, 118.

20. *Ibid.*

21. Charles S. Whiting, *Creative Thinking*, Reinhold Publishing Company, New York, 1958, p. 1.

22. John Dewey, *How We Think*, D. C. Heath and Company, Boston, 1910, p. 6.

23. By permission from Jerome Bruner, *The Process of Education*, Harvard University Press, Cambridge, 1960, p. 58.

24. Harrison G. Gough, "Imagination—Underdeveloped Resource," in Sidney Parnes and Harold Harding (eds.), *A Source Book for Creative Thinking*, Charles Scribner's Sons, New York, 1962, pp. 218, 219.

25. Jerome Bruner, *op. cit.*, pp. 13, 14.

26. Rutherford Platt, "The Mystery of our 'Sixth Senses'," *Reader's Digest*, 83:77, September, 1963.

27. John E. Arnold, "Education for Innovation," in Sidney Parnes and Harold Harding (eds.), *op. cit.*, p. 128.

28. Carleton Lake, "Color as Love, A Portrait of Chagall," *The Atlantic Monthly*, 201:73, June, 1958.

29. From S. L. Vygotsky, *Thought and Word*, The M. I. T. Press, Cambridge, 1962, p. 119.

30. Charles Van Riper, *Speech Correction, Principles and Methods*, 4th ed., © 1963. Reprinted by permission of Prentice-Hall, Inc., Englewood Cliffs, New Jersey, 1963, pp. 3, 4.

31. By permission from S. L. Vygotsky, *Thought and Language*, edited and translated by Eugenia Kaufman and Gertrude Vakar, The M.I.T. Press, Cambridge, 1962, p. 125.

32. Elliot W. Eisner, "Fostering Creativity in the Classroom," *The Instructor*, 79:92, May, 1963.

33. By permission from Alex Osborn, *Applied Imagination*, rev. ed., Charles Scribner's Sons, New York, 1957, p. 318.

34. *Ibid.*

35. By permission from G. Polya, "How to Solve It," in Sidney Parnes and Harold Harding (eds.), *op. cit.*, p. 253.

36. William J. Gordon, *Synectics: The Development of Creative Capacity*, Harper & Brothers, Publishers, New York, 1961, pp. 33, 34.

37. By permission from John W. Lincoln, "Developing Creativeness in People," in Sidney Parnes and Harold Harding (eds.), *op. cit.*, p. 274.

38. By permission from E. Paul Torrance, "Creative Thinking Through School Experiences," in Sidney Parnes and Harold Harding (eds.), *op. cit.*, pp. 32, 33.

39. *Ibid.*, p. 46.
40. John V. Irwin and Majorie Rosenberger, *op. cit.*, pp. 281, 282.
41. *Ibid.*, pp. 306, 307.
42. By permission from Paul A. Carmack, "Evolution in Parliamentary Procedure," *The Speech Teacher*, 11:38, January, 1962.
43. Donald K. Smith, Andrew T. Weaver, and Karl R. Robinson, "The Field of Speech: Its Purposes and Scope in Education," Official Document of Speech Association of America by action of the Administrative Council in Denver, Colorado, August 18, 1963, Section 4.

8

Improving the Child's Speech

It is so easy to think of words as words rather than as thoughts or messages; to view words only as sounds or coordinations rather than as carriers of communication.

Charles Van Riper

A student is identified as a speech handicapped person when his speech interferes with his communication. When this definition is understood the teacher will approach the improvement of individual sounds and words with the objective of total communication. This implies an understanding of articulation and pronunciation in relation to language development. Articulation is concerned with the formation of individual sounds of the language, pronunciation with the choice and combination of those sounds acceptable to the society in which he lives. Unless the child can form the individual sounds correctly he will have difficulty in pronunciation of individual words. Expressive vocalization and articulation depends on the coordinated functioning of all speech organs working with the interpretative concepts of the mind.

"Of all man's civilized activities, none requires a greater degree of coordination than speech. Considering all of the muscles which act in breathing, phonation, resonance, and articulation, vocalization involves hundreds of muscles, all of which have to be moved in split-second timing and always in relation to at least one other muscle. For example, in producing the "b" sound of English the adjustments of lips, jaw, soft palate, and vocal folds require action of no less than 19 muscles in addition to those involved in breathing; and all these muscles must act with the right amount of tension, at the proper speed, and in exactly the right sequence. No doubt many sounds require an even more complex pattern. At an average rate of 175 words per minute, with an average of 5 sounds per word, and a minimal average of 19 muscular movements per sound, a speaker produces in excess of 16,625 *disciplined and refined movements per minute*. It is not difficult to appreciate the importance of a sound nervous system and a healthy developed musculature to the activities of civilized man. We can understand that good coordination is characteristic of better speakers, while ineffective speaking and poor coordination are highly related."[1]

Most children take this complex process in their stride. By the time they come to school they are able to speak so they can make their needs known. For this reason teachers too often fail to realize the needs of the children who are not so fortunate. To know when to help a child with his speech, what kind of help to give, and how to provide such help is essential for the teacher in the elementary school. Learning how to identify speech defects is essential for the prospective teacher.

In the average classroom some five to ten per cent of the children are unable to communicate effectively. They need special help. The teacher will begin by organizing activities on the basis that what is good for the normal is good for the child with speech problems. Although some children may need individualized help from a speech therapist they should not be excluded from group speech activities. The admonition of Van Riper, "Speech therapy cannot be carried out in a vacuum. The ebb and flow of communication, the give and take of messages, these are the opportunities for learning to speak as others do"[2] should be heeded.

In many schools the development of each child to his maximum potential is interpreted to include speech development. In such schools there is a team approach to helping the child with speech difficulties as well as the child with other handicaps and the child with need for speech improvement rather than speech correction. The team is concerned with the speech development of *all* children. Thus there is a concerted effort of speech and hearing therapists, classroom teachers, administrators, special teachers, and parents. The classroom teacher plays a distinct role in helping each child with his speech improvement. Specifically this requires a knowledge of:

(1) Defective speech, (2) types of speech disorders, (3) identifying speech and hearing defects, (4) helping the child with a speech handicap, (5) the development of normal speech, (6) techniques of speech improvement in the classroom, and (7) a professional relationship between the classroom teacher and the speech therapist.

WHAT IS DEFECTIVE SPEECH?

"Speech is defective when it deviates so far from the speech of other people that it calls attention to itself, interferes with communication, or causes its possessor to be maladjusted."[3]

Such a definition is of significance to the classroom teacher as well as to the speech therapist. It brings to the fore the responsibility of the teacher to share in the improvement of the speech of every child in the classroom. True, "The pattern of the child's speech is established before he enrolls in school. In most instances he speaks adequately for his level of maturity. Various authors give widely differing percentages of the elementary school children who are handicapped in their oral communication skills because of speech disorders. Some have called handicapped only those who need the services of a trained speech therapist; others have included all who speak in a way to be noticeably "different" from their associates. The most conservative of them estimate that at least five percent must have speech correction if they are not to suffer serious drawbacks in life. If mild speech problems are included, the estimate runs as high as 25 per cent."[4]

Richard states, "The speech handicapped represent the largest group of exceptional children. Speech difficulties range from slight problems to cases of severe disability. The main types include: articulatory defects, stuttering, voice disorders, retarded speech development, organic disorders such as cleft palate and cerebral palsy, and the speech problems of the hard of hearing. Because of the increased interest in developing speech therapy programmes in the Canadian schools, large numbers of children are now freed from the crippling effect of a speech handicap."[5]

With such proportions of children requiring help in speaking effectively the task of the classroom teacher in identifying the speech defective is facilitated if he is aware of the speech behaviour that hinders effective communication: speech that is *conspicuous,* speech that has poor *intelligibility,* speech that is *unpleasant.*

Conspicuous Speech

Conspicuous speech calls attention to itself and is characterized by a speech pattern that varies from the norm to the extent that, for the developmental level of the child, it is inappropriate. It does not include the child of four who refers to the red wagon as "da wed waddon". The child of eight, however, who says the same thing would be considered defective in his speech. Also, if the speech differs radically from the cultural group of which one is a member, it is conspicuous and could be classified as defective speech.

Poor Intelligibility

Poor intelligibility interferes with communication. It may be the result of either organic or psychological problems. It is characterized by such speech patterns as dysphonia, cleft palate, excessive nasality, cluttering, stuttering, jargon, sound substitutions, sound omissions, lisping, and idioglossia (baby talk). In each of these cases the speaker is unable to communicate effectively.

Unpleasant Speech

Unpleasant speech is characterized by vocal elements which are unpleasant to the listener or physical manifestations which are distasteful to the observer. Examples of the former would be gutteral, extreme variations in pitch or mono-pitch, nasality, hoarseness, harshness, huskiness, breathiness. Physical characteristics would include secondary stuttering, excessive saliva, muscular contractions of spastics, facial grimaces.

This type of speech may not be unintelligible, but it can contribute to emotional maladjustment and personality problems that in turn intensify the speech defect. If children are criticized for unintelligible speech; if they are laughed at for conspicuous speech, it is possible for them to become so concerned over the affective aspect of trying to speak that they feel rejected and become emotionally upset and disturbed. "A severe speech defect, because it provokes rejection and other penalties due to its communicative unpleasantness, causes a loss of self-esteem, in ego strength."[6]

Goldberg contrasts defective speech with good speech:

DEFECTIVE SPEECH

1. Defective speech is unintelligible or indistinct.
2. Defective speech draws attention to itself because it is conspicuous in its difference from the usual.
3. Defective speech lacks ease, clarity, and fluency.
4. Defective speech interferes with communication.
5. Defective speech hinders normal social adjustment.

"Defective Speech" is generally regarded as the type of speech that is marked by one or more of the above characteristics.

GOOD SPEECH

1. Good speech is pleasing to the ear and conveys its message with clarity and distinctness.
2. Good speech has agreeable voice quality pitched at a level suitable to the age and sex of the speaker.
3. Good speech is rhythmic, fluent, and free from hesitations, repetitions, and interruptions.
4. Good speech is clearly articulated, clearly enunciated, and correct in pronunciation and usage.
5. Good speech has sufficient carrying power to be easily heard within a reasonable distance from the speaker.
6. Good speech is flexible and animated.
7. Good speech is easy, unrestrained, and confident.[7]

The often frustrating and seemingly interminable task of aiding the speech handicapped child to reach *his* potential can be made enjoyable if the teacher is knowledgable and skillful in this vital area of the child's development.

TYPES OF SPEECH DISORDERS

"Spasmophemia, rhotacism, uranoscolalia, lambdacism, rhinolalia, sigmatism, idioglossia, and bradylalia. Do not worry: we do not intend to inflict such a heavy burden of polysyllabic jaw-breakers upon your tender memory. Translated, in sequence, these terms refer to stuttering, defective *r* sounds, cleft-palate speech, defective *l* sounds, excessive nasality, lisping, delayed speech characterized by jargon, and speech which is uttered too slowly."[8]

This is not the complete list of speech disorders; it is simply cited to point up the necessity for becoming familiar with those which are common to the children enrolled in our schools in order that: (1) the teacher can learn to identify them, (2) recognize the symptoms which characterize the speech of children who need special help, (3) refer to the speech therapist or speech clinic those which require such help, and (4) plan a program of speech improvement for *all* children in the classroom. This should include both the children whose speech is developing normally and those whose speech is defective. In addition to special help, the latter should be included, when possible, in all the speech activities.

A helpful classification of speech disorders based on the behaviour itself is that of Van Riper who divides the disorders into four major categories: *"articulation, time* (or rhythm), *voice,* and *symbolization* (language). This fourfold classification, it should be understood, refers to the *outstanding* features of the behavior shown. Thus even though his stuttering causes certain sounds to be distorted, we place the stutterer in the second category because the major feature of his disorder is the broken timing of his utterance. The person with aphasia often shows articulation errors, broken rhythm, inability to produce voice, but the outstanding feature of aphasia is the inability to handle symbolic meanings and language. Therefore, we would place aphasia under disorders of symbolization or languge."[9]

Articulation

Among articulation disorders are those characterized by substitution, omission, addition, and distortion of speech sounds. Baby talk or infantile perseverance is a disorder which also fits this category. The chief characteristics of articulatory disorders are distorted, substituted, omitted, or added speech sounds.

In the very young child this all passes as a normal part of learning to speak. As he enters the elementary school, however, he is expected to make himself more clearly understood. When his language pattern develops into a "self-language" which is incomprehensible to all except his fond mother he is in need of special help. The child flies into a temper tantrum at school because he is not understood when he says, "Taw uh Dwamma Doody toh tay me tow." It is the rare teacher who can translate the jargon into "Call up Grandma Coodry to take me home." In the situation of this type the emotional scene which ensues wears out the teacher and frustrates the child. Although all teachers would consider this a serious articulatory problem, most feel that the problem of articulatory disorders in general are relatively unimportant. However, in the personality development of the child the need to be understood is imperative. It is therefore essential to aid the child to overcome his difficulty. Articulation problems present a challenge to the classroom teacher. They are the most prevalent problems of the speech difficulties and the ones which the classroom teacher should be equipped to handle. Any articulatory problems which persist into the second grade should receive individualized attention— the more severe ones by the speech therapist if one is available. Kindergarten children and first graders benefit most from group speech activities in the regular classroom. Individualized help should usually be casual.

Disorders of Time and Rhythm

Children differ in their tempo in speaking, in their fluency, and in their pattern of speech. Good speech is characterized by fluency of speech without an undue amount of um's and uh's, ah's, hesitation, false starts and repetitions. When the timing of sounds and syllables is so far off the standard that speech is unintelligible, unpleasant, or conspicuous, there is a defect of rhythm. In stuttering and cluttering these deviations are serious enough to cause problems in communication.

Stuttering. Stuttering is a nonfluency which has become habitual and noticeable. Symptoms which give evidence of stuttering include: blocking on sounds, repetition or prolongation of words or syllables, repetition or prolongation of sounds, and spasms of the speaking mechanism in severe cases. Stutterers differ in the stimuli which motivate stuttering. At times they speak with comparative or complete fluency. The teacher should distinguish between the nonfluency which is common with all children and stuttering which becomes habitual nonfluency. The teacher and other adults should not demand such perfection in speaking that they change the normal child's pattern of nonfluency into a pattern of stuttering.

Primary stuttering. In this stage of stuttering the child's speech is broken by an excessive amount of repetitions of syllables and sounds, or at times by the prolongation of a single sound. Fortunately the child seems unaware of his difficulty, is not embarrassed, nor does he appear to be conscious that it is a problem. He goes jauntily along making the effort to communicate. An excerpt from a parent's letter illustrates this primary stuttering:

> I would appreciate some advice about my daughter. She is almost three years old, and has always been precocious in speech. Four weeks ago she recovered from a severe attack of whooping cough and it was immediately after that when she began to show some trouble with her speech. One morning she came downstairs and asked for orange juice and it sounded like this: "Wh-wh-wh-wh-where's my orange juice?" Since then she has repeated one or two words in almost every sentence, sometimes repeating twice, and sometimes eight or nine times. It doesn't seem to bother her but I'm worried about it as it gets a lot worse when she asks questions or when she is tired, and I'm afraid other children will start laughing at her. One of her playmates has already imitated her several times. No one else in our family has any trouble talking. What do you think we should do? Up to now we have just been ignoring it and hoping it will go away.[10]

If extreme non-fluency continues or grows worse it would be wise to consult a speech therapist. Unfortunately primary stuttering does not always remain in its primary form, nor does it always "go away". If it gets worse the child as well as the parent becomes disturbed. As a result he reacts by becoming tense, fearful of some speaking situations, and concerned about saying certain words and sounds. This starts a vicious circle. The more he is afraid, the more he stutters, and the more he stutters the more he is afraid to talk. When he reaches this point he has moved into the stage of secondary stuttering.

Secondary stuttering. Secondary stuttering takes on a variety of forms. The teacher should be aware of the varied evidences of this speech disorder. Such behaviour includes: spitting, grunting, pounding oneself, protruding the tongue, speaking on inhalation, waltzing or jumping, or merely staring glassily when in the throes of what is called a"spasm" or a "block".

Stutterers may react to an emotionally laden word. For some reason or another a particular word sends them into an agony of fear which "brings on" the spasm. It is possible for some stutterers to find a synonym for the difficult words, and learn to correlate bodily movement with the act of speaking the word and thus be able to communicate successfully. Unless this is accomplished severe stuttering can create stress which may result in a nervous breakdown.

There are many instances of stutterers who have been able to "live with" their problem. One such example involves a young lad who went into secondary stuttering when he discussed the farm. Both of his parents were professional people and looked forward to his following a professional career. Instead, the lad hoped to become a farmer, much to the disappointment of his family. In an interview with him at his home and in the presence of both parents the relationship between certain words such as "farmer" brought to light the conflict which was at the root of the problem. Once the word brought on contortions and struggle which immediately blocked all communication. After the problem was analyzed the parents were happy to allow the stutterer to plan his own future. As a result he is a successful, happy individual. As it turned out when the pressure was removed he became interested in the teaching profession.

Cluttering. Cluttering is garbled speech. It is frequently confused with stuttering. Cluttering nevertheless has distinctive elements. The major features are: (a) the excessive speed of speaking; (b) disorganized sentence structure; (c) omitted or slurred syllables and sounds. The clutterer speaks in a garbled manner without being aware of his problem. The speech of a clutterer has been described as a torrent of half articulated words, following each other like peas running out of a spout. The flow of his speech is hard to listen to.

Voice Disorders (Dysphonias)

Voice disorders have to do with faults of pitch, quality, or intensity. In each of these elements of speech, abnormalities can be found, and there are individuals with voices which may be defective in all three.

Pitch disorders. Pitch disorders include: too-high pitch, too-low pitch, monotone, pitch breaks, and stereotyped inflections.

We all have recollections of individuals—children and adults—whose defects in pitch proved to be a handicap. For example, the high-pitched, strident voice of

Joanne who made all the children turn to look at her; the low-pitched husky voice of Charles whose ability to simulate a fog horn in creative dramatics proved highly unpopular in other class situations. An extremely high-pitched voice in a man is definitely a handicap socially, communicatively, and economically. The expressionless voice of the teacher is often a cause of lack of success in the classroom. Droning on during a class or in delivering a lecture is an invitation to students to catch up on their sleep. Incongruities between the physique and the voice of an individual are often startling to the listener. A case in point is the two-hundred-pound football player who retains a high, piping, shrill child's voice.

Pitch breaks are frequent in the adolescent boy, whose voice is "changing". The break may be up, it may be down. It may turn a flip-flop without warning. Often the self-consciousness of the adolescent can be traced to the fear of a "voice break" and leads to an unwillingness to talk. Much of the so-called taciturn behaviour of the adolescent is related to problems of pitch breaks.

Disorders of Voice Intensity. Defects of intensity are readily recognizable; the *too loud* voice, the *too weak* voice, no voice at all (aphonia), peculiar *stereotyped patterns* of emphasis, loudness or inflection. The extremely loud voice may be caused by a hearing problem or a personality problem. Extremely soft voices may be the result of a feeling of inadequacy, insecurity, or lack of confidence. When a beginning teacher or a student teacher is criticized for the very soft voice—it may be pointed out that success in the teaching experience may bring a more appropriate voice quality. The strident voice of the veteran teacher may turn the budding teacher against the profession, and a too thin voice may change a room of confident young children into anxiety-prone youngsters who cry, whine, and have other problems caused by a lack of trust in the adult with a child-like voice. The strain of being in a classroom with a teacher whose voice is barely audible or harshly strident is evident in children who appear emotionally worn out by the end of the day. The teacher must set an example of appropriate intensity as well as appropriate usage.

Disorders of Voice Quality. There are as many different voices as there are different faces. If one listens carefully he will learn that even where voices apparently sound the same, discriminating listening will distinguish differences, however subtle. The student who listens to a recording of his own voice for the first time is often shocked and is unable to believe that the voice is really his. Some students are so discouraged after listening that they are ready to seek help in voice improvement. Among the types of voices that cause discouragement because of their unpleasant quality are those characterized by: hoarseness, raspiness, harshness, nasality, tenseness, denasality, breathiness, or throaty, guttural, and pectoral qualities.

Overstrain due to screeching, yelling, shouting, wrong use of the throat muscles, incorrect breathing, exhaustion, can cause unpleasant voice quality. Malnutrition, illness, impairment, and imitating poor models—these, too, can be significant factors in producing unpleasant voices. Teachers will find that children tend to imitate their voices—good or bad. This sets a direct responsibility on the teacher to provide a good model.

Symbolization Disorders

Some children are able to perceive but are unable to translate into linguistic formulation. The general term for all disorders of symbolic formulation and expression is known as *dysphasia*. The extreme form (aphasia) is seldom met in the classroom. In a mild form it occurs occasionally as a pronounced reading, writing, or speaking disability. "Such persons find it difficult to use or comprehend linguistic symbols, whether they be written or spoken. In the motoexpressive type of aphasia, the case may say "bum-bum-bum" for "cigarette", and "bum" for "shoe". Another aphasic may grope for words in attempting to say "pencil" but say "eraser" or "pen" instead. Yet he knows his errors the instant they are spoken."[11]

Unfortuately, children with problems of this type are all too frequently classified as hard-of-hearing or mentally retarded. When the problem relates to failure in using or comprehending spoken symbols it should be dealt with by a speech correctionist.

The problem of bright children who have been unable to learn to read and write because of Specific Dyslexia (specific language disability) which makes it impossible for them to perceive and/or record accurately the symbols of the printed page, has only recently been recognized by educators.

Delayed speech. Delayed speech which is a marked retardation in the child's use of language may or may not belong in the category of symbolization disorders. Van Riper suggests a relationship when he points out "Injuries to the brain have often, in young children, interrupted speech development or retarded it. . . . It is also certain that many children who are mute or speak in an unintelligible jargon or gibberish have been called 'brain-damaged' when they were entirely normal individuals who just had not been taught to talk. Delayed speech often approximates the pattern of a very severe articulation disorder and some cases, so diagnosed, probably belong in this category."[12]

Other children suffer from delayed speech or persevere in baby talk because parents learn the language of the child instead of teaching them to imitate adult language. Betsey was an example of this lack of parental teaching. At three and a half Betsey was speaking a language which no one but Mother could understand. Instead of expecting Betsey to speak so she could be understood, her mother translated the language and Betsey enjoyed the power the little game gave her. Not until a new baby arrived and Mother was too busy to take the time to translate Betsey's every whim did she feel motivated to speak clearly enough to make her wants known. When she finally did, she discovered that the language everyone could understand was far more satisfactory than the limited communication of the past.

Wendell Johnson lists the following common factors in delayed speech development:

1. Mental subnormality.
2. Illness and physical impairment, such as brain injury or paralysis.
3. Lack of sufficient speech stimulation, as in homes where no one coos or babbles to the baby, or where the members of the family talk very little among themselves.
4. Impaired hearing.
5. Inadequate or disturbing or inconsistent rewards—even a certain amount of misplaced punishment—for the child's early attempts at speech.
6. A pattern of rewards and in general a relationship of such a nature that he gets along so well without speaking that he lacks sufficient motivation for attempting to learn to speak.
7. Intense shock, fright or shame, experienced over a sustained period or on one or more crucial occasions.[13]

Multiple Speech Disorders

Some speech disorders are multi-oriented. Among defects which almost always have multiple features of abnormality are: cleft palate, cerebral palsy, deaf and hard-of-hearing, and foreign accent.

Cleft-plate speech. The cleft may go through the teeth ridge, hard palate, and soft palate. The speech of such an individual is characterized by articulatory errors, hypernasality, and faltering, laboured rhythm. Surgery at an early age is often recommended. When surgery is not indicated obturators (an appliance used to close a cleft or gap) are recommended.

Cerebral palsy. Cerebral palsied children may have hearing losses resulting in part from the cerebral palsied condition in addition to voice problems, and articulatory difficulties resulting from impaired musculature. Most of these children will be found in special education classes. Since this problem is due to a brain injury which affects the coordination of the muscles it is particularly handicapping to a child.

Deaf and hard-of-hearing. These children, too, are the victims of multiple disorders. The congenitally deaf are lacking in language and symbolization. These children will not be found in the regular classroom. The voices of the hard-of-hearing are abnormal in pitch, intensity and quality; their rhythms are unusual; they make many articulatory errors. Both language and social development of the child with hearing loss may be retarded because of lack of stimulation of a "speaking" environment.

IDENTIFYING SPEECH AND HEARING DEFECTS

Regardless of the type of speech and hearing program which operates within a given school system, the teacher's observations will continue to play an important role in identifying the children who need therapy. Although the more progressive school systems and teacher training institutions have assumed their responsibility in providing for the needs of speech handicapped children, the classroom teacher still has a vital role to play.

"Because of the increased interest in developing speech therapy programmes in Canadian schools, large numbers of children are now freed from the crippling effect of a speech handicap.

"The therapist assumes responsibility for the speech programme, provides in-service training, conducts therapy sessions for the severe speech cases and serves as a consultant to the classroom teacher. Within recent years teachers have been contributing to the early development of good speech habits in children, the prevention of speech defects, and the improvement of minor speech problems. This is accomplished by applying in a learning situation certain skills acquired through in-service programmes and speech correction courses in teacher-training institutions."[14]

Testing and referral procedures for identifying speech and hearing problems vary from school to school. Even schools which have speech therapists often use teacher referrals rather than screening speech tests given by the speech therapist to identify children with speech disorders. Hearing tests, too, are supplemented by teacher observations. It is essential therefore that every teacher should be sufficiently familiar with the observable symptoms of speech and hearing problems to be able to identify and refer such children to a speech and hearing therapist, or to other designated personnel. To help the classroom teacher determine which pupils have speech or hearing handicaps the inventories below are presented.

Speech Inventory[15]

Pupil's Name _____

The speech difficulties checked below have been observed.

    I. Articulation
        1. Can hardly understand him _____
        2. Omits certain sounds _____
        3. Uses "baby-talk" _____
        4. Substitutes wrong sounds for right ones, such as "w" for "r" _____
        5. Has a foreign accent _____
        6. Has "sloppy" speech _____
        7. Distorts certain sounds _____
        8. Protrudes tongue for s-z sounds _____
        9. Sounds which appear inaccurately made: p-b-m _____ wh-w _____
                t-d-n _____ h _____ y _____ k-g-ng _____ f-v ————
                        th _____ l-r _____ s-z _____ ch-j _____
      vowels _____

    II. Voice
        1. Usually has weak voice and can hardly be heard in class _____
        2. Has a very monotonous voice ————

3. Is too breathy when talking _____
4. Is throaty and guttural _____
5. Has a husky, hoarse voice _____
6. Sounds too nasal _____
7. Is too high pitched _____
8. Speech lacks variety and life _____
9. Usually talks in a whisper _____
10. Usually talks too fast _____ too slowly _____

III. Fluency
1. Repeats initial sounds, syllables, and phrases _____
2. Blocks sometimes and can't get words out _____
3. Speech is jerky _____

IV. Other Problems
1. Has cleft palate _____
2. Has cerebral palsy _____
3. Appears to be hard of hearing _____
4. Very poor oral reader _____
5. Avoids speaking in class _____
6. Appears tense and uncomfortable much of the time _____
7. Has symptoms of nervousness _____
8. Unusually shy _____
9. Frequently too aggressive _____
10. Does not co-operate well in the group _____

Hearing Inventory[16]

Pupil's Name _____

The hearing difficulties checked below have been observed.

I. Physical symptoms
1. Frequent earaches _____
2. Running ears _____
3. Faulty equilibrium _____
4. Chronic colds _____

II. Speech and voice symptoms
1. Omission and substitution of certain sounds of speech _____
2. Mispronouncing common words _____
3. Other speech defects _____
4. Voice lacking in intonation pattern _____

III. Behavior reactions in the classroom
1. Request for repetition of words _____
2. Turns one side of head (better ear) toward speaker _____
3. Inattentive in class discussions _____
4. Watches teacher's lips _____
5. Shows strain in trying to hear _____

6. Unusual mistakes in taking dictation _____
7. More than normal use of hands to make wants known _____
8. Frequent mistakes in following directions _____
9. Low achievement for age _____

IV. Some signs that may indicate hearing impairment
1. Irritability ——
2. Child appears more intelligent than work indicates _____
3. Temper tantrums _____
4. Inferiority complex _____
5. Child is tense _____
6. Child sometimes appears dull _____

Following the identification of the child with a speech and/or hearing problem the teacher refers him to the speech therapist, or to the principal who contacts the designated personnel. More and more the cooperative efforts of teachers, parents, speech and hearing therapists, doctors, psychologists, and other personnel are utilized in diagnosing the problem and undertaking a program of therapy.

HELPING THE SPEECH HANDICAPPED CHILD IN THE CLASSROOM

A speech or hearing handicapped child should receive therapy from a speech and hearing therapist in the school or in a speech and hearing center in a near-by hospital, community agency, or university. However, the role of the classroom teacher is an extremely important one in the therapy program because the child spends so much more time within the classroom than he does with a speech and hearing therapist. "A classroom teacher provides the best possible help for a speech or hearing handicapped child when she adjusts her teaching of speaking and listening to meet the handicapped child's needs in the same way in which she provides for individual differences of nonhandicapped children. Speech handicapped children should be encouraged to participate in all speaking and listening activities of the classroom."[17]

Logan and Logan further emphasize need for understanding by the classroom teacher in dealing with the speech defective child.

First of all, the teacher must understand that the child who has difficulty in his speech usually differs from the rest of the children in no other respect. The same range of intelligence, the same likes and dislikes will be found in those who speak easily and those who have problems in speaking. Differences in personality are usually the result not of any basic differences in the children but the frustrations and misunderstandings brought about by their speech problems. . . . If the problem he faces in communication difficulties could be understood there would be fewer extreme differences in his behavior pattern. Co-operation with the parents, speech therapists . . . and the child himself is essential to make sure that both the goal and the methods for reaching the goal are mutually understood.[18]

In making provisions for the speech handicapped child the teacher should have some guideliness which will aid in helping a child with a specific handicap during the time he is in the regular classroom. Not only must the teacher arrange for the speech handicapped child to have special help, he must also include him in the regular speech program and encourage him to participate in the speech improvement activities.

Helping the Stutterer

The child who suffers from occasional or habitual nonfluency needs more than anything else to be in an environment in which he feels accepted, valued, and secure. It is especially important for him to be a part of the classroom activities, to be successful in endeavors he chooses, and to know that he is free to participate when he feels comfortable about speaking and is free to refrain when circumstances cause too great anxiety. The classroom teacher can best help the pupil who stutters by giving him opportunity for oral communication in an environment in which acceptance, warmth, empathy, and approval predominate; free from discrimination, fear, tension, and disapproval. As self-evaluation on creating a classroom climate in which the stutterer can most successfully achieve the teacher might ask himself these questions: How do I feel about such factors as: (1) the importance of a warm accepting, nurturing environment? (2) pressure for academic achievement? (3) a democratic role for the teacher? (4) an authoritarian figure for the teacher? (5) need for providing for individual differences? (6) importance of a rigid timetable? (7) negative discipline? (8) positive reinforcement? (9) working with parents and the speech therapist? (10) the child in the classroom who stutters? (11) significance of oral communication in the total program?

It is well to remember the old adage "Nothing succeeds like success". Thus the teacher creates an environment in which a child is able to succeed in as many areas of the curriculum as possible. A child should not be merely accepted but valued, and be guided step-by-step toward reaching his potential not alone in speech activities but in every phase of his development. As the child develops a greater sense of his own worth as a person as well as a speaker, he is well on the road toward success in minimizing the handicap of stuttering.

Helping the Hard-of-Hearing

The development of speech is normally dependent upon auditory impressions. Impaired hearing involves, potentially or actually, a degree of distortion of auditory perception. The hearing handicapped child in the classroom should be provided with the instruction in speaking and listening which have been discussed in the preceding chapters. It is essential that he be given opportunity to participate in speaking activities of all types plus participation in activities in rhythms, dramatics, improvisation, and choral speaking.

This child has the same physical, social, emotional needs as well as intellectual needs as other children. Most of the suggestions for the stutterer will benefit the child with a hearing problem also. Special attention is required to keep him in top physical condition. Medical attention for even minor respiratory problems or ear infections is imperative.

The classroom teacher who is concerned with helping this child is alert to signals such as: earache complaints, running ears, stupid expression, poor speech, poor spelling, need for teacher to repeat questions, and watching the speaker with a special intentness.

The teacher should give consideration to the following responsibilities for helping the child:

1. Seating the child as near as possible to the instruction area
2. Allowing the child to move around the room when the instructional area shifts
3. Making a special effort to be certain that the child hears what is said
4. Helping the other children in the class assume a positive attitude toward the problem
5. Including the child in regular and extra-curricular activities of the class

The Cleft-palate Child

What the cleft-palate child needs often more than speech improvement activities is help with his psychological and cosmetic problems. These problems may interfere with his development of adequate speech even when surgery has corrected the physical abnormality. The most important point for the classroom teacher to remember is the need to create an environment in which the child gains acceptance, security and achievement—not rejection, over protection, and criticism.

The Cerebral Palsied Child

The majority of cerebral palsied children will attend special classes or schools. They will receive daily speech and hearing therapy. If possible they should also have opportunity for daily speaking and listening activities in the regular classroom. Many times the less severely handicapped cerebral palsied child attends the regular classroom. He may need special attention to the development of language concepts, vocabulary development, vocal and articulation skills. Dramatization, puppetry, choral speaking all lend themselves admirably to helping children with problems caused by cerebral palsy. If these children are to develop in communication skills the teacher and class must exert patience as well as understanding.

Delayed Speech Development

Here, especially, the child must be helped to develop language concepts and vocabulary through listening and speaking activities. Dramatic activities stressing bodily action and rhythmic movement are valuable in stimulating children's development of linguistic skills. Because the classroom teacher must work with the handicapped child for the larger part of the day it is evident that the handicapped child must be encouraged to participate with other children in discussion, dramatic activities, and choral speaking.

The greatest help the classroom teacher can give to the speech handicapped child is that of creating a climate in which the child is secure, accepted, and valued. He does what he can to aid the child in understanding and accepting his difficulty. He assists him in adjusting to his school environment. He encourages him to take part successfully in speech situations. As a result of the teacher's efforts, the child not only attains better social adjustment, develops a positive image of self, but learns to live with his handicap as he improves his communication skills.

SPEECH IMPROVEMENT

From the first breath of life, beginning with the birth cry, the child continues to express through vocalization feelings, wants, and ideas. He is not born with speech; this he acquires through the use of muscles and organs that have biological functions far removed from speech. The quality and purpose of human sounds undergo changes as the child responds to and learns to control his environment through language. "Even in the crying and wailing of infants the short, sharp inhalation and prolonged exhalation so fundamental to true speech are being practiced. Lip, jaw, and tongue movements involved in the production of all of the speech sounds in all human languages are repeatedly performed. The early awareness of these movements and their accompanying sounds provides the foundation for speech readiness."[19]

The child during the first two months has a variety of types of cries. He cries in protest against being left alone, against being hungry, or just "because". Soon he learns the pleasure of making sounds other than those of crying. Near the sixth month the child enters the stage of random vocalization, or babbling. Here he first uses the variety of vowels and consonants that will lead to the development of language. As crying is a form of protest, babbling is an expression of the child's delight. Other factors being equal, the happy child has a better opportunity of developing speech skills than the protesting, crying one.

During this babbling stage the child utters a wide variety of sounds. Many of them seem very strange to us. Only a phonetician or linguist can distinguish them. However, many a proud parent can "interpret" the sounds without any difficulty. Those that the child finds bring the most pleasant response, he keeps. The others eventually will be lost. The baby should be encouraged in this prelingual phase of his speech development. He is forming patterns now for true speech.

About six months later he enters the next phase of his speech development. He has apparently become entranced with the sound of his own voice. He repeats sounds that are pleasurable to him. As he listens to himself he gains skill in making selected sounds at will. This leads him into the next stage of development, echolalia.

In this echolalia stage the child consciously tries to repeat the sounds made by his mother or other adults. Here is the beginning of the child's native speech. Sounds that he has been making but that are now not given to him by the adult tend to disappear. He retains only those sounds that bring response from the people upon whom he depends.

By the time the child is two years of age, he should be talking. He will have learned the names of those who are near him and the objects and actions that concern him. The jargon he has used in imitation of the adult's speech in his effort to capture their fluency and intonation pattern is rapidly vanishing. Instead, he has become concerned with communication with the adult world. This means that he must use the oral symbols that are meaningful to them. At first he uses mostly the nouns which are the names of people and objects he can see, feel, and hear. Sixty five percent of the words used between thirteen and twenty-seven months are nouns. By the time the child is three or four years of age, only twenty percent of his words are nouns.

The visibly made sounds are the first to appear in the child's meaningful speech. The labials (lip sounds), p, b, m, h, and w, are used in connection with the vowels that have appeared and have been practiced during the jargon and echolalia stages. The next to appear are the front tongue consonants, t, d, and n. The back-of-the-tongue consonants are usually next, k, g, ng, y. The l, f, v, th, sounds, which are more difficult, are comparatively late in appearing; s, z, r, and sh are the last.

Speech Improvement in the Classroom

Speech improvement as distinguished from speech therapy is that part of the speech program that aims to develop every phase of the speech of every child, normal, or handicapped, to the best of which each is capable. Many minor problems common to most children can be eliminated in the classroom by the regular classroom teacher who understands the basic problems and who has a wealth of exercises and activities from which to choose to meet specific needs.

The ability to think develops before the ability to express ideas. The ability to express ideas develops before the ability to read. For this reason it is imperative that a planned program for the improvement of speech be instituted in the primary grades and continued throughout the elementary school. Experiments have shown that where children are having difficulty with articulation this sequence of learning the sounds has been successful—first the child is helped to distinguish and make the sound in isolation, then to use the sound in nonsense syllables, then in unfamiliar words, and finally he is guided to establish the habit of using the sound correctly in familiar words.

As an aid to adults in fostering speech development during the preschool and primary years, Hanson cites speech norms and suggests games for each age to stimulate the development of specific speech sounds. The chronological age norms represent the *outside* limits of consonant maturation; many children will have acquired these phonemes by earlier ages.[20]

GAMES: SOUNDSCOTCH. A hopscotch diagram should be drawn on paper, sidewalk or floor. Each square should be named for a sound in a word. The child hops from square to square saying each sound as he does so. He is not permitted to advance to the next square until he utters the sound in the preceding. If he is nonfluent, however, no penalties should be attached for a failure to comply. (Note: For older misarticulates or stutterers the sounds may be printed in the squares.)
3½—p, m, w, h, b

SOUND TOSS. A funny picture of an animal or clown is required. Holes should be left or cut for the eyes, mouth, ears and nose and the spaces given names. The child should aim the chip or play coin toward a hole (different values may be assigned each target) and if his chip goes through one, he must say its sound name to get credit. (The holes, of course, have been captioned after difficult or feared sounds or words.)
4½—t, d, n, k, g, ng, y

GAMES: FISHING. Vari-colored slips of paper, to which small clips have been fastened and representing the child's problem words or sounds (mispronounced or stuttered) should be prepared. If the children are older, the words or sounds should be printed on the slips. A dime store magnet is fastened to a line. The child is then instructed to drop his "line" (the magnet) by the "fishing pole" (pencil) into the "pond" (area containing the word or sound slips). If the paper and clips are sufficiently light, they will adhere to the magnet, and constitute the child's "catch", which can serve many different purposes. In the ear training stage, he has "caught" a fish when he recognizes his sound in a word, or discriminates a good production or a poor production of it by his parent, or pronounces it correctly himself. Should he be nonfluent, then he is asked to say the word or sound in a phrase or sentence. However, in whatever manner the stutterer pronounces his "fish" he should not be directly corrected. The parent or teacher can improve any incorrect sounds of potential stutterers by example and simply saying the sound or word after him correctly. If the nonfluent child seems to be having particular difficulty with certain sounds or words, the pond can be filled with more of these; in this way there will be practice on the poor words or sounds but without making the child conscious of being "taught". Those extra "p" or "t" or "d" words simply happen to be his "haul".

SOUND LADDER: The instructor should draw a ladder and name or print each rung with a sound or word difficult for the misarticulating child. To climb the ladder the child must identify or pronounce correctly, etc., each rung. If he is nonfluent he may simply be asked to name the rung to climb the ladder, and if he makes any speech attempt credit should be given. If he does not wish to climb it, he should not be forced.
5½—f

GAMES: SOUND HIDE AND SEEK. This game may be played several ways depending on the nature of the child's problem. If he is misarticulating sounds, and in the ear training stage, a picture or object may be hidden in the room, the child sent to look for it, and the correct version of the sound used by the teacher as he approaches its hiding place, the error production if he moves away. If the child sometimes mis-pronounces a sound, but has reached the stage of producing it with occasional success, he may hide the picture or object while the parent or teacher looks for it and he signals their nearness to it by producing it himself in the correct manner. If the assistant moves away he speaks it incorrectly. It should be pointed out quickly here that it does no harm, and actually helps, for the child consciously to produce the sound incorrectly at times. However, this technique called negative practice, should be used only with his awareness that he is deliberately producing an error. Later, with the older stutterer, negative practice is used in therapy in a form called voluntary stuttering; it is not, however, commonly used with the nonfluent young-ster. At this age, mere speaking of the word or sound is sufficient and helpful.

6½—v, th-(unvoiced), sh, 1, zh

GAMES: RIDDLEREE—I SEE SOMETHING THAT BEGINS WITH. This old favorite may be used for continued practice on particular sounds or words giving trouble to the child who misarticulates or stutters. The former should be corrected for errors in response but no comment should be made on the quality of the speech attempt of the stutterer or nonfluent child. With this game, as with others used with stutterers, elimination of the fear of speaking and increasing talking time are the primary objectives.

SOUND SPINNER. The teacher should construct a cardboard circle with a spinner and divide it into squares, named or printed after the child's difficult or feared sounds or words. The youngster spins and where the spinner stops he must say the sound or word in that square (or the parent or teacher may pronounce it if he is still at the ear training stage.) The young stutterer, again, should not be forced to verbalize but encouraged to do so in the "spirit of the game" to comply with the "rules." In this and other exercises, the regulations calling for a spoken response (for points or a turn or a move, etc.) should be clearly outlined and reiterated before the game begins; they should be followed, too, as if part of a ritual, with the mis-articulates. If her tone is kept light and gay, the teacher may even remind the stutterer at first of the "rules" but if he does not comply should not be insistent. It will help in securing compliance, however, if the "rules" of the game are printed, read and made to seem an *intrinsic* part of the activity from the start of the game.

PIN THE SOUND. This exercise is a version of the one above and similar to the old birthday party favorite, *Pin the Tail on the Donkey*. In this case, a map or picture of some scene should be substituted. The different areas should be given the names of words or sounds produced incorrectly, whether misarticulated or stut-tered. The child is given a tail, a shape of a state, a tree, or merely a slip of paper, blindfolded, and told to try to pin the tail on the donkey, or the state on the map in its proper location. Where he pins the form he must say the word or sound written in that area (or the name which the teacher has assigned it.) Different areas may be given different values but pronouncing the word is a condition of earning points. The stutterer, if he forgets to say the word, may be gently, gaily reminded of the "rule" but not compelled to follow it.

7½—s, z, r, th—(unvoiced), ch, j, wh

GAMES: BANKING. This is a popular game with many possible variations. Play money (coins or bills), colored slips or chips may be used as rewards. If a child identifies a sound or pronounces it correctly in isolation, nonsense syllable or word, or if a stutterer, simply speaks the word, he is "paid" with money or chips. Difficult words may earn bigger bills or coins or more slips. If he mispronounces a word or fails to identify sounds he forfeits his turn or pays the parent or teacher from his "roll" or "stack". (The only exception to this procedure is in the case of a stuttering child who is not to be corrected for any speech errors but only encouraged to talk. With a nonfluent youngster, it is sometimes helpful to deflect attention from the *speaking* act, to emphasize the thinking of a sentence in which the sound or word may be used). In this, and preceding games, MAKE SPEECH FUN! This last suggestion, again, applies equally to the misarticulating child although the latter may be corrected directly and the former only very lightly and indirectly.

ADDITIONAL GAMES. The following will be effective at any age level, with the child who misarticulates or stutters.

MISSING. Objects or pictures should be placed on a table. These should bear sounds or words which the child mispronounces or repeats or fears. He should then be requested to close his eyes, while parent or teacher removes one of the items. When he opens his eyes, he should try to guess what is "missing". (Through repetition of the "s" in missing, each round of the game, sufficient practice on his phoneme is afforded, that if it is the one defective, the items themselves need not also contain the sound.)

TIC-TAC-TOE. This is a convenient game for the busy parent or teacher. To place an X in his square (or preferably the letter or some symbol representing his sound, or the word itself), the child must perform some speech task, identifying or recognizing a sound, or if a stutterer, simply produces it or a problem word. A row of his sounds or words constitutes a win and he should say "bingo" or, perhaps one of his defective sounds or words if this has been agreed upon earlier.

SOUND SCAVENGER. Several pictures, some containing his error sounds or words, others not, are placed about the room. If he is misarticulating the child should be required to return with pictures containing his sound and perhaps pronounce same, if he is ready; if he is a stutterer he is asked to find a particular picture and then say the word to earn points in a game. Riddle-like directions as to the location of the pictures may be used to add interest.

SOUND AUTHORS. A series of flash cards, using defective or anxiety-laden words or sounds should be prepared. The game is then played like the traditional Authors, only with four sounds or words of a kind comprising each "book". This pastime is always valuable in stuttering therapy but should be employed with misarticulates only when the child has passed the ear training phase and is pronouncing words.

SITUATIONAL PRACTICE. The parent or teacher may send the stuttering child (and the misarticulate, too, when he has reached the stage of pronouncing words) on errands around home, school or store which will require use of the difficult sounds or words.

ANY GAME. While the ideal speech activities are those in which the speech task is central almost any game can motivate practice. In order to take a turn or make a move, the youngster must perform some specified speaking or listening act, whether recognizing a sound in a series of nonsense syllables or in words, or pronouncing it correctly himself. The stutterer, of course, need merely use such in a phrase or sentence.

In a program in which improved speech for all is the objective the responsibility for organizing the class and developing the activities is left very often to the classroom teacher with or without guidance from a speech therapist.

Van Riper and Butler reinforce this view: ". . . It is being realized that speech improvement practices and procedures should not be the sole property of the speech teacher or the speech correctionist in the public schools. All children will benefit from some phase of speech improvement, and it is the classroom teacher who is acutely aware of the need for this type of instruction. She recognizes the indistinct, hesitant speech of the shy child; the rather halting, stumbling speech of the poorly coordinated child; the loud, strained tones of the aggressive child. . . so the basic responsibility remains with the classroom teacher."[21]

If the program for speech improvement is to be successful it must go beyond the mechanics of speech drills into the area of meaningful language and exciting activities. It should have as its ultimate goal the objective of helping children improve their voice and speech. This goal is achieved through helping them to organize and verbalize their thoughts—to be able to think on their feet.

THE ROLE OF THE TEACHER

The key task of the classroom teacher in meeting the speech needs of children centres around organizing, planning, and directing activities which contribute specifically toward speech improvement. Some elementary teachers are well prepared for this responsibility. Others, however, need help in developing activities which will meet the goals of speech improvement for *all* children. The following are suggested to facilitate the establishment and implementation of a successful speech improvement program: determine the specific needs of the pupils; plan purposeful activities consonant with the needs; develop procedures that will achieve the purposes; build an activities and materials file; and present an example of good speech.

Determining Specific Needs of Children

The average kindergarten child does not yet have mature speech. Although maturation will take care of many speech problems, some will persist. Therefore throughout the elementary school years a short speech improvement period for all children several times a week is recommended. In the kindergarten and primary grades emphasis should be placed on group games and rhymes. Children who are already proficient in speech will benefit from these games and those who have difficulties can participate without any feeling of being singled out or pressured.

The chart opposite will be useful for all grades in determining the specific defects children have and should be considered in working out a speech improvement program.

Phonatory Defects

A. QUALITY
   1. Nasal (positive nasality) .... _____
   2. De-nasal (negative nasality) .... _____
   3. Breathy (aspirate) .... _____
   4. Hoarse-husky .... _____
   5. Strained and harsh (strident) .... _____
   6. Throaty - guttural .... _____
   7. Falsetto (juvenile voice) .... _____
   8. Weak - thin .... _____
   9. Tremorous .... _____

B. PITCH
   1. General level high (above average) .... _____
   2. General level low (below average) .... _____
   3. Monopitch .... _____
   4. Pitch spasmodic, uncontrolled .... _____

C. INTENSITY
   1. Too weak .... _____
   2. Too loud .... _____
   3. Spasmodic, uncontrolled .... _____

Articulatory Defects

A. SPEECH SOUNDS
   1. Omitted .... _____
   2. Substituted .... _____
   3. Added .... _____
   4. Defective .... _____
B. ORAL INACTIVITY (indistinct articulation) .... _____
C. SLOW, LABORED .... _____
D. RAPID, SLURRING .... _____
E. ARTICULATION BELOW AGE LEVEL .... _____
F. FOREIGN DIALECT .... _____
G. REGIONAL DIALECT .... _____

Linguistic Defects

A. SPEECHLESSNESS .... _____
B. SPEECH CONFUSION, SEARCH FOR WORDS .... _____
C. CANNOT UNDERSTAND WORDS .... _____
D. CANNOT WRITE WORDS .... _____
E. READING BELOW GRADE OR AGE LEVEL .... _____

Defects of Rhythm

A. ABNORMAL REPETITION OF SOUNDS .... _____
B. ABNORMAL REPETITION OF WORDS .... _____
C. SPEECH BLOCKS .... _____

D. ABNORMAL HESITATIONS .... _____

E. CLUTTERING, IRREGULAR RHYTHM .... _____

General Observations

A. TICS, FACIAL GRIMACES .... _____

B. EXCESSIVE STAGE FRIGHT .... _____

C. UNUSUAL POSTURE OR BODILY MOVEMENT .... _____

D. ABNORMALLY SHY, UNRESPONSIVE .... _____

E. BELLIGERENT, NEGATIVISTIC .... _____

F. OTHER PROBLEMS .... _____

Planning Purposeful Activities

Meeting the needs of children in speech improvement requires planned, purposeful activities. Once the teacher has determined the needs of the children (with the help of the speech therapist if one is available), a specific program for speech improvement can be drawn up relating needs and objectives.

The Major Goals in Speech Improvement

1. Improve the speech of all children. All children can improve in at least one area: volume, inflection, usage, articulation, etc.
2. Eliminate speech problems such as infantile speech, lisping, indistinct speech and careless use of voice such as too loud or too soft. This program also helps the child with a severe problem.
3. Develop a good phonic background. It helps to improve habits of listening and increases the attention span, and helps articulation.

Specific Goals

1. Develop the attitude that the speech improvement period is fun time. Remember the enthusiasm of the children is directly parallel to that of the teacher.
2. Develop the ability to relax.
3. Develop good coordination. Big muscle coordination must precede fine muscle coordination.
4. Improve the ability to listen.
   a. Gross sounds
   b. Speech sounds in isolation, nonsense syllables, words, simple sentences, poems, games.
5. Develop the use of a pleasant and audible voice.
   a. Develop the recognition of gross differences in quality, volume, pitch and rate: the Big Billy Goat Gruff and the Little Billy Goat Gruff; the Big Bad Wolf and the Little Pig.

b. Develop an awareness of the voice to use when speaking to one, a small group, or the entire class.
6. Develop the correct use of the speech sounds. One sound should be stressed at a time.
   a. Develop the use of the articulatory mechanism.
   b. Encourage the use of natural weak forms in all speaking activities.
   c. Endeavor to correct marked deviations.

Approach

1. Direct. There needs to be a specific period for speech improvement in order to develop the correct techniques and to develop correct attitudes.
2. Integrated. It will be necessary to integrate the correct habits and attitudes towards speech with the entire curriculum.

Developing Procedures

The classroom teacher is in a strategic position to correct articulatory errors as they appear in classroom activities. Opportunities for children to participate in speech activities in a relaxed classroom atmosphere is the first step toward improving the child's speech.

In such an atmosphere and with the rapport between teacher and child developed through being an accepted member of the group, the speech handicapped child as well as the child with normal speech will benefit from a program of activities designed to improve speech. The teacher may then use the following speech activities and stories as a channel through which a speech improvement program may be planned in correlation with the lessons, exercises and games suggested in this chapter.

Although speech improvement lessons are developed in a variety of ways, it is important that every lesson begin with relaxation exercises as a prelude to the specific drills which are developed in the lesson. The exercises which follow are carefully planned to implement the objectives of the speech improvement program.

The scope of the program in speech improvement is both comprehensive and balanced. It includes provision for activities increasing the agility of the tongue, lips, and jaw for both the consonants and vowels. Through games, jingles, stories, poems, dramatics, and exercises children improve voice quality and speech ability.

Guidelines for Speech Improvement

1. Each lesson should start with RELAXATION. It is difficult to get all children to relax. Relaxation is the basis for good speech. Suggestions:
   a. Raggidy Doll. The teacher reads this rhyme aloud and then re-reads it (better

to say it from memory), while the children interpret with arms, head and bodies. Parts of this may be used in emergencies to start lessons when for some reason the room has been under special tension.

> Let's play rag-doll
> Don't make a sound
> Fling your arms and bodies
> Loosely around
> Fling your arms! Fling your feet!
> Let your head go free!
> Be the raggest rag-doll
> You ever did see.

b. Playing Rag Doll. This requires the use of "play-magic", which the teacher makes by waving her arms. With one wave the feet turn to rags, at the second wave, the knees, then the back, arms, elbows, hands, neck and head, in the order given. The teacher then goes on a tour of inspection, gently shaking arms, shoulders, head, and lifting knees to be sure all are relaxed. Some she will find "made of paper", some of "wood", and some of "rags" —but highly starched. Then with one magic wave the room must be awakened and the exercise repeated.

c. Playing Scarecrow. "Magic" is again utilized as in "Rag Doll"; this time, in order to turn the children into scarecrows as in the "Wizard of Oz". This exercise is done standing with arms at right angles, stiff and tense, the hands, head, chest are limp. At a signal the wind blows, the scarecrows wave gently.

d. Floating. Have the children lie with their backs on the floor, face upward. Tell them to imagine that they are floating in the water. When given the command to "float" direct the children to lie with arms at right angles with the body, heels together and at rest. Go to each child, lift his arm or leg to see if it falls of its own weight. The speech of the teacher must be slow and quiet. Compliment each child when he is relaxing or improving. If children are seated at desks direct them to stretch their arms forward, to place their heads on the desks and relax when given the command to "float". Go to each child to see if he feels relaxed.

e. Flowers. Let each child play that he is a flower. The kinds of flowers may be chosen according to the season of the year. Tell the children to imagine that the wind comes along and causes them to nod their heads very slowly, down around to the right shoulder, back to the left side and front. Let the jaw drop. The wind blows a little harder and the body gently sways in the direction the head is moving.

f. Let the children play elephant. They stand, bend from hips, allowing head and arms to drop limply, and sway loosely from the ankles.

2. Develop correct breathing. Encourage the children to close their lips and to breathe with a quiet rhythm. Develop deep breathing but do not encourage gasp-

ing in a great amount of air. Deep breathing means taking an adequate supply of air and expanding the lower region of the chest.

Suggestions:

a. Pretend you have a little candle for a birthday cake. Hold it up and blow it out.

   Pretend you have a larger candle. Hold it farther away and blow it out.

   Pretend you have a big candle. Hold it at arms length and blow.

   Do not permit noisy blowing.

   The breathing will be deeper each time. There will be more chest expansion.

b. Blow a balloon up. Each blow will require greater chest expansion.

c. Blow the candles on a birthday cake. Pretend they all go out except two and then one. The blowing will start with great chest expansion and end with little.

d. Provide the students with bright paper pin wheels. Who can keep his pin wheel spinning the longest? The fastest? Who can blow a "soft south wind" and make the wheel spin slowly for a long time? Give each student a turn to come before the class to show how steadily and long his wheel will go. By placing your hands gently on the student's ribs you will be able to test his ability to expel air evenly. The muscles should contract evenly and gradually.

e. Have the student hold the pin wheel close to his lips and talk to it. "Where are you going little pin wheel?" "Why do you whirl so fast, little pin wheel?"

f. Have the student place a two-inch square of light paper against the wall, mouth high and try to keep it there by blowing a steady stream of air against it.

g. Have the student imitate the long-drawn-out tooting of a distant train— (distance will require less volume) tu-u-u, tu-u-u.

h. Ask whether they have ever watched a dog breathe, and have them open their mouths and pant as a dog does on a very hot day while they put their hands on their stomachs and feel the rapid motion of their bodies.

i. Have the student's inhale slowly. 1-2-3-4-5; exhale on whispered "choo, choo, choo", as an engine would leave the depot (teeth closed, air is to be forced through).

j. Inhale slowly and steadily, 1-2-3-4-5; cool burned fingers by blowing cooling breath through small lip opening on fingers, 1-2-3-4-5.

k. Repeat Exercise j, warming cold fingers through the open mouth.

l. Teach the students to hold a tone while your hand is raised and to stop the instant you lower your hand. Varied exercises may be use to develop breath control. The exercises should be graduated as the students develop (for example gradually increase the time of holding a steady tone or increase the number of short tones given at one breath).

m. The game of laughing may be played during the dramatization of the Mother Goose rhyme "Hey diddle diddle." Show the students how the little dog laughed. Place one hand on your diaphragm while you give quickly and forcibly "Ho, ho, ho, ho." Be sure that your muscles go in and out vigorously. Have the children place their hands on their diaphragm and test each individually to see which is the best dog who "laughed to see such sport."

n. Have the students practice whispering several sentences. This will assist in securing deep, controlled breathing and will improve the enunciation as well.

o. Have the students place their hands on chest and diaphragm. Have them imitate a pricked balloon; the sound "puh".

3. Encourage greater flexibility of speech organs.

   Suggestions:

   a. Tongue

   Have visual aid material: A clown, baby, cat, dog, pumpkin with an open mouth. Use a tongue blade painted red to encourage the children to look, follow and imitate the movements you make with it.

   Have the children make the watch sound (T) and use the tip of tongue, then make the coughing sound (K) and use the back of the tongue. Make the tongue rock both ways (T-K) and (K-T) several times.

   Have the children say these with exaggerated tongue action. Following the drill work have the children repeat these poems with "normal" tongue action.

JACK IN THE BOX

Jack jump out,
And Jack jump in!
Jack jump up,
And Jack jump down!

Shake your head!
Look out and in!
Go in and shut,
The cover down!

LAPPING MILK

Little kitty laps her milk,
Lap, lap, lap!
Her tongue goes out,
Her tongue goes in,
Lap, lap, lap!

Little kitty likes her milk,
Lap, lap, lap!
Oh, see her tongue
Go out and in,
Lap, lap, lap!

A FARMER WENT TROTTING

A farmer went trotting,
Upon his grey mare,
Bumpety, bumpety, bump!

With his daughter behind him
So rosy and fair,
Bumpety, bumpety, bump!

A raven cried "Croak!"
And they all tumbled down
Bumpety, bumpety, bump!

The mare broke her knees,
And the farmer his crown
Lumpety, lumpety, lump!

The mischievous raven
Flew laughing away,
Bumpety, bumpety, bump!

And vowed he would serve them
The same the next day,
Lumpety, lumpety, lump.

THOMAS A TATTAMUS

Thomas A Tattamus took two T's
To tie two tups to two tall trees,
To frighten the terrible
Thomas A Tattamus
Tell me how many T's there
    are in all that.

DOTTING THE ROOF

My tongue can dot
The roof of my mouth;
Dot__dot__dot.

It touches the front
And middle and back;
Dot__dot__dot.

Can your tongue dot
The roof of your mouth?
Dot__dot__dot.

Can it touch front,
And middle and back?
Dot__dot__dot.

THE TWO CROWS

There were two crows sat
    on a stone,
Fal, la, la, la, lal, de
One flew away, and then
    there was one
Fal, la, la, la, lal, de
The other crow finding
    himself alone,
Fal, la, la, la, lal, de.

DICKERY, DICKERY DOCK

Dickery, dickery, dock!
The mouse ran up the clock!
The clock struck one, and
    down he ran;
Dickery, dickery, dock!

b. Lips

    Suggestion: Use visual aids material: clown, babies, cats, dogs with lips in open spread or rounded positions.

    Read the following poems first with exaggerated, then normal lip action.

TU-WHIT'. TU-WHOO'.

The owl by day can't see, 'tis said!
    OOoo, OOoo, OOoo!
He sits and blinks, turns his head,
    OOoo, OOoo, OOoo!

But when the stars come out at night,
    Tu-whit, tu-whoo, tu-whoo!
He calls his mate with all his might,
    Tu-whit, tu-whoo, tu-whoo!

THE CHEE-CHOO BIRD

A little green bird sat on a fence rail,
    Chee-choo, chee-choo, chee!
Its song was the sweetest I ever have
    heard,

Chee-choo, chee-choo, chee!
I ran for some salt to put on its tail,
    Chee-choo, chee-choo, chee!
But while I was gone, away flew the
    bird,
Chee-choo, chee-choo, chee!

BAA, BAA, BLACK SHEEP

Baa, baa, black sheep,
    Have you any wool?
Yes, sir, yes, sir, three bags full;
One bag for Bobby,
    And one bag for Bill,
And one bag for Betty,
    Who lives on the hill.

PUMP, PUMP, PUMP

Pump, pump, pump, pump,
Water from the spout;
Plish, plosh, plish, plosh,
Water gushes out.

Pour, pour, pour, pour,
Fill the doggie's pan;
Pump, pump, pump, pump,
Quickly as you can.

BROWN BIRDIE

Little brown birdie is bobbing his head,
   Bobbety, bobbety, bob.
Looking for something behind the shed,
   Bobbety, bobbety, bob.
If his dinner will be a fat bug or worm,
   Bobbety, bobbety, bob.
Whichever it is, I think it will squirm,
   Bobbety, bobbety, bob.

PETER, PETER

Peter, Peter, pumpkin eater,
Had a wife and couldn't keep her,
He put her in a pumpkin shell,
And there he kept her very well.

PITTY PATTY POLT

Pitty Patty Polt
Shoe the wild colt;
   here a nail
   and there a nail,
Pitty Patty Polt.

THE LITTLE BIRD

Once I saw a little bird
Go hop, hop, hop,
I said, "Little birdie,
Will you stop, stop, stop?"

He looked me up and down
With a peep, peep, peep,
And across the grass he went
With a leap, leap, leap.

BUBBLE BATH

Bubble bath, bubble bath
   In a white tub
Hear the little bubbles go
   Bub, bub, bub.

THE BIRCHES

The little birches, white and slim,
   Gleaming in the forest dim,
Must think the day is almost gone,
   For each one has her nighty on.

c. Jaw

Suggestions: Use visual aids material: clowns, cats, dogs, etc., with closed and open mouth.

Read the following poems first with exaggerated, then normal jaw action.

JOHN COOK'S GREY MARE

John Cook had a little grey mare,
   Hee, haw, hum;
Her legs were long and her back was
   bare,
   Hee, haw, hum.
John Cook was riding up Shooter's
   Bank
   Hee, haw, hum;
The mare she began to kick and to
   prank,
   Hee, haw, hum.
John Cook was riding up Shooter's Hill,
   Hee, haw, hum;
His mare fell down and made her will,
   Hee, haw hum.
The bridle and saddle were laid on the
   shelf,
   Hee, haw, hum;
If you want any more, you may sing it
   yourself,
   Hee, haw, hum.

BOW! WOW! WOW!

Bow, wow, wow, whose dog art thou?
Little Tom Tinker's dog, bow, wow,
wow.

THE OLD BLACK CROW

An old black crow flew into a tree.
    Caw, caw, caw!
And what do you think he could see?
    Caw, caw, caw!
He saw the sun shine on the lake.
    Caw, caw, caw!
And tiny splashes fishes make.
    Caw, caw, caw!

THE OLD BILLY GOAT

In a lot near our school
    Is an old Billy Goat.
      Baa, baa, baa!
He has a long beard
    And a warm wooly coat.
      Baa, baa, baa!
The children at noon
    Throw him bits of their lunch.
      Baa, baa, baa!
And laugh as they watch
    Old Billy Goat munch!
      Baa, baa, baa!

FROG'S CHORUS

"Yaup, Yaup, Yaup!"
Said the croaking voice of a frog:
    "A rainy day
    In the month of May
And plenty of room in the bog."

"Yaup, yaup, yaup!"
Said the frog as it splashed about:
    "Good neighbors all,
    When you hear me call,
It is odd that you do not come out."

"Yaup, yaup, yaup!"
Said the frog: "It is charming weather.
    We'll come up and sup
    When the moon is up,
And we'll all of us croak together."

THE JOLLY LITTLE CLOWN

I'm a jolly little clown,
    Yak, yaw, yah!
I can smile and I can frown,
    Yak, yaw, yah!
I can drop my jaw far down!
    Yak, yaw, yah!

4. Develop listening habits. Listening is as important as speaking. Have children:
   a. Close their eyes and see how many sounds they can identify.
   b. Listen to gross sounds such as: a horn, whistle, bell, rhythm band instruments.
   c. Listen for loud and soft sounds: clap hands, stamp feet, chord on a piano, etc.
   d. Listen for fast and slow sounds: play the piano, walk, clap hands, etc.
   e. Listen for high and low sounds: play a key on the piano or harmonica, talk
      with high or low pitch.
   f. Play musical chairs. Listen when the music starts and stops.
   g. Take turns asking, "Who am I?" Children with eyes closed try to guess.
   h. Imitate the inflection of the teacher when she says a word (yes—no—good
      morning) using a happy, sad, or pleading voice.
   i. Listen to a story and dramatize it using appropriate voices for the giants,
      fairies, etc.
   j. Tell a story. Listen to see if: the sequence was right, the facts correct, the

correct voice used, the characters were impersonated correctly, and sentences were used.

EXAMPLES OF SPEECH IMPROVEMENT LESSONS: PRIMARY GRADES

Every speech improvement lesson should have a specific purpose related to the needs of the children in the group. It should be carefully planned so that the purpose, procedure, and development will be in harmony with good principles of teaching.

In the second grade class where there was a general tendency toward careless, slovenly speech the teacher decided to teach a lesson emphasizing distinct enunciation.

Purpose: To develop distinct enunciation through awareness of movements of the jaw and lips for the vowel sounds.

Materials:

Traditional song: "Old MacDonald Had a Farm".

Procedure:

Teacher: Let's sing a song we all know, "Old MacDonald had a Farm". Ready————
Teacher and Children: "Old Macdonald had a farm, E-I-E-I-O.
And on this farm he had some ducks, E-I-E-I-O."
Teacher: Let's find out what we do with our lips and mouths when we say the vowels in the song. What do we do when we say "E"?
Child: We smile, our mouths are almost closed shut.
Teacher: Let's all say "E" and be sure we are smiling.
Children: "E"
Teacher: What do we do when we say "I"?
Child: We open our mouths wide.
Teacher: Let's open our mouths wide and say "I"
Children: "I"
Teacher: What do we do when we say "O"?
Child: We round our lips.
Teacher: Let's all pucker our lips and say "O".
Children: "O"
Teacher: Now let's all sing E-I-E-I-O again. Sing it distinctly.
Children: "E-I-E-I-O"
Teacher: Now let's sing it fast.
Children: "E-I-E-I-O"
Teacher: Now that we know the first part of the song and can sing it distinctly, let's list some of the animal noises we can include in the song. I will write the words "smile", "open" and "round" on the chalkboard.

Give me as many animal noises as you can. Tell me which column to write them in.

Children:

Smile	*open*	*round*
chick-chick	quack-quack	moo-moo
peep-peep	gobble-gooble	oink-oink
neigh-neigh	baa-baa	caw-caw

Children: Meow-meow belongs in all three columns
Teacher: Let's say the words in the "smile" column.
(Children repeat "smile" column)
They do same with the "open" column and the "round" column.
Teacher: This time let's make it harder. We'll do one word in the smile column, one in the open column and one in the round column. We'll do this for all the words and end with "meow-meow." (Children repeat sounds after the teacher.) They then sing the entire song about Old MacDonald, using all the animal noises and singing distinctly.

Evaluation:

Teacher: Did we achieve our purpose?
Child: Yes, because we used our mouth and lips to form the vowel sounds correctly and therefore we learned to enunciate more clearly.

It is often effective to interchange activities involving music, oral reading, and choral speaking in teaching a lesson on enunciation to motivate interest in accurate articulation. Children enjoy singing their way to better speech.

This can apply to teaching of specific vowels, dipthongs or consonant sounds as well.

Speech Improvement Lesson in a Third Grade[22]

1. Alphabet of Sounds   *Game:* Circling Sounds
   Material: Volleyball or small softball
   Instructions: Children form a circle; sounds are reviewed. Then the ball is tossed haphazardly from one child to another. Each succeeding child must produce a different sound in isolation. If he repeats a sound said by the person just before him, he is out of the game. Sound must be produced at the same instant the ball is caught.
2. Voice Production   *Game:* Be an actor
   Material: None
   Instructions: Unison speech activity. Teacher gives each sentence, children repeat. "I feel cross today". "I am so sleepy". "I can hardly wait for Christmas." "I wish I didn't have to go to school." "I feel happy inside."
   Demonstrate voice qualities—cross, tired, excited, etc.,
3. General Speech Improvement   *Game:* Teacher Makes a Mistake
   Material: None

Instructions: "I'm going to be a third-grader now and show you different ways of talking." (Act out and have children tell you your mistake—talking with hands . . . , in a monotone, too fast, too loud, too soft, etc.,

Correlating speech improvement with other areas of the curriculum enhances a child's enjoyment of speech and improves his skills in speaking. Among the areas that combine readily with voice improvement are:

Rhythms—poems for skipping, galloping, clapping, rocking

Art—tell about pictures

Music—good articulation and rhythm

This should help to develop: Poise

A favourable attitude toward speech

Good habits of socialization

Listening habits

Big and fine muscle coordination

Awareness for better voice

Awareness of speech sounds

Better articulatory patterns consistent with chronological and physical maturity

Use of sentence to express ideas

SPEECH IMPROVEMENT IN THE INTERMEDIATE AND UPPER GRADES

Teachers who work with speech in the elementary schools sometimes find themselves confronted with sixth, seventh and eighth graders for whom speech improvement has lost its appeal. Motivations used with success and delight in the lower grades have lost their magic. They are confronted with vital needs which demand a fresh and broader approach.

"How can we lead these older children to a realization of the tremendous importance of speech to an individual, both in his career and in his personal life"?[23]

Activities

A persistent problem that confronts the intermediate and upper grade classroom teacher or the speech therapist is that of organizing, directing, and evaluating an effective program in speech improvement. A well organized speech improvement program for a fifth grade class which has been reported by Kupferer gives an excellent suggestion for an intermediate grade teacher who does not want to use the same exercises, games, drills, etc., used in the primary grades. The work was divided into three units and was supervised by a speech consultant but taught by the classroom teacher over a period of 16 weeks. The activities presented were organized in such a way that the speech improvement activities of the first unit were the basis of the applied speech activities in the second unit and integration with other curriculum areas was the core of the activities of the third unit.

I. First Unit: Basics of Voice and Diction[24]
    A.   Lesson 1—Introduction
        1. Discuss: What is a good voice?
        2. Demonstrate: How do we get a good voice?
        3. Have first class practice.
    B.   Lesson 2—Recordings ($\frac{1}{2}$ of the class)
        1. Have students deliver a short talk.
        2. Record each student's voice.
        3. Play back the recording.
        4. Discuss the results of the recording in terms of the introductory questions.
        5. Suggest to each student that aspect of his speech pattern on which he should work.
    C.   Lesson 3—Recordings (completed)
    D.   Lesson 4 and 5—Directed Speech Practice
        1. Present choral speaking material as an instrument for group practice and speech improvement.
        2. Demonstrate the ways in which choral speaking can be used in practicing the "basics" of good speech.
        3. Use a variety of selections for practice in the different aspects of voice and speech and the major sound difficulties.
II. Second Unit: Applied Speech Activities (Putting the basics to practice in structured speech situations)
    A.   Lesson 6—Giving a talk
        1. Discuss delivery of a talk: What does the good speaker do?
        2. Present a sample outline for speech preparation.
        3. Have the students give examples to fit sample outline.
        4. Assign a speech, making use of some phase of the classwork for the next lessons.
    B.   Lessons 7 and 8—Listening and Evaluation
        1. Discuss standards of good listening.
        2. Decide: what are we listening for now? (Content, Organization, Voice and Speech)
        3. Hear the prepared talks.
        4. Discuss the speeches in terms of item #2.
    C.   Lessons 11 and 12—Choral speaking
        1. Review notes on the basic steps in getting a good voice.
        2. Review some directed practices, checking on the progress of individuals.
        3. Present choral speaking techniques in order to work for grouping, emphasis, and expression, as well as for good voice and diction.
        4. Have the class do some choral speaking for expression and interpretation.

    D. Lessons 15 and 16—Final Speech Session.
        1. Introduce "Casey At The Bat."
        2. Practice the poem co-ordinating all the skills and practices done in speech.
        3. Record the poem as the final speech performance.
III. Third Unit: Integrated Work (Working with the classroom teacher on class projects involving speech to foster carry-over)
    A. Lessons 9 and 10—Language Arts and Reporting.
        1. Help the classroom teacher in relating book reports, reading aloud, preparing an assembly program, etc., to the fundamentals of speech previously presented.
        2. Comment on the class work in which speech is used, regarding the effectiveness of the application of the basics.
    B. Lesson 13 and 14—Other Subject Matter areas
        1. Work with the class teacher in relating the basics of speech to oral work in an arithmetic lesson or a social studies class discussion.
        2. Help the students to realize that they must use good speech all of the time.

Methods of Teaching: This outline was developed in the following manner. Each student was asked to keep a speech notebook. Such a record helped the students and the teacher in evaluating growth and noting the sequence of lessons. It also helped them to review and to apply what was learned in speech to the other curriculum areas. It helped them see the relationships between speech improvement lessons, applied speech activities, and integrated learning experiences.

Basics of Voice and Diction: In lesson one the student was asked to discuss the question *"What is a good voice?"* The teacher gave illustrations of voices with faulty speech. The students entered into the discussion, contributing positive qualities of voice. One class listed the following qualities in their notebooks as an outgrowth of this discussion.

A good voice is one that is:

(1) Loud enough to be heard; (2) Clear so that all may understand what is said; (3) Pleasant sounding to the ear; (4) Smooth flowing; (5) Used with expression and variety.

Having determined the qualities of a good voice, the next problem discussed was *"How do we get a good voice?"* The speech consultant presented basic elements in developing a good voice. This he did through demonstration and practice as he illustrated each step. As a prelude to every speech improvement activity a short session of relaxation and breathing exercises should be run through quickly.

First, there must be a good *support of tone*. The students sat straight and tall; pushed down with their feet sitting well back on the chair, and "gripped" the floor, thus giving the proper support to their voices. The class practiced: "Fee-fie-foe-fum", and "Boomly-boomlay-boomlay-boom." Several members of the class gave sentences being sure they had the proper support to the voice.

Secondly, there must be a good *focus of tone*. The students were asked to think of using their lips as a megaphone to get the sounds forward on the lips. They practiced saying, "Oh, what a beautiful morning," each student feeling the forward protrusion of the lips on the lip sounds.

Third, there must be a smooth *blending of tone.* They linked their words by holding on to the tone from sound to sound until the end of the phrase was reached giving a quality of blending similar in effect to a legato touch on the organ as one holds one key until the next has been sounded. Materials containing the nasal sounds were practiced. They also used some Sing and Say exercises.

Fourth, fullness of tone is essential. They opened the mouth on vowel sounds and held on to the nasals, so that a full, round tone was effected. The fifth graders were excited with the quality of resonance this exercise gave.

Finally, it is important to include *all final consonants or word endings.* Nothing is more indicative of slovenly speech than the failure to complete the final endings of words. To attain the objective, they practiced materials containing tongue-tip sounds and final voiced sibilants. This promoted clearer articulation and sharper diction. The students put this second list into their notebooks showing its relation to the first.

The second phase of the fifth grade course presented here was the recording of each pupil's voice. On the basis of the established criteria (support of tone, blending of tone, fullness of tone, and final consonants) the students and teacher evaluated each voice. The speech consultant pointed out areas in which the child needed to work for smoother tone, more support of tone, or clearer focus. General vocal characteristics were also noted.

At this point in the course, the sessions were devoted to direct group speech practices, with choral speaking used as the medium. For example, in the poem *Ticking Clocks,* by Rachel Field, the first verse ends with "plenty of time, there's always plenty of time." This was used for focus of tone and tip-of-tongue exercises. The second stanza concludes: "Time will tell, yes, time will tell." This was used for blending of tone. The third verse concludes with "Time and tide, solemnly, Time and tide." This lent itself to the development of resonance of tone. In these activities, the class practiced first as a group, then the boys and girls divided, then row upon row. In choral reading for interpretation, the objective differs from this type of work. These lessons were designed to equip the teacher with methods and techniques which could be used in working with the entire class in applying the five basic steps for good voice and diction as outlined above.

Applied Speech Activities. Preparation and presentation of reports and talks was one of the important applied speech activities. The students were concerned with outlining, topic sentences, supporting evidence, and giving all types of oral reports. The student was helped to organize a speech outline providing for an *introduction* containing an interesting opening sentence; a *body* which divides the topic in sub-topics supported by many interesting details; and a *conclusion,* which is a summary. Students were assigned talks with the assistance of the class teacher and they were evaluated as to content, delivery, and voice and speech.

Integrated Work. During the lessons of the third unit the class integrated speech with other curriculum areas. There was a speech specialist, so he planned with the classroom teacher to assist the class in some project on which they were working which involved speech, in order to integrate the speech work into the regular classroom lessons. Some examples in which integration took place are:

1. *Play Production Activities*. The teacher pointed out the necessity of good tone, support, and focus in order to have projection and clarity in the auditorium.
2. *Songfest*. To make the lyrics seem more clear, the teacher reminded the class that the good articulation they had achieved in the speech practice sessions could be obtained in singing by applying the basic techniques.
3. *Science Demonstrations*. The students chose to prepare demonstration "speeches" with emphasis on having good opening sentences.
4. *Wall Chart*. In one fifth grade the teacher made a speech reminder list and placed it on the wall. Its items included: eye contact, sufficient volume, appropriate rate, clear diction.
5. *Geography Research Reports*. Evaluations included speech, eye contact, stance as well as content.
6. *Language Book*. Language arts activities correlated well with speech sessions.

The integrated speech activities listed above indicated that the fifth grade teachers were mainly interested in improving and developing the speech skills of their youngsters. Moreover, the following examples of carryover without the assistance of the speech teacher suggests that many of the teachers continued doing it.

1. *Social Studies Reports*. Evaluation carried on by the class and teacher included a discussion of voice and speech production.
2. *Speech Arts: Choral Speaking*. The speech consultant listened to the class performance of a poem. The five basics were applied with no assist from the speech teacher. The class teacher had prepared the class on his own making application of the techniques of good speech.
3. *Whether or Not: A play*. The youngsters wrote their own play and included their own poetry which they had used for speech practice. This helped them project their voices on the stage.
4. *News Reports*. One fifth grade took the choral speaking techniques used for the practice of the "basics" and used these techniques as they gave their news reports.
5. *Support of Tone*. In practically all of the fifth grades, the teachers expected their students to "sit tall", "grip the floor", and "Use a strong voice".[25]

In examining the opportunities for speech improvement in the intermediate grade classrooms it is evident that the underlying philosophy "speech for all" implies that this must be implemented with selected activities, effective methodology, and tools for evaluation in order to achieve the objective. It implies, too, that a program of "speech for all" requires a balanced approach which takes into consideration activities centered on speech improvement, speech development, and which encourage the correlation and integration of speech with other curriculum areas as well as with the language arts.

SPEECH IMPROVEMENT IN THE UPPER GRADES: AN EXPERIMENT THROUGH DISCOVERY TO DELIGHT

To impress upon upper grade students the significance of the fact that even though we live in a democracy our society does still recognize what Bernard Shaw dubbed "vocal class distinctions" requires ingenuity. Most students do not believe that careless, incorrect speech can be a real barrier to success, blocking one's career and one's fullest self-realization in his personal life. To counteract this attitude Nurk turned to the story of *Pygmalion* and *My Fair Lady*. She found in them a dramatic medium for motivating children in these grades to consider speech improvement in its proper perspective.

Introduction. She introduced the unit on *Pygmalion* to the children by discussing the concept of the changes that stories undergo through the ages. As life and civilization change, each age leaves its imprint on its old favourites.

She approached the basic idea of change by relating an anecdote of a youngster who, when asked to choose a bedtime story, begged eagerly for "the cat and the fiddle and the cow that went into orbit around the moon." The appreciation of the sixth graders for the changes civilization wrought on the simple Mother Goose rhyme led readily into the discussion of a story which was older than the oldest Mother Goose rhyme. The story to be considered dated back to the time of the "Golden Age of Greece"—some four thousand years ago.

Background. Discussion followed, centering around the knowledge the children had of Ancient Greece, the Greek's love of beauty, appreciation of the arts, and the architectural style of their buildings. They saw the role that the sculpture played during that period. They learned that many of the great stories of that age logically centered around sculpture. This led into the story of Pygmalion, the King of Cyprus, who was a gifted sculptor. When his search for the perfect woman ended in repeated disappointments, he decided to create a perfect woman through his art. He worked several years, carving from rough, crude stone a beautiful woman. Pygmalion fell in love with her beauty, and prayed that the gods would bring her to life. His prayer was answered and she became his Queen.

The story of Pygmalion has been retold through the centuries. George Bernard Shaw, the English playwright, decided to write it into a modern play. Not being a Greek, nor living in a "Golden Age of Sculpture", he did not choose a sculptor as the hero. The questions the teacher asked to involve the children in the solution of the problem were: "Whom do you think he would make the hero of this modern story?" "What kind of an age is this"?

In the discussion that ensued the children began by suggesting "atomic age"; "space age"; following this they were asked the question, "What new development has permeated the private life of our whole society"? Further analysis lead to the conclusion that the basic and most fundamental things that radio and television give us is speech. Thus they agreed that this is the age of speech.

In answer to the question, "How do we know this"? the children answered, "Never in any age has speech been so important. There is no profession or field of endeavor in which speech is not important in this era. If one achieves in any area, be it architecture, biochemistry or politics, he must be ready to present his accomplishments and convictions through the medium of speech to millions at a time, as well as in person. This is, indeed, a speech age!"[26]

Having through analysis and problem solving arrived at the conclusion that the significance of speech in our age is of inescapable importance, a very real motivation for speech improvement was immediate.

Procedure for Development. At this point the class was ready to return to its original question, "Whom do you think Shaw would make the hero of his modern story? Who, in a radio and television age would be searching for the perfect woman? The television producer, the radio announcer? No, the speech professor! And when he could not find her—how would he go about trying to create a perfect woman?"

The class concluded that he would accomplish his goal by giving her such perfect speech that she could travel in any society she chose. Although ideas of physical beauty have changed since the days of Greece, there is no way to camouflage incorrect and unpleasant speech. The perfect woman must have beautiful speech.

Activities. The class was introduced to Professor Higgins and Eliza Doolittle, and the plot of Shaw's play. They listened to the recordings of the musical *My Fair Lady.* They listened for the distorted vowels heard in the early selections of the record. They listened critically for the following high points:

(1) Professor Higgin's conviction that speech determines our class distinctions; (2) The contrast of the speech of the streets with the professor's speech; (3) The contrast in values held by Eliza and the professor; (4) Eliza's hatred of the professor for his relentless drill and correction; (5) The professor's joy and delight when Eliza began to "get it"; (6) Eliza's joy when her speech no longer condemned her to the gutter, when the professor could invite her to accompany him to social functions; (7) The changes that occurred in the speech of the characters as the story developed.

Evaluation. Evaluation followed after listening to one side of the record. This involved such questions as the voice qualities which characterized the gutter girl (specifically voice, articulation, and vowel quality). What characterized the speech of the professor as a well-educated, cultured person? (Voice, articulation, diction).

They discussed the speculation among the guests that Eliza was really a Hungarian Countess, thus reinforcing the idea of the social importance of speech. "These basic truths, coupled with vivid examples of contrast in voice quality, range, articulation and diction make this story and the records of *My Fair Lady* a treasure chest for one working to inspire and challenge upper elementary and junior high pupils to appreciate and to strive for excellent speech".[27]

Children might well take the original play of Bernard Shaw and use it for a creative project in reader's theatre. Projects of this type will be discussed in the chapter "Appreciating Literature Through Experiencing".

ACTIVITIES AND MATERIALS FILE

A comprehensive and usable collection of activities and materials for use in a speech improvement program is essential. Such a file will include not only those which are specifically speech-oriented but also materials and activities which can be integrated with other curriculum areas.

The speech improvement program should be an integral part of the classroom activities, it requires a dual approach—direct and integrated. The direct teaching focuses on speech and voice improvement per se—the integrated utilizes all curriculum areas for speech improvement. For example, ear training in relation to phonics offers an excellent activity in which source materials may come from the phonics in reading. A music period may stress vocalized rhythm and variations in pitch and volume. It may emphasize the use of distinct enunciation. Spelling gives the teacher an opportunity to introduce new words with emphasis on accurate articulation. Units in language arts and social studies may centre around such communication skills as using the telephone, speaking over the radio, or appearing on television, actual or simulated. Creative art, too, can be integrated with speech improvement. Frequently children tell the class the story "behind the picture," or read the caption for the teacher. Creating rhythms and dramatizing stories stimulate speech improvement spontaneously. Stories for such activities should have strong action and strong sensory appeal: *The Three Bears, Angus and The Ducks, Millions of Cats, The Story About Ping, Curious George,* are some examples.

Speech improvement integrates readily with science. For example, children can begin a scientific study of the voice organs. Such a study involves the use of films, charts, and models of the throat, mouth, and nose, to see how sounds are produced and resonated. This will help them understand what happens to the vocal organs when they yell at a hockey game.

A file of available recordings, films, and film-strips is useful in the speech improvement program.

Many business concerns make available free materials that are excellent for use in the program.

Materials from children's literature can make a great contribution to speech improvement and provide a readily available source for the teacher. Many of the poems and stories stimulate the child's flow of thought so that his speech patterns improve without his being too conscious of the response.

"At the right moment a child will yield his mind with ease to a story or poem which delights him. The focus is there without push or strain."[28] Children will enter into the experiences of the characters of the story and repeat with the teacher the repetitive phrases or repeated words which normally they might not attempt to articulate.

The right poem at the right time for the right group of children is the watchword of the effective teacher.

Especially conducive to speech improvement are the folk tales and rhymes handed down from one generation to another by word of mouth. The innate rhythm found in the "speaking them down" rather than "writing them down" from one person to another makes them ideal for speech practice.

Poetry is rich with immediate and direct fulfillment of most of the requirements for good speech practice. "Poetry goes directly to the crystal-clear imagery of an experience. A very essence which makes it poetry is the rhythm and often its verbal repetition."[29]

The following poems have been used successfully in speech improvement practice.

FAIRIES?

Are there really truly fairies
Out on our garden walk?
Are there really truly fairies
And can they walk and talk?
Are there really truly fairies?
    Of course there are!

Why only just this morning
When I went out to play
I heard a tiny fairy say
Come out with me and play.
Are there really truly fairies?
    Of course there are!

At first I thought I heard him
Behind the big oak tree
But when I ran to see
There was no one there but me.
Are there really truly fairies?
    That's what puzzles me!
                Lillian Logan

ADVENTURE

When I adventure to the zoo
I always look for someone new,
A lion, tiger or a goat
In cage, in den or on the moat.

I get so used to those I know

Annie, the elephant and slow Old Joe
The long-nosed anteater, and the lion.
I near forgot the porcupine

If you should stand so close to me
I'd tell you what I'd like to see,
Some-one very wee, about my size
Who stares at me with friendly eyes.

That seem to say, "I'd like to play
A game of hide and seek today
But I am me and you are you
And that would never, never do."
                Lillian Logan

MUSIC BOX

I have a little music box,
    It plays the sweetest tune
In tones so lovely, soft and gay—
    Tinkle, tinkle, tinkle.

I close my eyes and listen,
    And pretend that I'm a dancer
Twirling lightly on my toes—
    Twinkle, twinkle, twinkle.

I won't forget that music box
    If I live to be a hundred,
A hundred years or more, I'll hear—
    Tinkle, tinkle, tinkle.
                Lillian Logan

DISCOVERY

Sometimes when I go out at night
I see the moon in all its light.
I wonder where it stays in day
And why it never goes away.

I ask my Mom, I ask my dad,
They look at me and say "My lad
When you grow up you'll understand
About the sky, the sea, the land."

How can I know when I am grown
If they just look at me and moan
And say, "What will he ask us next?

I guess we better get a text."

About everything under the sun,
Then when he asks another one
Of those questions that so puzzle us
We'll know, and there'll be no more
  fuss."

It's not the answer I have found
That makes my brain go round and
  round,
It's finding out all by myself,
Or wondering and discovering.

Lillian Logan

EXERCISES FOR INTERMEDIATE AND UPPER GRADES

The following suggestions for voice improvement are particularly geared to the needs of the intermediate and upper grade children.

Relaxation Exercises

Relaxation is basic for good voice production. Begin all speech improvement drills with relaxation exercises.

1. The purpose of the first exercise is to help the students get the "feel" of relaxed muscles by having them first tense the muscles as tightly as possible, and then relax them. Have the students stand with an erect posture (but not stiff). "Tense the toes as tightly as possible. Tighter! Tighter! Tighter! Now relax." Using the same instruction, give the order of tenseness and relaxation as follows —ankles, legs, thighs, back, stomach, chest, shoulders, arms, hands, neck, face. Allow the students to stand with a relaxed posture briefly before moving to the next exercise.

2. Hold the head upright. Relax the muscles of the neck and let the head fall forward with the chin resting on the chest. Let the head fall of its own weight. Do not pull it forward.

3. Repeat, letting the head fall forward, then rotate it slowly to the left shoulder, let it fall back. Let the jaw drop from its own weight. Repeat several times.

4. Lean from the waist and let the shoulders and arms hang limply. Drop the head and let the jaw hang open. Repeat.

Lip Exercises

1. Trill with the lips as long as the breath holds out. Repeat several times.
2. Bite lower lip lightly with upper teeth. Bite upper lip with lower teeth. Repeat 5 times.

3. Place lower lip in the mouth as far back on the tongue as possible.
4. Holding the lower lip motionless, extend the upper lip outward and upward to touch the nose. Close the lips firmly. Repeat five times.
5. Protrude the lips, and make the vowel sound *oo*. Repeat five times.
7. Protrude the lips and instead of saying *oo*, suddenly blow air through them. (If done correctly a whistle will result.)
8. Draw the corners of the mouth back as if about to smile and say *ee*. Immediately follow that by protruding the lips and saying *oo*. Repeat rapidly ee-oo-ee-oo. Repeat 3 times.
9. Say the following vowels, being sure to note that the position of the lips changes for each one. Repeat, first slowly, and rapidly: oo-oh-aw-ah-ay-ee. Repeat 3 times. Repeat with the following: ah-aw-oh-oo-oh-aw-ah. Glide both of these groups without sound.
10. Say each of the following lines clearly and in one breath:
    bah-bah-bah-bah-bah   Repeat in turn, with each of the lip consonants:
    bay-bay-bay-bay-bay
    bee-bee-bee-bee-bee   P,B,M,F,V,W.
    boh-boh-boh-boh-boh
    boo-boo-boo-boo-boo
11. Open the mouth wide as for *ah*, then round the lips as for *oo*; then stretch the lips as for *ee*; return to the position for *ah*. Thus: (Repeat each 10 times.)
12. Repeat with exaggerated lip action: wah-fah-wah-bah; wah-lah-wah-mah. Repeat 10 times.
13. Repeat with exaggerated lip action, again normally, but noting lip action.

Jaw Exercises

1. Relax jaw, opening mouth as in a sleepy yawn. Open on one count, close on one count. Repeat five times.
2. Fix your eyes on some object in front of you, drop your jaw and follow action by protruding it—that is, first movement down, second movement forward and upward. Repeat 3 times.
3. Fix your eyes on some object in front of you, and without allowing your head to make the slightest movement, drop your lower jaw. Repeat 5 times.
4. Move the jaw from side to side in two counts. Repeat 10 times.
5. Drop the jaw down; push it to the right, then upward, to the left, then down, in a circular movement. Repeat 5 times.
6. Repeat slowly the following vowels, noting change in the position of the lower jaw: ah-ee-oh-aw. Repeat 5 times.
7. Speak the following vowels, allowing the jaw to fall for each vowel:
   ah—oh—oo—ee—uh—a
8. Say the following sound combinations, opening the mouth wide, then closing it completely. Repeat 10 times.

yah-yah-yah-yah   rah-rah-rah-rah
pah-pah-pah-pah   bwah-bwah-bwah-bwah
bah-bah-bah-bah   mah-mah-mah-mah

9. Read the following sentences, letting the jaw fall at every possible opportunity. Read them again, this time in a natural manner; sense the movement of the jaw as you read.
   1. Father ran to the barn.
   2. Howard sat down on the rock.
   3. "Bow-wow," barked the black dog.
   4. The class grasped at the chance for a holiday.
   5. The basket was half filled with grass.
   6. The jackdaw cawed raucously in the orchard.
   7. He argued ardently for arbitration.
   8. He had a weak heart and hardening of the arteries.
   9. Paul yawned as the clock struck five.
   10. He found out how to plow the ground.
   11. The famous legal array dismayed the alien.
   12. The author took a long jaunt.
10. Read often and practice dropping the jaw at every opportunity.

Exercises for Velar Control

1. Open the mouth as for ah. Exhale first through the mouth, then through the nose, keeping the mouth in position for ah.
2. Open the mouth for ah. Put the tongue tip against the lower teeth, and repeat UNG-Ah, trying to sense the lowering and raising of the velum as the syllables are sounded.
3. Say AHMPMAH slowly. The velum should lower for m, rise for p and lower again for m. Having become conscious of the movements of the velum as the sounds are uttered, try to raise and lower it silently.
4. Pronounce the following clearly and slowly, trying to sense the rising and lowering of the velum:

ah-ung-ah	oh-hung-oh	ump-ma	ah-gar
ah-ong-ah	oo-ung-oo	ump-ma	ah-gar
ee-ung-ee	i-hung-i	ump-ma	ah-gar
ah-hung-ah	ah-sah-ah	ing-ick	
ay-hang-ay	ah-sah-ah	ing-ick	
ee-hung-ee			

5. Pronounce the following: The velum is first lowered and then raised:

mmmmm-bee	nnnn-dip
mmmmm-bill	nnnn-deck

mmmm-bat	nnnn-dock
mmmm-ball	nnnn-dove

6. Pronounce the following: The velum is first twisted and then lowered:

b-man	d-nod
b-mee	d-nap
b-my	d-not
b-may	d-nip
b-mad	d-new
b-moo	d-nice

7. Pronounce the following:

snack, snag, slack, crack, crag, mack, mag, rag, rack, sag, sack.

Bring Eva, coming in, teasing Emma, pouring oil, looking old, saying all, strong arm, Long Island.

SPEECH DRILLS FOR NASALITY (FUNCTIONAL RHINOLALIA APERTA)

Nasal quality, or nasality, is characterized by undue nasal resonance of non-nasal voiced sounds. It is noticeable in vowels, especially if the vowel is preceded by an "h" sound, or if a nasal sound is adjacent to it.

This series of drills should be used in the order given, and the teacher should make sure that a given drill is mastered thoroughly before going on to the next drill. The lists of sentences given merely indicate the scope of that drill; hence both the student and the teacher should construct other sentences of the same type for use in that drill.

1. *To learn to distinguish between nasality and normal quality*:

In the following pairs of sentences, the first favours normal quality while the second favours nasality. Do not attempt to eliminate nasality but rather simply read them aloud to learn to know nasality when heard. Listen especially to the vowels.

This is the house that Jack built.
Many and many a year ago in a kingdom in North America.

You put the foot rule above the law books.
Jane rang the triangle and the cranky men came to dinner.

"Let's eat supper with Ruth," suggested Betty.
"I'm in the chain gang," exclaimed Dan angrily.

2. *To learn to use a larger, rounder mouth opening*:

The following should be practiced aloud, reading at a rapid rate and exaggerating the mouth movements:

    (a) Nonsense syllables:

Combine the vowel "ah" (a) with "p", "b", "t", "d", and "s", as

Pa-pa-pa-pa-pa-pa	ta-ta-ta-ta-ta-ta	da-da-da-da-da-da

(b) Sentences:

Jack laughed as Bobby fell, but Bobby had the last laugh.
Ask the cop whether Popeye or Pluto played at the Palace.
Ted stopped Paul as Paul tackled the cop at Bob's party.
Bobby bought pop bottles at Robert's Hot Dog Shop.
Dutch robbed the hock shop while his pals watched.

3. *To perceive velar position and movement*:

Place the tongue in the position for "k" and build up air pressure in the back of the mouth. But instead of releasing the "k", lower the velum quickly so that the air escapes through the nose with a noticeable voiceless click. Repeat many times noting the sensations of the velum.

Repeat the drill, using the positions of "t" and "p".

4. *To achieve non-nasal nonsense syllables*:

Place a cold mirror against the upper lip under the nostrils. Note that breath escaping from the nose causes moisture to condense on the mirror. Use this for final check on nasality of vowels.

Repeat the following nonsense syllables many times, listening carefully for nasality and checking frequently with the mirror:

ki-ku-ki-ku-ki-ku	ke-ko-ke-ko-ke-ko	kae-ko-kae-ko-kae-ko
ti-tu-ti-tu-ti-tu	te-to-te-to-te-to	tae-to-tae-to-tae-to
pi-pu-pi-pu-pi-pu	pe-po-pe-po-pe-po	pae-po-pae-po-pae-po
(i as in key)	(e as in pet)	(ae as in cat)
(u as in too)	(o as in toe)	(o as in paw)

5. *To achieve non-nasal words*:

Read aloud many times the following words, keeping the velum raised and making sure that the vowels are not nasalized:

cook	coat	cuff	toot	tote	tuck	pooch	pope	puff
cool	cope	cut	twos	taupe	tut	poof	poke	pup
coot	coke	cup	tooth	toast	tough	poop	post	puck

6. *To achieve non-nasal words when associated with nasal sounds*:

Begin by uttering the sounds separately with a pause between them, prolonging each sound. Then lessen the pause until the two sounds are joined. Finally, pronounce the syllable in a normal manner. Check all vowels for nasality.

A. Vowel in final position:

m long pause   i ("e" as in me)
m short pause   i
mi prolong both
mi say naturally

Combine all the vowels with "m", "n", and "ng" in the same manner.

B. Vowel in the initial position:

                              i   long pause   m
                              i   short pause   m
                              im prolong both
                              im say naturally

Combine all the vowels with "m", "n", and "ng" as above.

   C. Vowel in the medial position:

                              m   long pause
                              m   short pause
                              mim prolong all sounds
                              mim say naturally
                              i   long pause   m
                              i   short pause   m

Combine all the vowels with "m", "n", and "ng" as above.

   D. Read the following word groups one row at a time. The vowels must not be nasalized. Note especially the third word, of each group.

pack	-	back	-	Mac	cap	-	cab	-	cam	pop	-	bob	-	mom
pate	-	bait	-	mate	tap	-	tab	-	tam	pap	-	Bab	-	ma'am
pet	-	bet	-	met	cat	-	cad	-	can	toot	-	dude	-	noon
tot	-	dot	-	knot	late	-	laid	-	lain	tight	-	died	-	nine
tip	-	dip	-	nip	tick	-	rig	-	ring	Tutt	-	dud	-	mud
tete	-	dote	-	note	rack	-	rag	-	rang	tat	-	dad	-	Nan

7. *To achieve normal quality in the use of sentences*:

   A. The following sentences increase in difficulty, therefore each should be practiced before going on to the next one. They are to be read in a normal conversational tone and manner. After each sentence has been mastered, they should be read as a group in the order given, making sure that the vowels of the lower ones are not nasalized. They should then be read as a group in reverse order.

     Joe Blow, the local show-off, posed as a rider at the rodeo.
     The bit was nicked by hitting it quickly and vigorously with a stick.
     Peggy said Ned wrecked several red and green sleds.
     The shock of the flogging robbed John of his strength.
     Our ancestors founded a new nation.
     The mangled remains of mammals make many museums memorable.
     Banging and clanging gongs rang to warn the remaining gangs.

   B. The following sentences alternate in difficulty. Check for the use of normal quality in each of them.

     Chang rang the wrong gong and mangled his ankle.
     The lucky cook put the cookies in the cup.
     Maidens and men came in their prime.
     Bustles were tucked away with shoes and rugs.

The clanking of the chains rang madly in the rain.
Bitter and swift is the death of a spy.

8. *To achieve normal quality in every-day speaking and reading*:

Read aloud prose and poetry selections, stories, articles, etc., listening carefully for nasalized vowels. There should be none of the latter.
Advice to the student:

You must now check constantly on your every-day speech, for the good speech habits you have learned must now be incorporated in all your speaking. Hence you must be very vigilant until these habits are well established and become an automatic part of your speech.

In using poetry and prose selections for voice improvement in the intermediate grades, both choral reading and individualized reading of the selections should be included in the program. The basic purpose of all reading should be interpretation. The students should not be permitted to read for drill purposes alone.

Literary Selections for Voice Improvement

Quality and Resonance Improvement
To the student: Read the following selection *out loud*, listening to your own vocal nuances as carefully as you can, keeping your jaw as flexible as possible, giving the vowels full tonal value, and being sure to produce an audible humming sound on all the m, n, and ng, sounds. (good nasal resonance).

WIND IN THE PINE[30]

Oh, I can hear you, God, above the cry
    of the tossing trees—
Rolling your windy tides across the sky,
    And splashing your silver seas
        Over the pine,
        To the water line
        Of the moon.

Oh, I can hear you, God
Above the wail of the lonely loon—
When the pine-tops pitch and nod—
    Chanting your melodies
Of ghostly waterfalls and avalanches,
Washing your wind among the branches
    To make them pure and white.

Wash over me, God, with your piney breeze,
    And your moon's wet-silver pool;
Wash over me, God, with your wind and night,
    And leave me clean and cool.

                         Lew Sarett

Flexibility and Variety Improvement

Communicate the contrast in this selection.

WHO HAS SEEN THE WIND?[31]

Who has seen the wind?
   Neither I nor you:
But when the leaves hang trembling
   The wind is passing thro'.
Who has seen the wind?
   Neither you nor I:
But when the trees bow down their heads
   The wind is passing by.

THE SPEECH OF THE CLASSROOM TEACHER

The teacher has a great responsibility in speech improvement in setting an example of speech that provides children with a model which they can emulate. His voice should be pleasant, free from harshness and strain. Articulation should be free from deviations and enunciation should be clear and distinct. Needless to say, the teacher should use speech which is appropriate in usage and contains clear diction ingredients. He should be conscious of the ingredients which go to make up good speech—quality, inflection, rhythm, and articulation. These are reflected in an integrated ,wholesome, self-reliant, and alert personality. The well-modulated, clear, distinct, pleasant, rhythmic speech of the teacher reveals a well adjusted individual who inspires confidence in the boys and girls he teaches. If the teacher recognizes that the voice mechanism is an instrument which is both the medium for communicating ideas to the students in the class, *and* a means of creating a climate in which speech is improved, it is likely that the goals of speech will be achieved.

A check list which has proved helpful to teachers in assessing their own speech follows:

Self-Evaluation

VOICE	Volume	Is my voice loud enough to be heard?
	Pitch	Am I using my optimum pitch? (It may be high, low or medium)
		Is the pitch flexible to denote change in meaning?
	Inflection	Does the voice glide from one pitch to another?
	Quality	Is my voice free from huskiness and nasality?
		Is my voice free from harshness and shrillness?
		Does my voice reveal fullness rather than breathiness of tone?
RATE	Tempo	Is my speech fast or slow?
		Does the rate vary with mood or emotions?
	Flowing	Is my speech normally uninterrupted?

		Is it free flowing?
	Smooth	Is my speech rhythmic?
		Is it free from repetition or undue prolongation?
ARTICULATION	Formation of	Are my habits of good articulation so well established
	Sounds	that I am not conscious of the mechanics of articulation?
		Do I produce the speech sounds accurately?

THE RELATIONSHIP BETWEEN THE CLASSROOM TEACHER AND THE SPEECH THERAPIST

The roles of the classroom teacher and the speech therapist are mutually supporting. If there is a speech therapist in the school system he shares with the teacher the responsibility for aiding those children whose handicap is of such a severe or specialized nature that it requires the help of a therapist. The presence of a therapist in the school system does not relieve the classroom teacher of the responsibility for the speech improvement of his children.

If there is a speech therapist, however, he works cooperatively in inaugurating, coordinating and implementing a speech improvement program.

The presence of the speech therapist serves to facilitate, enhance and enrich the speech improvement program. The activities suggested in this chapter do not require the services of a speech therapist. The procedures for motivating and directing activities for speech improvement can be satisfactorily handled by the classroom teacher as a phase of the three-part program in speech: development of speech skills, directed speech improvement lessons, and integrated activities.

Irwin points significantly to the importance of the close-working relationship with the speech therapist when she states: "The teacher with a background of classroom teaching plus training in general speech with knowledge of speech improvement and rehabilitation techniques is probably the type of person to handle the speech improvement program. . . . The public-school speech therapist will work with the classroom teacher to correlate speech rehabilitation with work done in the classroom . . . and plan with the teacher, who is interested, specific lessons which will develop acceptable speech in the classroom."[32]

The classroom teacher works with all the children in the classroom on problems which are not so complex or difficult to change as the speech disorders handled by the speech therapist.

A promising note regarding the role of the classroom teacher in speech improvement and a trend in preparing her for that role is sounded by Richard. "A few of the more progressive teacher training programs in Canada include courses in speech education. Adequate training prepares the teacher to assume responsibility for carrying out an active speech improvement program which includes not only general classroom activities but the skills necessary to identify problems, initiate the appropriate referrals and co-operate and contribute to the clinical work of the speech and hearing therapist."[33]

CONCLUDING STATEMENT

Because most children speak easily when they enter school, good speech is taken as a matter of course. Some teachers, it is true, are concerned with the problem of impaired speech and hearing and their relation to the child's progress in other class activities. However, all too often, unless the teacher is aware of the significance of speech as a medium of communication and self-expression, the child with speech problems is neglected.

Unfortunately, neglect of speech problems blocks progress educationally as well as socially. Living in a society in which communication skills are so vital in meeting the social, educational, and vocational demands of to-day's world, the ability to communicate effectively and to express ideas clearly and distinctly within the limits of individual aptitudes and abilities is imperative.

Schools have a responsibility to bring every child to his maximum potential in speech as well as in other communication skills. A program for speech improvement provides ample opportunities for every child to develop good speaking and listening skills. In addition, there must be a program for helping the child with specific handicaps of speech and hearing. A planned, consistent course of speech improvement should be carried out in the regular classroom.

Every classroom teacher must have an understanding and knowledge of (a) defective speech, (b) types of speech disorders, (c) techniques for identifying speech and hearing defects, (d) ways of helping a child with a specific type of speech handicap, (e) the development of normal speech, (f) speech improvement procedures in the classroom, and (g) relationships between the classroom teacher and the speech therapist and/or other personnel responsible for meeting the needs of speech handicapped children in the elementary school.

The estimate of speech disorders in the elementary school population ranges from 5 to 25%. Some of these disorders require the services of a therapist. The remainder, however, can be helped by the classroom teacher. Early in the school year an analysis of the speech and hearing of the children in the room should be made. Errors in articulation, ability to discriminate between speech sounds, quality of speaking voice, fluency in speech, delayed speech, and problems of a more serious nature are recorded. By early identification of those who need special help, the teacher can initiate the speech improvement program. The teacher who is knowledgeable about the various disorders in speech can cooperate and contribute to the work of the speech therapist if there is one. If there is no one to whom she can refer children with handicaps, it is the duty of the principal to take the responsibility for contacting the proper agencies.

In the primary grades speech improvement is largely group oriented. Group learning provides spontaneous stimulation and motivation. The activities suggested in this chapter are effective in helping children improve their speech skills and attitude. Through the use of good resource materials the teacher can integrate speech improvement with the language arts and other curriculum areas.

The importance of the teacher's voice cannot be overestimated in the total program. The teacher should set a model in voice and speech which is worthy of imitation and emulation. The teacher with a pleasant voice, an interesting and lively manner of speaking motivates children to effective speech.

The teacher who creates a relaxed, friendly, democratic atmosphere in which children are free to communicate, to exchange ideas, and to express them without fear of cutting criticism contributes to confidence in developing adequate speech skills.

"Oral communication", says Henning, "is like the motor in that it can be developed, improved, and made more efficient in its operation."[34] It is the responsibility of the school, particularly the classroom teacher, to initiate and direct a program of speech improvement so that every child will be able to use speech with greater skill, effectiveness, and anticipation than before he entered the class.

REFERENCES

1. Horace Rahskopf, *Basic Speech Improvement*, Harper & Row, New York, 1965, p. 217.
2. Charles Van Riper, *Speech Correction: Principles and Methods*, 4th ed., © 1963. Reprinted by permission of Prentice-Hall, Inc., Englewood Cliffs, New Jersey, 1963, p. 2.
3. *Ibid.*, p. 16.
4. By permission from Lillian M. Logan and Virgil G. Logan, *Teaching the Elementary School Child*, Houghton Mifflin Company, Boston, 1961, p. 771.
5. By permission from Isabel Richard, "Special Services of the Elementary School," in Joseph Katz (ed.), *Elementary Education in Canada*, McGraw-Hill Company of Canada Ltd., Toronto, 1961, pp. 149, 150.
6. Charles Van Riper, *op. cit.*, p. 18.
7. By permission from Edith B. Goldberg, *Mending the Child's Speech*, F. A. Owen Publishing Company, Dansville, 1959. The Instructor Handbook Series, p. 7.
8. Charles Van Riper, *op. cit.*, p. 14.
9. *Ibid.*, pp. 18, 19.
10. *Ibid.*, p. 25.
11. *Ibid.*, p. 32.
12. *Ibid.*, p. 33.
13. Wendell Johnson, *Children with Speech and Hearing Impairment*, U.S. Department of Health, Education and Welfare, Bulletin No. 5, Washington, 1959, p. 11.
14. Isabel Richard, *op. cit.*, p. 150.
15. Ruth Irwin, "How Can a Speech and Hearing Program be Initiated?" *Bulletin of the National Association of Secondary School Principals*, 34:173, November, 1950. Reprinted by permission of the *National Association of Secondary School Principals*, 1950. Copyright: Washington, D.C.
16. *Ibid.*
17. By permission from Wilbert Provonost, *Speaking and Listening*, Longmans, Green and Co., Toronto, 1959, p. 302.

18. Lillian M. Logan and Virgil G. Logan, *op. cit.*, p. 772.
19. Charles Van Riper, *op. cit.*, p. 75.
20. Jane Hanson, "Fostering Speech Development During Pre and Primary School Years: Norms and Speech Games," Special Educational Services, Evansville College, Evansville. (Mimeographed.)
21. From *Speech in the Elementary Classroom*, by Charles Van Riper and Katherine Butler, Harper Brothers, New York, 1955, pp. 5, 6.
22. *Ibid.*, pp. 170, 171.
23. By permission from Maude Nurk, "Motivating Speech Improvement in the Upper Grades," *The Speech Teacher*, 9:301, November, 1960.
24. By permission from Albert F. Kupferer, "A Voice and Diction Course for Grade Five," *The Speech Teacher*, 9:297-298, November, 1960.
25. *Ibid.*, pp. 299, 300. (Adapted)
26. Maude Nurk, *op. cit.*, p. 302.
27. *Ibid.*, p. 303.
28. Marjorie Carey, "Children's Literature - Creative Speech Practice," *Today's Speech*, 7:27, November, 1959.
29. *Ibid.*, p. 29.
30. Lew Sarett, *The Box of God*, Henry Holt and Co., New York, 1922, p. 21.
31. Christina G. Rosetti, *Sing Song*.
32. By permission from Ruth Beckey Irwin, "The Role of the Speech Therapist in the Speech Improvement Program," *The Speech Teacher*, 9:288,289, November, 1960.
33. By permission from Isabel Richard, "Children's Speech," *The Journal of Education of the Faculty of the University of British Columbia*, 10:63, January, 1966.
34. James H. Henning, *Improved Oral Communication*, McGraw-Hill Book Company, New York, 1966, p. 230.

9

Guiding Reading in the
Primary Grades

As children talk, so shall they read.

Helen Hickok

"The basis for reading is spoken language; if a child can understand and use spoken words well, he has demonstrated the capacity for dealing in symbols. In a society highly dependent on spoken and written words, early education must be concerned with the development of language skills, including preparation for success in beginning reading."[1]

Before the child can extract meaning from the printed page, he must be able to bring meaning to the printed page. This demands richness of experience and development of communication skills. The interaction between experience and language is constant. Spoken language is an index to the child's understanding of the world about him—the world of people, places, and phenomena. Spoken language is one of the communication skills essential for successful living in today's complex world. Systematic instruction in oral language is the responsibility of the elementary school.

Children must be equipped to deal critically, intelligently, and creatively with an enormous amount of printed material. Learning to read is a complex process. Pupils are led step by step to develop inquiring attitudes along with the mechanical skills of reading. They learn to understand ideas, examine them, and to decide whether or not they are valid. They learn, too, to think of reading as a way of communicating with great minds of all ages, a way of expanding horizons, increasing understanding, and developing insights.

Every child should bring to reading a rich and varied experiental background, a fluency in oral language, a degree of emotional, social, physical, and mental maturity *plus* a desire to read. The eager pupil and the skilled teacher are the best combination for teaching reading.

"The skillful and perceptive teacher knows how to light a fire in a child's mind. She knows the kindling points of interest. Her own behavior initiates those activities which, when nurtured in refinement, can carry the child well beyond 'where he is'."[2]

Most children come to school with the belief that learning to read is an exciting adventure. The effective teacher capitalizes on their interest, curiosity, and desire to learn and provides a program geared to their needs. The teacher must: (1) be aware of the inter-relatedness of the language arts, (2) utilize linguistic factors in teaching reading, (3) understand the nature of the reading process, (4) understand reading development, (5) be familiar with current approaches to reading instruction, (6) organize a reading program, (7) help children master reading skills, (8) provide for individual differences, (9) evaluate the reading program.

INTER-RELATEDNESS OF THE LANGUAGE ARTS

Children enter school with widely varying language experiences. Some come with a vast fund of "capital stock" for the teacher to tap in initiating into the reading process. They have already made a significant growth in speaking and listening. Others come from impoverished backgrounds and have limited skills in the language arts. Each teacher must build on whatever background of language skills the child has and on the basis of the child's individual needs.

Research findings give evidence of the significance of the inter-relatedness of the language arts and the sequence in which the language skills develop. Loban's[3] study of the language development of 338 children from kindergarten through high school contains evidence of the extremely close relationship existing among the language arts: listening, speaking, reading, and writing. He reports that the group of pupils who were high in general language ability were also high in reading ability, while those who were low in general language ability were also low in reading ability.

Burrows has shown that when writing is preceded by oral language activities, all forms of written communication are appreciably improved. All children need a great deal of experience in oral language activities before they can be expected to write. Research makes it clear that "the quality of children's writing can be little different from the quality of oral language they use."[4]

Reading vocabulary requires two important factors: the ability to identify the word and the knowledge of its meaning. Robinson shows the relationship between reading and other language arts: "Reading vocabulary is built on listening and speaking vocabularies, with word identification added."[5]

Strickland concurs with this evidence since she found that pupils who ranked high in silent reading comprehension skills tended to use longer sentences or "utterances" when speaking and also used more "moveables" and elements of subordination.[6]

Armstrong asserts: "Oral langauge must be used continually and related constantly to reading if the teacher is to make full use of the amazing language competence that the child has when he comes to school. . . . A total language approach is the key to better reading. The concept of the unity of the language arts has been well supported in theory if not in classroom practice, and the evidence that language competence is the single, most important factor in reading success is overwhelming. Language is the essence of reading readiness."[7]

Thus an effective program in the language arts is based on the concept of inter-relatedness. Activities should include both integrated experiences and separate teaching of the skills of communication. The strands of the language arts are so closely interwoven that development in one leads to greater skill in each of the others.

The inter-relatedness and the commonalities of the language arts form a logical basis for planning the learning experiences. For example, each of the language arts depends upon the process of thinking and the expression of ideas for success. Growth in each depends upon experience with language and conceptualizing in an environment that is both stimulating and supporting.

As a prelude to success in reading, the child must have fluency with words. The foundation for reading is laid by providing the child with experiences in his physical and social environment which stimulate and give meaning to the symbols of language. As he develops meaning through experiencing, he is building a speaking and thinking vocabularly; as he learns to express ideas through oral language, he is developing the tools he will use to master the symbols of written language—reading and writing.

Experience, ideas, and the mastery of tools of communication—these are essential to each of the language arts. These are the threads which form the design for creative expression of ideas. The formula for weaving the threads of the language arts into a design for creative expression is $E + W + T + C = CE$.

E Experiences—stimulate children to think

W Words—convey ideas, experiences and ideas take flight

T Tools—clarify meaning

C Creativity—expresses individuality

$\overline{CE}$ Creative Expression—the individual expresses his thoughts imaginatively, spontaneously, and with originality.

LINGUISTIC FACTORS IN EARLY READING INSTRUCTION

"It is doubtful whether a child can become a fluent reader, comprehending fully what he reads, without a good oral language foundation and continued attention to oral language improvement."[8]

When the child comes to school he has already developed some skill in the use of oral language. If the first experiences in reading lead him to see the relationships between oral language and printed symbols reading becomes meaningful. Consequently, success is more likely to follow. The child who is learning to read succeeds more readily if he is taught to relate the speech patterns he already knows to the symbols in the written language which he is trying to decode.

Learning to read, as every teacher knows, does not take place in a linguistic vacuum. It cannot take place outside the context of language. The fact that beginning readers already have gained a modicum of control over the spoken language does not negate the teacher's responsibility for continued experiences in developing the spoken language skills throughout the process of learning to read.

All too frequently teachers fail to provide time in the daily program for the activities designed to improve speech skills. They fail to realize the significant role oral language plays in learning to read. To skimp on time for speech activities in the belief that "reading is more important" is self-defeating. Time given for oral language is time given for reading since oral language experience is actually an integral part of learning to read. A good rule for the teacher is—Do not begin reading instruction without first taking into account the child's status in speech. Develop oral language skills prior to and along with reading experiences if you want your children to read effectively.

The study of linguistics has implications for instruction in reading. It reveals that "when a child is ready to learn to read, the *only* new skill he must master is the skill generally referred to as word perception—the ability to respond to written symbols with the appropriate sound. The other skills generally described as reading skills, comprehension, interpretation, vocabulary development, and so forth—are largely developed by children in the process of listening to language rather than in reading. That is not to say that development of such skills is not in any way aided by learning to read. It is simply to say that such other skills are obviously employed in responding accurately to oral language as well as to written language."[9]

The teacher should make use of the linguistic skills children already possess—skills of oral usage and listening. He should relate them to the new skills to be acquired in writing and spelling along with reading instruction. Composing sentences for the experience charts helps children develop "sentence sense." Writing (composing stories) reinforces the general linguistic skills related to reading with meaning.

Thus teaching reading in a language-oriented, linguistic centered program is more rewarding to the teacher than relying upon mechanical word drills, and motivates children to develop the essential reading skills of extracting meaning from a variety of syntactical patterns.

Reading is more than word-calling. It is an experience in which sounds are associated with meaning. Meaning is expressed not only by single words but by units of phrases and sentences. This is the language-centered approach to reading.

"Comprehending the meanings of phrases or sentences is the central problem of the reader. The ability to comprehend such meanings is developed by the child's experiences primarily and mainly with the oral language. The more extensive the child's experience in the language of speech, therefore, the better equipped he is likely to be in getting an author's meaning."[10]

As the oral aspects of the language provide the basis for achieving success in learning to read, so too does a growing mastery of the written symbols of language help the child develop interest in and sensitivity to the many facets of language; structure and form, rhythm of the language, translation of sounds and concepts into symbols that hold meaning for the reader, as well as for the writer. As the child gains in the command of oral and written language he finds an open door to adventure. He develops an understanding of man and his universe, and gains a greater insight into his dreams and aspirations.

THE NATURE OF READING

Never in educational history has there been such a great interest by such a variety of individuals and groups in the problem of reading. There was a time when primary teachers were lone voices crying in the wilderness about the importance of teaching children to read. Now they are no longer alone. Today teachers at all educational levels, the lay public, and governmental agencies are uniting in their efforts to improve reading instruction.

In order to cope with the demands of our technological age new methods, new approaches, new materials for reading instruction are being tested. This concern for reading has resulted in incorporating principles and practices as well as theories and concepts from other disciplines.

An understanding of the key concepts concerning the nature of reading is a prerequisite for teaching reading successfully. The psychological, sociological, physiological, neurological, and pedagogical aspects of the reading process must be considered in developing a program whereby children can be successfully taught to read.

Key Concepts in the Nature of Reading

Reading is rooted in experience. The more you bring to a book, the more you will take from it. The initial focus must be on experience. The child extracts meaning from the printed page in proportion to the meaning he brings to it. Broad experiences and reading are mutually reinforcing. The teachers and parents have a responsibility to provide the experiences children need—both first hand and vicarious. Time spent in teaching word recognition and comprehension skills is wasted if the child has not had a broad enough range of experiences.

Reading as responding. "Reading is something we do, not so much with our eyes as such, as with our knowledge, our interests and enthusiasms, our hatreds and fondnesses and fears, our evaluations in all their forms and aspects."[11] Children respond to the printed page at three levels—word-calling, comprehension, and the creative level. The effective teacher endeavors to bring all children to the creative level.

Reading is reaction. Reading is reaction to the graphic representation of sound symbols in terms of *recognition* and *understanding*. Whether oral or silent, reading involves reaction to the abstractions of symbols that represent sound. Even at the most elementary level in teaching reading, two fundamental skills must be developed. They are *recognizing* words and *getting meanings from them*. In the earliest stages of reading instruction children learn to recognize the symbols that represent things and ideas. "The act of reading, is a matter of using the stimulus of the marks on the page to recreate speech."[12]

The teacher should provide ample experiences with the oral language before he attempts to teach children to react to the written symbols. The average child by the time he enters the elementary school is no stranger to oral language. Experience in speech is intimately related to the process of learning to read.

Reading is a native language process. If reading instruction is tied closely to speech the child will be more successful in reading. If the teacher begins with familiar materials from the child's spoken language, the more familiar the better, the child senses the relationship between his native language expression and the reading process. Thus he sees that the way he talks, which requires the use of oral symbols, is related to the way he must translate the written symbols in order to make the meaning clear. "Instruction should relate to the total speech system, dealing with the fluctuating relations between letters and sounds of actual speech. It should rest heavily on intonation, and the students should be provided with intonation contours rather than be permitted to puzzle out their own. The teacher should talk out in normal speech patterns what is on the page and encourage the children to do so also. No reading singsong should be permitted to develop."[13]

If children are encouraged to read as they speak with appropriate inflections, the word-droning—the bane of the primary reading class—will be held at a minimum.

Reading is complex. Reading is such a complex activity that any assertion that there is just one approach to teaching is as ridiculous as it is dangerous. A realization of the complexity is the foundation for progress. "Anyone who has taught reading realizes that it involves physical, psychological, intellectual, and emotional responses. In the physical realm there are sensation and perception; in the psychological, abstract symbols are clothed with meanings; in the intellectual, critical thinking is a major goal; and in the emotional there is the nature and intensity of the reaction to the material presented by the writer."[14]

The reading process involves perception (perceiving the words clearly), recognition (recognizing each word and its meaning), comprehension (understanding the meaning of words, sentences, and paragraphs and sensing relationships among the ideas), interpretation (making an accurate analysis of the meaning of the material read), evaluation (determining the adequacy of the ideas in the light of predetermined criteria), and utilization (using the ideas for a purpose). Research and empirical evidence attest to the complexity of reading and that it is not a unitary skill. Rather, it has components of word-recognition skills, comprehension abilities, interpretative skills, and attitudes involving critical thinking and evaluation. The simple ability to recognize words will not meet the demands of modern life.

Reading is a tool for communication. Through reading the child communicates with great minds of the past as well as the present. Through reading he enters into experiences which otherwise would be closed to him. Words merely serve to convey the ideas set forth in a book. They come to life only as the reader brings meaning and experience to them. To the degree that he can unlock the printed symbol and associate it with meaning, is the recognition process effective in communicating ideas.

Reading is creativity. The creative reader brings to the reading material the skills of comparison and synthesis, the ability to see new relationships and to arrive at conclusions based on an "educated hunch". He anticipates outcomes, projects beyond the obvious, and "reads between the lines". The creative reader gains new insights, new understandings, and new appreciations of the ideas revealed in the printed page.

Reading is a developmental task. Society expects every child to learn to read during the first grade. It is one of the developmental tasks. Havighurst defines a developmental task as: "a task which arises at or about a certain period in the life of the individual, successful achievement of which leads to his happiness and to success with later tasks while failure leads to unhappiness in the individual, disapproval by the society, and difficulty with later tasks."[15]

This concept implies that at the time the task is presented the child will have sufficient maturity to achieve success when the opportunity to learn is provided. Unfortunately, however, this assumption is not consistent with our knowledge of individual differences. The teacher of beginning reading must reconcile the expectations of society with his own understanding of child development and learning. Each child learns at his own rate of growth, and in terms of his own needs, abilities, aptitudes, interests, and ways of learning. Unless a child recognizes that reading will meet his immediate needs he will not be motivated to learn to read.

Reading is for specific purposes. People read for specific purposes. Reading serves at least four purposes in the life of an individual: reading for information, reading for enjoyment, reading to solve problems, and reading to evaluate. Reading stimulates thinking, creates broadened interests, and contributes to personal and social adjustment.

Reading is developmental in nature. Reading is a continuing process. It takes years to become what is known as a "mature" reader. Characteristics of a mature reader are cited by Gray and Rogers: "The mature reader has enthusiasm; reads widely and intensively; comprehends and interprets words, ideas, moods, and feelings; makes use of ideas gained in reading; reads critically and evaluates the material; integrates ideas gained in reading with previous experiences; adjusts pace to the occasion and the demands of interpretation; and discriminates in the selection of material and interpretation of the selection."[16]

Reading development progresses year by year, not in a series of separate steps but in patterns which emerge almost imperceptibly as one moves from stage to stage. The lack which college students show in attempting to meet the demands of the curriculum is in part the result of a lack of understanding of the importance of reading as developmental in nature *throughout* the individual's life.

STAGES IN READING DEVELOPMENT

Reading ability must be developed gradually and systematically. One ability is built upon another; one skill is interrelated with another; each phase merges into another. Each skill must be introduced at the time it is needed, related to skills already acquired, and re-introduced at a higher degree of competence at succeeding levels of development. As the child progresses through the elementary school he needs to refine, perfect, and master abilities and skills introduced earlier. He develops new skills as they are needed.

The conscious planning in the school program to provide for continued emphasis on this important linguistic skill at an ever-deeping and broadening level truly makes it an element of organization helping to tie together the language arts curriculum. Reading serves usually both as an element of vertical organization, and as an element of horizontal organization, since reading is commonly emphasized in the content areas of the curriculum as well as in the language arts.

Continuity in reading development is concerned with what happens to the learner as he moves from level to level, from phase to phase, from stage to stage in the reading program as he engages in an expanding variety of reading activities. "Continuity emphasizes children's needs and problems as well as their purposes for and their uses of reading; that is, continuity is based upon what we know about human development and learning."[17]

Research and empirical evidence indicate that children normally go through a sequence of stages in their development of reading abilities. However, it is important to point out that the general categories of stages presented are merely descriptions giving a general idea of a child's reading progress. These are not discrete stages, but merge into one another. Furthermore, children vary widely in their rate of progress through the various stages. At any one educational level or at any one grade level children will be at several different stages of reading progress or in combinations of two or more. Continuity in reading development is facilitated if an entire school system plans for the reading program from kindergarten through the secondary years.

In a desire to delineate the concept of stages, some school systems have made specific designations and spelled out specific skills to be mastered at each step in reading development. For example, they have spelled out children's achievement in reading and study skills in the primary grades, not in the typical stages of readiness, initial reading, and the transition stage in fundamental skills but in eight to twelve "reading levels" or "growth levels". This system is used both in graded or ungraded primary and intermediate units. Frequently the "reading levels" are related to corresponding texts in the basal reading systems. An understanding of the stages of development in reading will give the teacher a bird's eye view of the developmental reading program: readiness stage, from birth to grade I; beginning-reading stage, later in grade I; initial stage of independent reading in grade II; the transition stage in grade III and early grade IV; the intermediate stage in grades IV to VI; and the advanced stages, (including grade VII and beyond.)

The Readiness Stage

In the pre-reading stage the child has his first association with phenomena in his social and physical environment. He learns that there is a relationship between language expression and the responses of others. He learns, too, that there is a relationship between sound and social responses. Then the sounds are linked to others, and the speech of adults, representing his first cultural contact, becomes important in setting sound patterns. He learns to associate the meaning of words with things—and words become for him symbols of objects. He continues to associate words with objects and later with actions. Eventually he learns to use words and expressions he hears. Words become important to him in controlling his social environment as well as in self development. He develops a number of abilities and skills in auditory perception and visual discrimination. In nursery school and kindergarten he is given continuous opportunity to develop language and conceptual skills. The teacher plans situations in which listening, story-telling, interpreting pictures, conversation, "talking-time", dramatization, discussion, and evaluation are integral parts of the daily program.

A premium is placed on oral activity and the child is encouraged to express his ideas. He tries his prowess at interpreting pictures, observing sequence in telling about events, following simple directions, identifying colours, and coordinating muscular activities. Through written communication in the use of captions on pictures, invitations to "Come and read", "Come and look", etc., children will have a desire to learn to read. Too, they are interested in composing stories of their own. On the basis of interest in the language skills it would seem that the early aspects of reading and writing should be included in the preschool experiences of some children. While there is an objection to insisting that every child be exposed to specific reading-readiness activities, there is no reason to deprive the child of language activities which are in harmony with his abilities, needs, interests, and desire to experiment. It is assumed that a good teacher will plan activities which will develop readiness for reading in a manner that does not destroy the child's enjoyment of reading when he is ready for the actual experience. On the other hand, it is equally undesirable to exclude instruction in reading and writing for those children who show the necessary maturity, *and* a desire to read.

Specific pre-reading training in skills required before the child is ready to read include: (1) training in auditory discrimination, (2) experience in visual discrimination, (3) establishing left-to-right sequence in reading, (4) training in listening, (5) developing vocabularly and clarifying concepts to be used in beginning reading material, (6) observing the relationships between letter form and the sound of the letter, (7) seeing the relationship between visual and auditory elements of words and phrases.

Beginning Reading (First Grade)

Most children are introduced to reading during this stage. True, there are children who begin reading in kindergarten, or at home before they enter first grade, but the majority have their initial experiences here. During this period they learn to use various techniques of word-recognition—context clues, word-form clues, and phonetic clues. They acquire skills of deriving information from printed symbols, discriminating between letter and word forms, distinguishing between initial sounds of spoken words, transcribing oral language patterns, using an initial sound together with oral context to supply an unknown word, listening for specific purposes, and reading from left to right. From the beginning children should learn to analyze new words flexibly, using various techniques for unlocking new words. Emphasis should be on reading for meaning—not on word recognition alone if reading is to achieve its purpose. From the first they should be challenged to react critically to what they read, and to interpret motives, behaviour and actions of characters in the stories. The greatest weakness during this stage is the tendency for teachers to allow children to become enmeshed in plodding along instead of reading for meaning.

Initial Independent Reading (Second Grade)

With this stage should come an increased desire to read, an interest in a variety of materials, and greater independence in word recognition, comprehension, and interpretation. Independence in reading thrives in an atmosphere in which the language arts are integrated, ongoing activities are provided which require mastery of skill in reading, creative activity is valued, and opportunities for language expressions are numerous. The interweaving of purposeful experiences in speaking, listening, reading, and writing is facilitated in a program which makes use of units of work and teacher-pupil planning. Independence in reading grows as time is allocated for instruction in reading skills, reading for a variety of purposes, learning to locate materials, and adapting reading techniques to the particular reading assignment.

Transition (Third and early Fourth grade)

The independence gained during the preceding stage merges into the greater independence and consequently increasing enjoyment in reading which characterizes the transition stage. Children now take more responsibility for reading on their own, and for reading longer stories which demand increasingly complex skills of word attack, comprehension, critical thinking, and interpretation. Emphasis shifts from reading comparatively short units to reading longer and more complex materials and demanding a shift in purpose and variety of material in the content fields. The school librarian makes an especially fine contribution at this level in finding just the right books for the right child at the right time. The challenge to the teacher is to provide materials for a wide range in reading abilities, reading interests, and individual projects. A good reading program demands books, books, and more books, if the child's desire to read is to be met.

Intermediate (Fourth to Sixth grades)

There are children who evidence their greatest spurt in reading during this stage: comprehension, reading for a variety of purposes, reading at appropriate speeds, reading fluently in the content fields, shifting method according to the demands of the material, reading for retention, enjoyment, interpretation, evaluation. Study skills such as skimming, summarizing, outlining, analyzing, giving critiques become increasingly important. Specifically, the teacher should expect to provide help needed in the following general areas: further training in phonetic analysis; development in structural analysis of words; emphasis on prefixes, suffixes, and roots through an inductive method; training in using verbal context to increase comprehension skills; training in the more mature use of study skills; more sophisticated use of the dictionary for word meaning and extension of vocabulary as well as pronunciation: increased development of critical and creative reading skills (analysis, comparison, interpretation, and synthesis).

Advanced—The Stage of Expansion (Junior High School)

The more mature talent of the junior high school student affords opportunities for continued growth in a wide variety of reading skills and abilities. Greater development in word study, comprehension abilities, critical thinking, and creative reading are demanded in understanding satire, tragedy, comedy, and irony. Greater attention should be paid to semantics as well as vocabulary development, word-recognition, phonetic and structural analysis of words. Emphasis is placed on refining the study skills, fluency and rate of reading, and adapting reading to specific purposes.

The Junior High School student should concentrate on the ability to organize logically, comprehend realistically, evaluate critically, appreciate aesthetically, and interpret creatively what is read.

Knowledge of the developmental sequence in reading will enable a school staff to organize a program in terms of the needs of the children enrolled in a particular school situation. Further, knowledge of the process of development in reading implies an understanding of the objectives of reading, of the sequential development of skills in the reading process, and ways of providing for the individual differences to be found in every school, in every educational level, and in every class. In the elementary school the teacher will find children at all stages of development as they progress toward maturity in reading. It is only as teachers individually, and teachers and educators on a school staff recognize landmarks on the road toward maturity in reading that they are able to plan and carry out a program of reading activities and linguistic experiences that will guide each child toward his highest potential—not only *in* reading but *through* reading. With such a knowledge it is possible to organize a sequence of reading experiences commensurate with the needs, abilities, interests, and aptitudes of children whether the administrative organization is based on grade levels, reading levels, or growth gradients.

CURRENT APPROACHES TO TEACHING READING

Among approaches to beginning reading are: language-experience, basal reader, individualized, phonic, linguistic, initial alphabet, multi-level reading, words in colour, and programmed instruction. Some of the approaches are relatively new; others have been developed over fifty years or more. Some have been in continuous use; others represent older methods in new apparel; and still others have only recently appeared and have not been tested sufficiently under controlled situations to form conclusive judgment. A longitudinal approach to research studies of reading allows for inter and intra-comparisons of approaches, methods, and evaluation techniques.

In becoming familiar with the basic ingredients of each approach the reader is in a better position to evaluate its effectiveness in the light of the needs of children in a given situation, availability of materials, and the willingness of the administration to cooperate. "Evaluation cannot be limited to the use of test results. Careful observation of children's overt reactions, their choice of a wide variety of reading materials, and demonstrated success in using these purposefully represent important evidence."[18]

Language Experience Approach

The language experience approach emphasizes the oral language background of the child as a basic ingredient in word recognition throughout the elementary grades. It is based on the premise that what a child thinks he can say, what he can say he can "write", what he writes he can "read". Here more than in any other approach to reading there is a developmental integration of the communication skills of listening, speaking, reading and writing. From the very first the child is encouraged to express his thoughts, ideas, and feelings. This approach to reading allows teachers to integrate and develop skills in all facets of language experience simultaneously and with equal emphasis instead of giving undue attention to any specific language skill.

Language experiences serve as the core of the program, thus contributing to balanced development of communication skills and attitudes. Van Allen and his co-researchers identified twenty language experiences which form the framework of the program. These comprise three major phases: (1) extending experiences; (2)

studying the English language; and (3) relating author's ideas to personal experiences.

Vital to the program is the creative expression of ideas. The child's own expression is encouraged through the use of a variety of media such as painting, speaking, and writing. The child is given opportunity to work individually with the teacher, in small groups, and in the total class group. In each situation he is encouraged to express and record his own thoughts, ideas, and aspirations, as well as to read and understand the thinking of others. "Student prepared materials are used as *basic* sources of reading, along with printed materials which are developed for general reading."[19]

The following overview of the language experience approach to teaching reading will clarify objectives of the design of 20 activities which are the core of this integrated language experience program.

Language — Experience Approach to Reading[20]

AN OVERVIEW

Throughout the child's school experiences there is opportunity and need to help him improve his language power through listening, speaking, reading, and writing. To do this, the child goes through a sequence of language experiences which are designed to enrich his experiences and improve his skills. Some of the most important skills which must be developed in children who are expected to live effectively in a democratic society are:

1. *Sharing Experiences* — The ability to tell, write, or illustrate something on a purely personal basis.
2. *Discussion Experiences* — The ability to interact with what other people say and write.
3. *Listening to Stories* — The ability to hear what others have to say and relate it to their own experiences.
4. *Telling Stories* — The ability to organize one's thinking so that it can be shared orally or in writing in a clear and interesting manner.
5. *Dictating* — The ability to choose from all that might be said, the *most important* part for someone else to write and read.
6. *Developing Word Recognition Skills* — The ability to attach sound and meaning to the words in our written language.
7. *Making and Reading Books* — The ability to organize one's ideas into a form that others can use. Also, the ability to use the ideas which others have shared through books.
8. *Developing Basic Sight Vocabulary* — The ability to recognize at sight, to spell, and to write automatically the words of highest frequency in our language.
9. *Expanding Vocabulary* — The ability to expand one's vocabulary — listening, speaking, reading, writing.
10. *Writing Independently* — The ability to write their own ideas and present them in a form for others to read.

11. *Improving Style and Form* — The ability to profit from listening to and reading well-written materials.
12. *Using a Variety of Resources* — The ability to recognize and use many resources in expanding vocabulary, improving oral and written expression, and sharing ideas.
13. *Reading Whole Books* — The ability to read books for information, recreation, and improvement of reading skills on an individualized basis.
14. *Reading a Variety of Symbols* — The ability to read in their total environment — clock, calendar, radio dial, thermometer.
15. *Studying Words* — The ability to find the correct pronunciation and mean- of words and to spell the words in writing activities.
16. *Improving Comprehension* — The ability, through oral and written activities, to gain skill in following directions, understanding words in the context of sentences and paragraphs, reproducing the thought in a passage, reading for detail, and reading for general significance.
17. *Outlining* — The ability to use various methods of briefly restating ideas in the order in which they were written or spoken.
18. *Summarizing* — The ability to get the main impression, outstanding idea, or the details of what has been read or heard.
19. *Integrating and Assimilating Ideas* — The ability to use reading and listening for specific purposes of a personal nature.
20. *Reading Critically* — The ability to determine the validity and reliability of statements.

The goals of broad language experience as stated above cannot be separated in an effective, efficient instructional program. To attempt to do so is to ask the child to do at an early age the most difficult tasks of the scholar — to integrate learnings into meaningful behaviour. *To take reading out of its rightful place in the total language-experience program is to ask children to do what is impossible for many of them.* Or it requires the teacher to use valuable time to put back together what did not need to be separated out in the first place.

Teachers can achieve their goals of reading instruction in many ways. Some of them require that reading be brought out for special attention to the neglect of the other facets of language development. Other teachers are able to leave reading in its natural place and work to develop skills in all facets of language experience at the same time and with equal emphasis.

This approach to reading is highly successful because children are introduced to reading as a developmental communication art related to the other arts of language. They are exposed to oral and written symbols through several avenues. There is more external stimulation and inner motivation to learn to read the products of their own thinking and writing.

Basal Reader Approach

The basal reader approach, in its most definitive sense, provides children with experiences which will help them learn *how* to translate printed symbols effectively and efficiently. This approach is used by well over ninety percent of the elementary schools as the major instructional tool in teaching reading. It provides a program whereby fundamental reading skills form the central focus of the program. These skills are those of analyzing, locating, interpreting, and comprehending written or printed symbols from the page. The objective of developing the basic skills involves direct, systematic instruction, usually on a daily basis. When properly used the basal readers serve as a spring-board from a skills development program to reading for information and enjoyment. Their usefulness lies in the carefully developed sequential organization for the development of reading skills and a controlled vocabulary. As the child progresses from one book to another the number and complexity of skills are gradually increased. To provide for differences in abilities, three groups are usually utilized. Pupils may advance through this sequential program at different speeds but all must follow the predetermined sequence.

In addition to the readers, basal programs also provide a corresponding number of ancillary materials—manuals, workbooks, phrase cards, filmstrips, parallel story books, etc. However, when school boards do not supply the required materials they limit the effectiveness of the program.

Although the instructional design of these basal series varies, the reading skills introduced in the first grade generally include those designed to build reading vocabularly, increase interest and appreciation of books; develop word recognition, comprehension, and critical reading; and develop oral and silent reading skills.

The teacher's manual gives directions and suggestions for direct teaching with appropriate related, and/or enrichment activities. These suggestions are directed toward major phases of the reading lesson: (1) *preparation* for reading—setting the stage and establishing a background for the story, discussing new concepts, and introducing new vocabularly, (2) *reading and discussion*—guided silent reading of increasingly larger units (sentences, paragraphs, stories) to answer specific questions, (3) *oral reading*—for interpretation, (4) *word analysis and comprehension building*—exercises in word analysis, phonetic analysis, and word meaning, (5) *enrichment activities*—the related creative arts of music, drama, art.

Basal readers serve as a spring-board for a logical skills development program to reading books for pleasure and information. The basal reading approach has its greatest value for the novice teacher who needs the security of following the carefully planned sequence of skills and content presented. Experienced teachers who use the basal series call upon their ingenuity and creativity in order to make reading more interesting for the pupil and more challenging for the teacher.

The Individualized Approach

Self-selection is the basis for the individualized approach to reading. The emphasis on the dynamic concepts of seeking, self-selection, and pacing produces results which delight children and amaze adults. The individualized methods are natural outgrowths of the result of child developmental studies. Individualized reading instruction is based on what is known about the differing rates at which children develop, sequence of development, and motivation for learning.

When children come to school some already read, some would like to read, and others have little interest in learning to read. These differences become more marked as the child progresses in school. The child before he comes to school has assimilated some of the language patterns of the culture in which he lives. He has learned to speak and may have learned to read. The individualized reading approach "takes" the child from where he is.

In individualized reading the teacher employs a cultural approach. Appropriate books for browsing are available from the beginning. There is conversation, story telling, and reading aloud. Simple labels and sentences help to identify things or experiences. The teacher provides in the classroom, a supply of books varied in range of difficulty and interest. "Ideally, there will be access to a larger supply. From the books children will seek according to their readiness, needs of the moment, and general interest. Rapid growers will seek many and difficult books, and slow growers, few and simple ones."[21]

Success and satisfaction for the learner are the motivating forces in this approach. The loss of face in being assigned to a slow group, being demoted from a higher group, or failing to please a teacher or admired adult is absent. The teacher does not set a standard for each child to achieve. He believes that each child is unique; each child will succeed in his own way, at his own rate, and in his own good time.

Practices in this approach vary widely. As it is conducted in some schools children learn basic sight words through experience stories, words and letter games, picture dictionaries, and other materials *before* formal book reading is experienced. In a relatively brief time they are able to select pre-primers and other books from a large collection of materials available to them and read at sight.

The pupil-teacher conferences which are an integral part of this approach serve as "contagious motivation". Skills are developed on the basis of needs of small groups as well as on an individual basis. A sharing period provides further motivation for children to discuss, read, and/or give a brief report of exciting parts of stories they have particularly enjoyed.

In a description of practice in using the individualized reading approach one teacher emphasized that the child's first experience with simple books should grow out of oral language experiences. "As all the language and first hand experiences are going on, I begin to introduce simple books. I read each one to the children. They discuss it and dramatize it before it is put on the library shelf. The children begin gradually to gravitate toward these books, tell each other the story from the pictures and begin to read the simple text."[22]

Books must be easily accessible to the children who are given ample time to browse through them, to recall their content, and to choose one they might wish to read. When the child is reading his first books (first in terms of expecting him to uncode the symbols in order to read them back), the teacher may sit with him or with a small group of children, each reading his individual book. She gives each one any necessary help, guidance, and encouragement. She supplies some words quickly, eases over other words, helps with recognition, pronunciation, and meanings. The child may read all of one book or a selected story from a collection of stories within a book. As he finishes a book he discusses it with the teacher or the children and is encouraged to take another.

As the child continues to read, the significance of the pupil-teacher conferences serves as "contagious motivation". Skills are developed on the basis of needs of small groups as well as on an individual basis. The teacher notes individual growth, she checks carefully the child's growth in *what* he reads as well as *how* he reads. She keeps a record of his problems, his skill needs, and when possible works on a particular skill needed by several children with a small group, rather than on an individual basis.

During the reading period while the teacher is having individual conferences with the children scheduled for that period, the other children carry on their reading lesson with a "helper" selected for the day to aid those having difficulty. These helpers are eager to give the time for this activity on a rotating basis and feel not the least deprived when on occasion they are requested to be the reading helper for the period.

Hunt summarizes typical common elements in the individualized reading approach:

1. Literature books for children predominate (rather than textbook series) as basic instructional materials.
2. Each child makes personal choices with regard to his reading material.
3. Each child reads at his own rate and sets his own pace of accomplishment.
4. Each child confers with his teacher about what he has read and his progress in reading.
5. Each child carries his reading into some form of summarizing activity.
6. Some kind of record is kept by the teacher or child or both.
7. Children work in groups for an immediate purpose and leave the group when that purpose is accomplished.
8. Word recognition and related skills are taught and vocabulary is accumulated in a natural way at the point of the child's need.[23]

In the individual reading, a child meets words naturally within the context of the story he has chosen to read. He learns them usually because he needs them to get the important ideas in his reading.

"Basically, the difference between the individualized reading program and the basal textbook program lies between reading instruction conceived as an intensive activity as contrasted to instruction based on broader extensive reading by children".[24]

Since children learn at different rates and in different ways the individualized reading program is based on the belief that learning is more effective and more efficient if the learner is allowed to progress at his own pace and to move ahead as fast and as far as his learning rate and capacity will allow him. Motivation to learn to read is a significant factor in success. The effectiveness of an individualized reading program is in large measure due to the positive attitude toward reading that such a program evokes, and the additional time spent in reading which accrues as a result of working on only those skills which each individual requires in his own reading development.

The enthusiasm which children in this type of program evidence toward reading, plus the number of books read and discussed, is obvious. Not only do children have an opportunity to read the books they want to read, they also gain deep satisfaction from their opportunities to share their books with others since they are not all reading the same texts.

Obviously, however, such a program requires understanding of the interests and motivations of the children, knowledge of evaluation skills, a large number of books varied in interests and difficulty range, and the ability to organize reading in a classroom in a new and somewhat unorthodox manner.

Phonic Approach

Reading with phonics is a system which aims to develop efficiency in word recognition by employing a multisensory approach and a sequential introduction of speech sounds of the English language. "A complete phonics program, this approach utilizes the 44 most frequently used speech sounds in English. It begins with the teaching of short sounds of 5 vowels and progresses to the study of 10 most frequently used consonants. In each early lesson a consonant is blended with the 5 vowels in pronouncing units or syllables, then word wholes. Progression is always from known to unknown, from simple to more complex. Words are always attacked at their beginnings, promoting left to right eye progression."[25]

This program of instruction in word recognition, asserts Wingo, "is designed for use with *all* basal reading series. . . . It has no grade level designation. Since it is a complete phonics program, it may be used in the kindergarten, primary, and intermediate grades. It should be introduced in kindergarten or first grade to establish proper word-attack skills for independent, fluent readers at the earliest possible age. Reading with phonics has proven of great use in the upper grades in creating awareness of the relation between speech sounds and printed letters, thus providing the disabled reader with a valuable reading tool."[26]

This is but one of the many approaches to the teaching of phonics at the present time. All approaches, however, fall into two general categories: (1) those that start the beginner directly in learning the sounds of letters of the alphabet and letter combinations, and (2) those in which the child is taught to recognize whole words for a short time as a preliminary to teaching phonics.

In the first method, "phonics first", the initial emphasis is on learning the sounds of the language. One method based on this concept provides a manual and three books for first grade and a manual and two books for second and third grades. The program includes the development of audio-visual perception, the application of phonetic analysis, the mastery of other word-analysis techniques, and the use of reading for meaning. The development of audio-readiness precedes the application of the sounds of letters and of principles governing their sounds. The program for the first grade is organized in the following sequence: (1) eight weeks of readiness work, emphasizing listening to sounds within words, (2) two weeks of instruction with the phonics primer, followed by six weeks of reading other primers, and (3) five weeks with the phonic first-reader, concluding with seven weeks of reading other first-grade level texts and supplementary materials. The readiness materials start with long vowels, then short vowels, then initial consonants; pre-primer reading is delayed until *all single* letters have been introduced.

Other phonic systems include the extreme in which the 26 letters of the alphabet are introduced on the first day. Drill on letter sounds in isolation follows. Some seventy phonograms, thirteen phonics rules, and twenty-six spelling rules are included, most of which are taught in the first grade. Approximately two to four weeks are used in learning the letter sounds, about six weeks is given to spelling of words, and then reading is started with regular primer material, while intensive work in spelling continues as new phonograms are introduced.

In the second method the child is taught to recognize whole words as a preliminary to teaching phonics. Instead of giving only isolated drill on phonics, phonics is taught in connection with words that give children difficulty. This practice removes phonics from the category of the much criticized method in which children eager to read are dismayed to find that "reading" consists simply of memorizing phonic elements as an exercise in itself.

Research, and modern educational psychology and philosophy make it clear that the concentrated phonics approach to teaching reading is diametrically opposed to what we know about learning. Teaching the child the sounds of the letters of the alphabet, then putting sounds together to make words, and finally putting words together to make sentences is in direct contrast to what we know about children's use of language when they come to school.

Recent studies and observation indicate that effective teachers reinforce phonics by teaching children other methods of "figuring out" how a new word is pronounced. Phonics is not fool-proof as a tool to use in ascertaining pronunciation. The method needs to be supplemented and checked by other word attack skills, using context clues, word-analysis, and dictionary skills. Most teachers use phonics as *one* method of unlocking new words.

The preferred method is an eclectic approach in which the teacher keeps the objective of teaching reading clearly in mind, e.g., to develop a love for reading. Thus the teacher is concerned with developing interest in reading, developing an attitude that reading is an exciting process of getting meaning from the printed page by bringing meaning to it, and that reading deals with ideas, not words; sentences, not letters and syllables.

Not all children benefit from phonic instruction. Dechant makes a pertinent observation: "The basic contribution of phonics instruction may be that it requires the child to visually study the words. Phonics instruction forces the child to look at all parts of a word and this may lead to a somewhat different Gestalt than is seen if the word were perceived strictly as a unit. . . . Through phonics the pupil may learn to more adequately scrutinize the configuration and this may develop the habit of being unsatisfied with a general, overall view of a word."[27]

Linguistics in Beginning Reading

Linguistics is opening new doors to the teachers of reading. Educators generally agree that the child when he goes to school is in full command of the system of his oral language–as presented to him by his family and his community—and it is so thoroughly a part of him that he uses it without conscious thought.

Lloyd states: "His speaking vocabulary, when he comes to school, is already old and already beyond measure; he needs only to learn how the words that he knows (their pronunciation varying as their place varies within intonation patterns) relate to writing and print. It is reasonable to assume that as he learned the syntax and vocabulary of speech through engaging in the processes of hearing and speaking, he will learn the grammar and vocabulary of writing through engaging in reading and writing, and not through dictionary study, word lists, and grammar. Our problem is to set him as free in reading and writing as he is in hearing and speaking."[28]

In defining his general stance on reading instruction Lloyd continues: "Reading instruction must be closely tied to speech in order to be successful. It should begin with familiar materials, the more familiar the better. It should not involve an attempt to change the children's speech, because that speech is the teacher's strongest ally; the child must learn to see the way he normally talks in the print on the page. . . . If reading actually is, . . a native language process, then the youngster who must carry to the page the signals that he finds on the page (if he is ever to find them there) can be helped to discover in his own free speech all he needs to make him a good reader."[29]

Lefevre emphasizes inter-relatedness of the language processes in order to achieve maximum reinforcement of skills, and major emphasis on the larger segment of language approach to reading. He states: "Children who are taught to read with main emphasis on larger patterns than words would be expected to devolop their own generalizations of spelling-sound relationships (phonics)—adequate for the purposes of reading—by a guided inductive process in the normal course of learning the graphic system. . . . In teaching children to read, we should analytically slice larger language segments into smaller ones only to the extent that the learning process requires it. This is the heart of the approach: moving as needed from larger to smaller wholes."[30]

In contrast to the use of larger speech patterns in the teaching of reading other linguists recommend the small unit approach. Fries describes current thinking on linguistics and reading in a concise summary indicating four essential features of an approach to beginning reading that applies linguistic knowledge:

1. The six-year-old school child understands spoken sentences in which the basic sentence patterns have, for their content, words that he knows. For the beginning reading material this child must recognize the written words in the sentence structures as those he already knows when he hears them spoken.

2. As the basic readiness requirement for beginning reading, the child must know the alphabet. He must be able to identify, by name, rapidly and accurately, the individual letters. He must also be able to determine immediately whether two sequences of two or three letters are alike or different in respect to both the individual letters that constitute each sequence and their order within each sequence.

3. English spelling, in its representation of English words, drastically shifted its basic principles from 1450 to 1600. It moved away from a representation that could be grasped in terms of correspondence between individual letters and individual sounds to a representation through spelling patterns. It made possible the "silent" letters of our etymological spelling as well as the differentiation, by spelling, of words having the same pronunciation.

   These developments in English spelling provide a basis for a very different approach to the teaching of beginning reading. It features specifically, even from the very early steps, the making of independent extensions of the matrices to build the pupil's ability to read hundreds of words he has never seen written before.

4. Reading for meaning requires the building of *situation* meanings out of the words and sentences read. Beginning books without pictures compel the pupils to read for meanings rather than guess at words after looking at pictures.[31]

Linguists themselves tend to teach in the manner they were taught rather than to incorporate the knowledge of descriptive linguists in their method. When this happens in the classroom instead of contributing to a child's development in reading the child's progress can actually be hindered. It is only when linguistic findings as a whole are utilized in a manner consistent with what we know about the way children learn language arts in a linguistically oriented environment, that our approach to teaching reading is effective.

What is perhaps the most concentrated sample of emphasis on the smallest basic sound units used in uttering words as a basis for reading instruction is that prepared by Bloomfield and Barnhart.[32]

In order to understand this method it is necessary to understand the basic concepts which underlie the approach. Beginners in reading begin not with the larger speech patterns, but with the smaller units used in structural analysis.

Phoneme - the smallest elemental sound that is recognized as being different from any other speech sound.

Word - the smallest linguistic unit that stands alone in conveying a meaning

Grapheme — a letter symbol for a speech sound (phoneme)

An example, typical of the reading material in this text appears opposite:[33]

had	can	cat	bag
lad	Dan	fat	nag
pad	man	hat	rag
sad	pan	rat	tag

Dan had a bat.

Has Ann a bag?

Ann had a bag.

Nat had a nag.

A fat cat had a rat.

A man had a hat.

Tab had a nap.

In beginning reading instruction the phoneme is used in presenting letter-sound associations for vowels and consonants. Only those words which are regular in the sense that each letter included represents the regular sound or phoneme the letter represents, as for example: *can, Dan, man, fan, pan, ran,* etc.. Initial sentences are developed from such words. Irregular words are not presented until the pupil has learned the regular words thoroughly. Even then the new words are used with previously learned regular words to facilitate reading of the printed lines.

On the basis of the rich experiences children should gain in reading, it is apparent that such emphasis on letter-sound association for vowels diminishes the experience and results in content which tends toward sterility, monotony and dullness.

There is little emphasis on developing comprehension skills at early stages of instruction in this approach because of the definition of reading which the authors suggest. Initial reading involves only the decoding of printed symbols, according to this method. For this reason the program does not include a systematic approach to the development of comprehension skills. The materials include nine readers with an accompanying manual for the teacher, nine workbooks to accompany the readers, and an ABC book designed to teach the letters of the alphabet prior to the work in the readers. The entire program is planned to be completed by an average class at the end of the second grade. Based as it is on the grapheme-phoneme correspondence, irregular words are not introduced until late in grade one.

Such an approach limits the initial reading experiences of children. It is well known that children relish opportunities to use words and to read words that do not fit into this program of reading. Reading is more than decoding. The approach to reading should be broad, interesting, and challenging to children in the initial experiences. Since children's language patterns at the time of school entrance are far more sophisticated and interesting than the material they encounter in the early reading, it would appear that they need to work with ideas which extend their abilities and horizons to develop effective reading and writing skills. To what extent does emulation of the language patterns in this approach mold and extend the child's learning potential and broaden his linguistic skills?

Teachers concerned with developing a love of reading may well question an approach which ignores basic educational and psychological principles concerning education of young children. They will, however, make use of the knowledge which linguistics has contributed in the broad sense, namely, the interrelatedness and developmental nature of the language arts.

Multilevel Reading Instruction

The basis for multilevel reading instruction, according to Parker, is founded on studies of reading process, children, and learning. Studies of *reading process* indicate the existence of specific reading skills essential for each child if he is to progress through the various stages of reading efficiency in a developmental sequence. These reading skills are on a continuum from easy to difficult, simple to complex. Studies of *children* indicate the unique design of development of each child thus demanding a tailormade program in reading instruction to meet his specific needs in acquiring needed skills in terms of *his* experiential background, cultural patterns, learning potential, and individual rate of learning. Studies of *learning* indicate certain cognitive processes.

The question to be answered is "How best to provide reading instruction for 25 to 30 pupils to meet their individual needs?" Parker's answer is—"Use multilevel materials and instruction". This program is widely known as the SRA approach or the Developmental Reading Program.

In this approach the teacher introduces the materials of the learning laboratory to the class and gives individual guidance. Following a placement test, each child starts on the skill track at a point where he can achieve success with effort. Continuous testing provides the pupil feedback, reinforcement, or redirection of his learning efforts. Self-programming enables the teacher to give individual help as needed.

The program requires that the child learn the names and sounds of the English alphabet, its phonic and structural sight-sound combinations, and linguistic word patterning as units of thought. From there he proceeds to decoding meanings from more complex (symbolic) units (paragraphs, stories, chapters).[34]

From this multilevel instructional approach, and paralleling the development of skills, each pupil moves readily into an individualized reading program, selecting books he can read, as a balance between acquiring skills essential in reading and applying these skills in reading for his personal and assigned purposes.

Initial Teaching Alphabet (*Augmented Roman Alphabet Approach*)

The Initial Teaching Alphabet, or ITA as it is known, was developed in England. It consists of 44 characters which provide each major phoneme of the English language with its own symbol. This eliminates the inconsistencies in the phoneme to symbol relationship in the English alphabet which consists of only 26 letters. It differs from other phonemic alphabets in that both ITA and its spellings were designed to simplify the transition of the regular alphabet *after* reading and language fluency are achieved. Sir James Pitman, of London, England, the author of the ITA, asserts that since it is a *meduim,* not a *method,* it can be used with any method of reading instruction. However, proponents of the system regard it as a distinct and unique *method* requiring special methodology as well as special materials.

The 44-letter ITA alphabet consists of 24 standard, lower-case, Roman letters ("q" and "x" are omitted) plus 20 additional characters. Each character has only one lower-case *form* and one *sound,* thus eliminating approximately 2,000 confusing spellings. The child, instead of being confronted with three separate symbols "A", "a", "ɑ", has only a single letter to decipher for a single sound. The unique feature is that there is only one shape for capital, lower-case, or script letters; the difference is in size only. Each character always represents its own sound.

The new alphabet has been used in remedial reading as well as in beginning reading in England since 1961, in the United States since 1963 with wide application. In England, the United States, Canada, Australia, Africa, Israel, and the U.S.S.R., young and old are said to have demonstrated that they can make an effortless transfer from ITA to the traditional alphabet and its spellings.

The regularity of the ITA and the more frequent repetition of the fewer syllabic forms are purported to enable the beginner to learn the mechanics of reading and writing more rapidly.

Conclusive evidence will not be available for some years, as it is the conviction of the originators that a ten to fifteen years period of testing should precede conclusive evidence.[35]

Two obvious weaknesses in the use of this approach are the need to make a transition from the regular script of the alphabet children are accustomed to seeing, and the need for specially prepared material for reading instruction which will have value only in this approach.

Words in Colour

Contrary to its name, colour is far less important than the trade name indicates, since all books and written materials are in black and white. Only the wall charts use colour. The use of colour is purported to solve quickly and easily the problems created by the grapheme-phoneme relationship in the English language without affecting the usual spelling of the words. Thus on the wall charts colour provides a clue and word imagery is said to be more vivid. "The many spellings of each sound occur in the same colour, and the many sounds of one spelling occur each in a different colour (each of the 47 sounds of English identified has its own colour). Examples:

late, way, they, eight, straight, veil, great, pail, (same sound so in same color) pat, was, village, any, fatal, swamp, all, ate, care (different sounds, so in different colors)."[36]

Originated by educator Caleb Gattegno as an experiment in Ethiopia for

UNESCO, this approach reduced the learning time in Amharic, Spanish, Hindi, and English.

Basic to the approach is the full and rapid extension of the linguistic skills already possessed by the learner. The cognitive processes involved in speaking are extended to include operations in related symbols (written language) or talk written down. This makes use of a unified or integrated approach to learning to read *plus* a new set of materials used in solving the problem of phoneme-grapheme differential in the English language. It claims that the techniques and materials of the approach allow the teacher to initiate challenging and enjoyable intellectual games which provide practice, without creating boredom through drill or strain through memorization, and to generate self-direction and creativity in the development and use of written language. This claim is not unique. It is equally applicable to a number of approaches used today by effective teachers. For children who have difficulty in distinguishing colour this approach merely adds one more obstacle to learning to read for meaning.

The Programmed Approach

In a technological age it is not surprising to discover the use of the teaching machine in improving reading instruction. Programmed instruction in reading as in other areas of the curriculum concerns itself with the individual learning of the student through the use of carefully, sequentially organized materials which break subject matter or skills into small learning units. Responses are called for in connection with each unit and answers are provided to which the student can refer immediately *after* he has made a response. Programmed material takes the form of separate worksheets, cards, tablets, workbooks, or textbooks.

Whatever form it takes, the "teaching machine" is the instrument or workbook which presents the individual student the program of questions and answers, problems to solve, or exercises to be performed, together with a feedback of answers so he may know immediately if he has been correct in his responses. Thus he has the opportunity to correct his errors immediately after he makes them. It is the preprogrammed set of exercises or questions presented that determines the learning the student does. The effectiveness with which the information or skill to be learned is organized, developed, and presented is the test of the program that utilizes programmed instruction.

An approach to reading based on programmed instruction is that developed by Sullivan. Goss gives a description of this approach:

> Recently, a new reading program, *Programmed Reading*, was introduced which promises to solve many of the problems. . . . Under this program, first grade pupils learn the alphabet. They then learn certain associated sound symbols, such as "a" as in ant, "m" as in mat, "n" as in man, "t" as in tan.
>
> After a prescribed number of these sounds are mastered the children progress to a primer workbook. When the child has finished the first three parts of this

Primer, he takes a Reading Readiness Test. If he scores 80 percent or above in this test, he starts Book I of *Programmed Reading*. If not, he takes a supplementary section of the Primer and is retested.

There are fourteen workbooks in the Programmed Reading Series, seven in Series I and seven in Series II. The two series correspond roughly to first and second grade levels. The children may read and work in these books as rapidly as their developing ability permits. Most of our children ask to take their books home so they may read and work in them during the evening.

Each volume features pages of self-contained response requirements under which a pupil verifies his own understanding of the material. After every fifty such responses, there is an in-book, diagnostic test. The teacher can check the results at a glance, verify the child's progress, and correct any misconceptions. The teacher also has the opportunity, at this point, of hearing each child read his test to her. This provides an excellent time to work on a one-to-one relationship with the child, praising his progress and thereby encouraging even better work in the future.

Some of the advantages of the *Sullivan Programmed Reading* are:
1. Each child may progress at his own ability level.
2. Since the children are all engaged in reading, the teacher has the time to help individual students.
3. The children are able to have a longer reading period since the three reading groups are eliminated.
4. The vocabulary is so controlled (the long vowels are not introduced until Book 8) that the children are able to sound out each new word they meet in their workbooks.
5. Punctuation is taught as a part of the reading program.
6. The pupils are able to write, spell and sound out each word they are able to read.
7. The child assumes more responsibility since he checks his own work, with the exception of the tests.
8. In a half-hour reading period, the average child makes between fifty and one hundred correct, written responses.
9. The material presented is interesting and challenging to the children. As the books progress, more factual material is presented in longer stories calling for greater comprehension.[37]

If such a program is to succeed in teaching children to read it must take into consideration the need for the child to develop in areas which go beyond literal comprehension. Developing skill in critical thinking, creative thinking, and creative reading are such significant parts of the reading process that a program such as this must be supplemented with group situations involving questions and discussion of material read and interpreted.

Smith adds a word of caution:

Programmed instruction may have some value in giving practice on word identification techniques, provided that several considerations are respected: (1) that these techniques are carefully developed by the teacher in terms of special needs before programmed practice is given; (2) that the programs are carefully worked out so that the child has opportunity to apply the results of practice provided on each frame to the identification of words containing the elements practiced in the reading of these words when embedded in context; (3) that the child is checked by the teacher through oral response on the results of his practice. . . .

The development of interest in reading and growth of taste and appreciation are important aspects of reading instruction. These are facets which do not lend themselves to routine practice and objective testing . . . programming would be of little value in promoting such growths. It is better to leave these to a wise, stimulating, artistic teacher.[38]

Programmed instruction cannot duplicate the role of the classroom teacher. It cannot carry on a good class discussion, nor can it discuss the pupils reactions to the reading. It cannot analyze the problems that the pupil is having. Handling discussion and questions, encouraging individual inquiry and discovery, motivating critical and creative reading—these are the areas which are neglected in a reading program that is centered too exclusively on programmed learning. Centering efforts on the individual student's learning is good. However, such efforts are more fruitful under the guidance of a knowledgable, effective teacher.

Current Approaches to Reading in the Upper Elementary and Junior High

As has been pointed out throughout the chapter, reading is a developmental process. Basic reading skills develop best in a carefully planned, effectively taught, and successfully learned design on the basis of needs of the growing, maturing individual. In addition to direct instruction and effective guidance in the reading period, elementary teachers must be concerned with giving instruction in reading in the content fields. As the child progresses through the elementary school into the junior high school it is important that the reading program be continued. It is necessary to include instruction in reading in the content fields as well as continuing the developmental reading program. This may take the form of: (1) individualized reading, (2) multilevel reading, (3) mechanized reading, and/or language experience.

Individualized reading. Individualized reading is characterized by a library-centered program based on the individual needs of each student. The teacher in cooperation with the librarian provides each child with books suited to his needs, abilities, and interests. The child makes the selection, reads it independently, and writes a report or book review. During the reading period the teacher plans conferences on an individual basis with children who require help. This period is followed by a class discussion in which the pupils discuss the books they have been reading. Thus speaking, listening, writing, and reading are integrated. Special help through group instruction of essential skills is given by the teacher, and guidance in problems in reading in the content fields is also provided, both on an individual and group basis.

Multi-level. Multi-level reading instruction, as has been pointed out earlier, provides an effective method of instruction for intermediate and upper grade children. Centered as it is on graded materials geared to the individual's learning rate and capacity, this program has many enthusiastic supporters, both among students and teachers. Administrators, too, are prone to look upon this method of reading instruction as beneficial, particularly to the student who has mastered the so-called basic skills to the point where he is motivated by the immediacy of the feedback in terms of his progress. The boon of the program for the student is the fact that he can proceed at his own rate. He is given responsibility in plotting his progress, and learns to evaluate his strengths and weaknesses.

Paralleling this multi-level reading instructional program, the pupil moves readily into individualized reading, selecting books at his level of ability, reading for enjoyment, for information, or for study. Thus he experiences a balance between acquiring skills and using those skills for a *specific purpose*.

Mechanized reading. Mechanized reading centers around various types of machines, mainly designed to increase speed in reading. Some students make progress in reading because of the novelty of the experience, the pressure to concentrate, or the desire to achieve. One type of machine which has received attention flashes a phrase on the screen for a small fraction of a second; the reader must respond with recognition of the meaning. Another type forces the reader to increase his speed by means of a lever or bar that moves down over the page at a rate slightly faster than his current reading rate. Opinions vary as to the lasting effect of machines of this type. However, no conclusive evidence has demonstrated their superiority over psychologically sound instruction under the guidance of well-qualified, competent, interested teachers.

Language skills. Verified by research and corroborated by experience in teaching, the concepts of interrelatedness of the language skills have significance for junior high teachers as well as teachers of the elementary grades. Correlation studies[39] show a strong relationship of reading ability to listening, or oral language development, to the knowledge of grammatical terms, and ability to manipulate syntactic structures, to breadth of vocabulary, to spelling, and to success in written composition.

Early asserts: "The fact that success in reading is dependent upon oral language development may be as pertinent in junior high as in primary grades, especially with students who speak a different dialect from standard English. . . . Even in classes where speech does not differ greatly from the norm, teachers are finding that the study of oral and written language patterns makes students more aware of the process of reading by helping them to see how syntax relates ideas."[40]

The Lasswell Formula is an example of a technique which serves reading and writing. "Reading teachers have borrowed this formula from a communications model to use it in teaching critical reading. Thus they teach readers to ask themselves: Who/Said/What/To/Whom Through What Channel/With What Effect? Turning the formula towards the student as writer instead of reader, he is reminded of the importance of 'voice' or point of view (WHO) and of Audience (TO WHOM). As a writer he controls the 'channel' through his choice of words and structure of the composition. Finally, he makes the decision of whether or not he has realized his purpose by testing WITH WHAT EFFECT on a real audience."[41]

In the light of the desire of the teacher to use the most effective approach for reading instruction at every level of growth, the implications of research, the observation and evidence of effective practice, and the willingness to provide the best type of reading instruction is a combination that should prove effective. In providing this quality of instruction, the teacher must be prepared to follow the advice of reading specialists who for many years now have urged "the language arts approach" to teaching reading as the most economical way of capitalizing on the interrelatedness of skills. "If this approach were taken in the junior high school the need for special reading classes would be open to question. . . . The theory is so reasonable that the challenge to every junior high school now is clear: to develop every teacher as a teacher, not of reading alone, but of language skills."[42]

Teachers frequently ask "What skills should the child master before he leaves the upper elementary grades (or junior high school) if he is to be successful in his senior high school years?"

At every reading level it is desirable that the child read widely, ranging from books that he reads for specific purposes in school, to books that he reads because he likes to read. Such wide reading, if encouraged, will develop vocabulary, increase fluency, broaden understandings, provide opportunity for utilizing skills, and open doors to adventure, knowledge, and the aesthetics.[43]

Specific objectives in reading skills and corresponding activities designed to achieve these skills during this developmental stage follow:

READING ABILITIES	LEARNING ACTIVITIES
Locating information	Solving real problems Giving oral reports Writing reports
Word-recognition skills Context clues Word analysis skills Phonetic clues Dictionary skills	Using appropriate method for dealing with unfamiliar words in meaningful situations
Vocabulary development Precise and vivid words Semantic interpretation	Word study coordinated with selections read Collecting synonyms, homo- nymns, antonymns Studying word structure, origin of words Interpretation of symbols
Organization and utilization of ideas gained in reading	Discussion of significant ideas Preparing oral and written outlines Giving reports, talks

Interpreting and evaluating	Problem solving
Critical reading	Discussing material read
Generalizing	Evaluating style of author
Evaluating	Finding clues to characters, plot, situations
Creative reading	Empathizing with the characters Making judgments concerning people and events Forming vivid images Ascertaining truth and error Projecting one's experience into the situation
Broadening interests	Individual reading projects Conferences with teacher Sharing books with others Reading widely for information, enjoyment, and problem solving
Developing taste	Establishing criteria Comparing books Discussing books Evaluating books read
Increasing fluency Adjusting rate to purpose and motive	Setting time limits Exercises in reading for different purposes Reading different types of material
Shifting gears	Demonstration of ability to shift gears in terms of content and type of assignment.
Utilizing content	Exercises in applying information gained in reading to: solve problem, relate information, share a creative interpretation, participate in a project, apply information read.

GUIDELINES IN EVALUATION OF READING METHODS

There is no royal road to reading. Children learn to read via many approaches. Many methods have been and are being used by effective teachers to bring children and reading together in a life-long relationship. Whatever methods are used it is essential that the teacher take responsibility for evaluating the method based on the specific needs of the children in each situation. It is essential, too, to keep in mind that objectives and evaluation are so closely related that in order to evaluate the effectiveness of any one method the teacher must keep in mind the primary objective of reading instruction: to develop the love of reading. Thus evaluation must take into consideration more than reading achievement. It must involve such considerations as the child's attitude toward reading, the choice of a wide variety of reading materials, the demonstrated success in utilizing his reading materials purposefully and effectively.

Dechant lists succinctly some observations pertinent to evaluation of reading methods:

> (1) Most children learn to read, regardless of the method. Many different roads can and do eventually lead to reading proficiency. (2) There are methods or specific teaching approaches that make a world of difference for the individual child. (3) The method that works best for a given child depends on the individual child. (4) The "best" method for *most* children has both an analytical *and* a synthetic emphasis. There are few pure configuration methods, and few programs ignore phonics completely. (5) Some teachers do not make use of the best that is available, but if the teacher is a good teacher, other factors often pale into significance.[44]

The key, of course, to effective reading instruction is the teacher. The effective teacher realizes the significance of using the research from child development, reading practices, sociology, learning, linguistics, language arts.

Research on methods of teaching reading—particularly beginning reading—is extremely popular and prevalent today. New approaches, new ideas, new methods need to be explored if we are to improve the teaching of reading to all children. However, reading programs should be based on reliable evidence that improvement will result. Both administrators and teachers have the right to expect reliable evidence of the advantages of any program, however enthusiastically it may be endorsed by other schools or teachers. Also they have the right to know the limitations and weaknesses as well. "The long-term superiority of a beginning reading plan needs to be established before it is adopted. In addition, it is essential to determine which plans are best for children with unique characteristics if schools are to develop maximal reading efficiency among all pupils."[45]

Every teacher needs to be aware that there is not just *a* method of teaching reading, but that there are many approaches which have been successful. Obviously a method which capitalizes on a child's native abilities, interests, and linguistic development as well as experiential background will be more successful in motivating a child to learn to read.

DEVELOPING BASIC READING SKILLS

"What are the basic reading skills?" "What other skills are essential in learning to read and reading to learn?" "What skills does an individual need if he is to be successful in reading in the content fields, reading for a variety of purposes, and reading with comprehension, critical evaluation, and creative interpretation?"

Questions such as these are inevitable in a discussion of guiding children's development in and through reading.

Unless the teacher has a clear-cut notion of what the reading skills are, he will fail miserably in guiding children in the development of these skills as they progress toward maturity in reading. If a child is to be successful in reading literature, science, social studies, mathematics—in any curriculum area where reading is an essential tool, if he is to successfully translate the graphic symbols on the printed page, he must be guided in the sequential development of the major skills demanded in the reading process. There are several broad categories of skills. Each category is further divided into sub-skills each of which has its unique and special characteristics and each of which is dependent upon and related psychologically or logically to intellectual and conceptual processes involved in reading. Thus to achieve competency in reading the child must master a number of different but complementary reading skills. The responsibility of the teacher is to guide the child step-by-step as he develops the necessary skills.

Regardless of the method of instruction, it is absolutely essential that the child have a comprehensive grasp of reading skills. In each approach, a carefully planned skill development program must be inherent in the instructional program. It is the teacher's task to be perceptive in sensing the specific needs of each child, and to be resourceful in helping children meet these needs.

"Perhaps nothing would contribute more to the improvement of reading instruction . . . than a keen awareness of the various reading skills on the part of teachers and a dedicated attempt to provide for their well-rounded development throughout the elementary grades."[46]

The major areas in reading skills which must be developed include: (1) word recognition, (2) getting meanings from symbols, (3) study skills, (4) fluency and speed. These areas are the foundation upon which subsidiary skills are based and are the nuclei around which these skills cluster.

What makes the teaching of reading so challenging is the complexity of the reading process, the varying rates at which children develop needed skills, and the intricacy of the design in which reading skills are interwoven, interlaced, and interrelated. An examination of the reading skills will provide the teacher with a better understanding of the unique characteristics of each, help him to differentiate between them, and utilize suggestions for helping pupils develop them effectively.

WORD RECOGNITION SKILLS

"An effective reading program must provide for specific instruction in word recognition. Word recognition skills include: a sight vocabulary in which the child recognizes a familiar word just as he identifies a familiar friend—by the way it looks; use of context clues—inferring meaning from context; use of word-form clues; phonetic analysis; structural analysis; and use of a dictionary."[47]

In helping children develop skill in unlocking new words, flexibility and suitability are watchwords. To limit a child by insisting upon one method of attacking an unknown word is to deprive him of the tools he needs in learning to read. Further, it is depriving him of the success that is so essential in beginning experiences with the printed word.

The techniques in the diagram below are the principal ones by which children learn to develop independence in word recognition. Techniques that have lasting value to children in unlocking unfamiliar words independently are shown on the right side of the diagram.

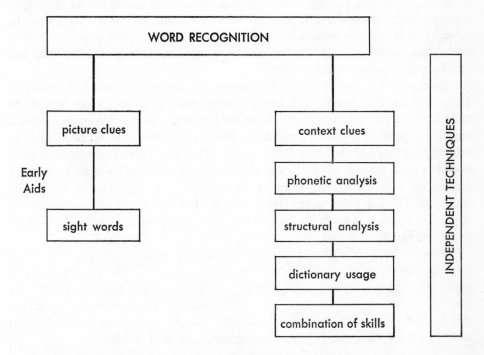

In order to pronounce a word a child sees he must be able to transfer the word symbol into sound. Good readers accomplish this through attending to a variety of skills almost simultaneously.

Picture clues and sight words. Picture clues and sight words are temporary aids in the recognition of unfamiliar words. Independence in reading becomes a reality only as the child begins to develop skill in other clues such as contextual, phonetic analysis, structural analysis, dictionary usage and a combination of skills. Sight words are those words the child recognizes by sight without the aid of any other word-recognition techniques. Adults use sight recognition combined with all other techniques they have learned in their progress toward maturity in reading.

The early stages in the reading program give the child opportunity to make use of picture clues and sight words. At this time he brings to the process of word identification his past experiences and makes use of a clue in the pictures. Sight words are best learned when they are used in meaningful sentences and when contextual clues are also considered. The child who has learned to read before he comes to school has made use of the whole word method of learning. This natural way of recognizing words is in harmony with the Gestalt concept of learning in contrast to concentrating in the beginning on memorization of small phonic elements. This is perhaps the most important function sight words serve in early stages of learning to read.

Sight recognition also serves the function of learning words that do not lend themselves to phonic analysis or structural analysis. Such words in fact often frustrate the child, particularly if teachers insist (as some do) that every word be attacked from a phonic approach—words such as *the, that, come, could, you, what, where, was, would,* etc. If these words are learned as sight words, the child can move readily into reading for meaning.

Context clues. Context clues help identify an unfamiliar word in a sentence. Using context clues can be as exciting as using clues in solving a mystery. If the child is taught to read for meaning *from the beginning*, he will be conscious of the meaning implied in a sentence and bring this insight, hunch, or educated guess to the task. This type of skill is definitely one which marks a growing independence in reading power. Several types of clues which help the child get the meaning through context are experience, comparison or contrast, familiar expression or cliché, and definition. The key point to remember is that the word has to make sense in the context in which it is used. Mature readers make much use of this clue in encountering new words.

Phonetic analysis. An adequate understanding of the science of sounds is essential for the teacher and child. Phonetic analysis is primarily a process of associating the appropriate sounds with the printed word forms. Relating the phonetic analysis to the reading lesson—not spending time in isolated drill—makes this method meaningful. In phonetic analysis the child perceives sound elements within the word—beginning letters, phonograms, consonant blends.

> The child who makes use of this skill can more readily figure out the pronunciation of many printed words the first time he sees them. Then he associates with the printed symbol the meaning or meanings that he has heretofore associated with the sounds of the spoken word.
>
> In order to use phonetic analysis successfully as an aid to word recognition, the child must identify the sounds that are used in our language and associate these sounds with the letter symbols that represent the sounds. Some forty-three separate and distinct phonemes, or sound units, are used in general American speech. Each of these is either a consonant or a vowel sound. The twenty-six letters of the alphabet are the written symbols that represent them. The difficulty lies in the fact that we have more sounds in our language than we have symbols. Therefore certain symbols are used to represent more than one sound. Each of the vowel symbols represents several vowel sounds. For example, the letter *a* represents a different vowel sound in *age, all, after, ago, bar.*[48]

Word identification. As a background for helping children identify the printed symbols the teacher should be familiar with the methods commonly used for word identification—synthetic, analytic, and analytic-synthetic.

Synthetic. The synthetic method starts with one of the word elements, letters (alphabet method), sounds (phonic method), or syllables (syllable method). These methods get their name because the letters, sounds, and syllables must be combined or *synthesized* to form words.

Analytic. Historically, the analytic methods of reading include: the word method, the phrase method, and the sentence method. These methods get their names because they begin by teaching the word, the phrase or the sentences. The larger units are broken down into their "basic" elements.

Analytic-synthetic or synthetic-analytic. The analytic-synthetic method begins by teaching the total word and then *more or less* simultaneously breaking it down into its phonemic or sound elements. The synthetic-analytic method, on the other hand, begins with the phonemes (sounds) and then combines these to form meaningful words.

Most teachers favour a combination or eclectic method of teaching word identification and recognition. Research and good practice demonstrate that most children learn more effectively through a multi-sensory approach to independence in attacking words. The good reader unconsciously interrelates, interwines, and integrates the analytic-synthetic methods.

Pooley emphasizes this tendency on the part of young readers as he points out: "One of the principle learning procedures at the early stage is the association of printed letters, singly and in combination, with the typical sounds they represent and the synthesis of these sounds into patterns which the child can recognize as the words he already knows. Some words he will learn as wholes, without the need for analysis; but, increasingly as he meets new words, the power to deal with them analytically in terms of sounds related to symbols is a valuable asset."[49]

Structural Analysis

Structural analysis clues are concerned with the units that make up the structure of a word, e.g., root, prefix, and suffix. These clues help children recognize: (1) the large number of words composed of basic roots to which endings such as s, ed, ing, and various prefixes and suffixes have been added, (2) compound words and contractions, and (3) words of more than one syllable which must be divided into pronunciation units before "sounding out" is possible.

The effective use of structural analysis in unlocking new words demands several sub-skills. The child must recognize words formed by the addition of inflectional endings to root words, and associate varied meanings with these endings. He must recognize words formed by the addition of prefixes and/or suffixes to root forms, and associate varied meanings with these structural elements. He must recognize syllables in words and use them as aids in pronunciation. He should be able to compound words he already knows to create a new word. Most children enjoy combining simple known words to form compound words, and to reverse the procedure.

Reading involves not only the ability to keep in mind the totality of a word, phrase, or sentence, to perceive the larger relationships, but also "to attend to individual words and at times, to parts of words. Perceiving in a general way the whole, but not discriminating clearly among its component elements (letters, words, phrases) may cause as much difficulty in reading as does concentrated attention on word-analysis and word-calling."[50]

The Dictionary

The classical joke about using dictionary skills in identification and recognition is the one in which the child points out that if he knew how to spell it he wouldn't have to look it up. Dictionary skills become increasingly useful to the student as he has need for: locating words in the dictionary, working out the pronunciation of words, and getting shades of meanings from words. These skills must be developed in such a way that the child sees the relationship among them and having learned the location skills, the meaning skills, and the pronunciation skills, he must learn to integrate them as quickly as possible. Later he will become familiar with syllabication and the understanding of diacritical markings.

Combination of Skills

No single method of word attack is effective in becoming a proficient reader. "The very fact that children are different and that they do not learn by the same methods ought to keep the teacher from putting undue emphasis on any one method. What is food for one may be poison for another."[51]

Dechant contends that what is important is the need for an economical method of word attack—one that helps both to identify the word with which the child is concerned and to use this present learning in the identification and recognition of other words. "The method should provide the maximum possibilities for transfer. It should help him to formulate inductively generalizations and rules that further aid word identification and recognition."[52]

Gibson summarizes the importance of a combination of skills as she states,

> Though configuration may be the method used in the early stages of reading, as vocabulary load increases, few children can continue to make the fine discriminations which become necessary if other means of word recognition are not available. As soon as words are grouped into sentences the child must be guided into using context clues in order to limit the number of possible correct responses. As he becomes proficient in associating sounds with letters, he should be trained to use both context *and* beginning letter sounds to think of a word that makes sense with the other words in a sentence. This is preferable to "sounding through" each word because the combination of phonics *and* context assures that the child will be made

conscious of the meaning of what he is reading from the early stages. In order to use phonic clues the child must be able to hear differences in letter sounds. This skill can be acquired by most pupils at an early age if teaching designed to develop auditory discrimination takes place. No attempt should be made to teach the use of phonic clues until the skill of auditory discrimination has been developed.

Structural analysis should be taught as soon as inflectional endings are needed. It is most essential that several different methods of word attack be used and that these be taught as early as possible. Though picture clues and sight words serve a very useful purpose as temporary aids in recognizing unfamiliar words the child will gain independence only as he begins to use other clues such as context, structural analysis and phonics *simultaneously*. There is a direct relationship between the mastery of reading skills and the automatic use of various methods of word attack. Good readers use a balance of all methods.[52]

In word-attack training it is interesting to note that the average and slow child gains more from concentrated training than the accelerated or bright pupil. The latter acquires his word attack skills through his every-day reading experience.

GETTING MEANINGS FROM READING

Until teachers understand the significance of the development of comprehension skills, there will be no reading in the real sense of the word. Pronouncing words is fruitless unless one brings to and gets from the printed symbols meanings and understanding.

There was a time in the primary grades when children were expected to learn to read; in the intermediate grades they were expected to read to learn; in junior high they were expected to read to evaluate; and finally in senior high they were expected to read creatively. Today, however, in order to equip children for life in a complex technological society we must teach them from the beginning the skills needed to read for meaning. Reading for meaning requires a child to master a cluster of distinctive skills, with experience in each of the skills at every level of reading, broadening and expanding his power to get meaning and interpret meaning in the books he reads.

"Reading is something we do, not so much with our eyes as such, as with our knowledge, our interests and enthusiasms, our hatreds and fondnesses and fears, our evaluations in all their forms and aspects."[54]

Developing skills of comprehension requires the mastery of a cluster of distinctive skills, with experience in each of those skills at every level of reading growth. We need to recognize the different categories of meaning-getting processes in reading. To do this we must break down the blanket term of comprehension. There are different kinds of comprehension which in turn call for the use of different mental processes. In the following diagram are graphically portrayed the specific meaning-getting processes which must be developed throughout the levels of reading growth if children are to read for meaning.

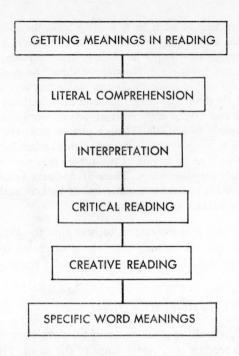

Reading involves the use of materials that are challenging and thought-provoking, so that each child will learn to use books to enrich his experiences, extend his horizons, broaden his understandings, develop his insights, and unlock the door to reading. Growth in reading is a complex, continuous process. Reading for meaning is the door to that process. An understanding of the elements involved in reading for meaning is the key that unlocks the door.

Comprehension Skills

Literal comprehension. Literal comprehension involves the skill of getting the literal meaning of a word, idea, or sentence in context. It is the level of comprehension which requires mere recall. There is no depth in this kind of reading, and yet all too frequently, practice in literal comprehension dominates the comprehension skills because teachers are content to use only the following techniques of meaning-getting:

1. Asking questions based directly on the text to elicit mere recall
2. True-false statements
3. Completion sentences
4. Multiple-choice responses

Among the types of questions which should be used in teaching literal comprehension are those which involve:

1. Getting the main idea

2. Recalling or recognizing details
3. Determining the sequence of events
4. Identifying things mentioned most frequently
5. Checking to understand the appropriate meaning

Interpretation. Interpretation goes beyond literal comprehension to supply meanings not directly stated in the text. It compels the reader to infer meanings which are not apparent in the words presented. The thinking skills involved are:

1. Drawing inferences
2. Making generalizations
3. Reasoning cause and effect
4. Anticipating outcomes
5. Making comparisons
6. Sensing motives
7. Discovering new relationships

Interpretation gives the child an opportunity to transcend the boundaries of a situation, and at the same time recognize the limitations imposed by the author.

Critical reading. Critical reading requires the reader to go beyond interpretation of what the author says and to give his personal reaction. It involves the reader in evaluating and making personal judgments as to the quality, accuracy, and plausibility of what is read. It requires that the reader make intelligent observations. Greater awareness in children can be encouraged through questions which elicit comparison with the child's own experiences, ask the author's purpose, or ask the child to react critically to the style of the author.

Creative reading. Creative reading goes beyond critical reading. It involves more than the ability to judge what one reads, both in terms of content and manner of presentation. Creative reading calls into play a child's imagination, his flow of ideas, his ability to project himself beyond the limitations of the situation. The child enters into the author's experience and makes it his own. "Creative reading is concerned with the production of new ideas, the development of new insights, fresh approaches, and original constructs."[55]

The child can interpret, in creative reading, ". . . the situations in the light of his experience, and understand analogies, allusions, figures of speech, connotations and denotations; he can reorganize the ideas he receives into a pattern that is unique and personal. He can express his reorganized learning through various media—word and song, gestures and action, materials and composition, through the very make-up of his personality."[56]

Specific Word Meanings

The skills of developing specific word meanings permeate all levels. For many years we have concerned ourselves with helping students to obtain word meanings from sentences and paragraphs. Only recently have we considered specific word meanings to be a reading problem. We have come to realize that lack of a single word may interfere with a student's ability to get the meaning of all, or part of a selection. The following activities will be effective in helping a child to develop skills in specific word meanings.

Methods of Developing Word Meaning

Through experience. Firsthand experience ranks highest as a technique in developing word meanings. Experiences build up a fund of clear, definite images which children use to relate the known to the unknown. The school can provide many experiences: direct experiences, with classroom activities and field trips, and vicarious experiences, through the various visual aids and sharing periods. Sharing of out-of-school experiences can be of specific benefit to our purpose when unfamiliar words are lifted from the conversation, presented on the board, and defined. The symbol should be associated with the experience to assure the child's knowing what he needs to know to interpret the symbol.

Through pictures. Collection of pictures to illustrate meanings of nouns, verbs, adjectives. Use all levels of picture reading: naming the objects in a picture, telling what is happening, interpreting the artist's idea.

Insert a picture in a sentence to replace a word; follow with a sentence containing the corresponding word.

Through literature. Enrich the vocabulary through stories read or told by teacher and pupils. Have pupils retell a story told by the teacher using new words meaningfully. Read poetry containing sensory images.

Through creative expression. Motivating situations for creative expression may include:

1. Asking pupils to create similes for the sound of crushing leaves, splashing waves
2. Making lists of favourite sounds, sights, odours, foods
3. Having pupils think of "the quietest thing you can imagine"
4. Setting up a "Touch and Feel" table where children handle various objects and volunteer words that tell how each object feels in their hands
5. Asking such questions as "What does it look like?" or "How did you feel?" to start children searching for *precise* descriptive terms that make word pictures for others to listen to or to read
6. Writing group experience stories, incorporating new words gained through the class experience
7. Writing original stories, with each child building up his own dictionary or card file of necessary words

Through comparison and contrast. (1) Help pupils discover the comparative forms of adjectives and draw illustrations, e.g. tall, taller, tallest. (2) Collect or match pictures illustrating synonyms, antonyms, homonyms. (3) Discuss the multiple meanings of a given word, e.g. ball, bar, run, iron, mine.

Through supplementary reading. Create an atmosphere that will encourage free recreational reading among pupils by:

1. Being familiar with many books so that the right book may be made available at the right time
2. Having an ample supply of books at various interest and ability levels on the library table
3. Encouraging children to bring their favourite books to school to be shared with class
4. Following children's interests in selecting books from the library and in choosing stories to be read
5. *Reading some prose and poetry each day*
6. Binding experience charts and original stories into book form and making them accessible
7. Providing definite times for recreational reading
8. Stimulating desire to read by providing for reporting, illustrating, or some other type of motivation

Through classification. List words under appropriate headings:

Things We Need in Art
Things We Take Home Today
People, Animals, Plants

Provide games based on this principle for children's free time.

Through dramatization. Action words (verbs) presented on word cards. Phrases may be used for the same purpose.

Through the use of proper terms. As children learn to read, they should be taught to use appropriate names for the concepts they encounter:

title	question mark	vowel
sentence	compound word	syllable
paragraph	consonant	prefix
period		etc.

This principle should be applied to other subjects in the curriculum, as well as to daily life in and out of school.

Through context clues. An unknown word may be defined in context. "First he *nibbled* on some *lettuce*." "Then he took a bite of *parsley*." "The little rabbit liked *(vegetables)*."

Meaning as an Aid to Word Recognition

The meaningful word is the one most easily recognized and longest remembered. That is why nouns present little difficulty to children, compared with articles and adverbs, for instance. By developing word meanings in a variety of ways we can increase their chances of being recognized on second meeting.

Through context clues. Several types of specific activities may be employed to promote skill in the use of context clues. These may involve group work or be used as individual seatwork.

Completion sentences are useful in helping to develop the ability to anticipate words:

The rabbit has a short..................

Apples grow on...................

In a similar exercise the child selects from a group the correct word to complete the sentence. The entire sentence should be read before the selection is made:

Bill laughed at the...................snowman.

(cat, cold, funny)

To give practice in using a context clue to choose the appropriate word from two or three with similar configuration, sentences such as this may be used:

Tom...............to the store.

(went, want)

Completion sentences in which there is more than one possible answer may be used, first as seen below, then with the first letter of the missing word supplied, showing that visual clues may be used to check meaning clues:

Mother called Joe to come and eat his...................

Through relation to objects and pictures. The device of labeling furniture, pictures and drawings, science and nature displays, number symbols, supplies, etc., brings meaning that aids recognition.

Those words with abstract meanings should receive special emphasis upon presentation and considerable repetition thereafter. Devices to give meaning can sometimes be worked out:

The word card showing *here* may be placed on a ledge near the reading circle while *there* is placed at the opposite end of the room.

Through comparison and contrasts. Exercises fixing the meaning of antonyms, synonyms, and homonyms also help to fix recognition patterns. Countless practice exercises can be devised to further both understanding and recognition:

The words can be matched with each other.

They can be matched with pictures.

They can be illustrated by pupils.

They can be used in sentences.

Through classifying. Familiarity with the meaning of words helps children recognize them in doing such exercises as:

Finding and listing names of children, animals, toys, food, etc.

Classifying words under certain headings, such as things that come in pairs, things we ride, etc.

Separating words and classifying them under two headings, as wild animals or farm animals, things we see or things we do.

Through the use of the chalkboard. The chalkboard is essential to the linking of word meaning with word recognition. The symbol should be associated with the experience to assure the child's knowing what he needs to know to interpret the symbol.

When an unfamiliar word is used in a story or conversation, for instance, it should be written on the board in order that visual imagery may be attached to meaning.

Lists should often be made for reference over a short period of time, even if there is to be no direct effort at teaching the words. What to take on our trip, words we use in arithmetic, workers we know, are some possible classifications. (An especially troublesome word may have an honoured place on the board for a while.) The reading group should face the chalkboard so that words can be written on it for use in the introduction and culmination of the reading lesson.

STUDY SKILLS

There was a time when concern for techniques and skills related to reading in the content areas was considered to be the province of the intermediate grades. From recent research, from observation, and from evidence gained in working with children, three categories of study skills emerge. These enable a child to read effectively and to study successfully in the different curriculum areas and academic disciplines. The study skills are defined as: (1) common reading skills, (2) common study skills, and (3) specialized techniques, including vocabulary and skills specifically required for reading in a particular subject area.

Smith differentiates between the common reading skills and the common study skills: ". . . the study skills in reading may be broadly defined as skills used when there is intention to do something with content read. A student may read the sports page to find out how the different teams are progressing, he may read a horse story or a book about space travel because it intrigues him, he may read a detective story to discover who stole the Black Diamond. In none of these cases is he going to do anything with what he reads. He isn't using study skills. But when he reads in his text in order to answer questions in class discussions, to make a report, to solve a problem, to conduct an experiment, to pass a test, he is reading for the purpose of doing something with the content. Now he is using study skills." See the following diagram.[57]

It would be realistic to refer to these study skills in relation to an educational task assignment. As a matter of fact the mature reader makes use of these study skills in reading for purposes outside the school as well as in educationally oriented

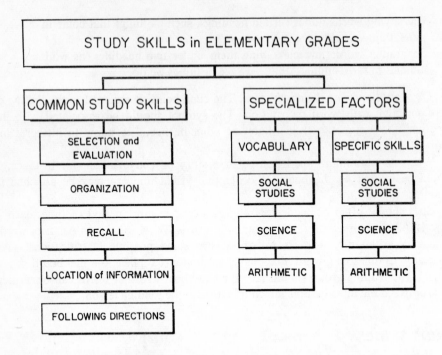

tasks. The authors hold that reading is a developmental process; that it takes a lifetime to achieve the goals of reading, and that study skills continue to be important throughout the life of the individual, and that whenever the reader reads in the content areas he *needs* to use the study skills in both categories of common study skills, and specialized techniques.

Common Study Skills

Regardless of whether a student studies social studies, science, mathematics, or literature he is required to use study skills. These skills are as basic to study in the subject fields as phonics and word structure are fundamental to word recognition.

Selection and evaluation. Selection and evaluation are concerned with the process students use when they select from the printed passage the sentence, word, or idea that is most pertinent to a specific purpose expressed in a question eliciting reasoning, critical, or creative thinking. Children should be taught from the very beginning to develop skills which call for thinking at a higher level than mere recall. They should learn to find in the written material documentary evidence to support a conclusion, a generalization, to prove a point, or make a judgment leading to a decision.

Organization. Organization is essential if ideas are to be presented in a logical, concise, and comprehensive manner. Children should learn early to classify, to arrange ideas and sentences in logical sequence, to put objects in correct order, and to arrange phenomena in appropriate categories. Outlining, summarizing, organizing data, taking notes, and learning to evaluate their appropriateness are all part of developing skills needed in proficient reading in the academic disciplines.

Other common study skills such as recall of information read, locating information, and learning to follow directions should be taught in a developmental design from the time children enter kindergarten. These skills should be an integral part of the language arts program.

Recalling information. Recalling information, fixing clearly in mind what one has read, is a skill which is important not alone for the child, but also for the adult. Information needed at a later time can be recalled by the child if the teacher utilizes the principles of learning, and provides the motivation, the need, and the purpose for the activity. However, expecting the child to memorize without a clear purpose is fruitless for the teacher, and frustrating to the child.

Locating information. Helping the child to learn how to locate facts and find information as he needs it is an essential task for today's teacher. He should be taught to make use of the table of contents, index, and glossary of individual books as well as the resources in the library.

Following directions. Following directions has been discussed as a skill in listening for information in an earlier chapter. It is the responsibility of the teacher to *make sure* that children understand the written directions *before* they begin to work. Reading the directions orally, writing the directions on the chalkboard, asking a child to tell what the directions say, discussion of the directions—these and other techniques can be used to ensure that *every child* knows what the directions say.

Specialized Factors

A knowledge of the cluster of techniques known as study skills is invaluable in teaching reading. It is equally important to have a knowledge of the specialized factors affecting reading in the content fields. Children need instruction and careful guidance in this area. Problems which face children in reading text book material in the content subjects are: "(1) technical vocabulary, (2) new and undefined concepts, (3) complicated explanations and careless writing, (4) too many facts in too short a space, and (5) lack of grading of difficulty level."[58]

In addition, the content subjects require a different approach from the easier reading of graded stories and material found in the basal and supplementary reading series. The content fields require intensive study rather than a more casual approach and demand much more time for reflection, discussion, and comprehension. The development of concepts which is vital for creative learning is facilitated by the use of visual aids.

Each of the content areas has its own specialized vocabulary and a learning process unique to its discipline.

Reading in the field of science. The area of science poses a problem for many students. The New York City Metropolitan School Study Council recommends a five-step approach which can be successfully used by elementary school children: "(1) readiness, (2) concept development, (3) silent reading—to find answers or discover, (4) discussion (oral or written), and (5) re-reading (silent or oral to check accuracy)."[59] They suggest further that to read science material successfully the pupils must apply the basic reading skills of (1) locating pertinent detail, (2) distinguishing between main ideas and supporting details, (3) visualizing, (4) following directions, and (5) drawing inferences. When children have perfected these skills they can use them successfully for reading in social studies, in word problems in mathematics, and in literature as well.

Reading in the social studies. If social studies is to be more than memorization of facts which may already be obsolete, the reader must identify central issues, make judgements on the basis of evidence from a variety of sources, and generalize from evidence in the content read. He needs to be familiar with the special vocabulary and to adjust his reading rate to the material as well as to the purpose. He must develop skill in thinking critically.

Umans suggests the following competencies for reading in the social studies:

1. Recognize and understand its vocabulary and note exact meaning.
2. Understand social studies concept by:
   a. finding main ideas in sentence, paragraphs, etc.
   b. noting how details support and illustrate main ideas
   c. organizing ideas and outlining for understanding, review, and presentation
   d. relating ideas and drawing inferences
   e. understanding time and space relationships
3. Read and study effectively by:
   a. adjusting rate and depth of comprehension to the purpose
   b. using survey methods such as SQ3R (Survey, Question, Read, Recite, Review)
   c. understanding visual and graphic materials such as globes, charts, graphs, diagrams
   d. using library skills to locate information for research
   e. taking useful notes.[60]

Reading in Mathematics. Special training in teaching children to read in mathematics includes, in the words of Spache, instruction in "(1) organizing details into working ideas, (2) recognizing relationships, (3) organizing processes to find solutions, (4) adjusting rate to slow speed to secure a high degree of comprehension, (5) understanding technical vocabulary and symbols, (6) understanding common words with mathematical connotations, or more precise mathematical usage, (7) locating and selecting related readings, (8) evolving procedures for problem solving."[61]

As children progress through the elementary grades, an increasing amount of instructional time is, as a general rule, devoted to developing reading skills and vocabulary in the content areas. This is indicated in the results of the *Harvard Report on Reading in Elementary Schools* by Austin and Morrison: "The percentage of schools systems which reported giving considerable time for this purpose increases from 17% for the first two grades (content subjects are not usually emphasized at this level) to 31 for grades 3 and 4, and finally 57 at grades 5 and 6. Conversely, the percentage reporting "little or no time" steadily decreases until it is less than 5 at the fifth and sixth grade level."

Relative Amount of Reading Time Devoted to Developing Reading Skills and Vocabulary in the Content Areas by Grades, as Reported in 759 Questionnaires[62]

AMOUNT OF TIME	GRADE LEVELS		
	1 & 2	3 & 4	5 & 6
	%	%	%
Considerable time	17.3	31.1	57.0
Moderate time	26.5	50.3	33.5
Little time	36.7	12.3	4.5
No time	14.5	1.1	0.1
No answer	5.0	5.2	4.9
	100.0	100.0	100.0

As an extension to the questionnaire data, an attempt was made during the field study to determine, in relation to the teaching of reading in the content areas, (1) the content subjects included, (2) the reading skills taught, (3) the barriers which prevented more extensive reading instruction, and (4) the adjustments made for superior and poor readers.

1. A few interviewees believed that reading skills and vocabulary were taught in all content subjects, and others named a wide variety of combinations. Yet, although every curriculum area was referred to at least once by name, social studies and science were mentioned far more frequently than the others.

2. When questioned on this point, administrators, supervisors and consultants named one item more than four times as often as any other: the development of the particular vocabulary for a given subject. Surprisingly, word analysis (perhaps because taught in conjunction with vocabulary development) was the second most frequently mentioned, followed closely by the general term "comprehension". Other skills reportedly developed were reference skills, selecting the main ideas, organizational skills, skimming, critical reading, and interpreting maps, graphs, and charts. . . . However, on the basis of their own observations, the study staff found only limited evidence that reading skills were being taught in the content areas. Apart from any consideration of the effectiveness of the teaching, only three reading skills — skimming, outlining, and map reading — were observed as

being taught with any degree of frequency. Comprehension was frequently tested, but for the most part there was only a parroting back of factual information.

3. From the responses voiced most often in the interviews, the teachers, it would appear, still suffer from the old educational disease, "inopia temporis". They reportedly do not have sufficient time to "teach everything" and, unaware that a dichotomy need not exist, feel it more important to cover the content than to teach the reading skills in the content areas. . . .

Almost as many respondents were of the opinion that the chief barrier to increased reading instruction in the content areas was put up by the teacher herself. They thought that teachers lacked adequate knowledge concerning reading instruction in the various areas and, to compound the problem, that teachers were none too interested in acquiring that knowledge.[63]

FLUENCY AND SPEED

Another most important skill in reading is that of shifting gears on the basis of content, purpose, and difficulty.[64] Unless the child learns early that reading must be adjusted to the purpose for which he reads and to the difficulty of the reading content, as well as the type of reading he is doing, he is in grave danger of developing a surface reading pattern, wasting valuable time, or reading too rapidly to savour the flavour of the story and the atmosphere of the narrative. Some material is meant to be read thoughtfully and reflectively, some material is meant to be read studiously; other material is meant to be skimmed lightly; and still other to be digested thoroughly.

A case in point is the illustration of the young man who went into a book store which dealt largely with the classics, and asked for *The Return of the Native* and a book on speed reading. It was obvious from the non-verbal as well as the verbal behaviour of the proprietor that she felt that reading for enjoyment and the reading of the classics (which to her were synonymous), and speed reading were incompatible.

Teachers should help children develop the ability to read for various purposes and approach the reading task in terms of the purpose. For example, they can give the students mimeographed excerpts from various sources to illustrate the need for different approaches in reading. A few paragraphs from narrative material can be written on a simple reading level, and then on successively more difficult reading levels, until the material to be read challenges the pupil to go beyond the usual level of difficulty—to stretch his mind as well as his skill.

Excerpts can be selected, too, from various subject fields, content areas, or academic disciplines, written on the level of difficulty children can manage. Children can be asked to read these materials—shifting gears in reading to meet the specific purpose for reading and nature of the material. They will discover that narrative reading requires a different speed, and attitude as well as a unique approach. The same is true of scientific and/or mathematical material, and the social studies. They will grasp the concept that some materials can be understood through a rapid, single reading; other materials require reflective, thoughtful reading interspersed with reflection before they are comprehended by the reader.

A study by Maney[65] reports that a generalized reading ability does not exist, and that content and purpose dictate the nature of the skills to be employed in reading a particular selection. To read material in the subject areas a student must set a purpose for reading so that he knows which facts to select and which to reject as unimportant for *his* purpose. Pupils must learn to vary the reading speed to achieve the comprehension demanded for the purposes for which they are reading at a given time.

Artley[66] reports that various studies clearly show that a particular field of knowledge makes demands for reading interpretation which do not duplicate those in other fields. The factors in each subject field or content area which determine the basic reading abilities are: (1) aim, (2) inherent nature of the material, (3) symbolism used, (4) characteristic methods of instruction, and (5) type of problem solved.

PERSISTENT PROBLEMS IN READING

The important objective is to develop a child's love for reading. In the struggle to develop basic skills this objective is often overlooked. Many teachers who are successful in teaching the basic skills have difficulty in achieving objectives dealing with the broad aims of reading.

Some of the persistent problems which, when solved, contribute to the broad objectives of reading are: oral reading, critical and creative reading, developing broad interests, providing for individual differences, and developing evaluation procedures.

Oral Reading in the Elementary School

It is essential to recognize that the significance of oral reading lies not in reading aloud as a diagnostic tool, but rather as a creative medium through which the child shares his appreciation of a selection of which he is especially fond.

With the increased emphasis on linguistics, the understanding of intonation patterns makes it easier to help the child learn to read with the same expressiveness with which he speaks. For years, teachers of reading have asked children to "read with expression" without giving them the techniques for doing so, and without understanding the relationship between spoken and written expressions. As teachers become increasingly sensitive to intonations, stresses, and junctures, and help children become aware of these elements in sentence structure, oral reading will begin to improve and to gain a place of significance again as an expressive art. Hatfield states: "Pupils may well be asked to prepare oral readings by first reading silently with attention to the expression the authors intended . . . even we teachers do not like to read publicly any material which we have not recently read to ourselves. This greater awareness of the speech values on the printed page may be invoked to increase enjoyment of literature, especially of poetry."[67]

Oral reading activities if properly guided contribute to the total development of the child, to his creative expression, and to his reading progress. It should be included in a well-balanced reading program. Educators concerned with creative development of the child are convinced of its role in helping children develop creative potential.

The use of the "barber shop" style of reading aloud (the "line a child") has brought a blight upon the practice of oral reading, as has also the practice of using oral reading for evaluating basic reading skills of word identification and comprehension. However, if used to develop the art of communication and an appreciation for the spoken word it can become an effective and enriching creative experience in the elementary classroom.

In oral reading the material is primarily manifestive. Here the reader shares the content with the audience. He and his audience are together looking at the material. As a result it is put within the realm of the audience. It must give the effect of the first time and of being shared. It is necessary for the student to know the material thoroughly. In the best sense it is necessary for him to "think the thought." He must know it so completely that it has become a part of his thinking. For this reason the greatest emphasis is placed on getting the meaning, absorbing the meaning, and then giving the meaning. In interpretation the reader, as an individual, recedes into the background. Once the student realizes this fully, it releases many inhibitions. The conception finally gained that *he* is not important, but that the material is all important opens a new vista of freedom and creative expression.

Critical and Creative Reading Skills

"While ample time is devoted in most schools to the identification of new words and to the beginning comprehension skills, higher level reading abilities are often neglected or treated only superficially in the intermediate grade curricula. If children are to become mature readers, they must become critical and creative readers."[68]

The effective teacher will use all available means of challenging children through questions which elicit more than acquisition of mere factual material. Instead, they can be motivated to reason, to discover, to project beyond the printed page, and to evaluate. It is the responsibility of the teacher to teach the critical and creative reading skills at levels appropriate for the child's development, and to find ways of stimulating thinking beyond the literal meaning of passages read.

Critical reading involves the processes of problem solving and evaluation. If children are taught from the beginning to evaluate and react to ideas in the light of the author's purpose, the development of these skills will be an integral part of the reading program. Asking such questions as "How does the author know this?" "Is this information as true today as when the book was written?" "Why are these facts important?" "Do other authorities take the same viewpoint?" "Do the biases of this author colour his presentation?" will help develop critical thinking.

For true creative reading to take place, the reader must recreate the material he is reading. He becomes a co-author, and a re-creator of whatever he reads. Through his own experiences, imagination, and projection he enhances and interprets the writer's meaning. Again, the teacher, through skillfull questioning, through development of imagination and through a creative approach to literature will help children develop such skills.

Developing Broad Interests in Reading

How does one help a child develop broad interests in reading? There is an old saying that developing broad interests in reading is much like catching the measles —from one who has them. There is also another old adage which says:

Read
    Read some more
Read some things you yourself enjoy
    Read and talk about it
Read very carefully some things
    Read on the run most things
Don't think *about* reading, but —
    Read!

Curiosity and the printed page are the warp and the woof in the design that leads to broad interests in reading. "Through books we can put on the shoes of swiftness, sense the power of subduing the elements, discover the secret virtues of minerals, sail the seas, fly across the mountains on a magic carpet."[69]

If we are to help children develop broad interests in reading we must help them experience in literature ways that begin with curiosity and end in enjoyment. If children are to enjoy reading, they must understand what they read. To understand they must have broad experiences—real and vicarious.

If reading is to be a broad as well as an exciting adventure, the teacher must know the children in his group, their interests and needs. He must know literature, so that he can make available the right book, for the right child, at the right time. In this way he opens the world of the imagination, the world of yesterday, of today, and of tomorrow.

Providing for Individual Differences in Reading Achievement

Providing for individual differences has unfortunately become equated with dividing children in one classroom into three ability groups. This practice is not only endorsed but almost venerated by an overwhelming number of administrators and teachers. "Used as a method to organize children into manageable numbers, ability grouping can serve as one means to an end. However, where this approach is adopted and no corresponding effort is made to adjust instructional techniques and methods for children both within and among groups, or where the plan becomes so rigid that flexbility and mobility cease to be essential elements, the organizational pattern serves as nothing more than an opiate lulling administrators and teachers into a sense of accomplishment and satisfaction which becomes, in fact merely chimerical."[70]

The wide range in reading achievement in the average classroom emphasizes the importance of making adjustments to meet individual differences. This calls for varied grouping practices, provision of materials on many levels of readability, individualized instruction, and other techniques which take into account the differences which exist within a class.

Plans for organization for the reading program to facilitate learning are many and varied. Through the years many plans have evolved as teachers attempted to operate on the premise that there is an inverse relationship between the number of children in the class and the amount of individual assistance each student can receive. In other words, the fewer pupils the teacher must teach, the more individualized the instruction can be.

Many plans to meet the needs of individual children with unrelated rates of learning, independent experiential backgrounds, and individual capabilities and interests have been used. These attempt to individualize instruction, curriculum, and learning materials. Some of these plans focus on the organization of the instructional units, others focus on organization of curriculum, and still others offer a combination of method and materials.

The Divided-Day Plan. One such plan, coming into favour after a forty-year evolution is becoming increasingly popular. Variously labelled as a divided-day, split-day, extended-day, and staggered day, it is designed to give the teacher more time per pupil to strengthen instruction.

Organized primarily for use in the primary grades it provides a reading period of one hour in the morning with half of the class, while the other half of the class arrives later and remains in school to receive instruction in reading after the first group has gone home. With a reduced teacher-pupil ratio, a more individualized reading program can be carried on. With split-day scheduling, there are four reading groups, two in the morning and two in the afternoon. The program can then be further individualized by providing appropriate books at the reading level of each child. The additional time spent with the teacher in the early stages of beginning reading contributes to an environment with less distraction as well as increased instructional time. Only half of the class is present at one time.

Nongraded Organization. In this type of organization sequential levels of reading growth are defined and presented as an aid to teachers in: (1) indicating the sequential development from one growth level to the next of the many skills, concepts, and activities a child must master in the course of learning to read; (2) in functioning as a yardstick to determine the reading growth stage of a child in order to define the point at which his reading instruction should begin.

Continuous progress in which pupils may progress through the first, second, and third years at their own rate characterizes the nongraded primary school. Grade lines are eliminated, and pupils are identified as primary. Slow learners may need a fourth year to complete the primary levels of achievement.

Since reading is a developmental process, reading instructional levels lend themselves to sequential and increasingly complex units. All pupils except kinder- gartners are grouped according to reading instructional levels determined by de- signed instruments of measurement. In the grouping the principal takes into con- sideration social relationships, emotional maturity, personality problems, and instructional needs. The result of this procedure is the formulation of groups. As the groups in different classrooms advance in reading, the picture changes. Further changes are made as pupils are promoted from one room to another at various times throughout the year. Evaluation is continuous and children are permitted to move ahead at their own rate and ability. Individualization of instruction is thus accomplished by removing the restrictiveness of gradedness.

The Joplin Plan. This plan is basically a method of grouping children for reading instruction homogeneously on an interclass basis. The plan involves the following successive steps: (1) measuring the achievement and needs of children in a reading program; (2) organizing the children into relatively homogeneous groups independent of their grade classification; (3) scheduling reading classes at the same period during the day throughout the school; and (4) dispersing pupils to reading classes where the instruction is geared to their reading level, not their grade level. Such a program emphasizes physical grouping arrangements in an effort to provide each child with the opportunity to read at his level of achievement.

Reading Levels. Children differ widely in reading achievement as they do in other abilities and characteristics. As they progress in the elementary school the reading level of the poorest and the best reader in grade four may vary from that of an average second grader to that of an average eighth grader. This means that plans must be made to provide for the differences in ability at any given grade level. One of the effective ways of managing this problem is that of providing reading mate- rials for the various levels of reading ability without designating the grade level as such. Reading series which avoid the use of grade distinctions are a boon to children who are sensitive about reading below "grade" level. Teachers plan to- gether to determine the specific skills, concepts, and competencies which are appro- priate for a child at a given reading level and through the necessary remedial and motivational techniques help each child to master the needed skills.

Individualizing reading instruction. Teachers who are looking for a solution to the problem of teaching every child to read have found that individualizing reading instruction brings rich rewards. While actual classroom procedures differ, these teachers have as a common goal: (1) freeing the children to develop their abilities at the peak of their rates of development, (2) allowing the children to pursue their own particular interests in reading, and (3) providing greater varieties of reading materials which would stimulate interest and challenge ability. Because teachers are convinced that this method is worth trying the enthusiasm with which they approach the problem is revealed in accounts such as the following from a third grade teacher:

> I spend an hour and a half each day in the reading program during the term. The children are free to select the books during the first hour and spend the remainder of the period on related activities. I would have preferred to have a larger library from which to select books, but since this was not possible, I enlisted the aid of the librarian at the Public Library and gave her a card file with the profile of each boy and girl in the class. This included — personality sketch, family background, peer relationships, hobbies, interests, achievement and three wishes.
>
> The librarian selected five books for each child at one time. During the eight-week period every child read the books selected for him, plus the additional ones from the room library, and other materials such as newspapers, magazines and pamphlets.
>
> All the children read their own choice of books during the first half hour of the reading period. They spend the remaining time on follow-up activities. Before the reading period begins I take time to explain the follow-up activities, select the "helpers" for the day and place the names of the children on the chalkboard who will have interviews with me. I interview about ten children during the ninety minute reading period. Each child gets approximately seven minutes of my time during the reading conference. The other twenty minutes are spent in answering questions from children in their seats.
>
> During the interview I check the following abilities on a chart for each child: initial sounds, middle sounds, ending sounds, word comprehension, word pronunciation, skimming, getting the main idea of the story, getting the main idea of a paragraph, understanding the plot, getting details, special needs, and reading conference data.
>
> The reading conference involves teaching reading skills, recording weaknesses, checking on comprehension, word attack skills, critical reading, oral reading, organizing groups who need help on similar skills, becoming perceptive to children's reading interests as well as abilities, and challenging each child to read for a variety of purposes.
>
> The physical arrangement of the reading class requires modification from time to time. I find that having two chairs for the conference facilitates the problem of time. The "on deck" chair is placed apart from the one where the child who is having the conference sits, thus assuring complete privacy. However, as soon as the reader returns to his seat the next child is "on deck" for the conference. Since the names of the children to be interviewed are placed on the chalkboard the problem of deciding when to come up is solved.

Such a plan is successful to the extent that the teacher feels secure about the program, he has sufficient books, he continually evaluates children's skills, and he has facilities for keeping records. Parents must be kept informed as to the objectives, procedures and outcomes of the program.

Organizing Combined Programs. Teachers who sense the need for both individualized and basic reading periods combine the best features of each type of program. The individualized reading proceeds continuously whenever children are not working on basic assignments. While the teacher is working with one group, the others will be completing workbook requirements and then spend the remaining time on free or independent reading.

In some classrooms the basal readers are used in the morning and the self-selected books are used in the afternoon. Basic and individualized work can be readily combined by scheduling the sequential skills activity in the morning and the self-selected individualized reading during the afternoon period. This has been found by many teachers to make an effective first attempt to the individualized reading. By incorporating extensive free reading and personal conferences into a sound basic reading program, these teachers have the security of knowing they are not neglecting the developmental reading program while at the same time they are capitalizing on the child's interests and need for individual attention in learning to read.

A suggested *Weeks Program*, combining basic and individualized reading follows on the next page.[71]

Regardless of the administrative organization which the school employs to solve the problem of individual differences, the teacher's responsiblity for individual instruction remains. There must be enough flexibility in grouping to allow children to experience success and satisfaction in reading if the child is to develop competency in one of the most important tools of communication. Among the special types of grouping that can be organized to motivate children to read are: self-chosen groups, interest groups, invitational grouping, skill grouping, recreational grouping.[72]

Finally, in providing for individual differences in reading among a group of children at any given developmental stage or chronological age the teacher may well consider the following suggestions:

1. Carry on a continuous program of evaluation of reading achievement.
2. Keep a complete and accurate account of each child's progress as he moves from grade to grade or level to level.
3. Provide a program of reading which utilizes a variety of required materials so each child will have material geared to his ability.
4. Use unit-type instruction for part of the reading program.
5. Develop a variety of supplementary reading, art and construction activities related to children's reading interests.
6. Utilize audio-visual and programmed teaching materials to free the teacher for giving help as needed.
7. Plan exhibits, book collections, scrapbooks, friezes, dramatizations, choral speaking, role-playing activities centering around books they have read.
8. Differentiate assignments based on the ability to achieve.

SUGGESTED WEEK'S PROGRAM, THREE-GROUP PLAN

Day	Min.	Group I (High)	Group II (Average)	Group III (Low)
MONDAY	20	Direct teacher guidance; new material	Work on individual problems, solo-team	Free reading; individual interests
	20	Committee work; planning of book reports	Direct teacher guidance: reading from text	
	20	Free reading	Reaction to story in art, drama, or writing	Direct teacher guidance: new story, guided reading
TUESDAY	20	Free reading; individual interests	Direct teacher guidance: discuss story or answer specific questions	Independent activities, work-study, games
	30	Direct teacher guidance: presentation of oral reports, drama	Committee work; individual work	Free reading; work on skills
	10	All-group activity: choral reading, story, dramatizations, etc.		
WEDNES-DAY	25	Reading related to unit of work	Work on individual needs: team, solo reading related to unit of work	Direct teacher guidance: silent-oral reading, work on skills
	25	Direct guidance: new story	Reading related to unit of work	Reading related to unit of work
	10	Help to the children from different groups who have a common need to practice a specific skill; others continue their activity		
THURS-DAY	20	Silent reading and reaction to story	Direct teacher guidance: discussion related to stories, planning of activities	Reading related to stories: help by pupil assistants
	20	Direct teacher guidance: discussion, oral-silent reading, work on skills	Developing activities related to readings (committee work, etc.)	Reading related to stories: help by pupil assistants
	20	Individual guidance on book selection for free reading, for unit reports, etc.; use of library aids		
FRIDAY	40	Free reading	Work on individual needs: team, solo; committee work; reading related to unit, etc.	Direct teacher guidance: discussion; plans for sharing with class
	20	All-group activity: library, dramatizations, storytelling, etc.		

9. Keep the groups flexible to allow for mobility.
10. Encourage varied types of grouping to supplement regularly organized groups.
11. Make use of team grouping and team teaching to facilitate learning.
12. Keep parents informed of the objectives, procedures and outcomes of the reading program.
13. Read to the children to motivate their interest in self-selection and reading for enjoyment.

Utilizing research findings, empirical evidence, experimentation and observation of teachers who are successful in providing for individual differences in reading achievement are indispensable in acquiring the aim of improving reading instruction for all children. The good teacher discovers the best features of each method, works out a way of teaching that is superior to any one method, and adapts the reading program to the children he teaches.

Variability in reading achievement has implications for teaching in the content areas as well as in the reading program. Failure to provide materials with varying levels of difficulty in science, social studies, or any other content area is inconsistent with what we know about differences in childrens' reading achievement. It is essential that materials in all areas of the curriculum are provided to meet the reading needs of students at both extremes of achievement as well as the "average".

The extent to which innovations in organizational patterns, approaches, or materials will bring about the desired goals in reading is dependent on such factors as: the extent to which a school staff plans cooperatively a developmental reading program based on an agreed-upon philosophy, defined objectives; the provision for the gradual development of needed skills for achieving the objectives, learning experiences and instructional provisions for children of varying abilities and interests, providing for the academically talented, the slow learning child, and children who need special help; instruments of evaluation of pupil progress; and a broad program of evaluation. It depends, too, on the opportunity a school staff has for creative teaching, for cooperative or team approach to some teaching areas, and an in-service program planned and endorsed by the teachers and supervisors cooperatively. Such a program takes into account the children, the teachers, the administrative staff, the parents, and the community.

It is the responsibility of the teacher who teaches reading to know the needs of individual children. Children differ not only physically, emotionally, socially, and intellectually, they also differ perceptually. One child is visually-minded, another orally-oriented, a third aurally-perceptive, another kinesthetically-centred. Children profit from methods emphasizing that sensory experience which is related to their way of learning. All children profit from making associations between the various sense organs in learning to read. They gain from obvious attention to relationships in hearing, seeing, speaking, and writing the symbols which they must clothe with meaning if they are to read with understanding.

Evaluation Procedures in Reading

Any teaching-learning process requires a continual appraisal of progress in terms of specific objectives set up cooperatively by teachers and pupils. Effective evaluation is not a "sometimes" or "term-end", or final examination schedule. Evaluation begins before the teacher enters the classroom in the fall; it begins when he decides on instructional objectives and basic teaching materials. It continues as the teacher gets acquainted with the children he teaches and discovers their reading abilities, interests, and needs. It does not end until he and the children evaluate the year's program in the light of each child's progress toward the defined goals.

The nature of the evaluation process and the procedures used to gain evidence of growth vary with the accepted concept of reading. If reading is conceived as the sounding out of words with little concern for their meaning and application in meaningful situations, evaluation is simple. However, if reading is to involve thinking and feeling, the use of the cognitive, affective and perceptual powers, and self-confidence in attacking new tasks with persistence, then evaluation must be based on these concepts.

A broad evaluation program includes: consideration of the child's comprehension, study skills, word-analysis and identification skills, appreciation of literary style, critical and creative reading skills, application of reading skills, reading interests, reading habits, shifting gears in reading, skills in reading in content fields and self appraisal. A variety of techniques of evaluation including observations of development, anecdotal records, work samples, analysis of student's oral and written responses to reading and related assignments, informal teacher-made tests and questionnaires, programmed reading materials, standardized tests of intelligence and reading achievement, and evaluative reports by teachers and pupils should be used. Not only should the teacher obtain evidence of the child's growth in reading, but he should be equally concerned with the more subtle aspects of development of the individual personality *through* reading.

Self-evaluation on the part of both the pupil and the teacher should be an integral part of the appraisal program. If the child early helps to set his own goals and assists in measuring his progress toward these goals; if he is a partner in gathering such evidence and clearly understands the purposes for reading and the reading experiences provided, it is understandable that he will move toward those goals with greater self-confidence and success.

If the teacher defines evaluation as the use of information for making decisions about educational programs, Cronbach's recommendation will be beneficial. He envisions "curriculum evaluation as encompassing general outcomes going far beyond content and formal testing and as including (a) assessments by scholars as to whether course content is consistent with contemporary knowledge, (b) systematic observation by teachers, (c) classroom process studies, (d) both proficiency and attitude measures, and (e) follow-up studies . . ."[73]

CONCLUDING STATEMENT

The main task of the educator is to organize a learning environment in which each child can develop to his maximum potential. This implies an educational setting and curriculum organization in which children are provided with experiences which motivate them to develop creatively, to solve problems, and to think critically. Such an objective implies, too, that every child must develop his powers to use reading as a tool for gaining information, solving problems, evaluating critically, and expressing creatively.

A program of this type offers a reading curriculum characterized by such factors as:

1. Understanding the inter-relatedness of the language arts of listening, speaking, reading, and writing.
2. Utilizing the knowledge of the development of the linguistic skill and the role of oral language in reading. Competence in the spoken language is a necessary base for reading *and* writing.
3. Broadening the concepts of readiness for reading to include readiness for each new reading skill introduced in the elementary school.
4. Introducing the child early in the primary grades to the skills involved in critical and creative reading.
5. Providing for individual differences on a broader base of method, materials, and media. If every child is to achieve power in reading, it is essential to adjust the reading program to individual needs, abilities, and interests.
6. Knowing a variety of approaches and methods in teaching reading. Knowledge of and experience with a variety of approaches in reading instruction enables a teacher to meet the needs of a particular group of children more effectively.
7. Developing skills in reading is an objective in every reading program. Whatever method is used, the following skills must be developed if a child is to become a proficient reader: (1) word identification in reading through context clues, word-form clues, phonetic analysis, structural analysis, and dictionary usage; (2) comprehension skills—literal comprehension, interpretative skills, critical reading, creative reading, and word meaning; (3) study skills including research skills, technical vocabulary, and specific skills related to content subjects; (4) fluency and speed—dealing with abilities to shift gears according to purpose and materials read.
8. Developing broad interests in reading. Through providing books to meet varied needs and interests, assigning reading for a variety of purposes, encouraging individual reading, library projects, free reading, the child is motivated to read widely with the result that his understanding of people, places, and phenomena develops simultaneously with his understanding of self.

9. Conceiving of evaluation as a shared responsibility. Today's teacher takes a dimensional approach to evaluation: (1) the child evaluates his own progress, (2) the teacher evaluates the extent to which he is helping children achieve individual and group goals in reading, and (3) the teacher and staff evaluate the extent to which the reading program is contributing to the goals of the language arts in meeting the needs of the children in communicating creatively.

Today's teacher must provide effective instruction and challenging materials in thought-provoking situations which challenge each child to read to enrich his experiences, extend his horizons, broaden his understanding, develop his insights, and unlock the door to learning.

REFERENCES

1. Donald Durrell and Alice Nicholson, "Preschool and Kindergarten Experience," in Nelson B. Henry (ed), *Development in and Through Reading*, The Sixtieth Yearbook of the National Society for the Study of Education, University of Chicago Press, Chicago, 1961, Part 1, p. 257.
2. Arthur I. Gates and Frank G. Jennings, "The Role of Motivation," in Nelson B. Henry, *op. cit.*, p. 122.
3. Walter D. Loban, *The Language of Elementary School Children*, Research Report No. 1, National Council of Teachers of English, Champaign, 1963, p. 87.
4. Alvina Burrows, "Helping Children to Listen and Speak", in Helen K. Mackintosh (ed.), *Children and the Language Arts,* Joint Publication of ACEI, ASCD, IRA, and NCTE, 1964, p. 17.
5. Helen M. Robinson, "Vocabulary: Speaking, Listening, Reading and Writing," in H. Alan Robinson (ed.), *Reading and the Language Arts*, University of Chicago Press, Chicago, 1963, p. 169.
6. Ruth G. Strickland, *The Language of Elementary School Children: Its Relationship to the Language of Reading Textbooks and the Quality of Reading of Selected Children*, Bulletin of The School of Education, Vol. 38, No. 4, Bloomington, 1962.
7. By permission from R. D. Armstrong, "Language: The Essence of Readiness," W. J. Gage Limited, n.d. (Pamphlet.)
8. By permission from Gertrude Hildreth, "Linguistic Factors in Early Reading Instruction," *The Reading Teacher*, 18:176, December, 1964.
9. By permission from Thomas J. Creswell, "Linguistics and Reading: Remarks on B. Robert Tabachink's Paper," in Alan Robinson (ed.), *op. cit.*, p. 109.
10. Gertrude Hildreth, *loc. cit.*
11. Wendell Johnson, *Your Most Enchanted Listener*, Harper and Brothers, New York, 1956, p. 123.
12. Ruth G. Strickland, "Implications of Research in Linguistics for Elementary Teaching," *Elementary English Journal*, 40:169, February, 1963.
13. By permission from Donald J. Lloyd, "Sub-cultural Patterns which Affect Language and Reading Development," in Bernard J. Weiss (ed.), *Language, Linguistics, and School Programs*, Proceedings of the Spring Institutes, National Council of Teachers of English, Champaign, 1963, p. 51.

14. By permission from Lillian M. Logan and Virgil G. Logan, *Teaching the Elementary School Child*, Houghton Mifflin Company, Boston, 1961, pp. 247, 248.

15. Robert J. Havighurst, *Human Development and Education*, Longmans, Green and Co., New York, 1953, p. 2.

16. William Gray and Bernice Rogers, *Maturity in Reading*, University of Chicago Press, Chicago, 1956, p. 56.

17. David H. Russell, "Continuity in the Reading Program," in Nelson B. Henry (ed.), *op. cit.*, p. 227.

18. Helen Mackintosh (ed.), *Current Approaches to Teaching Reading*, NEA Elementary Instructional Leaflet, NEA-Department of Elementary-Kindergarten-Nursery Education, Washington, 1965, p. 4. All articles from this symposium are reprinted with permission of the Department of Elementary-Kindergarten-Nursery Education and the author.

19. *Description of Three Approaches to the Teaching of Reading: Monograph 2*, Department of Education, San Diego, May, 1961, p. 19.

20. By permission from R. Van Allen, *Language — Experience Approach to Reading*, Department of Education, San Diego, 1963. (Mimeographed.)

21. Willard C. Olson, "Individualized Approach," in Helen Mackintosh (ed.), *Current Approaches to Teaching Reading*, op. cit., p. 2.

22. Marcella K. Draper and Louise H. Schwietart, "Individualized Reading: A Dynamic Approach," in May Lazar (ed.), *A Practical Guide to Individualized Reading*, Board of Education, City of New York, 1960, p. 98.

23. By permission from L. C. Hunt, Jr., "Philosophy of Individualized Reading," in J. Allen Figurel (ed.), *Reading and Inquiry*, Proceedings of the Annual IRA Convention, Vol. 10, International Reading Association, Newark, 1965, pp. 146, 147.

24. *Ibid.*, p. 148.

25. Charles E. Wingo, "Phonic Approach," in Helen Mackintosh (ed.), *Current Approaches to Teaching Reading*, op. cit., p. 2.

26. *Ibid.*, p. 3.

27. Emerald V. Dechant, *Improving the Teaching of Reading*, © 1964. Reprinted by permission of Prentice-Hall, Inc., Englewood Cliffs, N.J., p. 193.

28. Donald J. Lloyd, *op. cit.*, pp. 48, 49.

29. *Ibid.*, p. 52.

30. By permission from Carl A. Lefevre, *Linguistics and the Teaching of Reading*, McGraw-Hill Book Company, New York, 1964, p. 7.

31. Charles C. Fries, "Linguistics in Beginning Reading," in Helen Mackintosh (ed.), *Current Approaches to Teaching Reading*, op. cit., p. 3.

32. Leonard Bloomfield and Clarence L. Barnhart, *Let's Read: A Linguistic Approach*, Wayne State University Press, Detroit, 1961.

33. *Ibid.*, p. 61.

34. Don H. Parker, *Schooling for Individual Excellence*, Thomas Nelson and Sons, New York, 1964.

35. Sir James Pitman, "Initial Teaching Alphabet," in Helen Mackintosh (ed.), *Current Approaches to Teaching Reading*, op. cit., p. 4.

36. Dorothea E. Hinman, "Words in Color," in Helen Mackintosh (ed.), *Current Approaches to Teaching Reading*, op. cit., p. 5.

37. Janet Goss, "A New Approach to Reading," *Journal of Programmed Reading*, 4:64,

pp. 1, 2. (Reprinted from the article, "A New Approach to Reading," by Miss Janet Goss, published by Webster Division of McGraw-Hill Book Company in *Journal of Programmed Reading.*)

38. Nila Banton Smith, *Reading Instruction for Today's Children,* © 1963. Reprinted by permission of Prentice-Hall, Inc., Engelwood Cliffs, N.J., pp. 84, 85.

39. Walter D. Loban, *loc. cit.*

40. By permission from Margaret J. Early, "Junior High: The Interrelatedness of Language Skills," in J. Allen Figurel (ed.), *op. cit.,* p. 33.

41. *Ibid.,* p. 40.

42. *Ibid.,* p. 34.

43. See also Harold M. Covell, *Teaching Canadian Children to Read,* J. M. Dent & Sons Ltd., Toronto, pp. 11, 12.

44. Emerald V. Dechant, *op. cit.,* p. 195.

45. Helen M. Robinson, "Assessing the Experimental Evidence for Various Beginning Reading Plans," *Educational Horizons,* 45:9, Fall, 1966.

46. Nila Banton Smith, *op. cit.,* p. 164.

47. Lillian M. Logan and Virgil G. Logan, *op. cit.,* p. 269.

48. *Ibid.,* p. 270.

49. By permission from Robert Pooley, "Reading and the Language Arts," in Nelson B. Henry (ed.), *op. cit.,* p. 41.

50. Jean Turner Goins, "Relation of Visual Perception to Reading," *Education Digest,* 24:44, September, 1958.

51. Lillian Currier, "Phonics or No Phonics," *Elementary School Journal,* 23:448-452, February, 1923.

52. Emerald V. Dechant, *op. cit.,* p. 193.

53. Betty Gibson, "Word Recognition Skills," *Primary Language Arts Outline Grades I-III,* Provisional, The Ministry of Education, Province of Manitoba, Winnipeg, 1966, p. 31.

54. Wendell Johnson, *Your Most Enchanted Listener,* Harper and Brothers, New York, 1956, p. 123.

55. David Russell, *Children's Thinking,* Ginn and Company, Boston, 1956, p. 283.

56. Helen Huus, "Critical and Creative Reading," in J. Allen Figurel (ed.), *op. cit.,* p. 117.

57. By permission from Nila Banton Smith, *Reading Instruction for Today's Children,* Prentice-Hall, Inc., Englewood Cliffs, N.J., 1963, p. 312.

58. William D. Sheldon, "Children's Experiences in Reading," in Virgil Herrick and Leland B. Jacobs (eds.), *Children and the Language Arts,* Prentice-Hall Inc.. Englewood Cliffs, 1955, p. 186.

59. New York Metropolitan School System, "Five Steps to Reading in Science, Social Studies and Mathematics," in Albert J. Harris (ed.), *Readings in Reading Instruction,* David McKay, Inc., New York, 1961, p. 319.

60. Reprinted with the permission of the Publisher from Shelley Umans, *New Trends in Reading Instruction,* New York, Teachers College Press, 1963. © 1963 by Teachers College, Columbia University, p. 27.

61. By permission from George Spache, *Toward Better Reading,* Garrard Publishing Company, Champaign, 1963, p. 287.

62. Reprinted with permission of The Macmillan Company, New York from *The First*

R: The Harvard Report on Reading in the Elementary Schools, pp. 48, 49. © The Macmillan Company 1963.

63. *Ibid.*, p. 49-50.
64. See Edward G. Summers, "Reading in the Secondary Schools," *Review of Educational Research*, 37:140, April, 1967.
65. Ethel S. Maney, "Literature and Critical Reading in Science," *Journal of Experimental Education*, 27:57-64, September, 1958.
66. A. Sterl Artley, "Critical Reading in Content Areas," *Elementary English Journal*, 36:122-130, February, 1959.
67. By permission from Wilbur W. Hatfield, "Will Structural Grammar Help?" *The English Journal*, 48:570-75, December, 1958.
68. Mary C. Austin and Coleman Morrison, *op. cit.*, p. 222.
69. Lillian M. Logan and Virgil G. Logan, *op. cit.*, p. 245.
70. Mary C. Austin and Coleman Morrison, *op. cit.*, pp. 4, 5.
71. Lillian M. Logan and Virgil G. Logan, *op. cit.*, p. 278.
72. See Paul McKee, *Reading: A Program of Instruction for the Elementary School*, Houghton Mifflin Co., Boston, 1966, pp. 245-251.
73. David A. Abramson, "Curriculum Research and Evaluation," *Review of Educational Research: Curriculum Planning and Development*, 36:392, June, 1966.

10

Toward Improved Written

Expression: Creative Writing

As imagination bodies forth
The form of things unknown, the poet's pen
Turns them to shapes, and gives to airy nothing
A local habitation and a name.

Shakespeare

As the child seeks outlets for his creative drive he is impelled toward those which bring him the greatest measure of satisfaction and reward. Through his successful ventures in creativity he becomes an integrated individual. Thus his creative activity contributes not alone to self-expression but toward self-realization.

In creative writing as in any creative activity the crux of the experience lies in the degree to which it is the spontaneous outpouring of the child's imagination, experience, and/or idea. The child who expresses his creativity through writing is exhilarated by the experience. Having tasted the deep delight of creating with words he rarely rests content, but repeats the experience again and again. His work tends to be spontaneous, sparkling, and scintillating. Because he is spurred on by the excitement of creating, his words dance as he stretches his imagination and follows where fancy leads. A flight of the imagination, a memory to be recorded, an experience to be recalled are the motivations that may spark the "creative itch" as Santayana terms it.

In creative writing it is possible to discern the working out of the creative process clearly. It is here that one observes both the effervescent power of the creative process as the words run over themselves and sparkle and glow, *and* the scrupulous polishing and perfecting of the expression. Fluency with words is not enough. The child must have something to say—something which he believes is important to express.

Although children create out of the imagination, the well must be replenished with fresh experience, literature which exposes them to rhythm, rhyme, beauty, and sparkling, scintillating words. Children need to balance impression with expression, intake with output. Carlson recognizes this need as she states: "Learning to use sparkling and spinning words involves an auding or creative listening to good literature. The child listens to the beautiful and descriptive words and phrases of prose and poetry. He becomes alerted to the original, the different, the unexpected quality of expression as contrasted with trite stereotyped clichés and hackneyed phrases. He grows cognizant of the 'crackling in carmine chasms', and the 'metallic splendour of purple waters'."[1]

Akin to composing music, writing has its distinctive movement, rhythms, and cadences. It flows along merrily until it comes to a resting point. The movement that follows is in contrast to it in tempo, mood, and rhythmic devices. There must be contrast and balance in the design. It may spring forth full blown like the romantic songs of Schubert; it may take weeks, months, even years, or may never reach fruition like his "Unfinished Symphony".

BEFORE THEY WRITE CREATIVELY

If every child were sufficiently free to originate ideas spontaneously and sufficiently skilled to express himself fluently in this medium, the teacher would merely provide a stimulating environment, a climate of psychological safety free from external source of evaluation, and say to the child "Create". However, even before the child has developed the manual dexterity necessary for writing he has the desire and ability to express himself creatively with words. At this stage he needs someone to capture and record the creative moment. This poem by Klaus is an example.

> In the country where I lived, there was no Shopper's Fair.
> But there were woods and trees and flowers everywhere
> In the country where I lived, way over there.
> Would you like to go with me to that other land?
> There are no roses at the door, and all alone I stand
> Waiting for Rosemary and Lee—in the country where I lived.
> There were woods and trees to see—
> But only one of me.[2]

Klaus, a five-year-old kindergartner who had arrived from Germany a few weeks earlier, expressed his loneliness to an imaginery companion. The teacher's discerning ear caught the loveliness of the "creative moment". The creative teacher is sensitive to moments such as this and stands ready to give whatever help is needed. This he can do when he understands the obstacles which confront children in writing creatively. He recognizes that children have such specific needs for creating with words as: opportunity for broad experiences, development of perception and imagination, experience with literature, skill in using words, and skill in communication.

CHILDREN NEED EXPERIENCES OUT OF WHICH TO CREATE

Without experience the child has little to communicate. How can he write graphically of the trees, the hanging leaves, the bare bough shaking in the winter winds—the boughs that only shortly before harboured nests of singing birds—when he has never seen them? How can he write of the crowded tenements with only the pavement for his playground when he has never seen them? How can he write of the first flowers of spring if he has not observed them as they push their heads up out of the ground and turn to the light? How can he write vividly of ocean liners if he has never been near the ocean? How can he write of the way he feels when he flies above the clouds in a jet if his feet have never left *terra firma*? It is when he experiences first-hand or vicariously that he writes most vividly. Experiences form a reservoir from which the child can draw in expressing himself creatively—experiences which make an impression so deep, so vital that he is not content until he has shared them.

CHILDREN NEED TO DEVELOP PERCEPTION AND IMAGINATION

By perception we mean the sharpened awareness of all that is around us. It goes beyond mere observation. "By imagination we mean the power of forming mental images which correspond to the experiences of the senses."[3]

Stephen Spender points out the relationship between imagination and memory. The poet should be able to think in images; he should have as great a mastery of language as a painter has over his pallet. "Imagination itself is an exercise of memory. There is nothing we imagine which we do not already know. And our ability to imagine is our ability to remember what we already once experienced and to apply it to some different situation. . . ."[4]

A child can develop his imaginative powers through experiences involving sense impressions. He should smell the rose, feel its velvety texture, experience the prick of its thorns. He needs to become aware of his kinesthetic sense to aid him in responding empathically to experiences involving muscular tensions. The child should develop an ever-increasing perception of and sensitivity to his environment.

Sensory experiences should not be limited to the traditional five senses. Lowrey and Johnson stress the value of others which are important in the development of the imaginative powers including the sensations of lightness or heaviness, temperature, equilibrium, emptiness or fulness.[5] In order to write imaginatively one needs "to feel the dancing, the running, and the galloping; the tense quietude, the agony of immobile suspense; or the slow resistless movement of ponderous things. Depth and vividness of appreciation lie in this response, through intimate sense imagery, to the things about me."[6]

All too often the teacher is concerned only with expository writing. The richness of writing creatively demands the ability to write out of the imagination. It requires not only the ability to recreate what one has experienced, but also the power of portraying mental images which correspond to the experiences of the senses—conceptions, notions, and fanciful ideas. Words become wings to take him on his flights of imagination. The young child does not distinguish between inner fantasy and outer reality as adults do. To him both are equally real and satisfying.

We like to think that children will write creatively if we give them rich experiences, teach them to perceive, help them to develop their imaginations, and utilize imaginative content. There still remains, however, the need to replenish the source of ideas. Literature which is characterized by imagination, spontaneity, brilliance, originality, rhythm, and clarity of style is one of the most effective means of accomplishing this end. Children can stretch the imagination and stand on tiptoe as it were to catch the stars as they twinkle in a world of words—words of colour, fire, and imagination—words that fall trippingly from the tongue and find a haven in the mind and heart of the child until he calls them forth to embody an idea or to clothe an emotion. The importance of literature is stressed by Herbert Spencer: "He who daily hears and reads well-framed sentences, will naturally more or less tend to use similar ones."[7]

Exposure to fine literature improves the child's acquaintance with words and thus increases his ability to express his own ideas. As he listens to and/or reads for himself from the treasury of literature he will develop not alone understanding, insight, and vocabulary, but he will assimilate into his design for living what he reads. Thereby it becomes an integral part of his personality. From fiction, biography, hero tales and legends, travel and adventure, from mythology and archaeology he will dip into the literary well and incorporate into his own thinking and creative expression the stuff from which dreams are born and writers are created.

Listening to his teacher and/or parents read good literature, and/or reading by himself, stories about the enchanted world of elves, gnomes, and goblins; the exploits of space men and astronauts; the heroes of Greek and Roman mythology; or the feats of everyday men of the work-a-day world will replenish the reservoir of ideas and stimulate creativity. "Through books we can put on the shoes of swiftness, sense the power of subduing the elements, discover the secret virtues of minerals, sail the seas, fly across the mountains on a magic carpet."[8]

CHILDREN NEED SKILL IN USING WORDS

Children love words. They love the rhyme and rhythm of words; they love the lilt and melody of words; they love their sparkle and spinningness. They love the feel of words as they roll off the tongue. They love their mouth-tickling quality as they dance with melody, mood, and movement. But words serve for more than to tickle the tongue or spark the imagination. They serve to communicate ideas. The child who sees in the right word the power to create a picture or portray an emotion has taken a big step toward creating with words. The discovery of the feeling for the combinations of words that set the imagination soaring is one of the spurs to creativity. This, coupled with the ability to say something worthwhile, is the essence of true creative communication. "Words are the vehicles that carry our verbal or written messages. Words are the verbal means of taking our listeners or readers along with us to our destination in communication. If the other person cannot or does not 'ride along' with the words we are using, he will not cover the same territory and hence will not understand what we are trying to express in words to him. . . . They are intended to be vehicles for the conveyance of ideas."[9]

CHILDREN NEED SKILL IN COMMUNICATING FEELINGS AND IDEAS

Mere facility with words will not ensure the effective communication of feelings and ideas children wish to express. If we really want a reader to share our emotion we do one of two things—or both. "We may say 'I felt like a million dollars—I had that wonderful feeling you get when the pain of a terrible headache suddenly leaves—I felt like writing a poem.' Or we may set about describing all the circumstances of yesterday's moment—the things about us, the events, what she looked like, what she said, what we said. Or we may use both methods. What we are forced to do to communicate our feeling is what the poet is forced to do."[10]

The writer must re-create the experience in such a vivid manner that the reader will experience the emotion the author intended. Whatever the inspiration for the creative writing, the emotion that touched it off may come suddenly unawares. To satisfy the creator completely the work must evoke a response from the listener. To the extent that the writer is able to reveal his emotion, his idea to another—to re-create an original experience in such a way that it expresses what he remembers of how he felt about the experience is the creative process completed and the creator satisfied. The artist, whether he reveals his art through marble, music, dance, or words must have guidance in handling the materials by which he expresses his concept and/or emotion. Added to this he must have the techniques for handling the material he uses to express his creative idea and recreate the emotion or feeling he wishes to convey. Fortunate is the child who creates spontaneously with words. "Little children are whole human beings with the capacity to think, to feel, and to express themselves. They develop in the use of language as they think new thoughts and acquire the words through which to express these thoughts. . . . Facility in the use of language and facility in thinking depend each upon the other. As thought is an essential in the use of language, imagination is the *sine qua non* of creative reading [and creative writing]."[11]

Emotions, sensory awareness, and imagination are the ingredients which go into creating with words. Combining these elements with children, experience, and expression the teacher becomes a catalytic agent who makes possible the process of creating.

In an experiment validating the idea that the development of sensitivity to environmental stimuli affects the quality of creative productions Littwin reports three methods he used in developing imaginative writing with three matched groups of seventh and eighth grade pupils. "Over a ten-week period, one group practiced writing vivid descriptions of pictures which they had previously studied; the second studied literary models containing words of sound, colour, and movement; and the third group practiced describing all the possible sensations, such as sight, smell, touch, and hearing, that they could experience in examining an object or situation. The group emphasizing perception through the various senses showed significantly greater gains on composition tests than did the other two groups."[12]

The Creative Process in Creative Writing

In creative writing the phases of the creative process can be clearly discerned. A re-examination of these from the viewpoint of creative writing will bring into focus the relationship of the teacher, the child, and the stimuli.

Cognition—awareness of a problem which can best be solved through writing
Conception—prelude to the moment of insight involving conscious and unconscious assimilation of ideas gained through observation, experience, memory, and/or the imagination
Combustion—the ignition of the spark, the idea takes fire
Consummation—perfection of the expression, the rewriting, and the polishing process
Communication—the sharing of the product.

Cognition. The child is aware of the wealth of ideas around him that are the source for adventuring in creative writing. As he explores the commonplace and the unusual, the sordid as well as the beautiful, the actual, the fanciful, the world of reality and the world of the imagination, he is moved by external stimuli or inner need to express. In a climate of psychological safety, rich experiencing, and effective guidance he is propelled into the phase of conception.

Conception. The fruits of creative imagination do not always spring forth full-blown, nor do they function by the clock. To tell the child, "You have half an hour in which to write a story" is to ignore entirely the law of creativity. There must be time for thought to take shape, for ideas to be "toyed with", looked at, and examined for possible development—and perhaps be discarded. For children who do not work rapidly under the momentum of original inspiration, or whose stimulus was not originally strong enough to carry the idea forward, the teacher accepts the delay, the uncertainties, the false starts, and with quiet encouragement, patient, skillful questioning, or simple suggestions, gives the needed help and confidence that is prelude to the high moment of creating.

Combustion. When the spark is ignited and the flame is kindled the child is catapulted into the "Eureka" phase by the sheer momentum of the idea. It is at this point that the previous experiences, the knowledge, the impressions, and the imaginings of the child merge. "Tinged with magic and flamboyant though it may sound, the concept of the creative flash is not a figment but is firmly rooted in experience. Too many great men have attested to such flashing insights and too many of us have experienced them ourselves in less notable connections to leave any doubt as to their reality."[13] Brief, satisfying, and swift is this creative moment. To be sensitive to such a moment is the mark of the creative teacher.

Communication. Communication is for some children the most exciting phase of the creative process. They are eager to share with others the product of their creative expression. The goal of their writing is the sharing. They are confident that their story or poem will be enjoyed, that their writing will be valued, and their ideas respected. Because the ideas, the style, and the form are theirs, because they have said just what they wanted to say in the way they wished to say it, or just

Formula for Guiding Creativity in Writing

PHASES OF CREATIVE PROCESS	THE CHILD	THE TEACHER
COGNITION	Becomes aware of the desire to write	Provides the stimulus for writing Creates climate for expression
CONCEPTION	Toys with ideas Considers several possibilities	Stands by to give help as needed
COMBUSTION	Discovers the ideas Starts to write	Provides encouragement
CONSUMATION	Completes the writing to his own satisfaction	Provides time, guidance, and encouragement
COMMUNICATION	Shares creative product if he chooses	Listens with interest, sensitivity, and courtesy Provides for publication of the writing Occasionally shares own creative product with group

because—they are confident that a sympathetic audience is waiting for their written expression.

In this sharing period, there is a discussion in terms of the child's purpose for writing; his own interpretation to the extent to which he feels he fulfilled his purposes. Not unless a child asks should the teacher evaluate his writing. Nor is evaluation of creative writing a responsibility of his peers. He shares with them for enjoyment, for exchange of viewpoints, for communicating ideas, feelings, and imaginings. He is still trying his wings, feeling his way, exploring with words ideas, and form. Creating is sometimes a lonely job.

Children differ in abilities in writing as they do in other creative activities. For some, the mere opportunity to write is enough. They get astride their Pegasus and ride into the wind across the prairie, over the dunes, and follow hidden trails. They are aware of the sights, the smells, the sounds—both real and imaginary—around them. They may see the rustling wheat in the prairies, smell the salt of the ocean, or hear the flutes of Pan playing in the marshes. What these children need is time, time to listen, time to think, time to imagine, and time to express. They move rapidly from cognition to communication in the writing cycle, each child writing in his unique manner.

The Creative Product

In these examples each child followed his creative muse in his own way. Some had a feeling for action, others for "painting" pictures of rare beauty, and still others for recreating half-remembered experiences.

APRIL WIND

April wind, April wind
   Tossing kites so high
Whipping wash hung out to dry
   You go whizzing by

April wind, April wind
   I wonder if you care
If all the clothes are torn to shreds
   And field flowers are stripped bare

April wind, April wind
   Blow with all your might
I love to hear you, feel you, touch you
   This lovely springtime night.
           Douglas—Kindergarten

In the wintertime I like to go out and play
And make a great big snowman every
   single day.
      Jonathon—Kindergarten[14]

IN WINTER

It was summer once,
   Then came fall.
But now comes what
   I like best of all.

I made a snowball big and round
   And rolled it softly on the ground,
I rolled it into a giant ball,
   Then I made another great big snow-
      ball.

I rolled it into a fat snowman.
   I got a carrot for a nose,
I got two cherries for the eyes.
   (He didn't even have a toe.)

But I got a curved stick for his mouth
   And I painted it fire-engine red.
And last of all, I put on his head —
   You're right—my father's stove-pipe hat.
      John Carlin—Kindergarten

If I had a horse I'd feed him hay
  I'd sing him a song most every day—If
    I had a horse.

And in the barn I'd stay far back
  Cause those hind feet can really whack!
If I *had* a horse.

Cheryl—First Grade

Oh the snow, the beautiful snow
  Filling the sky and the earth below;
Over the house tops—over the street
  Over the head of the people you meet.
    Dancing
      Flirting
        Skimming
Beautiful, beautiful, snow.

Pamela—Second Grade

The scent of apple blossoms in spring
  And burning leaves in autumn
The sound of footsteps in the snow
  And sand slithering through my hand—
    in summer

Greta—Third Grade[14]

The snow falls
    Softly
From heaven,
Cloaking the waiting earth
    With beauty.
Softly it comes down
Like fairies
    On fragile
Crystal wings.

Nancy—Fifth Grade[14]

It's a sign of the season when the crocus
  pokes through
And covers the prairies with its dazzl-
  ing hue,
And every little boy and girl
  Picks a bouquet for his Auntie Pearl.

It's a sign of the season when pussy willows bud
And the streams well up and sometimes
  flood
And the frogs come back from under-
  ground
  To jump and play with a leap and a
  bound.

It's a sign of the season when each morning
  You are awakened without an alarm
  clock's warning
By the cheerful "Cheerup, cheerup,
  cheerup"
  Of a robin who sings in a nearby tree.

It's a sign of the season when the gentle
  rain
  Softly beats on the glistening window
  pane
To wash the winter's smog away
  And lift up the flowers that grow in
  May.

What season have I been singing of?
  The very best that life can bring.
It's the season that makes me laugh and
  sing.
  Of course you've guessed it—it's here.
It's Spring!

Rosemary—Fifth Grade

THE ROLE OF THE TEACHER IN GUIDING CREATIVE WRITING

Although these children expressed their creative urge spontaneously through the written word, others find this a difficult medium of expression. It is the responsibility of the teacher to give the needed guidance in each case. Most children need specific guidance as well as opportunity if they are to reach their potential. This is most effectively accomplished in an atmosphere in which each child can express his ideas freely, knowing that he will not only receive appreciative comment on writing which gives evidence of vivid expression, originality, awareness, imagination, and invention, but also recognition for his best efforts even when he falls short of the goal he has set for himself. Children need a teacher who understands each phase of the creative process and stands ready to give the needed help.

Such a teacher is cognizant that his role includes: (1) conscious awareness of the effect of the teacher's attitude toward creative writing, (2) an effective approach to guiding writing, (3) spurs to creative writing, and (4) evaluation procedures which foster creative writing.

The Attitude of the Teacher

A good teacher knows that the acquisition of skill in writing is a developmental process, interrelated with and dependent upon the process of physical, social, emotional, aesthetic, and intellectual growth. A good teacher realizes that helping students write creatively is a day-by-day process that requires not so much teaching the mechanics of writing, but sympathetic understanding and guidance. As the child develops confidence in writing he will recognize his need for direct instruction in organization and other writing techniques.

A good teacher takes pleasure and shares in the delight and joy of discovery which comes to the student as he gains power in expression of ideas. He treats their works or creations as tenderly as if they were his own. He is constantly reminded of the value of creative expression because he too experiences the rewards of his own creative writing.

A good teacher recognizes that in guiding the truly creative child his chief function is that of creating an atmosphere wherein creativity can flourish. He provides time for writing, plans rich experiences which furnish a fund of ideas, stimulates through reading good literature to the children, and teaches them the needed skills of writing.

A good teacher guides creative writing in a way that enables children to set and achieve their own goals and attain self-realization through writing. This guidance is determined by his understanding of children, his knowledge of writing, his skill in knowing when to give direct instruction, and when to stand back and merely provide a place for creative expression to take place.

An Effective Approach to Creative Writing

In creative writing emphasis is on the expression of the idea, feelings, and imagination of the writer. It is that kind of writing in which the child, in one way or another, expresses his feelings, ideas, or reactions to an experience, real or imaginary. Creative writing is concerned with artistic self-expression, whereas expository writing is concerned with functional communication. Creative writing appeals to the senses and emotions; expository writing to common sense and logic.

Guidelines for Creative Writing

**PROVIDE THE
MOTIVATION**

To guide creative writing successfully the teacher should be familiar with stimuli to creative writing. Prairies, weather, seasons, stars, night, birds, fish, streams, wheat fields, lakes, fire—any of these may stir a response in children. Any of the exciting experiences from real life, literature, or the imagination can serve to ignite the spark that results in creative writing.

**PROVIDE FOR
EXCHANGE OF
IDEAS**

Not all children are self-starters—some need to have a push. They need opportunities to get their ideas from others. They need time for the exchange of ideas, to talk, to think through before they are ready to write.

**HELP CHILDREN
EXPRESS IDEAS**

Children may have ideas, but they need words to express them. Through vocabulary development children will be stimulated to find the exact word or phrase that fits the expression. To help children increase the pool of words from which they draw in writing, the teacher may:

1. Keep a list of colourful phrases and descriptive words in a file box
2. Play word games in which children pantomime the meanings and shades of meanings of words
3. Keep a list of shining words, and trite words
4. List on a chart various categories of words such as colourful, gay, tranquil, sad, angry
5. Describe common, every-day occurrences in interesting, exciting, and vivid ways.

**ENCOURAGE
NEW IDEAS**

When a child expresses an idea in a unique way he should be commended for it and the expression added to a big book of "Unique Ideas".

**GUIDE THE
WRITING**

The teacher should circulate among the children and give them help and encouragement when they need it.

**PROVIDE FOR
SHARING THE
WRITING**

Sharing or publishing creative work stimulates some children to write both more frequently and with greater discrimination. Publishing the work of children in a mimeographed or printed form is an incentive to further writing.

**EVALUATE THE
CREATIVE
WRITING**

The teacher does not mark up the child's creative writing with red pencil. This does not preclude, however, a discussion with the child which leads him to make suggestions for improvement. Among the questions such a discussion may bring forth are:

1. Did you enjoy writing it?
2. Does it say what you wanted it to say?

3. Is the content original?
4. Are you giving an old idea a new twist?
5. Has the writing imagery, comparison, rhythm?
6. What sensory appeals did you use?
7. Are there enough colourful and descriptive words?
8. Are there too many descriptive words so that the meaning is obscured?
9. Could you improve this if you wrote a second draft?

If the child is satisfied with the first draft in creative writing, he should be permitted to choose a new subject for his next creative writing experience.

The following is an example of how one teacher applied these guidelines.

PROVIDE THE
MOTIVATION

"Let's pretend that the whole class is suddenly transported to the pampas of Argentine. You have seen the pictures of the pampas, the gauchos or cowboys in the books on the library shelves. You remember the films, pictures, and exhibits of Argentine artifacts.

PROVIDE FOR
EXCHANGE OF
IDEAS

Now close your eyes, and when you have a picture that you see clearly in your mind's eye, will you exchange ideas? Who has a starter for a cowboy adventure story? I'll write your ideas on the chalkboard."

John: A cowboy was hunting stolen cattle and came upon the rustlers unaware.

Susan: A cowboy was caught in a blizzard with his cattle and he rescued a baby calf from the wolves.

Tom: A cowboy - - - -

(As soon as the children finish sharing ideas they choose the one they want and start writing.)

HELP CHILDREN
EXPRESS IDEAS
AND ENCOURAGE
NEW IDEAS

(Some children have difficulty in expressing the ideas even when they get the basic thought for the story. When this happened the teacher continued in the following manner.) "How would you describe the great plains of the Argentine?"

Tom: The rich stretches of the pampas.

Mary: Grass flowing in the wind like a sea.

Susan: The mahogany faces of the cowboys from living with the wind and the sun.

Isabel: The easy way the gaucho rides his horse and the long, easy lope of the steed.

GUIDE THE
WRITING

(During the writing the teacher circulates among the students, giving a helpful word here, an encouraging smile there, helping the child observe, feel, imagine. She draws out *his* ideas, then helps him express them.)

"What a delightful sense of humour you have."

"You have a genius for invention."

"You are an artist with words."

"I like the way you are developing the story."

"Tell me what you want to say and maybe we can get it down on paper."

(The teacher continues to circulate among the children, encouraging, praising, suggesting.)

In the early grades creative writing takes the form of group stories, poems, or short plays, first dictated to the teacher and then as the child gains skill in handwriting the creative work is in the child's own writing.

PROVIDE FOR
SHARING

When the children finish their writing they drop it into the Treasure Chest in the writer's corner. Once a week it is opened and the stories are shared. At the end of a term the children compile their own anthology of creative writing, each child choosing what *he* considers to be his best work. It is mimeographed. The children might even have an "Author's Tea" when another grade, or the parents, are invited and the authors autograph their work.

Spurs to Creative Writing

There are many spurs a teacher can use to stimulate creative writing. He should keep in mind the needs, abilities, interests, and experiential and developmental level of the children in his group; those whose creative spark has never been kindled, those whose flame is burning low and needs rekindling, and the talented whose flame would burn more brightly with guidance.

Many spurs can act as catalysts for creative expression. The expressive and descriptive language found in literature contributes to stimulation of creative writing. The stories children themselves write, although they may not be examples of literary excellence, nevertheless often carry the vigorous action children demand and are worthy of a hearing and act as a stimulus to the group. No matter how simple the stories may be from an adult standpoint, the wise teacher treats the children's stories with respect, as treasures to be shared if the author so desires. If the teacher can read the story expressively, lending it the appropriate dramatic interpretation, the child achieves the satisfaction that comes from being an author.

A Serial Story. Starting a story and sharing it episode by episode with the class is another spur to creative expression. The teacher can ask children for suggestions for the next episode, or invite designated children to carry on with the episode for the day. In this experience children frequently use puppets to present the day's adventure.

Tall Tales. The natural outgrowth of the oral telling of tall tales is the written expression. Most children have a desire to exaggerate in a legitimate manner. In the lower grades children can take a cue from "And To Think I Saw It on Mulberry Street". Paul Bunyan and Chinook Tales are enjoyed by intermediate and upper grade students. Burrows suggests, "Once a wave of these yarns has got going, almost everyone in a class is likely to have a try. In most groups observed, the tall tale is forsaken once children have gained some confidence and courage to try other kinds of invention."[15]

Sensory Experiences. Sensory experiences are a good source for motivating creative writing.

1. Auditory. Sounds are mysterious. Children love to listen to and express the sounds they hear. A group of children who experimented with sounds listened to some thumb tacks falling into a pan (They were unable to see the source of the sound.) This is the result as each wrote what he heard: popcorn popping, tiny rocks falling, beads breaking, tacks bouncing, marbles falling, buttons dropping, big hail balls, pumpkin seeds falling into a pan, money jingling, shotguns popping, pencils dropping, crayons drawing, chalk writing, electrons going all over.

Listening to music is another excellent auditory "spur" to creative writing. Many children have oral contributions to make about what they hear in music. Saint-Saëns' "Carnival of the Animals" was played, after a statement that the music was written to remind us of different animals. The music was then replayed, and the children wrote as they listened. Most of the writing consisted of disconnected sentences. Some of the results follow:

> The ostrich with a beautiful tailfeather is dancing. A baby duck and a mother duck are lost. A butterfly flying in the air. A little blue bird. A mad tiger hunting food. A beautiful swan that is as white as snow. A little red squirrel jumping from tree to tree.

On another occasion, Debussy's "Afternoon of a Faun" brought out the following story:

> Once upon a time there was a husband and wife robin. Mother Robin was waiting impatiently for her eggs to hatch. One sunshiny day they did hatch, that is, all except one. Mother Robin worried and worried and waited and waited.
>
> After about four days the last egg finally hatched. Now the family was really worried for the baby did not look like a robin at all. The more Mother Robin looked at him the madder she became. Finally she could stand it no longer and she kicked him right out of the nest.
>
> Soon it was almost time for fall and the robin couldn't fly yet so he sadly watched the others fly by overhead. A solid red bird was up in the tree watching and when he saw how sad the little bird was he chirped a shrill "Hello!"
>
> Little Robin was glad to find someone to talk to and when he told the bright red bird his story the other bird laughed harder and harder. Soon Little Robin was so bothered by the strange actions of his friend that he stopped talking and started crying.
>
> "There is no need to cry," chirped the bright bird. "You are very lucky, really. I could have told you right away that you are not a robin at all but a cardinal, so there!"

The story spread and other cardinals came to help Ugly Robin learn to fly. He was so happy and he learned quickly. Before the really cold days came, he joined his kinfolks and flew quickly away.

The music that will inspire creativity is plentiful. The following is merely a suggestion:

Debussy	*The Afternoon of a Faun, The Submerged Cathedral*
Elgar	*Pomp and Circumstance*
Gershwin	*Rhapsody in Blue*
Gounod	*Funeral March of a Marionette*
Grieg	Ase's Death from *Peer Gynt* Suite
Grofé	*Grand Canyon* Suite
Haydn	The 'Toy' Symphony, Andante from The 'Surprise' Symphony
Herbert	*March of the Toys*
MacDowell	*Woodland Sketches*
Mendelssohn	*Spring Song*
Pierne	*March of the Little Lead Soldiers*
Poldini	*The Waltzing Doll*
Ponchielli	*Dance of the Hours*
Prokofief	*Peter and the Wolf*
Ravel	*Pavan for a Dead Infanta*
Rimsky-Korsakof	*Scheherazade*
Saint-Saëns	*Animals' Carnival, Danse Macabre*
Schumann	*Papillon, The Wild Horseman*
Smetana	The Molda
Strauss	*Pizzicato Polka, Blue Danube Waltz*
Stravinsky	*Firebird* Suite
Tchaikovsky	*Nutcracker* Suite
Wagner	*Ride of the Valkyries*

2. Kinesthetic. Children are intrigued by the feel of objects. The teacher may have each child come to his desk, reach into a box, feel an object (one that has an unusual shape or texture), and then return to his seat to write his reactions to the experience giving his sensations and description of the experience.

3. Olfactory. Have the children recall and write about their most pleasant odour, their most unfortunate experience with odours, and/or an exciting story about tracing an unusual and unknown odour to its source.

4. Gustatory. Have the children describe the taste of a favourite food without naming it. Have the other children guess what it is. Write the most vivid words and phrases on the chalkboard to use in the self-chosen writing activity.

5. Visual. Pictures offer excellent avenues for evoking creative expression. Children view a picture, discuss it, look at it again, and then write. Only fine examples of art should be used. The instructor can also have a file to which

children may go to select a picture. Questions may be written at the bottom of the picture to stimulate writing. A vocabulary may be provided on the reverse side of the mounted picture. For example, if a child selected a picture showing a clown in a gay costume and a spirited pose the questions might read: "What trick do you want me to do?" "What do I do with my time in the winter season?" "Do you suppose I am as happy as I look?" On the reverse side such words might appear as—clown, trick, tent, circus, joke, etc. The picture file should include pictures of animals, children, life in other countries, seasonal scenes, and others to provide motivation for writing.

BEAUTY

This picture gives me a feeling of beauty. When I look at it I can see a bison and a fox terrier. In the corner of the painting I see a fish. It seems they are in a golden wheat field. The color makes it seem realistic.

It gives me a feeling of being in the country on a warm sunny day looking out over a field. I can feel the warm gentle breeze. The smell of wheat is coming my way. In the background I see mountains. The colors used in painting let the features stand out.

I have seen modern art before and some of it I did not like. This is one of those pictures I like. This picture has made an impression on me. I think it shows a great deal of beauty.

Debra Spoon, age 11
Jacobs School, Findlay, Ohio.

Debra had found it difficult to put her ideas into words. However, the impact of the visual image of the painting brought the first expression she was willing to share. Hitherto she had made comments such as "Tear it up, I don't like it".

AN ODDITY

I like the picture because of its lightness and darkness. I think its tones are very nice.

It reminds me of a valley or a cliff with shrubs, or sticks and bushes on each side. At the top of it there are burned stumps and logs. It looks as if there has been a fire.

It also makes me think of three antelopes in a wheat field. Maybe the animals that I see are really buffalo but whatever they are they almost seem to come alive.

I like the brush marks in it—the way they go. Some of them are curved and some are straight. If I could name it, I think I would call it "Dead End", because it looks like the end of the world with the cliffs and shrubs silently standing there. Even the sky or air seems to look a sickly yellow, afraid to move.

Though the picture has very little rhythm or proportion I still like it.

I wonder what the artist had intended it to be when she put it together.

Terry Richardson, age 12
Jacobs School, Findlay, Ohio.

(Picture by E. Falk, yellow background with brown imaginative animals.)

Terry reacted favourably to the stimulation of the picture and was freer in expressing his ideas—although he felt he could not quite trust himself to express his feelings.

6. Word pictures and descriptive phrases. Painting word pictures is an activity which children enjoy. For example, the teacher might give a word and the children respond with descriptive phrases or synonyms. These should be put on cards and placed in a file where children can refer to them when they are writing.

Examples:

snow: soft and crisp and white
        drifting lazily through the air
        sailing along the boughs of the tree
        covering the country side with feather-light flakes

waves: rolling endlessly toward the shore
        crashing thunderously against the grey rocks
        sending countless sprays of foam skyward
        galloping out into the lost horizon
        white caps rolling in for sleep

softness: snow flakes floating softly by
           bits of dainty, frilly lace

whiteness: new fallen snow
           a billowy white cloud
           a field of daisies

quietness: a quiet lullaby
           a cooing dove
           a velvet glove

darkness: a gathering storm
           a thundercloud
           a sky at dusk
           a gloomy cave

sharpness: a clap of thunder
           a blue jay's cry
           a crow's caw
           an eagle's scream

As children develop their imagery and become aware of their ability to paint pictures with words they can be guided to discover relationships between such categories as softness, darkness, freshness, sharpness and project the picture into a situation in which they might integrate the various elements. As one child said during an experience with this word-painting: "I don't know whether to get out my paints and paint a picture of a stormy beach or write a story describing a storm—not that I ever saw one like I'm going to describe—but I have the words that can paint the picture."

Frequently after a group experience of developing concepts, the individual children will be motivated to express their own unique creative work.

The two examples illustrate the group composition and an individual expression:

> Snow, snow everywhere,
> Snow on the ground but we don't care.
> Snow on the pond, snow on the hill,
> So come and play with us if you will.
>
> Snow, snow, soft and white
> Falling, falling pretty and bright.
> Snow, snow everywhere,
> Snow in our hair,—but we don't care.
> Third Grade—Harwood School, Evansville, Ind.

> I looked into the valley
> And almost like a dream
> So clear so white so starry bright
> So beautiful and clean
>
> The sparkling snowflakes
> Like fairies dancing on a knoll
> Had clothed the valley with their light
> The brightly, swirling, falling snow
> Jane—Third Grade

Poetry: A Spur to Creative Writing

Another effective spur to creative writing is poetry. However, if poetry is to be used as a motivational factor it must be read to the children by a teacher who loves poetry and who can read it well. Only after listening to a wide variety of poems read well and learning to read it themselves with skill and understanding are the children ready to create their own in the form demanded by the idea they wish to express. They also should be encouraged to experiment with various poetic forms, such as Haiku, couplets, and limericks.

Most children have a natural feel for the poetic. In the early grades they should be encouraged to follow this inherent sense. As they gain experience in using "their" poetic form they should be encouraged to experiment with a wide variety of forms. In this way they will discover that the content determines form.

For example, a primary grade teacher read "If Only" by Rose Fyleman. It was not difficult for the children to think of what they would like to buy if only they had some money. This poem practically writes itself with any primary or intermediate group of boys and girls—especially at Christmas time.

A fourth grade teacher who had allowed complete freedom in choice of poetic form in an experiment to broaden the children's writing experience form introduced the couplet by reading Rosetti's "What is Pink?" After hearing and discussing the poem the children tried their hand at writing questions about various colours and then supplying their own answers with descriptions in the couplet form.

> What is white? Clouds are white
> See them in the morning light.
>
> What is blue? The sky is blue
> It's the very loveliest hue.
>
> What is red? Blood is red
> See it running down your head.
>
> What is pink? A rose is pink
> Fresh and cool as a big, big drink.
>
> What is green? The grass is green
> Softest velvet ever seen.
>
> What is black? The night is black
> Dark, mysterious and black.
>
> What is gray? A cat is gray
> Lying on the soft mown hay.

The lyricism as well as the imagery is often the result of listening to poetry read aloud by the teacher or another adult. Children are able to immerse themselves in the content of the poetry and simultaneously are motivated to avail themselves consciously or unconsciously of the tools and literary devices of poetry. The older they are, if they have been writing happily, the more they incorporate the literary devices they find in the well loved poems.

> I saw a broken moon go down,
> In the slithery stillness of night
> I watched it slowly disappear and
> Finally drop from sight
>
> I watched a broken dream slip by
> In the willowy flight of dawn
> And thought how surely one bright night
> The moon would laugh once more.
>
> Jean, age ten

The following poem was written by a highly gifted eighth grader.

> BEYOND[16]
> What is more awful than a door?
> Doors are opaque; one cannot see through them.
> One can only hear, and imagine—and dread.

"Come," you say, "it is not so bad as that!"

But put your eye to the keyhole.
All you see is pressed in the mold of the keyhole;
Its shape leads you astray.

"I see perfectly, plainly;
I see the leg of a chair, and a little
Pool of light: there must be a lamp above."

What color is the lamp? Crimson? . . . You do not know!
What is in that shadow?
What is it the shadow of . . . You cannot see!
The side of the keyhole obscures!

"But," you say, "one can listen."

Come closer. Place your ear hard against the painted wood;
Press your ear until it becomes warm; and listen.
"Yes, I believe it to be true," a gruff voice says.
"It's a lie!" says another.
That's all you hear;
They always contradict each other on that side of the door!

Let me tell you something: you and I
Who have never been there,
Know more about that room than its inhabitants;
They are not sure of anything, but we know
That there is the leg of a chair with a lamp above,
And that they contradict each other.

Whenever teachers ask, "What motivates children to write?" one might well answer: "Whatever interests them deeply". They like to write about themselves, their pets, quiet lovely things, sensory experiences, biography, nature, people, their environment, make believe, the jet age.

Applegate suggests: "I know of no subject that will fail to bring poetry from children provided it is an interest of their age level. A child's poem is a talked-out feeling, and only on subjects which have feeling will children write effective verse. Fine poems only pop out when they have the push of emotion behind them. But so facile are children's imaginations that they have feelings on the strangest subjects. No teacher ever has to teach a child to write poetry; it lies in his interests unborn. The teacher is merely the midwife."[17]

Such results in writing, using words to paint pictures, come not from a vacuum. They are the result of an environment rich in experiences, filled with poetry read aloud, poetry spoken in choral reading, creative movement, and rhythmic expression, coupled with time for discussion, for development of ideas, for experimenting and creating with words and sharing writing with others.

Literature

There are books and stories a teacher reads to the class which somehow automatically spur children to creative expression. This expression may take the form of creative dramatics, a painting, or at other times it emerges in creative writing. A group of third graders, after listening to the story *The Little Red Lighthouse and the Great Gray Bridge*, discussed the possibility of finding an old land mark in their community that had outlived its usefulness. They found it without too much trouble: an old hitching post at "Five Points." The rings for the horse's reins were still attached. Such questions arose as, "How does the hitching post feel in this day of jets, planes, helicopters?" This was the stimulation for numerous stories about *Hiram, the Hitching Post*, with as many endings as there were authors in the class.

In the collection *Patchwork Plays*, Rachel Field points the way for creative writing using an Aesop fable as a starter. In "Miss Ant, Miss Grasshopper and Mr. Cricket", she presents a dramatization of the well known story of the ant and the grasshopper with a new character and a happy ending. However a group of sixth graders were dissatisfied with this version of the story for their puppet play and rewrote the ending.

In *Children and Books*, May Hill Arbuthnot includes two poems written by upper grade pupils as a sequel to "Nancy Hanks" the poem by Rosemary Carr Benét. Nancy Hanks asks:

> "What's happened to Abe?
> What's he done?"

The children answered the questions in the poems they wrote. In order to answer the questions they tried to find information about Lincoln not included in the Benét poem.

Canadian writers offer a challenge to children's imagination—the book *Great Canadian Writing*, an anthology of Canadian writing edited by Claude Bissell, has a wealth of material that will challenge the intermediate and upper grades.

The Group Story

No great literature has been produced by a group. However, many children feel more secure in writing if they can participate in a cooperative venture. Group composition can be used throughout the elementary school to improve as well as to stimulate written expression. It offers the opportunity to share ideas, to develop a colourful and descriptive vocabulary. It acquaints children with proper punctuation, correct form, usage, construction, capitalization, and paragraphing while the story is in the process of composition by children and teacher.

The teacher who is concerned with helping every child develop his potential takes every opportunity to provide him with varied media of creative expression. Each child should have some experience in working with written expression as a creative media. He must, of course, discover the particular medium which suits his mode of expression and his need for expression at a particular time. Winged words can readily become the Pegasus for a child to adventure with words in a group situation, whereas he might well be too timid to venture in a solo flight. For such a child particularly, the security of the group carries him along. In the group he is able to contribute ideas without being responsible for an entire composition. For such children the cooperative story is both satisfying and rewarding.

Listening to a well-loved story, planning an imaginery trip, taking an excursion on the ferry, a train, or a plane ride over the city—any of these may be the spark that catapults a group into a cooperative writing venture. Children contribute their ideas rapidly, spontaneously, and generously as the teacher takes on the role of a scribe and writes on the chalkboard as the ideas come. As rapidly as the story unfolds the teacher records it. Depending upon the impact of the experience, the background of the children, the skill in using words and ideas, the teacher directs attention to such elements as development of the plot, picturesque language, exciting climax, and originality of expression. Even pre-school and kindergarten children enjoy the experience of being authors as evidenced by the following writing.

THE LITTLE TRAIN THAT BROKE DOWN
by A B C Playschool

A little train was loaded with people, and it was broken down. The wheels wouldn't go around—they were stuck, and the engine wouldn't make the train go. The train was going to California with boys and girls who wanted to visit Disneyland. They thought the train was too full of people; that the load was too heavy. So, some of the people got off, but the wheels still wouldn't go around and the engine wouldn't make the train go. The engineer got off and walked around the train, and, what do you know, one of the wheels was missing.

Johnny, whose daddy rode in the caboose, was riding in the caboose with his daddy. Johnny thought he saw the wheel lying way down the track, so he asked his daddy if he could go see, and his daddy said he could. So Johnny ran down the track as fast as he could go, and sure enough, it was the wheel. Johnny tried to pick up the wheel, but it was too heavy to carry, so he rolled it down the track. Then they had to find a bolt to hold the wheel back in place.

Just then they heard another train coming. They were afraid it might hit them, but it was on the other track and it stopped to help them. The mechanic on the other train brought his tool box out and helped get the wheel back on.

When they got the wheel back in place, the engine went "chug-chug," the whistle blew,"toot! toot!" The conductor called, "All aboard for Disneyland!" The wheels went round, and they all got to Disneyland after all.

A group composition by four-year-olds in nursery school in cooperative group effort with their teacher Twila Hills, Findlay, Ohio.

LITTLE JOE

Once upon a time there was a boy by the name of Little Joe. He lived on a farm with his mama and papa and his three pets, a dog, a kitten, and a parakeet.

One day Little Joe's papa bought him a new pop gun. He took his three pets out into the woods to see if his pop gun worked. As he walked through the woods, he met a cougar. The cougar said, "Gr-r-r-r! I'm going to eat you up, Little Joe."

Little Joe said, "Please don't eat me up, Mr. Cougar. I'll give you my dog and with him to follow you around, you will be the grandest cougar in the woods."

Said Mr. Cougar, "Of course I'll let you go on if you give me the dog." And he went off saying, "Now *I'M* the grandest cougar in the woods."

As Little Joe went on, he met another cougar who wanted to eat him up. So Little Joe said, "Please do not eat me up, Mr. Cougar. I'll give you my kitten and with her to ride on your back, you will be the grandest cougar in the forest."

This cougar was not so sure he wanted the kitten. However, he decided to take her and off he went saying, "Now *I'M* the grandest cougar in the woods."

As Little Joe went on, he met another cougar who said, "Gr-r-r-r, I'm going to eat you up."

Little Joe said, "Please do not eat me up. I'll give you my parakeet."

Mr. Cougar said, "What would I do with a parakeet?"

"You could have him sing to you and be your friend," said Little Joe.

"Why, of course," said Mr. Cougar, "and now *I'M* the grandest cougar in the woods."

Going deeper into the woods, Little Joe met another cougar. This fourth cougar said, "Gr-r-r-r! I'm going to eat you up, Little Joe."

"Please do not eat me up, Mr. Cougar," said Little Joe; "I'll give you my pop gun".

And so the fourth cougar went off with the pop gun tied to his tail. He was saying, "Now *I'M* the grandest cougar in the woods."

Walking further into the woods, Little Joe was very sad. Then he heard all this noise. He looked around to see the four cougars chasing one another around a rock. Little Joe said, "Don't you want my pets and pop gun any more?"

The cougars were so afraid that one might get away, they just held on to each other's tails saying, "Gr-r-r-r". They got so hot they turned to tar.

The pop gun got untangled and flew right into Little Joe's arms. He gathered up his pets and hurried to his farm.

Little Joe's papa was coming home from town with a pail on his head and he saw the tar the cougars had made. He said, "I could use this tar to mend our silo and walls." So he picked up the tar and carried it home.

There he plugged up all the holes in the silo. Now all the cows, horses, and pigs would have enough food for the long, cold winter. There was plenty so the cows had fifteen bushels, the horses had twenty bushels, and the pigs had one hundred and five bushels of grain.

> First Grade—Hahn School, Wayne, Nebraska.
> Supervising Teacher—Vesta Wright.

Older children, too, find the cooperative story fun on a slightly more mature basis. They enjoy dividing into groups of three or more pupils to create an entire story or a sequence of episodes which can later be woven into a story. They work in groups of their own choosing, discuss the story or episode which they wish to take responsibility for writing, decide what form it should take and begin.

Through pooling ideas, dictating to a scribe selected by each group, taking turns to be a scribe, children who might otherwise fail to experience this form of written expression find satisfaction in being authors too.

In guiding such an endeavor, the teacher moves from writing group to writing group, discussing and giving encouragement and help where it is *really* needed, eliciting ideas from the group, and being a good listener when ideas are flowing spontaneously. At times he gives direct instruction to the combined groups by pointing up common problems, literary devices, and asking the class for solutions and suggestions. At other times giving direct instruction to small groups is more valuable.

While there are those who believe all writing should be of an individual nature in the intermediate and upper grades, there is merit in group activity in which children collaborate as authors. Cooperative effort can be a stepping stone to individual activity as well as a different way of expressing ideas.

Enjoying the Writing of Others

Children may be overwhelmed by the skill and perfection of the professional writer and become discouraged with their own efforts. The wise teacher provides examples of fine creative writing by children across the country.

The stories that follow are typical examples of what children write in the average classroom when they are given time, encouragement, and guidance.

READY FOR CHRISTMAS

Once upon a time there was a little squirrel who didn't have any food to eat. He had eaten everything except one little hazelnut. That one last nut he must save for his Christmas dinner. So he put on his raincoat and went for a walk in the woods. He walked and he walked, but as the sun set in the west, he found he had no nuts to carry back to his home. All at once he looked up and who should he see but a little lady with a fairy wand. She didn't say a word, but led him straight to a little house that had a pleasant look. He followed her and peaked in at the window. Lo and behold a woman who looked very much like the lady in the woods was baking a Christmas cake. He could hardly believe his eyes when he saw the little lady had six beautiful pecans ready to put in to the batter. He made a squirrelly noise. The little lady, thinking it was the telephone ringing, left the kitchen to answer the phone. This was his chance. He grabbed the pecans and stole away.

The little lady came back to the kitchen to find the pecans gone. So the little lady sat down and cried. "There will be no fruitcake for Christmas!" Ever since little squirrels go hunting for nuts early, so they have enough to last all winter, and little ladies baking fruit cakes for Christmas use raisins when there aren't any nuts.

As for the little squirrel, merrily scampering up the hill with the nuts, he chuckled to himself, "I'm ready for Christmas. Are you?"

Phyllis Gass—5 years old. Henry Reiss Kindergarten, Evansville, Ind.

A GRUMWUFF

Once upon a time there was a grumwuff. Before I tell you the story you must know what a grumwuff is. A grumwuff, so I've been told, is a furry pink animal with no arms and legs. It sits on your shoulder all day, even when you're playing ball or brushing your teeth. Since it doesn't have any legs, a grumwuff just bounces from place to place.

That is, a proper grumwuff does. But this grumwuff wasn't happy bouncing from place to place, so he said: "I will ask the gods to teach me to fly". And that he did. And that they did. And on a summer's evening when the sun is sinking in the west you may see a streak of pink against the sky—a streak of fluff that wings across the sky. And you will hear the wind sigh: "Grumwuff-grumwuff-Grumwuff— . . . There he goes!"

Mary Becker—6 years old.

THE LOST PEARL

Once upon a time there was a Queen who had a neclace with dimonds and one big pearl in the middle. One day she was looking over the pond to see her pretty reflection in the water, when suddenly her neclace broke, splash, splash, SPLASH! That was the big pearl. The Queen ordered some men to look for the dimonds. They brought out dimonds and dimonds and dimonds, but not the big pearl. A man was fishing one day and caught a big fish. That fish had ate the pearl. His wife sewed it on his jacket. There it is on the old man's jacket—to this very day. [Spelling and usage are Connie's]

Connie—7 years old. School District No. 67, Duncan, B.C.

THE SIX-INCH MONSTER[18]

Once there was a monster that was about six inches high. If you got a ruler and measured him you would find that he was exactly six inches high.

And you could measure him because he was very polite. That is, if you could ever find him. I know where he lives and I visit him sometimes. He has a lot of money that he has hid somewhere. He digs holes and put it in. He has a lot of holes with money in it. Because he is so little and couldn't handle very much at a time. He told me where a pot of gold was but that little monster had just dug it up to give it to someone for helping him. That monster is really just an overgrown fairy. I've been calling him a six inch monster because he plays so many tricks.

Once I went to visit him to get some butter. When I knocked at the door I listened for a while. And all I heard was that little monster trying to teach his dishes how to sing. Then I knocked again and he opened the door and gave me some butter right in the face.

He said, "That is what you wanted, isn't it?" So I never tried to borrow anything from him again. And once I lost my purse and I told the little six inch monster about it and the next day I went to visit him. He came out with a big thing (anyway it was big to him) on his back.

I asked him what it was and he said, "It is your purse." I took it off his back and it was my purse. He said he took a long walk but it was just a few steps away. He said he had to cross an ocean, but it was really just a little puddle. He said it was too long to go around. But the funny thing about it was he had fun. [Spelling and usage is Phyllis']

Phyllis Ormand—8 years old, third grade.

LUCKY DAN

What strange and mysterious experiences I have been having. For months I have been cold and all shriveled up in the dark soil under the snow near my brothers and sisters. One day we began to feel warmer and we started to stretch upward as though we were being drawn. One day a wonderful thing happened. I became so large that my head popped up a little, my arms stretched way out and I had a first chance to look around. I was sitting on a beautiful soft green blanket and near me were many lovely yellow flowers. They all seemed so much taller and more beautiful than I. It was such a frightening experience. There were many giant feet that came close and sounded so much like thunder. They made me shake and I wished I could go back into the soil. One day a huge lady came with a basket and a sharp thing that hurt so badly when she cut as she tried to destroy all my family and friends. Somehow she didn't notice me and I was relieved to hear her go away and never come back. I was beginning to feel so much better when a machine which made a horrible noise and a man whose voice I had heard go by often, came close again and again to snip off our heads. I should be glad now that I never grew very tall, for again I was left. The beautiful warm sunshine and gentle breeze made me feel so wonderful. Many days went by, then one day my coat of gold seemed to become dry and I felt different than I had ever felt before. I became so light and I was white now and looked something like down. Not long after, a gentle breeze came by coaxing me to come along. It coaxed and pushed and coaxed and finally I felt myself flying through the air like a fairy. I felt so light I wanted never, never to stop again.

Phyllis Reeder—10 years old. Findlay, Ohio.

THE MISSING TOOTH

Once there lived a very poor family. The family was made up of an old man and his young grandson, Punco. Punco had a little bull named Pekelo.

One morning Punco got up early for today Punco and Pekelo were going fishing. As Punco sat eating his food, Pekelo devoured his food . . . which was half Punco's that he was sharing.

When Punco returned home, his grandfather said to him, "Punco, we have no more food. We will have to sell Pekelo."

"No, I will never sell Pekelo," said Punko.

"But you must," replied the grandfather.

"Run, Pekelo, run!" shouted Punco.

Pekelo understood, but since he had been very young his eyesight has not been good. He ran right into a big tree. Punco ran over to the tree.

"Are you hurt, Pekelo? Are you hurt?"

Pekelo gave Punco a big smile. Punco saw that the bull had knocked one of his teeth out. Punco looked on the ground for Pekelo's tooth. He found it.

"Pekelo, I will put a hole in this tooth and put it on a string. I will put it around my neck and when grandfather takes you away I will always remember you."

About 17 years later when Punco was a full grown man he was going to fight a very mean bull. Punco sat in his room thinking about when he was a little boy. Then he heard his cue to go out. He walked in to the pen very straight. The pen door swung open and the biggest bull Punco had ever seen charged out. The bull hated the sight of the man with the red cape. The bull was going to attack Punco. Punco drew his sword. Then the bull stopped and gave Punco a big smile. Punco saw that one of his front teeth was missing. Punco pulled his tooth out from around his neck. Punco put his arms around his lost Pekelo.

Then Punco heard the crowd howling boo, boo. Punco and Pekelo walked out of the pen together.

"Pekelo, if it hadn't been for your missing tooth, I might have killed you," said Punco.

Punco was a little sad because the people didn't like him as a bull fighter, but he did find Pekelo and he was very happy for a long time.

Zelma Anderson—11 years old. West Elementary School, Mt, Vernon, Indiana.

A RING

The low clouds hung like ragged folds in a gray dress. Nowhere did the sun peek through with its warmth and comfort. The sunlit green had seeped out of the trees and they stood back, silhouetted against the sky. Beyond the trees a small bright flame rose and fell as the rain drizzled down.

Nestled in her coat, a young girl sat nearby, her face brightening and darkening with the fire. Between her fingers she carefully held a small ring. As her full blue eyes looked lovingly at it, she smiled. The ring was old and the silver had tarnished. The stone was chipped and worn, but as the flames leapt again it was flecked with gold.

Although it was no longer beautiful, her feelings for the ring continued to shine in her eyes.

Susan Paxton—13 years old. Vancouver, B.C.

THE ARSONIST

Hunched under the lee of the towering building the man tried to keep himself warm against the squalling wind and rain, and the night which coated him in a black jacket. Suddenly a flashlight moved its beam to the man. His mask thrown off, he stabbed through the wind and night leaving the searching beam to dash itself among the spidery trees that covered the spot. From the spot a fire sprang its clawing hands into the wood. It soon brightly illuminated the fleeing trees and the human form that quickly was swallowed by the night.

David Poskitt—13 years old. Balmoral Junior Secondary School, North Vancouver, B.C.

Questions. Thought provoking questions may also be used to develop the art of thinking, feeling and expressing. How would you feel standing in a room completely filled with your favourite colour?

This question presented to a class of fifth grade boys and girls in a creative environment brought the following response:

> "Pink is the color I like the best,
> If I were a bird I'd put pink in my nest.
> Babies wear pink and so do you,
> I'm not a baby but I like pink too.
>
> Look out in the yard with spring in the air
> And put a pink cherry blossom into your hair.
> Roses are pink and so are carnations
> Pink is the favourite all over the nation."[19]

Expressions follow closely on the heels of strong impressions when teachers are sensitive to the phenomena in the environment, to the child's innate urge for expression and are skilled in asking questions which spur creative expression.

A question which always evokes creative expression is one dealing with weather. "What tells you that Jack Frost is just around the corner?" Responses include: "silvery spider webs struggling to hold up fresh dew drops", "turning on defrosters when starting the car in early morn", "the cat resuming his customary cold weather habit of sleeping with his tummy against the hot-air register."[20]

To the question "What does Up mean to you?" the following responses were written: A ten-year-old, "Up depends on whether you're a bug or an elephant". A seven-year-old girl, "Up is as high as you want it to be". A twelve-year-old boy, "Up is as high as you feel when something nice happens to you". An eight-year-old boy, "Sun, stars, and Pluto are what some people think are high, but nobody knows if there's anything higher than heaven". A nine-year-old girl, "To an ant, a wheat stalk must be as far as up".[21]

Integrating the arts. Stimulation for creative writing is where you find it. A sixth grade teacher came up to a group of children who were manipulating the potter's wheel. As a child worked the treadle, others in the group responded to the rhythm by tapping, clapping or otherwise reacting to the rhythm. Someone began humming a few notes. The group joined in spontaneously. The teacher went to the chalkboard and wrote the melody on the board as the children created it. They added to the notes and melodic pattern until someone said, "That's it."

Each child wrote his *own* words to the melody on the basis of the rhythm of the potters wheel. Here was creativity—music and poetry intertwined. Here is one example.

Hear my wheel turn round and round
Listen to the humming sound whrrrrrrr, whrrrrrrr, whrrrrrrr,
See my wheel spin round and round
As if my foot never left the ground—whrrrrrr, whrrrrr, whrrr.

Children write because they have a desire to express their ideas, their feelings, their imaginations. The teacher is there to clear the track, to encourage each child, to stimulate his thinking, to help him develop the skills he has a need for, and to give the recognition that will make him eager to write, eager to improve, and eager to express through the medium of the written word.

Literary Devices

The young child plays with words for the joy he finds in the sound and rhythm. As he matures, however, he senses a need to develop techniques for expressing his creative ideas more effectively. It is at this point that the perceptive teacher will introduce him to various literary devices upon which he can draw. This implies that the teacher will himself be well versed in the various literary devices and will be at ease in pointing them out to children in their literature as well as helping them become skillful in their use. As the artist learns to use the whole spectrum of colour, so the weaver of tales learns to use words to express precise meaning as he develops his unique writing style.

Techniques which add colour to a writer's palette. Unless the child is in command of a variety of literary devices his writing tends to be sterile and stereotyped. Robert Frost once said, "All the fun's in how you say a thing." The following devices can serve as tools for saying it in vibrant, rich, colourful language.

1. Figures of Speech. Figurative language is a picturesque comparison designed to make vivid an idea or to illlustrate a thought. The expressed likeness of the simile and the implied likeness of the metaphor intrigue children. "Old as Methuselah", "tall as a stringbean", "time's winged chariot", "starry vaults of the heaven", "jumping on the bandwagon", "sly as a fox", "eyes bigger than his stomach', "slow as molasses in January," "innocent as a dove", are some that come readily to mind. Good writing makes use of figurative language. "I saw him [Napoleon] in Russia, where the infantry of the snow and the cavalry of the wild beast scattered his legions like winter's withered leaves. I saw him at Leipsic in defeat and disaster—driven by a million bayonets back upon Paris. . . . And I saw him at St. Helena, with his hands crossed behind him, gazing out upon a sad and solemn sea."[22]

Children enjoy completing such phrases as:

as soft as	The wind howled like a ....
as loud as	Jack was as restless as ....
as happy as	All day long I've been as busy as ....
as sad as	This gadget is as useless as a ....

as stern as	She turned green with ....
as quiet as	The doctor was tied ....
as gentle as	He put his foot in ....
	He was a .... in the fight.

The simile is commonly used by children in their writing. The metaphor is seldom found. The use of the metaphor will make children's writing even more vivid. "Metaphor is at the root of extensions of meanings in our language. One simple illustration is the use of words for the parts of the body in everyday speech: *hand, heart, head, foot, arm, toes.* Even young children learn to use these word metaphors as they speak of the hands of the clock or the foot of a sock. From our feet comes the extension of meanings of the word *foot* to include *foot of the mountain, foot of the class, foot it to town, footwork,* and so on. Such words may range from the literal and concrete (the valvular human heart) to the most abstract: *the heart of the matter, giving one's heart away, putting one's heart into the effort, a heartless girl.* Such words stand not only for physical objects (the human heart) but for very abstract phrases that have a physical referent (*heart of the matter*). Metaphor is the device by which we use words which signify objects in the physical world to imply a comparison and to express the unknown in terms of the known. It has been called the device by which we express the inexpressible."[23]

2. The Historical Present. Transporting the reader into the past by means of the present tense is an effective literary device commonly used in television, radio, and documentary films. It is especially liked by elementary school children, particularly when they can present some historical episode which has significance in their social studies or literature class.

3. Inverted Word Order. One of the most widely quoted phrases using this technique is that of John F. Kennedy. "Ask not what your country can do for you—ask what you can do for your country." Although all sentences contain parts of speech or classes of words these need not necessarily always follow in the SVO (subject, verb, object) sequence. Experimenting with word order is a worthwhile activity for the embryo writer.

4. Rhythm and Rhyme. Children should be encouraged to listen to the rhythm and flow of language. As teachers read aloud children become aware of the singingness, the rhythm and the rhyme of poetry, and the flow of prose. They should be led to appreciate good literature by hearing it read by a teacher who reads it beautifully. They thus become aware of the elements of style. At times they should be encouraged to write in the style of a chosen author as a means of developing their own.

5. Alliteration. The repetition of the same initial sound in successive words is euphoneous. Witness the effect of "wild, woolly west," "let me languish in loneliness," "purple pansies preening in the picture window," "soft slumbering summer," "lonely leaf," "wide, wonderful world."

6. Assonance. Somewhat similar to alliteration is the repetition of the same

sound in successive words although in different positions within the word. Whereas alliteration generally involves consonants, assonance usually is related to vowel sounds. "Dennis the menace", "more bounce to the ounce," "molten-golden notes", "I like Ike".

7. Imagery. Images are an integral part of the writer's stock in trade. They may be classified in several different ways, but a useful way is classifying them according to the kinds of sensations involved. The most important from the standpoint of the elementary and upper grades are: images of sight (visual), images of sound (auditory), images of movement (kinesthetic), images of touch (tactile), images of taste (gustatory), images of smell (olfactory).

8. Antithesis. A form of comparison that lends colour to the written word is sometimes compressed and a graphic statement in which ideas are set off one against the other and in which opposites are brought close together is often effective. "A man is never so tall as when he stoops to help a little child."

The wise teacher knows that developing skill in expressive writing does not come easily. It is a gradual process. The creative idea should be put on paper as quickly as possible. However, as the child matures he discovers that much refinement and rewriting is necessary before he is ready to share his work with others.

WRITING STORIES

Ideas for writing stories come from many sources—from half-remembered experiences, from bits of conversation, from stories heard or read, from experiences real or imaginary. At times ideas erupt spontaneously. At other times they remain beneath the surface and refuse to come until someone has provided the stimulus.

Getting the Story Started

If the child knows what he wants to write the teacher should step aside and let him write. However, for the child who is having difficulty the effective teacher will have at hand a number of useful techniques to help him get started.

The idea box. Children respond readily to the "Idea Box". The teacher may need to provide the initial supply of ideas. The children should be encouraged to replenish the "Idea Box" before the list is exhausted. Sometimes a committee of children is chosen to gather, screen, and catalogue the ideas. Titles that "strike oil" are:

The Lonely Stegosaurus	A Horse for Henry
Witches Brew	First Prize for ....
Fire! Fire!	The Bear that Couldn't Hibernate
Lost in a Storm	The Missing Link
The Hidden Valley	A Lucky Fall
A Falling Star	An Exciting Discovery

The Little Lost Bunny
A Bear in the Camp
The Biggest Fish I Ever Caught
The Man with Balloons
The Time I Almost Drowned

The Time I was Rescued
The Tall Tale to End All Tales
The Night of the Big Blizzard
The Rescue at Sea
A Plane Crash
The Mysterious Box

Let's pretend. Children enjoy pretending to be someone or something and then tell what would happen if they were—a football, a tea kettle, an eyebrow, a tooth, a turtle, an airplane, a shoe. For the older children this leads naturally to imaginative writing relating to the historical past. Such suggestions as—If I were:

Travelling across the mountains in a covered wagon a hundred years ago
A rider for the Pony Express
A member of the Hudson Bay exploring party
A pioneer in the province in which I live
An astronaut
A cowboy on a drive to market
A hockey star who has a bad season

Sentence starters. Children of all ages enjoy sentence starters. As with the idea box, they should be encouraged to contribute. Older children should develop a file of their own. These sentence starters have been contributed by children:

If my ruler were only a magic wand I
The day I went to the moon I
On my last visit to the circus the lion
If I could go to any place in the universe I would
I feel proud when
I was walking along the beach at Point-No-Point when suddenly
My hair stood on end as
Our entire house seemed to explode as
If I could have one wish I
If I were in Never-Never Land I
We never thought a stray puppy could cause such a rumpus.
Teddy Bear sat at the table slurping his
The hinge creaked behind me!
The old woman and the girl walked slowly up the street.

Phrases. Sometimes a phrase is all that is needed to get the story under way. Sometimes a single phrase will be given. Sometimes two or three will be given to be included somewhere in the story. Several exciting stories were based on these three phrases: "a twisted old tree", "faint blue hills", "a tumbed down shack".

Phrases that suggest moods for the stories are often helpful. Try the following suggestions:

Write a story using some of these phrases that give you a lonely feeling:

faint toot of an engine	empty and quiet
longing for the sight of someone	aching heart
sad and anxious eyes	homeless
shut in by towering trees	surrounded by stillness
lengthening purple shadows	steady downpour of rain
mirrorlike surface of the sea	disappointed sighing
	landing at the airport in deep fog

Write a story using some of these phrases that give you a gay feeling:

flowers turning to the sun	white cottages freshly painted
wishes coming true	a rainbow bridge in the sky
squirrels scampering	boys whistling while fishing
a shining blanket of white snow	birds singing in the trees

Write a story using some of these phrases that give you a spooky feeling:

shutters banging back and forth	dark mysterious shadows
sudden hooting of an owl	round and smiling moon
sighing, sobbing wind	branches bending and groaning
creeping closer and closer	black and scary night
anxiously listening	listening and shivering
high, terrifying scream	strange, unusual footprints

Complete the story. **Some children need more than phrases and ideas. If the actual story is started they may find it easier to complete it.**

One evening I was walking through the jungles. I was all alone. The night had many noises. All of a sudden I came to a bend in the road and there I saw...

The night was still, broken only by shrill screeches of the owl. The black, shabby house looked forbidding in the pale moonlight. The leaves on the trees made eerie rustling sounds as a faint breeze blew in the night air. Suddenly I thought I heard ....

Into the dark, cold den he crawled for the third time, slowly and painfully. On he crawled to the end of the cave where the great wolf was lying very still. Was she really dead or was she just stunned? He wondered if he dared approach any nearer. Cautiously he held the torch nearer her nose.............................

The King lay stretched in the warm sun on the east side of the cabin. At times he moaned. His legs jerked as he dreamed of rabbits racing through the tall grass. The Princess eyed him from the corner, then hobbled over, squatted down, and playfully whacked the King on the nose with her wooden leg.............................

Story based on a picture. All teachers should have a file of pictures. At times a single picture may be shown and all children write stories inspired by the one picture. They enjoy hearing how each reacted to the one scene. At other times the children should be encouraged to find pictures of their own and write a story using the pictures to illustrate it. For the children who do not have a source of pictures the teacher may have a table or cupboard with magazines and catalogues that the children may cut up.

Developing the Story

After children have had some experience in writing stories they will recognize the need for specific guidance in developing a story line. First of all, a story must have a beginning. Traditionally "once upon a tme" was all that was needed to get the writer off to an exciting start. Today's children use a wide variety of starting sentences. The opening sentences should lead into the statement of the conflict or problem that requires a solution. Specific and interesting details are introduced and developed as the story moves to its climax. The problem is solved as a result of the climax. The ending should be brief. The writer should be helped to keep his focus on the climax and to refrain from introducing extraneous and/or superfluous details and incidents.

Evaluating the Story

In the initial story writing experiences at any grade level the attention should be centered on the structure of stories, including such elements as an interesting beginning, a sequential development of ideas, a high point or climax, an effective ending. As these basic elements are mastered the child's attention should be directed to the novel ideas, ingenuity, and other personal and imaginative qualities. It is only when teachers themselves understand these additional qualities can they help the child evaluate his own writing.

There are several scales for rating written compositions which are helpful to the teacher and pupil in discussing and evaluating written expression. Yamamoto at the University of Minnesota issued a scale and scoring manual for evaluating imaginative stories. "The Yamamoto scale has six major divisions to evaluate organization, sensitivity, originality, imagination, psychological insight, and richness. The illustrative subdivisions under various categories are useful to the teacher in planning the writing conference."[24]

Originality	*Imagination*	*Richness*
choice of topics	richness of imagination	expression
ideas	fantasy	ideas
organization	abstraction	emotion
style of writing	identification	curiosity
sense of humor	reasoning	fluency

A widely used scale is that developed by Torrance in what he called "Supplementary Scoring Guide for the Evaluation of Originality and Interest". Part I evaluates originality. Part II assesses the interest of imaginative stories.[25]

Originality
picturesqueness
vividness
flavor
personal element
original solution or ending
original setting or plot
invented words or names
other elements such as
unusual twist in style or
   content

Interest
conversational tone
naturalness
use of quotations
variety of kind of sentences
variety in length of sentences and
   structure
personal touch
humor
questions and answers
feeling of characters

One point is awarded for each interest item that appears in an original story. Samples of stories are given in the Torrance Scale.

Carlson prepared an analytical originality scale as a part of a doctoral dissertation, *Stimulating Children in Grades Four, Five and Six to Write Original Stories.* The Carlson Originality Scale has five divisions: Story Structure, Novelty, Emotion, Individuality, Style of Stories. Examples of the subdivisions of these categories follow:[26]

Story Structure

unusual title
unusual beginning
unusual ending
unusual plot

Novelty
novelty of names
novelty of locale
unique punctuation and
   expressional devices
new words
novelty of ideas
novel devices
novel theme
quantitative thinking
new objects created
ingenuity in solving
   situations
recombinations of ideas
   in unusual relationships
picturesque speech
humor
novelty of form
inclusion of readers
unusual related thinking

Emotional Aspects

unusual ability to express emotional depth
unusual sincerity in expressing personal problems
unusual ability to identify self with problems
   or feeling of others
unusual horror theme

Individuality

unusual perspective sensitivity
unique philosophical thinking
facility in beautiful writing
unusual personal experiences

Style of Stories: includes seven items:

exaggerated tall tale
fairy tale
fantasy turn-about of characters
highly fantastic central idea or theme
fantastic creatures, objects, or persons
individual story style

The creative teacher will use this scale to bring into focus some of the characteristics of creative writing in an individual writing conference with a child, *not as an effort to evaluate the child's writing*. It can well serve to teach children the difference between clichés and fresh, vivid writing. As Carlson points out "Teachers in elementary and secondary schools, concerned with the mechanical elements of written expression, may fail to recognize unusual qualities of thought, style, and form. Creative pupils may abandon novel modes of expression if they are not valued by the teacher...."[27]

Developing Style in Writing

Each individual's writing is the expression of his personality, experience, and ability. Phrasing, tempo, content, and form determine his style. Just as the artist combines the elements of colour, form, and design to personalize his conception into a visual creation, just so does the writer use his materials to create his own inimitable work of art in written expression. "Style", says Lee, "is the significant contribution of the individual artist, whether his tools be the power of the word, the brush, or the sculptor's knife. We recognize the personal touch in athlete and artist alike. It is what gives him his color, his particular conformation. . . . It is the means by which the artist achieves an end...."[28]

What the writer does with the elements unique to the process of writing creatively; what he does with the materials—the vocabulary, the words, and the ideas, and how he manipulates and shapes these determines his style.

It is within the province of the teacher to help the child to develop his own style, to become cognizant of the worth of his own expression, to be confident of the importance of what he has to say, and to develop skills as he needs them. Not limiting oneself to imitation, nor copying the manner in which another expresses his ideas, but becoming confident through increasing skills in using words—is the key to successful writing. The teacher's manner as well as his words tell the child "You have something to say—say it in your own words—don't look to anyone else. Follow your own inner impulse". Chagall expressed this sentiment when he asserted: "You listen silently and the sacred power that is within you dictates and you obey; and that is what is called creation."[29]

Children should be encouraged to play with ideas, to choose topics for writing which appeal to them, and to experiment in finding new ways of expressing ideas, new relationships between ideas, and connecting links among experience, imagination and creative communication.

A perceptive teacher is ready to motivate, nurture, and guide children in their written expression. He maintains a fine balance between standing back and allowing the child to express his ideas and helping him develop the needed skills.

A perceptive teacher realizes when a child is in need of learning skills which will enable him to see relationships between experience, communication and the nature of the subject. He will help the child become familiar with such styles as narrative, historical, or argumentative.

The elements of composition must be mastered. As an artist masters colour and design, as a dancer masters body and movement, as a musician masters form, harmony and melody, so the writer masters words and their ways. As the writer writes expressing himself in his own way, style becomes the outer clothing for his inner thoughts.

EVALUATION OF WRITTEN EXPRESSION

In considering evaluation of written expression it is necessary to focus on evaluation of creative writing separately from expository writing. Each must be evaluated in terms of the purpose of the writing. The purpose of creative writing is artistic self-expression. Thus the focus of evaluation is the child. Strickland supports the idea of self-evaluation on the part of the child in writing. "It would appear that the key to good work may lie not in the standards the teacher sets for the children's writing, but in standards each child is helped to set for himself, because those are the standards he takes with him out into life after he leaves the realm of the teacher's authority."[30]

The teacher who is concerned with helping children become confident writers will begin with writing experiences which focus on what the child wishes to say and his purpose for saying it. As the child matures he will discover that form is determined by the content. The content should be emphasized above the form while children are trying their wings in written expression. "It is impossible to correct or improve a child's expression until he offers enough of it to work with. When it is flowing as freely as he is capable of at the time, he is ready for help with form and correctness."[31]

Self-evaluation and self-confidence go hand-in-hand. If self-evaluation is to be meaningful every child should have a folder in which he can keep his writing. This will enable him to see his own growth. It will also enable him to evaluate his own writing.

Questions the Child Asks Himself

As the child is growing in self expression through writing with a teacher who helps him lift his sights without causing him to lose confidence he assumes a large share of responsibility for evaluation of his own work and will in time become his own best critic. Some of the questions the child asks as he evaluates his work are:

Did I say what I wanted to say—not approximately but as precisely as possible?
Did the words run trippingly along with rhythm, grace, and spontaneity?
Were the words blended with artistry, strength and finesse?
Were the words briskly alive?

Will they ignite the imagination of the listener and thrust him forward on a journey of adventure, anticipation and enjoyment?

Did the writing communicate my feelings as well as my ideas?

Did the style express my personality, *my* ideas, and *my* feelings?

Will the listener recognize the style as my own?

Did I show improvement in the use of the tools and techniques of writing?

Did the experience of creating with words bring me a feeling of exhilaration?

Did anyone else enjoy what I had written?

Periodically each child should be invited to bring his folder of creative writing to a conference with the teacher. This will include all the writing he may have done. These questions may be used.

Questions for the Child and Teacher to Discuss in Conference

Do you feel that you said what you wanted to say?

Did you really know enough about your subject to write about it—either real or imagined experiences?

Did your choice of words express your ideas clearly, vividly, and precisely?

For your stories were your plot structures clear and plausible?

Did you use imaginative, vivid language, and appropriate rhythms in your poems?

Did you use variety in sentence structure in your prose?

Have you any suggestions or questions about the mechanics and form?

Do you enjoy writing?

What are your next writing plans?

There are important questions, too, which the teacher must ask himself if he is to carry out the objectives of a creative writing program in the language arts curriculum.

Questions the Teacher May Ask Himself

Do I provide a climate for creative expression?

Do I recognize each child's need for creative expression in writing?

Do I allow freedom to create while at the same time providing the needed tools and techniques when the child requests them?

Do I provide time, encouragement, and opportunity for children to experience, discuss, and create through written expression?

Do I help each child establish a purpose for writing?

Do I share the child's enthusiasm when he brings me some of his writing?

Do I understand the difference between guiding creative writing and teaching the techniques of composition?

Do I point the way toward improving the writer's craft without destroying his creativity?

Do I help each child develop his own style of writing?

Do I allow children to become their own critics?

Do I occasionally share some of my own creative writing with them?

Do I make provision for sharing and publishing the works of children who are ready for this experience?

Do I tread a fine line between giving needed encouragement, recognition, and praise for the child to continue his creative efforts, and offering subtle suggestions and techniques for improvement to enable him to raise his sights in harmony with his growing needs and abilities?

Although self-evaluation and teacher evaluation are vital for the success of a creative writing program, they are not in themselves adequate. The total staff should be involved in the evaluation of the program.

Questions for the Staff About the Creative Writing Program in the School

Has the school as a whole established objectives for a long range creative writing program?

Are our objectives consistent with the socio-economic level of the community?

To what extent are we as a staff achieving our objectives?

Are there occasional staff conferences for the improvement of teaching creative writing?

Are there opportunities for action research in this curriculum area?

Are the parents kept informed of the purposes as well as the products of the creative writing program?

If the objectives of the creative writing program are to be met evaluation must be comprehensive and continuous; it must focus on the individual—his needs, abilities, and interests; and it must be a cooperative enterprise. "The entire school staff as well as the parents and the community should be concerned with evaluation. . . . Children can have a part in setting up goals, in working together to achieve them, and finally in evaluating progress. When the child knows where he is going, what he is expected to do when he gets there, and how to judge whether he has accomplished what he set out to do he is well on the way. . . ."[32]

CONCLUDING STATEMENT

What makes the difference between writing that is spontaneous, sparkling and scintillating, and writing that is dreary, drab, and dull? How the child expresses his creativity in writing is dependent upon such factors as native capacity, degree of perception, ability to absorb, aptness in seeing relationships, fluency with words, aptitude for the miracle of words, and skill in portraying through written expression the images he sees in his mind's eye.

How the child expresses his creativity in writing is dependent, too, upon the skill and insight of the perceptive teacher. Such a teacher creates an environment of psychological safety in which children are free to express ideas; provides stimulating experiences; allows time to explore, experiment and create; supports children during the creative activity, provides them with the needed skills and tools; helps them in making words come alive; motivates them to become more aware, more perceptive, and more sensitive to people and phenomena; plans opportunity to share the writing products; and guides children in evaluating their own writing in terms of the goals they set for themselves.

The teacher must be aware of the phases of the creative process through which the child progresses as he moves from cognition to communication and is there to give the needed encouragement and help. Creative writing, the teacher knows, is personal, individual, and imaginative.

The locus of evaluation is the student. Since the purpose of creative writing is artistic self-expression, evaluation must be based on the extent to which the child grows in his own ability to express his ideas in a manner satisfactory to him at any given point in his development.

When the child has had sufficient time to experiment, to explore, to create with words, he is ready to consider seriously the discipline of the writer—form. He becomes concerned with organization, style, and convention as well as invention in writing. Until he reaches this point through writing frequently and confidently—he is not ready for external evaluation.

Children vary as widely in linguistic development as they do in other phases of development. The perceptive teacher recognizes this and plans his writing program to meet individual differences. The spiral curriculum facilitates planning. At every level it is important to provide each child with freedom to invent before he becomes concerned with the conventions of the discipline.

Children differ; so will their experiences in writing. There are those who move quickly from experience to expression; there are others who need stimulation plus encouragement; and there are some who need motivation and direct help. Not all children will find in writing their favourite mode of creative expression. *But* all children can know to a degree the delight that begins with curiosity and ends in wonder—of putting into words how he felt on that afternoon in the first storm of summer which began by watching a dark cloud come from out of the west, cover the sun and send peals of thunder, shafts of lightning, and torrents of rain, where moments before he heard birds singing, saw clouds floating lazily across the sky as he lay on the velvet green grass. Such a child, in the final phase of creating—finds the communicating of his idea to another the capstone of the experience. In the words of Herrick, "The process of communicating through the appropriate symbols, ideas, feelings, thoughts and/or emotions involves intellectualizing. . . . Transmitted ideas via language arts evoke emotional responses. Words and ideas take on an emotional quality; they engender certain moods, feelings or attitudes."[33]

REFERENCES

1. Ruth Kearney Carlson, "Sparkling and Spinning Words," *Elementary English,* 41:55, January, 1964.
2. By permission from Lillian M. Logan and Virgil G. Logan, *Teaching the Elementary School Child,* Houghton Mifflin Company, Boston, 1961, p. 335.
3. By permission from Wright Thomas and Stuart Gerry Brown, *Reading Poems,* Oxford University Press, New York, 1941, p. 748.
4. Stephen Spender, "The Making of a Poem," in Brewster Ghiselin (ed.), *The Creative Process,* The American Library, New York, 1955, pp. 121, 122, 123.
5. Sara Lowrey and Gertrude E. Johnson, *Interpretative Reading,* Appleton-Century-Crofts, Inc., New York, 1942, pp. 26-59.
6. Clarence T. Simon, "Appreciation in Reading," in Gertrude Johnson (ed.), *Studies in the Art of Interpretation,* Appleton-Century-Crofts, Inc., New York, 1940, p. 26.
7. Herbert Spencer, *Philosophy of Style,* Pageant Press, New York, 1959, p. 15.
8. Lillian M. Logan and Virgil G. Logan, *op. cit.,* p. 245.
9. Leland Jacobs, "Teaching Children More About Words and Their Ways," *Elementary English,* 41:33, January, 1964.
10. Wright Thomas and Stuart Gerry Brown, *op. cit.,* p. 746.
11. Sara Lowrey and Gertrude E. Johnson, *op. cit.,* pp. 20, 21.
12. By permission from E. Paul Torrance, "Creative Thinking Through School Experience," in Sidney J. Parnes and Harold F. Harding (ed.), *A Source Book for Creative Thinking,* Charles Scribner's Sons, New York, 1962, p. 34.
13. H. Herbert Fox, "A Critique of Creativity in Science," in Myron A. Coler (ed.), *Essays on Creativity in Science,* New York University Press, New York, 1963. p. 133.
14. By permission from Lillian M. Logan, *Teaching the Young Child,* Houghton, Mifflin Company, Boston, 1960, pp. 332, 333, 334.
15. Alvina Trent Burrows, "Children's Experience in Writing," in Virgil Herrick and Leland Jacobs (eds.), *Children and the Language Arts,* Prentice-Hall Inc., Englewood Cliffs, 1955, p. 228.
16. By permission from Paul Witty (ed.), *The Gifted Child,* D. C. Heath & Co., Boston, 1961, p. 106.
17. Reprinted from *Easy in English* by Mauree Applegate. Copyright © 1960 by Harper & Row Publishers, Incorporated, New York, p. 262.
18. Lillian M. Logan and Virgil G. Logan, *op. cit.,* pp. 335, 336.
19. Margaret S. Woods, *Thinking, Feeling, Experiencing: Toward Realization of Full Potential,* Department of Elementary-Kindergarten-Nursery Education, Washington, 1964, pp. 20, 21, 22. Reprinted with permission of the Department of Elementary-Kindergarten-Nursery Education and the author.
20. *Ibid.*
21. *Ibid.*
22. Walter W. Stevens, "Attention Through Language," *Today's Speech,* 11:23, November, 1963. A quote from *The Liberty of Man, Woman and Child.*
23. By permission from Mary Elizabeth Fowler, *Teaching Language, Composition, and Literature,* McGraw-Hill Book Company, New York, 1965. pp. 54, 55.
24. By permission from Ruth Kearney Carlson, "An Originality Story Scale," *The Elementary School Journal,* 65:366-371, April, 1965.

25. *Ibid.*
26. *Ibid.*, pp. 368-371.
27. *Ibid.*, p. 373.
28. Sherman E. Lee, *Japanese Decorative Style*, The Museum of Art, University Circle, Cleveland, 1961, p. 2.
29. Carelton Lake, "Color as Love, A Portrait of Chagall," *The Atlantic Monthly*, 201:73, June, 1958.
30. By permission from Ruth Strickland, "Evaluating Children's Composition," *"Children's Writing: Research in Composition and Related Skills*, National Council of Teachers of English, Champaign, 1961, p. 64.
31. *Ibid.*
32. Lillian M. Logan, *op. cit.*, p. 145.
33. Virgil Herrick and Leland Jacobs (eds.), *op. cit.*, p. 156.

11

Teaching Expository
Writing

Writing, when properly managed, is but a different name for conversation.

Lawrence Sterne

The child is fortunate to be in an environment where he is challenged to express his ideas, thoughts, and feelings creatively and to begin his writing as a means of creative self-expression. He has been encouraged to explore his world through his senses, to formulate his impressions, to express them through language—first oral and then written. In an environment which is challenging, nurturing, receptive to ideas, and under the guidance of a sympathetic, creative teacher, he takes great pleasure in communicating his ideas. The wise teacher recognizes the need to allow the freedom of creative expression, both oral and written, as a prelude for the more strict discipline and conventions involved in expository speaking and writing.

Once the child begins expository writing he must, of necessity, become more concerned with such skills as: developing a sense of form; organizing and developing a sentence, paragraph, or essay; becoming increasingly aware of style in writing; and mastering the tools of handwriting, spelling, punctuation, capitalization, grammar, and usage. The child who through oral language has developed many of the skills he needs in communicating ideas and experiences with coherence, organization, and confidence is ready to apply these skills to expository writing.

If the teacher sees writing as a dynamic, developmental process that takes time, practice, encouragement, motivation, and direct teaching of skills in terms of each child's developmental pattern the child will grow in power in written expression. As children grow in the arts and skills involved they learn to organize their ideas, choose the precise word which conveys a specific meaning, select the form they wish for the content, and to shift gears as readily and easily in writing for various purposes and functions as they do in oral expression.

Expository writing is that writing which the child employs to fulfill a practical or utilitarian need—to report, to record, to review a book, to write a letter, to transmit specific information or beliefs. He learns to observe the conventions and skills of handwriting, spelling, usage, punctuation, and capitalization. He concerns himself with form as well as content from the initial experiences in expository writing. Organization of ideas, clarity of expression, development of style, proofreading, and re-writing are integral parts of expository writing. Evaluation is based on these factors and proceeds from three sources—the child, the teacher, and the group.

The teacher must create a climate by providing experiences which give children a springboard for writing. These will include such things as trips, films, recordings, discussions, and debates as well as broad literary experiences which give children insights and broaden horizons. Through literature they become aware of the style of the various authors, the world of words and of ideas. In a linguistic oriented environment the child has opportunity for oral language activities as a prelude to writing. There is time for expression of ideas, direct teaching of needed skills, opportunity for evaluating, and sharing the writing products. Expository writing provides the opportunity to teach children writing techniques and to develop the essential skills. Writing is both a creative art *and* a communicative skill.

EXPOSITORY WRITING IN THE PRIMARY GRADES

Expository writing, unlike creative writing, is *factual, functional,* and *utilitarian.* It is writing for the purpose of communicating information, ideas, or facts. When the child has something to say which he wishes to be preserved he is ready to write. He knows that when he talks it is quickly forgotten; when he writes his ideas are recorded.

Children need an environment in which writing is valued. They need a classroom organized on the premise that children need time to grow, to experience, and to develop. They also need time to write. They cannot write in an environment in which they are hurried, harassed, or pressured. Tension and good writing are antagonistic.

A developmental approach to writing will facilitate the realization of the objectives of writing with accuracy, truth, logic, organization, and correct mechanics.

Objectives of Expository Writing

To provide experiences which will stimulate children to express ideas, record facts, and compose reports.

To establish a purpose for each writing assignment.

To provide opportunity to write on a variety of topics and use a variety of forms of literary expression.

To provide direct teaching of form, organization, mechanics, and correct usage in a functional setting.

To set standards of evaluation that motivate each child to become increasingly competent in improving his writing.

To help children form the habits of the writer: proofreading, re-writing, and analysis of one's own writing.

Developmental Steps in Teaching Expository Writing

Children do not enter the primary school as full-blown writers. They develop ability first to express their ideas orally. Developing skill in expository writing progresses through several steps, each of which requires motivation, guidance, and evaluation from the teacher.

1. Composing and dictating experience charts or stories to the teacher who acts as a scribe.
2. Dictating and copying messages.
3. Learning skills needed in writing through directed practice.
4. Developing independence in writing to communicate facts, ideas, and happenings.

Composing and Dictating Experience Charts or Stories

Children are eager to talk about exciting group experiences and many times wish to keep a record of the happenings. Wise teachers use this built-in motivation and plan such activities as excursions both on and off the school grounds to stimulate a writing experience. Acting as a scribe, the teacher elicits from the children a group composition which includes the main points of interest, the exciting adventure, and the culminating point of the experience.

Children learn to organize ideas, develop interest, and record their impressions. The teacher encourages them by accepting their statements, approving their expression of ideas instead of putting words into their mouths. He asks thought-provoking questions, as well as questions which elicit recall. Thus through this medium he stimulates thinking, encourages recall, and motivates expression of children's ideas.

Dictating and Copying

As soon as the children have the necessary handwriting skills for copying from the script on the chalkboard or newsprint, the teacher can begin helping them in written expressions by eliciting from them expressions such as "Happy Birthday", "No School Thursday", "Home and School Wednesday", "To Mother".

Until their handwriting skills approach their linguistic skills the teacher continues to be the scribe. He helps them organize their ideas which he writes on the chalkboard for them to copy. Thus, in a functional, meaningful setting children learn to organize ideas, express them clearly, logically, and fluently.

Directed Practice

As the children participate in writing messages they begin to see the need to learn the mechanics of composition. When this need becomes evident the teacher calls attention to such items as placement and capitalization of the title, capitalization at beginning of sentences and proper names, punctuation, margins, and spelling of difficult words.

Mechanics are important in factual writing for this type of writing is written primarily for someone else to read. Some children pick up the needed skills earlier than others because of their developmental readiness, interest, and special concerns. Practice must be geared to the needs of the children as well as the abilities of individual children to benefit from direct teaching and directed practice.

Independence in Writing

Children vary, too, in the time required to become independent in writing. Some teachers respond to the child's desire to move ahead in writing independently by using such techniques as the following:

The unfinished story. The unfinished story is developed cooperatively by the group, following a group experience such as a trip to the fire station or a farm. It is written on the chalkboard by the teacher. The end of the story is left for each child to write in terms of his own reaction to the experience.

An unfinished letter. A letter is started by the class and written on the chalkboard by the teacher. The last part is left unfinished for the individual response of each child.

Writing captions. Children enjoy writing titles for pictures on the bulletin boards, and for movies that they create from their favourite stories. Experience in writing captions teaches children to be brief, provocative, and relevant.

Illustrating a process. (A series of pictures which describes a process).

The teacher asks the children to fold a large sheet of paper into six or eight sections—which becomes the frame for each picture the children create. They write captions and the description of the process at the bottom of each picture. Experience in awareness of the need of the exact sequence in a particular process is gained through this technique.

Activities for Expository Writing

Many meaningful activities for purposeful, factual writing, as well as for developing skill in written usage based on correct oral usage, must be provided if the children are to be motivated to sharpen the tools for writing. The following activities challenge children to communicate effectively through written expression, and at the same time encourage development of the mechanics of writing and the level of language usage.

Group Activities
Composing experience charts and cumulative stories
Writing captions for movies and illustrated stories
Writing letters, invitations, and thank-you notes
Keeping a record of daily plans, weather, etc.

Formulating problems for a unit of work in social studies
Planning and listing questions to be answered during an excursion
Listing names of characters and scenes in dramatizations
Listing room duties, committee assignments, books read
Outlining plans for a party, games to be played, rules for the games
Composing new articles, summaries, and book reports

Individual Activities
Writing captions, and labels
Writing messages on gift cards
Observing and recording daily temperatures
Writing daily news items
Keeping records of library reading
Explaining arithmetic games
Framing questions for interviewing people: the nurse, custodian, policeman, fireman, fire chief, librarian, postman, the inspector, student teacher
Keeping a personal spelling list
Making a picture dictionary
Writing descriptions based on incidents in the social studies or other reading materials
Writing experiments in science

Group and Individual Practice in the Mechanics of Writing
Using correct manuscript form, correct margins, heading papers according to plan
Capitalizing the names of people, the school, first word of a sentence, "I", names of months, days, holidays, titles of stories, poems, pictures, etc.
Capitalizing names of towns, countries, provinces, streets
Capitalizing Dr., Mr., Mrs., Miss

Using Correct Punctuation
Teachers should help children become skillful in using
    Period at the end of sentence, initial, or abbreviation
    Question mark in interrogative questions
    Apostrophe in single contractions, in possessive case
    Quotation marks at the beginning and ending of the direct words of others in the stories they write
    Exclamation point at the end of a sentence that has strong feeling

Correct Usage
    The school must take responsibility for helping a child understand levels of usage. Appropriateness is the criterion for using specific levels of usage. In the primary grades children will learn to use correctly such forms as: saw, seen; did, done; went, gone; come, came; ran, run; eat, ate; wasn't, weren't; has,

have; hasn't, haven't through an *oral* approach—*not* through filling in blanks which have little relation to the language they use in speaking.

Providing the child with a model of good English, reading literature of high quality, taking an oral approach to usage, and helping children use language appropriate to the situation will go far in improving a child's sense of fitness in written expression.

In expository writing the basic conventions of written expression are taught and practiced in terms of a functional setting, a purposeful activity, and individual readiness for the activity.

EXPOSITORY WRITING IN THE INTERMEDIATE GRADES

Expository writing in the intermediate grades broadens both in scope and purpose. Children are eager at this period to preserve the fruits of their labour in written expressions. They are becoming more aware of the need for critical thinking, organization of ideas, correct sentence structure, clearer diction, improved style, and a wider variety of types of writing experiences. They anticipate new challenges and enriched experiences. Teachers should capitalize on this attitude, their growing maturity, and broadened experiential background by providing many varied and challenging experiences in writing. A broad curriculum will give many opportunities to develop writing skills. Some activities which challenge their interests and demand improved writing skills are writing social and business letters, book reviews, news items, feature stories, and editorials.

Letter Writing

Letter writing can be a challenging adventure or a dull routine chore. If children are taught that letter writing is a natural mode of expression which involves such elements as: writing in a conversational style, planning the organizational pattern, using vivid description and imagery, including news which will interest the reader, and observing conventional forms, they find it exciting. Applegate attests to the importance of letter writing: "An effective letter can get you a job; a weak letter can lose you a job. A good letter can make you a friend; an angry thoughtless letter can lose you a friend. A letter that has kept the other fellow in mind can straighten out misunderstandings; a letter you write when you see only your side of a question can plunge two people deeper into misunderstanding."[1]

Since letter writing is an activity that will continue throughout the life of the average individual, learning to write them in such a way that they give pleasure to the reader as well as the writer is an achievement worthy of time and space in the language arts curriculum. Artistry in letter writing goes beyond stating the facts—reporting the news; it recreates in words, pictures, and actions what the writer experienced.

A couplet which wisely suggests how to start a letter contains more truth than poetry:

> Don't begin your letter with an apology—
> It will do no good, and it's bad psychology.

In letter writing the student should understand the conventional forms of a letter and the function each serves. Social letters are written in an informal conversational style about things of mutual interest to the writer and reader. Business letters are more formal. Precise information should be given. The letter should be concise, legible, and brief. The value of learning to write, and the importance of writing such letters as thank you notes, congratulations, and invitations should be impressed upon all students. The written word of appreciation is even more rare than the spoken word—and valued more because of its rarity.

Writing letters to pen pals in other parts of the world has become an integral part of social studies as well as the language arts program in many schools and has led to greater understanding of other cultures and people.

Reporting Information

In the intermediate grades the student has many more demands for reporting information. Among these are: writing summaries of books, speeches, articles, motion pictures, television, or radio programs; summarizing discussions carried on in student councils, class or club meetings; writing research reports based on interviews, wider reading on specific topics, personal experiences. The student should follow the suggestions for organizing such information in much the same manner he would organize it to report orally to the group.

News Writing

News writing is one of the most challenging activities which motivate writing in the elementary school. Children become so intrigued with collecting and reporting news in the school newspaper that they have been known to publish a weekly newspaper in the summer holiday to "keep their hand in" as it were until school opens again. Applegate gives ten reasons for a school to publish a newspaper:[2]

1. Appeals to all children, whether they are imaginative or not
2. Provides all the children in the classroom with a job
3. Is live (not book) language work
4. Makes children feel important
5. Builds school spirit
6. Interprets the school to the community and the community to the school
7. Gives purpose to language classes
8. Tends to improve spelling
9. Gives a variety of writing experience
10. Is "Democracy in action"

From the child's point of view, publishing a newspaper is fun. From the teacher's point of view it is work. However, it is an excellent motivating device for language arts, and an effective way of helping children learn to work together, to set standards, to take responsibility, and to write for a purpose.

The student editor of one elementary school paper gave this list of suggestions to each staff writer:

News is where you find it.

News is anything that interests the reader.

News should contain answers to questions *What? where? why? when? how? who?*

Any rare happening is news.

Facts must be accurate, relevant, and unbiased.

A news story must have a *lead* line.

A feature story is a newspaper highlight, and must be unique as well as interesting.

An editorial states the opinions of the writer on a timely issue in an effort to persuade the readers to his point of view.

All copy must be on time.

Publishing a newspaper may be work, but it is fun.

Using newspapers as an avenue for teaching expository writing gives students opportunity to practice expository writing and also to examine it. The daily newspaper is one of the very best sources because it makes use of expository writing: the news report, the feature story, and the editorial. In addition it molds public opinion and forms the basis of critical analysis and evaluation of writing in the upper elementary grades.[3] A unit on newspapers and magazines is an excellent motivation for expository writing. The teacher can organize this unit around such topics and activities as: getting acquainted with newspapers, writing captions and headlines, writing a news report, writing classified advertisements, learning to write an editorial, and organizing a newspaper.

Getting acquainted with newspapers. Students should study the format of a newspaper to discover the many sections that go to make up a daily and/or Sunday newspaper. Ask the students to examine the newspaper for its daily features, the variety of topics included and the type of news which appears on page one. Provide the students with a formula for studying the questions answered by each news item: When? Who? What? How? Where? What happened? and Why? This is another way of stating the usual time, name, event, manner, place, result and cause items.

During the period of study and analysis students should have access to local newspapers as well as some of the more illustrous examples of newswriting in order to look for such characteristics as simplicity, clarity, vividness and conciseness in the writing. The students should be encouraged to study the writer's style which distinguishes his writing from that of another individual.

As soon as students are ready to move into the next unit they should be encouraged to try their hand at giving evidence of their ability to report a good news story within their realm of experience. It might be a sports event, a party, a debate, a play, a school party, or any news event of interest to the readers.

Writing a news story. A news story is a report: one that gives accurate and objective information about a specific event. Personal bias and personal reaction to the news story interfere with effective reporting. Like all good news stories there are three main divisions to consider: a headline, a lead, and a body. The headline printed in large black type is a title meant to be eye-catching. It also gives the reader a brief summary of the content of the article. Writing headlines can be exciting. Emphasis should be on clear, precise, concise, economical writing. The students should study the style used by good writers and become aware of the almost telegraphic style they adopt. Evaluation should be a part of each writing assignment whether one is engaged in writing captions, headlines, news reports or other types of news writing.

Related to news reporting are activities such as personal interviews with well known personalities in the community, visiting celebrities or government officials. The same principles apply for effective interviews which are to be printed in the newspapers as apply to carrying on successful interviews as a speech activity. The student who has learned in a speech class the type of questions to ask, the behaviour appropriate for the situation, and the organization of material will bring such knowledge to the writing assignment for the school paper.

In the discussions which follow the news reports the student has an opportunity to report an event from his viewpoint. No two students who observe the same event will have the identical experience. No two students will write it up in exactly the same manner. This is to be expected. However, the importance of accurate, objective and reliable reporting is emphasized throughout the newspaper activity. Again emphasis is placed on the importance of answering correctly such questions as Who, What, When, Where, Why and How of the happening. Guidelines for writing a news story include: (1) choosing a subject of general and personal interest, (2) presenting the most important information in the heading, (3) writing the story impartially, and (4) reporting the events accurately. That names are spelled correctly and dates and statistics are accurate, goes without saying.

Classified advertisements. Classified advertisements too, furnish motivation for expository writing. The study of advertisements in the daily paper, magazines, and weeklies, will furnish the reader with a format based on psychological motivations. As the student listens to advertisements over the television and studies the examples in the classified ad section in the papers he should become aware of the need for logical thinking as well as clear, concise and honest writing.

Writing an editorial. Editorial writing requires more sophisticated skills than the other types of writing discussed. Here the student is expected to make full use of his powers of critical thinking, reasoning, and logic in presenting his point of view on an issue of significance to the readers. Although the editorial page is not always read first, it is one of the most important parts of a newspaper and should be studied carefully by novice newspaper writers. Most editorials are written with one or more of the following purposes in mind: (1) to present certain facts and to comment on them, (2) to put forth arguments for and/or against a particular course of action, and (3) to influence public opinion. This necessitates that the writer be aware of his facts when he makes assertions. It is not simply a vehicle for "getting things off one's chest". Indeed, any opinions expressed should be based on fact. Documented evidence is important in writing an effective editorial.

Before starting out to write an editorial the students should study the format used and look for such elements in the construction of editorials as: the introduction, the body of fact, opinion, and reason which motivated the writer to address himself to the topic at hand, and a summary of the facts of the case.

In planning an assignment on editorial writing it is important to give consideration to the topic. Subjects which have vital interest to the students as well as to the community at large will evoke better writing than subjects in which students are only mildly interested. The following illustrates topics which can stimulate effective editorial writing.

1. Announcing tryouts for the spring play
2. Reading good books
3. Good behaviour in the auditorium
4. Friendliness to the new student
5. The teams in next week's hockey game
6. Honesty is the best policy
7. Consideration for minority groups
8. Integrity to stand up for one's convictions
9. School corridor rules
10. Second-rate citizenship
11. Our town needs an athletic field
12. Truancy and petty crimes are the result of lack of discipline in the home

Using the local newspaper to discover topics of vital concern to the citizenry is an avenue to bringing the composition assignment and a functional situation together in a meaningful fashion.

Before students write on topics of vital concern they should carry on research, interviews, discussion in order to produce an editorial that is characterized by the behaviour of the newspaper writer—careful thinking, accurate information, and skillful presentation of the facts and a specific point of view on an important issue.

In initial experiences it may be necessary for the teacher to provide ideas for editorial writing. Later the students will discover for themselves points of interest, areas of controversy, and comments which have within them the kernel of an editorial. An example of such a statement which provides a clue to the treatment of the material and which has been effectively used by a seventh grade class is the following:

1. Of all the sports in our physical education program, swimming is the most valuable.

   How is the word valuable used here? Why do you believe swimming is valuable in that sense?

2. Success in today's world is influenced more by whom you know than by what you know.

   Define success. In what way would it be influenced by people and by knowledge?

Organizing a newspaper. When students are becoming skilful in various types of writing which a good newspaper provides, they enjoy the experience of organizing a real newspaper. It can be set in any period of history the class decides. In conjunction with a social studies unit it might well become a newspaper of the past—thus involving much research into past history; it might, on the other hand, be set in the present scene.

Whatever the decision for the period of time, the newspaper gives excellent motivation for expository writing, and research. It also provides the embryo author, historian, or social scientist with motivation for perfecting the craftsmanship so essential in good newspaper writing.

The extent to which schools go into the publishing business varies with the situation. If the project is to be an extensive one, it will be important to select an editorial committee, a production committee, a publicity committee, and a financial committee.

As each set of sheets is rolled off the press, there must be room for them, there must be a place where they can be assembled, and finally there must be a plan for distribution of the finished product. Teachers may motivate newspaper writing with a minimum expenditure of financial means; however, they cannot motivate it without a maximum expenditure of time and energy. Those who have tried it are convinced that it is worth both the time and energy involved.

Getting acquainted with magazines. In addition to making use of newspapers as a motivation for good writing, teachers are finding magazines stimulate interest in writing as well. Some magazines published primarily for adults interest teen-agers. Others written especially for teen-agers have been popular for decades.

A magazine is a source of knowledge as well as entertainment. A good magazine will include articles by outstanding writers on topics such as people in the news, problems of concern, and sports and hobbies. Among the magazines which can be read and enjoyed by students are *Junior Scholastic, National Geographic, Nature, Popular Mechanics, Popular Science Monthly, Reader's Digest, Teen Digest.* Other magazines which are of interest are *Consumer Reports, Better Homes,* government pamphlets, *Home Handyman.*

Students can make use of such magazines in preparing research on specific topics, and will find that in gathering statistics and other supporting material for an essay, such technical, scientific, business and consumer magazines are helpful.

Other assignments related to magazine activities are the assembling of an ideal teen-age magazine from poems, articles, features, and stories of high literary quality. Another could be to select the contents of a magazine from the writings of the members of the class. There should be variety in content, quality in style, and unity within diversity.

Written Book Reports

A book report should be interesting. Unfortunately, however, too many are dull, routine, and uninspired. One purpose of a book report is to create the desire on the part of other students to read the book. Some suggestions for successful book reports are:

1. Organize the report on the development of plot
2. Organize the report on the development of characters
3. Organize the report on the use of descriptions
4. Analyze the central theme
5. Compare the protagonists
6. Write the report in the form of a letter to the author giving what was liked and what was disappointing
7. Select the most exciting episode and tell why it was chosen
8. Find recurring words that are especially significant to the story. Show how they were effective in creating mood, developing characterization or moving the story along
9. Analyze the story in terms of cause and effect
10. Compare this story to one in a similar theme by a different author

As a guide to the writing of the book report the pupils may develop a brief form which they may use as an outline in working out the report or review:

My Book Report
Title ....
Author .... Illustrator..........................
Characters essential to the development of the plot ....

....
The most exciting episode ....
The conflict ....
The resolution ....
The epilogue ....
My reaction to the story ....

The most important task of the intermediate grade teacher in teaching expository writing is that of helping children raise their sights as they establish goals and evaluate their progress toward those goals. Individual children can be motivated to:

Establish goals which are attainable but stretch their capacities
Write well when they have a clear purpose for writing
Write for pure enjoyment if there is time, encouragement, and guidance
Write clearly, logically, and intelligently if they have direct teaching
Write imaginatively, spontaneously, and vividly if they have caught the "spark"
Project themselves into their writing *if* the environment is supporting
Improve their expository writing by rewriting and proofreading

Evaluate their own expository writing

Recognize and appreciate good writing of other children, of established authors, and their own writing

It is the responsibility of the teacher to motivate each child to achieve loftier aims and more satisfying experiences in writing. In the section on speech many types of activities which stimulate oral expression were presented. These are also effective in stimulating written expression. Activities which have their origin in social situations, or situations with social implications, serve to motivate children to write.

As they develop the habits of rhetorical and mechanical skills needed in expository writing, they automatically use these competencies in their creative writing without losing the spontaneity which characterizes creative expression.

Sequence in the Intermediate and Upper Grades

In establishing a well rounded sequential program for written composition it is essential to take into consideration the findings of research which make it clear that there must be provision for recurring experiences with concepts and skills at higher levels of organization and complexity. Schools have abandoned the idea that the elementary school child should study the sentence, the junior high school child the paragraph and the senior high school student the essay. Since writing at any educational level deals with ideas beyond the sentence, the emphasis on deepening and broadening of the concept is essential.

Sequence in composition should introduce children to problems of expressing ideas in various forms. From the beginning the child must be taught to relate his ideas to the appropriate organization in terms of the purpose of writing. It is the teacher's responsibility to provide direct teaching and guided practice in writing in order that the child may grow in the efficiency with which he manipulates the form of the sentence, the paragraph and the longer composition. This is frequently planned in the course of study for the entire school.

Sequence in writing should also consider and make plans for a balance of all important aspects of writing. This is to say that attention should be centered on ideas, organization, diction, style, and usage. Avoid an *over-abundance* of time given to the mechanical problems of handwriting, spelling, and punctuation— important though these are.

If teachers are to vitalize the area of expository writing it is essential that each school agree on sharply limited areas of emphasis at each instructional level and hold students responsible for minimum essentials necessary before they are ready to attack the next level of skills.

Agreement on the scope and sequence of activities by an entire school staff assumes teachers who are knowledgable about the growth and development of children, the organization of activities, the development of needed skills, and the methods of teaching which are effective at each educational level.

Not only must there be an understanding of the broadening scope of the activities in the intermediate and upper grades; there is also a need to plan for the sequence in these writing activities. There are a number of ways in which the sequence is organized to help children develop essential skills in written composition. In the plans illustrated below scope and sequence of activities in various writing experiences common to pupils in the elementary school have been successfully used: (1) levels, (2) grades, (3) junior high.

Levels in Teaching Composition[4]

If the program is arranged by levels rather than by specific grades it enables pupils to attack the assignments and to experience suggested learning activities on the basis of their readiness for the task rather than on the basis of their grade level. Some pupils may never progress beyond the third or fourth level; others however will be ready for the kinds of writing suggested for levels five or six before they complete the elementary school. Teachers will select materials and/or assignments from the levels on the basis of needs, abilities, experiential background of the children in the class.

The sequence or "horizontal" arrangement of the program provides for development over the period of years the child spends in the intermediate and upper grades. The scope or "vertical" arrangement of the program suggests the kind of writing activities which the pupils might reasonably be expected to deal with during a specific year. "The series of writing tasks, then, should provide opportunity for the development of the Brunerian promise that the foundations of any subject may be taught to anybody at any age in some form and is therefore both spiral in its arrangement in progressively difficult assignments and sequential in the development of important writing skills."[5]

In the following chart the sequence of writing activities proceeds from simple to complex, from easy to difficult, from brief papers to longer ones, and from assignments focusing on the child's world of experience to increasingly challenging topics demanding research, critical thinking, and creative interpretation. Such a sequence of learning experiences takes into account current research in child development and language learning. It takes into consideration the child's progression from the stage of exploration and freedom during his early years, the stage of precision in his middle years of childhood, and finally into stages of generalization as he moves into adolescence.

Grade Sequence in Teaching Composition

Many schools are still structured on the basis of grade organization. In planning a sequence for such organization the staff as a whole meets to clarify its philosophy, define its goals, and plan activities which will be appropriate for EACH GRADE LEVEL.

In the examples on page 359ff. the teachers cooperated to make clear the relation-

Levels in Teaching Composition

KINDS OF WRITING	LEVEL ONE	LEVEL TWO	LEVEL THREE	LEVEL FOUR	LEVEL FIVE	LEVEL SIX
Simple Exposition Skills: using clear, concise, specific language; following logical order; writing directions or accounts of processes; writing clear definitions	Giving directions for a simple act or process: tying a shoe, starting an outboard motor . . .	Writing definitions of everyday words (*door, chair, pencil*) and comparing with the dictionary definition. Writing personal definitions of abstract words: *happiness, friendship, beauty* ("What ___ means to me")	Same, with more complicated topics: directions for going from a known location to an unknown; processes such as developing a film, changing a tire.	Explaining the organization and work of a club or group: Boy, Scouts, PAL, Boys' Clubs, etc.	Describing and explaining the function of a well-known activity to someone who has not had experience with it: a pep rally, a square dance, a religious festival or ceremony	Clarifying the meaning of complex abstractions (*democracy, liberalism, prejudice, integrity*) by giving many specific illustrations and exploring the diverse meanings of these terms
Narration Skills: handling of different kinds of detail; selection of detail to develop one central theme	Accounts of family or school incidents, of family trips or celebrations; narratives of personal experience or incident			Describing an incident for vivid narration; selecting details for vivid narration to convey a single theme	Describing an incident from a particular point of view; selecting details about complex event to	
Reporting Skills: using the language of fact with clarity and precision	Factual reporting of simple incidents, school trips, accounts of firsthand observations, family or school incidents. Writing reports of class meetings, keeping notes on class discussion and assignments			Reporting discussions of controversial issues in student council or committee meetings, town meetings, community groups. Factual reporting of speeches and events. Note-taking on lectures, assignments, and readings		
Description Skills: use of concrete words, selection of detail to support a single impression; accurate use of language	Brief papers describing familiar scenes, places, or persons	Descriptions emphasizing sensory impressions with concrete detail	Descriptions of place or scene to evoke mood; character sketch to emphasize a dominant trait	Longer papers of more complex descriptions: a holiday celebration, a person, a group of people in action	Description of something minutely observed: an animal, bird, flower, anthill. Technical descriptions, as of laboratory equipment, mechanisms, etc. Description of the dramatic, the violent, the unusual: an accident, a storm, a street fight, a group in a moment of crisis	
Library Reports Skills learning the techniques of summarizing, paraphrasing, and interpreting reference materials for reports; learning the differences between honest borrowing and pla-	Brief reports on the history and derivation of one word	Report on the history of a custom, a superstition, place names, or similar language investigations	Investigation of topics suggested by assignments in the study of language and literature; report on a mythological, Biblical, historical, or other reference in literature	Report on an aspect of the history of the language or of a point in changing usage	Using reference materials to gather and organize a report on an investigation related to work in language: the invention of the printing press, the development of the	Biographical report on a person who made significant contribution to a development of language: Braille, Caxton, Gallaudet, Helen Keller; teachers, inventors. Bio-

KINDS OF WRITING	LEVEL ONE	LEVEL TWO	LEVEL THREE	LEVEL FOUR	LEVEL FIVE	LEVEL SIX
giarizing; gaining skill in documenting sources and mastering conventional form in footnoting and bibliography					alphabet, manuscript writing, code systems, Biblical analysis, problems in translation from a foreign language	graphical paper on the works of a single writer or group of writers: the Bronte sisters, Frost, Dickens, Emily Dickinson
Writing about Books Skills: dealing with literature from the critical and analytical point of view rather than the retelling of plot; writing honest reactions to literature; searching for author's purpose and theme; examining dominant tone, mood, symbolism	Personal reactions to characters and situations in books; agreement or disagreement with the choices or decisions characters make	Observing the steps through which a character changes or develops	Comments on the relationships between characters; observing the writer's description of place and character	Observing the conflict between forces in the piece of literature; analyzing the author's purpose; discussing the relation of the endings to the development of character and action	Discerning the writer's theme and how it is illustrated in the book; observing and analyzing stylistic characteristics	Analyzing the writer's central symbols in the book; developing thematic statements made by the author; commenting on books which illustrate a universal human plight or illuminate a major literary theme. Analysis of a literary theme developed in several readings, both fiction and non-fiction (for instance, the theme of racial injustice)
Argument and Opinion Skills: practice in supporting opinion and argument by adequate evidence, in logical thinking and writing. The audience for the early years may be the writer's classmates; later, receptive adults; lastly, he may address an unknown audience: contemporaries outside his own school, **unknown adults**	Papers on such topics as "I believe my parents (teachers, etc.) are wrong about . . .", pro or con arguments on problems of allowances, dating, chores, homework, school responsibilities or rules; letters to editors of school paper on school or teen-age problems	Arguments pro or con school requirements, policies, punishments, rules	Pros and cons of cheating, school and civic issues. Matters of school policy, changes needed, etc.	Pros and cons of personal standards and values	Argument and opinion about national or international issues; political, social, ethical, or moral issues; questions of human rights, educational goals, questions of values and beliefs. Papers should offer specific illustrations and deal with specific situations	

KINDS OF WRITING	LEVEL ONE	LEVEL TWO	LEVEL THREE	LEVEL FOUR	LEVEL FIVE	LEVEL SIX
Critical Writing and Analysis Skills: exercise in critical thinking and writing about problems increasing in complexity; analysis of mass-literary and mass-media sources to develop awareness of logical fallacies, semantic traps, propaganda techniques, and of stylistic features of literature	Practice in critical analysis of advertising appeals, TV stereotypes in family and western programs	Analysis of commonly used abstractions: *success, integrity, school spirit*	Analysis of the reality of characters in literature, credibility of motivation and dialogue, consistency of fiction or endings of drama	Analysis of newspaper editorials and mass-media materials for balance of fact and judgment; examination of such materials for validity of evidence. Analysis of a prejudice, a deeply held belief, an important value	Interpretation of a passage from literature, an aphorism, a parable, a folk saying, a well-known quotation, or a general truth. Interpretation of a poem or a short story. Critical review of a TV program, a play made from a book, or the film version of a classic	Critical analyses of some difficult poems, short stories, plays, and novels, with emphasis on theme, symbolism, structure, and style
Exercises in Style Skills: developing sensitivity to a variety of styles in literature through "trying them on" in practice. Although the student's major problem in writing is to develop a style and voice of his own, occasional attempts to write paragraphs or brief bits modeled after well-known stylists may help him develop an ear for style, and perhaps increase his own command of language. The writing of paragraphs modeled on the sentence patterns of a prose passage from literature may develop sensitivity to word order, syntactical patterns, and choice of words	Writing brief paragraphs in Madison Avenue English, sportswriters, or TV commercial language, or *Mad* magazine satire	Writing dialogue in the style of movie or TV romances, westerns, or mysteries; teen-age fiction or popular magazine romance; trying *New Yorkers* or *Timestyle*	Writing a well-known piece (a fairy tale, fable, or parable) in several styles	Attempting pieces of character description, dialogue, or action, modeled on the prose of Hemingway, Salinger, Lardner, Conrad	Attempting writing closely modeled on paragraphs from 18th, 19th, or 20th century prose masters: Johnson, Lamb, Stevenson, E.B. White, Mencken, and others (the teacher can find a wealth of examples for models)	

ship between the goals, the stimuli, and the activities which would motivate children toward the accomplishment of defined aims. For specific assignments such as are illustrated here, the committee brought together their finds on methodology, research or curriculum guides, their own ideas, experience and ingenuity in planning sequences of writing activities for an elementary school.

Sequential Composition Program[6]

Grade 4

GOAL	STIMULUS	ACTIVITY
To write a friendly letter	Date Greeting Message Closing Name	Learn and practice using the five elements of a friendly letter
To rephrase ideas found in reference books	Use material from social studies, science, *Britannica Junior, The World Book* Stress on accurate information, organization, encouragement of manipulation of sentence	Make independent selection of useful, important words and copy for use in a report Reduce a paragraph to a single sentence Summarize one to three pages in a short paragraph

To write a paragraph with a topic sentence	Personal experience
	
	Opinion
	
	Feeling
	
	Summary of textbook material for reporting
	
	Autobiographical experience
		Begin with experiences common to all, such as—
		    My birthday party was a big success.
		    Our (family, school) trip to ....
		    .... was really an adventure.
		I felt proud when........
		
		Five new words in my vocabulary are ....
		....
		We are a family of (no. in family).

To write main idea of a chapter in a book, one to three sentences	Independent r e a d i n g Material from social studies, science	Emphasize facts or opinions of author Use this skill in essay-type answers to questions

(Sequential Composition Program continued)

GOAL	STIMULUS	ACTIVITY
To write a topic outline using phrases for headings		Outlines based on social science
Grade 6		
To make a bibliography	Report on recreational reading—*English Is Our Language*	Compile lists of favorite books
	Organization or reorganization of room library	Select a theme, such as horses or heroes, and make bibliographies
		List six to eight books by author, title, place of publication, publisher, and date
		Share lists with class
		Prepare a list of books not now in school library that students wish to see purchased
To take notes from reading, listening, observing	Class or school newspaper	Interview a student, friend, or teacher, listing— Who was interviewed Date Questions and answers
	Interview of a story character	Imagine an interview with a character in a story or an imaginary character, such as— Pecos Bill Paul Revere Paul Bunyan A mermaid
	Subject matter film Television at home or school	Report on film or filmstrip, listing— Name or subject of film Main ideas
	Newspaper Magazine Story	Listen to material read by teacher and take notes

(Sequential Composition Program, continued)

GOAL	STIMULUS	ACTIVITY

	Poem
	Field trip
	Science experience
		Take notes from science experience or field trip, listing—
		    Subject or reason for trip
		    Date and place
		    Main ideas or learnings

To make a three-step outline using notes taken from observing, reading, listening	Oral report from topic outline	Use Roman numerals for topics Capital letters for sub-topics Arabic numerals for additional details
Grade 8		
To write a descriptive paragraph	Discussing not only the hastily spoken words of Philip Nolan, who stormed and said, "Damn the United States! I wish I may never hear of the United States again!" but angry words others may have uttered. (What lies behind any angry word, an angrier word, and finally the extreme explosion of anger that ends a friendship? Are people really uncontrolled? Are they pushed by anger into making extreme statements they don't really mean?) See Sandburg's poem "Primer Lesson."	Write in chronological order an incident you remember in which you spoke words in haste or in anger that you were not able to take back.
To study sentence variety through use of compound and complex sentences	Reviewing the actions of some of the children in relation to their parents.	Think about yourself in relation to your friends. Are you satisfied with the

(Sequential Composition Program, continued)

GOAL	STIMULUS	ACTIVITY
		relationship? Dissatisfied? Write a composition analyzing these relationships.
To reinforce giving reasons or opinions	Centering a discussion around discipline in the home. Asking questions such as the following: How were you brought up? How should boys and girls be punished? Rewarded?	
To reinforce the importance of specificity To reinforce the importance of order in writing	Learning how Braille was invented; the assembly line was originated; printing was invented.	Choose as a topic something you have done and can do a good job of explaining to someone else.
To analyze statements and quotations for interpretation in oral and written compositions	Sample quotations, such as— "We should pray not for lighter burdens but for stronger backs."— Theodore Roosevelt "Cutting remarks usually are made by people who aren't sharp." — Country Parson "The man who lets himself be bored is even more contemptible than the bore." — Samuel Butler	Analyze and discuss your selected quotation, supporting your thinking by example and exposition.
	Sample statements, such as— "Rhetoric may be defined as discovering the possible means of persuasion in reference to any subject whatever." — Aristotle "To influence his audience, the speaker needs	Explain your selected statement as clearly and concretely as possible.

(Sequential Composition Program, continued)

GOAL	STIMULUS	ACTIVITY
	knowledge of the world." — Cicero "There are some things which depend not on the teacher but on the learner." — Quintilian	
To study the classical rhetorical principles of invention (content), disposition (organization), exposition (style), memory (remembering, not memorizing), and pronunciation (delivery) in oral and written composition	Terms used in classical rhetoric to be defined. Examples: *invention, disposition,* and *exposition*	Define your selected term from the standpoint of classical rhetoric.
To study the classical rhetorical principles of invention (content), disposition (organization)	Classical rhetorical terms to be explained Examples: *memoria, pronunciation*	Explain your selected classical rhetorical term in the light of the modern speech course.

Junior High

Some school systems organize on the junior high school plan. During the elementary years the pupils have had much experience and practice in the physiological, psychological, and creative aspects of writing—handwriting, spelling, simple sentence structure, simple forms of exposition, brief narratives, and creative writing of poems and stories. In the junior high school years their skills in writing must keep up with their increasing needs for written expression. Minimal goals for each grade level are suggested with considerable specificity.

Grade Seven

Students should review the paragraph, both narrative and expository. This involves beginning a paragraph with an interesting, specific topic sentence. They should review the principles of topic outlining through a major division and several sub-topics. Outlining for writing makes use of the types of organization learned in the speech classes—chronological, spatial, cause and effect, and so forth.

The students will refine their writing of social and business letters. They should practice in a meaningful situation the techniques of narration and exposition by relating experiences and reacting to the world about them. Their writing should be geared to the reader and emphasis should be on real communication.

Expository writing activities should include: preparing brief reports based on reference reading; writing reports for social studies and science classes; taking notes, summarizing information, and evaluating their writing.

They should avoid the stereotyped book report which consists mainly of retelling the plot of the book. They should be taught to look at books in terms of finding something specific on which they wish to base their report. For example, they might be asked in the assignment to relate the incident most interesting to them or to give their reasons for their dislike of a particular character in the book. They might be asked why the main character decided not to influence another character, or to tell why they thought the punishment meted out to the villain was justified. The assignment should be such that it will lead to a greater interest in books, and to the development of permanent reading habits.

Grade Eight

A review of the types of composition previously taught enables the student to make the transition between grades seven and eight and to regain his former writing ability following the summer holidays.

Writing assignments should include the topic outline, the narrative and expository paragraphs. If the descriptive paragraph has not been taught, it should be introduced now. First emphasizing colour, then sound, and moving to a variety of other sensory impressions as motivations in writing, is an interesting sequence for the student. Throughout the year emphasis should be on the narrative, expository, and descriptive paragraphs. If pupils gain proficiency in writing a variety of paragraphs, they will have an excellent foundation for writing longer compositions of different kinds. Since nearly all the principles of good writing can be utilized in a paragraph, competence in writing such units is vital before they begin to write longer papers. Individual choice of a subject for writing often results in improved writing through better handling of subject matter.

Report writing. Students should continue report writing based on reading of at least two or three references and incorporating them into the report. They need practice, too, in writing book reports that go beyond the summaries of book plots. They should focus on comparison—similarities, and differences, between characters or books. Further practice in narrative, expository, and descriptive writing should emphasize developing ability not alone in synthesis of material but also in writing techniques.

Grade Nine

In order to be aware of the aims of the years following the elementary school a brief glance at the ninth grade program is in order. The year should begin with a review of the topic outline, and include a variety of paragraphs chiefly expository and descriptive, and introduce précis writing for accelerated students.

Expository paragraphs developed by example, incident, reasons, comparison, contrast.

Descriptive paragraphs developed by various sensory impressions and maintained by consistent points of view.

Writing specific and interesting topic sentences as introductions to paragraphs and writing coherent paragraphs by tightening transitions between sentences.

Practice in writing expository paragraph required in essay examination.

Expository theme of two paragraphs. Serves as a bridge between the paragraph and the longer theme.

Skill in writing an effective opening paragraph is an important prelude to competency for writing a longer paper. It must be specific and interesting, yet act as a controlling purpose or *thesis sentence* for both paragraphs. For example, "Swimming is an excellent sport because of the fun and exercise it provides", would help to give organization to the theme, with the first paragraph developing "fun" and the second "exercise". The teacher would teach the problem of connecting paragraphs with a proper transition. With the writing of a two-paragraph theme students are introduced to the problems confronting them when they write a longer theme:

Selecting and limiting a subject
Determining the purpose
Planning the paper in outline form
Phrasing an effective opening sentence
Developing paragraphs adequately
Connecting the paragraphs
Creating an effective title

Both the scope and sequence of all writing activities must take into account the varying linguistic abilities and experiential background of the students at every educational level.

THE ROLE OF THE TEACHER

The most important factor in a successful writing program is the teacher. To the extent that the teacher assumes the responsibility for implementing the goals of writing in terms of the children he teaches will they develop power in written expression. Teaching practical, functional, and utilitarian writing involves: setting the stage, putting the program into practice, providing for individual differences, and designing an effective evaluation program.

Setting the Stage.

Good writing does not come naturally to the child. He must be *taught* to write clearly, concisely, and accurately by a teacher who is knowledgeable about the characteristics of good writing, of the literary heritage of expository as well as creative writing, and who is skilled in methods of teaching writing. Such a teacher combines knowledge of children and of motivation of children in setting the stage for the writing program.

The teacher creates an environment which is linguistically oriented, in which there is time for the discussion and exploration of ideas. The children are secure in the knowledge that their best efforts are appreciated. They are motivated to master the technical skills necessary for clear writing.

Providing firsthand experiences. The more firsthand experiences available to a child the more likely he is to use these as a springboard for written expression. He uses these experiences as a basis for his expository writing.

Developing background for writing through literature. In the initial experiences the children provide the content and the teacher provides the form. Children's firsthand experiences are limited. Providing them with vivid, well-written literature gives them a backlog of ideas out of which to write.

Establishing purposes for expository writing. If a child is aware of the purpose for which he is writing and the audience with whom he is communicating there is a greater incentive to write with clarity, correctness, and with logical organization. In a linguistically oriented classroom there are numerous opportunities to write notices, invitations, thank-you notes, daily news reports, business and social letters. It is well that the child as well as the teacher be conversant with the objectives of the program.

Providing time and encouragement. Teachers frequently ask children to write a paper, a paragraph, an essay, or a story without giving them time to proceed logically through the steps in writing. It is better to give fewer assignments, to make fewer writing demands and give the child *time* for ideas to ripen, for thoughts to jell, for sequence to develop than to force the children into inferior work because of lack of time for preparation. Children need more than time, however. They need encouragement. Writing is a lonely job, and a word of encouragement is worth much in providing incentive for continued writing.

Putting the Program into Practice

In teaching expository writing there must be an understanding of the interrelatedness of the language arts in the composition process and the role of the teacher in directing the activities and evaluating progress. The entire staff must plan the scope and sequence of learning experiences in writing as an integral part of the language arts program. Too often teachers assign topics which require research without giving the student time for the research, the planning, the discussion necessary before he is ready to approach the writing problem. In an effective program writing is an integral part of the student's language arts curriculum and he is given time to plan and prepare for his assignments.

The process of writing may be viewed as a design consisting of six phases in which a teacher and the students work cooperatively toward the finished product.

A design for the composition process. To avoid the too common frustration resulting from teaching expository writing it is evident that there is a need for a practical, basic, effective plan for the teacher. One such plan involves six phases: (1) thinking, discussing, and reading; (2) planning the writing; (3) writing the first draft; (4) proofreading, evaluating, and revising; (5) direct teaching of the needed language skills; (6) sharing the final copy.

This plan is applicable at all educational levels. It integrates all the language arts. In this design the composition process is the culmination of various language skills. A writing program based on such a design makes it possible for children to develop and grow in writing through a program which is taught systematically, sequentially, and spirally from the pre-writing experiences in the kindergarten through the elementary, junior, and senior high school. This process is basic to all forms of expository writing since it involves gaining ideas through thinking, discussing, and reading; organizing ideas in a manner appropriate to the material; writing the first draft; evaluating and rewriting; and finally sharing. The direct teaching of the skills of organization, usage, sentence construction, punctuation, vocabulary development, spelling, and handwriting will be determined on the basis of immediate needs. Skills appropriate for each grade level are contained in the curriculum guides and/or the basic language arts textbook series which a particular school system uses.

"The pedagogical truth about instruction in writing lies somewhere between twentieth-century emphasis on the joy of learning and the classical emphasis on disciplined thought and precise expression. On that middle ground the teacher of composition takes his stand."[7]

The following account of a series of lessons based on one assignment planned to help children develop writing skills using this design involves all aspects of the language arts program.

PHASE I   THINKING, DISCUSSING, AND READING
The teacher introduced the children to the assignment: "Select your favourite fictional character such as Tom Sawyer, Caddie Woodlawn, Cinderella, Alice in Wonderland, Casey at the Bat or one of the characters from *Aesop's Fables* and write a description of the locale of the story." A brief discussion of favourite characters followed. The characteristics of fictional characters and the impact of environment on character were discussed prior to the reading of the story.

PHASE II   PLANNING THE WRITING
Characteristics of the characters were reviewed. The elements of the descriptive paragraph were pointed out. Punctuation was reviewed and proper page form and literary style were stressed. A number of characters that were discussed were placed on the chalkboard. Each student chose one about which to write.

PHASE III   WRITING THE FIRST DRAFT
Writing was not new to these children. In their creative writing they had worked with both characterization and description as a part of the

story. Now they brought this background to the expository writing assignment which stressed the *elements* of both characterization and description rather than the creative aspects. The teacher was not surprised to see each child go directly into the writing of the first draft.

PHASE IV PROOFREADING, EVALUATING, AND REVISING

The children proofread their essays, and those who were satisfied with the result read them to the class. After each was read, the boys and girls told what they liked about it and where they thought improvements could be made. Revision was the next step. This consisted of revision of content, sequence, expression, etc. Next, they made corrections dealing with mechanics through the use of a directed, step-by-step look at the proofreading chart. They used symbols to indicate mechanical errors to be dealt with. The final draft was written from the corrected draft and turned in to the teacher. She had an opportunity to give help to eight students during this one writing period. More conferences were scheduled with other students at a later date.

PHASE V DIRECT TEACHING OF NEEDED LANGUAGE SKILLS

This phase of the composition process involves teaching thoroughly some of the essential language skills. These were selected from those which the pupils were having difficulty with in their compositions. This lesson emphasized the use of descriptive, colourful adjectives. The children were shown the importance of adjectives in effective writing. An essay involving description was read to the class and the children were asked to identify adjectives. Children discussed colourful adjectives in relation to the five senses. They suggested words in describing nouns the teacher had written on the board. Then they wrote sentences using colourful language. Several children read what they wrote:

> the crisp salad on the table
> freshly washed air
> the glowing pallet of Pinnochio's master
> thunderous pounding of the surf
> glossy-smooth sunset color of grapefruit
> pigeon-toed woman
> virgin eyes of the morning sun
> unseasoned potatoes

Other children were asked to portray in pantomine the adjective modifying the noun being discussed. The remainder of the class attempted to guess what was being "described" in pantomine.

PHASE VI SHARING THE FINAL COPY

When the children had completed the final rewrite incorporating the language skills they accumulated during the direct teaching and the writing conferences, they were given a period in which to share. Sometimes the author read his own, sometimes the teacher read it for him. The compositions were filed in individual pupil folders and the class was ready to begin another basic, six-phase composition process.

Note the comparison with the phases of the creative process in creative writing:

cognition, conception, combustion, consumation, and communication—the five phase process in which children move from an awareness of the *need* to *communication* or sharing the product. Direct teaching of the language skills in the expository writing carries over into the creative writing which children do as they gain mastery of the skills and techniques of the craft of writing.

Making assignments. In an effective writing program making assignments is a challenging, creative task—not a dull, dreary chore. Too many teachers rely on prepared lists of topics without consideration of the interests, abilities, and needs of the students. When the children are involved in selecting their own topics the literary quality of the writing improves.

Children will write about almost everything under the sun and one of the stimulating techniques in planning topics for writing assignments is that of having them think up possible topics for each letter of the alphabet. The following list resulted from a brainstorming session:

Allowances: How do you spend your allowance?

Books: Write about a character from a book you have recently read.

Brainstorming: Define brainstorming and tell how you could demonstrate it to your classmates.

Colours: What is your favorite colour? Why?

Dinosaurs: Write an essay about the types of dinosaurs and their demise.

Enemies: Who do you regard as the enemies of man?

Friends: Describe your best friend.

Games: Explain the rules of your favourite game.

Heroes: Describe your hero.

Island: Write a paragraph about the island you would like to visit.

Jobs: What jobs do you do around the house? What do you like best about them? Least?

Knowledge: Which subject do you like best? Why?

Lost and Found: Relate your experience with a treasure you lost and found.

Music: What is your favourite type of music? Why?

Nature: What outdoor sport do you most enjoy?

Opera: Describe a night at the opera.

People: Do you believe people are funny? If so, why?

Quotations: Select a favourite quotation and write a paragraph explaining what it means to you.

Radio: Write a script for a radio sports announcer announcing the most exciting play in a hockey tournament.

Sentence: "As the sentence was pronounced the prisoner fainted." Use this as a sentence starter.

Titles: My First Day in a New School, Halloween, A Bout with the Measles, It Happened Only Yesterday, The Day at the Circus, The Hardest Problem I Have.

Universe: If you could go anywhere in the universe where would you go, how would you travel, and whom would you take along?

Vacation: The most exciting incident in my vacation.

Winter: Describe the most memorable scene on a winter's day.

X-Ray: Write a science fiction story about an X-Ray that can see into the minds of people.

Yarn: Tell the biggest yarn you have heard.

Zoo: Tell about your most interesting day at the zoo.

Guiding Principles in Expository Writing Assignments

The assignments must be difficult enough to make the student reach higher than he thought he could and stimulating enough to make him *want* to write. Haphazard assignments, flung out as the bell rings, are an invitation to false and superficial response. Making good assignments in writing is an art.

A good assignment evokes the best from the writer and gives the teacher the best chance to be helpful. It asks for nothing that the teacher cannot, with effort, understand well enough to criticize intelligently, both in form and in content. The vacuous subject, "What I did on my summer vacation," fails because the poorest student learns little from treating it, and the best finds in it no stretch for the mind.

A good assignment aids learning and requires a response that is the product of discovery. The lackluster writer is primarily one who has not discovered anything worth saying. The assignment therefore must touch the outer edge of the student's knowledge and incite him to go further, and it must guarantee that going further will give him the chance of discovering something he did not know before.

To provide that invitation and guarantee that discovery, *a good assignment furnishes data to start from.* "Let us assume. . . ." it begins; or "Assuming the following things to be true, write. . . ." It may set conflicting data, such as "A penny saved is a penny earned" and "Penny wise, pound foolish".

A good assignment may take the form of, or be constructable into, a proposition. The conversion of a theme "topic" into a proposition is helpful because it gives students something definite to work against. "The view from my window" has the virtue of inviting invention but the serious fault of giving the writer nothing to control his attention.

Translated into propositional form: "That the view from my window makes me dread (or welcome) getting up in the morning"—the same topic suggests a focus and even a tone for the writer to exploit.

A good assignment limits either form or content or both. By limitation the teacher reduces the choices that a writer must make. He stakes out the limits within which the writer may exercise his freedom and thus makes it possible for him to compare results. When he reads the papers he will be sure to consider not only the satisfactoriness with which the limited element is managed but the ingenuity the student has shown in managing what was left free.

Wherever feasible, a good assignment will stipulate the audience to be ad-

dressed. To inculcate the habit of considering audience, the teacher may vary the stipulations and begin with fairly simple exercises. "Write a letter to the governor arguing that. . . .", "Write a petition to the student council requesting that. . . .", "Write an essay on the proposition that . . . for submission to *Harpers'*, *The Reader's Digest, Atlantic Monthly, Field and Stream*."

As his sense of audience is sharpened, as the matter of appropriate style and content becomes clear to him, the student should be more and more frequently expected to define his own audience, and eventually to define it not in so many words, but by tone and content alone.

Assignments should vary in kind. The Commission holds that there is no sacred pattern of progression, from description through narration to argument, for instance, nor any from matters of daily living to outpourings of the heart or ruminations of the spirit. The précis, the summary, the parody, the imitation of a master are all valuable exercises. The expository essay should be the staple of the student's education . . . it allows the best definition of problems and permits the most helpful exercise of informed criticism by the teacher; it provides the best classroom exercise because its discipline is the best understood.[8]

Developing an assignment. All good writing starts with an idea. Although words are the units of the idea, one seldom thinks in terms of individual words or sentences. These are merely the media through which ideas are expressed. The thought unit of the basic idea (the paragraph) is the key to good writing. Once the idea is down on paper it may be necessary to search for a more precise word, a more expressive sentence, or a more coherent or dynamic structure. Getting the idea down is imperative. If, however, the teacher's first concern is with words and structure the idea may never take shape.

One profitable way to approach the teaching of expository writing is to consider the component structure of prose—the essay, the paragraph, the sentence, the word—as these are shaped and controlled by the varying demands of the four elements of the writer, subject, purpose, and audience. Such an approach might conceivably "take off" with reading and analyzing selections of expository prose—usually complete essays rather than isolated passages.

Such analysis will point up the fact that good writing does not come from the mechanical application of rules but rather as a result of a series of choices involving the demands of the writer, subject, purpose, and audience. As the student experiences the writing of others he is required to pay particular attention to the ways in which organization is determined by the writer's purpose, his acquaintance with his subject, and his awareness of the audience for whom he is writing.

The student who has a background in composing speeches throughout the elementary grades finds the problem of organization in writing to be negligible. If he has had practice in organizing his thoughts into logical oral expression he will discover that the principles of rhetoric are equally applicable to written expression.

Techniques for teaching students to write paragraphs effectively include *analysis of paragraphs* written by professional authors of the daily paper and weekly journals in addition to those by great writers of the past. In studying and analyzing this writing the students will discover that a paragraph is the rounded development of an idea; that the paragraph is effectively composed when a thought is fully or exhaustively explored; that a paragraph is more than a group of sentences loosely tossed together, that it, in fact, represents the careful, thoughtful shaping of an idea the kernel of which is expressed in the opening sentence. Through this inductive method the topic sentence is introduced, and, again by studying the paragraphs of successful writers, students can see clearly the role of the topic sentence in the development of paragraph organization. They will see that the content determines the form as it does in creative writing. *Content and form cannot be separated.* What a writer says is not really separable from the way he says it.

Among the organizational patterns for developing a paragraph are: (1) Definition, (2) specific instances, illustrations, anecdotes, (3) description, (4) comparison and contrast, (5) cause and effect, (6) need—plan (7) analogy, (8) restatement, and various combinations of these patterns.

At times it may be helpful to suggest topic sentences which will spark the idea and at the same time suggest the organizational pattern.

The following suggestions illustrate organizational design.

1. No one should have been surprised by the recent election results. (Cause and effect. Why not surprised? I was.)
2. Trying out for a school play is a grueling experience. (Specific instances, illustrations. Is it? Show me.)
3. Though on the surface they might seem to have much in common, the soldier and the sailor have vastly different responsibilities. (Comparison and/or contrast. How are their duties different or alike?)
4. The term "abstract painting" has been subjected to many nonobjective misinterpretations. (Definition. What do *you* say it is?)
5. "The quality of mercy is not strained." (Analogy. Remember how Shakespeare did it: "It droppeth as the gentle rain from heaven.")
6. Does today's student need more or less education than his parents received? (Cause and effect. Give reasons for your position.)
7. Courage and wisdom often go hand in hand. (Analogy. Definition, illustration or comparison and contrast. Get these concepts out into the open where you can deal with them.)[9]

Providing for Individual Differences

The teacher's guidance is perhaps the most essential part of the actual writing process if each child is to develop power in expressing interesting, worthwhile ideas. A child does not learn to write by being told to write. The teacher must be there to suggest as well as to encourage; to help the child try out his sentences orally; to help him discover omissions in content as well as in form; and to demonstrate acceptable punctuation, mechanics, spelling, grammar, and usage.

An analysis of children's writing, even in the primary grades, reveals a wide divergence in the expression of an idea, in organization, interest value, sentence structure, style, spelling, handwriting, capitalization, punctuation and usage. Some have already learned to write thoughtfully, clearly, concisely, critically, interestingly, legibly and creatively as well as with honesty, simplicity, and confidence. For these the process of composition is such that they can now concentrate on content and the expression of ideas. It is important that the teacher recognizes the importance of supervision and guidance when children write. The responsibility of giving needed help makes it imperative that the teacher be there to help individual children as well as groups with form, punctuation, construction, correct usage, and spelling during the writing period. Children will require varying degrees and kinds of help. Some pupils will be ready almost immediately after an assignment is given to proceed, others will need more specific motivation. Some will be finishing their work while others are just getting well under way. Some will be proofreading and others rewriting or recopying.

If the teacher observes that several children are having difficulty with the same problem—punctuation or capitalization, spelling or usage, he may give direct teaching to these pupils as a group in terms of their specific needs. At other times the teacher may use the writing conference as a means of individual guidance in writing.

The individualized reading conference is well known. Teachers are less familiar with the individualized writing conference. In such a conference the teacher assumes the role of the interested reader and comments upon the worth of the writing. He follows this by assuming the role of an editor. In this role he elicits from the child—he does not tell him—ways in which he could say better what he wanted to say. The teacher encourages the child to "speak freely about his ideas, with emphasis on *reliving the experience* which motivated the writing. The most common mistake which the novice makes in a conference of this nature is the well-meaning attempt to tell the pupil what to write."[10]

It is during the writing conference that a teacher often discovers a child's specific needs and is then able to plan direct teaching of needed skills.

EVALUATION

Expository writing is concerned with functional communication. It is utilitarian and practical. It is a service-type writing which grows out of individual and group needs. Therefore, it must be evaluated on the extent to which the writer meets certain standards of skills and abilities.

Self-Evaluation

In becoming a writer the student must take more and more responsibility for evaluating his own work *before he* presents it to be evaluated by the teacher or group. Among the specific points to be evaluated are organization, content, mechanics, and style. In helping the child gain in skill in self-evaluation the teacher should establish certain ground rules for learning to proofread and re-write before turning in a written assignment. One practical plan for this activity follows.

1. After the material for the paper is assembled the child writes a rough draft, keeping in mind the *organization* of the paper. He may use chronological order (sequence of events), cause and effect, need and plan, and so forth.
2. The child then assesses the paper for the development of the *content*.
3. He checks it for the *mechanics* (spelling, handwriting, punctuation, grammar, usage.)
4. He re-reads it to see if the *style* is appropriate for the purpose.
5. Following this, the final draft is written and presented to the teacher or the group for evaluation. This last draft is carefully written in terms of organization, content, mechanics, and style.

Children gain skill in writing not only through self-evaluation, but also through group evaluation. The teacher selects papers which illustrate not only common problems but also successful handling of the specific points which have been under consideration. By using an overhead projector it is possible for the teacher to analyze for the class content, good points, faults, ambiguity, incompleteness, and improvement.

As the child progresses through the elementary school the objectives of writing are broadened and in turn the expectations of the quality of the writing are heightened. Children who have been schooled in the importance of being precise with the use of facts, logical in drawing conclusions, and skilled in organization of ideas in both speech and written language will follow the tradition of good writers: clarity, brevity, simplicity, care in the use of writing techniques and conventions.

Expository writing for the upper elementary and junior high school pupils should be evaluated in terms of their growing skills, abilities, and needs.

Specific elements to be emphasized at this level include:

Invention (Content). Content is the most important facet in expository writing. As defined by Cicero, invention [content] is the effort of the writer to find out what he should say. "The concept of invention includes the entire investigative undertaking, the idea of the *status* and the modes of persuasion—logical, emotional, and ethical—in all of their complex inter-relations."[11]

Disposition (Organization). "Disposition covers the concept of arrangement, of orderly planning and movement of the whole idea."[12] This concerns the plan for the paper as a whole and the development of the specific parts—the introduction, the body and the conclusion.

Style. Style embraces, "the concept of expression in language, resulting, basically, from the choice of words and their arrangement or composition."[13]

To paraphrase Cicero, the purpose of expository writing is to prove what we maintain to be true, conciliate those who read; and that we produce in their minds whatever feeling our cause may require.

Mechanical errors. Mechanical errors still must be checked and effort should be made toward habitual usage of correct spelling, punctuation, grammar, and diction and elimination of specific problems.

Group Evaluation

British educationists have devised a plan to relieve the English teacher's load while enhancing students' critical faculties. Responsible teachers have wholeheart-edly embraced the plan, which makes use of what is called "writing workshops".

This program places more responsibility on the pupil for self-criticism and evaluation. Several times a year, the teacher allows each student to choose the composition he regards as his best up to that time. This composition is then evaluated by the teacher.

In the meantime, the other compositions he has been writing have all been read and appraised in the various writing workshops. Organizing these workshops in-volves writing partners, a board of editors and teacher involvement.

Writing partners. Each student is provided with a writing partner chosen by the student or assigned by the teacher. Each student, then, has a writing partner to proofread his or her rough draft of a composition. Each writing partner checks his partner's composition for:

1. logic,
2. punctuation,
3. paragraphing,
4. choice of words,

Other points are added as the student's knowledge of writing techniques develop.

When the first draft has been written, the writing partner suggests changes, deletions or both, and the revised copy of the composition is written. His final copy is collected and read by the class's Board of Editors.

Board of editors. It is essential in guiding the board of editors in their function to select a small group who can work well together. Some teachers choose four students and set up with them standards for evaluating the compositions written by their peers. They use the criteria established in the class for each type of writing assigned. For example in writing news reports they watch for organization and logic in writing; how, when, where, who, etc., must be answered in the article.

In working with the editors it is essential that the elements of good writing be understood by the editors. Such elements as clarity, critical thinking, diction, vivid words, specificity in choice of known, etc., should be checked.

It is important too that the editors be prepared to defend their evaluation of a composition in terms of the compositions they evaluate as best and "runnerup". As they read, they should make notes which they can use in defending the choices they made. These notes include such phrases as: good diction, good sentence structure, good lead topic sentence, excellent imagery, etc. The editors should make suggestions for improving the writing, but they should select the most important point for improvement in a particular manuscript.

It is important that the editors read well orally since they will read the selections they chose to the entire class. They should be ready to defend their choice to the members of the class in the period following the oral presentation.

A final point for improving the writing through a workshop writing project is the importance of the teacher's own writing. If the teacher writes a composition on the chalkboard while the children are writing at their desks, he can provide the children with examples of the use of punctuation, vocabulary and style in his own writing. Creative teachers inspire creative writing in children.

Self-Evaluation for the Teacher

The responsibility of the teacher for helping children to express themselves fluently and accurately in writing cannot be overemphasized. This he does by helping children develop their powers of observation. He guides them in selecting and organizing material wisely. He teaches them to compose clear and effective sentences, paragraphs, and essays. He motivates them to work toward accuracy in spelling, punctuation, capitalization, usage, and handwriting in harmony with their level of maturity. The teacher might use the following criteria for self-evaluation— Do I implement the goals of written expression by stimulating in children:

A desire to write and recognize the value of writing for clarifying one's own ideas, for sharing news with distant friends and relatives, for carrying on business or making plans at long range, for sharing, recording, and preserving facts, ideas, and experiences, and for exchanging messages and social courtesies?

Careful observation, alert listening, sincere feeling, and clear thinking as essential elements in good writing?

Skill in preplanning and critical thinking as means to selecting and ordering ideas, information, or experiences in logical or chronological order or in storytelling for the sake of suspense and interest?

Skills in letter writing for practical purposes with attention to content, form, and manner of expression appropriate for the intended purpose, recipient, or occasion?

Power to think clearly and logically, differentiating main from subordinate ideas, and mastery of the skills needed to make them clear to others?

A sense of personal integrity in writing and a willingness to stand by what they have said?

Curiosity about words, their origins, their multiple meanings, their varied forms, and their relation to reality as a means of avoiding mere verbalism or semantic misinterpretations?

An interest in the use of fresh, concrete, and pictorial words to convey ideas?

Mastery of sentence sense and a feeling for variety in sentence order together with an understanding of the capitalization and punctuation related to the sentence?

Understanding of the paragraph as an organized unit of thought and ability to use it effectively?

Facility in handwriting and accuracy in spelling, capitalization, and punctuation for making their ideas clear to others?

Appreciation of the qualities of successful writing through attention to the improvement of a few elements at a time?

A sense of responsibility for self-evaluation and proofreading organization and form before submitting it for group or teacher evaluation?[14]

CONCLUDING STATEMENT

Expository writing is that writing which the student does for a practical, utilitarian purpose. He has to write to keep a record, to transmit needed information, to communicate ideas to another person. This type of writing then, demands that the writer write with clarity, organization, correct form and mechanics and that he develop a style which is appropriate to the writing task and in harmony with his own growing needs for expression.

The child seldom writes better than he speaks. Therefore it is essential that he have much opportunity for oral language expression before he is faced with the task of putting his ideas down on paper. Writing is a process which requires the blending of the language arts of speaking as well as the act of logical thinking and the motor act of handwriting. The pupil who is effective in expository writing must be well versed in expressing his ideas logically, succinctly, and interestingly. He must have the spontaneity which comes as a result of much opportunity for creative oral expression in which his ideas flow freely and spontaneously.

The problem of organization of ideas, of selecting a topic, developing the topic, researching the topic, and using the knowledge of composition he has learned in composing a speech will be of inestimable value in expressing his ideas in written form.

The knowledge of the objectives to be attained, direct teaching by the teacher of specific skills needed in using various forms, encouragement to develop individualistic style, and the responsibility for evaluating his own writing, will tend to help the elementary school child find in expository writing an outlet for expression throughout the educational years and into adult life.

Writing, like speaking, and the other language arts is a developmental process. It takes experience, time, opportunity, practice, specific skills, and direct teaching to become a writer. It takes ideas, logically organized, clearly expressed, and interestingly composed. It takes thoughtful research, accurate observation, precise discrimination in choice of topic, form and style. It takes writing, proofreading, rewriting and polishing to develop from an embryo writer to a satisfied author.

Significant features to emerge from recent research have implications for the classroom teacher:

> . . . elementary pupils need many opportunities to grapple with their own thoughts in situations where they have someone to whom they wish to communicate successfuly. Instruction can best aid the pupil's expression when individuals or small groups with similar problems are helped to see how *their own* expression can be improved. The instruction would take the form of identifying elements which strengthen or weaken communication, increase or lower precision of thought, clarify or blur meanings. For the pupils the approach would usually be through models, meaning, and reasoning, rather than through the application of rules . . . .
>
> Instruction can yet do more than it has with *oral language*. Many pupils who lack skill in using speech will have difficulty in mastering written tradition. Competence in the spoken language appears to be a necessary base for competence in writing and reading. Modern equipment for recording and studying the spoken word makes possible marked advances in such instruction.[15]

"The discipline of correct form learned in practical writing along with spontaneity and colorful expression enjoyed in personal writing constitutes a healthy balance of learnings. Encouraging children to take pride in correctness and clarity in business-like writing along with freedom and originality in personal writing brings results: children who savor writing for its own sake."[16]

An effective program for teaching expository writing may be based on a few basic principles:

Writing Is for Reading

Unlike creative writing which may be read only by the author, expository writing is meant to be read by someone else. The purpose of mastering the form as well as the content of writing is clear to the child when he knows that what he is writing is meant to be read by an audience—his class, his friends, his family as well as his teacher.

Writing Is Based on Experience

In expository or factual writing, what the child has experienced plays an important role. Motivation for writing is higher if the child realizes that what he is writing is related to some experience he has had, or some experience he will encounter in which written expression is necessary. In all of the expository writing the child's experience will become a valuable asset as he writes.

Writing Improves Through Guided Practice

Practice in writing is essential if the writer expects to develop fluency, skill, style and control over ideas he wishes to express. Children who feel insecure about writing frequently have not had sufficient opportunity to express ideas orally and lack encouragement in creative writing. The child who begins his written composition experiences via the creative writing avenue has little fear when he is asked to write something of a practical or functional nature. The empty page is a challenge!

Meaning Supercedes Form

The child must first be concerned with saying something he has to say before he is concerned about form in writing. The primary objective in expository writing in the elementary and upper intermediate grades is the communication of ideas. In a developmental program in which the child has a purpose for writing, he will first determine what to say and *then* give his attention to the form in which it will be meaningful to the reader. Thus the need for organization, accuracy, clarity, and economy of words will serve the purpose of communicating one's ideas to another in such a way that the little black marks the writer puts on paper will have meaning for the reader.

Oral Language Activities Should Precede Writing

Written communication is enhanced when preceded by a rich background of oral activities. Opportunity to talk about what they are going to write about is essential. Few children write better than they talk. Children at all educational levels, especially the less verbal children need many speech experiences before they write. The quality of children's writing can be little different from the quality of the oral language they use. Children who are more proficient in oral language development are significantly more successful in writing.

Researchers including Strickland, Burrows and Loban recognize the significance of oral language as a prelude to written expression.

Composition in oral and written expression are closely related. The techniques of preparing a talk can be successfully used in organizing written expression. The student will discover that learning to compose using the written word is akin to composing a speech. The elements of organization, the ability to select, organize and compose using written symbols of communication are similar to the skills he is already familiar with through his experiences in speech or oral language activities.[17]

REFERENCES

1. Reprinted from *Easy in English* by Mauree Applegate. Copyright © 1960 by Harper & Row Publishers, Incorporated, New York, p. 395.
2. *Ibid.*, p. 328.
3. See Fred E. H. Schroeder, "How to Teach a Research Theme in Four Not-So-Easy Lessons," *English Journal*, 55:898—902, October, 1966.

4. From *Teaching Language, Composition, and Literature* by Mary Elizabeth Fowler. Copyright © 1965 by McGraw-Hill, Inc. Used by permission of McGraw-Hill Book Company, pp. 159-161.

5. *Ibid.*, p. 157.

6. By permission from Leonard Freyman, "Developing a Sequential Program," in Arnold Jewett and Clarence E. Bish (eds.), *Improving English Composition*, National Education Association, Washington, 1965, pp. 36-40.

7. By permission from College Entrance Examination Board, New York, *Freedom and Discipline in English: Report of the Commission on English of the College Entrance Examination Board,* 1965, p. 106.

8. *Ibid.*, pp. 93-97. (Adapted.)

9. See Edwin H. Sauer, *English in the Secondary School,* Holt, Rinehart & Winston, New York, 1961.

10. *Ibid.*, p. 130.

11. Lester Thonssen and A. Craig Baird, *Speech Criticism,* The Ronald Press Co., New York, 1948, pp. 79.

12. *Ibid.*

13. *Ibid.*

14. By permission from Alfred Grommon (ed.), *Education of Teachers of English,* Appleton-Century-Crofts, New York, 1963, pp. 36, 37. (Adapted.)

15. By permission from Walter D. Loban, "The Language of Elementary School Children," *Research Report No. 1,* National Council of Teachers of English, Champaign, 1963, p. 89.

16. Alvina T. Burrows, "Composition—Newer Approaches," *Grade Teacher*, 81:99, April, 1964.

17. See Ruth E. Reeves, *Ideas for Teaching English: Grades 7-8-9,* National Council of Teachers of English, Champaign, 1966.

12

Mastering the Tools of Language: Usage and Grammar

Language is a tapestry of culture representing the people who use it and have made it.

Priscilla Tyler

Before a student leaves the elementary school, he should have developed the ability to think clearly, and to communicate in good spoken and written English. He should also develop the habit of listening critically and appreciatively.

To achieve these goals, the elementary school should organize a continuous, well articulated program of experiences with language. Such a program must include specific instruction in using the accepted forms of the English language, and the conventions and mechanics of written expression (punctuation, capitalization spelling, and handwriting.) It should in fact, train the student to become sensitive to appropriate ways of communicating his thoughts in acceptable oral and written English.

The ability to use these tools effectively is developed primarily *not* through mechanical exercises but through practice in the understanding, expression, and communication of meanings and purposes which grow out of or arise naturally in the life of students. Through practice in meaningful situations mastery of language becomes an exciting adventure; not a set of rules which have long since lost their vitality. The teaching of usage and grammar should proceed on the basis of a well-articulated plan in which the staff agrees on a common vocabulary and the sequence of instruction in the details of grammar and usage. Students should learn to discuss the syntax of the sentence in the agreed upon vocabulary for English grammar. Instruction in the use of the English language cannot be left to chance nor incidental learning. Teaching in other areas of curriculum should reinforce direct instruction in the use of English; it cannot replace it. A detailed program to develop the student's ability to master the tools of language in order to communicate effectively must be carefully planned and carefully implemented throughout the entire elementary and secondary school program.

Whereas, in the past, emphasis has been largely on the written form of language, it is becoming apparent that proficiency in oral language should both precede and accompany instruction in written expression at every educational level. As Trim asserts, ". . . this view, that writing equals literacy, was perhaps adequate for the age of the three R's, of the railway train and the printing press and the penny-posts. It is anachronistic in the age of petrol and jet engines, telephones, radio and television, disc-and-tape-recording. There can be no doubt that the full effect of these still recent inventions has yet to be felt. I am convinced that we shall all conduct more of our business in *speech* with a wider range of partners and that writing will find a more restricted place in the ecology of language. Increasingly through speech shall we have to instruct, entertain, and persuade our fellows, and in turn receive instruction and entertainment whether to be persuaded or not."[1]

The charge to teach millions of students to think, speak, listen, read and write effectively in English is indeed a challenge. However, it is a hard fact that a democratic society depends for its very life upon the ability of each of its citizens to think clearly, to listen critically, to speak fluently, and write effectively in his native tongue. Recent research has implications for the teacher which point the way toward improving the ability of each child to master the tools of language as an instrument of thought and creative communication.

WHAT RESEARCH SAYS TO THE TEACHER

Those who are responsible for guiding children's development in the mastery of language will find the following generalizations concerning the improvement of teaching grammar, usage, handwriting, spelling, and the conventions significant. They reveal implications from linguistics and experimental research in the areas of improving communication skills which will help improve the teaching of the tools of communication.

Certain fundamental facts and conclusions drawn from recent research in language study, if applied, will influence the teaching of English in the elementary school.

Children's Language Patterns Are Set By the Time They Reach School Age

Long before the child comes to school, he has learned to sort out sounds, to control sentence patterns, to recognize and manipulate structural meaning, and in some cases to apply such linguistic devices as derivation, functional change, and analogy. "By the time a child is six years of age, and before he has begun to read, he has as good a knowledge of grammar as he has of vocabulary or pronunciation; and this is very considerable. Yet, he cannot define a sentence. He has never heard of the parts of speech. He has not met the terminology of technical grammar. But he has as thorough a knowledge of fundamentals as he has of anything."[2]

The studies of Noell,[3] Smith,[4] Strickland,[5] Loban[6] and others confirm the fact that most children beginning school have already learned to use whatever sound system, grammar, and vocabulary are characteristic of their home and neighbourhood. Strickland and Loban in recent reports indicate that vocabularies and speaking habits are almost completely set by school age and Wilson[7] points out that the child may already have discovered from his grandfather's speech that languages change and from his mother's corrections that adult's language is sometimes irrational and often arbitrary.

Children Learn and Strengthen Command of Language Through Speaking and Listening

Greatly increased time must be provided in the classroom for developing skills in listening and speaking by giving children many and varied experiences in conversation, group discussion, reporting, story telling, giving talks, and practicing the conventions of spoken English. Neglect of oral language, over-emphasis or premature emphasis on reading and writing, and/or lack of challenging oral activities interfere with the child's ability to develop language power.

Oral Language is Basis For Achievement in Other Learning Areas

A recent experimental study by Strickland[8] has provided evidence that there is a higher relationship between speaking and listening than between speaking and any other tested variable. She found too that relationships between speaking and oral reading of sixth grade pupils indicated that pupils who ranked high in oral reading interpretation used fewer short utterances than pupils who ranked low.

Burrows[9] found that children's writing activities were enhanced when preceded by a series of oral activities during which the children were encouraged to talk freely about what they are going to write.

Her research showed too that the quality of children's writing can be little better than the quality of the oral language at their command. Loban[10] provides further evidence of the correlation between proficiency in oral language and written expression.

Vocabulary Growth is Measured by Ability to Produce Contrasting Meanings

In early vocabulary studies, size of vocabulary and sentence length were emphasized. Recent research takes the length of the phonological unit as a measure rather than words the child knows. "We would now measure the child's first progress in learning to talk, not by counting the number of 'words' he is said to know, but by the degree to which he has achieved the production of and responses to the functioning contrasts by which words are identified."[11]

Appropriateness Rather than "Correctness" is the Aim in Teaching Usage

In-so-far as language exists to convey meaning, to impart feeling, to establish rapport, usages do not differ absolutely in quality or effectiveness as between "correct" and "incorrect", "bad" and "good". Teaching methods and the emotional reactions of teachers should be organized on the facts about language already known in part by the student. Language is an integral part of his cultural heritage.[12]

Children are taught today that there are functional varieties and social levels of usage. The sensitive teacher takes into account the child's self-concept and family loyalty in teaching usage.

The Way to Improvement in Usage is Through the Oral Approach

Usage or choice of words is largely dependent upon such variables as social class, experiential background, audio-lingual instruction, and what is happening at the moment. One cannot depend solely upon the study of grammar to make significant change in usage. Rather, improvement comes as a result of "tuning in" on correct forms of oral usage.[13, 14]

Pooley demonstrated this concept and showed that the common practice of attempting to improve the oral and written grammar and usage of children by having them learn rules and fill in blanks was the least possible effective approach. He discovered that language patterns in need of modification must first be practiced orally if desirable habits are to be established. He concluded that only after the individual uses language correctly at the oral level can he profit from a knowledge of the rules of good language usage.

More recent research supports this view. Loban's study is a case in point. He showed that what teachers do to motivate language experience which demands elaboration and precise thought leads to more effective usage than does undue attention to errors. It is his conviction that the teacher must motivate children's interest in the variations in language usage and conventions *before* using that interest as a springboard for lessons sensitizing pupils to the implications of such variations.[15]

Usage and Grammar Should be Taught in a Meaningful Context

Frogner in an early study found that students who approach problems of sentence structure from the standpoint of communication of ideas perform better on tests of grammar and sentence structure than those who are taught to approach such problems through grammatical definition.[16]

Kraus, in a study comparing three methods of teaching sentence structure found that the method which related the instruction to the needs of the students in terms of actual errors made in compositions achieved results in one-third the time spent on the other two methods—all using the thought approach.[17]

Strickland points out,

> Our present teaching of English grammar presents many problems. Every teacher knows that it is not only time consuming but also completely ineffective. Our language textbooks begin at the third or fourth grade to single out the "errors" for correction and to work on parts of speech and the structure of sentences. Attempts are made to simplify vocabulary by calling nouns "naming words" and

verbs "action words" which serve only to add confusion. Definitions add abstraction and further confusion. Children who talk glibly about astronauts, auxiliary rockets and planetary exploration scarcely need this kind of simplification if the terminology has usefulness to them.

Language is a major interest of children. They acquire new words and new expressions from television and a wide variety of sources. They enjoy manipulating language. Of course, all of this is done orally, as they learned their language from the beginning.[18]

Writing is Facilitated by Automatic Control of the Technical Skills

In teaching for mastery of the tools of writing it is important to consider the approaches which best achieve maximum efficiency so that handwriting, a subordinate skill, is so thoroughly mastered and unconsciously performed that it never interferes with the communication of ideas. "Legibility, ease and simplicity of writing, as well as comfort and economy of time are prime considerations in the teaching of handwriting."[19]

The Tools of Communication Must Be Considered as a Unit

Because of the complex interrelationships among grammar, usage, punctuation, and other conventions of writing, they must be considered as a unit. Punctuation should be taught in conjunction with sentence patterns. Meaning is clarified by the attention to the signals of grammar, the juncture patterns which prescribe punctuation, and by conventional forms of recording which help the reader interpret what the writer has tried to communicate.

Writing Is a Secondary Symbol System Based on the Speech Symbols

Learning in the language arts involves grasping the interrelationships of two distinct symbol systems for communication of ideas. "In societies that have writing, all normal adults have a working command of the spoken language, but only a minority have a comparable command of the written language."[20] The experience of the human race gives evidence that speech in some form is existent in every human society, but a large number function without an accepted system of writing. Speech is acquired first and largely without conscious effort, whereas the understanding of the writing system is a much later phenomena and requires extended and intensive study.

The Teacher Should be Open to Innovation in Teaching Usage and Grammar

In the absence of any one definitive grammar, it is important to study all grammars and select experimental patterns for testing in the classroom. The distinction between "traditional grammar" and linguistic grammar is beginning to blur and soon may become irrelevant. So, too, are the once sharply drawn lines between the transformational-generative position and the "old-line" linguists. "Ways are being found to incorporate certain of the newer findings into other general schemes."[21]

Therefore in teaching language skills teachers should capitalize on the children's interest and fascination with language and be on the alert for ways to utilize findings from research. Since at the present time the only safe generalization that can be made from research is that, regardless of the approach, the basis for instruction should be the language pattern of the children themselves, the teacher should make language exciting by taking into consideration the prime objective of teaching grammar, i.e., to improve the students' speaking and writing. If such an aim is facilitated by a specific approach it is not expecting too much to ask the teacher to be knowledgable about grammars, to be open-minded about trying a new approach, and to make use of the findings of research in teaching children.

The problems reported by Hogan[22] are still facing us: (1) the gap between research and theory on the one hand and school programs on the other, (2) the tendency to duplicate inferior research experiments, (3) the problems of sequence and articulation, (4) the determination of appropriate reading materials at each grade level, (5) the need for research on modern approaches to language study and their relation to ability to compose, and (6) the major issues in evaluating composition. These problems become challenges to the teacher who understands the significance of his role in the language arts.

The teacher is not the guardian of the language, protecting it from change, defending the status quo against the split infinitive and double negative. Nor can he make himself the keeper of "pure" language by legislating the forms pupils may use or forbidding them to use certain "incorrect" forms outside of the classroom. However, the question does arise, "How should I teach children in the elementary school to speak and write correctly if usage is relative and there is disagreement on what is right and wrong"?

It is the responsibility of the school in a democratic society to give each student as firm a grasp as possible of the standard spoken and written English as he is capable of attaining since command of "middle class" English is imperative for economic advancement and social status. It is the responsibility of the teacher to establish good patterns of usage through example, appropriate methods of correction when the student deviates from accepted forms, and direct instruction in the use of the language.

The teacher needs to have a clear understanding of the place of the tools of oral and written expression in the totality of the language arts curriculum in the elementary school. As a member of the staff, the teacher should be conversant with the sequence as well as the scope of language activities and the extent to which these rely on the mastery of the tools of writing and speaking for effective communication.

Fowler asserts: "The study of language stands at a new frontier. It has wide horizons; it draws on a range of materials of a vitality and richness and flexibility undreamed of in an earlier era. It emphasizes creation rather than dissection. Instead of handing the student a narrow list of prohibitions to memorize, the teacher sends him to language in use—his own and that of others—for the purpose of exploring, discovering, observing, and finally creating an infinite variety of patterns of language possible for the users of English.

In many English classrooms today, the student looks at his language not as a series of sentences in his grammar book to be diagrammed, a list of pitfalls of usage to avoid, or words to fill in the blanks of workbooks, but as a vital form of human activity. . . ."[23]

Such a concept opens new vistas for the child: his eyes are alert for the new words, the vivid phrase, the colourful image; his tongue acquires fluency that comes from rich experiences in oral language; his ear discerns differences which stem from a broad range of experiences.

Developments in language and linguistics have opened the door to a number of grammars of English representing differing points of view about language, different analyses of English, and the structure and inner workings of the language. Each has contributed something of value to the material used in today's schools.

Putting the program into practice involves an understanding of: (1) terminology of usage, (2) guidelines for teaching usage and grammar, (3) approaches to teaching grammar, and (4) promising practices in teaching grammar effectively.

TERMS OF USAGE

In order to teach usage and grammar, spoken and written, the knowledge of the terminology is essential.

Language. Language as used by the linguist refers to speech and its recorded forms. Written language is an attempt to record the stream of sound shaped by the inhabitants of a specific culture in a series of written symbols.

Grammar. Grammar is the study of the structure and function of the sentence: parts of speech; subject, verb, object, etc; case, gender, mood, voice, etc; sentence, phrase, clause; and associated matters of consonance and agreement. Exluded are the mechanics of writing and problems of usage not related to structure. Terminology varies with different approaches to the teaching of English. Pooley distinguishes grammar as an inventory of the choices open to the user of the language.[24]

Standard English. Standard English is the dialect of educated speakers, those prominent in business, and in public and cultural affairs of the community. Standard English is " . . . the English that with respect to spelling, grammar, pronunciation, and vocabulary is substantially uniform though not devoid of regional differences, that is well-established by usage in the formal and informal speech and writing of the educated, and that is widely recognized and acceptable wherever English is spoken and understood."[25]

Good English. "Good English is that form of speech which is appropriate to the purpose of the speaker, true to the language as it is, and comfortable to speaker and listener. It is the product of custom, neither cramped by rule nor freed from all restraint; it is never fixed, but changes with the organized life of the language."[26]

Usage. Usage is "the term employed to cover the full range of choices and discrimination in the use of language. Usage makes choices, expresses preferences, takes sides, creates standards. The bases upon which choices are made, preferences are expressed, sides are taken, and standards are set up is the concern of usage."[27]

In a later publication Pooley reiterates: "I am willing to stand upon this definition still. Usage is to grammar as etiquette is to behavior. Behavior simply notes what people do, etiquette sets a stamp of approval or disapproval upon actions, or sets up standards to guide actions. The specific business of usage, therefore, is to determine what choices and what discriminations are made in the use of English, and then to analyze the forces, social and psychological, which determine the choices. In practical terms, usage is the study which notes the variety of choices made in the use of English, observes the standards set up by such choices or created to influence such choices, and attempts to evaluate the validity of such standards."[28]

Usage is the way people use language. Correction thus becomes a matter of helping children become aware of and sensitive to social acceptability and appropriateness much as one teaches a boy to remove his hat in church and a little child to say "Please" and "Thank you".

Colloquial usage. "Colloquial, properly interpreted, is a label indicating a functional variety, not a level of the language, nor was the term, as used by lexicographers, ever intended as a condemnation."[29]

That teachers too frequently interpret colloquial as substandard usage is evidenced in the following:

> Even teachers of English frequently misunderstand the application of the label *colloquial* in our best dictionaries. Some confuse it with *localism* and think of the words and constructions marked "colloquial" as characteristic of a particular locality. Others feel that some stigma attaches to the label "colloquial" and would strive to avoid as incorrect (or as of a low level) all words so marked.
>
> The word Colloquial, however, as a label in a modern, scientifically edited dictionary, has no such meaning. It is used to mark those words and constructions whose range of use is primarily that of polite conversation of cultivated people, of their familiar letters and informal speech, as distinct from those words and construction which are common also in formal writing.[30]

Substandard usage. Substandard usage is used widely in certain locales and socio-economic levels. American language varies in word choice from the "middle class" to the culturally disadvantaged group in the community: "drownded; hisself." Substandard usage calls attention to the speaker's lack of education, and for this reason is the chief concern for the teacher in the program of improvement of usage.

Disputed usage. Disputed usage includes "the items of language use which are widely current, which are often heard in public speech and frequently appear in print, yet are condemned by many textbooks and are disliked by conservative teachers, editors, and other language-conscious people." Pooley continues with several examples of disputed usage:

1. *Proven* as a participle of prove. Condemned as illogical formation. Now fully acceptable.

2. *Data* as singular. "I had a hard time collecting this *data.*" Condemned in the singular because it has a latin plural. Now widely used in high level journals. Has become a singular collective noun.

3. The *reason* I came late is because I wanted to. . . . It is condemned by practically all handbooks. Yet it has a long and honorable history and is used by reputable writers today. Why condemn it?[31]

GUIDELINES FOR TEACHING USAGE

The purpose of language is effective communication. With that as the criteria the following suggestions are pertinent in teaching usage.

Stimulate the student to explore the varieties of ways in which one can express the same idea.

Find ways of expressing an idea in patterns of formal, colloquial, and substandard usage.

Lead the student to discover the varieties of levels of expression used in literature to establish a *tone* or mood.

Help the student to become sensitive to the appropriate level of usage in specific situations.

Help the student develop appreciation of the shades of language usage. In society, the well mannered person is the one who is sensitive to all aspects of a situation and behaves in a way that is appropriate to the specific situation, formal when it is appropriate, informal where it is desirable, and familiar when acceptable. English usage is exactly the same: "to say the right thing in the appropriate manner in a suitable tone of expression is the ideal for which we are striving."[32]

Teach the use of the dictionary and handbooks in mastering acceptable usage. Acceptable usage must be substituted for substandard usage as the child is motivated to change. Before a change occurs the child must see a purpose for the change. He must be motivated *before* he will make the effort.

The teacher should set an example of socially acceptable usage, and gear his teaching to the needs, abilities, and linguistic level of the students. The method of ear training in usage is more effective than merely correcting the student's written work, for the errors in written usage are the reflection of the unconsciously retained speech patterns.

Children bring to school a wide assortment of speech habits and patterns of usage. Those from home where cultured speech is an integral part of the environment, where usage errors have been corrected since infancy, will need little direct teaching. Others, less fortunate in background, bring to school patterns which do not measure up to the expectations of the school and society outside the home. The latter will need specific help in gaining control over the language and learning to substitute acceptable English for the undesirable.

The program in usage should be based on the application of two simple principles—How much social penalty does the usage item bear? How frequent is its use? Thus at any grade level or educational level the basic curriculum in usage should consist of those items which carry heaviest social penalty and are most frequent in use. It is therefore possible for a staff to make lists at each level, from observation of the spoken and written English of the children, of the items of usage most in need of instruction, and of those items which may be left untaught at that level. Although the needs of individual children will vary, the objective is to help each child to reach at least the established minimum acceptable level in spoken and written English.

Minimum Goals in Usage

A suggested developmental list of standards of minimum acceptability in usage for elementary school children follows.

1. The elimination of all baby talk and "cute" expressions.
2. The correct uses in speech and writing of *I, me, he, him, she, her, they, them.* (Exception, *it's me.*)
3. The correct uses of *is, are, was, were* with respect to number and tense.
4. The correct past tenses of common irregular verbs such as *saw, gave, took, brought, bought, stuck.*
5. Correct use of past participles of the same verbs and similar verbs after auxiliaries.
6. Elimination of the double negative: *we don't have no apples,* etc.
7. Elimination of analogical forms: *ain't, his'n, hern, ourn, theirselves,* etc.
8. Correct use of possessive pronouns: *my, mine, his, hers, theirs, ours.*
9. Mastery of the distinction between *its,* possessive pronoun, *it's, it is.*
10. Placement of *have* or its phonetic reduction to *v* before *I* and a past participle.
11. Elimination of *them* as a demonstrative pronoun.
12. Elimination of *this here* and *that there.*
13. Mastery of the use of *a* and *an* as articles.
14. Correct use of personal pronouns in compound constructions: as subject (Mary and *I*), as object (Mary and *me*), as object of preposition (to Mary and *me*).
15. The use of *we* before an appositional noun when subject; *us,* when object.
16. Correct number agreement with the phrases *there is, there are, there was, there were.*
17. Elimination of *he don't, she don't, it don't.*
18. Elimination of *learn* for *teach, leave* for *let.*
19. Elimination of pleonastic subjects: *my brother he; my mother she; that fellow he.*
20. Proper agreement in number with antecedent pronouns *one* and *anyone, everyone, each, no one.* With *everybody* and *none* some tolerance seems acceptable now.

21. The use of *who* and *whom* as reference to persons. (But note, *Who did he give it to?* is tolerated in all but very formal situations. In the latter, *To whom did he give it?* is preferable).
22. Accurate use of *said* in reporting the words of a speaker in the past.
23. Correction of *lay down* to *lie down*.
24. The distinction between *good* as adjective and *well* as adverb, e.g. He spoke *well*.
25. Elimination of *can't hardly, all the farther* (for *as far as*) and *Where is he (she, it)* at.[33]

This list of twenty-five kinds of corrections to make, constitutes a very specific standard of current English usage for today and the next few years. Some elements in it may require modification within ten years; some possibly earlier. Conspicuous by their absence are these items which were on the usage lists by which many of us were taught; which survive today in the less enlightened textbooks:

1. Any distinction between *shall* and *will*
2. Any reference to the split infinitive
3. Elimination of *like* as a conjunction
4. Objection to the phrase "different than"
5. Objection to "He is one of those boys who *is* . . ."
6. Objection to "the reason . . . is because . . ."
7. Objection to myself as a polite substitute for I as in "I understand you will meet Mrs. Jones and myself at the station."
8. Insistence upon the possessive case standing before a gerund.[34]

How Can Usage be Taught with Culturally Deprived Groups?

One of the persistent problems middle class teachers have in teaching the so-called culturally deprived child is the dilemma of teaching standard English to children whose dialect is discovered to be functioning as a primary language. The following illustration of a teacher in an elementary school in a disadvantaged area is a case in point.

> One day after class, as she was putting her hat on to leave for the day, one of her students approached her with the compliment, "That's sure a tough hat you got on."
> The teacher, who had heard enough "Hip" spoken among her charges tried the time-honored approach to correcting the boy: "Don't say tough, say pretty or nice." The boy thought about that for a moment, then concluded: "Okay, but that pretty hat sure is tough."
> That might have been the end of this particular story except that this particular teacher also gave some thought to the exchange.
> First, she realized that she had come up against a case of linguistic inversion— a social situation in which a dialect was the primary language.
> Second, and most important, the teacher recognized that by attempting to correct her student's speech in the conventional way, she had confused him about

the nature of the avowed teaching objective. Worse, she had antagonized him. To the student's mind, the teacher had been asking him, not so much to learn something, but to reject something—his primary language, the slang, the non-standard "Hip" spoken in his home, among his friends and neighbours. The result was hostility—a determination by the student to *not* learn— expressed, with just the necessary touch of humor, in the put-down phrase, ". . . that pretty hat sure is tough."

In short, this teacher had hit on a truth fundamental to the fact of language: One's primary language, because it is primary, is not to be denied lightly, for it is, in very basic ways, one's own self. Asking the disadvantaged child to suppress the language he brings to the learning situation is equivalent to demanding that he suppress his identity, and all the defenses that go with it. . . . [35]

Once this teacher was aware of the truth, she took a new approach to teaching standard English. She made a game of it, the *Dialect Game*. She asked the students to explain the meaning of a word heard frequently in their vocabulary—in *their* language. Then she proceeded to ask them how to explain "cool" in the language heard on TV.

Some of the answers she received were "calm", "casual", "collected", to which she added the more formal "nonchalant".

As a result of this new approach the students who had previously gone to sleep during English classes became interested. They became aware that they were play-ing a game—"digging the teacher's jive".

As a consequence, they increased their vocabulary and found new ways of expression in a context which did not demand rejection of their own language. In short, they were learning standard English as they might learn a foreign language, a second language. As they continued this approach to language they learned about language itself: its forms and the social role language plays. By approaching Standard English as a foreign language, they became aware of the untranslatability of much of the language *per se*. They discovered the reason for incorporating foreign phrases intact, without translation, for example *esprit de corps, coup d'etat*. They discovered, too, that many of the "Hip" words and phrases that make up their primary language have been accepted for usage in Standard English conversation. "Knowing this, they were in a position to equip themselves with a basic sense of linguistics style, which can be simply defined as the ability to choose among words and phrases according to their social appropriateness."[36]

Basic to such an approach to the student's primary language is the acceptance on the part of the teacher of the student's non-standard primary language and utilizing it as an avenue to that other languaage which, in more formal circum-stances, can produce more effective communication and gain for the student en-trance into a wider society.

Thus the teacher takes the child *as* he is, *where* he is, and *builds* on what he brings to the classroom with him. He does not *take away from* the pupil. Under such an approach the student's sense of identity grows, his self-concept grows, and his sense of language—all language—grows. This is the beginning of a love of language and its literary form.

Usage must be taught in an oral language context before the child is introduced to the study of formal grammar. It is in relation to oral language that the child is first concerned with expressing his ideas. In the daily linguistic experience the interplay of language which goes on within the school during the five hours of formal instruction is by no means as extensive or as natural as the communication which takes place on the playground or in the home. Long before the child is consciously concerned about learning the rules and regulations which are an integral part of the grammar lesson in many schools, if he is in a linguistic-oriented environment, he is becoming aware of the need to select his usage in terms of the situation and the audience.

If students are taught to speak and to write in a functional setting, if they are motivated by a real situation in which these skills are required, they have the distinct advantage of discovering generalizations instead of memorizing rules.

APPROACHES TO TEACHING GRAMMAR

Teaching grammar in today's schools offers greater challenge and greater opportunity for decision making than did the teaching of grammar in the past. Today's teacher no longer asks merely, "How shall I teach grammar?" Rather, he is confronted with such questions as: What is grammar? Which grammar shall I teach? How shall I put the grammar program into practice? What are some promising practices in teaching grammar? How shall I evaluate the effectiveness of my teaching?

The right place of formal grammar in language teaching is still debatable. The traditionalists hold that proficiency in writing or speaking can be acquired by learning a set of grammatical rules to which the language is supposed to conform, and mechanically applying these rules in writing or speaking.

On the other hand there is a growing belief that there are more effective ways of teaching language skills. The modernists use an inductive approach to grammar which gives the pupil the opportunity to formulate generalizations that are helpful to him in understanding the workings of language, and from his own writing he discovers such principles as he finds necessary to overcome the difficulties which confront him.

"Many schools have discarded the teaching of formal grammar as it used to be taught. Emphasis is being placed more and more on the love of good writing for its own sake, for what it can do to enrich and inspire the understanding of life itself. Students are encouraged to do their own writing and understand the mechanics of written language first hand rather than by vivisecting someone else's novel."[37]

Teachers who approach language with the same spirit of discovery that is used in the "new" science and mathematics will discover that both they and their students will find that study of language is exciting, exhilarating, and enlightening. As in the "new math" the teaching of language today requires the mastery of new terms, concepts, and operations.

TERMS USED IN THE STUDY OF GRAMMAR

Grammar. Grammar is the study of the structure of the language. It involves the study of the sentence—what it consists of, how it patterns for clear communication, and what signals are necessary to convey intended meanings. Grammar is the behaviour, not the etiquette, of the language. It includes three main branches: morphology, syntax, and phonology.

Morphology. Morphology is the study and description of the formation of words. It includes inflection, derivation, and compounding. For example, the addition of *s* to form the plural of most English nouns or the *ed* suffix showing past tense of verbs.

Morpheme. A morpheme is the smallest portion of an utterance that expresses meaning.

Syntax. Syntax is a study of word order in meaningful communication, and ways in which words are arranged to form sentences. This involves the study of the variety of sentence structure, modification and subordination of words and phrases, clauses and independent elements.

Phonology. Phonology is the study of the sound system of a language, of the stresses, pauses, intonations and the melody of speech.

Phonetics. Phonetics is the systematic study of the sounds of a language.

Phoneme. A phoneme is a group of similar sounds distinctively different from any other group of sounds. For example, the "t" sound in *not, button,* and *tap* varies in each word, but is recognized as a "t" sound.

Allophone. The allophone is a submember of a phoneme. It is the term applied to the variations such as the variations in the utterance of the "t" sound in the example above.

Grapheme. A grapheme is a single letter or combination of letters that represent a phoneme, e.g., the grapheme "gh" of *hiccough* represents the phoneme (sound) "p". It could be the "d" in the word *day* or the "ay" which represents the phoneme (sound) "a".

The purpose of the study of grammar is improved communication by a careful consideration of the ways in which ideas may be structured within a sentence. Thus evaluation becomes the measurement for testing the ability to structure ideas into a sentence in a way which improves communication of ideas. To teach coordination, subordination, order, and modification requires some simple machinery—the basic sentence elements: subject, verb, modifier, connective, phrase, subordinate clause, and main clause.

Traditional grammar. The traditional grammar (often called formal grammar) is well known to English teachers. This grammar is an analysis of the language according to classifications and definitions based on Latin grammar and formulated in the Middle Ages and the Renaissance to meet the needs of scholars concerned with the study of classical languages rather than of the vernacular. Largely *prescriptive,* traditional grammar presents rules and regulations as to the correct way words should be used. The new grammars in contrast are descriptive; they formulate generalizations about language on the basis of its use and describe the way it works.

Structural grammar. Structural grammar analyzes the living spoken language to ascertain the basic structure of English sentences, the stress and intonation patterns which signal meaning, and the words which operate as signals to indicate parts of speech.

Transformational or generative grammar. Transformational or generative grammar, as it is often called, has been claimed to be the most significant development in linguistics in the past thirty years. Generative grammarians assert that if preschool children of limited intelligence can generate thousands of new sentences based on the early sentence structures they have learned, there must be an underlying process which can be explained and taught. Basically, transformational grammar makes clear those relationships that the native speaker of a language perceives intuitively.

Roberts identifies elements of transformational grammar thus: *"Kernel sentences* are the basic, elementary sentences of the language, the stuff from which all else is made. *Transforms* are the 'all else' structures drawn from the kernel to produce all the complications of English sentences."[38]

STRUCTURAL GRAMMAR

In order to understand one new approach to grammar the teacher should be familiar with the basic concepts inherent in the term "structural grammar". Lefevre conceives of the English language as consisting of four subdivisions on which he bases his program of structural grammar. "Intonation, sentence patterns, structure words and word form change. Each has its place in understanding the system by means of which we communicate with one another through vocal symbols."[39]

1. *Intonation.* Intonation means the speech rhythms and melodies of native speech; a "foreign" intonation marks the foreigner: we recognize his as non-native more by his intonation patterns than by his smaller speech sounds. Intonation gives the over-all configuration to the spoken sentence; it is very important in the "silent" language related processes of writing and reading.

The elements of intonation are levels of pitch, degrees of stress (loudness, or accent), and junctures (or pauses). These three elements pattern together in overall intonation patterns.

2. *Sentence Patterns.* The typical English sentence pattern has a subject (Noun part), a verb (Verb part), and a complement (Completer). Four important sentence patterns exist for making statements, the "declarative sentences" of school grammar. These patterns may be infinitely expanded and varied by inversion, by

substitutions within patterns, and by pattern transformation, such as passive constructions. Other common patterns are questions, requests, and commands.

3. *Structure Words*. Structure words (function words) primarily show grammatical and syntactical relationships within sentence patterns. The most important structure words are noun markers, verb markers, clause markers, phrase markers, and question markers.

4. *Word-form Changes*. Word form changes include the *inflectional endings* of the four word classes, or parts of speech (noun, including the forms of pronouns; verb, adjective, and adverb); they also include the *derivational prefixes* and *suffixes* that modify the meanings of words or convert words from one form class to another. (For example, the *y* suffix converts the noun *steel* to the adjective *steely*.) [40]

Intonation

The teacher can make use of knowledge of intonation in teaching children to read by having the children read silently to get the meaning before reading aloud. They also should read their own writing aloud, listening for normal intonation patterns, sentence patterns, word order, grouping, phrasing, general movement, and rhythm. The oral approach to teaching punctuation is one of the by-products of a knowledge of intonation. The writer may use intonation as a rough guide in punctuating. Since written communication is not reinforced by rhythms of sounds, punctuation serves to provide the reader with clues to syntactical relationships.

Sentence Patterns

Formulas can be presented to pupils which challenge them to go beyond the common categories of subject, predicate, and complements. For example NVN (Man bites dog), the most common pattern in English. *N* stands for *Noun part, V* stands for *Verb part,* and the second *N* for *Noun Completer.* Such sentence parts may be expanded almost indefinitely.

Although there is lack of agreement among linguists as to the number of sentence patterns which can be called "basic", the concept that certain structures or patterns recur with great frequency and that innumerable sentences can be built on these patterns is inherent in both structural and transformational grammars.

Students who are introduced to the form classes and the basic function words, can go on to construct a rich variety of sentence structures on these models.

The most commonly used patterns appear below.

Pattern 1. The first, irreducible sentence pattern is that of NV (noun-verb or subject-predicate): *children run, birds fly, dogs bark.*

Any number of verbs may be substituted for *run*

Children *play*
Children *laugh*
Children *cry*

Any number of nouns may be substituted for *children*

    Men run

    People run

    Horses run

Verb phrases may be substituted for *run*

    Children *are running*

    Children *have been running*

    Children *might have been running*

This sentence pattern (NV) is the simplest structure of the English language.

    Pattern 2. The formula for pattern 2 is NVN (noun-verb-noun complement).

    N   V   N

    Horses eat hay

    Cows eat hay

    Children eat candy

    Men build houses

    Women buy hats

    Jane studies violin

Verb forms (verbals) may be substituted for either noun in the pattern. For example, in the sentence *"Walking* builds health" you may substitute *"To exercise* builds strength".

Subject-predicate word-groups (subordinate clauses) may be substituted for the noun complement in the pattern N-V-N. For example:

    Children eat ice-cream.

    N   V   N

    Children eat *what they like.*

    Dogs chew bones.

    N   V   N

    Dogs chew *whatever they can find.*

It is also possible to substitute a subject-predicate word-group for the subject noun in this pattern.

    Judy   helps mother.

    N   V   N

What you are doing helps mother.

The third and fourth most often used patterns in our language involve linking verbs of two types: noun-linking verb-adjective and noun-linking verb-noun.

    Pattern 3. The formula for pattern 3 is N LV Adj.

    N LV Adj

    Gary is studious.

    Boys are rough.

    Cities are crowded.

The linking verbs in English are verbs which couple the subject and the complement. Among the most frequently used linking verbs are forms of *to be, become, seem, look, taste, smell, feel.*

Pattern 4. The formula for pattern 4 is N LV N.

N	LV	N
Miss Smith	is my	teacher (friend, neighbour, counselor).
The building	is a	college (church, store, factory, office).
My cat	is a	Siamese (Persian, show cat).

Pattern 5. The formula for pattern 5 is N V N (D)N. This pattern uses a transitive verb and two objects, the first indirect and the second direct:

(D)N	V	N	(D)N
Mother	gave	me	a bicycle.
Flowers	give	me	hay fever.
He	brought	Jim	the telegram.

Once children master these basic patterns they are ready for practice in expanding sentence patterns through such techniques as compounding, modification, subordination, or *headword*. [The term used by linguists to denote nuclei or "that which is modified".] Roberts uses the term *S group* to denote subordinate clauses: Conlin uses the term *headword*.

Expanding Sentences. Sentences may be expanded through the addition of words and groups of words which add to but do not change, the basic structure of the sentence pattern. This is accomplished through compounding, modification and subordination.

1. Compounding. The sentence may be compounded by compounding subjects, predicates, and/or objects. *Birds fly.* . . Birds and bees fly . . . Birds, bees, and mosquitos fly . . . *Birds fly* . . . Birds fly and hop . . . Birds fly, hop, and sing. *John plays golf* . . . John plays golf and tennis . . . John plays golf, tennis and hockey . . . *John plays golf, tennis and hockey; reads poetry and drama; and enjoys swimming and riding.* Whole sentences may also be compounded. *John plays golf and tennis, but Henry studies violin, organ, and piano.*

2. Modification. Another method of expansion is modification. Here the student can begin expanding patterns by adding word modifiers: adjectives, adverbs, determiners, and intensifiers, and proceed to add prepositional phrases, participial phrases, and dependent clauses. Experimentation should begin with simple patterns at first.

The three pretty girls were walking home.

John suddenly saw the *three pretty girls.*

He discovered that *three pretty girls* were on the bus.

After students have experimented with simple sentence patterns they may proceed to more complicated methods of sentence expansion such as the following.

3. Subordination. Among the structures frequently modifying noun headwords are relative clauses beginning with *who, which,* or *that.* Adding clause modifiers after the noun headword offers innumerable possibilities for expansion.

The boy   *who was in my class*   went to Europe.

The examination *which was administered in the gymnasium* was difficult.

Children in the elementary school find enjoyment as well as challenge in the realization that sentences can be made to express thoughts with increasing clarity and interest by the addition of movables of a variety of sorts. For example, that simple subject, predicate sequence, "Tom came", can be expanded by the addition of movables that tell where, when, why, how and for what purpose, as in the following examples: "Tom came home yesterday to visit his parents". "Yesterday, because it was their anniversary, Tom came home to visit his parents and surprise them with the gift of a new car." Thus children learn how to weave longer sentences, how to blend ideas together by starting with a simple formula and expanding it. They soon recognize that a simple sentence pattern can develop into well-constructed longer sentences. They find that intonation and meaning determine punctuation within the written sentence.

The child subconsciously uses a wide variety of sentences long before grammarians impose their definitions and restrictions upon him.

Robert Frost expressed this in a letter to a friend.

> A sentence is a sound in itself on which other sounds called words may be strung. You may string words together without a sentence-sound to string them on, just as you may tie clothes together by the sleeves and stretch them without a clothes line between two trees, but—it is bad for the clothes. The sentence-sounds are very different entities . . . they are as definite as words. It is not impossible that they could be collected in a book. . . .[41]

Structure Words

There are some three hundred structure words classified under the categories of noun markers, verb markers, intensifiers, phrase markers, conjunctions, subordinators, and question markers. They are used with greater frequency than all other words in the language. They are often the most difficult for children to learn in reading and yet they must be mastered for effective communication.

Noun markers. This category includes the articles (a, an, the) the bugbear of beginning readers. It includes the cardinal numbers; the possessive pronouns and such words as *another* and *most*. Any word that marks a noun or signals that a noun is coming, no matter how far down the line, is a noun marker.

Verb markers. Sometimes called auxiliaries, verb markers include the forms of *be, do,* and *have,* as well as the models such as *can, could, may, might, must, shall, should, could, will* and *ought to.* Other models which serve as verb markers are *get, go, keep, and start.*

Intensifiers. Intensifiers such as *very, quite, rather,* and *somewhat* pattern readily with adjectives and adverbs. Children enjoy completing sentences using intensifiers. For example, in the frame: He was very . . . ; He walked very . . . ; He looked somewhat . . . ; they can insert *interesting, wonderful, honest, attractive* in the first frame; *rapidly, vigorously,* or *slowly* for the second, and *grave, tired, dejected,* or *worried* for the last.

Phrase markers. Prepositions signal the coming of a noun in the sentence. Nine prepositions used in more than ninety per cent of all prepositional phrases in order of frequency of use are: *of, in, to, for, at, on, from, with* and *by.*[42]

Conjunctions. The system of conjunctions (linking words) serves to connect or join words and word groups. Coordinating conjunctions linking equal grammatical units include *and, but, for, nor, so, yet* and pairs such as *either—or, both—and.*

Subordinators. The system of linking words which commonly joins subject-predicate word groups includes those commonly known as relative pronouns (*who, which, what, that, whoever, whatever, whichever*) and basic subordinating conjunctions (*after, although, as, as if, since, that, unless, until, when, whenever, where, wherever, whether, while*). This basic series of function words links an *independent* subject-predicate word group to a *dependent* (subordinate) subject-predicate word group.

Question markers. Question markers are those that begin questions or signal that question patterns can be anticipated. Such words as *how, however, when, who, where, which* are commonly used either in regular or inverted order.

Word-Form Changes

Word-form changes have two main divisions: (1) grammatical inflections of the four word classes or parts of speech; and (2) derivational prefixes and suffixes.

The literate individual must be accurate in his use of inflections in nouns, pronouns, adjectives, adverbs, and verbs. The ability to use these forms with discrimination is often the difference between being judged literate or illiterate.

The subsystem of derivational prefixes and suffixes, whereby roots shift from one word to another is important for understanding the precise meaning in reading and for the exact choice of words in writing. In an integrated language arts program children are introduced to these changes in spelling as well as in writing experiences.

The student who comprehends the four subdivisions of the structure of language—intonation, sentence patterns, structure words, and word-form changes is well on the way toward understanding the unit of effective communication—the sentence.

TRANSFORMATIONAL GRAMMAR

In contrast to the analytical bases of structural grammar, another new grammar holds that any and all English sentences are capable of being generated by a set of explicit and vigorously applied rules. Through   transformation rules the few simple basic types of sentences may be combined into all the remaining sentences conceivable.

This recent development in the study of grammar is what is referred to as transformational grammar. Although transformational grammar is often referred to as generative grammar the terms are not synonymous. "The term *generative*", asserts Marckwardt, "is concerned primarily with the purpose of grammatical study, which according to its adherents is to formulate a grammar of language in such a fashion that it will generate all of the grammatical sentences of a language and none of the ungrammatical ones."[43]

Transformation relates to technique rather than purpose. It is one of the modes of operation of the generative grammarians who conceive of language as consisting of a number of kernel sentences. Thus, by employing a number of transformations, such as the change from active voice to passive, or a number of successive transformations, they hold that a large number of sentence, clause, and phrase patterns may be generated.

> Basically, transformational grammar makes explicit those relationships that the native speaker of a language perceives intuitively. . . . A sound grammar should be able to account for these intuitive relationships. Traditional grammarians have noted them in their compendiums of language, but the structural linguist seems to have ignored them, focusing his attention on procedures for dividing and labeling sentences.
>
> Chomsky found that a more powerful device than the listing of sentence frames, form-class, and function words was necessary in order to account for human language. The key unit of language is the sentence. We are able to create or generate an infinite number of understandable sentences.
>
> The underlying structure of any sentence (S) consists of a position for a noun phrase (NP) acting as the subject, an auxiliary phrase containing at least the unit TENSE, and one for a verb phrase (VP), sometimes containing a noun object. We can write this as a sentence formation "rule":
>
> [I]S = NP — Aux. — VP
>
> These positions underlie *any* sentence of English, though the positions may be filled by transforming sentences into clauses and inserting them into the subject and post-verb positions, for example:
>
> | What worried me | was John's being sick. |
> |---|---|
> | (Something worried me) | (John was sick.) |
>
> . . . But let us start with a very simple sentence. The noun phrase consists of a noun place and a place for a determiner (words like *the, this, two, some*). The verb phrase must contain a verb, and possibly another noun phrase. Our sentence is *The boy saw the dog.*
>
> We can represent the formation of this sentence in an ordered set of rules called a Phrase Structure Grammar:
>
> [I]S → NP — Aux — VP
>
> We can represent the formation of this structure in an ordered way called a Phrase Structure Grammar:
>
> 1 S → NP — Aux — VP
> 2 NP → Det — N
> 3 Aux → Tense
> 4 VP→ V — NP

5 Det → the
6 N → boy, dog
7 Tense → Past
8 V → see

This structure can also be represented by a family tree diagram with Sentence (S) at the top, dividing to the three branches—NP, Aux, and VP. Each of these branches in turn is subdivided, as the formation rules show. But this is not a very powerful grammar. Using it we can produce or "generate" only four sentences:

The boy saw the dog.
The dog saw the boy.
The boy saw the boy.
The dog saw the dog.

—not very useful, it seems. But we can make the grammar generate eight sentences by changing rule 7 to read

[7] Tense → Past/Present

so that the present tense can also be used for each of the sentences. Allowing another verb, "like" makes our grammar generate sixteen sentences. Other nouns can be added, the verb category subdivided into transitive, intransitive verbs, and so forth, and the noun phrase in rule 4 made optional for some verbs:

[4] → V (NP)

SIMPLE TRANSFORMATIONS

Soon our grammar is generating thousands of sentences. But it cannot generate all and only the grammatical structures of English. The complex ones, with their complex interrelations, require a more powerful kind of rule. Our grammar should show that *The boy saw the dog* has the same underlying structure as *The dog was seen by the boy* and, hence, the same basic meaning.

In the passive the auxiliary word *be* does not change the meaning. It acts as one of the pointers which indicated to us that it was the boy who did the "seeing" (i.e. was the "logical subject") and the dog that was seen (i.e. "logical object"). What the relation is between these two sentences is seen by a comparison of their arrangement. The first is structured

$$NP_1 - Past - V - NP_2$$

The second is structured

$$NP_2 - Past - BE - En - V - by NP_1$$
$$\text{was} \qquad \text{seen}$$

In the second, NP_1 though the grammatical object of the preposition, actually bears the same intuitive relation to its verb as does NP_1 to the verb in the first sentence. Logically both are the *subject* of the verb, just as "dog" is logically the *object* of the verb in both sentences.

Since the grammatical and logical relations are identical in the first sentence, it is reasonable to assume that this structure is the primary one. We can describe the second as a rearrangement or *transformation* of the first. To transform the first structure into the second, we may simply interchange the two noun phrases, insert *be* and the past participial ending (denoted *En*) before the verb, and *by* before NP_1, as shown. This type of transformation, operating on single sentence-structures, is called a *singularly* transformation.

COMPLEX TRANSFORMATIONS

Phrase Structure rules (often called Formation Rules) may also produce two structures like those underlying *John is eager* and *John pleases someone*, but transformational rules combine these kernel structures into one: *John is eager to please*.

The logical relation between *John* and *please* in the transformed sentence is the same as the grammatical one in one of the underlying ones—subject and verb. On the other hand, the two kernel structures underlying *It is easy* and *Someone pleases John* can be combined into *It is easy to please John* and then to *John is easy to please*.

In these two transformed sentences *John* is the logical object of the verb, *please*. And, sure enough, in one of the kernel structures we find the same verb-object relationship shown grammatically. Such transformational rules, combining two or more sentence-structures are called *generalized* transformations.

GRAMMAR AND MIND

The rules described so far are only a small, slightly simplified part of the incredibly systematic set of rules capable of generating all the sentences of English, rules that reflect man's own incredible capacity to generate a rich system of language. Research is still going on. It is believed that the same kinds of rules can generate any human language. Turkish, Hebrew, Japanese, Mohawk, Spanish and Russian are among the languages already being described in this way.

More important perhaps is the probability that whatever structure is common to all language is an innate property of the human mind. Knowledge of this kind may lead us eventually to a deeper understanding of the great and amazing powers of the human mind, through which language functions.[44]

Transformation of Basic Sentence Patterns

According to its proponents, transformational grammar is full of promise for clarifying students' concepts about how the language operates. Briefly, the key concept of transformational or generative grammar is that the language consists of kernel or basic sentences and transformed sentences built on these basic patterns. The direct description in terms of phrase structure is limited to a kernel of basic sentences (simple, declarative, active, with no complex verb or noun phrases) deriving all other sentences from these—by transformation, possibly repeated.

The rules are formulas for building sentences. They provide a theoretical model of how native speakers construct quickly during conversation, a never-ending succession of sentences each of which conforms perfectly to the requirements of his own language. The passive construction derives from a kernel sentence.

Kernel (basic) sentence. *John ate the apple.*
Passive transformation: *The apple was eaten by John.*

The transformational rule: make the second noun (*apple*) the subject; add a form of the (*be*) verb, plus-*en* (sign of past participle), plus *by*, plus the original subject (John). The formula for the transformational rule is:

Object + be + Vt + en + by + subject.

Other transformations on the simple kernel sentence *John ate the apple* are:

John was eating the apple.
Did John eat the apple?
John didn't eat the apple.
Who ate the apple?
What did John eat?

Simple transformations which students may practice, illustrated in sentences are:[45]

TRANSFORMATION	BASIC, KERNEL OR SOURCE SENTENCE	TRANSFORMED SENTENCE
Passive	He broke the vase.	The vase was broken by him.
Yes/no	The girl has lost her book.	Has the girl lost her book?
WH question	He will show something.	What will he show?
DO	He likes olives.	He does like olives.
Imperative	You will close the door.	Close the door.
Negative	He can walk the dog.	He can't walk the dog.
Expletive IT	The girl is lost.	It is a girl who is lost.
Expletive THERE	Three bears were here.	There were three bears here.

Students may find the following pattern helpful in filling in the subject-predicate, and subject-predicate-object patterns:

Someone or *something* *did something* *to* *somebody* or *something*
→ (sometime, someplace, in some manner, for some reason.)

The appeal of transformational grammar, while not as widespread as that of structural grammar, lies basically in its constructive approach. It makes possible cumulative progression from the basic and simple, to the complex and complicated, in a way that is as obvious as it is intriguing to the student. One sentence leads readily into another.

It puts emphasis on essentials as the children explore fundamental relationships. However, the classroom teacher who is looking for an easy approach to the teaching of grammar will find that transformational grammar formulas themselves, to be accurate and workable, are elaborate and complex, rather than short and simple. Obtaining a relatively precise and systematic description of English through the use of a small set of kernel sentences from which more complicated patterns are derived, demands a concentrated effort. However, in the words of Gleason,

It must also be said that some of the complexity which many people see in a transformational—generative grammar is really only strangeness. A quasi-algebraic notation is not a usual form of expression for many in the English-teaching profession. It may repel, confuse, or frighten some. It can, however, be learned by anyone who will give a little time to the task. Learning a new form of expression can be rewarding, as anyone knows who has really studied a foreign language. English teachers might profitably think of the generative notation as a foreign language worth acquiring. It will open up to them a new world of thought and put into a new perspective their old ways of speaking about language. . . .

Generative approaches are of a recent development. New and better ways of handling various details of structure are appearing. Very likely we have not yet found the best form for stating many of the facts. More succinct and more revealing formulations will certainly continue to be discovered. English, like every other natural language, is complicated. A description of any sort, if it is to be true to the facts, must be intricate. A generative grammar underscores this because it can so easily pass difficulties by in silence.[46]

Politzer asserts ". . . . we can predict that the concern with transformational grammar, coming as it does at a time in which self instruction and programmed learning are also an important interest, will lead within the next ten to fifteen years to the creation of more teaching materials, characterized by extremely careful step by step presentation of grammatical structures."[47]

METHODS IN TEACHING GRAMMAR

In the past grammar has too often been taught as a body of incomprehensible rules handed down with authority to be learned without question—often with a minimum of explanation. This is no longer adequate. Today's emphasis on inquiry should arouse the student's curiosity about his language and how it functions. However, this requires a change in the method of teaching grammar. At least two things can be done to achieve the change. *First,* the student should be introduced to the techniques by which grammatical formulations are arrived at, and shown how these statements are rooted in observations of language itself. This is most easily accomplished by what is known as "inductive teaching," the method whereby students are led to discover principles for themselves. Since the data is readily available and generally familiar, grammar is a suitable subject for this method of learning. *Second,* students must not only be led to be critical about language, but equally critical about our understanding of language. At appropriate places they must see that there is more than one way to describe a significant point of structure, to analyze a particular group of sounds, and to explain a specific concept in verbal expression. By the time a student enters high school he should be aware of the major approaches to syntax. The educated teacher should be conversant with linguistics. He should become familiar with such names as Bloomfield, Jepersen, Roberts, Fries, Chomsky and others who contribute to the ever-expanding understanding of language.

As Gleason points out, "Grammar must . . . be expanded to become a full study of the English language comprehending both its structure and the variation of its patterns. English is a special case of that most intriguing phenomena, language. It is best understood in this framework. The need, then, is to broaden the language curriculum beyond English. The syntax, phonology, dialectology, and historical development of the student's own language are clarified—and hence most easily taught—from a perspective of general linguistics. Contrasts with other languages can frequently illuminate points as no amount of discussion restricted to English can possibly do."[48]

In the matter of teaching grammar in the schools says Chomsky:

> My impression is that grammar is generally taught as an essentially closed and finished system, and in a rather mechanical way. What is taught is a system of terminology, a set of techniques for diagramming sentences, and so on. I do not doubt that this has a function, that the student must have a way of talking about language and its properties. But it seems to me that a great opportunity is lost when the teaching of grammar is limited in this way. I think it is important for students to realize how little we know about the rules that determine the relation of sound and meaning in English, about the general properties of human language, about the matter of how the incredibly complex system of rules that constitutes a grammar is acquired or put to use. Few students are aware of the fact that in their normal, everyday life they are constantly creating new linguistic structures that are immediately understood, despite their novelty, by those to whom they speak or write.[49]

In teaching grammar the dilemma of freedom of expression versus correct form may be solved by placing the emphasis in the primary grades upon spontaneity of written expression, and introducing only those terms and concepts the child needs in order to be effective in oral and written communication. Children vary in their needs for formal instruction in the terminology of grammar and practice in identifying, naming, and using the parts of speech or functions of the sentence. Terminology should be introduced as children ask questions involving the use of grammatical terms such as, "What is that word called?" "How is it used in this sentence?"

If the program is planned with a view to relate these learnings to significant experiences, most of the mechanics and tools of language can be learned effectively. Learning to speak and write well becomes synonymous with *wanting* to speak and write well.

A Formula for Teaching Grammar Effectively

The challenge of a functional approach to teaching grammar involves a change in method, emphasis, and attitude. It is imperative that grammar be reoriented toward analysis, the observation of data, and the framing of descriptions. That is, we must teach not only a body of facts and theories but also a technique—a technique by which the body of facts and theories can be augmented as needed. The content of the syllabus for the new grammar must include only the most general principles, particularly those rooted in the nature of the subject itself.

The inductive method. The inductive method has been applied in various ways ranging from the use of problem-solving of a simple type to free-wheeling investigations of language, following whatever students suggest. The problem-solving techniques suggested in the chapter on speech will provide practice in genuine analytic processes and thus train the students to observe language scientifically. Grammar presents many interesting and instructive problems, of varying degrees of complexity, which can be the basis of discovery of principles rather than mere memorization of rules.

Formal instruction should begin with principles antecedent to the definitions of parts of speech. Just as in modern mathematics the student is introduced to number concepts rather than beginning a study of addition as a manipulation of numbers and a set of "arithmetic facts", here the student is introduced to grammar as a part of the study of language as a whole.

Inductive teaching of grammatical concepts although slower, less precise, and more demanding of patience and careful planning on the part of the teacher than in deductive teaching, brings better results. This type of teaching leads to understanding and application much more readily than does mere memorization of rules. The following diagram illustrates inductive teaching in grammar.[50]

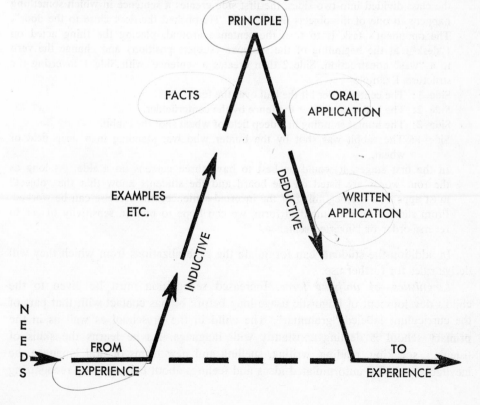

The following points should be noted:

1. Motivation should be from felt needs of pupils and should grow out of pupil's previous experience.
2. Teaching should be inductive. Pupils derive their own rules or principles from an examination of a number of carefully chosen examples. The teacher elicits rather than tells; guides rather than directs.
3. The first application of the principle should be oral so that re-teaching can readily be done when necessary. The first written attempts should be largely successful so that right patterns will become established.
4. The teacher should know in advance what transfer she expects from grammar to oral and written composition.
5. Drill lessons begin at the apex of the triangle with a review of work previously taught, and are largely deductive in nature.

In a Sixth Grade Classroom

Problem: Understanding Inverted Sentences

The teacher places four words on the board: *ball, window, desk, bird.* With the class divided into two sides, the first side creates a sentence in which something happens to one of the objects listed, as in "He pushed the desk close to the door". The opponent's task is to turn the sentence around, placing the thing acted on ("desk") at the beginning of the sentence (subject position) and change the verb to a "was" construction. Side 2 then creates a sentence, with Side 1 inverting the structure. Example—
Side 1: The centerfielder hit the ball over the fence.
Side 2: The ball was hit over the fence by the centerfielder.
Side 2: The hunter standing in a deep field of wheat shot the rabbit.
Side 1: The rabbit was shot by the hunter who was standing in a deep field of wheat.
In the first stages, it would be best to have three persons on a side. As long as the four words are listed on the board and the students know that the "object" must appear at the beginning of the inverted sentence, this exercise can be worked. From success in this simplified form, we can hope to build a sensitivity of ear to reverse-order or "inverted sentences".[51]

In addition the students can formulate the generalizations from which they will derive rules for further use.

Linguistics—A unifying force. Increased recognition must be given to the child's development of linguistic usage long before he has contact with that part of the curriculum labeled "grammar". The child in the preschool as well as in the primary school is dealing constantly with language. As he learns the skills of listening, speaking, reading, writing, spelling and new forms of oral language, he inevitably picks up unformulated ideas and feelings about language. By recognizing the importance of the role of oral language instruction *prior* to other language arts; by improving of the teaching of phonics so that it will take advantage of our best phonetic and phonemic understanding; by seeing relationships between spelling, writing, reading, listening, and speaking; by giving increased attention to sentence structure in beginning reading; and finally by utilizing foreign language instruction in the elementary grades improvement may be anticipated. The roots of effective communication are laid in the preschool and primary grades. Every element in the language arts curriculum must be re-examined in the light of its contribution to basic linguistic understanding as the foundation for creative communication.

> *Changed attitude toward grammar.* Traditionally, it (grammar) has been looked on largely as a tool useful in the teaching of correct speech and writing, but of no independent intellectual value. It has been a Cinderella consigned to scouring the grimiest pots in the composition classroom. . . . If prescriptive notions of correctness are abandoned and if language is approached inductively against the background of a broad set of fundamental principles, attitudes toward language will inevitable improve. There is one essential additional step. We must also develop a critical attitude toward the tools with which language is investigated and the framework within which it is discussed. We must not simply replace naïvete about English with dogmatism about linguistics. A critical approach to language must turn back on itself and examine its own instruments. An educated person needs to understand not only the nature and function of language but equally the nature and function of grammars, for these also have their strength and limitations, and our understanding of language is inevitably colored in various ways by them. . . .
>
> The contrast of one grammar with another can give us much insight into the nature and functioning of grammars.[52]

Utilizing the findings from research. As teachers become conversant with the findings of research and become open-minded about experimenting in the classroom they will find new and effective ways of teaching grammar in much the same way that they utilize research from other curriculum areas. An example of research carried on in which the attempt was made to compare the results of traditional and structural approaches to grammar gives insight into some of the challenges as well as the problems of experimentation in the teaching of grammar.

An Experiment in Teaching Grammar

In a seven-month study comparing the structural and traditional approach to teaching grammar at the junior high level, the accepted definition of grammar agreed upon was "grammar is the study of the sentence—what it consists of, how it patterns for clear communication, and what signals are necessary to convey intended meaning." Grammar, in other words, was to be considered as the *behaviour,* not the *etiquette,* of the language.

As the lessons were planned, the basic viewpoints, the basic differences between the approaches were under constant study. In the group taught by the traditional approach, the emphasis was on definition and classification of words and word-groups. These were used as criteria for identification of the words and word groups. Meaning was used as guide to the structure of the English sentence. Prescription rather than description guided the pupils in their study of the language.

The students analyzed or diagrammed "ready-made" sentences. They were taught punctuation through a study of rules and of sentences which showed the application of these rules.

The method in the traditional approach was deductive as contrasted with the inductive method in the structural approach. In the structural classes the emphasis was on sentence "patterns". Sentences were classified according to their patterns—the position of words in sentences; phrases and clauses, were identified by their structure and position. In short, the English language was *described*. Stress was placed upon what the language communicates through its structure.

Another difference between the two approaches was the opportunity the students in the structural group had in creating their own sentences according to suggested formulas rather than working with "ready-made" sentences.

Too, attention was given to the importance of various oral or sound signals in the language. As the students studied punctuation they were made aware of the part intonation plays upon sentence meaning.

Finally, the teaching methods of the two approaches were different. Instruction in the structural approach was inductive. The text books used were Roberts' *Patterns of English* for the experimental groups and *Building Better English*. (Harper and Row) books for the control group.

Significant results of the study as summarized by Klauser were:

1. On the basis of tests administered, the pupils in both groups at each of the three grade levels made significant gains in achievement. There were, however, no significant differences in the gains made by the groups being compared. We can say, therefore, that both approaches to the teaching of grammar were effective.
2. In the ninth and the seventh grades, the pupils studying grammar by a structural approach made more significant gains in understanding effective writing than did the groups studying grammar by the traditional approach. . . .
4. In the seventh grade the group studying grammar by a traditional approach made more significant gains in accuracy of writing than did the experimental group studying structural grammar. . . .
5. The eighth and ninth grade groups studying grammar by a structural approach seemed more enthusiastic and interested than did the groups at the same grade levels studying grammar by a traditional approach. This conclusion is based on the attitude—questionnaires, which required the checking of ten items under the two major headings of "I liked grammar because. . ." and "I did not like grammar because. . ." Pupils also had the opportunity to give reasons other than those stated; on the final questionnaire an additional part (C) asked for the following information:

Grammar this year was
1. More interesting than before.
2. Just as interesting as before.
3. Boring.
4. Easier than before.
5. Harder than before.
6. Neither easier nor harder than before.

Answers to part (C) of the final questionnaire indicated that twenty-three of the twenty-five ninth graders studying structural grammar found it *more interesting* than the traditional grammar previously studied, and none in this group found structural grammar *boring*, fourteen found it *harder*, whereas three found it easier. . . . Among the eighth graders, thirteen from the experimental group in contrast with seven from the control group found grammar *more interesting* than before; six of the experimental group found it *boring*; nine of the experimental group found it *harder* . . .

6. Seventh graders in both groups had positive attitudes toward grammar. Those in the structural class asked to continue with structural grammar the next year.
7. The teachers of the three levels liked many of the features of the structural approach and expressed a desire to use this approach, perhaps with some modifications, again. . . .
8. There was no evidence that either the traditional or the structural approach which was used would be more appropriate for a particular grade in junior high school. Superior teachers can achieve good results regardless of what approach they use. . . .

The following conclusions seem valid: (1) Since pupils of the structural grammar indicated that it aroused their interest in the English language and taught them "new and exciting things" about it and since no such statements were made by those studying traditional grammar, we can feel that the study of structural grammar made an important contribution. (2) The teachers who taught both kinds of grammar felt that the structural emphasis on the studying of sentence patterns and the writing of original sentences resulted in better understanding of sentences than the traditional methods of diagramming, identification, and classification. (3) Since in a period of only seven months a new method (the structural) produced as good results as a conventional method (the traditional), continuation of a structural approach for a longer period seems feasible.[53]

On the basis of studies such as this it would appear that the teacher should inform himself about the various approaches, and experiment with them in the classroom. The emphasis upon functional and interesting features of the structural approach is a catalyst which stimulates teachers to try it in an effort to arouse enthusiasm for learning about language on the part of *both* student and teacher. Other teachers have found transformational grammar fully as challenging. A willingness to learn and an open mind about new methods characterizes the creative teacher.

An Experiment in Teaching Transformational Grammar

. . . a class of 19 seventh-graders attending the George Peabody College Demonstration School in Nashville, Tennessee, was put together from a class of
35 sixth-seventh,- and eight-graders who had come from different schools in the
Nashville area to do extra work on composition in the summer. These students
had an above-average IQ of 118.6, with a range from 91 to 138. . . .

For the class, the experimental technique involved the use of audio-lingual
drills based on a transformation grammar and centered around an unedited version
of Stephen Crane's "The Open Boat." During the month, the students and the
instructor read the entire short story together, generally with the instructor reading each sentence and the students repeating each, reading in unison after the
instructor's model. This choral reading provided diversion for the students, a relief
from the routine of practicing audio-lingual drills. It, undoubtedly reinforced the
effect of the drills; furthermore, it provided a linguistic context for them.

The drills themselves focused on the process by which two sentences combine
to produce a third, more complex sentence. . . . The instructor gave the students
two sentences such as the following: "Their eyes were fastened on the waves"
and "The waves swept towards them." They then combined these two sentences
to produce a third sentence: "Their eyes were fastened on the waves which swept
towards them." Similarly, they took two cue sentences such as "They could hear
the surf breaking on the shore" and "They could not see the land." They then
combined these into a single response sentence: "Although they could hear the
surf breaking on the shore, they could not see the land." They also practiced the
production of sentences with post-nominal modifiers such as: "The injured captain,
lying in the bow, was dejected. The surf's roar, dulled by the sound of the wind,
was thunderous and mighty. The men in the open boat experienced a subtle brother-
hood." At first, the students produced these sentences primarily in oral drills, hence
the name, audio-lingual drills. This oral practice was intended not only to strengthen
the student's command of sentence structures but also to increase his vocabulary.
Selected vocabulary items from the story were included in each drill.

In the class hour, not fewer than ten sets of cue sentences and not more than
fifteen were drilled every day. To start the drills, the instructor wrote two cue
sentences on the blackboard and showed the students how these cue sentences
formed a third response sentence by writing it on the blackboard also. Then the
instructor merely read the remaining cue sentences and requested individual
students to combine them into the appropriate response sentence. Each student
recited in turn. If a student gave the response sentence correctly, the entire class
repeated it in unison; if it was not correct, the teacher modelled the correct response
for the students to repeat in unison.

At the end of the class hour, the instructor read five sets of cue sentences,
and the students wrote the responses. These daily written exercises were collected
and graded by the instructor for spelling and for the student's correct performance
of the exercise. During the exercise, the teacher put the spelling of unfamiliar
words on the blackboard. If the student did not know the spelling of any word,
it was supplied on request. In spite of this, there were some spelling errors in the
papers; students can even misspell the words on the blackboard before them.

Many students found it possible to produce error free papers consistently, and as a result, daily before class they peppered the instructor with questions: "Did I make a hundred today?" Evidently, students looked forward to receiving their corrected papers. Furthermore, students who were doing the exercises badly at the beginning of the class improved appreciably on the written exercises as the class progressed, so that the gap between the poor students and the good students narrowed.

Thus, each class period was divided into six different activities, each using from five to twelve minutes of class time:

1. Review of oral drills of the previous two class sessions. The instructor conducted this review in the same manner as the original presentation of the drills.
2. Review of the written exercises from the previous day. The papers from the previous day were distributed so that the student could observe their progress. They then kept a record of their errors in a notebook.
3. Practice of the drill for the day. This exercise generally required a full ten to twelve minutes or longer. Sometimes, the exercise took the form of a competition with two teams matching each other's ability to correctly form the response sentences.
4. Reading from Stephen Crane's "The Open Boat". On some occasions, individual students read a sentence or two; most frequently, however, the students participated in a choral reading.
5. Review of the cue sentences for the day. If time permitted, the class reviewed the sentence patterns for the day in the same manner in which they originally practiced them.
6. Practice in writing the response sentence. Generally, the practice involved only five sets of cue sentences. . . .

To discover whether the drills had indeed changed the writing habits of the students, the investigator counted those structures which the students had practiced extensively in class. Improvement was then measured as the difference in the number of drilled structures between pre-test and post-test. By this measurement, the class as a whole showed positive gain; they wrote 57 of these structures on the pre-test and 79 on the post-test for a gain of 22. Six students showed more gain than the entire class. These students wrote 20 of the drilled structures on the pre-test and 49 on the post-test for a gain of 29. Thus, the exercises had succeeded in changing the linguistic behavior of at least some of the students. . . .

Furthermore, the use of audio-lingual drills can provide a systematic method for the strengthening of the student's command of the vocabulary and structures of formal written English. Traditional methods of teaching composition generally neglect this aspect of the teaching and learning of writing. Besides this, the drills provided the context in which spelling could be taught without depending on the negative approach of merely correcting the errors of students. The exercises in writing carefully controlled structures permitted the teacher to supply the correct spellings to the students.

. . . the use of audio-lingual drills in a composition course is effective not only because these drills help to alter the student's language behavior; it is also effective because students can work on the acquisition of new structural patterns and of new vocabulary, and on the mastering of English spelling. . . .[54]

Regardless of the choice made in the approach to teaching grammar students have a need to understand the nature and structure of the language they speak. Traditional grammar, with its innumerable rules, definitions, generalizations, and abstractions poses almost insurmountable difficulties for the child of culturally disadvantaged socio-economic level, or a child of average or below average intelligence. Both structural and transformational grammar challenge the student to experiment with the parts of language to see how it works.[55]

Whether the approach is traditional, structural, or transformational the mastery of the language involves an understanding of: (1) the word classes (parts of speech); (2) basic sentence patterns; (3) operations of modification, coordination, and subordination; (4) the intonation patterns, pitch, pauses, stresses which act as signal systems in English; and (5) the mechanics involved in transcribing oral language into the written word: punctuation and spelling.

In one way or another, the teacher must come to grips with the idiosyncracies of the English language while he deals with the structure of the language as it is, rather than as it would have been, had it remained a highly inflected language. In other words, he will have to make explicit those grammatical devices which children subconsciously recognize and utilize from the time they first begin to speak in meaningful utterances. Somehow, he must find a way to help children discover grammar as an exciting vital part of the curriculum—a language in which *if* one begins with an oral approach one may sense the humour of the following verse:

We'll begin with box, the plural is boxes,
    But the plural of ox should be oxen, not oxes.
Yet the plural of mouse is never meese.
    You may find a lone mouse or a whole nest of mice,
But the plural of house is houses, not hice.
    If the plural of man is always men,
Why shouldn't the plural of pan be pen?
    The cow in the plural may be called cows or kine,
But a bow if repeated is never called bine;
    And the plural of vow is vows, not vine.
If I speak of a foot and you show me two feet
    And I give you a boot, would a pair be called beet?
If one is a tooth and a whole set is teeth,
    Why shouldn't the plural of booth be called beeth?
If the singular's this and the plural is these,
    Should the plural of kiss be written kese?
We speak of a brother, and also of brethren,
    But though we say Mother, we never say mothren.
Then the masculine pronouns are he, his, and him,
    But imagine the feminine: she, shis and shim!
So English, I think that you all will agree
    Is the funniest language you ever did see.

                                    Author Unknown

REFERENCES

1. By permission from J. L. M. Trim, "Speech Education," in Randolph Quirk and A. H. Smith, (eds.), *The Teaching of English*, Oxford University Press, London, 1964, pp. 66.
2. Franklin Bobbit, *The Curriculum of Modern Education*, McGraw-Hill Book Co. Inc., New York, 1941, p. 258.
3. Doris L. Noell, "A Comparative Study of the Relationship Between the Quality of the Child's Language Usage and the Quality and Types of Language Used in the Home," *Journal of Educational Research*, 46:161-67, November, 1953.
4. Henry Lee Smith, Jr., "Linguistic Science and the Teaching of English," *Inglis Lectures*, 1954, Harvard University Press, Cambridge, 1958.
5. Ruth Strickland, *The Language of Elementary School Children*, Indiana University Press, Bloomington, 1962.
6. Walter Loban, *The Language of Elementary School Children*, Research Report No. 1, National Council of Teachers of English, Champaign, 1963.
7. Graham G. Wilson, "The Structure of English," in G. W. Ford and Lawrence Pugno (eds.), *The Structure of Knowledge and the Curriculum*, Rand McNally & Co., Chicago, 1964, p. 74.
8. Ruth Strickland, *op. cit.*, p. 86.
9. Alvina Burrows et al., *They All Want to Write*, 3rd ed., Prentice-Hall, Inc., Englewood Cliffs, 1965, p. 221.
10. Walter Loban, *op. cit.*
11. C. C. Fries, *Linguistics and Reading*, Holt, Rinehart and Winston, Inc., New York, 1962, p. 64.
12. Martin Joos, "Language and the School Child," *Harvard Educational Review*, 34: 209, Spring, 1964.
13. Robert C. Pooley, *Teaching English Usage*, Appleton-Century-Crofts, New York, 1946.
14. Robert C. Pooley, *Teaching English Grammar*, Appleton-Century-Crofts, New York, 1957.
15. Walter Loban, *op. cit.*
16. Ellen Frogner, "Grammar Approach versus Thought Approach in Teaching Sentence Structure," *English Journal*, 28:518-528, September, 1939.
17. Silvy Kraus, "A Comparison of Three Methods of Teaching Sentence Structure," *English Journal*, 46:275-281, May, 1957.
18. By permission from Ruth Strickland, "Implications of Research in Linguistics for Elementary Teaching," *Elementary English*, 40:170, February, 1963.
19. Virgil E. Herrick et al., *Handwriting in Wisconsin: A Survey of Elementary School Practices*, University of Wisconsin, School of Education, Madison, 1951, p. 114.
20. David Reed, "A Theory of Language, Speech, and Writing," *Elementary English*, 42:846, December, 1965.
21. H. A. Gleason, Jr., "What Grammar?" *Harvard Educational Review*, 34:271-273, Spring, 1964.
22. Robert F. Hogan, "English," in Glenys G. Unruh (ed.), *New Curriculum Developments*, Association for Supervision and Curriculum Development, NEA, Washington, 1965, pp. 16-27.

23. By permission from Mary Elizabeth Fowler, *Teaching Language, Composition, and Literature*, McGraw-Hill Book Co. Inc., New York, 1965, p. 164.

24. Robert Pooley, *Teaching English Grammar*, Appleton-Century-Crofts, New York, 1957, p. 49.

25. Webster's New *Third International Dictionary*, G. & C Merriam Co., Springfield, 1961.

26. Robert C. Pooley, "A Perspective on Usage — Standard vs. Substandard," in *Language, Linguistics and School Programs*, National Council of the Teachers of English, Champaign, 1963, pp. 65, 66. Reprinted by permission of the National Council of Teachers of English and the author.

27. *Teaching English Grammar*, by Robert C. Pooley. Copyright © 1957 by Appleton-Century-Crofts, Inc. Reprinted by permission of Appleton-Century-Crofts, Division of Meredith Publishing Company.

28. Robert C. Pooley, "A Perspective on Usage — Standard vs. Substandard," in *op. cit.*, p. 64.

29. By permission from College Entrance Examination Board, New York, *Freedom and Discipline in English*: *Report of the Commission on English of the College Entrance Examination Board*, 1965, p. 33.

30. *The American College Dictionary*, Random House, Inc., New York, 1964, p. 19a.

31. Robert C. Pooley, "A Perspective on Usage — Standard vs. Substandard," in *op. cit.*, p. 69.

32. *Ibid.*, p. 70.

33. *Ibid.*, pp. 67, 68.

34. *Ibid.*

35. By permission from Frank Riessman, "Digging the Man's Language," *Saturday Review*, 49:80, September 17, 1966.

36. *Ibid.*, p. 81.

37. Janet Lunn, "What About English?" *Quill and Quire*, 32:36, March-April, 1966.

38. Paul Roberts, *English Syntax: An Introduction to Transformational Grammar*, Harcourt, Brace & World, Inc., New York, 1964, p. 1.

39. Carl Lefevre, "A Concise Structural Grammar," from the November, 1965 issue of *Education*. Copyright, 1965 by the Bobbs-Merill Company, Inc., Indianapolis, Indiana, p. 132.

40. Carl Lefevre, *op. cit.*, p. 132.

41. Robert Frost, *Selected Letters of Robert Frost*, Lawrence Thompson (ed.), Holt, Rinehart and Winston, Inc., New York.

42. Verna L. Newsome, *Structural Linguistics in the Classroom*, The University of Wisconsin Press, Madison, 1961, p. 31.

43. Albert H. Marckwardt, "The Structure and Operation of Language," *Language, Linguistics, and School Programs*, Proceedings of the Spring Institutes, 1963, National Council of the Teachers of English, Champaign, 1963, p. 26.

44. Roderick A. Jacobs, "A Short Introduction to Transformational Grammar," *Education*, 86:138-141, November, 1965.

45. Adapted from unpublished materials presented by John Mellon at the Linguistics Workshop, NCTE Convention, Miami Beach, Florida, 1962.

46. From *Linguistics and English Grammar*, by H. A. Gleason, Jr., Copyright © 1965 by Holt, Rinehart and Winston, Inc., New York, p. 298.

47. Robert L. Politzer, "The Impact of Linguistics on Language Teaching: Past, Present and Future," *The Modern Language Journal*, 48: (reprint), March, 1964.

48. H. A. Gleason, Jr., "What Grammar?" *Harvard Educational Review*, 34:280, Spring, 1964.

49. Noam Chomsky, "The Current Scene in Linguistics: Present Directions," *College English*, 27:595, May, 1966. Reprinted by permission of the National Council of Teachers of English and the author.

50. By permission from E. B. Brooms, "The Teaching of Grammar," *Macmillan Bulletin for Teachers*, March, 1956.

51. By permission from John Maxwell, "Creative Language Teaching: Grammar and Usage," in Verna Anderson, et al., (eds.), *Readings in the Language Arts*, The Macmillan Co., 1964, p. 276.

52. From *Linguistics and English Grammar*, by H. A. Gleason, Jr. Copyright © 1965 by Holt, Rinehart and Winston, Inc., New York, p. 493.

53. Adapted from Lucile Klauser, "Structural or Traditional Grammar?" *Delta Kappa Gamma*, 31:42-44, Summer, 1965. By permission of the Delta Kappa Gamma Society and the author.

54. James W. Ney, "Applied Linguistics in the Seventh Grade," *English Journal*, 55:7, October, 1966. Reprinted with the permission of the National Council of Teachers of English and the author.

55. See William W. West, "Written Composition," *Review of Educational Research*, 37:165, April, 1967.

13

Mastering the Tools of Writing: Punctuation, Spelling, and Handwriting

One may not move a mountain, but one *may* preserve a state
By cultivating commas.
. . . . And tomorrow is too late!

Be gentle to the comma with its curly
    little tail:
Though dainty and diminutive, its
    power turns one pale!
It causes much confusion when
    neglected or misplaced,
So slur it not in ignorance, nor
    hobble it through haste!
Expressions parenthetical (*however*
    or *said he*),
All nominatives of address, appositives
    aussi,
Inverted-order clauses, which come
    before the main,
The members of a series (Lizzie,
    Annabel, and Jane),
Long phrases introductory containing
    verbal parts,
All nonrestrictive elements ("His
    hobby, whi*ch is arts*—"),
Dates, addresses, in detail (10
    Broadway, Hartford, Conn.,
Or Saturday, June 1, '36), and, last to
    ponder on,
The parts of compound sentences ("Ike
    hops but Willie flies")
All these require commas tucked in
    their interstices,
One may not move a mountain, but
    one *may* preserve a state

By cultivating commas.... And
tomorrow is too late![1]

Although the mechanical conventions of transcribing speech into writing consume a great deal of time which many feel might more profitably be devoted to reading and written composition, one of the marks of an educated person is competence in the mechanics of English.

However, much of the drudgery associated with punctuation and spelling can be minimized if the program is planned in such a way that the student sees the purpose for learning. The staff should organize a sequential program in which the child develops skill through functional, meaningful situations, and motivated practice in a classroom in which the language arts program is based both on integrated experiences and specific teaching of needed skills.

It is the responsibility of the elementary school to help each child to achieve a mastery of the conventions and mechanics of writing.

In the teaching of punctuation, as in the teaching of usage and grammar, handwriting, and spelling, every effort should be made from the very beginning to link punctuation with the expression of ideas, to make pupils feel that the presence or absence of a comma may change the meaning of a sentence. The student should especially be made aware of the distinction between restrictive and non-restrictive modifiers. As children grow in awareness of language and its subtleties, they should learn the use of the semi-colon as the mark of logical relationship in thought between independent elements.

Always there should be a functional setting in which the learning and use of a particular rule, definition, and operation can emerge. An awareness of the function the mechanics of expression serve in communicating ideas acts as a catalyst for mastering them.

To a degree punctuation symbolizes the pauses we make in our speech, but only to a degree. In transfering the oral communication to the written expression the natural pauses of speech can be a guide to punctuation. With practice, it is possible to hear those pauses in the inner ear. But correct punctuation not only reflects the grammatical structures of sentences, but also the particular conventions of the times.

The conventions of punctuation, like the conventions of etiquette, have to be learned. Punctuation, however, is not merely a series of rules; it is an additional means of clarifying expression. The prose style of the writer is very largely controlled by his use of punctuation marks where no rule clearly applies. Two rules of thumb which have helped experienced writers are: "When in doubt, don't". "When in doubt use common sense". However, these suggestions are not for the novice writer. The novice needs to learn and use the rules.

DO'S AND DON'TS IN PUNCTUATION

A few simple reminders will facilitate the learning process in punctuation.

1. *Do* recognize that writing is recorded speech. Since the intonation, stress,

and pause patterns of the human voice in speech are the original source of our system of punctuation, realize that awareness of intonation assists remarkably in punctuation. Learn the basic intonation patterns of English and let them work for you in punctuating.

2. *Do* learn the basic syntactic structures and sentence patterns of English. Unless one recognizes English sentence structure, clauses, phrases, verb and noun clusters, adjectives, and adverbs, it is well-nigh impossible to make much progress with the rules of punctuation. Once the basic structures are known, the task of gaining a command of punctuation is relatively simple.

3. *Do* observe current usage in punctuation. Much can be learned by reading text books, daily newspapers, magazines, stories, and so on.

4. *Don't* overpunctuate. When in doubt leave it out. There is more truth than poetry in that statement. There has been a change in the conventions of punctuation in recent years. Of the numerous rules for the comma in some composition handbooks, only five or six are commonly used in good contemporary writing and publishing. Learn those first.

5. *Don't* try to learn all the rules of punctuation individually. As in spelling, a large percentage of errors can be dealt with by using a basic group of concepts and guiding rules. Master this basic group before worrying about the so-called finer points of punctuation.

A DIMENSIONAL APPROACH TO THE CONVENTIONS OF WRITTEN EXPRESSION

The Primary Grades

The conventions of written expression are best learned in conjunction with other language skills in a functional setting. Textbooks and curriculum guides offer well-worked out sequences for teaching the skills of written expression. If these are incorporated into the writing program most children will have developed some competency and many will have mastered the minimal requirements by the time they leave the elementary school.

In the primary grades the child is introduced to the need for these conventions as a part of his written expression. The following outline presents a guide for minimum objectives.

Writing in the First Grade

A. Use correct manuscript form
   1. Head paper in correct form
   2. Leave prescribed margin
B. Use capitalization correctly
   1. Distinguish between capitals and small letters
   2. Capitalize the first word in a sentence

    3. Capitalize greeting and complementary closing of letter
    4. Capitalize names of people and places
    5. Capitalize Mr., Mrs., Miss, Dr., Rev., Msgr.
    6. Capitalize the word "I"
    7. Capitalize the first word of each line of a poem
    8. Capitalize the name of a day, the name of a month
C. Use correct punctuation
    1. Use a period at end of sentence
    2. Use a question mark at end of sentence
    3. Use exclamation marks
    4. Use a period after Mr. or Mrs. and other abbreviations

Writing in the Second Grade
A. Use correct manuscript form
    1. Head papers correctly
    2. Leave prescribed margins
    3. Write neatly
B. Use capital letters correctly
    1. Review items for first grade
    2. Capitalize titles of books, stories, poems, songs
C. Use correct punctuation
    1. Use a period after initials in proper names: H. A. Smith
    2. Use a question mark after a direct question within the sentence: "Will you be ready?" the man asked.
    3. Use a comma after the greeting in a letter
    4. Use a comma after the closing in a letter
D. Spell correctly with the teacher's help

Writing in the Third Grade
A. Use correct manuscript and correct cursive form
    1. Review skills for second grade
    2. Use correct form in writing social notes and letters
B. Use capital letters correctly
    1. Review rules learned in first and second grade
    2. Use capitals for such abbreviations as CBC, RCMP, UNESCO, BBC
    3. Capitalize each word in the name of a street
    4. Capitalize each word in the name of a town or city
    5. Capitalize each word in the name of a province or state
    6. Capitalize the titles of plays
    7. Capitalize the titles of rulers
    8. Capitalize the name of a pet
C. Use correct punctuation
    1. Review items listed for earlier grades
    2. Use a comma to separate the name of a town or city from the name of a province or state

3. Use a comma to separate the number of a day of the month from the number of a year (July 1, 1967)
4. Learn the skills in using the apostrophe—contraction, possessive singular
5. Use a comma to set off short direct quotations: "We are ready," called the girls.
6. Use a comma to separate words in a series: John, Jack, Jim, and Jerry are cousins.
7. Use a colon:
   Before a long series: Mother bought: meat, vegetables, milk, jello and cake.
   To separate the hour from the minutes (2:30 A.M.)
   To denote examples (A proper noun should be capitalized: Martha).
8. Use quotations marks:
   In a quotation with the descriptive element preceding the quotation. He cried, "Get a new player on third base!"
   In a quotation when the descriptive element follows the quotation. "Get a new player on third!" he cried.
9. Use a semicolon:
   To replace the conjunction in coordinate clauses.
   (Mary was sad; Jim was happy.)
D. Spell correctly with the aids provided by the teacher
   1. Develop the dictionary habit
   2. Use other aids, such as a personal list, a spelling text list, a class list
   3. Progress in mastering homonyms
E. Expanded vocabulary
   1. Add new words to writing vocabulary
   2. Use descriptive words
   3. Recognize literary and rhyming quality of words
   4. Use writing terms as sentence, capitalization, period, question mark, comma, apostrophe, greeting, closing, margin, heading, indent, paragraph, contraction, imperative, intonation, subordination, expanding sentence, hyphen

The above outline is merely a skeleton which comes alive only as a group of children and their teachers discover the excitement of making language live. When challenging activities are geared to the needs, abilities, and interests of the children the mechanics and conventions of written expression become the tools for effective communication.

The Intermediate and Upper Elementary Grades

It is important for the teacher to keep in mind that the mastery of the tools of written expression is a developmental process. Understanding the developmental progress expected of the average children in the elementary grades is important if the teacher is to assume responsibility for guiding this phase of the language arts program.

Writing in the Intermediate Grades

A. Use the approved form for written work
 1. Use manuscript lettering for charts, maps, posters, etc.
 2. Use approved heading for papers
 3. Use required indentation of paragraphs, margins
 4. Demonstrate habitually legible handwriting
 5. Proofread before handing in written work.

B. Review and maintain skills learned in the primary grades in the use of capitals: address, heading, salutation, complimentary closing of letters; first line of poetry, first word of a sentence; the word I, names of persons, pets; days of the week, holidays, months; names of cities and towns, states, provinces, streets and avenues; titles of stories, songs, plays, books, persons; abbreviations such as Mr., Mrs., Dr., CBC; names of rivers, a country, a school.

C. Learn new capitalization
 1. Introduce in Grade 4: First word in direct quotations, first word in exclamations, first word of topics in outlines, initials, names of characters, words referring to people of a country
 2. Introduce in Grade 5: Geographical names, names of clubs, names of companies, names of programs, proper nouns, rural routes, sacred names, divided quotations consisting of more than one sentence
 3. Introduce in Grade 6: The names of newspapers, names in headlines, names in bibliographies, direction words in addresses, first word of details in outlines, proper adjectives, the departments of government, and historical events

D. Use correct punctuation
 1. Maintain skills learned in the primary grades in the use of punctuation: comma in dates; after greeting and closing of letter; period after abbreviations and after numbers in listing; apostrophe for contraction and possession; quotation marks; exclamation point
 2. Introduce in Grade 4: A colon after greeting in a business letter
 3. Introduce in Grade 5: Extension of the use of apostrophe for possession; comma in direct address; hyphen in separating word at end of line; dash between page numbers in an index
 4. Introduce in Grade 6: Comma to set off words in apposition; between last name and first name or initials of a person when last name is given first; question mark following any interrogative sentence being quoted in a direct quotation; exclamation point following any exclamatory sentence being quoted in direct quotation

E. Maintain the habit of checking spelling in writing and skill in finding how to spell a word needed in writing. Extend throughout the intermediate grades: a study of homonyms; use of contractions and possessives; spelling of plurals ending in *s* and *es*, words changing final *y* to *i* before *e*, *es*, words dropping final *e* in adding *ing*, *er*, *ed*, or *y*.

1. Introduce in Grade 4: Plurals changing *f* to *v*; doubling the final consonant in adding suffixes like *ing, ed, est* (to keep short vowel sound)

2. Introduce in Grade 5: Plural of words ending in *o*; words keeping the final *e* in adding suffixes like *ness, ment*; plural possessives; words with *ie* and *ei*

3. Introduce in Grade 6: Adding prefixes like *un, im, dis*, capitalizing pronouns, and adjectives formed from proper nouns

When children write they should be encouraged to make use of the dictionaries, to utilize the vocabulary lists readily accessible, to see clearly the models of legible handwriting before them, and to have within view examples illustrating the form required in their writing. When children have clear concepts of the goals to be achieved, when they are given direct teaching, time to write, they will master the needed skills.

A dimensional approach to the conventions of written expression offers a broad base for evaluating pupil progress. An inventory or check list whereby the student can keep a record of his own strengths and weaknesses enables him to identify readily areas in which he needs help. The following plan has been used successfully with students for self evaluation. Each pupil is provided with mimeographed sheets like the one below which he keeps in his writing folder.

NAME .... GRADE .... DATE ....

Mistakes I make in writing.

(Write your error on the blank line and your
correction immediately below.)

Sentences

Fragments ....

Comma splices ....

....

Run-on sentences ....

....

Verbs ....

....

Pronouns ....

....

Word Division ....

....

Capital Letters ....

....

Punctuation

Commas ....

Semicolons ....

Colons ....

Quotation marks ....

Apostrophes ....

Spelling ....

Other Mistakes ....

Writing in the Upper Grades

Most students enter junior high school with some basic concepts of punctuation. They recognize and use the minimal system: beginning sentences with capital letters, ending with a period or a question mark, commas to set off words in a series. Many know far more than this, of course, and others are still in relatively shaky command of capitals, periods, and commas. The student needs first to learn the various marks which signal the basic sentence patterns of his writing.

As he begins to expand basic sentence patterns by compounding, he may, in some related lessons, learn how to punctuate such structures. If, as is suggested here, the emphasis is on having him write his own sentences, learning the punctuation system for these takes on significance as it becomes closely related to meaning and structure.[2]

A. Punctuating by intonation patterns

The teacher who understands the significance of the oral approach to the communication skills will readily see the value in training children to hear intonation signals in speaking and use these to provide them with useful clues to punctuation. Often when a child is having difficulty in punctuating a sentence the teacher will ask, "How would you say that?" The intonation and pause pattern provides a clue for punctuation. This technique is especially helpful in punctuating restrictive and nonrestrictive clauses. Fowler suggests the following as the most useful clues in this connection.

1. The falling juncture signalling the end of a declarative sentence and calling for a semicolon or period:

↘
                        We are going to dinner.

2. The level juncture signalling the restrictive clause or phrase versus the rising inflection and the three stresses which signal the nonrestrictive clause.

/   /   /

My sister, who lives in Texas, owns a Thunderbird.
(Three stresses, slight rising juncture marked by commas).

→

My sister who lives in Texas owns a Thunderbird.
(Level juncture; no distinctive pauses; no punctuation).

3. The comma after long introductory clauses or phrases, sometimes called sentence modifiers:
Because he never thought of anyone but himself, most people did not like him.
Since we are driving down to the shore on Tuesday, we will bring the beach chairs with us.[3]

B. Intonation and sentence structure

One of the difficult problems in punctuation is that of the semicolon between two independent clauses without a conjunction. Here too, attention to intonation and recognition of structure may help. Fading or falling juncture indicates the end of a thought unit. Too, often the sentence fragment is the result of inattention to the oral sentence melody. The student thus cuts into two structures one that should be punctuated by a comma. In *reading the sentence aloud* the falling juncture makes clear the structure and the desired punctuation.

She was a popular student. A girl who had been active in every important organization of the school.

Often, too the comma splice, joins two independent structures which require the semicolon:

We didn't expect anyone this afternoon, we were not prepared for guests.

C. Punctuating by structures

Once the student has some basic concepts of punctuation gleaned from his functional writing of letters, reports, and essays, he is ready for more complicated activities. Obviously until he is in command of the various symbols which signal the basic sentence patterns of his writing he is not ready for more complex assignments.

As he begins to compose his own sentences, learning the punctuation system takes on added meaning as it is related closely to structure and expression of his own ideas. He sees that compounding subjects, predicates, adverbs requires the separating comma to make his meaning clear.

She was pretty, gay, and charming. (pretty and gay? Or pretty gay?)

Teen-agers like hamburgers, ice-cream, and pickles. (Not ice-cream with pickles).

D. Punctuating interrupted patterns

One of the chief systems of punctuation is that which marks off the structural elements of the sentence: subordinate from main structures, words and modifiers in unexpected places, modifiers of word groups placed between, before, or after basic NV, NVN or linking verb structures. Students should be taught the basic patterns and observe the ways of setting off clauses and phrases. As students work with expanding sentence patterns, NV, NVN, they discover that modifiers, verb or noun clusters, phrases, or clauses may interrupt the basic pattern. They find that such words or word groups are commonly set off by commas to indicate an interruption of the basic structure:

Interrupting word: *He displayed, nevertheless, a fine attitude toward criticism.*

Appositive phrase: *His sister, a fine pianist, is studying modeling.*

(Added information interrupting the NVN pattern.)

Subordinate clause: *We started out and, because we had forgotten our change, went back home.*

(Clause interrupting compound sentence.)

Punctuation also sets off introductory word, clauses, and phrases to indicate the beginning of the main structure:

Instead, we went right home.

Instead of going to the movies, we went back home.

It should be made clear to the student that a single comma *never* separates the basic structural elements of the sentence: Subject and predicate, predicate and object, or linking verb and complement.

TEACHING THE CONVENTIONS OF WRITING

Teaching the conventions of writing involves more than providing the motivation and opportunity. It requires that the teacher:

Plan carefully meaningful situations that will involve the specific skill

Provide for application and self-evaluation

Encourage and supply special practice on the basis of individual needs and abilities

Integrate the learning of the specific skill, item, or convention with other learning activities in the language arts and in other curriculum areas.

A student must see a reason for and have opportunity to apply his newly acquired skill in a functional, real situation. He should evaluate the extent to which he is successful in that application. For example, if he is to use his new knowledge in writing letters effectively, he must have time to examine his performances to discover things he needs to do in order to improve in his communication skills.

Because children differ in their ability to learn and apply new skills it is necessary for some to have special practice exercises in using those items which they find difficult to master easily. This special practice should be planned on the basis of individual needs. The particular items on which special practice is needed are those which are matters of habit formation and which are essential for practically all writing activities. Specifically, this involves writing good sentences, using capital letters and punctuation marks, using words effectively, and organizing paragraphs clearly.

To help children understand the inter-relationships of the language arts and the need for effective communication of ideas in all schoolwork, as well as to provide further practice in a variety of situations, there should be opportunity for using skills learned in the language arts in other areas of the curriculum such as social studies, science, and so on. For example, in writing a report, or writing a letter in connection with social studies, the child must use correct mechanics in his written communication. In such an application of a specific written or oral activity, the child should be expected to apply the skills he has learned and to adhere to the standards which have been set for him not only in the language arts class, but in other curriculum areas.

In the following illustrations the principles suggested above are clearly seen:

Using Capital Letters and Punctuation Marks: A Third Grade

PLAN:

The children had been learning the purpose for using capital letters and punctuation marks. In the course of their study they received a letter from a pen pal who had written without using such clarifying marks. They were perturbed by the letter in which every word started with a capital and a number of the punctuation marks had been omitted. The teacher used the letter as a starting point for an assignment in using capital letters and punctuation marks. "Which words should begin with capital letters?" "Where should punctuation marks be placed in the letter from John?"

603 Elmwood Avenue
Victoria B C
January 6 19—

Dear Third Grade

What Do You Think I Got For Christmas My Dad Gave Me A Puppy Called Rover I Am Going To Enter Him In A Pet Show Next Monday At Woodmere Park. My Mother Gave Me A New Bicycle My Sister Gave Me A Piñata. What Did You Get For Christmas Please Write

Your Friend
John

APPLY:

Directions: On a sheet of paper copy John's letter. Use capital letters *only* where they are needed. Put in the punctuation marks which have been omitted.

EVALUATE:

Use the rules on the bulletin board to help you check your paper. Correct any mistakes you find. Hand your paper in.

PRACTICE:

Write a letter centering around one of the following situations:
1. Your uncle sent you a present for Christmas. Write him a thank-you letter.
2. Your best friend has moved. Write telling him the news of his friends and their activities.

3. Write an invitation to a party you are having for your birthday.
4. Write a letter to one of your friends about the things you are seeing on your holiday trip.

INTEGRATE:

Write a report of a trip (real or imaginary) you took to a neighbouring province. Such a report should enhance the study of the neighbouring province in your social studies class. Other suggestions for teaching capitalization and punctuation in meaningful situations are: Rewrite the following paragraph using: 6 Sentences, 10 Capital Letters, 5 Commas, 4 Quotation Marks

mary reached into the large bag and pulled out a santa claus suit and held it up it was bright red with black fur trim billy could see that there was a set of whiskers and a cap and shiny boot made of black leather isn't it lovely she said to billy the minute i saw it i thought of you im sure it will be a perfect fit she said laughingly.

In teaching punctuation and capitalization it is well to keep in mind that the important thing is the communication of an idea, or feeling to be aroused in the reader. Punctuation marks are there to help the words evoke that response. Teaching children to punctuate properly involves a combination of examples and rules, as in learning the salutations for friendly letters and formal letters, analysis and imitation of the punctuations we see in our reading, and opportunity to experiment with the various techniques in learning how to punctuate and capitalize.

As we begin to relate punctuation to oral expression it will become clearer to the child that there is *no one* way of punctuating; that a knowledge of several approaches is extremely useful.

INTERMEDIATE AND UPPER GRADES

Intermediate and upper grade children need a change of pace and more complex activities to challenge their interest in this phase of the writing program.

Some motivations for teaching the new elements at the intermediate grade levels include such activities as the following:

T.V. and punctuation. A television program in which each punctuation mark appears and is questioned concerning its function and activities; this can be adapted to the program "What's My Line?" format with each punctuation mark appearing as a guest; the Master of Ceremonies commences by a remark: "Our first guest does four things [or ten if it's the comma]. Let's name them all in order to identify him completely."

Punctuate trick sentences such as the following:

The fight over the boys came home
This is the story of walter who has not heard the story through it walter gained lasting fame a beautiful girl and a glorious name he also gained one autumn day on the muddy field in gridiron play the team was losing the clock moved fast any play

could be the last of the game injured walter then called his own signal explaining men ill take the blame if we dont score he ran a full ninety yards or more

Dictation. To make sure the punctuation habits of students are deep-seated and automatic teachers find frequent dictation a motivating device and excellent means for practice. Farrell suggests dictating to students while they copy it *verbatim* at their desks or at the blackboard. The students insert all punctuation marks and all capital letters; they decide when a sentence ends and when to start a new one; in longer passages they make their own decisions about spelling as well. This is the procedure:

> Mr. McCorkell reads the passage aloud three times; once so that the students may learn the length and gist of it; a second time very, very slowly so that they may write it; a third time fairly quickly so that the students may check their writing.
>
> Mr. McCorkell's methods of correction vary: (1) each student corrects his own work. (2) The students correct each other's work. (3) Mr. McCorkell corrects all the passages. (4) Two or three careful students, chosen by Mr. McCorkell, form a committee to check the passages.
>
> A numerical mark is given to each paper. The procedure is simple. Mr. McCorkell counts the number of words in the passage, say 100. He then divides by 5. This gives him the total mark possible for the passage. If there are 100 words, the possible mark is 20; if there are 25 words, the posible mark is 5.[4]

Dictation can be used in a number of ways to improve the mechanics of writing: spelling dictation, anecdote dictation, homonym dictation, poetry dictation.

Abbreviations. What do the abbreviations stand for in the following sentences?

(a) The U.S.S.R. does not look with favour on the DEW line of MLF.

(b) Danny Kaye has done a great deal of work for UNICEF, a branch of UNESCO, which in turn is a specialized agency of the UN.

(c) I found a kitten riding under the hood of my GM truck and I took it to the SPCA.

(d) Write the abbreviations for Alberta, Florida, Prince Edward Island, Quebec, Alabama, Maine, Manitoba.

(e) What are the abbreviations for: company, limited, association, pages, Doctor of Philosophy, postscript, manager, pound (money), pound (weight), ounces, prescription symbol (as used by doctors and druggists) parallel, triangle?

(f) Give the abbreviations for the days of the week.

(g) Give the abbreviations for the months of the year.[5]

(h) Have students investigate abbreviations in current newspapers and magazines. Compare them with newspapers and magazines of earlier times.

Discovery through research. Have children research and report on a Formula for Punctuation System. An example follows:

> Although man has been speaking for ages and has been practicing alphabetic writing for over 3,000 years, he has punctuated in the modern sense, for less than

250 years. As yet he has not perfected a system of ideal punctuation. As it now stands, the symbols of punctuation are as follows:

(a) For *linking*, use:
        ; semicolon
        : colon
       — linking dash
       - linking hyphen

(b) For *separating*, use:
       . period
      ? question mark
      ! exclamation point
      , separating comma

(c) For *enclosing*, use:
      , . . . , paired commas
      - . . . - paired dashes
      (. . .) paired parenthesis
      [. . .] paired brackets
      " ; ; ; " paired quotation marks

(d) For *indicating omissions*, use:
      ' apostrophe
      . omission period in abbreviations (or dot)
      — omissions dash
      . . . triple periods (or dots)
      . . . . quadruple periods (or dots)[6]

If the teacher is concerned about helping children master the mechanics of writing he will keep in mind the importance of: (1) knowing why punctuation is necessary, (2) what must be taught at each educational level, (3) teaching in harmony with principles of effective motivation, (4) organizing learning activities with imagination, (5) using a functional approach in teaching, and (6) utilising knowledge from research in linguistics and English which have implications for teaching.

Major ideas emanating from research and educational theory stress the significance of creating an environment which motivates and develops the oral and written expressive abilities of the students. The goals of the teacher, the teaching style he adopts and the objectives to be achieved by the students must be clear not only to the teacher but to the student who comes to recognize the mastery of the skills as a vehicle for creative communication of ideas. It is a tragedy as well as a truism that many men and women with significant ideas, yes, even with sublime ideas, have failed to develop skill essential to communicate them to others.

TEACHING SPELLING CREATIVELY

"Who does not remember the enlivening effects of the spelling matches of his boyhood? So intensely was their attention concentrated upon the subject in hand, that grown men remember distinctly the very words missed by themselves and others in some remarkable contests."[7]

Methods of spelling have changed since the days when our forefathers "spelled down" in the little country school house. But have we in our emphasis on spelling simply as a tool, lost something of the emotional involvement that was once an integral part of the experience of learning to spell? Can we in our technological age recapture some of the excitement, some of the challenge, and some of the competitive spirit that pervaded the spelling program? Can we blend it with what we are learning from research in making use of the clues we have gained about the interrelationships of the language arts, and what we are discovering from linguistics and creative learning to revitalize the teaching of spelling?

Insight into the relationship between a child's affective response to a learning situation, his joy in discovery, and his need to have a purpose for learning makes it possible for today's teacher to teach spelling even better than the teacher of yesteryear. Cannot spelling be retrieved from the dull, plodding routine of the daily utilitarian task to the enriched, creative conquest of new words and through them new ideas?

How well a pupil learns to spell depends largely upon his interest and attitude. His interest and attitude toward spelling determine what he will do toward attempting to learn, how hard he will try, and how persistent he will be in his learning effort. Today's teacher has available the benefit of research to guide him. In an effective program the child's interest will be captured. His attitude toward learning to spell will be a positive one. He will have a motivation for learning to spell. Words which have meaning and value for the student will be selected. The practice of words will be limited to those he cannot spell and he really needs. He will be helped to develop individualized study habits. He will be guided in using self-evaluation techniques. Materials which have inherent appeal for the pupil develop not merely an effective spelling method but facilitate a creative approach to teaching spelling. A teacher must take the responsibility for discovering the key to unlock each child's interest in learning what he needs to know. Spelling is one of these needs.

> Correct spelling is evidence of good manners. It is a matter of courtesy to spell correctly so that reading is easier, just as it is courteous to speak distinctly so as to be easily understood. Accurate spelling is one of those things that stamp one as cultivated, neat, accurate, painstaking. The candidate for a new job is judged by the spelling in his dossier no less than by the polish on his shoes.
>
> In the public eye, inaccurate spelling is so generally associated with illiteracy, that the results school children achieve in spelling have been known to influence public attitudes toward the school. Some laymen judge the quality of the entire program by how well the children can spell.[8]

THE STATUS OF SPELLING IN THE CURRICULUM

Noah Webster's "Blue Back" *Speller* with its long lists of words developed primarily for formal practice in word pronunciation as a prelude to reading, dominated not only the curriculum but also the social life through the "spelling bee" centering around the exercises in Webster's book. The theory of formal discipline was replaced during the early 1900's by the social utility concept. This was used to justify the continuation of the long, difficult lists of spelling words. It was assumed that after years of drill the pupil would eventually be ready to use spelling as a tool for writing.

In the 1920's and 30's emphasis on factors of interest and learning through meaningful activities gave a new direction to the teaching of spelling. Now the learning to spell to express ideas became an important factor.

In the current scene emphasis is on the interrelatedness of all the language arts. The authors believe that all language skills, including spelling, develop best in an atmosphere of meaningful and creative learning activities, such as writing communications that have a purpose, planning a script for a play, writing for the school newspaper. However, a belief in the interrelatedness of the language arts does not preclude the need for systematic instruction of spelling as a distinct discipline as well as the correlation of spelling with other curriculum areas.

Today's high school and college students are evidence that spelling is not being taught as effectively as it should be in the elementary schools. Indeed, according to Petty, "Disturbing as it may be, there appears to be evidence that teaching practice has tended to remain influenced far more by habit than by research evidence."[9]

The spelling textbook series used in spelling programs obviously influence the actual procedures followed in the classrooms. The extent to which these textbooks utilize the available research determines the spelling program in the schools. Unfortunately, some textbook series tend to reinforce traditional practices and procedures and result in a cycle of practices which have little validity in the light of current research.

This practice tends to limit the spelling power of children. In today's schools the goal must be to develop the maximum potential of every child in every curriculum area. Spelling lists in recent years have tended to include less than 4,000 words. The actual word lists and grade levels suggested for teaching particular words varies considerably from list to list. Recent research points to lack of agreement among authors of spelling textbooks.[10] Such disagreement makes it imperative that the individual school system carefully study the textbooks in the light of the needs of the pupils who will be using those textbooks in their spelling activities.

Although research has established the superiority of the test-study procedure of instruction, it has been ignored by many teachers. The test-study procedure calls for beginning the unit of instruction with a test which identifies for each pupil words he does not know how to spell. This helps build favourable attitudes toward spelling as does the corrected test. The corrected test focuses upon specific spelling problems through having each student check his own test. This has been shown to be the most efficient single procedure for learning to spell.[11, 12]

A procedure in widespread use is the contextual presentation of the spelling words. Such a presentation is purported to aid the child to learn the meaning of the words, however, most of these presentations simply use words rather than develop their meanings. Since these words are normally in the children's speaking, comprehension and reading vocabularies, any so-called development of meaning is largely a waste of time, both for teacher and pupil. The list presentation of words is more efficient and fosters a more favourable learning "set".[13]

Despite the fact that early studies pointed out the futility of expecting improved spelling merely as a result of increasing the time devoted to teaching spelling,[14] time allotments have recently been increased in many schools. As a matter of fact, no more than seventy-five minutes a week should be given over to spelling instruction and there is evidence that even less time accomplishes equal achievements. In most schools, spelling is taught five periods a week, primarily because of the ease of administering such a program. However, particularly if the corrected test technique is used, fewer periods may be as satisfactory.

There are students who find spelling difficult and there are those who find it relatively easy to learn to spell. Thus people often reach the inevitable conclusion "You're either a born speller or you're not."

To ask a good speller for the answer to the question, "How did you learn to spell," is not much help. He might not remember; he might have had a good teacher in the third grade; he sounds out words; he looks up words in the dictionary; he traces the words with his fingers as he spells; he memorizes them; he visualizes them in his mind's eye. The reasons may all sound fine, but are they the real answers? Some of the studies which shed light on the subject follow.

WHAT RECENT RESEARCH SAYS TO THE TEACHER

The superior teacher always makes use of research findings to improve and vitalize his teaching.

Russell[15] reported that poor spelling ability in grades five and six is closely related to poor auditory discrimination and visual differences, although high spelling ability is not necessarily related to superior discrimination. Furness[16] emphasized the importance of correct pronunciation—including articulation, enunciation, and syllabication.

Russell[17] later reported that auditory abilities and spelling achievement appear to be related.

1. Some auditory abilities are significantly related to spelling abilities at the percent level of confidence.
2. Some verbal auditory skills are significantly related to both spelling and reading ability; these abilities involved recognition of word parts rather than whole words.
3. Relationship of listening comprehension of paragraphs to spelling scores was low.

Damgaard[18] in studying auditory acuity and discrimination differences in spelling concluded that the pitch, loudness, and rhythm with which spelling words were presented influenced the results. Timbre of the teacher's voice did not influence results.

Rea[19] studied oral-aural training with 207 second graders and found that the teaching of principles in regard to the application of phonemes in contextual writing did produce greater transfer of learning to similar tasks than was evidenced by training which emphasized either the visual or the haptical approach (based on or relating to the sense of touch).

Psychological Factors Are Involved in Learning to Spell

There is an emotional factor in learning to spell as well as a motivational factor. Among the points Furness[20] cited concerning psychological determinants of spelling success were:

Ability to spell seems to be contingent upon two processes—recognition and reproduction.

The older the child, the more difficulties and discouragements were encountered, but these old attitudes can be replaced with new ones.

Indifference, carelessness, and distaste for intellectual drudgery are major factors in poor spelling, especially for the student with a high IQ.

The skilful management of incentives is unquestionably more important than techniques of instruction.

There is a Close Relationship Between Spelling and Reading

The relationship between spelling performance and reading ability has significant implications, particularly in dealing with the poor reader. Plessas and Petty[21] found that the poor reader had a special problem in learning to spell. They point out that although good spellers are usually good readers and poor spellers are often poor readers, not all poor spellers are poor readers. Implications for the teacher of spelling in dealing with the poor reader are: (1) children should not be expected to learn to spell words they cannot recognize; (2) persistent failure in spelling can only reinforce undesirable attitudes toward spelling; and (3) there is little evidence to suggest that spelling instruction promotes growth in reading.

Many skills and abilities are common to reading and spelling. Reading and spelling are two facets of the language arts, not discrete fields. Each is based on oral language skill. Stauffer[22] points out:

The correlations between reading and spelling are relatively high

The best single measure of a child's readiness for reading is how well he talks

Spelling rules, like phonetics, should never be taught in isolation

Self-study skills are important in spelling and reading

For best results, spelling instruction should be integrated with instruction in the other language arts and correlated with the different curriculum areas

As a rule of thumb, avoid asking a child to spell a word he cannot read, regardless of the curriculum area in which it occurs.

Teaching spelling through reading should be avoided. Russell[23] maintains that teaching spelling through reading interferes with the thought getting process in reading. There is no basis for emphasis upon learning to spell through reading; in fact, certain techniques in learning to spell may interfere with reading comprehension. Gilbert and Gilbert[24] photographed eye movements of students while they were reading materials containing key spelling words. They concluded that many fixations during the eye movements in reading may indicate spelling reactions, thus affecting comprehension of printed matter. Emphasis on spelling can create a problem if a reader consistently focuses attention on the letters in words rather than on the meanings of these words during the reading process.

The Role of Phonic Skill Development

Aaron[25] found that ability in the spelling of phonic syllables seems to be predictive of spelling achievement. Newton[26] concluded that of the abilities and skills investigated, the ability to spell phonic syllables was the greatest contributor in learning to spell.

The controversy over the value of phonics in teaching spelling is a continuing one, with extensive claims being reported concerning the "regular" representation of *phonemes.*[27]

Some studies indicate that phonetic rules do not apply to a substantial percentage of *words* pupils are called upon to spell.[28, 29, 30] The position of many is that some teaching of sound-to-letter and letter-to-sound relationship may prove of real value.[31]

Cues from Linguistics for Teaching Spelling

By far the most exciting cues for vitalizing spelling come from the linguists. "Typically, the teaching of spelling has been predicated on the assumption that there is little relationship between the way words are said and how they are spelled so that each word requires a separate act of learning. Consequently, lists of spelling words for class study have been selected largely on the basis of the utility of these words in children's and adult writings."[32]

Statistical analysis of phoneme-grapheme correspondences, on the other hand, suggests a considerably different rationale for spelling instruction. Research initiated by Hanna[33] in 1950, undertook to test the spelling consistency of the 3,000 most frequently used words in children's writing. It was discovered that phonemes (sounds) of the 3,000 words are regularly represented by certain graphemes (letters) approximately 80% of the time.

More recently, with the use of computer technology, the Stanford (University) spelling research project attempted to analyze the orthography using linguistic techniques. These studies, corroborate the findings. A study of more than 17,000 words reveals a relatively consistent phoneme-grapheme (sound-to letter) relationship. By relying on phonological cues alone more than 8,300 words can be spelled correctly from the spelling list of 17,000 words. The basic question concerning the Stanford Study is the extent to which the findings will have utility in spelling methods. [34, 35, 36]

"What has been demonstrated at this stage of the research", assert Hodges and Rudorf, "is that the orthography reflects the structure of the oral language upon which it is based. It suggests that regularities exist in the relationship between phonological elements in the oral language and their graphemic representations in the orthography, and that a pedagogical method based upon aural cues to spelling may well prove to be more efficient and powerful than . . . methods which rely primarily upon visual and hand learning approaches. . . . From these Stanford research studies, one evidently can hypothesize that even a limited knowledge of the phonological relationships between the sounds and the letters of the orthography can provide the power to spell literally thousands of words and that other abilities relating to morphology and syntax may give pupils the ability to spell the vast majority of the words in their oral vocabularies."[37]

Obviously the cues from linguistics will still require the student to memorize certain of the words which depart markedly from the basic alphabetical nature of the orthography. More consideration must be given to the problem of determining which words should be selected to help the pupil arrive inductively at the generalizations that will guide him in translating oral cues into writing. The extent to which the child is able to make use of the most efficient method of learning to use spelling as a tool for writing more effectively is the measure of the good spelling program. The answer may well be found in a linguistically-oriented language arts program.

PROBLEMS TEACHERS FACE

While researchers continue to explore, teachers continue to be faced with three basic problems: determining readiness for spelling instruction, selecting words that should be taught at various grade or educational levels, utilizing effective methods of teaching and vitalizing the spelling program.

Readiness for Spelling

When is a child ready to learn to spell? "Some children can spell a few words before they come to kindergarten. At home they have scribbled on writing paper and sent a letter to Grandma. When they get to kindergarten, they want to put their names on their work, write messages to Mother, and spell out their names and the names of their best friends. Many of them learn to print during the year. A number of them become interested in spelling games: "How do you spell _____?" "I see a little girl whose name is M-a-r-y." "Will J-o-h-n go to the desk and bring me a b-o-o-k?"[38]

This informal experience with sound and letter in no way suggests that every child in the kindergarten is ready to learn to spell. The child is ready when he evidences certain abilities which are related to spelling—auditory discrimination, visual discrimination, muscular coordination, perceptual readiness, social and emotional control, intellectual curiosity, and mental maturity. Beginning spelling instruction implies a readiness to integrate the skills of listening, handwriting, perception, and visualization for the purpose of communicating something through the written word.

Not until a child is able to discriminate sounds, associate sounds and letters, coordinate eye and hand, demonstrate muscular control of the instrument for writing, and has something important to say which motivates him to written expression does he give evidence of readiness. When a child associates the sounds he hears in words with letters he recognizes, when he reads words with comprehension, when he writes legibly, formal instruction in spelling can begin.

A basic program of formal instruction according to Hildreth should be initiated when the pupils have achieved

> A mental age of 7½ years or more
> A speaking vocabulary of some 5,000 words
> The ability to enunciate words distinctly
> Ability to recognize and pronounce 300-400 of the commonest words met in reading
> A beginning in phonetics—the commonest letter-sound combination
> The ability to write the letters of the alphabet correctly
> The ability to copy simple words correctly
> The ability to write a few simple words from memory.[39]

With the emphasis on the oral approach to written expression it is obvious that the teacher must make sure that the child "hears" the sounds in the words he is learning to spell. A basic program of instruction in spelling should help the child: (1) hear, speak, and think these sounds clearly so that he is able to distinguish between them; (2) recognize that words he uses in communication are made up of sequences of individual single speech sounds (phonemes) blended together; (3) recognize that in the written form of our language each sound is represented by one or more letters of the alphabet; (4) develop an automatic association of a written letter with each of those sounds which is very commonly represented by a single letter; and (5) develop skill in manuscript writing in order to form letters legibly in a reasonable amount of time without undue pressure or stress.

Initial experiences in spelling should be based largely on words that are familiar to children in their speaking and listening vocabulary and are spelled in a phonetically regular manner. Words of high utility value that are not spelled phonetically should be introduced as needed but kept to a reasonable minimum.

In the linguistic environment the child learns to spell in the same manner in which he learned to speak. He listens and imitates. When his eyes are filled with print, his ears conscious of sound, his muscles ready to form letters, and his ideas crying out to be recorded in permanent form, the child is ready to learn to spell.

Selecting Words to be Studied

As children progress in their linguistic development and do more writing, there will be some basic words which they will need to learn. Three widely used practices for selecting spelling words in the primary grades are: (1) selecting the words all children need to learn as they progress through the grades; these are found in the best of current spelling textbooks; (2) developing a list of spelling words which the class needs in its current activities, and (3) choosing the words that are important for individual children to learn for specific purposes. These words include family names, place names such as address, and words that are required in personal and expository writing. Children need these individual lists to fit individual needs. Each child also develops and keeps his own list of basic words that are difficult for him.

In the primary spelling program many common words are mastered. The child is also encouraged to use unfamiliar words and spell them to the best of his ability. As he writes, phonetic skills developed in the basic reading and spelling program help him to some extent in spelling these new words. The teacher should be prepared for "creative spelling" in creative writing since the child's speaking vocabulary outreaches his spelling vocabulary. The new words that he uses in creative writing become a part of his personal spelling list.

In the intermediate grades words to be studied will come from several sources: (1) a prepared spelling list taken from the textbook series being used in the school, (2) the list of words compiled by the teacher who foresees in a particular assignment words the children will be using, (3) a list of "spelling demons," (4) frequently misspelled words from the children's day-to-day writing and on words misspelled in special subject areas, and (5) a combination of a prepared list and an individual list for each child. However the words to be studied are selected, it is the responsibility of the teacher to provide for individual differences among children and to make the study of spelling interesting, challenging, and exciting.

Once the list is determined it is important for the teacher to help children in the intermediate grades develop the ability to analyze spelling words phonetically and structurally. Children should associate the sounds of letters with the visual forms, and become skilful at adding prefixes and suffixes to root words, and at hearing and seeing parts or syllables in words. They should have direct teaching and practice in forming plurals, possessives, and contractions; they should become familiar with homonyms, compound, and hyphenated words. Spelling power grows with direct instruction, regular practice, and application in meaningful writing activities.

In the grades seven through nine lists in spelling continue to be made up of (1) basic lists from the spelling series, (2) "demon" lists, (3) special subject matter lists, (4) vocabulary development lists, and (5) an individual list of words each student frequently misspells.

Methods of Teaching Spelling

Spelling power cannot develop in a vacuum; it develops together with language power as children are motivated to express their own ideas clearly and fluently in speaking and writing. Learning to spell is a developmental process; it is a complicated process. If children were to delay writing until they were competent in spelling the words they need to use in their written compositions much of the motivation for writing would have disappeared. Children should not be forced to wait until they have learned to spell the words in a selected spelling list before they are free to use them in their writing.

The responsibility of the teacher is two-fold: to motivate children to develop spelling power *and* to teach children to become independent in their study of words. In order to accomplish these aims the teacher must have a clear understanding of what is involved in learning to spell. Learning to spell depends upon how accurately a child hears and says the sounds in a word, how clearly he visualizes the written form, the extent to which he has muscular control, and his personal involvement in learning to spell. Because of individual differences in children, a method of study that combines aural-oral, visual, and kinesthetic imagery with an inductive approach, and an understanding of psychological factors is necessary.

An illustration of the elements that comprise the spelling process are shown in the chart below:[40]

Spelling in Action

PRODUCT
Behavioral Competencies—Physical
Aural acuity
Oral refinement
Visual sensitivity
Haptical proficiency
Behavioral Competencies—Psychological
Knowledge of Spelling Principles
Ability Deductively to Apply Generalizations
Mastery of Spelling Irregularities

A brief examination of methods of teaching spelling will be important in solving the persistent problem of how to teach spelling effectively, efficiently, and creatively.

The textbook approach. The spelling textbook has traditionally formed the basis of the spelling program. In this method the textbook dominates the program.

It determines what will be studied (content), the scope and sequence, and to a great extent the procedure. Its main advantage is that it gives to both the teacher and pupils a well articulated, over-all plan for developing spelling skills throughout the elementary grades. Its chief disadvantage is that it may devitalize the spelling program into routinized, sterile, and rote learning.

In using the textbook method a plan similar to the following is generally used. In planning the procedure the teacher must keep in mind both the teaching and learning process.

FOR THE TEACHER
1. *Introduce the word.* (Recognition and meaning)
   Teacher says the word
   Teacher writes the word on the chalkboard
   Children point to the word in their books
   Children use the word orally in meaningful sentences
2. *Identify the letters* (visual and auditory imagery)
   "What letters are needed to write the word?"
   "Do you see any new letter in this word?"
   (If children answer yes, the teacher writes the new letter on the board demonstrating the proper formation of the letter)
   Children practice the letter (teacher gives help where needed)
   Teacher repeats, "What letters are needed to write the word?"
   "Jane, Jim, all the boys, all the girls, row two, row five, etc., say the letters with me, fingers pointed to the word and eyes taking a photo of the word."
   "Who can name the letters without glancing at the book?" (spell the word)
3. *Write the word* (visual and motor imagery)
   Teacher writes the word on the board calling attention to the details of letter formation (Using ruled lines sets example of letter formation and size of letters)
   Teacher writes the word again and a third time if needed to strengthen visual imagery and "reinforce" the learning. Children write the word once (Compare with the teacher's example)
   Repeat until the word has been written several times
   Teacher gives help where needed
4. *Use the same procedure* for teaching the next word
5. *Review*
   Have children spell orally words learned during the previous spelling lesson
   Children recall and spell orally words learned on any previous day
6. *Check Test*
   If time permits, children may take a written trial of words learned thus far (in a given week)

The child in learning to spell follows this sequence of six steps.
FOR THE CHILD
1. *Look* at the word.   Look at it from left to right
                                 Notice anything in the word you did not expect to be there

2. *Pronounce* the word.	Be sure to pronounce it slowly and distinctly
	Say the letters to yourself
3. *Visualize* the word.	Close your eyes and visualize the word
	Look at it again
	Do you see it in your mind's eye?
4. *Write* the word.	Write the word without looking at it
5. *Check* the spelling.	Did you get it right?
	Check with the word on the chalkboard or with your word list.
	If misspelled, write the word correctly.
6. Use the word.	Write a sentence using the word
	Check the spelling in a sentence[41]

With the advent of linguistics on the spelling scene a new formula which emphasizes the aural-oral approach is used. The child is told to:

Listen to the Word
Pronounce the Word
Visualize the Word
Discover the Word Patterns
Spell the Word
Write the Word
Check the Word
Use the Word

The teacher who uses a linguistically oriented spelling series develops a lesson through a sequence of aural-oral activities, sounds and patterns, structure and meaning, check point, word knowledge, and word challenge.

1. *Aural-oral Activities*

   Ask pupils to pronounce words after you. Help pupils discover the specific item that you plan to teach. Write words on chalkboard and let volunteers identify the item that has been introduced.

2. *Sounds and Patterns*

   Have pupils turn to their books and follow the written exercise and identify the sounds and patterns in the spelling words.

3. *Structure and Meaning*

   Have pupils do the exercise centering around the structure and meaning of the words. Use the dictionary as suggested in the spelling text.

4. *Word Knowledge*

   Have pupils write sentences using the new words.

5. *Word Challenge*

   Enrichment activities in using the words learned.

6. *Post Test*

   Subsequent to enrichment activities children are tested by dictation of sentences containing the word list.

An integrated spelling-writing approach. Obviously spelling instruction, when integrated with fictional and creative writing, demands a technique different from that used in a textbook centered spelling program. It is fostered in an environment in which each child is secure as he writes, and is assured that in his writing, misspelled words are temporarily acceptable, and that he will have time to make the necessary additions or corrections *after* the writing is completed.

Suggestions for techniques and prepared materials which are helpful in allowing each child to do his best creative writing, and in encouraging personal responsibility for correct spelling and in developing ingenuity in locating and using information, follow:

TECHNIQUES:

Permit a child to write only the first letter of a word which he cannot spell, leaving a space for the word to be completed after the writing has been finished.

List on the chalkboard a group of class-dictated words to be used as needed.

Place topic words on a chart for copying as needed. Attractive and appropriate pictures drawn or pasted on the chart make it a joy to use. The chart may be stored for use at a future date when the same topic is being explored in greater depth. Additional words may be added at that time.

Direct the child to find the word in a book where he remembers having read it.

Help him personally if other avenues of self-help fail.

MATERIALS:

The "Writer's Corner" contains a number of picture dictionaries, writing paper, pictures of interest to children, previously used charts, and books pertaining to topics currently being discussed. Word charts related to areas of interest to the children are prepared and filed in appropriately labeled envelopes. The children will use these as spelling helps when engaged in independent writing.

The children construct individual dictionaries with several pages reserved for each letter of the alphabet. Under the direction of the teacher, they enter words which are important enough to be mastered. . . .

[In such a setting, spelling,] as incorporated in a dynamic writing program, is carefully planned to promote continuous progress in writing proficiency and in the development of an expanding vocabulary. The word lists for mastery, when kept within the maturation level of the child, increase writing power and lead to satisfactory learning experience. The use of functional materials develops desirable work habits and self-reliance.[42]

Obviously in this program it devolves upon the teacher to determine content and skills in accordance with the needs and interests of the children and the demands of the total curriculum. Skills are developed as they are called for by specific projects. Children are free to explore writing opportunities and to broaden their vocabularies beyond a ready-made list of words. Care must be taken not to leave gaps in children's mastery of words within their maturational level. This program when used by an effective teacher fosters a high degree of interest in and quality of writing.

Individualized spelling: In the individualized spelling program each child selects words from the authorized grade list which children are supposed to know by the end of the year. The words are alphabetized and graded 1 through 10 according to difficulty. Each week each child selects as many words from the list as he feels he can successfully learn in that week—thus making his individual weekly list. Any words missed on the final weekly test are added to the following week's work. When he learns to spell the words on one graded level correctly, he is allowed to go on to the next graded level.

A weekly program illustrating this method follows:

> *First day*: Each child prepares his list. (This is done by the child selecting from the complete list those words he wishes to study according to the level he is on. In addition, his individual list includes words misspelled from the previous week and words that he may have needed to have spelled in Social Studies, Creative Writing, etc.)
>
> *Second day*: Each child practices his words (using the accepted method—look at the word, look away, write the word, *etc.*) In addition, the teacher gives help with spelling rules, associations, *etc.*
>
> *Third day*: Each child has a partner to whom he gives a practice test and from whom he receives a practice test: the test is corrected by the tester by comparing it with the list in the notebook.
>
> *Fourth day*: Same as the second day except the child is expected to pay particular attention to the words missed on the Practice Test.
>
> *Fifth day*: Final test.[43]

In summarizing the effectiveness of such a program Eisman points out that the children in the Individualized program were working on the average from .8 to 1.5 grades higher in spelling than children in the Group Program. The advantage of this program is that the student may work at his own rate and learns to spell by the method most effective for him.

Word mastery: the spelling-vocabulary partnership. Although inability to spell and to use words effectively and correctly may handicap the elementary student in effective writing it is at the junior high level that the problem becomes acute. "Junior high students are frustrated because their own performance does not meet the demands of their critical judgement. They are extremely conscious of their incompetencies and are baffled by their inability to write at the level of their thinking. In the classroom they will usually stumble along, but the product of their efforts suffers from imperfectly expressed ideas and a lack of clarity and continuity. Such students must be taught word mastery to achieve satisfactory growth in their writing ability."[44]

Certain specific skills are introduced, reviewed and expanded in the junior high school. As a guide to help teachers in developing a word mastery program in grades seven through nine the following list is presented:

> WORD ANALYSIS: Heavy stress is placed on word attack skills and understandings in the junior high school. Study of suffixes, prefixes, and root words is fundamental to teaching spelling and vocabulary.

PRONUNCIATION: Although the lack of consistency in the spelling conventions of English is misleading, a valuable means of improving spelling is the study of pronunciation, including a review of phonics and syllabication. Pronunciation merits special emphasis in the junior high school, for this is a time when student exuberance often lead to careless speaking habits.

DEMON LISTS: A list of commonly used, frequently misspelled words has an important place in the junior high school program. In addition, each student can be encouraged to develop a list of words he frequently misspells.

DICTIONARY: A continued, day-by-day emphasis on independent use of the dictionary is essential. Acceptance of the individual responsibility for learning correct spelling is fundamental to a growth program in this area.

PROOFREADING: Continued practice in proof-reading can pay real dividends in the word mastery program. There is little doubt that students can spell correctly many of the words they misspell. There is also little doubt that students can recognize many misspellings of words which they have not yet learned to spell. These words can be learned with the help of the dictionary.

SPELLING RULES: A few carefully selected spelling rules can be helpful to students; however, the limitations of this deductive approach are apparent to the skilled teacher. A number of handbooks give rules suitable for inclusion in a word mastery program. Hook's "Guide to Good Writing" is one excellent source.

HOMONYMS: The study of homonyms is an important, although not major part of the word mastery program. In addition to the study of homonyms, attention will be given to words of similar sound and structure. Errors in writing related to similarities of words are often a result of inattentiveness and spontaneity, characteristics of many junior high students.

The preceding list is not complete, but it includes many methods of teaching and studying word mastery skills in the junior high school. It indicates that perhaps the most common cause of problems is lack of attention to detail. It suggests that word mastery is most effectively developed through understanding word meaning and the techniques of word analysis, but it also suggests other methods to be used in a successful program of word mastery.[45]

A discovery approach. The discovery approach is particularly effective in a program emphasizing independent study. A master list of possible questions is provided to guide the student in the problem of "looking at a word" in such a way that it will give practice in phonetic, structural, and meaning analysis as well as in usage practice. "It is intended that from this list", says Blake, "under the teacher's guidance, a pupil will discover those questions which provide for more efficient independent study of words of the type habitually missed. With guidance, a pupil will discover those questions which he must apply to every word week after week in order to bring about improvement in spelling ability. He would eliminate those questions which do not contribute to [his] spelling growth."[46]

Blake feels that such a chart as the one listed below is useful, but inadequate in guiding independent word study.

Hear the word correctly
Look at the word
Say it aloud to yourself
Close your eyes, look away, try to visualize it
Look at the word and study it again
Write the word
Check the spelling
Write the word three to five times

Blake suggests in addition that questions dealing with four categories be developed. The categories and an illustrative question from each are listed.

Phonetic analysis e.g., Does the word contain a *sound* that might be spelled in more than one way? (phone; near)
Structural analysis e.g., Is this a compound word?
Meaning e.g., If this word can be dramatized, can I do so?
Usage e.g., Do I understand the word and its synonyms, antonyms, and homonyms well enough to use them in my speech and writing?[47]

Teaching spelling creatively. While the various methods of teaching spelling are successful with some children, others are leaving the elementary school and the high school without the mastery of the tool of spelling. Although it would seem that the findings of research should enable every child to learn to spell, it is a fact that some children who spell words correctly on spelling tests cannot apply this knowledge in their writing. "Although it would seem that with the aid of a dictionary any normal child can learn to spell, this does not appear to be the case. Some students, regardless of the care they exercise, consistently make a few spelling errors when writing. Perhaps this must be accepted."[48]

An ally to teaching spelling effectively which but few teachers have recognized is that of combining the findings of research in the dynamics of communication, linguistics, and learning with a creative approach to teaching spelling. "Through a creative approach to teaching spelling," asserts Margaret Woods, "learning seems to be a highly personal matter. To a great degree, desire to learn is facilitated when feelings are brought into full play."

"Boys and girls can tell us much about effective ways of learning. They continue to show us that the imaginative process inherent in one method of teaching spelling causes children to feel compelled to communicate and to arrive at understandings which prove a potent source of new ideas, clear-cut actions, new understanding and new powers. The potential lies within, silently, but hopefully waiting to be enticed."[49]

In the description of the creative approach to teaching spelling the author reinforces the answer the artist Cizek gave when asked—

"How do you do it?" we asked at last,
"But I don't do it", he protested. . . .
"I take off the lid, and other art masters
Clap the lid on—that is the difference."

The Creative Approach in a Sixth Grade Classroom

MOTIVATION:

"Just suppose you were among the first to land on the moon. A sign on the post nearest the point of landing contained bold letters spelling out one word:

SUPERCALIFRAGILISTICEXPIALIDOCIOUS

What meaning might that sign have for you?"

Challenged by an avid curiosity, a keen desire to discover a clue, children conjectured the following:

"It might mean quarantine."
"It might be a special moon plant."
"It might say, 'Parking lot full, go home' !"
"Well, it might say, 'Welcome' ."
"When I use my imagination, it could be most anything . . . danger . . . surprise . . . adventure . . . This is really having fun while you're learning!"

ENVIRONMENT:

In this room the environment is such that the learner feels impelled to satisfy an avid curiosity and in doing so, responds with improved learning. Sincerity in expression, enthusiasm for learning, depth in thinking, flourish in such an environment which tends to build in academic learning as well as ethical character.

Natural but successful ways of learning rely upon hidden sources of power occasionally belittled and ignored by baffled adults . . . . boys and girls consider imagination as a patent source of courage and confidence to achieve success. . . . One effective means of helping children achieve success in spelling relies heavily on use of the imagination. . . .

PRESENTATION:

"How many experienced difficulty in getting a clear picture of the word chosen? Alright, take a second look. Close your eyes again." For some, need for double-checking is necessary since power to grasp meaning and arrangement of letters varies with intellectual abilities and background of experiences. "There are a number of ways we could let the class know which word has been selected. How? . . . Yes, through written expression; through verbal expression. . . . Yes, through drawing a picture. But this time, let's try a different approach. . . . Let's think about how we might "show" the word chosen through expression of movement and feeling. If you remember our imaginary trips and how real they seemed to us you will have an idea. . . . Without making a single sound, let's communicate to the class in such a way that they will be able to recognize the word you have selected."

"When you have a good audience, begin." Cliff begins when he has had eye contact with every member of the class. Sometimes when a check is made by the teacher, understanding of a good audience means "folding one's hands in one's lap," "sitting still," "paying attention," "being quiet while someone's talking". Now, however, understanding is shared by the total group. Good listening habits begin to develop to the point that hush spreads over the room when someone steps up in front of the class to speak, for there exists a self-committment to listening carefully and critically. Should it be difficult to achieve the quiet hushed mood prior to presentation, constant praise for those ready to listen encourage the reluctant to cooperate. "I like the way so many of you are ready to listen."

Sylvia attempts to show the word, "scale" by stepping on an imaginary scale and appearing quite surprised and pleased at what she observed.

"Which word do you think Sylvia chose to show? . . . Why? What actions were convincing?"
"Because she lifted her foot and then the other and put them both down at a time on something small. Then she looked down and waited and watched. I think she was pleased with what she saw. The word was *scale*". . . . Since the word possesses added meanings, the teacher asked, "Who can think of a way to show this word, possibly as another part of speech?"

Fred proceeded to prepare bait for a hook and managed to catch a large fish. The group watched as he proceeded to *scale* the fish, careful to move the knife away from him as he removed the scales. Interest was high as the word, *scale* was shown. Used in this manner it was labeled a verb. . . . Pamela imagined she was a concert pianist in the midst of putting forth great effort in her daily routine of practicing. . . . Daryl carefully demonstrated safety measures on an imaginary crevasse prior to an attempt to reach the top of a mountain. Each interpretation of the word, *scale*, was identified as a specific part of speech.

With clear-cut movements, Ron communicated a feeling of danger ahead as he moved stealthily from tree to tree, constantly on the watch for the enemy. "I think that the word is 'danger' because of the way Ron moved."

"It might have been, but it doesn't happen to be the word Ron chose to show." Encouragement by discussing the "why" enables the hesitant one to look further and to see why his choice was justified.

"Cliff? Yes, why did you think the word was stealthily?"

"Well, the way Ron's eyes moved quickly and stopped . . . then he was all ears. When he took another step, he looked first to see if there was anything that might crack under the weight of his foot. . . . It's more than cautious." "Can anyone think of a time when you had to move stealthily?"

Brenda's reply, "I did when I heard somebody on the front porch when I was home alone. I tried to get to the window to peer out without being heard. It was such a relief when I discovered that the wind had blown over an umbrella."

Judy added, "I had to move very stealthily once when I had to kill a big rattlesnake. I didn't want to let him see my movements."

The time seems right for spelling of the word *stealthily*. "Now, will all of you please write the word, stealthily, at your desks? I like the way some of you are tempted to look at the word on the chalkboard but I can see that you are not doing so." Encouragement for quality action tends to promote higher standards of responding.

When the class has written the word at their desks, Judy is encouraged to spell her word. Class members check her spelling against theirs. Occasionally moved by excitement of learning through such natural and normal processes, a child encounters difficulty in the actual spelling of the word. Sometimes a second chance to spell is necessary. Even a third.

The teacher's encouraging remark, "That is a difficult word to spell. . . . I can remember when I used to miss that word. Class, what do you think we can do to be helpful?"

Members of the class automatically sound out the word which is the beginning of success, particularly for a reluctant speller. "This way you learn how to spell because you can do the best you know how to do and nobody grumbles. Besides, you're given a second chance."[50]

To better understand the lesson presented, the rationale for this method of teaching is presented below with an evaluation by children and teachers who have used it.

METHOD:
The process of teaching spelling creatively utilizes a method which:
1. Cultivates a readiness for spelling [at every level]
2. Fosters in the child a desire to spell correctly
3. Respects the wide span of spelling abilities within a given class
4. Challenges the quick to spell and brings success to the reluctant speller
5. Provides for the expression of the word first through non-verbal communication
   —then through written communication
6. Words are selected in terms of needs, interest and subject matter.

PROCEDURE:
1. Listing of words on the chalkboard
2. Choice and discussion of a number of the words listed
3. Picturing the word in the "mind's eye"
4. Doublechecking the word by taking a second look at the word on the board
5. Showing the word through action and feeling (non-verbal communication)
6. Recognition of word and reason for recognition
7. Praise for clearcut actions and reactions (dramatization)
8. Written spelling of a word by children at their desks
9. Checking of spelling by children as contributor spells.

EVALUATION BY CHILDREN:
Children who have experienced spelling sessions taught creatively state:

"When you spell this way you can see the word in your mind's eye. It's easy then."

"This way of spelling, the word becomes a real person or thing, and then it means something to you."

"When I spell this way it gives me courage to get up in front of the room."

"This way, you can spell with smart kids and not feel like a heel when you spell."

"When you learn to spell this way it seems like magic and magic makes you work."

"This way of spelling, the word gets inside of you and you get inside the word, then you understand."

"This way you really learn to spell because your whole self gets mixed up into the learning before it settles into your head for good."

EVALUATION BY TEACHERS:
Evaluation of this approach to teaching spelling has consisted of pointing to such advantages as the following:

Increased self-confidence among the reluctant-to-spell.

Equal benefits in the form of challenges activate keen interest on the part of the quick to spell.

Excellent means of vocabulary building.

Use of oral expression as motivation for written expression which follows serves to make spelling "come alive".

Provides new motivation and at the same time helps students gain insight into hitherto unknown and even abstract words.

Puts children at ease prior to the spelling experience.

On the debit side teachers who were quick to point up advantages of the creative approach felt that spelling with this approach was time consuming, but worth a try.

Intuitive appraisal of children and teachers along with records kept of children's progress in the mastery of spelling taught creatively, spells SUCCESS for children with a wide span of spelling abilities.[51]

Not until children are stimulated to take pride in words correctly spelled and legibly written, not until they become aware of the significance of accuracy in all written work, not until they sense the "magic" in spelling will the aims of instruction be accomplished. Each teacher must find ways of challenging the children he teaches. From the methods of teaching spelling presented it is evident that there is no one way guaranteed to meet the needs of each child in learning to spell. The wise teacher makes use of the findings of research that facilitate the process of learning to spell, uses methods that take into consideration individual differences of children, motivates children through purposeful written work to improve ability to spell and write correctly, uses games, dramatization, competitions and spelling matches to stimulate interest in spelling accurately, impresses upon children the social as well as the utilitarian aspects of spelling, supplements basic texts and graded word lists with individual lists and written work geared to the child's individual needs and interests, and concentrates on teaching efficient techniques of word study.

Once a child learns that spelling can be mastered; that spelling a new word involves finding clues, discovering relationships, and figuring out generalizations; he will look upon spelling as an ingredient in written expression that not alone helps him to write more fluently, but also brings a touch of magic into the program of written expression.

It is the task of the teacher to teach each child to listen as well as to speak, to read as well as to write, and to spell as well as to think. The mechanics or tools of language must become automatic in order that the child is not hampered in his ability to think, or in his power to express ideas by the limitations of the tools through which experience is expressed. Spelling is such a tool. As a tool it has a discipline of its own, which must be understood by the teacher in order to teach the child to acquire and use it effectively.

TEACHING HANDWRITING DEVELOPMENTALLY

The problem of teaching children to write legibly is a serious one. "An estimated million letters yearly end up as 'dead letters' in United States Post Offices because poorly written names or numerals make delivery impossible; and most of the 400,000 Federal income tax refunds totaling millions of dollars were delayed in the Spring of 1958 because Internal Revenue personnel were unable to read the handwriting of the claimants."[52]

Handwriting is all too often the most neglected, the least understood, and the poorest taught subject in the elementary school. "Evidence has been presented that as high as 30 per cent of all school systems have no handwriting program and as many as 50 per cent of all schools have no separate handwriting period."[53]

Years later Enstrom deplores that "handwriting has hit an all-time low. The problem is one that our schools can ill afford to ignore, for poor handwriting creates a host of difficulties."[54]

Although most teachers admit the importance of good handwriting, the common complaint is "There is no time to teach it". But can teachers ignore it? How can they afford the tedium and the waste of time involved in trying to decipher poorly written papers? Surely the time and effort involved in helping children write legibly pays dividends for the teacher in time saved and for the child in the personal satisfaction in the quality of the handwriting. This may well give the child the needed impetus for creative and/or expository writing.

Creative expression and skill in handwriting are, in a sense, intimately related. Long before the child has developed the muscular coordination necessary for writing down his ideas, he is expressing his thoughts creatively. In order to enable him to record his own ideas as they come to him it is necessary for him to develop the mechanical skills of handwriting. Two aspects of written expression—the skill involved in the mechanics of handwriting and the creative elements in the expression of ideas—must be developed if the child is to achieve his potential in written communication.

The teacher who keeps before him the goal of creative written expression will not be satisfied until he has taught the child the skills he needs in writing down his own thoughts. This responsibility on the part of the teacher makes it essential that he understand: the developmental nature of the process of handwriting, key concepts about handwriting, issues in teaching handwriting, procedures which are indicated by research in the field of handwriting, and the persistent problems.

THE NATURE OF HANDWRITING

Handwriting is a developmental process. It is actually one of the graphic arts, but because it is used as a tool for communication, it is usually taught in the language arts curriculum. It requires time; time to develop the necessary maturation, muscular coordination, and experiential background to understand its use in the expression of ideas.

Each child has his own design for development. This is as true of fine-muscle coordination, a prerequisite to handwriting skill, as it is in other phases of physical development. The small-muscle coordination of some first graders is so well developed that they have little difficulty in reproducing a sample of the teacher's manuscript writing or from the practice books. Others, however, whose small muscle development is progressing at a much slower rate, have difficulty in reproducing even the simplest straight lines, curves, and circles. Writing expectations of children in the primary grades must be realistic in terms of the developmental nature of growth in the process of writing. The child should not be pushed into writing too soon.

Before children are given writing instruction they should participate in activities that involve the large muscles—work with easels, finger paint, clay, scissors and other materials which aid in developing coordination. When the child shows readiness for writing with chalk, pencil, or crayon he is taught on an individual or small group basis.

In the intermediate grades the child gains greater control over both large and small muscle activities, and eye-hand coordination. His handwriting tends to become smaller. The teacher must be alert to individual needs of boys and girls as they work to achieve legibility and reasonable speed.

The urge to write well comes spontaneously if the child has a motivation for the drill and practice which are an integral part of learning the skill of handwriting. He will not, however, write well by merely being told to write well. Motivation, plus a readiness for the mechanical problems involved, provision for individual differences, an appropriate attitude, effective writing materials, direct instruction, and a continuous analysis of the writing are essential to success.

KEY CONCEPTS

An examination of the studies of handwriting and the recommendations for developing the skills involved reveals some key concepts that are invaluable to the teacher.

The child is the focus for making decisions about the most effective methods of teaching handwriting. It is the responsibility of the teacher to tailor the system to the individual needs of each learner.

Handwriting is more a graphic art than a language art. Where possible it is best taught in cooperation with the art teacher. Handwriting is a complex sensory-motor skill involving interrelationships of motor coordination, letter formation, words, symbols, and ideas in effective language patterns.

Handwriting skill comes from direct teaching and correct practice.

Handwriting is developmental. The process must be presented sequentially, with ample practice.

The goal in handwriting is legibility. Simplicity of letter formation, economy of time, and ease in writing contribute to this goal.

Provision should be made for the left handed child.

Copying to learn the formation of letters is preferable to tracing.

Handwriting is an expression of individuality. No two individuals have the same walk, the same posture, the same handwriting. Individuality in handwriting should be encouraged within the framework of legibility.

Evaluation should be based on the child's developmental level; measuring the child's ability to adapt writing techniques to a variety of writing assignments, a variety of speed requirements, and a variety of qualities of excellence as he progresses up the educational ladder.

The teacher's own handwriting, his understanding of the developmental nature of handwriting, and his skill in handwriting procedures are important factors in the successful teaching of handwriting.

Quality of handwriting is not related significantly to intelligence. Improvement in handwriting quality comes as children are motivated to diagnose their own writing needs, to evaluate their own progress, and to receive direct help with their handwriting problems.

ISSUES IN TEACHING HANDWRITING

Some of the issues in the teaching of handwriting that concern the teacher are: (1) When should instruction in handwriting begin? (2) Should both manuscript and cursive writing be taught? (3) Should practice on letter forms and handwriting movements occur in isolation? (4) How should handwriting be evaluated? and (5) How can instruction be individualized to meet individual differences?

Readiness for Instruction

The young child is interested in scribbling, painting, drawing, modeling, constructing, and other similar activities without being aware that they are pre-writing activities. It matters little to him that these activities develop muscular coordination of his fingers, hands, and arms. For him these are media for self-expression and for communication of ideas.

The teacher capitalizes on such manipulative experiences. It is through such activities that the child gains the needed development and control over the tools used in writing.

Another type of readiness experience is that designed to develop the child's ability in the use of oral language. There is little point in trying to teach the child to write before he can express his ideas orally. In the preceding chapters emphasis has been placed on the importance of providing varied and challenging activities which motivate the desire for communication and creative self-expression. Listening to stories, chanting rhymes, dictating stories and letters, writing the daily news, composing songs—these are experiences which lead to a readiness for writing. As children watch the teacher act as a scribe and write down their story, poem, letter, or invitation, the chalk becomes a magic wand. Out of this experience grows the desire to take the place of the teacher as the scribe.

Some children now are ready for those experiences which are specific pre-writing activities. During this stage children are introduced to the rudiments of manuscript through circles and sticks. They are encouraged to experiment at the chalkboard with drawing all the things they can think of that can be made from circles and lines. Among the responses are clocks, doughnuts, balls, bubbles, jack-o-lanterns, cats, Christmas trees, ornaments; and place settings of plates, knives, forks, and spoons. Children soon combine circles and lines and draw wagons, stick figures, animals, geometric designs, etc., As the teacher observes a child or group of children who appear to give evidence of interest in going beyond these preliminary steps he can safely introduce manuscript writing if the following conditions of readiness obtain:

1. Facility in the use of crayons, scissors, paint brush, and pencils in a variety of self-chosen activities
2. A persistent interest in learning to print his own name
3. Ability to copy simple geometric or letter characters
4. The establishment of hand dominance
5. Interest in group or individual written expression
6. A sense of personal need to learn to write

Teachers have found simple, informal devices helpful in reinforcing their judgement as to which children are ready to gain from handwriting instruction. One such device consists of a sheet of paper, at one side of which is printed or mimeographed a series of geometric forms such as:

The teacher provides the children with pencils and asks them to copy each figure four times on the blank portion of the sheet. The copying is freehand with no time limit set. If the child can copy most of the characters successfully, with reasonably correct proportions and steady lines, he is giving evidence of motor readiness for handwriting. If he loses interest in the project, or finds it difficult to copy, he is giving evidence that he is not at this point ready for handwriting instruction.

The teacher will find that as children give these signs of readiness and are ready to write their names, copy dictation from the chalkboard, progress from left to right on writing paper, or newsprint, and write captions on the pictures they draw, writing instruction can begin. The teacher must expect individual differences in readiness for writing, in interest in writing, and in the amount of supervision needed. Some children are ready for formal instruction in writing in the first grade, while others should not be given formal instruction until later.

Manuscript and Cursive Writing

Manuscript writing has a distinct advantage for children who are learning to write. This form is relatively easy because it is made up of circles, straight lines, and combinations of lines and circles. Each stroke of a letter is formed separately and there is no need to join letters to form the word. Then, too, manuscript writing resembles the print children are accustomed to in their books.

More than 90 per cent of the schools begin handwriting instruction with the manuscript form. Most schools teach both forms so this issue is largely one of evaluating the consideration which should be given to custom in the continuance of teaching cursive writing. There is a growing trend toward the maintenance of skill in manuscript form throughout the elementary school years. Schools that teach either manuscript or cursive style exclusively are in the decided minority. Upper grade teachers approve the change-over to cursive because they are not familiar with instructional procedures in manuscript and have no copy books for the pupils.

The evidence concerning the merits of manuscript, versus cursive writing is inconclusive. Cursive writing tends to deteriorate with speed. Manuscript writing deteriorates less under pressure. However, cursive writing is considered the socially accepted form. Therefore it continues to be taught.

Research has yet to determine that cursive writing is superior to manuscript. It is essential that greater guidance be given during the transition from manuscript to cursive, for it is at this time that many of the handwriting cripples are developed. Instead of laxity during this important step, greater attention should be given to this phase of the program.

A child will need practice and guidance as well as direct teaching in making the transition to cursive writing and continued practice and direct teaching in mastering cursive writing. There is evidence that the transition, if it is to come, should be postponed beyond grade two and be a gradual process rather than abrupt.[55]

In the majority of public schools the transition to cursive is made in grade three.

The transition to cursive writing should not be dictated by the curriculum guide, the course of study, nor the handwriting series. The dangers of teaching cursive writing to children before they have mastered manuscript are apparent from research of Herrick and Jacobs,[56] Strickland,[57] and others. For slow learners or immature sensitive children the changeover may be painful indeed.

Readiness for the Transition is Indicated by the Child's Behaviour

Among indications of evidence for readiness for cursive writing are: (1) adequate physical development so there is coordination of muscles of the arm, hand, and fingers, (2) ability to write all the letters of the manuscript alphabet from memory, (3) ability to read simple passages written in cursive style of writing, (4) ability to copy a selection in manuscript maintaining quality and reasonable rate of speed, and (5) a desire to write in cursive style.

Transition from Manuscript to Cursive

There is a growing tendency for children to continue manuscript writing while they are making the transition to cursive. Thus in their written composition they may be using the manuscript form for ease and fluency in writing, while learning to form the letters of the cursive alphabet.

Teachers who take into consideration the emotional, mental, and muscular elements involved in the transition to cursive writing as well as the visual ability needed to discriminate between minute differences in letters and letter formations make the decision to change to cursive on the basis of the best interests of the individual child. The program must be flexible to allow for individual differences in muscular coordination, desire to change, and willingness to apply oneself to the task.

It should be remembered that for the child learning the new system of writing there is an abrupt shift in motor skills. It is not simply a matter of joining the letters but of learning new letter strokes, new proportions, and slant. Some letters differ considerably from the manuscript style. The pen is not lifted from the paper until the end of the word, and there are connecting strokes linking the letters within the words. Too, letters that the child is accustomed to write beginning at the top in manuscript writing begin at the baseline in cursive writing, or there are reversals in letter formation. Examples can be seen in such letters as b and d, f and h, l, k, r, s.

Cursive writing is not a spontaneous development from unjoined manuscript. Joining must be taught and practiced. Unless there is direct instruction in the transition process, unless that teaching is persistent and thorough, some children become confused and never fully recover their original legibility and speed.

A growing number of schools are questioning the validity of making the changeover. They are asking: "Is this changeover necessary?" One proponent of retaining manuscript throughout the elementary school gives an answer to this question.

1. Manuscript style writing is a practical, serviceable hand for all mature writing needs.
2. Changing over involves lost motion and in some cases actual distaste for writing.
3. The time and effort needed for mastering the new cursive style can be devoted to written expression and composition work.
4. Difficulties due to the fact that upper-grade teachers do not pay much attention to [teaching] handwriting are avoided.[58]

Should Practice on Letter Forms and Handwriting Movements Occur in Isolation

In essence this issue revolves around the question of a functional approach versus learning the letter forms in isolation in large group sessions. It may become an issue in those schools which have no time set aside for handwriting, and thus give little if any formal handwriting instruction. In the functional approach the direct instruction in handwriting skills is incidental and grows out of the child's felt need to form specific letters. There are those who favour the functional approach, who believe that group practice should be supplanted by individual instruction governed by a diagnosis of handwriting deficiencies and related to the individual pupil's instructional needs.

On the other hand, Cole asserts: "Handwriting is allied to athletic skills. One needs the same physical basis for producing a good script that one needs for hitting a ball, or rolling a hoop, or jumping a rope; namely, good muscular control, relaxed nerves, good eyesight, and excellent co-ordination between hand and eye. . . . The main thing to grasp is that handwriting is purely a muscular tool, without content or end in itself, and without any fixed relation to intellectual development."[59]

If this line of reasoning is followed the system of training children to write would follow a course something of this nature:

1. Base the teaching upon careful imitation of a good model, allowing only such minor variations as are necessary because of a pupil's age or size.
2. Continue the practice of simple skills under close supervision until the pupil can execute a series of movements perfectly.
3. Teach self-diagnosis and self-correction, until you feel sure that the pupil has the habit of self-appraisal.
4. Then introduce intensive practice, but without competition.
5. Permit no strain or pressure. If the pupil voluntarily tries to hurry, stop him.
6. Wait for nature to take its course in the development of speed.[60]

Children learn to write under either method. The wise teacher recognizes that either extreme is undesirable. If writing practice is identified only with penmanship drills, push-and-pull exercises, with mechanical aspects that have no relation to linguistic experience, efforts to improve the child's writing will be dimmed. On the other hand, if instruction is left to chance and the child's "needs", he may be seriously limited in his ability to use handwriting as a tool. The recommendation is to provide the child with motivation for writing through making writing a functional skill, serving his purposes of communication from the beginning. Unless the child masters handwriting through direct teaching, motivation to express ideas will be of little avail. A judicious planning of the handwriting program as an aid to written expression is the answer to the dilemma. In other words, the functional approach to writing must be strengthened through directed practice.

How Should Handwriting Be Evaluated?

Many schools evaluate children's writing on an informal basis rather than through the use of commercial handwriting scales. One reason for this, of course, is the emphasis currently on individuality of handwriting. Handwriting scales should provide for self-diagnosis and should reflect current trends toward the cultivation of a natural, comfortable, personalized style of handwriting.

An examination of commercial handwriting materials reveals that there is a growing tendency toward providing for individual differences. Some, unfortunately, continue to neglect the individualized instructional procedure. This is particularly true with respect to the emphasis given rhythmic count in forming letters.[61]

A perceptive teacher will allow variance, however, even if the school system is making use of a handwriting series which fails to consider adequately individual needs. If the teacher builds into the program diagnosis and self-evaluation as an integral part, provision will be made for individual differences. Adjusting instructional procedures requires taking into consideration: (1) the objective of legibility, ease, and simplicity of writing, (2) comfort, (3) economy of time, (4) differences in abilities of the pupils, and (5) awareness that pupils should develop "personalized" style of writing. It is imperative to develop programs which provide for individuality.

In evaluating growth in handwriting the following basic principles should obtain: (1) evaluation should be based on objectives which are clearly understood by the child, (2) evaluation should be continuous and interrelated, (3) evaluation should be a cooperative enterprise—involving both the child and the teacher, (4) evaluation should involve self-appraisal of progress in achieving defined objectives.

In evaluating handwriting growth it is of utmost importance that the child know the specific objectives and the criteria upon which his writing is judged. He should know whether he is trying to improve a specific skill in handwriting or writing to express ideas. Each purpose is legitimate. If the purpose is to improve his handwriting skill, he concentrates on that specific objective. He needs to have an individualized check list or progress chart which he can use in evaluating his own progress. As he improves through directed teaching, through planned exercises in handwriting, he enjoys charting his own improvement. Procedures such as the following are useful in initially motivating self-evaluation and pride in improvement.

An Evaluation Procedure: First Grade

Circulate around the room when children are writing. Check with them points such as the following. (In time they can learn to ask and answer these questions themselves)

1. *Height and size of letters*
   a) Are capital letters all the same size?
      Are they twice the size of small letters?
   b) Are small letters the ratio of 2 to 1?
      Are tall letters twice the size of small letters? *b, h, k, l, f?*
   c) Is the small *t* one and a half times the size of small letters?
      Are extensions below the line the length of a short letter?
      ex. *g, p, j, y.*
      When first graders write they make the capitals and tall letters two spaces high.
2. *Alignment*
   Do all letters rest on the base line?

3. *Spacing*
    a) Is the space between two fat letters narrow?
    b) Is the space between two thin letters wider?
4. *Circular letters*
    Are the circular letters like circles?
5. *Parallel Strokes*
    Are all down strokes straight and parallel?
6. *Vertical down strokes*
    Are *k*, *v*, *w*, *y*, and *z* the only letters that do not have vertical and straight down strokes?

Under such procedure it is evident that self-evaluation can become an integral part of the program. When the teacher and children both know what the goals and expectations are, the teacher can help children evaluate their own progress. A progress chart such as the one opposite can be inaugurated and used throughout the elementary grades.

PROCEDURES FOR TEACHING HANDWRITING

Handwriting is important to the child to the extent that it helps him do something that *he* considers worthwhile. For this reason each handwriting lesson should involve a purpose—a situation which requires writing. This motivation is the focus of instruction. However, the child and the teacher who recognize writing as a tool also are aware that in order to be useful tools must be kept sharpened. A child is motivated to learn to write when he has something to say which he wants recorded.

Introducing Manuscript

Many children first become interested in writing manuscript as they watch the teacher writing on the chalkboard. Seeing the teacher act as a scribe when they have a story to tell, news to report, or questions to formulate furnishes the needed motivation. They enjoy going to the chalkboard and imitating the teacher's behaviour. There is a similarity in the movements of writing and easel painting. The chalkboard provides for the use of the large muscles; another advantage is the ease with which the teacher can demonstrate and supervise activity in writing. The music staff liner, by inserting chalk in the first, third, and fifth holders, provides guidelines for the writing. As a group of children give evidence of readiness for writing the teacher can invite them to the chalkboard. As new groups begin their writing experiences at the chalkboard the others will work at their tables. A carefully planned handwriting experience will include the following elements: (1) visualization, (2) analysis, (3) practice, (4) evaluation, (5) correction, and (6) application. These components so essential in an effective teaching-learning experience are illustrated in the following example from a primary grade.

The children in Miss Meredith's room were interested in sending out invitations

MY PROGRESS REPORT

NAME_____

GRADE_____

	OCT.	NOV.	DEC.	JAN.	FEB.	MAR.	APR.	MAY	JUNE
Letter formation and size	NI*	S*							
Spacing: within words									
Spacing between words									
Spacing between sentences									
Alignment									
Slant									
Line quality									
Letter joinings									
Letter endings									
Margins and arrangement									
Rate of Writing									
Neatness									
Position and Movement									

Key: NI = Needs Improvement
S = Satisfactory

for "Open House" at their school. Miss Meredith had prepared the invitations to parents but had left a blank line for the children to write their own signatures. She had prepared a 3 × 5 card with each child's name in manuscript.

VISUALIZATION. "I wonder how many of you can read your own name? How many can read each other's name? Good. As I hold up the card, the person whose name appears on the card will come up and call on another child who is ready to read it. After all the cards have been read, you may each have your own name card."

ANALYSIS. "How many of you have a name that begins with the letter 'A'? Allen, show us at the chalkboard how you make the capital letter 'A'. That's right, you started at the top. That is exactly the way I write it. Thank you, Allen. Does anyone have a small 'o' in your name? Flora, will you come up and show us how to make a small 'o' and then write your whole name. Remember, the letter 'o' is the letter that is a complete circle. That's right, it starts at the two o'clock position, doesn't it? Thank you, Flora."

"George, will you come up and write your name? What letter does George have in his name that he writes in two ways? That's right, a 'G'. Will you underscore the capital 'G' as you write it? Let's watch as he forms each letter. Can you see the difference between the capital 'G' and the small 'g'? For the rest of the time each of you will write his name at his table except those in Mary's group. Remember, it's their turn to work at the chalkboard today."

PRACTICE. "Be sure to look at your name card before you start to write. Those at the chalkboard be sure to use your guide lines. Remember, your capital letter is twice as tall as your small letters. When you have finished be sure and check with your name card to see if you made each letter correctly. Those at your tables may practice in your writing book."

EVALUATION. "How many of you made all the letters right? How many have all the letters resting on the base line? How many left space between letters? How many need to correct your writing?"

CORRECTION. "Write your name again, making the corrections that are needed. Use your name card as a model while you correct it."

APPLICATION. "As soon as you have copied your name correctly write it on the line in your invitation that I put on your table. Remember, when we write for someone to read, we write the very best we can, don't we?"

In teaching handwriting lessons it is essential to have a clear idea of the elements of visualization, analysis, practice, evaluation *and* application in order to make the writing task as interesting, efficient, and effective as possible. Skills a child uses, he remembers.

As children progress in their work in beginning manuscript writing they should be led to formulate guidelines which form the basis of their self-evaluation. One group of primary children developed the following guides.

1. We begin at the top of the letter when we write.
2. We make all our letters with straight lines and circles.
3. We move from the left to right in making letters, e.g., in making small *d* we make the circle first, then the straight line. In making the letter *b* we make the straight line first, then the circle.
4. We make all capital letters two spaces high and all small letters one space high.

5. We space circle letters close together, circle and straight letters farther apart, and straight letters farthest apart.
6. We space words four fingers apart for chalkboard work, two fingers apart for newsprint, one finger apart on our writing paper, and the space of the letter O when we write on ruled paper with smaller spaces.
7. We write so our writing can be read.

Handwriting series vary not only in the way the letters are formed and in the sequence in which the letters are introduced, but also in their approach. When there is no specific system required by the school, the staff will need to develop a sequence and system based on the needs of the children. Two systems using different approaches are shown on the pages 464 to 469.

In planning the instructional program in manuscript writing for the first grade the findings from a recent investigation dealing with the relative difficulty of the fifty-two letter forms should prove useful to teachers and curriculum workers.

Letters of the Manuscript Alphabet Arranged in Order of Difficulty[62]

ORDER OF DIFFICULTY	LETTER	ORDER OF DIFFICULTY	LETTER
1	q	27	K
2	g	28	W
3	p	29	A
4	y	30	N
5	j	31	C
6	m	32	f
7	k	33	J
8	U	34	w
9	a	35	h
10	G	36	T
11	R	37	x
12	d	38	c
13	Y	39	V
14	u	40	F
15	M	41	P
16	S	42	E
17	b	43	X
18	e	44	I
19	r	45	v
20	Z	46	i
21	n	47	D
22	s	48	H
23	Q	49	O
24	B	50	L
25	t	51	o
26	z	52	l

The Manuscript Alphabet

Introduction—Research proves that children are interested in writing something. However, they must first be taught how each letter is formed. Practicing the letters, themselves, should be kept at a minimum, with most of the writing period devoted to practicing words, phrases and sentences. To establish readiness, simple exercises, related drills and fundamental exercises should be practiced at the beginning of each writing period.

Descriptive Count—Rhythm plays an important role in teaching writing. While a numerical count cannot be given in print writing, describing each stroke as the pupils write it aids in the formation of the letter. Such teacher direction helps develop smooth, rhythmic strokes. The following analysis lists the sequence of strokes and the descriptive count for each letter in alphabetical order for easy reference.

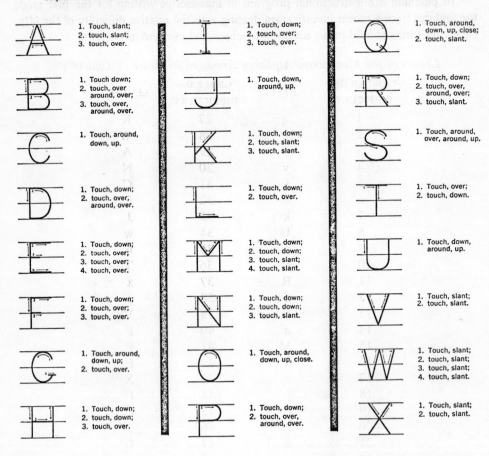

A
1. Touch, slant;
2. touch, slant;
3. touch, over.

B
1. Touch down;
2. touch, over around, over;
3. touch, over, around, over.

C
1. Touch, around, down, up.

D
1. Touch, down;
2. touch, over, around, over.

E
1. Touch, down;
2. touch, over;
3. touch, over;
4. touch, over.

F
1. Touch, down;
2. touch, over;
3. touch, over.

G
1. Touch, around, down, up;
2. touch, over.

H
1. Touch, down;
2. touch, down;
3. touch, over.

I
1. Touch, down;
2. touch, over;
3. touch, over.

J
1. Touch, down, around, up.

K
1. Touch, down;
2. touch, slant;
3. touch, slant.

L
1. Touch, down;
2. touch, over.

M
1. Touch, down;
2. touch, down;
3. touch, slant;
4. touch, slant.

N
1. Touch, down;
2. touch, down;
3. touch, slant.

O
1. Touch, around, down, up, close.

P
1. Touch, down;
2. touch, over, around, over.

Q
1. Touch, around, down, up, close;
2. touch, slant.

R
1. Touch, down;
2. touch, over, around, over;
3. touch, slant.

S
1. Touch, around, over, around, up.

T
1. Touch, over;
2. touch, down.

U
1. Touch, down, around, up.

V
1. Touch, slant;
2. touch, slant.

W
1. Touch, slant;
2. touch, slant;
3. touch, slant;
4. touch, slant.

X
1. Touch, slant;
2. touch, slant.

*By permission from *Peterson Directed Handwriting*, The Peterson System, Inc., Greensburg, Pa., 1963.

y	1. Touch, slant; 2. touch, slant; 3. touch, down.
z	1. Touch, over; 2. touch, over; 3. touch, slant.
a	1. Touch, around, down, up; 2. touch, down.
b	1. Touch, down; 2. touch, around, down, up.
c	1. Touch, around, down, up.
d	1. Touch, around, down, up; 2. touch, down.
e	1. Touch, around, down, up; 2. touch, over.
f	1. Touch, around, down; 2. touch, over.
g	1. Touch, around, down, up; 2. touch, down, around.
h	1. Touch, down; 2. touch, around, down.

i	1. Touch, down; 2. dot.
j	1. Touch, down, around; 2. dot.
k	1. Touch, down; 2. touch, slant; 3. touch, slant.
l	1. Touch, down.
m	1. Touch, down; 2. touch, around, down; 3. touch, around, down.
n	1. Touch, down; 2. touch, around, down.
o	1. Touch, around, down, up, close.
p	1. Touch, down; 2. touch, around, down, up.
q	1. Touch, around, down, up; 2. touch, down, around.

r	1. Touch, down; 2. touch, around.
s	1. Touch, around, over, around, up.
t	1. Touch, down, around; 2. touch, over.
u	1. Touch, down, around, up; 2. touch, down.
v	1. Touch, slant; 2. touch, slant.
w	1. Touch, slant; 2. touch, slant; 3. touch, slant; 4. touch, slant.
x	1. Touch, slant; 2. touch, slant.
y	1. Touch, slant; 2. touch, slant.
z	1. Touch, over; 2. touch, over; 3. touch, slant.

1234567890

Descriptive Count 1—Touch, down. 2—Touch, around, slant, over. 3—Touch, around; touch, around. 4—Touch, down; touch, over; touch, down. 5—Touch, down, around; touch, over. 6—Touch, down, around, loop. 7—Touch, over, slant. 8—Touch, down, around, over. 9—Touch, around, up, down. 0—Touch, around, down, up, close.

4

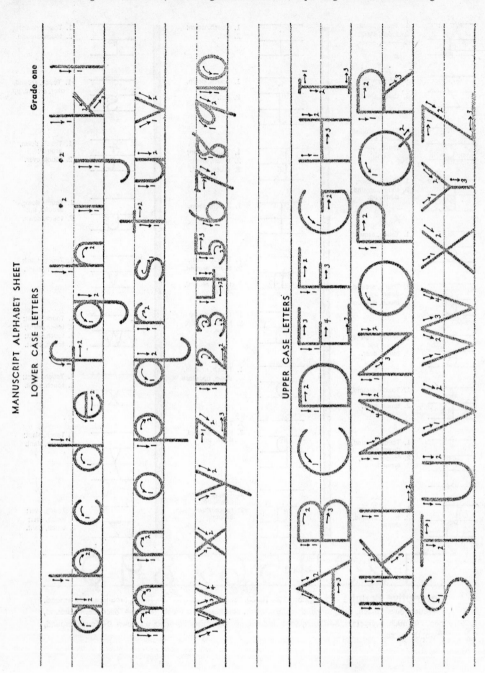

MANUSCRIPT ALPHABET SHEET

LOWER CASE LETTERS

UPPER CASE LETTERS

Grade one

*By permission from *Guiding Growth in Handwriting*, The Zaner-Bloser Company, Columbus, Ohio, 1958.

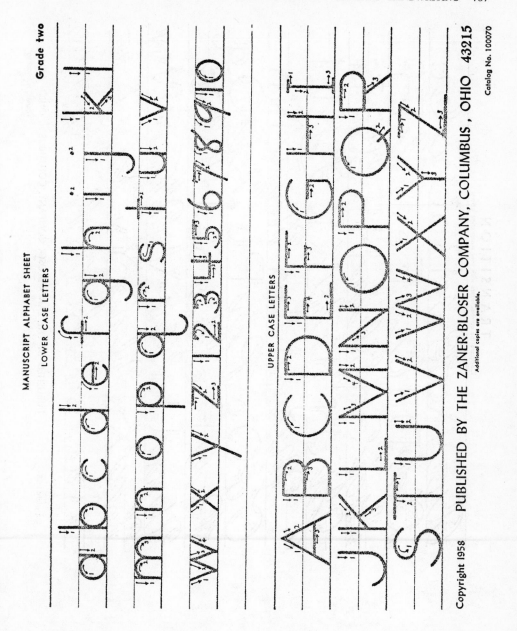

MANUSCRIPT ALPHABET SHEET

Grade two

LOWER CASE LETTERS

a b c d e f g h i j k l
m n o p q r s t u v
w x y z 1 2 3 4 5 6 7 8 9 10

UPPER CASE LETTERS

A B C D E F G H I
J K L M N O P Q R
S T U V W X Y Z

Copyright 1958   PUBLISHED BY THE ZANER-BLOSER COMPANY, COLUMBUS, OHIO 43215

Catalog No. 100070

Additional copies are available.

*By permission from *Guiding Growth in Handwriting*, The Zaner-Bloser Company, Columbus, Ohio, 1958.

TRANSITION

Compare the cursive letters with your manuscript letters.

Copyright 1958

PUBLISHED BY THE ZANER-BLOSER COMPANY, COLUMBUS , OHIO 43215

Catalog No. 100080

*By permission from *Guiding Growth in Handwriting*, The Zaner-Bloser Company, Columbus, Ohio, 1958.

Grade three

CURSIVE ALPHABET

Aa Bb Cc Dd Ee Ff
Gg Hh Ii Jj Kk Ll
Mm Nn Oo Pp Qq Rr
Ss Tt Uu Vv Ww Xx
Yy Zz 1 2 3 4 5 6 7 8 9 10

MANUSCRIPT ALPHABET

ABCDEFGHIJKLMNOPQR
STUVWXYZabcdefghijklm
nopqrstuvwxyz 1234567890

Copyright 1958

PUBLISHED BY THE ZANER-BLOSER COMPANY, COLUMBUS , OHIO 43215

Parker Zaner Bloser

*By permission from *Guiding Growth in Handwriting*, The Zaner-Bloser Company, Columbus, Ohio, 1958.

The letters are ranked in order of difficulty as indicated by the frequency of error in two samples per child. The five most difficult letters were q,g,p,y,j. Information such as that from the above finding should be taken into consideration when planning the sequence of introducing manuscript letters for direct instruction. It should serve to indicate the possibility of more individual help when children are writing words using letters difficult to make.

A sequence of introducing manuscript letters which has been successful with some teachers in planning for teaching letters with similar characteristics is shown.

Category I   o,c,a,d,e ....circles and straight lines

Category II   O,C,G,Q, ...circles and straight lines

Category III   i,l,t,f,u, ...straight lines and half circles

Category IV   I,L,T,F,E,H, straight lines

Category V   b,p, ... straight lines and reverse curves

Category VI   P,B,P,D,U, ..straight lines, reverse and half circles

Category VII   n,m,r,h, ... straight lines and half reverse circles

Category VIII   j,g,y, ... circles, straight lines, half circles, and half reverse circles

Category IX   S,s, ... half circles and reverse circles

Category X   v,w,x,k,z, ... slanting strokes and straight lines

Category XI   M,N,K,A,V, slanting strokes and straight lines

The Transition to Cursive Writing

The shift from manuscript to cursive writing is generally made in the third grade, when most children have developed muscular coordination, visualization, and eye-hand coordination required to maintain a smooth flow of movement from letter to letter. In making the transition the teacher must plan specifically in terms of the readiness for the change and the need for direct teaching of the steps in the transition. Demonstrating at the chalkboard, the teacher can simplify the change-over by using the following steps:

1. Write the word in manuscript   COW

2. Use dotted lines to indicate the joining strokes   COW

3. Retrace the dotted lines   COW

4. Slant the letters and join the letters without lifting the chalk.   *cow*

As children imitate the teacher in writing the cursive form they will shortly be able to eliminate step 3 and use only three steps in changing from manuscript to cursive writing.

1. Write the word in manuscript   eat

2. Use dotted lines to indicate the joining strokes   *eat*

3. Slant the letters and join without lifting the chalk (or pencil)   *eat*

In this method the procedure is characterized at first by moving from manuscript forms to joined manuscript writing, then to vertical cursive, and finally to slanted cursive.

In teaching the child to make the transition it is helpful if both teacher and children recognize differences between manuscript and cursive forms and their implications. Some letters in cursive are formed differently from manuscript—the child will need help in learning how to form these letters. The pencil is not lifted after each letter in cursive writing as it is in manuscript—the child will need help in joining the letters in a word. Cursive writing is characterized by a slant—the child needs help in changing from vertical writing to the proper slant of cursive writing. Cursive writing looks different from manuscript writing—some children may have to learn to read cursive writing.

"Most teachers have found that periods of fifteen to twenty minutes per day over a period of four to six weeks are sufficient to help third and fourth graders make the transition from manuscript to cursive writing. Helping children to continue their development in handwriting, of course, should not cease after this initial period of instruction."[63]

Teaching Cursive Writing

Among the problems that children have in forming cursive letters are:

Failure to keep loop letters open: b,e,f,g,h,k,l,q,y,z.

Failure to use strokes instead of loops on letters: d,i,p,t.

Failure to close letters: a,o,d,s.

Failure to cross the t; dot the i; and the j.

Failure to round the tops of m,n, and h so they are not mistaken for other letters.

While it is important for the teacher to develop a positive attitude toward handwriting and to be aware of the elements that make for legibility, it is also important to know the errors which block progress for many children. Among the most troublesome and frequent offenders are: (1) faulty endings; (2) incorrectly made undercurves; (3) mixed slant; (4) failure to give letters proper slant; (5) incorrect formation of the initial stroke of such letters as the capitals W,H,K; (6) incorrect endings in final, h,m,n; and (7) failure to retrace the downstroke of t, d, and p.

The transition to cursive writing demands visualization of the new form of such letters as b,e,h,f,r, and s. These differ appreciably from the manuscript form. The teacher should begin instruction with cursive letters which more nearly resemble their manuscript counterpart. Writing in cursive style involves the ability to see the image of the letter forms in the mind's eye, to analyze the strokes involved, to feel the muscular movement in writing them, and then to make the necessary relationships. Until this process becomes automatic, handwriting is not an efficient tool for expression.

Whether the intermediate grades continue to teach manuscript or cursive there is need to provide the child in the intermediate grades opportunity to use his skill in manuscript writing as well as cursive. Posters, labels, items on charts provide a need for continuing to use manuscript. In this way the manuscript skills he learned are not lost. More and more in business and industry the skills of manuscript or block printing are an asset to the individual. The initial objectives of writing still obtain in the intermediate school, legibility, ease and speed, and in written assignments neatness and attractiveness of the finished copy. The responsibility of the teacher is to take the child from where he is when he enters the intermediate grades and help him develop these qualities together with motivation for improvement.

How the teacher does this will depend upon the handwriting program in the school. In a school in which there is a definite time scheduled for handwriting individual as well as group needs can be met. Too often, however, handwriting like grammar, is relegated to a specific period. It is an isolated skill divorced from the rest of the curriculum. Until such time as the elementary school furnishes typewriters for all students handwriting will remain an essential tool in every class.

The use of commercially prepared material facilitates instruction of a specific drill type and allows the teacher to use the language arts time for applying the skill learned in a brief fifteen minute handwriting lesson.

Group instruction might well begin at any intermediate grade level with a self-evaluation lesson which emphasizes the objectives of the handwriting program.

The most important goal of handwriting is legibility. The intermediate grade teacher should begin the instructional program with a writing lesson which gives evidence of the child's handwriting ability. Each of the elements of good handwriting are analyzed by teacher and student and the self-evaluation form remains in his notebook throughout the succeeding lessons.

How Well Do I Write?[64]

A. Here is how I write when I am in a hurry:
(Write: "this is a sample of my writing")

....

B. Here is how I write when I do my best writing:
(Write: "this is a sample of my best writing")

....

C. I would grade my hurried writing: (Circle one grade)

Excellent   Good
Fair   Poor

I would grade my best writing: (Circle one grade)

Excellent   Good
Fair   Poor

D. Here is my analysis of my handwriting:

	Excellent	Good	Fair	Poor
1. Slant Do all the letters have the same slant?	——	——	——	——
2. Spacing Are the spaces between words uniform?	——	——	——	——
3. Size Are all small letters approximately ⅓ space tall?	——	——	——	——
Are all tall letters almost a space tall?	——	——	——	——
4. Alignment Do all the letters touch the base line?	——	——	——	——

5. Loops ....
   Are l, f, h, k, b, well formed?   _____ _____ _____ _____
   Are g, y, z, j (lower loops) well
   formed?   _____ _____ _____ _____

6. Closing ....
   Are a, d, g, o, p, s closed?   _____ _____ _____ _____

7. Roundness ....
   Are m, n, h, u, v, w, y well rounded
   on top?   _____ _____ _____ _____

8. Stems ....
   Are all the downstrokes straight in
   the stem letters *p, b, r*   _____ _____ _____ _____

9. Retraces ....
   Are t, i, d, m, n retraced?   _____ _____ _____ _____

10. Endings ....
    Are all my words ended with good
    finishing strokes?   _____ _____ _____ _____

Teaching handwriting cannot be left to chance in the intermediate and upper grades. Provision must be made for handwriting instruction as an integral part of any effective language arts program.

Helping the child to write legibly at this level as well as in the primary grades involves acquiring uniformity of slant, of height of the various types of letters, of forms of similar letters, endings, and spacing. As each individual child compares his own writing with the master copy, or with samples of his own previous writing he is helped to see that he needs to close his "d" and his "g", that he must make his "h" more than twice as high as his "n", and he must dot his "i" and cross his "t" if he wants his writing to be easily read. He must be encouraged to observe, to compare, to evaluate, and in so doing to decide whether his writing is better, has made no improvement, or is poorer.

A lesson designed to be used in an intermediate grade as a motivation for self-analysis and self improvement follows:

Capital letters—The "Cane" Family. There are 11 capitals that start with a "cane". This is the family:

Write a line of each of these cane letters. Start the "cane" just a little below the top line for your capital letters. Then swing around as if you were making a letter e upside down. Then swing down with a straight line until they touch the base line you are writing on. These are H, K, M, N. Other letters start the same way and then curve before they come to the base line. Look at the model to be sure you are right.

Now write each of the following words twice. Start each word with a capital letter:

Help   Keep   Much   No   West   Use   Very   Question

When you have finished, compare your capitals with the model. Put a check mark above any that need improvement. Then write these letters three times, trying to make each as nearly perfect as possible.

Now check to see if your capitals have the proper slant. How well did you write?

Excellent .... Good .... Average .... Poor ....

If you had difficulty with any capital letter, practice it. Write it as many times as you can during this period.

For those who had no errors compare sentences using words beginning with the capitals as shown in the previous diagram.

Alignment. One of the characteristics of good writing is alignment. Good writers try to have all of their letters rest on the base line. A few letters have lower loops that go half a space below the line—f, g, j, p, z, y. All of the others are written directly on the line. Because of a difficult joining stroke there are letters that start above the line, but some part of every letter written always rests on the base line. This makes the writing legible and neat.

Write the following proverbs twice, concentrating on alignment. See how many other elements of good writing you observe as you write.

Time lost is never found again.

Waste not want not.

A penny saved is a penny earned.

Always lend a helping hand.

Do a good deed every day.

Where there is a will, there is a way.

Now check your alignment. Circle any letter that fails to rest on the base line. Place an asterisk above any word where all the letters rest on the base line. Now practice writing the words that had any circled letters. Check all of the writing of the proverbs against this scale.[65]

	Excellent	Good	Fair	Poor
How good was my alignment?	....	....	....	....
How was the slant of my writing?	....	....	....	....
How was the spacing between words?	....	....	....	....
How were the finishing strokes?	....	....	....	....
How were the letter sizes?	....	....	....	....
Summary of my evaluation				
Total	....	....	....	....

Commercial handwriting scales also may be used to help children appraise their progress. Jill may compare her handwriting with the model and with the writing she did last month. She can note her progress and also what specific item she needs to improve, with help from the teacher. For example, the teacher might ask, "Will it help if you change the slant of the b?"

Teachers should be familiar with the standardized handwriting scales. Among the widely used scales are:

Ayers Measuring Scale for Handwriting, Princeton, N.J., Educational Testing Bureau Service, grades 2-8.

Evaluation Scales for Guiding Growth in Handwriting, Columbus, Ohio., Zaner-Bloser Company, Grades 1-9.

Other suggestions for vitalizing handwriting instruction in the intermediate and upper grades which experienced teachers have found challenging are:

Have a writing clinic in which the best writers act as consultants for forming specific letters, and for diagnosing writing problems.

Plan a writing exchange program with other schools in the city, region, or another country.

Collaborate with the art department in lettering for making posters.

Organize a Frank Laubach Week—"Each One Teach One", where each child teaches another child or the group how to make one letter.

Encourage children to write the titles of their poems and creative stories in their best handwriting.

Put poems, jingles, and rhymes having unusual combinations of letters on the chalkboard for children to copy.

Make an Animal ABC alphabet for the first grade writing corner.

Make a chart grouping letters for cursive writing lessons

     Upper loop letters

     Lower loop letters

     Intermediate letters

Vary the procedure of the handwriting lesson so the element of surprise is an integral part of learning.

PERSISTENT PROBLEMS IN HANDWRITING

Ease and speed in writing. Because of the ever increasing demands for writing from the intermediate grade child the writing often deteriorates. The teacher who is concerned with the quality of writing will not stress speed unduly. Not until the child's basic letter forms are so well established that writing has become automatic should pressure for speed be placed upon him. The teacher must take into consideration individual differences in deciding if certain children are in need of motivation to increase speed while maintaining legibility. For ease in writing teachers may allow the child to continue to use manuscript writing in taking notes or in his personal writing. Some school systems teach typing in the elementary grades and encourage children to type their assignments.

Neatness in writing. The problem of neatness in writing is one that must be considered. A standard format should be decided upon by the staff and adhered to by each child. Children should learn to use margins, good spacing of words, and to use the writing instrument with a fair degree of ease and competence. Once they have learned to use the pencil with reasonable speed, they will need to learn to use a pen in order to develop skill in this medium as well. Writing instruments noted in the Wisconsin Survey, in 1951 in order of frequency of use were:

Grade III Adult pencil, chalk, mechanical pencil, beginner's pencil, crayon, ball point pen, fountain pen, pen and holder

Grade IV Adult pencil, fountain pen, ball point pen, mechanical pencil, pen and holder, chalk, crayon, beginner's pencil

Grade V Fountain pen, adult pencil, pen and holder, ball point pen, mechanical pencil, chalk, crayon

Grade VI Fountain pen, ball point pen, adult pencil, pen and holder, mechanical pencil, chalk, crayon.

In an ideal elementary school the materials for writing instruction included crayons, chalk, beginner's pencils, adult pencils, speed-ball pens, fountain pens, pen and holder sets, 8½ by 11 sheets of lined paper with lines 1 inch, ¾ inch, and ⅜ inch apart, unlined paper, writing easels, typewriters, and chalkboard.[66] Today the ball point pen is the most commonly used writing instrument.

Perhaps the most important factor to remember regarding neatness, legibility and speed in writing is that studies reveal that speed of writing is a relative and highly individual matter. If a student is forced to write faster than his usual comfortable rate, the legibility of his handwriting will almost certainly deteriorate; the most legible handwriting is that of pupils with the greatest degree of fine motor control of the hand. Neatness in writing is influenced by personality, motivation, sex, and environmental factors.

More and more emphasis is being placed on the importance of developing individuality of handwriting rather than "copper plate" perfection. Slavish similarity to the model is giving way to emphasis on legibility and neatness. Good writing is that which is easily written and easily read.

Upper grade students as well as primary and intermediate grade children need to be cognizant of the objectives of handwriting if they are to improve their skill. A checklist prepared by upper grade pupils follows next as an aid to self-analysis, self-evaluation, and self-improvement. The pupils mark the check sheet once every two months on the basis of a critical analysis of their own handwriting. The key to the list is: + for improvement, — for retrogression, and X if the quality remained the same.

It is the responsibility of staff to make sure that every child who moves from the elementary school is competent in the basic rudiments of handwriting. A useful tool in achieving this goal is a review of basic letter and number formations.

My Handwriting Chart[67]

DATE	SEPT.	NOV.	JAN.	MAR.	MAY
1. Capitals should be at least twice as large as small letters.					
2. The difference between o's, c's and a's should be clear.					
3. The round parts of m's, n's, and u's should be clear.					
4. The loops on f's, j's, g's, and y's should be clearly drawn below the line					
5. Loops should not intercept writing on lines above and below.					
6. T's should be crossed and i's dotted (not with a circle).					
7. Letters should not be crowded together.					
8. Letters should all slant in the same direction.					
9. Words should be separated by clearly defined spaces.					
10. A page of manuscript should have pleasing margins.					

Lefthandedness. Since some 5 to 10 per cent of the population fall into the left-handed category, most teachers will eventually have to face it. The teacher should assure the child that lefthandedness is not an uncommon occurrence. If he is to be of help to the child he must know why he gradually brings his hand around to the upside-down position. This is because the natural way to draw a horizontal line is from the middle of the body outward. A right-handed person naturally draws a line from left to right. The left-handed person draws the line naturally from right to left. Also, the natural way to draw a circle is counterclockwise for the right-handed child; clockwise for the left-handed. Since our language is written with left-to-right progression and since most ovals in cursive writing are made counter clockwise, it is unnatural for the left-handed child to write in the same manner as the right-handed child. Also, the right-handed child can more easily read what he is writing than can the left-handed child. The left-handed child tends to smear what he has written unless he gets his hand out of the way. Only as he twists his wrist around and writes upside-down can he see what he writes.

Here are, for your review, both the small and capital cursive letters.

Here is a good, simple lettering alphabet. It may be used for labels, cataloging cards, tickets, parcel tags, map lettering, signs, drawings, etc. It is a modified manuscript form.

A B C D E F G H I J K L M
N O P Q R S T U V W X Y Z

a b c d e f g h i j k l m n o p q r s t u v w x y z

Drummond gives the following suggestions to help the "leftie" keep his wrist straight instead of crooked.

> Provide lots of writing on the chalkboard. It is practically impossible to use the upside-down style at the board.
>
> Make sure the paper is properly placed on the desk. For manuscript, paper should be square with the desk. For cursive, the bottom right corner should be pointed at the body. . . .
>
> Permit lefties to continue manuscript writing indefinitely. Their writing is almost always more legible before they learn to write cursive than afterward. As the left-handed children change to cursive, though, watch like a hawk the placement of paper.
>
> Encourage children to hold pencils or pens so that the top of the writing instrument is pointing over the shoulder of the same arm.
>
> Encourage lefties to develop a writing slant which feels natural and good. The slant will, undoubtedly, be a bit backhand compared to generally accepted handwriting styles because it's natural that way. . . .
>
> Furnish lefties with pencils which have slightly harder lead than that used by right-handers. Harder lead will not smear as easily. . . .
>
> When ink is used, be sure that all lefties have a good nonskip ballpoint pen which has a high-quality nonsmear cartridge.
>
> Encourage lefties to learn to type. Most classrooms should have type-writers to encourage children to write creatively. With lefties, the need for typewriters is even greater.[68]

If primary teachers will take responsibility for giving the left-handed child a good start, teachers in higher grades could give help in improvement of writing and using writing as a tool for communication.[69]

The Teacher Evaluates His Teaching Practices

If there is to be improvement in handwriting instruction self-evaluation by the child is not sufficient. It is equally, if not more important for the teacher to evaluate his teaching of handwriting. This he can do by asking questions such as:

Are my expectations of children's writing based on individual ability and development?

Do I help pupils set individual and realistic goals?

Do I plan the handwriting lesson in such a way that enthusiasm for *writing* is maintained?

Do the pupils see real purposes for writing legibly and with reasonable speed?

Does my own handwriting exemplify high standards?

Do I put increasing emphasis on pupil evaluation of individual handwriting needs and motivation toward self-improvement?

Do I value individuality in handwriting as an avenue of self-expression and encourage it?

Do I see the need for integrating handwriting with the other curriculum areas as well as teaching handwriting as a specific skill?

Do I enjoy teaching handwriting as a tool, not as an end in itself?

Do I enjoy teaching handwriting?

Self-Evaluation: the student-teacher evaluates his experiences:

1. Do I know how to use Teacher-prepared or commercially designed work sheets efficiently for instruction in handwriting?
2. Am I successful in teaching handwriting to a small group with similar needs?
3. Am I able to teach handwriting at the chalkboard (primary grades)?
4. Have I learned how to guide children in the transition from manuscript to cursive writing?
5. Have I skill in teaching drill lessons using the handwriting text?
6. Can I direct self-evaluation through tests, handwriting scales, overhead projector examples, the handwriting text, and examples of the child's own handwriting?
7. Am I competent in teaching remedial lessons to children with poor handwriting abilities?
8. Am I convinced that mastery of handwriting as a tool is essential for the elementary school child?

Among the factors which are essential to a handwriting program in the elementary school are an understanding of: the developmental nature of the process of writing; key concepts about handwriting; issues concerning handwriting; procedures for teaching handwriting; and a dimensional approach to the persistent problems.

Handwriting is a developmental as well as a personal skill and a child's ability will depend largely on his muscular coordination, his attitude toward writing and the quality of the instruction. Well-planned practice-periods throughout the elementary school with review of previously acquired skills to ascertain which children need re-teaching and specific teaching will aid in strengthening the child's control and encouraging his efforts. Handwriting, to be an effective tool, must become so spontaneous that the writer's attention will focus upon the ideas to be expressed, not upon formation of letters. As practice continues the pupil learns to become increasingly self-sufficient in evaluating his own writing with respect to letter formation and slant, spacing, alignment, size and line quality. This means that teachers must strive continually to find better ways of teaching handwriting that combine legibility with speed, motor skill with social purpose, and basic principles with individual variation.

CONCLUDING STATEMENT

The need for mastering the mechanics of writing (punctuation, capitalization, spelling, and handwriting) is based on the premise that the mechanics of writing must be developed in a sequential order. Ability to express oneself effectively through the written word does not develop automatically. It grows gradually; but it needs nurture, guidance, *and* direct teaching. Recognition of the inter-relatedness of the arts of language, although it serves as a motivating force for writing, does not preclude the direct teaching of the mechanics and skills essential to the effective expression of ideas.

The complexity of written expression makes it desirable to focus on basic principles which contribute to growth in written expression.

Writing is an art, an art concerned with the creation of ideas, not merely with the structuring of ideas; writing is a craft and as such requires knowledge of form, modes of expression, and understanding of rhetorical principles; writing is a skill and as such demands mastery of the mechanics, the conventions, and the tools; writing is for communication. As a tool for communication it requires the habit of craftsmanship.

REFERENCES

1. By permission from Herbert R. Mayes, "Trade Winds," *Saturday Review,* 49:12, October 15, 1966.
2. From *Teaching Language, Composition, and Literature* by Mary Elizabeth Fowler. Copyright © 1965 by McGraw-Hill, Inc. Used by permission of Mc-GrawHill Book Company, p. 200.
3. *Ibid.,* p. 201.
4. By permission from John Farrell, *The Creative Teacher of Language*, McGraw-Hill Company of Canada Limited, Toronto, 1965, pp. 266, 267.
5. Adapted from *Ibid.,* p. 274.
6. Adapted from Paul S. Anderson, *Language Skills in Elementary Education,* The Macmillan Company, New York, 1964, pp. 403, 404.
7. By permission from Lillian M. Logan, *Teaching the Young Child,* Houghton Mifflin Company, Boston, 1960, p. 202.
8. Gertrude Hildreth, *Teaching Spelling,* Henry Holt and Company, New York, 1955, p. 2.
9. Walter T. Petty, "Handwriting and Spelling: Their Current Status in the Language Arts," *Elementary English,* 41:839, December, 1964.
10. Wilbur S. Ames, "A Comparison of Spelling Textbooks," *Elementary English*, 42:150, February, 1965.
11. Ernest Horn, *Teaching Spelling: What Research Says to the Teacher*, Department of Classroom Teachers and American Educational Research Association, Washington, 1954.
12. Thomas Horn, "Research in Spelling," *Elementary English*, 37:174-177, March, 1960.
13. *Ibid.,* p. 177.
14. Thomas Forna, The *Psychology and Teaching of Spelling*, Catholic Education Press, Washington, 1934.
15. David Russell, "Second Study of the Characteristics of Good and Poor Spellers," *Journal of Educational Psychology*, 46:126-141, March, 1955.
16. Edna Furness, "Mispronunciations, Mistakes, and Methods in Spelling," *Elementary English,* 33:508-11, December, 1956.

17. David Russell, "Auditory Abilities and Achievement in Spelling in the Primary Grades," *Journal of Educational Psychology,* 49:315-19, December, 1958.
18. Thelma L. Damgaard, "Auditory Acuity and Discrimination Differences as Factors in Spelling Competence," Unpublished Doctoral Thesis, Stanford University, Stanford, 1956.
19. Thelma Rea, "Disciplines in Oral-Aural Discrimination as a Factor in Developing Power in Spelling," Unpublished Doctoral Thesis, Stanford University, Stanford, 1958.
20. Edna Furness, "Psychological Determinants of Spelling Success," *Education,* 79:234-39, December, 1958.
21. Gus Plessas and Walter T. Petty, "The Spelling Plight of the Poor Reader," *Elementary English,* 39:463-466, May, 1962.
22. Adapted from Russell G. Stauffer, "Relationships Between Spelling and Reading," *Education,* 79:206-10, December, 1958.
23. David Russell, "Spelling Ability in Relation to Reading and Vocabulary Achievement," *Elementary English Review,* 23:32-37, January, 1946.
24. Luther C. Gilbert and Doris Wilcox Gilbert, "The Improvement of Spelling Through Reading," *Journal of Educational Research,* 37:13-23, February, 1944.
25. Ira E. Aaron, "The Relationship of Selected Measures at the Fourth and Eighth Grade Levels," *Journal of Educational Research,* 53:138-43, December, 1959.
26. Bertha Newton, "A Study of Certain Factors Related to Achievement in Spelling," *Dissertations in Education,* University of Missouri Bulletin, Columbia, Study 41, 1960, pp. 134-36.
27. Paul R. Hanna and James T. Moore, Jr., "Spelling: From Spoken Word to Written Symbol," *Elementary School Journal,* 53:329-337, February, 1953.
28. Patrick J. Groff, "The New Iowa Spelling Scale: How Phonic is It?" *The Elementary School Journal,* 62:46-49, October, 1961.
29. Walter Petty, "Phonetic Elements as Factors in Spelling Difficulty," *Journal of Educational Research,* 51:209-214, November, 1958.
30. Loretta J. Sah, *A Study of Spelling Performances,* Master's Thesis, Sacramento State College, 1964.
31. Ernest Horn, "Spelling," in Chester W. Harris (ed.), *Encyclopedia of Educational Research,* The Macmillan Company, New York, 1960.
32. By permission from Richard E. Hodges and E. Hugh Rudorf, "Searching Linguistics for Cues for the Teaching of Spelling," *Elementary English,* 42:527, May, 1965.
33. James T. Moore, Jr., "Phonic Elements Appearing in a Three Thousand Word Spelling Vocabulary," Unpublished Doctoral Dissertation, Stanford University, Stanford, 1951.
34. Paul L. Garvin and Edith C. Trager, "The Conversion of Phonetic into Orthographic English: A Machine Translation Approach to the Problem," *Phonetica* (to be published), cited in Richard E. Hodges and E. Hugh Rudorf, *op. cit.,* p. 527.
35. Richard E. Hodges, "An Analysis of the Phonological Structures of American Hyphenated English Orthography," Unpublished Doctoral Dissertation, Stanford University, Stanford, 1964.
36. *Phoneme-Grapheme Relationships Basic to Cues for Improvement of Spelling,* USOE Cooperative Research Project No. 1991, Stanford University, Stanford. (To be available from the United States Office of Education.)

37. Richard E. Hodges and E. Hugh Rudorf, *op. cit.*, p. 532

38. By permision from Virgil G. Logan and Lillian M. Logan, *Teaching the Elementatry School Child,* Houghton Mifflin Company, Boston, 1961, p. 348.

39. Gertrude Hildreth, *op. cit.*, p. 50.

40. By permission from Paul R. Hanna and Richard E. Hodges, "Spelling and Communications Theory," *Elementary English,* 40:485, May, 1963.

41. See Maria Montessori, *The Montessori Method,* tr. by Anne George, Frederick Stokes Co., New York, 1912.

42. By permission from Robert Pooley, *Teaching Speaking and Writing in Wisconsin,* Wisconsin English Language Arts Curriculum Project, Department of Public Instruction, Madison, 1966, pp. 15, 16.

43. Edward Eisman, "Individualized Spelling: Second Report," *Elementary English,* 40:529, 530, May, 1963.

44. Robert Pooley, *op. cit.*, p. 69.

45. *Ibid.*, p. 70.

46. Howard Blake, "Studying Spelling Independently," in Robert E. Chasnof (ed.), *Elementary Curriculum: A Book of Readings,* Pitman Publishing Company, New York, 1964, p. 318.

47. *Ibid,* pp. 320-321. (Adapted.)

48. Robert Pooley, *op. cit.*, p. 70.

49. By permission from Margaret Woods, "Success in Spelling: A Creative Approach," *Resources for Teaching and Learning,* The Official WDAVI Journal, April, 1965, p. 17.

50. *Ibid.*, pp. 16, 17

51. *Ibid.*, p. 17. (Adapted.)

52. Robert O'Brien, "The Moving Finger Writes—But Who Can Read It?" *Saturday Review,* 42:8, July 18, 1959.

53. Fred M. King, "Handwriting Practices in Our Schools Today," *Elementary English,* 38:483-486, November, 1961.

54. E. A. Enstrom, "The Decline of Handwriting," *The Elementary School Journal,* 66:22, October, 1965.

55. J. Kendrick Noble, Jr., "Handwriting Programs in Today's Schools," *Elementary English,* 40:510, May, 1963.

56. Virgil E. Herrick and Leland Jacobs (eds.), *Children and Language Arts,* Prentice-Hall, Inc., Englewood Cliffs, 1955, Chapter 12 "Children's Experiences in Handwriting".

57. Ruth Strickland, *The Language Arts in the Elementary School,* Heath and Co., Boston, 1957, p. 362.

58. Gertrude Hildreth, "Manuscript Writing After Sixty Years," *Elementary English,* January, 1960. Quoted in Verna D. Anderson et al., *Readings in the Language Arts,* The Macmillan Co., New York, 1964, p. 165.

59. By permission from Luella Cole, "Reflections on the Teaching of Handwriting," in Verna D. Anderson et al., *op. cit.*, p. 201.

60. *Ibid.*, p. 202.

61. Virgil E. Herrick (ed.), *New Horizons for Research in Handwriting,* Report of the Invitational Conference on Research in Handwriting, University of Wisconsin Press, Madison, 1963.

62. By permission from Edward R. Lewis and Hilda P. Lewis, "Which Manuscript Letters Are Hard for First Graders?" *Elementary English*, 41:858, December, 1964.

63. Virgil E. Herrick, "Manuscript and Cursive Writing," in Robert Chasnoff (ed.), *Elementary Curriculum: A Book of Readings*, Pitman Publishing Co., New York, 1964, pp. 314, 315.

64. Nathan Naiman, "Handwriting Blitz," in Verna D. Anderson et al., *Readings in the Language Arts*, The Macmillan Co., New York, 1964, pp. 176-177.

65. *Ibid.*, p. 187.

66. Virgil Herrick et al., *Handwriting in Wisconsin: A Survey of Elementary School Practices*, School of Education, University of Wisconsin, Madison, 1951, p. 114.

67. By permission from *Some Evaluation Techniques in Language Arts for Teachers and Pupils*, Portland Public Schools, Curriculum Publication LA-38, Portland, n.d., p. 6.

68. Harold D. Drummond, "Suggestions for 'Lefties'," from *The National Elementary Principal*, 38:15, February, 1959. Copyright 1959, Department of Elementary School Principals, National Education Association. All rights reserved.

69. A complete set of writing exercises for the left-handed child learning cursive writing can be procured from Dr. Warren Gardner, Interstate Press, 19 North Jackson Street, Danville, Illinois. See also: E. A. Enstrom, "The Little Turn That Makes a Big Difference," *Elementary English*, 43: 865-868, December, 1966.

14

Appreciating Literature

Through Experiencing

For sooth, he cometh to you with a tale, which holdeth children from play, and old men from the chimney corner.
Sir Philip Sidney

In our anxiety to teach children to read, to prepare them for living in a technological, computer oriented society, is it possible that we fail to cultivate in them an appreciation for good literature? Are the schools yielding to external pressures to emphasize reading primarily as a utilitarian tool and neglecting reading as a means of developing moral and ethical values through literary experiences? The teacher of literature must be dedicated to a consuming interest in ideas and in the aesthetic and moral values of the literature he is to teach. If he is to communicate the riches of the literary heritage—past and present—he must be a person who makes literature live.

Literature is a means by which children widen horizons, heighten awareness, develop the imagination, stimulate thinking, discover meanings, expand vocabulary, develop sensitivity to words, and grow in understanding of both other people and themselves. As children come in contact with the cultural heritage of the past and present through literature, they are guided to appreciate the gifts of past generations and of other peoples, and so understand better the cultural milieu in which they live. Familiarity with the classics and their well-loved characters and plots aids children in understanding the many allusions to literature in everyday speech.

Children enjoy listening to stories and poems long before they are able to read for themselves. The wise adult fills their lives with books and provides numerous opportunities to experience literature. Discussing the characters, the plot, the events, times and places; participating in choral reading, reader's theatre and dramatization are avenues through which children grow into appreciation of the best in literature. A teacher skilled in interpretation, and sensitive to the needs and interests of the children, is able to bring life to literature.

Effective teachers recognize the significance of literature to the child and the role it plays in a well-planned language arts curriculum. They take the long view and plan learning experiences in such a way that by the time the child leaves the elementary school he has experienced literature which is balanced in scope. They include the best of poetry and prose both past and modern, fictional and factual,

486

imaginative and realistic, informative and nonsensical. When children and literature are brought together by a teacher who has knowledge, appreciation, and enjoyment of literature; knowledge, understanding, and interest in children; *plus* perception, skill, and competence in teaching, children develop a life-long interest in reading.

Teachers need to remember too that the quality of their teaching will be determined ultimately by their qualities as human beings. The task of the teacher in literature is to select the poems, novels, plays, paintings, music, philosophies and ideas which can affect the student and make an adjustment between his present values and those of the writers, artists and thinkers.

WHAT IS LITERATURE?

Literature is Experience

Literature is life as seen by the author. It is interpreted by the reader who brings to the printed page his own experiences, rich or limited. Literature is a way of looking at life, of questioning life, of structuring the components of life in such a way that what might seem ordinary, mundane, or menial may become suddenly extraordinary, exciting, and/or elevating.

Literature is both Creative and Recreative

The writer paints a picture, portrays a scene, and develops a concept with words as clearly as an artist does with paint and brush. The skilled reader, as interpreter, recreates first in his mind's eye images and ideas as vivid, as real, and as urgent as they were for the writer himself. As he reads, the words construct for the listener the time, the place, the scene, or situation. To the extent that mood, situation, character, place, or time are made vivid, arresting and exciting, the listener as well as the reader can find adventure, mystery, nonsense, fancy. He can live in times and places he has never known except through books.

"In education through the literary arts, there are three principal components in the art of learning—the writer, the student, the teacher. They are in the midst of a creative process. The writer has seen one or another part of life in a certain way. With the talent he can command, he writes about it, discovering a literary form which will convey his total meaning. . . . As a creative artist in the medium of education, the teacher invents a style of his own to convey to his students the meaning he finds in the book. . . . The student enters this process, bringing whatever he can do it, and if the process is successful, he projects himself into the life and mind of the writer, and learns from the writer and the teacher something more than was possible before, something he could not find by himself."[1]

Literature is Art

Art is the distillation or abstraction of an experience, real or imaginary, portrayed through a chosen medium, and restricted or enhanced by the experience, perception and skill of the artist. Literature, like the other arts is such an experience. A literary experience evokes response through identification. Creative teachers use many and varied methods for aiding the child in identification.

Through literature as an art form the child experiences, he identifies, he becomes a part of the content, a part of the world of ideas. By bringing to the student literature as art, the meaning of art is discovered through their own experiences.

Literature is a Key

Literature is a key that unlocks doors, that opens windows, that helps a child understand people and phenomena he encounters. He identifies with the characters and "becomes" and grows as he lives with the heroes of yesterday and of today. Through biography, hero tales and legends, as well as stories of modern times, the child develops an affinity with people, a sensitivity to their joys and sorrows, an understanding of situations, and periods of history. The world becomes more meaningful through folk tales, picture books, regional stories, stories of other lands, the world of nature and of machines.

A child will grow in an environment in which there is much creative experience with literature. He will grow in stature as a person, he will grow in competence as a reader, he will develop taste for good literature through many contacts with writers who use words with imagination, discrimination, and taste. The world of books broadens the child's horizons, gives him understanding and empathy, provides him with insight into human relationships. Good books provide him with clear standards of right and wrong, show him conflict and ethics of human behaviour.

Teachers have two major responsibilities to the child in literature: first, to become keen judges of what distinguishes good literature from second rate; and second, to discover what literature appeals to different children at various age levels.

WHAT ARE GOOD BOOKS FOR CHILDREN?

Good literature for children like good literature for adults mirrors the minds of men and the ever swifter pace of change in the universe. Books reach across the years and make the past come alive and real. They make the future seem as near and real as the present. Children respond to books on the basis of the experience and background they bring to the reading.

Children are pastmasters at rejecting books which they do not like, as countless well-intentioned parents, grandparents, librarians and teachers have discovered. A book may be considered a juvenile classic by the experts, but if it does not touch the child, if it is beyond his understanding, if it is too far removed from his interests he will be indifferent to it.

In deciding what is a good book for children in the elementary school the following characteristics will serve the teacher as broad guidelines:

In a good book the child can identify with the main character. Admiring a hero of one of the great sagas a child might well say, "If I had lived in those times, woe to the evildoers!"

If on the other hand the main character lives in the present time, the reader might think, "I know how he felt. If my parents were to go to Pakistan, I would venture forth just as he did. I too, would save the village from terror and destruction."

A good book is true to life. Being true to life involves such elements as realism, honesty, and integrity in developing the plot, and the characters. It is at this point that many stories of adventure and mystery fail because of their falsity, shallowness, sentimentalism and/or sleaziness.

A good book is true to facts. If it is an informative book it is important that the facts are accurate. Even science fiction should be based on what is now known and the potentialities of technology. If the author writes about a section of the country, a specific vocation or avocation he must have the necessary background to make the characters plausible, the setting true to life, and the action logical in terms of the mores of the region.

A good book is true to type. Fictionalized biography and biographical fiction have their place, but they should not make the pretense of being biography. Modern writers of juvenile biographies of the childhood of the hero are careful to examine the facts before committing them to the printed page. Biography based on inaccurate, slight or non-existent facts should not be included among the books recommended for children.

A good book has literary style. If children are to develop taste in literature they must be provided with books that embody the elements of good writing. In poetry there should be rhythm; in fairy tales there should be cadence, the building up to the climax. In good fiction there is understanding, communication, and dialogue that rings true. Visual imagery, colourful language, choice words and phrases are important if a book is to live for children.

A good book has a dominant theme. There must be an underlying theme which motivates every episode and action. The theme may be simple, but it should have sufficient backbone to stand up firmly and support the whole structure.

A good book has richness of detail. A good book is more than a series of statements of facts. It recounts the events and episodes that lead up to the main event. It gives detailed and needed background of information to aid the reader in understanding and interpreting the actions of the characters. A book should give the reader the feeling of moving through the story in step with the character, empathizing with him all the way.

A good book, in short, offers identification, is true to life, sticks to the facts so far as they are known, is honest, and is true to its type. A good book is written in a style worthy of its content, has choice language and vivid imagery, a dominant theme, and richness of detail. Whether fact or fiction, imaginative or realistic, a good book speaks to the child. It may tickle his funny bone, set him to chuckling, move him to pity, motivate him to achieve, thrill him with hope and courage, inspire him to be like the hero, and keep him hanging in mid-air of suspense. It should enrich his life, and help him to understand better both life and his own actions. It should catapult a student out of the world of things into the world of imagination and bring him back better able to understand himself and the world in which he lives.

What Are Children's Interests?

Adults have made attempts to discover the reading interests of children in order to try to make available to them books which will meet their interests and needs at particular developmental levels. From 1893, when M.B.C. True reported "What My Pupils Read," to the present time there have been more than two hundred studies made to determine the amount and nature of voluntary reading preferences and activities. In 1925 Terman and Lima concluded that there are certain well-defined tendencies in reading interests that change as the child's experience grows and as his imagination and reasoning powers develop. They identified a number of factors which contribute to the development of reading interests: age, health and physical development, school environment, home training, mental ability, and sex. Both boys and girls were found to enjoy animal stories, but boys preferred adventure and vigorous action while girls liked fairy tales, poetry, and "sentimental" fiction. Boys read more nonfiction than girls. The amount of reading increased from age six to twelve or thirteen and showed a gradual decrease from that point on. Sex differences in reading choice were increasingly apparent after age nine.[2]

Norvell[3] in 1958 investigated the reading interests of more than 24,000 children in Grades III-VI. He found the following elements in the books favoured by boys: animals, humour, courage and heroism, and patriotism. They regarded as unfavourable elements: description, didacticism, fairies, romantic love, sentiment, girls or women as leading characters, and physical weakness in male characters.

Elements favoured by girls were: lively adventure, home and school life, human characters, domestic animals and pets, romantic love, sentiment, mystery, the supernatural, and patriotism. Disapproved elements included violent action, description, didacticism, boys and girls younger than the reader (except babies), and fierce animals.

It was found that many selections classified as juvenile literature increased in appeal to a high point and then declined. Many Mother Goose Rhymes were enjoyed as late as Grade VI; others were rejected as early as Grade III. *Aesop's Fables* and fairy tales were particularly popular in Grades V-VII; myths, legends, and hero and folk tales were most popular in Grades V-VII. Sex differences in children's choices in reading appeared early, and although girls seemed to enjoy many boy's books, boys rejected almost all girls' books. Some adult magazines were popular with both boys and girls.[3]

A later study of reading interests indicated that the first grade children's preference in reading ranked as follows: (1) make believe, (2) happiness, (3) humour, (4) adventure, (5) history, (6) family, (7) anxiety, and (8) today's world. Adventure and history ranked highest for boys while humour and family ranked second and fourth for girls.[4]

Some implications from studies are: Children read all types of material. Some is poor writing, some is reasonably good and the rest is literature. Teachers have the responsibility of guiding children into broader interests and to raise the level of their enjoyment *if* they are to help them develop taste and appreciation.

Children's preferences in books and stories are influenced by such factors as mental age, cultural background, sex, maturity, appeal of the book, and recommendations from others.

Both boys and girls choose selections that are biographical, that deal with animals and nature, that relate adventure, and that contain humour and nonsense. Girls often read selections intended primarily for boys, but boys rarely read those obviously intended for girls. Preferences of girls and boys reading interests appear in the table below.

Preferences of Boys and Girls Reading Interests[5]

CATEGORY	MEAN PERCENTAGE OF YES RESPONSES	
	Boys (1,000)	Girls (942)
Adventure	77.3	63.3
Animals	67.4	60.2
Fine and Applied Arts	36.1	61.7
Family Life and Children	44.0	62.0
Fantasy	68.3	76.1
Famous People	65.7	50.9
Machines and Applied Science	70.9	35.4
Personal Problems	61.1	72.9
Physical Science	72.3	57.0
Plants	45.4	54.4
Social Studies	70.0	69.4
Sports	75.4	65.7

Children read juvenile magazines and as they mature they read some adult magazines. Boys show a preference for sports and mechanics, and girls for home life, movies, and early romance. Comic books are popular and are read extensively, chiefly because they are easy to read, are readily available, relate humour and adventure, and are light and entertaining.

Prose is much more popular than poetry, fiction is more popular than non-fiction. However, children enjoy poetry read aloud *if* the teacher reads expressively. They enjoy particularly poems of a narrative type. Ballads are high on the preference list.

The spread of children's reading interests over grade levels is wide. Preference is related more to maturity than to sex and the great and varying individual differences in choices are more significant than any differences associated with groups in terms of sex, age, intelligence, or cultural background.

Although the results of investigations of children's reading interests give the teacher a clue to the books, stories, and poems boys and girls liked best and the characteristics of selections and subject areas which most appealed to them at the time the studies were made, this does not relieve the teacher of studying the specific needs and interests of the children in his class.

How Shall We Select and Teach Children's Literature?

Anyone who has been on a committee to evaluate and select the best books for children is well aware that this is not a simple task. True, there are certain criteria one can draw up: Books selected must be written in good literary style, ethically sound, true to life, universal in appeal, attractive in format, give evidence of knowledge of children's interests and needs, and satisfy the innate curiosity of the reader. Having drawn up a list of criteria, the task remains to find books that will meet it. However, in spite of the help such criteria give, there still remains the unpredictable variable—the individual child.

Every teacher would profit from looking at the lists which indicate the best judgment of a group of specialists—librarians and teachers working with children and children's books over a number of years deciding which books should be salvaged from the old well known and much loved ones and which of the new books should be included because of their rich significance for today's child.

Dora Smith compiled the following list which she hopes may serve as a guide to elementary schools aiming to develop a well rounded literature program.

The Children's Literary Heritage[6]

Aesop and the Fables
   The Blind Men and the Elephant . . . Lillian Quigley . . . Scribner 3-5
   The Fables of Aesop . . . Joseph Jacobs . . . Macmillan K-6
   The Hare and the Tortoise . . . Il. Paul Galdone . . . Whittlesey K-3
   The Miller, His Son, and Their Donkey . . . Il. Roger Duvoisin . . . McGraw 2-4
   Once a Mouse . . . Marcia Brown . . . Scribner K-3
American Folk Tales
   America Sings . . . Carl Carner . . . Knopf 5-9

The Fast Sooner Hound . . . Arna Bontemps and Jack Conroy . . . Houghton 2-5

Grandfather Tales: American and English Folk Tales . . . Richard Chase . . . Houghton 5-9

Jack and the Three Sillies . . . Richard Chase . . . Houghton 2-4

Jack Tales . . . Richard Chase . . . Houghton 4-6

Journey Cake, Ho! . . . Ruth Sawyer . . . Viking K-3

Mike Fink . . . James Bowman . . . Little 6-9

Ol' Paul, the Mighty Logger . . . Glen Rounds . . . Holiday 4-9

Paul Bunyan and His Great Blue Ox . . . Wallace Wadsworth . . . Doubleday 6-8

Paul Bunyan Swings His Axe . . . Del J. McCormick . . . Caxton 4-6

Pecos Bill, the Greatest Cowboy of All Time . . . James Bowman . . . Whitman 6-9

The Rainbow Book of American Folk Tales and Legends . . . Maria Leach . . . World 5-9

Rip Van Winkle and the Legend of Sleepy Hollow . . . Washington Irving . . . Macmillan 6-9

Uncle Remus: His Songs and Sayings . . . Joel C. Harris . . . Appleton 5-8

With a Wig, With a Wag, and Other American Folk Tales . . . Jean Cothran . . . McKay 3-5

Yankee Doodle's Cousins . . . Anne Malcolmson . . . Houghton 5-9

Andersen, Hans Christian

The Emperor and the Nightingale . . . Il. Bill Sokol . . . Pantheon 3-5

The Emperor's New Clothes . . . Il. Virginia Lee Burton . . . Houghton 2-5

Fairy Tales and Stories . . . Tr. Signe Toksvig . . . Macmillan 5-7

It's Perfectly True and Other Stories . . . Tr. Paul Leyssac . . . Harcourt 5-8

Seven Tales . . . Tr. Eva LeGallienne . . . Harper 2-5

The Steadfast Tin Soldier . . . Il. Marcia Brown . . . Scribner 1-4

The Swineherd . . . Il. Eric Blegvad . . . Harcourt 2-5

The Ugly Duckling . . . Il. Johannes Larsen . . . Macmillan 2-4

The Arabian Nights

The Arabian Nights . . . Andrew Lang . . . Longmans 5-7

The Flying Carpet . . . Il. Marcia Brown . . . Scribner 4-6

English Folk and Fairy Tales

Chanticleer and the Fox . . . Barbara Cooney . . . Crowell K-4

Dick Whittington and His Cat . . . Il. Marcia Brown . . . Scribner K-3

English Fairy Tales . . . Joseph Jacobs . . . Putnam 4-6

English Fairy Tales Retold . . . Flora A. Steel . . . Macmillan K-5

Favorite Fairy Tales in England . . . Virginia Haviland . . . Little 2-5

The Golden Goose Book (The Three Bears and the Three Pigs) . . . Il. L. Leslie Brooke . . . Warne K-1

The Old Woman and her Pig . . . Paul Galdone . . . McGraw K-2

French Fairy Tales

Cinderella or the Glass Slipper . . . Charles Perrault . . . Scribner K-3 Il. Marcia Brown

Favorite Fairy Tales Told in France . . . Virginia Haviland . . . Little 2-5

French Legends, Tales and Fairy Stories . . . Barbara L. Picard . . . Walck 5-8

Puss in Boots . . . Charles Perrault . . . Scribner K-3 Il. Marcia Brown

Puss in Boots . . . Il. Hans Fischer . . . Harcourt K-3

Stone Soup . . . Il. Marcia Brown . . . Scribner K-3

German Fairy and Folk Tales

Favorite Fairy Tales Told in Germany . . . Virginia Haviland . . . Little 2-5

Household Stories . . . Grimm, Jacob and Wilhelm . . . Macmillan 4-6

More Tales from Grimm . . . Told and il. by Wanda Gág . . . Coward 4-6

Rapunzel . . . Grimm, Jacob and Wilhelm . . . Harcourt 2-5 Il. Felix Hoffman

The Shoemaker and the Elves . . . Grimm, Jacob and Wilhelm . . . Scribner K-4 Il. Adrienne Adams

The Sleeping Beauty . . . Grimm, Jacob and Wilhelm . . . Harcourt K-3 Il. Felix Hoffman

Snow White and the Seven Dwarfs . . . Grimm, Jacob and Wilhelm . . . Coward 2-5 Il. Wanda Gág

Tales from Grimm . . . Told and il. by Wanda Gág . . . Coward 4-6

The Travelling Musicians . . . Grimm, Jacob and Wilhelm . . . Harcourt 2-4 Il. Hans Fischer

Norwegian Folk and Fairy Tales

East of the Sun and West of the Moon . . . Asbjörnsen, Peter C., and Jörgen E. Moe . . . Macmillan 5-7 Il. Hedvig Collin

East o' the Sun and West o' the Moon . . . Gudrun Thorne-Thomsen . . . Row 4-5

Norwegian Folk Tales . . . Tr. Pat Iversen and Carl Norman . . . Viking 4-7

The Three Billy Goats Gruff . . . Il. Marcia Brown . . . Harcourt K-4

Folk Tales from Many Lands

Beyond the Clapping Mountains (Alaska) . . . Charles E. Gillham . . . Macmillan 4-5

The Dancing Kettle and Other Japanese Folk Tales . . . Yoshiko Uchida . . . Harcourt 3-5

Heather and Broom (Scotland) . . . Sorche Nic Leodhas . . . Holt 4-7

Jataka Tales (India) . . . Ellen C. Babbitt . . . Appleton 4-5

Once the Hodja (Turkey) . . . Alice G. Kelsey . . . Longmans 4-6

The Shepherd's Nosegay, Stories from Finland and Czechoslovakia . . . Parker Fillmore . . . Harcourt 4-7

Tales from Silver Lands (South America) . . . Charles J. Finger . . . Doubleday 5-7

The Tangle-Coated Horse and Other Tales (Ireland) . . . Ella Young . . . Longmans 6-8

Thirteen Danish Tales (Denmark) . . . Mary C. Hatch . . . Harcourt 3-5

The Three Sneezes and Other Swiss Tales . . . Roger Duvoisin . . . Knopf 4-6

The White Stag (Hungary) . . . Kate Seredy . . . Viking 6-9

Collections of Fairy Tales

Anthology of Children's Literature . . . Edna Johnson, Evelyn R. Sickles, Frances Eichenberg . . . Houghton K-8

The Arbuthnot Anthology of Children's Literature . . . May H. Arbuthnot . . . Scott K-8

The Arthur Rackham Fairy Book . . . Arthur Rackham . . . Lippincott 4-6

The Blue Fairy Book . . . Andrew Lang . . . Longmans 4-6

Chimney Corner Fairy Tales . . . Veronica S. Hutchinson . . . Putnam 3-5

Chimney Corner Stories . . . Veronica S. Hutchinson . . . Putnam 3-5

Mostly Magic (Vol. 1 of Through Golden Windows) . . . Phyllis Fenner . . . Hale 1-5

Time for Fairy Tales, Old and New . . . May H. Arbuthnot . . . Scott K-8

Told Under the Green Umbrella . . . Association for Childhood Education . . . Macmillan K-3

The Wonder Book . . . Howard Pyle . . . Harper 4-7

Great Hero Stories—The Bible

A First Bible . . . Il. Helen Sewell . . . Walck 4-8 Ar. Jean W. Maury

The Bible Story for Boys and Girls—Old Testament and New Testament . . . Walter R. Bowie . . . Abingdon 5-8

The Christ Child . . . Maud and Miska Petersham . . . Doubleday K-4

David . . . Maud and Miska Petersham . . . Macmillan 3-5

Joseph and His Brethren . . . Maud and Miska Petersham . . . Macmillan 3-5

Ruth . . . Maud and Miska Petersham . . . Macmillan 3-5

Also stories of Moses and, where possible, stories of parables like The Talents and The Sower

Greek and Roman Gods and Heroes

The Children's Homer: The Adventures of Odysseus and The Tale of Troy . . . Padraic Colum . . . Macmillan 6-9

The Golden Fleece and the Heroes Who Lived before Achilles . . . Padraic Colum . . . Macmillan 6-9

The Golden Touch . . . Il. Paul Galdone . . . McGraw 2-5

The Gorgon's Head (Perseus) . . . Ian Serraillier . . . Walck 6-9

The Heroes . . . Charles Kingsley . . . Macmillan 5-8

The Iliad of Homer . . . Alfred J. Church . . . Macmillan 6-9

The Odyssey of Homer . . . Alfred J. Church . . . Macmillan 6-9

The Odyssey of Homer . . . Barbara K. Picard . . . Walck 6-9

Stories of the Gods and Heroes . . . Sally Benson . . . Dial 6-9

A Wonder Book and Tanglewood Tales . . . Nathaniel Hawthorne . . . Dodd 5-7 Il. Maxfield Parrish

Norse Gods and Heroes

Adventures with the Giants . . . Catherine F. Sellew . . . Little 4-7

The Children of Odin . . . Padraic Colum . . . Macmillan 6-9

The Thunder of the Gods . . . Dorothy Hosford . . . Holt 6-9

Hero Stories of Many Lands

The Apple and the Arrow (Switzerland) . . . Mary & Conrad Buff . . . Houghton 4-7

The Book of King Arthur and His Noble Knights . . . Mary MacLeod . . . Lippincott 5-8

The Boy's King Arthur . . . Sidney Lanier . . . Scribner 6-9

By His Own Might (Beowulf-England) . . . Dorothy Hosford . . . Holt 6-8

The Adventures of Don Quixote de la Mancha (Spain-Cervantes) . . . Leigh Barret . . . Knopf 6-9

The Golden Treasury Of Myths and Legends . . . Anne T. White . . . Golden 6-9

The Heroes of the Kalevala (Finland) . . . Babette Deutsch . . . Messner 6-9

The Merry Adventures of Robin Hood of Great Renown in Nottinghamshire . . . Howard Pyle . . . Scribner 5-9

Pilgrim's Progress . . . John Bunyan . . . Lippincott 6-8

Robin Hood . . . Carol Oman . . . Dent 5-6

Some Merry Adventures of Robin Hood of Great Renown in Nottinghamshire . . . Howard Pyle . . . Scribner 5-7

The Story of King Arthur and His Knights . . . Howard Pyle . . . Scribner 6-9
The Story of Roland (France) . . . James Baldwin . . . Scribner 6-9
Tale of the Warrior Lord (Spain) . . . Merriam Sherwood . . . Longmans 5-6

Poetry-Nursery Rhymes

Joan W. Anglund, Il. . . In a Pumpkin Shell . . . Harcourt K-2
L. Leslie Brooke, Il. . . Ring o' Roses . . . Warne K-3
Marguerite DeAngeli, Il. . . Book of Nursery and Mother Goose Rhymes . . . Doubleday K-3
Feodor Rojankovsky, Il. . . The Tall Book of Mother Goose . . . Harper K13
Blanche F. Wright, Il . . . The Real Mother Goose . . . Rand K-3
John Langstaff . . . Frog Went A-Courtin' . . . Harcourt K-3 Feodor Rojakovsky, Il.
Peter Spier, Il. . . The Fox Went Out on a Chilly Night . . . Doubleday K-2
Maud and Miska Petersham, Il. . . The Rooster Crows: A Book of American Rhymes and Jingles . . . Macmillan K-3
William Cowper . . . The Diverting History of John Gilpin . . . Warne 5-6
Randolph Caldecott, Il. . . A Frog He Would A-Wooing Go . . . Warne K-5

Individual Poets

Robert Browning . . . The Pied Piper of Hamelin . . . Warne 5-8 Kate Greenaway, Il.
Walter de la Mare . . . Rhymes and Verses: Collected Poems for Young People . . . Holt 2-7
Eugene Field . . . Poems of Childhood . . . Scribner 3-5
Rose Fyleman . . . Fairies and Chimneys . . . Doubleday 4-6
Edward Lear . . . The Complete Nonsense Book . . . Dodd 1-6
Henry W. Longfellow . . . The Children's Own Longfellow . . . Houghton 5-8
A. A. Milne . . . Now We Are Six . . . Dutton 1-4
A. A. Milne . . . When We Were Very Young . . . Dutton K-4
A. A. Milne . . . The World of Christopher Robin . . . Dutton 1-4
Robert L. Stevenson . . . A Child's Garden of Verses . . . Scribner 1-4

Collections of Verse

May Hill Arbuthnot . . . Time for Poetry . . . Scott K-7
Association for Childhood Education . . . Sung Under the Silver Umbrella . . . Macmillan K-4
John E. Brewton . . . Under the Tent of the Sky . . . Macmillan 4-8
Helen Ferris . . . Favorite Poems Old and New . . . Doubleday K-8
Mildred P. Harrington . . . Ring-A-Round . . . Macmillan K-4
Blanche J. Thompson . . . Silver Pennies . . . Macmillan K-6
Louis Untermeyer . . . Rainbow in the Sky; An Anthology of Modern Poetry . . . Harcourt K-6
Louis Untermeyer . . . This Singing World for Young People . . . Harcourt 5-9

Modern Classics

Louisa M. Alcott . . . Little Women . . . Crowell 5-9
James M. Barrie . . . Peter Pan . . . Scribner 4-6
Margery Clark . . . The Poppy Seed Cakes . . . Doubleday 2-4
Samuel Clemens . . . The Adventures of Tom Sawyer . . . World 6-9
Daniel Defoe . . . Robinson Crusoe . . . Scribner 6-9
Charles Dodgson . . . Alice's Adventures in Wonderland and Through the Looking Glass . . . Macmillan 4-7

Kenneth Grahame . . . The Wind in the Willows . . . Scribner 5-7
Lucretia P. Hale . . . The Complete Peterkin Papers . . . Houghton 4-8
Will James . . . Smoky, the Cowhorse . . . Scribner 6-9
Rudyard Kipling . . . The Jungle Books . . . Doubleday 5-7
Rudyard Kipling . . . Just So Stories . . . Doubleday 4-6
Charles Lamb . . . Tales from Shakespeare . . . Macmillan 6-9
Hugh Lofting . . . The Story of Dr. Dolittle . . . Lippincott 4-7
Hugh Lofting . . . The Voyages of Dr. Dolittle . . . Lippincott 4-7
Jack London . . . The Call of the Wild . . . Macmillan 7-9
George Macdonald . . . At the Back of the North Wind . . . Macmillan 5-7
A. A. Milne . . . Winnie-the Pooh . . . Dutton 3-5
A. A. Milne . . . The World of Pooh . . . Dutton 3-5
Beatrix Potter . . . The Tale of Peter Rabbit . . . Warne K-3
Robert L. Stevenson . . . Treasure Island . . . Scribner 7-9
Jonathan Swift . . . Gulliver's Travels . . . World 7-9
Johann D. Wyss . . . The Swiss Family Robinson . . . World 5-8

Recent Classics for Children

Carolyn S. Bailey . . . Miss Hickory . . . Viking 4-6
Ludwig Bemelmans . . . Madeline . . . Viking 1-3
Claire H. Bishop . . . The Five Chinese Brothers . . . Coward 1-3
Carol Ryrie Brink . . . Caddie Woodlawn . . . Macmillan 5-7
Jean de Brunhoff . . . The Story of Babar . . . Random 1-3
Virginia L. Burton . . . The Little House . . . Houghton 1-4
Virginia L. Burton . . . Mike Mulligan and his Steam Showel . . . Houghton 1-3
Elizabeth Coatsworth . . . The Cat Who Went to Heaven . . . Macmillan 4-7
Meindert De Jong . . . The Wheel on the School . . . Harper 4-7
Marie H. Ets . . . Play With Me . . . Viking K-1
Marjorie Flack . . . The Story about Ping . . . Viking K-3
Marie Ets and Aurora Labastida . . . Nine Days to Christmas . . . Viking K-3
Ruth S. Gannett . . . My Father's Dragon . . . Random 2-4
Doris Gates . . . Blue Willow . . . Viking 5-8
Hardie Gramatky . . . Little Toot . . . Putnam K-2
Thomas Handforth . . . Mei Li . . . Doubleday 1-3
Marguerite Henry . . . King of the Wind . . . Rand 5-8
Marguerite Henry . . . Misty of Chincoteague . . . Rand 5-8
Eric Knight . . . Lassie Come-Home . . . Winston 6-9
Robert Lawson . . . Rabbitt Hill . . . Viking 3-6
Munro Leaf . . . The Story of Ferdinand . . . Viking 1-4
Robert McCloskey . . . Homer Price . . . Viking 4-7
Robert McCloskey . . . Make Way for Ducklings . . . Viking K-2
Marjorie K. Rawlings . . . The Yearling . . . Scribner 7-9
Keith Robertson . . . Henry Reed, Inc. . . . Viking 5-8
Kate Seredy . . . The Good Master . . . Viking 5-7
Dr. Seuss . . . And to Think That I Saw It on Mulberry Street . . . Vanguard K-3
Elizabeth G. Speare . . . The Witch of Blackbird Pond . . . Houghton 7-9
Armstrong Sperry . . . Call it Courage . . . Macmillan 5-8
James Thurber . . . Many Moons . . . Harcourt 4-5

Pamela L. Travers . . . Mary Poppins . . . Harcourt 4-7
Lynd Ward . . . The Biggest Bear . . . Houghton K-3
E. B. White . . . Charlotte's Web . . . Harper 4-6
Laura Ingalls Wilder . . . The Little House Books . . . Harper 6-9

Even a cursory glance through this list of books reveals a broad scope of children's literature. The prospective teacher will find many of his favourites here and a challenge to new reading. It is in the interest of the children that he be able to select wisely books and stories on the basis of the particular experiential background of interests, needs, and temperament of his group.

The Heritage of Prose

Prose is the language of everyday conversation. Because of this many teachers find the reading of prose more natural. "Once upon a time . . ." immediately gains the attention of the listeners. It is out of words that the reader creates those pictures that captivate the listeners. Teachers should familiarize themselves with representative prose selections from each of the categories.

There are often occasions for reading fables. Best known are *Aesops Fables*. These vary in difficulty of reading and in demands of maturity of the reader thereby meeting the growing and varied abilities and interests of children throughout the elementary school. These stories which invest animals with human traits to point a moral came to be called fables. With the passing of time they have found a place in children's literature.

Folklore is an integral part of every nation's heritage. McNeer and Ward's *The Canadian Story* contains anecdotes and legends built around the lives of colourful and diverse peoples who played important roles in Canadian history. These absorbing stories of human interest tales concerning Hiawatha, Evangeline, Count Frontenac, the "Mounties", and countless less-known characters, in conjunction with the exceptionally fine illustrations stimulate genuine interest in the study of life in a rigorous era.

American folklore is characterized by the braggadocio of such heroes as Paul Bunyan and Pecos Bill. The stories grew with the telling and the fine line between the legendary and real is often a thin one. The folk-tale however, remains an avenue through which man voices his achievements, ambitions, dreams and protests.

Some of our best loved tales of imagination were created by Hans Christian Anderson. "Intermingling folk-lore and fantasy", says the *Toronto Public Library Books for Boys and Girls*, "Hans Christian Anderson's fairy stories are unique in children's literature because of their variety, their dramatic completeness, their delicate humor, their original and beautiful imagery, and their wisdom distilled from the heart."[7]

In its truest sense a fairy tale is the product of an individual in contrast with the tale which evolved from the "folk" and was handed down from mouth to mouth and generation to generation.

Although the endings are not always happy and a sense of sadness pervades many of the Anderson stories, there is the feeling throughout that life is good and that in the end everything will be all right, that good will triumph over evil. There is even a sense of humour in the ending of *The Emperor's New Clothes*. Among the well known collections, Eva La Gallienne's for young readers and Paul Leyssac's and Signe Toksvig's for intermediate and upper grades are exceptional for fluency in translations and appropriateness of their illustrations.

The Arabian Night Tales have long fascinated children with their magic, touch of mystery, and enchantment of the East. In Andrew Lang's version of *The Arabian Nights,* the stories of "Sinbad the Sailor," "Ali Baba and the Forty Thieves", "Aladdin and the Wonderful Lamp", and others provide much enjoyment for intermediate grades. "The Flying Carpet" in Marcia Brown's arresting edition has strong pictures in absorbing Oriental designs which in an age of supersonic aircraft and flyng saucers hold a peculiar fascination for children.

From the English come some of the best known of all folk and fairy tales. *The Golden Goose Book* of Leslie Brooks with its charming pictures of "The Three Pigs" and "The Three Bears" continues to enchant children in today's kindergarten and primary grades. The atmosphere of the English rural scenes makes these tales excellent ones with which to introduce the fairy tales. There are numerous picture books of individual stories which are very popular with children in the beginning reading stages.

We have come to know Cinderella through the French fairy tales. Among the perennial favourites of Perrault are "Cinderella", "Little Red Riding Hood", "Beauty and the Beast". These stories, however, are best when read or told to the children. The difficulty of the language of some of the tales makes it all but impossible for weak readers to enjoy them at a time when the stories are psychologically suitable for them.

Eleanor Farejon has a long version of Cinderella that is almost a novel, *The Glass Slipper*. A favourite with intermediate and upper grade children, Cinderella is excellent for dramatizing.

If it hadn't been for the scholarly German brothers Grimm—Jakob and Wilhelm, the world's most enchanting fairy tales might have disappeared forever. Their *Household Tales* were adapted from old folk tales rather than created like those of Anderson. Such favourites as "The Bremen Town Musicians", "The Elves and the Shoemaker", "Hansel and Gretel", "Rapunzel", "Tom Thumb", "The Frog Prince", and "Sleeping Beauty", are told in a way that appeals to children. The rewarding of virtue, the confounding of vice is handled with dispatch and with assurance.

Wanda Gag's retelling of "Snow White and the Seven Dwarf's" is enchanting with the diminutive dwarfs, the musical, rhythmical telling, and the childlike quality which is utterly devoid of the sophisticated treatment given by other artists.

From Scandinavia comes the folk literature of the ogres, giants, trolls, the charming ladies and devoted lovers. "The Three Billy Goat Gruffs" has long been a favourite with primary children as has "East o' the Sun and West o' the Moon."

Gudrun Thorne-Thomson, the famous Norwegian story teller of the Carnegie Library School, captures in her retelling of the stories from *East o' the Sun and West o' the Moon* the spirit of the Norwegian folk heritage. Correlating the music of Grieg with the literature gives children further insight into the cultural heritage of these people. The "Peer Gynt Suite" is exceptionally valuable in this connection.

The eight volumes of *Folk Tales from Many Lands* is typical of the numerous collections which have in recent years enriched the field of children's literature. As the world shrinks it is important to understand other cultures and other peoples. The teacher should be concerned with helping children appreciate not merely literature but also cultures of other lands.

Gods and Heroes have long been a subject for writers. The great hero stories of the Bible such as Moses and the Promised Land, David and Goliath, Daniel in the Lion's Den, Joseph and His Brethren, have laid the foundation for the Judea-Christian ethic, with its emphasis on moral heroism and the worth of the individual.

An early encounter with the Petershams' *The Christ Child*, selected passages from the Christmas story, illumined in gold, blue, and rose, provides children with a great literary experience.

The Myths of the Greek Gods—Zeus, Poseidin, Apollo, Athena, and many others—have survived in all their grandeur. Children enjoy them in the upper intermediate grades and junior high school. Their acquaintance with the gods of Olympus and their intervention in the affairs of men introduce them to concepts and allusions they will meet in much of their later literature.

Kingsley's "The Heroes", and Sally Benson's *Stories of the Gods and Heroes* are helpful in understanding the epics. Individual children will vary in their readiness for such reading. The responsibility of the teacher is to plan a program in which the individual interests of children are broadened.

Myths and legends about great human heroes, hero tales and epics evolved in the days of man's greatest wondering about himself and his origin. Religion, magic, and explanation of life were intermingled. Out of this came great epics and stories. *The Illiad*, and *The Odyssey* of which Church's version has been a standard for many years, challenge able readers in the intermediate grades. Padriac Colum's *The Adventures of Odysseus* and his *Tale of Troy* are well paced and related with vigour. The teacher could well read them aloud to a class. Some individual children select such literature if it is available.

A favourite hero of English speaking children is Robin Hood. Howard Pyle has an excellent way of telling the story enabling pupils to relive the old days of Sherwood Forest and Nottingham Castle. His illustrations, too, are delightful. Some pupils, however, will enjoy reading the less demanding Carol Oman version, and leave the Pyle version to be read by the teacher during the story hour.

Other heroes are Beowulf, the Finnish heroes of the Kalevala, Roland of France, the Cid, and Don Quixote of Spain. Not to be missed is the story of

Christian in Paul Bunyan's *Pilgrim's Progress*. Although written for adults it is relished by young students.

The Heritage of Poetry

Introducing children to poetry can be both challenging and exciting. Poetry is readily appreciated by a child because the poet and the child are kin in the sense that the child like the poet sees with the imagination, hears with the ear of the musician, and shares what he sees and hears. For every occasion there is a poem. The teacher who makes poetry an integral part of the day's activities will teach children that what we call the music of the words in poetry is actually what we hear through our thoughts and feelings. In a classroom in which a sensitive teacher has guided children into the wonder of words poetry begins in awe and ends with delight.

In every library should be varied and appealing editions of Mother Goose. The Mother Goose Rhymes hold interest for children above the primary grades if interpretation includes opportunity to dramatize, to develop themes for a poetry program, to combine with other creative arts, and to delve into the historical background of the rhymes. The aim is to stimulate the imagination, to broaden the horizons, and to motivate response.

The teacher should keep up with the ever growing body of new offerings in children's literature, both prose and poetry. Fortunately there are sources of information and evaluation of new books. Among these are the reviews of books in the *Horn Book, Elementary English, The Reading Teacher, Saturday Review, School Library Journal, Association for Childhood Education,* and in the children's book sections in newspapers such as the *New York Times* and the *New York Herald Tribune, Vancouver Sun, Winnipeg Tribune,* Toronto *Globe & Mail, Montreal Gazette.*

How Shall We Teach Children's Literature?

Individuals interested in the teaching of children's literature have long held that such instruction can extend the pupil's experience, develop his taste for literature, stimulate him to acquire high ideals and moral or spiritual values, develop an understanding of other peoples, and broaden the scope of his reading interests. Whether such goals are achieved depends on the selection of the material and on meaningful learning experiences. In all too many elementary schools pupils' experiences in literature are limited to memorizing facts. Word study, rhythm, sentence structure, style, names of figures of speech, and other structural elements can be made important in aiding the students to understand and appreciate literature. It is the conviction of the authors that in developing appreciation of literature every aspect of the program should focus on the child's experience with the literature itself. The teacher utilizes the content as an avenue to deepening, broadening, and enriching children's experiences. By careful planning the teacher leads the child to project himself imaginatively into various times, places, and situations. This may be accomplished in various ways.

Guiding principles. Fostering delight and hearty enjoyment of literary selections through experiences is the basis for developing appreciation and taste in literature.

1. Literature should be approached in such a way that the pupil comes to the experience anticipating that here is something to be enjoyed.
2. The approach to literature should be both creative and analytical.
3. The teacher must provide for a wide selection of books in order to help children broaden their interests in reading.
4. The reading of good literature to children and by children should be an integral part of the curriculum.
5. The teacher himself should have both an understanding of and appreciation for the literature he teaches.
6. Creative activities of many kinds should evolve directly from the child's experience with literature.
7. The best basis for developing taste and appreciation is the exposure to good literature over a long period of time.

WHAT ARE SOME CREATIVE EXPERIENCES WITH LITERATURE

Creative teachers are using many and varied experiences to vitalize the literature program in the elementary classroom. Here the teacher is not concerned primarily with reading ability but with guiding children to appreciate and enjoy literature through varied experiences. In developmental reading the teacher is concerned with the question, "What is Johnny doing in reading?" In literature he is concerned with the question, "What is reading doing for Johnny?" The teacher must ask himself, "Can I teach so enthusiastically, so effectively, so creatively that Johnny will under my guidance:

1. Share the real and imaginary experiences of the author
2. Extend and enrich his own experiences
3. Broaden the scope of his interests by bringing him in contact with a wide range of literature in a wide variety of situations
4. Develop insight into his own personality and problems
5. Develop discriminating taste and a permanent love for good literature
6. Express creativity through literature?"

Oral Interpretation

Reading aloud is the most fundamental method of bringing children and literature together. The child's first introduction to literature of necessity is an oral one. Yet how often we hear teachers say "There isn't time enough to read aloud to children". When one examines the importance of a regular "read-aloud period", one may well ask if he can afford not to take the time. If literature is an interpretation of life, and creative reading is an interpretation of literature; it follows that the creative reader is really an interpreter of life through the medium of literature. The teacher sets the standards for reading aloud. Even in the child's beginning experiences with reading he should be encouraged to read interpretatively as he reads aloud to the group.

If the teacher is to make literature live for children, he must understand the fundamentals of oral interpretation both for himself and for the children he teaches.

It is through the interrelationship of the writer who creates the work of art, the oral interpreter who recreates the work, and the work of art itself that the creative process is set in motion again and again. It is when the oral interpreter recreates what the writer has set down in print that the listener shares in the creative process. The creative process is not completed until the product (the writing) is shared with another human being. In oral interpretation the interpreter becomes a creator in his own right.

When the young child who has faith in his own powers of creating reads aloud he has such a vivid imagination that all he has to do when he is moved by literature which stirs within him concrete imagery—is merely to recreate it. It is not necessary for him to have experienced everything he reads in order to appreciate it. He brings to literature a rich imagination which makes him capable of enjoying much he cannot comprehend or much of what he has never experienced except vicariously. This is particularly true in poetry and accounts for his enjoyment of poems which many times adults are sure he cannot understand.[8] It accounts, too, for his affinity with nonsense poems.

To enjoy poetry one must read with the imagination as well as with the experience, and a child has the imagination.

Intermediate and upper grade teachers are familiar with the reaction of the child who brings to his reading the excitement and enjoyment that comes from having first-hand experience with a place, a phenomena, a person. As the child grows and learns the meaning of specific words, he brings to the reading a more mature power of interpretation. He becomes aware of the power of a word to create a picture or portray an emotion. As he brings to each new experience with literature an explorer's attitude of discovery, new realms of enjoyment and creativity will constantly be opening to him.

To bring to the literature a freshness, a spontaneity, a re-creation of the author's inspiration requires understanding, preparation, and skills which create "the illusion of the first time". This is achieved through a combination of understanding the meaning of the work, feeling the emotion, and sharing with another the ideas, emotions, and feelings which originated in the mind of the author and are communicated through the oral interpreter.

The effective oral reader understands the meaning of the literature he is interpreting, is sensitive to characterization, and is willing to experiment until he discovers the interpretation that for him is "right". When he integrates body, voice, and feelings into an organic whole he recreates for the listener the ideas, feelings, and emotions of the writer shaded by his own personality.

It is only when the oral interpreter understands the poem through his own background and imagination and recreates it in relation to his own experiences through an interrelation of voice, body, and inner voice that he achieves true creativity.

The intellectual and emotional experiences are joined in oral interpretation of literature. The teacher or child who reads interpretatively is actually interpreting life itself.

Storytelling

Storytelling is one of the best avenues for the development of the imagination and the manifestation of creativity. It is in storytelling that the art of communication receives its greatest challenge. It is here that the good oral communicator is in his element. He senses the need to put his listeners at ease as he invites them to share his inner world of delight, excitement, and suspense. Whether the child participates in this experience as a listener or as a teller of tales is immaterial. In either case he requires the full powers of an awakened imagination coupled with his skill of communication in order to express his creative urge, just as surely as the artist expresses in colour, the musician in song, and the dancer in movement. "Words used by the tale-teller are as colors used by the painter. Forms grow out of the materials of the tale and the teller's reaction to them." Sherwood Anderson proved this statement repeatedly in the tales he told.

There are those in the elementary classroom whose imaginations are so well developed and whose skills in communication so effective that they have within them the ability to hold the group of listeners as they proceed to transport boys and girls to the magic land of make-believe. Through the imagination, the development of the senses, the skill in using words, the ability to paint imagery pictures the teller spins his tales to the enchanted listeners.

It is in storytelling that the teller who has perfected the requisite skills invites the listeners to come with him and share his inner world, his delight in the story, his excitement at the development, and the mystery of what is about to unfold. He conveys the feeling that there is something here that demands every ounce of the listener's attention and every ounce of the teller's energy, skill, and imagination in the telling. It is here that he can transmit to the listeners a feeling, too, of security and safety as they empathize with the teller.

Encouragement of the child as he tells stories he has heard, or weaves new ones out of the figment of his imagination will help him develop confidence in his ability to share with others his joy in storytelling, whether as a weaver of tales, a teller of tales, or as a listener of tales.

In order to develop the ability to tell stories creatively there are certain guidelines.

Guidelines for Storytelling

1. Develop powers of awareness of the world in which you live; use your imagination and improve your ability to communicate what you see, feel, think, and imagine.
2. Select a story which appeals to the basic motivations of the audience. They like stories that deal with other human beings, their triumphs, joys, difficulties, struggles, sorrows, and final victories. They like stories that touch their heart strings, tickle their funny bones, and bring a tear to the eye, a smile to the lips, or a hearty laugh to all the listeners.
3. Always have the story clearly in mind before you try to tell it. Develop the ability to see with your inner eye in order that the audience shares with you your interest, excitement, and pleasure in the story as it unfolds.
4. Organize the story in logical sequence. If it is long, be sure the points are interesting and each leads logically to the next. Build to the climax. Plan the ending.
5. Get the attention of the audience from the beginning by making it interesting right at the start.
6. Don't retrace your steps obviously if you have forgotten some important point. Improvise and bring it in logically, or add it as an "aside" to the audience.
7. Increase your vocabulary so you are never at a loss for words. Don't break the continuity of your story as you search for a word that should be on the tip of your tongue.
8. Enjoy telling the story and work toward improving your ability to hold your audience.
9. Make the characters come alive. Differentiate between the characters by voice and action.
10. Remember that the storyteller is an interpreter, not an actor.

Storytelling can become a motivation for developing the powers of awareness, extending the imagination, improving the skills of communication, understanding the needs, feelings, and viewpoints of other people, places, and times. It can become, too, a powerful means for revealing social and emotional problems as children identify with characters they discover, create, or re-create. For some the magic of storytelling becomes the avenue for expressing creativity and thus for moving toward self-realization.

Preparing a story. The teller of tales does not memorize the story in detail. Rather he learns the sequence of the important events, memorizes specific lines essential to the style, and fills in the details afresh each time he tells the tale.

A story well told is as a series of pictures unfolding. Here is an example of learning a story by pictures. *The Bremen Town Musicians* from the Brothers Grimm is a great favourite with children. Here are the pictures as they develop naturally in the mind's eye of the story-teller.

An old donkey is the first character to be introduced. He has worked hard all his life. Now that he is too old to work his master has turned him out.

He takes the road to Bremen. He will become a town musician. On the road he falls in with Growler, the old dog, who has fallen on bad times.

Together they travel and meet up with Whiskers, the old cat. No longer able to catch mice, the cat overhears his mistress saying she will drown him.

They come to a barnyard. They hear the old cock on a post bemoaning his fate. He failed to crow "fair weather" for Lady's Day, so he is to be served up for the holiday dinner.

The donkey persuades all of them to come with him to Bremen and organize a band. Their spirits rise. They are no longer outcasts, abandoned by their masters.

That night they take shelter in the woods. The cat and cock go up a tree, the dog and donkey lie down under it. Aloft the cock spies a light. It may offer better shelter.

Making their way cautiously through the woods the four find a barn where robbers are hiding. They are feasting around a table.

"Good fare for us", announces the donkey. It is high time to start trying out their prowess as musicians. On the donkey in turn mount dog, cat, and cock. Together they bark, caterwaul, and crow.

Terrified, the robbers flee. The four take over the barn. They feast, then settle down for the night each in his accustomed spot.

The robbers return. One of them attempts to discover what has happened. As he tries to find his way in the dark he is scratched by the cat, bitten by the dog, clawed by the cock, and kicked by the donkey. Terrified he tells the others that the place is bewitched. That is the last they see of the robbers.

The four, left in peace, end their days in comfort and plenty.

"The Bremen Town Musicians" illustrates every point in a good story; it is brief; it is colourful; language is simple; introduction is brief; it develops logically; it ends quietly after the climax, and it satisfies. The story has a single central theme—and lends itself well to telling and later to dramatizing. Easy to learn and delightful to tell it is a favourite with children.

When to read and when to tell a story. Picture stories should usually be read from the books because the illustrations are an integral part of the story. Illustrations should be large enough so the children grouped closely around can see as the teacher holds the book open, facing children at their eye level, turning the pages as the story unfolds. The teacher should know the story well enough so he can share it with the children while holding the book for them to see. He should avoid constantly shifting the book from reader to audience. If the illustrations are small the story should be read first, then the pictures can be shown later as the book is passed around or placed on the library table.

Stories which depend upon exact wording of the author as do some of the fairy tales should be read rather than told. For example, *The Fisherman and His Wife* is most enjoyed when the verse repeated throughout the tale is given in exact wording.

The teacher should make a point of adding several folk tales each year to his repertoire. Telling stories creates an atmosphere of direct communication with the listeners that cannot be achieved in reading aloud except by the most experienced student of oral interpretation.

Storytelling can be a many-faceted activity in the elementary school. Children who hear a teacher tell stories are often inspired to try storytelling. Various techniques for motivating this type of activity can be used. Children can tell the stories during the story hour to the class or to their reading group. In individualized reading programs children frequently tell parts of stories they have read to whet the taste of the listener to read the entire story. Children in the intermediate and upper grades gain valuable experience in storytelling to primary grade children during story hour in the school or public library. Children often write their own stories with a great deal of dialogue as tales to be told rather than read.

Through storytelling children become acquainted with a great variety of literature. In the process of choosing a story to tell they will read many. They should learn to tell them in the storyteller's style. The storyteller tells the tale as if it were happening *now*. Such telling involves the ability to keep in mind the setting, happenings in sequence, problem, characters, climax, and ending.

Experience with Poetry

Poetry is meant to be spoken and heard. Poetry is for enjoyment, not for dissection. Through listening to poetry children become aware of the sounds and symbols, the movement and moods, the rhythm and rhymes. The child instead of viewing the literature parade from the traditional Mother Goose Rhymes to the stanzas of Auden with boredom, will experience poetry with delight.

If poetry is to become an integral part of the literary heritage it must be planned as carefully as any other phase of the literature program. It is highly unlikely that a group will casually develop a liking for poetry. It is more likely to occur in a classroom in which the teacher himself is enthusiastic about poetry and has a genuine liking for it. He has a wealth of poems at hand that fit the occasion or the mood of the moment. Poetry for young children should be for fun-filled experiences, entertainment and enjoyment, not for teaching rhyme schemes, figurative language, or metrical arrangements. Rather, the teacher pre-plans to recreate the sensory impressions, the word pictures, the mood, and the characterizations.

Reading poetry to the children makes it a pleasurable experience. In an atmosphere in which the teacher creates a mood *before* he introduces the poem, the readiness for listening is there. The teacher may simply talk about a familiar experience related to the poem; he may ask the children to react to the central idea of the poem; he may interest the children with the tongue tickling words and phrases of the poem; he may have the children predict the content from the title; or he may simply begin to read the poem without a single introductory remark. He creates the mood for listening by setting the tone in the spirit of the poem, light, gay, or pensive; boldly adventurous, or timidly withdrawing; strong and vigorous or playfully fanciful. It is through the invitation to listen that the child's attitude is shaped. For the teacher the invitation to listen to the poem is in itself a creative act which he should perhaps plan even more carefully than the introduction to other literary experiences.

Children should be encouraged to read poems in the classroom. Young children often learn their poems through repeated saying of their favourites—not through required memorization. Intermediate and upper grade children usually memorize the poems they have in choral speaking simply from the repetition during practice. Children memorize the poems they truly want to remember. Many are committed to memory from the sheer joy of saying them again and again. Pressure to memorize assigned poems has been a contributory factor to the dislike many children have for poetry.

Dramatizing poetry is another way of experiencing poetry. Since poetry is filled with numerous sensory images and rhythm, it is a natural avenue for creative expression. As children act out the poem they gain greater insight into its meaning.

Choral speaking enhances children's enjoyment and appreciation of literature through group experiences with poetry. Like group singing, it builds *esprit de corps*, releases creativity through a group enterprise, and develops children's taste in literature.

CHORAL SPEAKING: AN ART FORM

The chief value of choral reading lies in the process, not in the product. There is joy in feeling, in interpreting, in recreating the mood and meaning of the poet as a part of a group. Choral speaking is again taking its rightful place in the language arts program. It was an integral part of early Greek drama. With the decline in popularity of Greek drama, choral speaking as an art form nearly vanished. Its modern revival came about at the Glasgow Music Festival in 1922 through the work of Marjorie Gullan of London. Its popularity soon spread to Canada and the United States as Miss Gullan lectured and trained verse choirs in both countries.

Many of the basic concepts held by Miss Gullan influence our approach to choral speaking today. New ideas have been added, greater flexibility in method has evolved, but the definition and spirit of Miss Gullan remain with us. Miss Gullan often stated that choric or choral speech is the speaking by a group of voices of various verses or prose. It serves as a medium for creating appreciation of prose and verse as well as a means of teaching good vocal practices without the counter attraction of stage fright. Choral speaking is a means not an end in itself. As a means it is invaluable; as an end it defeats its purpose.

Key Concepts about Choral Speaking

Informal, incidental choral speaking is universal. The sports cheering section, mass chants in political rallies, congregational prayers, response to the Mass, responsive readings, pledge of allegiance, toast to the Queen are all examples of choral speaking.

Choral speaking as a creative experience knows no age limit. It is enjoyed by the pre-school child and the senior citizen alike.

Interpretation is a group product rather than an individual dictum.

Material should be of excellent literary quality, be within the perceptual understanding and interest of the group, and be objective rather than subjective in nature.

The poem, not the director, should be the focus of attention.

Values of choral speaking. Choral speaking has both educational and psychological values. Among the educational values are that it: develops literary appreciation; stimulates imagination; improves oral reading and comprehension; develops a sense of rhythm; helps in analyzing ideas and abstract concepts; increases vocabulary and perception of meanings; improves speech skills; develops listening ability; and provides a treasure-trove of poems.

Among the psychological values are that it: develops poise, enthusiasm, tolerance; provides avenue for achievement; provides outlet for emotional expression in an acceptable form; helps aggressive child to blend his ideas with others; aids timid child to build a positive image of self; provides for the individual's need for recognition; builds awareness of value of cooperative enterprise; and develops desirable teacher-pupil rapport.

Division of voices for choral speaking. There are several ways of dividing the voices for choral speaking. An understanding of the effects that may be gained by a creative use of these divisions will enhance the choral speaking experience.

The main divisions or types of choral speaking widely used in the elementary schools are: refrain, antiphonal, unison, sequential (line-a-child or line-a-choir), and dramatized choral speaking.

The *refrain* with solo and group arrangement is one of the most popular types of choral speaking. In the refrain an individual recites the narrative and the group responds with the refrain. At first the teacher may take the solo part and the class responds with the refrain. Later different children read the solo lines.

Antiphonal choral speaking capitalizes on contrasting voices. The most common division is into high and low voices. When the group gains experience a third division may be added—the medium voices. In the upper grades separate grouping of the boys and the girls utilizes the natural contrasts in their voices. Antiphonal choral speaking is recommended when the poems contain considerable contrast.

Probably the most difficult form of choral speaking is *unison*. Exactness and precision are required in the rate of speaking, phrasing, pausing, emphasis, inflection, and pronunciation. There is little attempt to direct the voice pitch of the group except in the matter of interpretation. Each member of the chorus speaks in his own normal key or pitch, allowing his voice to move up and down the scale in response to the ideas or moods to be expressed. Harmony results from the blend of voices and unity is gained by the group interpretation.

In the *sequential* or line-a-child division each child reads a separate line. Each child should be well acquainted with the whole composition in order to achieve the proper mood and timing. It is essential for the child to respond at the precise and proper time.

Dramatized choral speaking provides an added interest for chidren to enjoy and experience literature. This form calls for the verse choir to speak while the action is being pantomimed by members of the drama and/or dance group. Dramatized choral speaking integrates the rhythmical movement of modern dance, portrayal of characters of drama, and reading by the speech choir. An understanding of each of these arts enables the teacher to blend them into a worthwhile experience for the children.

In developing such an experience the entire class plans the arrangement of the material for the verse choir and the choreography for the performers. The procedure is somewhat similar to that of creative dramatics, but has the added dimension of choral speaking. Poems which are highly rhythmical or have an unusual beat that stimulate creative dance movements, ballads, and poems that suggest definite actions are most effective for this activity.

INTRODUCING CHORAL SPEAKING IN THE CLASSROOM[9]

To introduce choral reading into the classroom, a teacher needs sincere enjoyment of poetry, an awareness of the instructional purposes, a knowledge of procedures and materials for choral speaking.

I. PROCEDURES
  a) Preparation before reading
    1. Careful reading of the selection
      a) Enjoy the thought of the poem
      b) Feel the rhythm without falling into sing-song
      c) Watch pronunciation of difficult words
      d) Note where enunciation must be especially clear

    2. Noting tempo and tones called for
      a) Reflect the mood of the poem
      b) Plan variety of tempo, tone, and arrangements, emphasis
      c) Note words to be emphasized

    3. Marking the lines of the poem to indicate readers
      a) A for all in unison
      b) BC, GC, for Boys' or Girls' Chorus
      c) BS1, BS2, etc., for Solo parts for boys

b) **Reading the poem**
   1. Start together on the first syllable at a sign from the teacher
   2. Speak in natural voice
   3. Subdue physical motions and emphasize the vocal inflection.
II. MATERIALS
   A. Selection according to purpose

   1. For *young* children, an activity rhyme and antiphonal reading
      e.g. *B.* Jennie come tie my
                 Jennie come tie my   (tying motion)
                 Jennie come tie my bonnie cravat

            G. I've tied it behind
                  I've tied it before   (tying motion)
                  I've tied it so often I'll tie it no more (finger shaking)

      e.g. *B.* "Where are you going, my pretty maid?" (bowing)
            G. "I'm going a-milking, sir," she said. (curtsying)

            B. "May I go with you, my pretty maid?"
            G. "You're kindly welcome, sir," she said.

            B. "What is your father, my pretty maid?"
            G. "My father's a farmer, sir," she said.

            B. "What is your fortune, my pretty maid?"
            G. "My face is my fortune, sir," she said.

            B. "Then I can't marry you, my pretty maid."
            G. "Nobody asked you, sir," she said.

   2. For shy children needing individual effort, a poem requiring sequential speaking, sometimes called line-a-child—
      e.g. *S1* Monday's child is fair of face,
            S2 Tuesday's child is full of grace,
            S3 Wednesday's child is full of woe,
            S4 Thursday's child has far to go,
            S5 Friday's child is loving and giving,
            S6 Saturday's child works hard for a living;
            A   But the child that is born on the Sabbath Day
                  Is fair, and wise, and good, and gay.

   3. For most children in elementary grades, a poem with narrative interest, vivid imagery, and strong rhythm
      e.g. The Pied Piper (selection)
            BC: Rats!
                   They fought the *dogs* and *killed* the cats,
                       And bit the *babies* in the cradles, (build up)
                   And ate the cheese out of the vats,
                       And licked the *soup* from the cooks' own ladles;
                   Split *open* the kegs of salted sprats,   (horror)
                       Made *nests* inside men's Sunday hats

> And even spoiled the women's chats   (climax)
>   By drowning their speaking
>   With shrieking and squeaking
> In *fifty* different sharps and flats.

GC: At last the people in a body
          To the Town Hall came flocking:
  A: "Tis clear," cried they, "our Mayor's a noddy;
          And as for our Corporation—shocking
          To think we buy gowns lined with ermine
          For dolts that can't or won't determine   (anger of mob)
          What's best to rid us of our vermin!"

Browning

4. For maturing children, a poem calling for appreciation of imagery and interpretation of thought
   e.g.   The Throstle

   GC: "Summer is coming, summer is coming
           I know it, I know it, I know it.
           Light again, leaf again, life again, love again."

   BC: Yes, my wild little Poet

           Sing the new year in under the blue.
           Last year you sang it as gladly.

   GC: "New, new, new new!"

   BC: Is it then *so* new
           That you should carol so madly?

   GC: "Love again, song again, nest again, young man,"

   BC: Never a prophet so crazy!
           And hardly a daisy as yet, little friend.
           See, there is hardly a daisy.

   GC: "Here again, here, here, happy year!"
   BC: O warble unchidden, unbidden!
           Summer is coming, is coming, my dear,
           And all the winters are hidden.

Tennyson

5. For children experienced in group reading, a poem that challenges their skill
   e.g.   The Musical Trust

Group 1:   There once was a man who could execute
             Old Zip Coon on a yellow flute,
             And several other tunes to boot,
             But he couldn't make a penny with his tootle-ti-toot.
             One day he met a singular quaint old man
             With a great big tuba, who solemnly said,

Group 2: "I've travelled wide and I've travelled far,
But I never made a penny with my oom-pah-pah."

Groups 1 & 2:
Then they met two men who were travelling
With a big bass drum and a cymbal thing
Group 3: Who said, "We've played since early Spring,
But we haven't made a penny with our boom-zing-zing."

Group 1: So the man with flute went tootle-ti-toot,
Group 2: And the other went oom-pah!
Group 3: While the men with drum and the cymbal thing
Went Boom-boom-boom, zing, zing!

All: And they travelled wide and they travelled far
Together they made the welkin ring
With their

Group 1:   Tootle-ootle,
Group 2:   Ooom-pah!
Group 3:   Boom, zing-zing!

All: And oh, the pennies the people fling,
When they hear the

Group 1: Tootle-ootle, ootle-ootle, ootle-ootle, oo
Group 2:   Oom-pah, oom-pah, oom-pah, oom
Group 3:   Boom, zing-zing, zing-zing!

Author Unknown

Teachers approach choral speaking with a group in various ways. Miss Hart's fourth graders planned to use "Roads" by Rachel Field for choral speaking. The motivation for selecting this poem was their keen interest in the new highway being build past their school.

Introduction: Miss Hart asked the children if they knew any poems about roads. Children responded by recalling poems about roads. Finally Miss Hart said, "The author of 'Roads',* Rachel Field, has some interesting ideas about them. Will you open your books and read the poem?"

Discussion: After reading the poem, the children volunteered their impressions. Miss Hart then asked for someone to read the poem aloud. They discussed the mood of the poem, the specific meaning of new words such as quays—bristly, foal—She asked such questions as, "What else can you name that is bristly?" "Where is the mountain?" "How does the poet picture the mountain?" "How does the punctuation help us classify meaning?" Various children then each read a couplet, discussing the couplet after each reading.

*From Rachel Field, *The Pointed People*.

"A road might lead to anywhere—
To harbours towns and quays,"

Children recalled trips they had made to Montreal, Halifax, San Francisco, New Orleans.

"Or to a witches pointed house,
Hidden by bristly trees."

This couplet started discussion of the witches house in "Hansel and Gretel."

"It might lead past the tailor's door
Where he sews with needle and thread,"

This aroused a discussion about experiences of sewing and one child contributed the fact that his father had his clothes tailor made. The discussion continued throughout the remaining couplets, concluding with the idea that after adventuring most people wish themselves back home again.

The children were ready now to suggest and demonstrate interpretations for various lines. The group selected the best interpretation and read it together. The children decided on an antiphonal arrangement of the poems by couplets. One child who read very well suggested that there be at least one solo couplet. The group agreed to try it.

The teacher directed the group in their chosen arrangement. They then evaluated their performance by responding to such questions as: "Did John's voice express fear of the witch?" "Did our voices show the excitement of searching and finding the treasure?" "Are we satisfied with our arrangement of the poem?" "Did we give the best possible interpretation?"

The class decided that on the next day they would try a sequence arrangement in which seven pupils would have solo parts—first, lines 1 and 2, second, lines 3 and 4, third, lines 5 and 6, and so on with the entire group coming in on a unison arrangement of the concluding couplet. The strength of Miss Hart's lesson lay in the fact that all the children were motivated to participate in the discussion, the interpretation, the reading, and the evaluation.

Children should be given the opportunity to determine the arrangement and the interpretation of poems for choral speaking. They will develop in perception and discrimination under a teacher who allows—even encourages them—to experiment.

Materials

In selecting materials for choral speaking an acquaintance with a wide range of poems, a knowledge of the interests and needs of children in the group, and an awareness of the special qualities that make a poem adaptable for choral speaking are essential.

Specifically, the material should: be within the emotional and intellectual understanding, and the interest range of the group; have literary value; have a wide appeal; be in a form which is adaptable to choral speaking; be objective rather than subjective in nature.

All of the materials suggested below have been enjoyed by children and teachers in the elementary grades. The arrangements are merely suggestive. An imaginative teacher and his children can modify them for their own group. They are arranged broadly in sequence of difficulty and developmental level of elementary school children. However, specific grade levels are not cited as children vary in background of experience as well as literary appreciation.

Nursery Rhymes provide an excellent means for introducing young children to choral speaking. Take for example, the well-known rhyme "Hickory, Dickory, Dock." Divide the group into two divisions: One group repeating the "tick-tock", "tick-tock", throughout the poem while the other group recites the poem in unison.

HICKORY, DICKORY, DOCK

Hickory, dickory, dock
The Mouse ran up the clock.
The clock struck one,
The mouse ran down,
Hickory, dickory, dock.

THE MYSTERIOUS CAT[10]

Girls	I saw a proud, mysterious cat,
Boys	I saw a proud mysterious cat
Solo 1	Too proud to catch a mouse or rat—
All	Mew, mew, mew.
Girls	But catnip she would eat, and purr,
Boys	But catnip she would eat, and purr.
Solo 2	And goldfish she did much prefer—
All	Mew, mew, mew.
Solo 3	I saw a cat—'twas but a dream,
Solo 4	I saw a cat—'twas but a dream,
Solo 5	Who scorned the slave that brought her cream—
All	Mew, mew, mew.
Solo 1	Did you ever hear of a thing like that?
Solo 2	Did you ever hear of a thing like that?
Solo 3	Did you ever hear of a thing like that?
Girls	Oh, what a proud mysterious cat.
Boys	Oh, what a proud mysterious cat.
All	Oh, what a proud mysterious cat.
All	Mew. . . Mew. . . Mew.

Vachel Lindsay

An adventurous group enjoys experimenting with this poem.

POOR OLD WOMAN

1   There was an old woman who swallowed a fly
All Oh, my! Swallowed a fly!
      Poor old woman, I think she'll die.

2   There was an old woman who swallowed a spider;
      Right down inside her she swallowed a spider;
1   She swallowed the spider to kill the fly
All O, my! Swallowed a fly!
      Poor old woman, I think she'll die.

3   There was an old woman who swallowed a bird
      How absurd to swallow a bird.
2   She swallowed the bird to kill the spider
1   She swallowed the spider to kill the fly
All Oh, my! Swallowed a fly!
      Poor old woman, I think she'll die.

4   There was an old woman who swallowed a cat,
      Fancy that! She swallowed a cat!
3   She swallowed the cat to kill the bird,
2   She swallowed the bird to kill the spider,
1   She swallowed the spider to kill the fly
All Oh, my! Swallowed a fly!
      Poor old woman, I think she'll die.

5   There was an old woman who swallowed a dog.
      She went whole hog! She swallowed a dog!
4   She swallowed the dog to kill the cat,
3   She swallowed the cat to kill the bird,
2   She swallowed the bird to kill the spider,
I   She swallowed the spider to kill the fly
All Oh, my! Swallowed a fly!
      Poor old woman, I think she'll die.

6   There was an old woman who swallowed a cow
      I don't know how but she swallowed a cow,
5   She swallowed the cow to kill the dog,
4   She swallowed the dog to kill the cat,
3   She swallowed the cat to kill the bird,
2   She swallowed the bird to kill the spider,
1   She swallowed the spider to kill the fly.
All Oh, my! Swallowed a fly!
      Poor old woman, I think she'll die.

7   There was an old woman who swallowed a horse!
All She died, of course.

This selection is an excellent example of Sequential or line-a-child division.

A modification of the line-a-child division is the cumulatve division. Timing is particularly important in this arrangement, as is building up to a climax. An additional person or group is added to each succeeding line of the poem. The entire group will be reading by the last line. An effective example of this type of division is "This is the House that Jack Built".

In a classroom of thirty pupils, for example, there could be three children added to each line as the poem progresses.

THIS IS THE HOUSE THAT JACK BUILT

This is the farmer sowing his corn,
That kept the cock that crowed in the morn,
That waked the priest all shaven and shorn,
That married the man all tattered and torn,
That kissed the maiden all forlorn,
That milked the cow with the crumpled horn,
That tossed the dog
That worried the cat
That killed the rat
That ate the malt
That lay in the house that Jack built.

WHISTLE, WHISTLE

Boys Whistle, whistle, old wife, and you'll get a hen.
Girls I wouldn't whistle, said the wife, if you could give me ten!

Boys Whistle, whistle, old wife, and you'll get a cock.
Girls I wouldn't whistle, said the wife, if you give me a flock!

Boys Whistle, whistle, old wife, and you'll get a coo.
Girls I wouldn't whistle, said the wife, if you could give me two!

Boys Whistle, whistle, old wife, and you'll get a gown.
Girls I wouldn't whistle, said the wife, for the best one in town!

Boys Whistle, whistle, old wife, and you'll get a man.
Girls Wheeple, whauple, said the wife, I'll whistle if I can!

THE PIRATE DON DURK OF DOWDEE[11]

Ho, for the Pirate Don Durk of Dowdee!
He was as wicked as wicked could be,
But oh, he was perfectly gorgeous to see!
The Pirate Don Durk of Dowdee!

His conscience, of course, was as black as a bat,
But he had a floppety plume on his hat
And when he went walking it jiggled—like that!
The plume of the Pirate Dowdee.

His coat it was crimson and cut with a slash,
And often as ever he twirled his mustache
Deep down in the ocean the mermaids went splash,
Because of Don Durke of Dowdee.

Moreover, Dowdee had a purple tattoo,
And stuck in his belt where he buckled it through
Were a dagger, a dirk and a squizzamaroo,
For fierce was the Pirate Dowdee.

So fearful he was he would shoot at a puff,
And always at sea when the weather grew rough
He drank from a bottle and wrote on his cuff,
Did Pirate Don Durk of Dowdee.

Oh, he had a cutlass that swung at his thigh
And he had a parrot called Pepperkin Pye,
And a zigzaggy scar at the end of his eye
Had Pirate Don Durk of Dowdee.

He kept in a cavern, this buccaneer bold,
A curious chest that was covered with mould,
And all of his pockets were jingly with gold!
Oh jing! went the gold of Dowdee.

His conscience, of course, it was crook'd like a squash,
But both of his boots made a slickery slosh,
And he went through the world with a wonderful swash,
Did Pirate Don Durk of Dowdee.

It's true he was wicked as wicked could be,
His sins they outnumbered a hundred and three,
But oh, he was perfectly gorgeous to see,
The Pirate Don Durk of Dowdee.

THE DUDE'S PLEA[12]

All   Oh, give me a horse so I can ride—
A western bronc let me bestride;
A horse with a flowing mane and tail
To blow as I gallop the prairie trail.

Oh, give me some spurs, a cowman's quirt,
A ten-gallon hat, a cowboy shirt,
A pair of chaps and I'm away
To ride and ride 'til the end of day.

Give me a trail that is winding, steep,
10   That follows the turns of a canon deep;
The roar of a river, a swaying breeze
That laughs and sings through the cedar trees.

Oh, give me a bubbling coffee pot,
The smell of bacon, sizzling hot,
Some lazy smoke and a campfire's gleam,
A cigarette and a chance to dream.

And after the day has changed to night
And we've reached the ranch with its food and light
At the end of a day in the saddle spent—
20　Oh, give me a bottle of liniment!

Helen Howland Prommel

The fun of this poem, to be spoken in unison, lies in a very breezy, confident, experienced nineteen lines, topped by a long pause and a painful, wailing line 20. The temptation to reduce speed and force on line 17 should be resisted in favour of the later contrast.

The Psalms are ideally suited for verse choirs. Psalm 24 offers many possibilities for arrangements, antiphonal being of the simplest and most effective.

PSALM 24

Solo-a The earth is the Lord's, and the fulness thereof;
the world, and they that dwell therein. For he
hath founded it upon the seas, and established it
upon the floods.

B-2　Who shall ascend into the hill of the Lord?
Or who shall stand in His holy place?

3　He that hath clean hands, and a pure heart; who
hath not lifted up his soul unto vanity, nor
sworn deceitfully.

Solo-b He shall receive the blessing from the Lord, and
righteousness from the God of his salvation.

B-2　This is the generation of them that seek Him, that
seek thy face, O Jacob. Selah.

G　Lift up your heads, O ye gates,

B　And be ye lifted up, ye everlasting doors
4　And the King of glory shall come in.
1　Who is this King of glory?
2　The Lord strong and mighty
3　The Lord mighty in battle.

G　Lift up your heads, O ye gates;

B　Even lift them up, ye everlasting doors
4　And the King of glory shall come in.
1　Who is this King of glory?
4　The Lord of hosts, He is the King of Glory. Selah.

TRANSCONTINENTAL[13] (A radio poem in six voices)
(Locomotive Idling)

1st announcer:
> The sun's going west. Do you want to chase the sun?
> Take the Transcontinental on Track Twenty-One. Go
> to the wicket, and buy yourself a ticket. Chicago,
> Omaha, Denver and the Coast.
> (Bell ringing)

2nd announcer:
> Want to see America for two cents a mile?
> America's a bargain. Do it in style. See what the Red-
> men lost and what the settlers won. See what the
> British risked with the Battle of Lexington. See what
> the French sold to Thomas Jefferson.

Together:
> Take the Transcontinental on Track Twenty-One.
> All aboard. All Board! All aboard!
> (train starting and under way)

High voices: (Quietly)
> Beneath the silt of the centuries,
> Beneath the salt tide that quarrels with the Hudson current,
> Beneath the clamor of the tugs and ferries,
> We move in the confident dark.

Low voices:
> Above the smear of oil in the sunset,
> Above the rhythm of steel on the river,
> Above the cattail plumes of the meadows
> We gather speed in the twilight.
> (Rail sounds: increased speed)

High voices:
> Black poles flicker past in the twilight,
> In a smoky second,
> Slow cinema of New Jersey marshes.
> Roof angles grow harsh in the final minute
> As the north sky is milked of its light,
> An hour is swiftly reckoned
> And a dozen counties in it
> As the moon rolls over chimneys and spires.
> A star dances along the telegraph wires. . . .
> F sharp to E in the treble clef
> Swaying to rhythm of grade and turn
> And half a continent is gone,
> With Capella in the dawn.

Low voices:

> What is there now to race?
> Not the fawn by the river bank
> Lifting a face of wonder
> To the flowing thunder of iron
> Not the casual crow
> Circling the high trestle and water tank
> In the murk of morning;
> Not the sad warning of the whistle,

(Whistle in distance)

> That cries "Be-ware," "Take care,"
> Then caroms with sadder echoes
> Down mountainside and meadow;
> Let us race the shadow of the train
> A fluid stain of darkness, lifting and falling
> Over tool shed and cinder bed.

(Rapidly and in rhythm of clicking rails) Line-a-child

1st:	I see a house
2nd:	I see a stable
3rd:	I see a weather cock
	Swing on a gable.
4th:	I see a goat
5th:	I see a sow
6th:	I see a collie
	Chasing a cow.
7th:	I see wheat
8th:	I see stubble
9th:	I see a field
	With a crop of rubble.
10th:	I see a school
11th:	I see a church
12th:	I see a young lad
	Bending a birch.
13th:	I see a highway
14th:	I see a road
15th:	I see rubber wheels
	Carrying a load.

All together:

> I see a state
> I see a nation
> I see a democracy
> At the railroad station.
>> (Engine panting)

High voices:

> Racing the horizon
> Is never a thrill

Without a hill,
Small as a mouse
Or an old farmhouse
On a windy knob,
Or best of all a long cloud,
A wind-puffed and down-tuft rabbit
To set the pace
For the slow chase
Over Sauk Center
Stencilled again and again like a habit;
Over the headstones of Spoon River;
Over the tassels of the corn that quiver
In the dusty wake of the train;
Over the forlorn
Vassals of the paupered soil;
Over the heart ache and the body pain,
Over the hunkies who toil
By the siding tracks,
Over the shacks . . . . . and the shacks.

Low voices:

Downgrade we go, past depot and tower,
Tracks all clear for eighty miles an hour.
The wheels are singing a song of the states
As we pass the crowd at the crossing gates.

Chorus: (Rapidly)

Missouri, Missouri, Missouri,
Montana, Montana, Montana,
Nevada, Nevada, Nevada.
                              (Train sounds)

High voices:

There will be uplands again,
And crouching buttes to follow, and fewer men,
But nothing to race but smoke on the canyon walls,
And the hollow shafts of sun
Drinking blue wine of the Sierra snows,
Or the vigil lights
Blinking green and white
As the engine crawls
Into the rocky side
Of the Great Divide.
          (Slacken speed to chugging effect)

Low voices: (Slowly)

Upgrade is slow, and we puff as we climb
And the thrust of the piston beats tardy time,

When the stacks are belching a thundercloud,
The double-header engines pant out loud.

Chorus: (Slowly)
Min-ne-so-ta, Min-ne-so-ta, Min-ne-so-ta,
Col-o-ra-do, Col-o-ra-do, Col-o-ra-do.
(Faster)
A-ri-zo-na, A-ri-zo-na, A-ri-zo-na,
(Faster) California, California, California.
(Bring train to stop, keep idling)

Low voices:
We will sprint with the dusk once more
For the dim shore of the Pacific
Before the sun touches the sea
In a hiss of golden steam,
And run upon quiet beaches
Only to see old men
Reach again and again
For the warm sand,
And let it fall from hand to hand,
Lost in a dream.

Chorus:
Fifty thousand towns all stitched together
By a double thread of silver glinting in the sun,
A quarter million of shining tether
Binding all the forty-eight states as one.
Three thousand miles and no stop for customs
Three thousand miles on one kind of money,
Three thousand miles on American slang,
Three thousand miles and only one ticket.
Freedom begins with the Boston & Maine,
Democracy ends with the old Santa Fe.

1st Announcer: (Sprightly)
Morning is coming.

2nd Announcer:
Who wants to meet the sun?

1st Announcer:
East Coast Limited on Track Twenty-One.

2nd Announcer:
All aboard. (Fading)   (Train starts. Fades.)

This poem lends itself readily in the development of a social studies unit on the United States in the upper grades.

Young children enjoy such poems for dramatizing choral speaking as the two

below. One group of children speaks the poems while the other group dramatizes
the action of the animals described in "Cat"[14] and "Jump or Jiggle"[15]

CAT

My cat
Is quiet
She moves without a sound.
Sometimes she stretches herself
   high and curving
On tiptoe.
Sometimes she crouches low
And creeping.

Sometimes she rubs herself
   against a chair,
And there
   With a miew and a miew
   And a purr purr purr
She curls up
And goes to sleep.

JUMP OR JIGGLE

Frogs jump
Caterpillars hump

Worms wiggle
Bugs jiggle

Rabbits hop
Horses clop

Snakes slide
Sea gulls glide

Mice creep
Deer leap

Puppies bounce
Kittens pounce

Lions stalk—
But—
I walk!

The following ballad has possibilities for dramatized choral speaking for intermediate grade children.

    Robbers: See the Robbers passing by, passing by,
               See the Robbers passing by, my fair lady.

 Neighbours: What have the Robbers done to you, done to you, done to you,
               What have the Robbers done to you, my fair lady.

     House: Broke the lock and stole the key, stole the key, stole the key,
               Broke the lock and stole the key, my fair lady.

 Neighbours: How many pounds will set you free, set you free, set you free,
               How many pounds will set you free, my fair lady.

    Robbers: Twenty pounds will set her free, set her free, set her free,
               Twenty pounds will set her free, my fair lady.

      Lady: So much money I have not got, have not got, have not got
               So much money I have not got, my fair lady.

    Robbers: Then off to prison you must go, you must go, you must go,
               Off to prison you must go, my fair lady.[16]

The teacher and the children read the ballad to decide how to interpret the
meaning, mood, and rhythm of the selection. Next they decide about the characterization and discuss the possibilities for dramatizing the ballad. The group first

responds with bodily movement and creative interpretation. The teacher or leader may guide the discussion by asking such questions as:

What characters are there in the story?

What type of people were the robbers?

How would they stand, walk, move, behave?

The children "try on" the characters: the Robbers, Neighbours, House, and Lady. The characters who have been selected portray the action while the verse choirs speak the lines.

Upper grade children will find a challenge in the following selection for dramatized choral speaking.

SIR PATRICK SPENS*

The king sits in Dumferling toune,
   Drinking the blue-reid wine:
"O Whar will I get guid sailor,
   To sail this schip of mine?"

Up and spak an eldern knicht,
   Sat at the kings richt kne:
"Sir Patrick Spens is the best sailor,
   That sails up the se."

The king has written a braid letter,
   And signed it wi his hand,
And sent it to Sir Patrick Spens
   Was walking on the sand.

The first line that Sir Patrick red,
   A loud lauch lauchèd he;
The next line that Sir Patrick red,
   The teir blinded his ee.

"O wha is this has don this deid,
   This ill deid don to me,
To send me out this time o' the yeir,
   To sail upon the se!

"Mak haste, mak haste, my mirry men all,
   Our guid schip sails the morne."
"O say to sae, my master deir,
   For I feir a deadlie storme.

"Late, late yestreen I saw the new moone,
   Wi the auld moone in hir arme,
And I feir, I feir, my deir master,
   That we will cum to harme."

*A modern translation may be found in Arbuthnot's *Anthology of Children's Literature*, 1961., p. 19.

O our Scots nobles were richit laith
   To weet their cork-heild schoone;
Bot lang owre a' the play wer playd,
   Thair hats they swam aboone.

O lang, lang may their ladies sit,
   Wi thar fans into their hand,
Or eir they se Sir Patrick Spens
   Cum sailing to the land.

O lang, lang may the ladies stand
   Wi thar gold kems in their hair,
Waiting for thair ain deir lords,
   For they'll se thame na mair.

Haf, owre, haf owre to Aberdour,
   It's fiftie fadom deip,
And thair lies guid Sir Patrick Spens,
   Wi the Scots lords at his feit.

A more ambitious project for children experienced in choral speaking in which dramatization can be an important element is "The Circus."

THE CIRCUS[17]

2 Red and yellow posters on a fence and vacant wall
2 Little green leaflets fluttering in the breeze
2 Boys cry and girls cry from every gate and hall:
G The Circus
B   The Circus
4   The Circus comes to town!
1 Run and get your savings bank;
1 Shake the pennies down!
G Oh Mother!
B Daddy!
3 Please!
2 Please!
1 Please!
B I'll be a good boy, I won't go catching fishes;
G I'll be a good girl, I will wash the dishes!
4 Oh, but we'll be good—Better than your wishes!
G Please Mother!
B Please Daddy!
3 Please!
2 Please!
3   Please!
2 Red and yellow posters, can they all be true?
4 SEE THE GREATEST SHOW ON EARTH
3 See the hip-hip-hippotamus and the gangaroo
3 (I know—kangaroo!)

    2 There is to be a cage of monkeys,
    2 And a big gorilla,
    1 (That's the way your mouth looked
    1 When you took sarsaparilla)
    3 And a bunch of diving seals
    3 Like a submarine flotilla!
    4 GIGANTIC, STUPENDOUS, THE GREATEST SHOW ON EARTH!
    G See the daring ladies   On the high trapeze,
  G1 This one hanging by her hands!
  G2 This one by her knees!
  G1 There's one hanging by her chin!
  G2 (Golly, 'spose she'd sneeze!)
    4 EPOCH MAKING, MARVELLOUS! THE GREATEST SHOW ON EARTH

(Calliope effect during this stanza to the tune of "Beautiful Ohio".)

        Group 1—TOOTLE TOOTLE; *Group 2* Sh- Sh- Sh- Sh; *Group 3*—OOM-
        PAH OOMPAH OOM-PAH. (Verse carried by small group of girls with
        solo boys and girls voice for two characters—Calliope off during their
        remarks)

        I hear the Calliope—that's the big parade.
        Off the street, boy! Down in front!
a   Wow! Hear the Lion roar! Rats, I'm not afraid!
b   Aw, shucks, who's afraid? afraid? afraid?
c   I am. I'm afraid!
abc   Never mind the wagons. There's nothing there to see
        But here comes the horses,
abc   Oh gee! Oh gee! Oh Gee!
        White horses, white horses, white horses!
a   I counted twenty-seven!
b   I counted thirty-three!
Solo B   "MARTHY 'TAINT SO GOOD A CIRCUS AS WE USED TO SEE"
Solo G   "NO HENRY: YOU'RE RIGHT: 'TAINT SO GOOD AS IT USE
          TO BE
a   Here comes the open cages; Hear the Hippo grunt—
b   See the tigers! Oh, the lions!
b   Watch 'em lash their tails in rage.
c   There's a leopard, slinky leopard,
c   Pacing up and down his cage.
a   Look, there's the monkeys, doing tricks
a   On a cunning little stage!
Solo B   "MARTHY, THE CRITTERS AIN'T SO WILD AS THE ONE WE
          USED TO KNOW"
Solo G   "NO, HENRY: THAT THEY'RE NOT. WHAT YOU SAY IS SO"
2   Clear the streets there boys! Then put'em down in front!
2   Red and yellow wagons croaking round the turn!
2   Boom tata rat-at-tat-boom!
2   Red and yellow banners in the sunshine burn!

(During this stanza—*Group 3* imitate a band with BOOM-BOOM-BOOM-to tune of "Stars and Stripes Forever" until end of the two solo voices.)

2		Red and yellow uniforms—
1		Boom tata — rat-a-tat! Boom tata-rat-tat!
2		Boom! Boom!
1 & 2		Boom tata rat-atat- Boom tata rat-atat!
		Tootle tootle tootle tootle
		Tootle tootle tootle toot!
		Tootle tootle toot!
		Boom tata-rat-atat! Boom tat-a-rat-tat!
		Boom!
Solo B		WELL MARTHY, THAT 'AIRE BAND AIN'T BAD, BUT THEN I'VE SEEN IT BEAT!
Solo G		YES, YOU CAN PLAY THE BIG HORN BETTER'N THAT. AIN'T IT MOST TIME TO EAT!
Babble	1	Boom tata-rat-a-tat Boom!
of voices	2	Red and yellow banners waving in the sun!
but each	a	I see the clowns
distinct	b	I saw them first!
	c	Oh, golly, see his nose!
	d	Keep your eye on the shortest one!
	e	I wish he'd grin at me!
	f	Hey, there, you, look this way!
	g	Isn't he the cutest thing!
	h	I'm going to be a clown someday!
	i	Didn't I—?
	j	I say I—
	k	No, I saw them first!
	2	Red and yellow banners flapping down the street
	3	Elephants go plodding plod-plodding in the dust.
	2	Boom tata rat tat. Boom tata-rat-tat-
	1	tweetle-tee tweet!
	1	Monkeys in the yellow wagons,
	3	Tigers in the red,
	2	A fat clown, a lean clown,
	2	Standing on his head.
2		Show begins in half an hour. Never mind the dust.
1		Zip-yip- yip- yipp-i-oodle
2 & 3		Umph-a-umph-a-umph-a-umph-a-umph!
4		Circus! Circus!
2		Red and yellow tents—get your fifty cents!
3		Boom tata-rata-tat! Boom tata-rat-tat! Boom!

BOOM- TATA-RAT- TAT (1)	*Solo B* — MARTHY? I AIN'T SO
BOOM- TATA-RAT- TAT (2)	YOUNG AS I WAS. I AIN'T
BOOM (3)	HALF SO SPRY!
BOOM (1)	*Solo G* — HENRY, THE CIRCUS AIN'T TO

BOOM (2)		BLAME. THE CIRCUS IS THE SAME:
BOOM (3)	*B & G*	THE FAULT IS, YOU AND I
BOOM (4)		WE AIN'T HALF SO SPRY
		YOU HAVE TO SEE A CIRCUS
		WITH A YOUNGSTER'S EYE

4   (loud) Ya-ay-ay! THE CIRCUS.

Choral speaking under the guidance of an enthusiastic teacher becomes one of the most effective ways of helping children develop skill and confidence in oral interpretation while at the same time providing an enjoyable avenue for appreciation of literature. Through choral speaking poetry moves from the inanimate page to become a living force on the tongues of the children who speak it.

Through the verse choir the members of the group will discover and express the essence of meaning and feeling in the subject matter. They all express the kernel which strikes the common responsive chord. They express only what all have recognized and can freely experience.

Readers' Theatre

Readers' Theatre is a new approach to a conventional custom. We have been "reading plays" for years. What, then, is so new about Readers Theatre? The challenge in Readers' Theatre is to create the dramatic impact of the theatre through the medium of oral interpretation. Nielson defines Readers' Theatre as ". . . that activity which involves oral interpretation of a carefully cut script, usually by three to five readers, without memorization, special costume, lighting, props, or sound effects, portraying their roles by means of vocal and facial expression alone, a narrator possibly providing transitional expository lines for clarification . . ."[18] The reader must enter into the script as spontaneously and enthusiastically as a young child enters into a dramatic play. The readers must not leave the audience with the impression that three to five people have been sitting holding scripts, each declaiming his own lines.

The advantages of Readers' Theatre become clear as one experiments with it. Without attention to set, costumes, or special effects, any number of worthwhile, readable plays and stories can come to life in the classroom in a most satisfying manner. The entire class may work concurrently and experimentally within the confines of the ordinary classroom. No special theatre or auditorium is needed. For example, a class of 35 can readily be divided into seven working groups, each member actively engaged in the reading-interpreting assignment. Children too shy or withdrawn, or lacking in dramatic ability, find Readers' Theatre within their powers, since the holding of the book and the group situation gives psychological support.

Readers' Theatre is a challenge to the imagination. Since it cannot depend upon the stage embellishments of drama it demands of the readers the ability to paint pictures so vivid that the listeners have the feeling of knowing the characters as real people. As for the listener, it develops his imagination as he visualizes the setting, the characters, and the action.

Readers' Theatre motivates excellence in reading skill. While there is no demand for acting ability as such, there is a great stress on effective oral interpretation, the use of the voice, and the accompanying facial gestures which make the reading come alive. Plays and stories of quality are much easier to read effectively and are more satisfying to both the reader and the audience. Although the teacher may use stories and plays from the children's reading series it is important that the script be carefully edited. Which scenes to use, which characters to include, and what kind of narration is best suited to this medium must be guided by such factors as: (1) time allotment for the reading, (2) theme of the play, (3) significant scenes and lines, (4) clarity of plot and characters, (5) variety of mood, (6) balance in the use of readers, and (7) climactic arrangement.

Narration for transitional bridges should be in keeping with the style of the play and should be kept at a minimum. The narrator is an important part of the production, and he must be selected on the basis of his ability to communicate clearly with the audience, catch and hold attention of the audience, and clarify and intensify each scene. This implies a sensitive, alert reader with a clear, flexible, and colourful voice.

For Readers' Theatre the intermediate grade teacher will find useful *Thirty Plays for Classroom Reading* by Donald D. Durrell and Alice B. Crossley. These are tested plays adapted for Readers' Theatre with clear instructions for the teacher and pupils. The teachers for grades five through eight will find equally effective for Readers' Theatre the same authors' book *Favorite Plays for Classroom Reading*, Boston: Plays, Inc., 1965. Each of these books includes a wide variety of adaptations from the classics, comedies, mysteries, historical plays, legends, and holiday material. In content and spirit the plays offer enrichment of ideas, aesthetics, and literary values.

The mechanics of presenting a Readers' Theatre performance are fairly simple. Readers may be seated on high stools behind lecterns, rising or facing front for each entrance and turning around on their stools when they are "off stage". If a platform is being used readers may be seated in a semi-circle on chairs, turning when offstage, and facing front when onstage. Readers may be seated at tables and remain in their places for the entire reading. Readers may stand in a semi-circle arrangement throughout the performance, with or without lecterns. If the cast is large they may all be seated on the platform, and come forward when they are "on stage".

Upper grade children prefer sitting on tall stools and reading from manuscript placed on music stands.

Readers' Theatre affords still another avenue for making good literature come alive. It offers training in creative communication and appreciation of theatre. It has a powerful appeal to those who enjoy dramatizing literature in any form.

Dramatizing literature. For many children creative dramatics is the most exciting avenue for experiencing literature—both poetry and prose. "The world and I" might well be the title of a child's creative activity in drama. Play is natural for a child. It is through play that he "tries on life". He moves, he dramatizes his ideas, feelings, and his imaginings long before he is able to verbalize. Through feeling, thinking, verbalization he moves from play to "the play".

The child who discovers creative dramatics as an avenue for expression early in life often continues fulfilling his need for creative expression through active participation in little theatre groups or solely as a spectator who understands and empathizes with the actors.

One has only to observe a group of children participating in creative dramatics to discover how much it contributes to the total development of the child—mentally, socially, emotionally, and physically.

The child develops his imagination as he thinks out solutions to problems presented in the dramatic situation. He tries on characters, improvises dialogue, decides how a scene should be played, determines the design for the stage setting, and evaluates objectively *after* the play is ended.

Because there is no written script the child is forced to use his imagination. It is as important for him to exercise his creative abilities as it is to exercise his muscles. Creative dramatics offers excellent opportunity for creativity in action.

The child develops socially through working effectively with others in the group, understanding the character he is portraying, appreciating cultural differences, and becoming increasingly aware of and sensitive to the feelings and needs of others. He soon learns that it is not enough to "walk through" the role. He must relate it to seeing and feeling if he is to be truly creative. He learns, too, that each member of the group has a responsibility to support and enhance the contributions of others and not to "steal the scene".

The child grows emotionally as he expresses his feelings, releases his tensions, and develops psychological stability through identifying with the characters he portrays. This is one avenue which permits him legitimately to release tensions and express negative emotions. He tries on new roles, identifies with desirable characters, and cooperates in group activities which are fun, exciting, and/or demanding.

For some, creative dramatics provides the first esthetic impact. They discover that beauty lies within them, waiting to be released. Here the child—the potential philosopher, artist, or poet—discovers the miracle of beauty, not alone in the unusual but in the common-place.

The child gains in poise, muscular coordination, and bodily skills through participating in creative dramatics. As he portrays various characters he must show that he feels the tensions, understands and depicts the characteristics of the strength of the evil giant, the power of the king of beasts, the fury of the hurricane, the agility of Robin Hood or Tarzan, and the weakness of the lame beggar treking along the country road. He develops command of his entire body as he creates a variety of characters and/or phenomena.

Through dramatizing literature a child becomes aware of the conflicts that confront others as well as himself. He grows in appreciation of drama as a means of self-expression.

Key Concepts in Creative Dramatics

Involvement is the essence of creative expression. In expressing creativity through any medium total involvement is important. In creative dramatics it is essential. The individual needs to feel, think, imagine, and enter into the experience completely. A total synchronization of thought, feeling, motion, and voice is required if he is to *become* the character he chooses to portray.

The creative process, not the product, is important. In creative dramatics it is the *experience* that is important, not the finished product. The creative process is concerned with ideas, the awareness of a situation, the development and the communication of feelings, the attitudes, and truths. Children proceed through the phases of the creative process from that moment of awareness to the final phase of communicating the idea to the group. Originality is rewarded, ideas are welcomed, thinking is stimulated as children are motivated to enter into the feelings as well as to think the thoughts of the characters with whom they are identifying as they express themselves creatively.

Creative dramatics develop understanding and empathy. Before one can portray a character he must understand the character, emotion, and cause-and-effect relationships of actions. He must concern himself with the motivations of the character. Understanding and empathy come as a result of projecting one-self into the thoughts and feelings of others. It is through this increased insight into emotions which are common to all people that empathy grows. Children readily, through their power to imagine, *become* the character they portray.

Originality, not imitation, is the heart of creative dramatics. All children are creative. If this creativity is recognized and valued children will be challenged to express original ideas growing out of their unique pattern of development. Originality may manifest itself in sequence of events, bodily movement, creative design of dance or rhythm, original turn of a phrase, stage design, or in costuming. As the child develops confidence in *his* ability to think, feel, express, and communicate creatively the inhibitions with which he may begin are shed.

The classroom climate contributes to the creative process. The optimum classroom climate is one of psychological safety which says, "We create conditions in which each child may succeed, but we also give him freedom to fail." In a climate of security children are quick to try out ideas, to respond, to experiment, to discover. Where originality is welcomed, children are valued, ideas are treasured, the shackles of conformity are released and children will create.

Creative dramatics serves as a vehicle for developing pupil-teacher rapport.

In an encouraging environment in which children and teacher express themselves creatively there is a minimum of misunderstanding, conflict, and negative behaviour. As the teacher participates in the creative process a bond of understanding and mutual respect is forged.

Ways to Dramatize Literature

Dramatic play. Dramatic play is the make-believe play of the young child. Spontaneous free activity, it boasts no plot, needs no audience, has no sequence. The child *is*, for that moment, the person, animal, or thing with which he has an impulse to identify. He shifts instantaneously from person, to animal, to thing.

Pantomime. Pantomime may be defined as the expression of thoughts, feelings, and emotions through bodily action. It is non-verbal communication. It is used alike by the uneducated and the literate.

Creative dramatics. Creative dramatics is an experience in which a group of children enact a situation based on life or fiction through creatively projecting themselves into the lives of the characters. It is distinguished from dramatic play by having a plot that builds to a climax. Since it is improvised it is never played the same twice.

Playmaking. The term playmaking is often used interchangeably with creative dramatics. It includes all forms of improvisation in drama such as dramatic play, pantomime, puppetry, and story dramatization. Impromptu, informal, and creative, it may be based on literature, history or it may be original in idea, plot, and character.

Puppetry. Puppetry, a form of creative dramatics, is especially valuable for the shy child who shrinks from performing in front of an audience. Here he can express his ideas and emotions through the voice and actions of the puppets. There are many types of puppets from the very simple stick puppets to the elaborate marionettes. One of the oldest forms of puppetry is the shadow play. "In the East it usually takes the form of a performance in which flat cut-outs, made of leather, tin, or cardboard, are held between a light and a cotton sheet."[19] The shadow play spread throughout the East. In Java actors took the place of the marionettes in the shadow plays. From this developed the dance-drama of the Orient. Teachers and children have unlimited possibilities for creativity through the use of puppets and shadow plays.

Children's drama. Children's drama differs from creative dramatics in form, purpose, and character. It involves a prepared script, a formal presentation, and memorization of set lines. The story is written by children or by adults for children. The actors are selected on the basis of ability to portray the characters. The settings and costumes should be authentic. The audience is entitled to a finished performance.

Children's theatre. Children's theatre is primarily for child audiences whereas creative dramatics is primarily for the child who participates. It provides dramatic productions with adult actors. Through the medium of drama children gain an understanding of life values drawn from the human experiences they see on the stage. The chief value of children's theatre is the vicarious enjoyment each child experiences as a member of an audience viewing a finished performance.

Guiding Children in Dramatizing Literature

He who would guide children to create drama must above all remember what it is to be a child. "It is to be so little that the elves can reach to whisper in your ear; it is to turn pumpkins into coaches, and mice into horses, lowness into loftiness, and nothing into everything, for each child has its fairy godmother in its own soul."[20]

The teacher's ability to recapture this make-believe of childhood is essential if he would be truly successful in guiding children in dramatizing literature. In addition, the teacher needs to know the procedures he can use. Although no two experiences are ever the same, in each creative dramatic experience there is a basic procedure. It involves creating a mood, developing an idea, planning the action, playing the story, and evaluating the experience. The creative process in drama, as in other avenues of expression, begins with cognition and ends with communication.

Creating the mood. The teacher may create the mood by capitalizing on the season, a holiday, a current interest, a recent experience, a favourite story or poem, and so forth. Teachers frequently use a picture, music, a question, or an experience to arouse immediate interest. If an eerie mood is demanded, for instance, a slightly darkened room will contribute indirectly toward this feeling as will music of a mysterious nature.

Developing an idea. Once the mood is created the children are ready to develop the idea, discuss the situation, and/or share the story. Given freedom of expression and time to develop ideas children often reach unexpected heights in creativity. The successful teacher contributes by presenting the material with such enthusiasm that it reaches inside the children.

Planning the action. Before children can dramatize they should plan the characters they deem essential to the play. Through pantomime and/or dialogue they try out their ideas singly or in groups trying to *feel* the characters they portray. The cast is chosen from among the children who have tried on the characters spontaneously, joyously, and with understanding. Whether the poem or story requires one scene or several the group will find the playing proceeds more smoothly if they determine ahead of time the number of scenes, the characters who appear in each scene, and the tone of conversation which will move the story along to the climax.

Playing the story. For children the moment for playing the story is the most exciting. Once these initiatory steps are decided the play should begin and move along without interruption to the finale. Each player is responsible for staying in character; each member of the audience is responsible for being a good listener.

When the play is finished the audience should show appreciation in relation to the effectiveness of the performance.

Evaluating the experience. Evaluation which begins with words of commendation and recognition leads to greater enjoyment and satisfaction on the part of the players and to greater appreciation on the part of the audience. "That was really good for the first playing." "I was very frightened when the ogre appeared." "What a pompous character the king was!" "You were certainly having fun creating the story." Such comments can precede more specific evaluation. There is *always* something good that can be found in a creative experience.

Specific elements to evaluate include characterization, pantomime, rhythmic movement, dialogue, teamwork, audience reaction, pacing, use of space, and time spent in preparing for the play. Praise for individual contributions is important, too. Such remarks may be: "Diane, you have given us excellent ideas today." "Genevieve, I'm glad you are thinking things through so well today." "Billy is the most imaginative person today. I am always surprised to hear the new ideas he comes up with." "John was such a pompous King. He used his own ideas in walking as he did." "I like the way Mary is original in her ideas. She was different from any godmother that we've had."

One good scheme for evaluation is:

GENERAL

1. What did you think made our play interesting?
2. What did you think was particularly good about the way we played it?
3. How might we improve it?

CHARACTERIZATION

1. Were the characters in our play thinking and feeling like the characters in our story?
2. Were they convincing?
3. How did they make you feel they were real?
4. Did everyone stay in character throughout the entire scene?
5. Did the characters interact with each other?

ACTION

1. Was the play interesting to watch?
2. If you did not know the story, could you tell what was happening?
3. Did we keep the story moving?
4. How do you think we might have helped it to move along a little faster?
5. Did we crowd the characters into too small a space or did we use the entire space?

STORY

1. Was the story exciting and interesting, or did it seem ordinary?
2. Did our play tell the story?
3. Did we have a good climax?
4. Did you like the way it ended?

DIALOGUE

1. Did the dialogue help to move the story along, or did the characters talk about things not needed in the play?

2. How did the characters help each other to keep the dialogue moving?
3. Did the dialogue seem to stop sometimes?
4. Did the dialogue seem real?

COOPERATION

1. Did we all work together to create the scene?
2. How did the audience help?
3. How did the characters who were off stage part of the time cooperate for the good of the play?
4. Did any character call attention to himself rather than help to make the play important?
5. Was there a good spirit among the cast?
6. How did the players help each other?

PACING

1. Did the play move along or did it drag?
2. If it dragged, what was the reason?
3. How might we improve it next time?

VOICES OF PLAYERS

1. Did the players project their voices so that the audience could hear without straining?
2. How might the players improve their voices next time?

AUDIENCE PARTICIPATION

1. Did the audience take the responsibility of being good listeners?
2. Did they help us do our best work?
3. Did they laugh in the "right" places?

TIME IN PREPARATION

1. Did we spend enough time in planning the play?[21]

The test of a creative dramatics experience is the eagerness with which the children want to engage in such an activity again and again. Given a teacher who understands the creative process and who is willing to experiment with techniques for releasing children's creativity through creative dramatics, children's imaginations will be fired. When children are filled with the desire to create, when they have something they want to say, and when they have a teacher who is eager to accept their expression, creative dramatics is a natural outlet for developing appreciation of literature.

Guiding a Creative Dramatics Experience

Creating the mood. As Halloween approached a group of primary children began bringing in pumpkins, masks, and other objects symbolic of the coming holiday. Miss Penney capitalized on their interest by reading a number of Halloween poems and stories. One day she darkened the room and played the recording of "Hall of the Mountain King" from the *Peer Gynt Suite* by Grieg. Jimmy commented, "This number makes me feel spooky."

Developing the idea. Ann said, "It makes me think about the poem of the goblin who became an elf." "That's 'The Goblinade',"[22] said George. "I know that poem. Let's play it." The children eagerly agreed and asked Miss Penney to read it again.

THE GOBLINADE

A green hobgoblin
    Small but quick,
Went out walking
    With a black thorn stick.

He was full of mischief,
    Full of glee,
He frightened all
    That he could see.

He met a little maiden
    In the wood;
He looked as fierce
    As a goblin should.

He crept by the hedgerow,
    He said "boo".
"Boo," said the little maid,
    "Where are you?"

"What," said the goblin,
    "Aren't you afraid?"
"I think you're funny,"
    Said the little maid.

"Ha!" said the goblin,
    Sitting down flat.
"You think I'm funny?
    I don't like that."

"I'm very frightening,
    You should flee."
"You're cunning," she said
    "As you can be."

Then she laughed again,
    and
Went away.
    But the goblin stood
      there
All that day.

A beetle came by, and
    "Well?" it said:
But the goblin only
    Shook his head.

"For I am funny,"
    He said to it.
"I thought I was alarming,
    And I'm not a bit."

"If I'm amusing,"
    He said to himself,
"I won't be a goblin,
    I'll be an elf."

"For a goblin must be a goblin
    All the day,
But an elf need only
    Dance and play."

So the little green goblin
    Became an elf,
And he dances all day
    And he likes himself!

Florence Page Jaques

Planning the action. Immediately following the reading Miss Penney said, "Now we're ready to plan the action. Have you been thinking about what goblins are like? How is this goblin different from other goblins? What could he do that shows he is different from other goblins? Do you remember what clues the poem gave us about the goblin?"

The children were vociferous in their responses. Among the suggestions were: goblins are mischievous, they could all be goblins, they could pretend they were carrying little black sticks; they could look for creatures to frighten. At first everyone was a goblin. Each had a different sized stick and tried in different ways to frighten the various creatures. Soon Ralph suggested that some could be the different kinds of creatures that live in the woods and that they could act out ALL the poem. Mary suggested that they needed a little girl and "Please, can I play that part?" Charles volunteered to be the beetle. The children suggested that Tony should be the goblin as he was the most frightening goblin in the group.

Miss Penney at this point interjected: "How many scenes should we have to make the action complete?" Obviously the children were "old hands" at creating a setting and immediately suggested four scenes: Scene one: The goblin meets the creatures in the woods. Scene two: Goblin meets maiden. Scene three: Goblin meets beetle. Scene four: Goblin becomes an elf. Peter volunteered to be the stage manager.

Playing the poem. "Characters in your places," said Peter in a stentorian voice. "Curtain ready!" Miss Penney motioned to Mabel and June who had not yet developed enough courage to play roles, but who liked to be the "curtain", to take their places at the centre of the stage. "Curtain!" cried Peter. A hush fell on the audience as Mabel and Jane parted the "Curtain" by each walking to her side of the room. The play was on! The children applauded spontaneously when the play was over and the "curtain" was again drawn. The children were now ready to evaluate their work.

Evaluating the experience. "Did we create a spooky mood?" "How well did we communicate our ideas?" "Did the characters feel their parts?" "What did you like best about the action?" were some of the questions that Miss Penney asked. Many details of action were commented on. The goblin received special praise. Miss Penney discouraged negative criticism. However, positive suggestions for ways in which the play could be improved by the next group to play it were encouraged. Among the responses were: "The little girl could have been doing something in the woods like picking flowers or gathering nuts." "The various creatures could have let us know who they were by the way they moved about." "The dialogue could have carried the story along better." "The beetle could have said 'Well' so the goblin knew he wasn't scared." "The goblin could have gone to see the fairy queen and request her to change him to an elf."

Suggestions for the Teacher

Capitalize on the imagination of the children. As the children *feel* the mood of the story, situation, or poem they are dramatizing, encourage them to express their ideas. Stir their imaginations to see more in the situation or story than appears on the surface. Use skillful questions to draw out *their* ideas. Instead of suggesting what to do, ask questions which will motivate *them* to think. As children express themselves in creative dramatics ideas will flow freely.

Give children freedom in playing. Every player should have a feeling of success each time he makes a sincere effort. Try to choose some children in each cast who are uninhibited, free, and imaginative together with some who are shy, withdrawn, and less imaginative. Such a question as, "Who would like to be the _____?" "What role would *you* like to play?" often motivates even the shy child to volunteer. Try to involve as many children as possible in each playing. Once the child has selected his role, let him develop it in his own way. The teacher may have to give some suggestions to the timid child, but the characterization should finally be the child's own.

Children's Drama

Children's drama, too, can be a creative experience. It is also possible to be creative even though the child is involved with a written script. The child becomes familiar with the role through putting himself in the character's place and seeing the world through the character's eyes. Such complete identification aids in understanding the meaning of the lines. Thus he is able to speak the lines so that they flow naturally and spontaneously. When children's drama is a truly creative process the child puts himself in the place of the character, experiences the world of the play, and integrates actions and speech—thereby communicating the author's intent to the audience.

Suggestions for the Teacher

SELECTING THE PLAY. In selecting a play (1) the script, (2) limitations of the stage, (3) the players, and (4) the audience must be considered.

The *script* may be written by a professional playwright or by the children themselves. It should have literary merit; students should not be forced to memorize lines that have no literary value. It should hold the interest through rehearsal; it should have universal appeal. It should be chosen by the teacher and group on the basis of a predetermined criterion.

STAGING LIMITATION. The size of the stage, the lighting equipment, and the resources for designing and building scenery—must be taken into consideration. With the interest in circle theatre little attention need be given to staging or scenery and yet an effective performance may be presented. If children are talented in art and there is time to build scenes, fairly elaborate settings can be designed which enhance certain plays—for example, *Heidi* and *The Emperor's New Clothes*.

An extremely important consideration is the talent, number, and availability of the *players*. There are plays that hinge upon the talent of a single player—a ballet dancer, a singer, or an emotional actress. If there is no such individual available it is well to select another play. Ideally, all rehearsals should be during school time. . . . If there are few children who can rehearse after school, and that is the only time possible, it will be necessary to choose a play with a small cast. If only one or two boys can stay after school the play choosen will have to have a predominantly feminine cast.

The final factor to consider is the *audience*. The director should select plays that the viewers will find interesting.

Children can be brought into the play selection group and given an opportunity to read, evaluate, and vote on the play to be selected—under the guidance of the teacher.

ORGANIZATION. The creative director knows what he wants the play to say; but he guides the children into understanding the roles they interpret, through discussion. He does not *show* them how to interpret. Directing is not telling. It is getting the player to understand and interpret the role as he "lives" it. He *is* the character.

If the play is complicated the director needs an assistant. He also needs committees to take care of business, staging, lighting, prompting, costuming, properties, ushering, and scenery. The director organizes and coordinates the functions of these committees.

CASTING. The director, or the director and committee, casts the players. Usually the time for tryouts is posted and those interested come at the prescribed time and read lines from the play. Players are chosen on the basis of ability for the part, reliability, cooperation, and willingness to work hard, take criticism, and work with the other members of the cast for the success of the play.

REHEARSALS. Everyone must know what is expected of him, what is to be accomplished by the group, and how the director hopes to accomplish it. The director must be thoroughly familiar with the play before rehearsals start. He studies the setting, the historical and geographical background, the meaning of the lines, the life of the author, and the subtleties and allusions in the play. He discusses the characterizations with the pupils. Then they read through the lines to get an idea of the voices they will use. At a later rehearsal they will "walk through" the lines holding their scripts, and block out the action. The characters mark the general action on their scripts so that they can memorize action and lines together.

GUIDES FOR ACTING

1. The actor should stay in character at all times.
2. The actor should not move on someone else's lines unless the move is a definite part of the action.
3. The actors must react to each speaker.
4. The actors should not turn their backs to the audience unless the action demands their doing so.
5. The actors should project to the back row of the auditorium but sound as if they were talking to someone on stage.
6. Exit lines should be delivered usually as the actor reaches the door exit.
7. The actor should remember that the stage is a picture and try to keep the "picture" in balance at all times.[23]

Both informal and formal drama have value for the child. Informal drama emphasizes the process, not the product; the expression rather than the impression; the journey rather than the destination. Formal drama stresses the product, the performance, and the destination. Children can be creative in both. The teacher who would guide these activities must understand the developmental nature of creative dramatics and relate it to the needs of the individual.

HOW AN APPRECIATION OF LITERATURE CAN BE DEVELOPED

Enjoyment of literature through meaningful creative experiences should lead into a deepening appreciation of literature. Appreciation requires more complex skills and greater knowledge than mere enjoyment. It depends upon our conscious effort to deepen our understanding by discovering all we can about the specific literary work—its form, style, structure, development. As involvement is combined with knowledge, appreciation is deepened. Appreciation does not "happen". It must be developed. Teachers should not stop with helping children enjoy literature. They have the responsibility of organizing literary experiences which lead the child from enjoyment through mental stimulation to appreciation.

Enjoyment of literature tends to be concerned chiefly with the sensory experiences whereas appreciation involves to a greater degree the cognitive factors.

One excellent method of developing the cognitive factors in literature is through units based on types of "pseudo-genres" of literature: folk tales, fanciful stories, animal stories, adventure stories, myths, fables, Other Lands and People, Historical Fiction, and Biography. The significant element in a unit is the degree to which it organizes learning activities which are socially significant, academically worthwhile, individually challenging, and combines subject matter and experience in a way that aids the pupil in developing appreciation of literature.

In the development of these units children discuss the characteristics of the works they encounter, their structure, motif, theme, and the style of the authors. Through discussion, discovery, inquiry, and research, they develop a greater appreciation of literature.

The teacher always keeps in mind that the most important objective of the program is the child's experience with literature itself. The primary grade units do not make heavy demands on the overt analytical capacities of children. The stories exemplify the basic principles of literary form and teach them in such a way that children perceive the principle by encountering the work. As the child matures he will develop the tools with which to verbalize and intellectualize about the works he reads. An oral-aural literary-centred classroom beginning in the primary school will result in the child's growing ability to enjoy, comprehend, verbalize, analyze, discriminate, and appreciate literature.

In such a program the child gains a rich literary heritage for enjoyment and appreciation as well as greater insight into the structure of his language and the forms in which it is written.[24]

CONCLUDING STATEMENT

The program in children's literature in the elementary school is concerned with helping pupils read widely, develop taste and grow in appreciation of the best in literature. The teacher must be familiar with the literary heritage and know how to capitalize on children's interests to bring children and books together. The attitude of the teacher should motivate interest in reading for enjoyment and growing in appreciation. An accumulation of knowledge will not burst into flame. The teacher must do something with the knowledge and that is what experiencing literature is all about.

Among the meaningful creative experiences with literature are: oral reading by the teacher and pupils, storytelling by teacher and individual children, choral speaking, readers theatre, creative dramatics, and children's drama. Using these creative experiences as a basis the teacher may proceed through units organized around basic types of literature, to develop skill in critical analysis which leads to appreciation of a constantly widening scope of literature and the language in which it is communicated. Thus involvement, knowledge and skills blend with discovery.

"From the very beginning of his education, the child should experience the joy of discovery. The discovery which he has to make is that general ideas give an understanding of that stream of events which pours through his life, which is his life. . . ."[25] The understanding which we want is an understanding of and appreciation for the best in literature.

A good literature program will provide children with a rich and lasting experience with the world's best literature, develop a permanent interest in reading a wide variety of material for enjoyment and appreciation, help children experience literature in such a way that contributes to creative growth and personal enrichment, and offer opportunities for the development of discrimination and taste in literature. To achieve such objectives the teacher must make literature an integral part of the language arts program and language arts an integral part of the total school curriculum.[26]

REFERENCES

1. Harold Taylor, "The Aims of Education," *College English*, 18:249, 250, February, 1957. By permission of the National Council of Teachers of English.
2. Lewis M. Terman and Margaret Lima, *Children's Reading: A Guide for Parents and Teachers*, rev. ed., Appleton & Co., New York, 1931.
3. George W. Norvell, *What Boys and Girls Like to Read*, Silver Burdett Co., Morriston, 1958.
4. Helen Rogers and H. Allen Robinson, "Reading Interests of First Graders," *Elementary English*, 40:707-711, November, 1963.
5. By permission from Bernice J. Wolfson, "What Do Children Say Their Reading Interests Are?" *The Reading Teacher*, 13:81, November, 1960. (A study examining the expressed reading interests of 2,000 boys and girls in Grades Three through Six in Norwalk, Connecticut Public Schools.)
6. Reprinted with permission of The Macmillan Company, New York, from "The Children's Literary Heritage", *Elementary English* by Dora V. Smith. Copyright © Dora V. Smith 1964, pp. 228-235.
7. Jean Thomson (ed.), *Books for Boys and Girls*, The Ryerson Press, Toronto, 1954, p. 25.
8. A group of kindergarten children enjoyed as their favourite poem Frost's "Stopping by the Woods on a Snowy Evening". They accepted the literal level of the speaker who stops at the lovely, lonely woods for a while and leaves when he suddenly remembers he has much to do before he can go to bed. To them the analogy with the death wish was farthest from their minds.
9. By permission from "Choral Reading in the Classroom", *Curriculum Bulletin LA-17*, Portland Public Schools, Portland, n.d.
10. Reprinted with permission of the Macmillan Company from *In the Congo and Other Poems* by Vachel Lindsay. Copyright The Macmillan Company, 1914. Renewed, 1942 by Elizabeth C. Lindsay.
11. Mildred Plew Meigs, *Child Life*, Child Life Incorporated, Boston, March, 1923. By permission of the author (Mrs. M. P. Ruckel, Trustee of Estate). By permission from Child Life Magazine, Copyright 1923, 1951 by Rand McNally & Company.
12. Marion Parsons Robinson and Rozetta Lura Thurston, *Poetry for Men to Speak Chorally*, Expression Company, Boston, 1939, p. 62.
13. By permission from A. M. Sullivan, *Three Choral Poems*, MacMullen Books Incorporated, New York, 1941, 1951, pp. 19-24.
14. By permission from Dorothy Baruch, *I Like Animals*, Harper & Brothers, New York, 1933.
15. From *Another Here and Now Story Book* by Lucy Sprague Mitchell. Copyright 1937, by E. P. Dutton & Co., Inc. Renewal, ©, 1965 by Lucy Sprague Mitchell. Reprinted by permission of the publishers.
16. By permission from Loren E. Taylor, *Choral Drama*, Burgess Publishing Co., Minneapolis, 1965, pp. 25-26.

17. Pearl William Walton from *Southern California Journal of Speech*, October, 1932, pp. 32-35.
18. By permission from Margaret Nielson, "Have You Tried Readers' Theatre?" in Leslie Irene Coger and Melvin R. White (eds.), *Studies in Readers' Theatre*, S and F Press, Vanderveer Station, Brooklyn, 1963, p. 9.
19. Kenneth Macgowan and William Melnitz, *The Living Stage,* Prentice-Hall, Inc., Englewood Cliffs, 1955, p. 299.
20. Sir Francis Meynell, *The Works of Francis Thompson*, Vol. III, Burns, Oates and Washbourne, Ltd., 1913.
21. By permission from Lillian M. Logan, *Teaching the Young Child*, Houghton Mifflin Co., Boston, 1960, pp. 344-345.
22. Florence Page Jaques, "The Goblinade" in Winnifred Ward, *Stories to Dramatize*, Children's Theatre Press, Anchorage.
23. By permission from Lillian M. Logan and Virgil G. Logan, *Teaching the Elementary School Child*, Houghton Mifflin Company, Boston, 1961, pp. 535-537.
24. See *A Curriculum for English*, Grades I to XII, the Nebraska Curriculum Development Center, University of Nebraska Press, Lincoln, 1966.
25. Alfred North Whitehead, *The Aims of Education and Other Essays*, Macmillan Co., New York, 1929, p. 3.
26. See Nathan S. Blount, "Bibliography of Research in the Teaching of English", *Research in the Teaching of English*, I: 98-125, Spring, 1967.

Index

DATE DUE
